DATE DUE

SEP 9 1990			
SEP 2 7 1990			

THE ORIGINS OF THE CULTURAL REVOLUTION

2 The Great Leap Forward 1958–60

Studies of the East Asian Institute

The research for this study was carried out at different times under the auspices of the Research Institute on International Change and the East Asian Institute at Columbia University and of the Royal Institute of International Affairs.

The Royal Institute of International Affairs is an unofficial body which promotes the scientific study of international questions and does not express opinions of its own. The opinions expressed in this publication are the responsibility of the author.

The Institute and its Research Committee are grateful for the comments and suggestions made by Mr John Gardner and Professor Stuart R. Schram, who were asked to review the manuscript of this book.

The East Asian Institute of Columbia University was established in 1949 to prepare graduate students for careers dealing with East Asia, and to aid research and publication on East Asia during the modern period.

This publication was prepared under a grant from the Woodrow Wilson International Center for Scholars, Washington, D.C. The statements and views expressed are those of the author and are not necessarily those of the Wilson Center.

THE ORIGINS OF
THE CULTURAL REVOLUTION

2 THE GREAT LEAP FORWARD
1958–1960

RODERICK MACFARQUHAR

Published for
The Royal Institute of International Affairs
The East Asian Institute of Columbia University
and
The Research Institute on International Change of
Columbia University
by
Columbia University Press

Printed in U.S.A.

Library of Congress Cataloging in Publication Data
(Revised for vol. 2)

MacFarquhar, Roderick.
  The origins of the cultural revolution.

  (Studies of the East Asian Institute)
  Vol 2—has imprint: New York: Published for the
Royal Institute of International Affairs, the East
Asian Institute of Columbia University and the
Research Institute on International Change of
Columbia University by Columbia University Press
    Bibliography: v. 1, p. 412–417.
    Includes index.
    Contents: 1. Contradictions among the people, 1956–1957— 2. The
great leap forward, 1958–1960
    1. China—Politics and government—1949–1976.
  2. China—History—Cultural Revolution, 1966–1969.
  I. Royal Institute of International Affairs.
  II. Columbia University. East Asian Institute.
  III. Columbia University. Research Institute on
Communist Affairs. IV. Columbia University. Research
Institute on International Change. V. Title.
  VI. Series.
  DS777.75.M32 1974 951.05   73-15794
  ISBN 0–231–03841–0 (v. 1)
  ISBN 0–231–05716–4 (v. 2)

c 10 9 8 7 6 5 4 3 2

FOR LARISSA AND RORY

Freedom does not consist in the dream of independence of natural laws, but in the knowledge of these laws, and in the possibility this gives of systematically making them work towards definite ends. This holds good in relation both to the laws of external nature and to those which govern the bodily and mental life of men themselves—two classes of law which we can separate from each other at most only in thought but not in reality. Freedom of the will therefore means nothing but the capacity to make decisions with real knowledge of the subject.

ENGELS, *Anti-Dühring*

CONTENTS

Illustrations

(Between pp. 238–239)

The sources of the photographs are: NCNA, 1, 2, 3, 4, 5; China Reconstructs, *6, 12*; Jen-min Hua-pao (*China Pictorial*), *7, 8, 9, 10, 15, 16, 17*; Chi-nien P'eng Teh-huai T'ung-chih (*Remember Comrade P'eng Teh-huai*), *11, 13, 14*.

PREFACE

This second volume of my projected three-part study of the origins of the cultural revolution appears long after the first, and it is perhaps worth restating my purpose; to examine the impact of the main events of the period 1956–65 on the thinking, actions and interaction of the Chinese leaders in order to understand why Mao decided to tear down and rebuild a regime he had done so much to create.

For me the delay has been frustrating but fortunate. During five years as an M.P., 1974–9, I managed to continue some research and writing, partly assisted by a grant from the Rockefeller Foundation, and with the use for a time of my old office at Chatham House; but the exigencies of an active political career did not really allow the leisure nor provide the tempo for ivory tower reflection on 20-year-old events in China. On the other hand, my years in Parliament gave me first-hand experience of perennial problems and processes of politics: the role of leadership; the relationship of leader to colleagues; the interaction of politicians and bureaucrats; the tortuous road from articulation through formulation to implementation of policy; the importance of party activists in the country to politicians in the capital; the behaviour of politicians under pressure when matters of urgent national interest are concerned; the continual conflict between conscience and compromise, personal conviction and party solidarity, self-respect and ambition; the often crucial part played by chance, accident, and luck. Britain is not China, Parliament is not the National People's Congress, the British Labour Party is not the Chinese Communist Party, and low-temperature British socialism of the 1970s was a far cry from the utopian communism of China's great leap forward in the 1950s. But I hope I have been able to examine the actions of Peking politicians with greater insight and understanding as a result of pursuing the same métier.

A second bonus provided by the delays in the writing of this book was the new material that began to flood from China at the beginning of 1979, a few months before I lost my seat in

Parliament. This has greatly enriched our knowledge of the great leap forward.*

In early 1980, I started full-time work on these new sources with the help of a generous grant from the Leverhulme Trust, whose Director, Ronald Tress, has kindly scheduled funding to allow me to avail myself of opportunities to pursue my research abroad.

Moving to Washington, D.C., with the assistance of a Fulbright travel award, I spent the 1980–1 academic year as a Fellow in the stimulating atmosphere of the Woodrow Wilson International Center for Scholars. James Billington, his Associate Director, Prosser Gifford, and their friendly and efficient colleagues provide one with a tempting intellectual feast of noon discussions, afternoon colloquia and evening dialogues, but are understanding when consumption must give way to production. There I wrote the final chapters of this book. Of the many others at the Wilson Center who also assisted me in that enterprise, I must single out Harry Harding, the founding secretary of the East Asia programme, and his assistant Lisa Wilson; Zdenek David and his staff, who were my umbilical cord to the library resources of the Washington area; Eloise Doane who taught me how to use a word processor and oversaw the production of my chapters; and Frances Hunter, who sat at the crossroads and ensured, when necessary, that the outside world did not impinge. My research assistants, Bonnie Glaser and Jeffrey Wang, generously took time from their own studies to examine and report on a great deal of material, and my third volume will also profit from their work.

I presented a draft of chapter 10 as my Wilson Center colloquium paper and benefitted greatly from shrewd critiques presented by the main discussants, Harry Harding and Thomas Robinson, as well as from comments by Doak Barnett, Cyril Birch, Henry Bradsher, Philip Bridgham, Maurice Meisner, Lyman Miller, Charles Neuhauser and Yao Wei. Helpful suggestions were also sent or given to me by Tom Bernstein, Jürgen Domes, Philip Emerson, Tom Fisher, Merle Goldman and David Bachman. John Fairbank, who spurred me to turn volume I into a belated Ph.D., read chapters and maintained a characteristic flow of generous encouragement and advice.

While I was in Washington, Wang Chi guided me through the Chinese holdings of the Library of Congress; Philip Emerson

*See Bibliographical Note.

saved me much time by lending me much material; and at the Center for Chinese Research Materials, presided over by P. K. Yü, Nailene Chou and Kwok-sun Luk assiduously informed me of their latest publications, including a valuable if heart-breaking eight-volume collection of hitherto unknown Red Guard materials. I also benefitted from conversations with Robert Barendsen, Robert Michael Field, Charles Freeman, Edward Friedman, James Graham, Carol Hamrin, Chün-tu Hsueh, Paul Kreisberg, Nicholas Lardy, Kenneth Lieberthal, Leo Orleans, Robert Oxnam, Lucian Pye, Robert Sutter and Richard Wich. Michel Oksenberg, who offered trenchant criticism of early drafts of early chapters, was a regular provider of insight and counsel.

Returning to Britain, I revised earlier chapters in the light of the new material. Chatham House's China Group, chaired by Basil Clarke, mulled over some ideas with me. Werner Klatt, having already commented on earlier chapters, now examined most of the later ones with his customary thoroughness; back at the time of the great leap forward, when I was chronicling it for the London *Daily Telegraph*, his advice had ensured that I was never in danger of accepting the grandiose production claims then made. And over the years, Stuart Schram, Kenneth Walker and Christopher Howe at the School of Oriental and African Studies have aided my understanding of this period in discussion and through their writings.

At Chatham House, Ian Smart and his successor as Director of Studies, William Wallace, had always maintained their confidence to any who doubted that my manuscript would finally turn up. When it did, Pauline Wickham efficiently took charge, securing as editor the very experienced and meticulous Judith Ravenscroft, who had earlier worked on *The China Quarterly*. When the time came to reply to editorial queries, I was fortunate to be teaching with Benjamin Schwartz at Harvard. Conversations with him and other colleagues, as well as the questions and comments of students, helped me to refine some issues, and the libraries of the Harvard–Yenching Institute and the Fairbank Center for East Asian Research enabled me to deal speedily with points of detail. However, the process of finalizing the manuscript for the press had to be slowed when two generous American scholars presented me with some important Chinese 'internal' publications, recently obtained; happily, these sources served to strengthen the argument rather than force its reconstruction. Needless to say, none of those to whom I have here extended my warm appreciation bear any responsibility for any mistakes and omissions.

Throughout the long years of gestation, my wife Emily has retained her faith in this project, been a fount of informed criticism on its content, and tried to ensure that I did not wreak excessive violence upon our shared language. Our children, Larissa and Rory, have tolerated my long absences at the typewriter and, more enthusiastically, have learned how to file the *People's Daily*. This book is for them.

Cambridge, Mass.   Roderick MacFarquhar

March 1982

ABBREVIATIONS*

ACFIC	All-China Federation of Industry and Commerce
ACFTU	All-China Federation of Trades Unions
APC	Agricultural Producers' Cooperative
CC	Central Committee
CCP	Chinese Communist Party
CDNCA	China Democratic National Construction Association.
CPSU	Communist Party of the Soviet Union
CPV	Chinese People's Volunteers
FYP	Five-Year Plan
KMT	Kuomintang
MAC	Military Affairs Committee
MTS	Machine Tractor Station
NCNA	New China News Agency
NPC	National People's Congress
PLA	People's Liberation Army
PSC	Politburo Standing Committee
SC	State Council
YCL	Young Communist League

* For abbreviations used in the Notes, see p. 337 below.

CHINESE NAMES

The Wade-Giles system of transliterating Chinese names is used in this book. The Pinyin equivalents of people's names referred to are given here.

Wade-Giles	Pinyin
An Tzu-wen	An Ziwen
Chang Ch'un-ch'iao	Zhang Chunqiao
Chang Fang	Zhang Fang
Chang K'ai-fan	Zhang Kaifan
Chang P'ing-hua	Zhang Pinghua
Chang Po-chün	Zhang Bojun
Chang Wen-t'ien	Zhang Wentian
Chao Che-fu	Zhao Zhefu
Chao Erh-lu	Zhao Erlu
Chao Tzu-yang	Zhao Ziyang
Ch'en Cheng-jen	Chen Zhengren
Ch'en Hsi-lien	Chen Xilian
Ch'en Keng	Chen Geng
Ch'en Po-ta	Chen Boda
Ch'en Yi	Chen Yi
Ch'en Yun	Chen Yun
Chiang Ch'ing	Jiang Qing
Ch'iu Hui-tso	Qiu Huizuo
Chou En-lai	Zhou Enlai
Chou Hsiao-chou	Zhou Xiaozhou
Chou Hsin-fang	Zhou Xinfang
Chou Li-po	Zhou Libo
Chou Yang	Zhou Yang
Chu Teh	Zhu De
Feng Pai-chü	Feng Baiju
Fu Lien-chang	Fu Lianzhang
Hai Jui	Hai Rui
Ho Lung	He Long
Hsiao K'o	Xiao Ke
Hsu Ch'i-wen	Xu Qiwen
Hsueh Mu-ch'iao	Xue Muqiao
Hsu Shih-yu	Xu Shiyou

Hsu Ssu-wen	Xu Siwen
Hu Ch'iao-mu	Hu Qiaomu
Hu Feng	Hu Feng
Hua Kuo-feng	Hua Guofeng
Huang Ching	Huang Jing
Huang K'o-ch'eng	Huang Kecheng
Huang Yen-p'ei	Huang Yanpei
Hung Hsueh-chih	Hong Xuezhi
Jao Shu-shih	Rao Shushi
K'ang Sheng	Kang Sheng
K'ang Yu-wei	Kang Youwei
Kao Kang	Gao Gang
K'o Ch'ing-shih	Ke Qingshi
Kuan Mu-sheng	Guan Musheng
Kung P'ing-mei	Gong Pingmei
Kuo Mo-jo	Guo Moruo
Liao Ch'eng-chih	Liao Chengzhi
Liao Lu-yen	Liao Luyan
Li Ching-ch'üan	Li Jingquan
Li Chung-yun	Li Zhongyun
Li Fu-ch'un	Li Fuchun
Li Hsien-nien	Li Xiannian
Li Hsueh-feng	Li Xuefeng
Li Jui	Li Rui
Li Po	Li Bo
Li Ta	Li Da
Li Wei-han	Li Weihan
Lin Piao	Lin Biao
Liu Ch'ang-sheng	Liu Changsheng
Liu Chien-hsun	Liu Jianxun
Liu Hsiao	Liu Xiao
Liu Jen	Liu Ren
Liu Lan-t'ao	Liu Lantao
Liu Ning-yi	Liu Ningyi
Liu Po-ch'eng	Liu Bocheng
Liu Shao-ch'i	Liu Shaoqi
Liu Shun-huan	Liu Shunhuan
Liu Tzu-hou	Liu Zihou
Liu Ya-lou	Liu Yalou
Lo Lung-chi	Luo Longji
Lü Hung-pin	Lü Hongbin
Lu Ting-yi	Lu Dingyi
Lung Wei-ling	Long Weiling
Mao Fu-hsuan	Mao Fuxuan

Mao Hsia-sheng	Mao Xiasheng
Mao Tse-tung	Mao Zedong
Nieh Jung-chen	Nie Rongzhen
P'eng Chen	Peng Zhen
P'eng Teh-huai	Peng Dehuai
Po I-po	Bo Yibo
P'u An-hsiu	Pu Anxiu
P'u Hsi-hsiu	Pu Xixiu
Sha Wen-han	Sha Wenhan
Shu T'ung	Shu Tong
Su Yü	Su Yu
Sun Yeh-fang	Sun Yefang
T'an Chen-lin	Tan Zhenlin
T'an Ch'i-lung	Tan Qilong
T'ao Chu	Tao Zhu
T'ao Hsiang	Tao Xiang
T'ao Lu-chia	Tao Lujia
Teng Hsiao-p'ing	Deng Xiaoping
Teng Hua	Deng Hua
Teng Tzu-hui	Deng Zihui
Tseng Chih	Zeng Zhi
Tseng Hsi-sheng	Zeng Xisheng
Tu Fu	Du Fu
Tung Pi-wu	Dong Biwu
Ulanfu	Ulanhu
Wang Chen	Wang Zhen
Wang Chia-hsiang	Wang Jiaxiang
Wang Hsueh-wen	Wang Xuewen
Wang Jen-chung	Wang Renzhong
Wang Kuang-mei	Wang Guangmei
Wang Kuang-p'ing	Wang Guangping
Wang Li	Wang Li
Wang Ming	Wang Ming
Wang Yang-ming	Wang Yangming
Wei Cheng	Wei Zheng
Wu Chih-p'u	Wu Zhipu
Wu Han	Wu Han
Wu Hsiu-ch'üan	Wu Xiuquan
Wu Leng-hsi	Wu Lengxi
Wu Po	Wu Bo
Yang Hsien-chen	Yang Xianzhen
Yang Hsiu-feng	Yang Xiufeng
Yang K'ai-hui	Yang Kaihui
Yang Ming	Yang Ming

Yang Shang-k'un	Yang Shangkun
Yang Yi-ch'en	Yang Yichen
Yao Wen-yuan	Yao Wenyuan
Yeh Chien-ying	Ye Jianying
Yueh Fei	Yue Fei

INTRODUCTION

A quarter of a century has passed since the great leap forward engulfed China, but its reverberations are still felt there. The leap was a catalyst for the emerging Sino-Soviet dispute; the split between Moscow and Peking still determines the shape of Chinese diplomacy. The leap represented the abandonment of a balanced development strategy; today, Chinese trace their economic problems back to that decision. The leap was premised on the mobilization of massed manpower and so led to the shelving of family planning; when that programme was revived 13 years later, there were 200 million more Chinese. The leap sparked a confrontation between the party leader, Chairman Mao Tse-tung, and the nation's senior serving soldier, Defence Minister P'eng Teh-huai; the tension between party and army still haunts the Chinese political system. The leap gave birth to a new social organization, the people's commune; its functions withered within a few years, but not until 1981 did Chinese economic reformers begin to talk about abolishing it lock, stock and barrel.[1]

The great leap forward took shape gradually. In the autumn of 1957 the Chinese leaders were disillusioned. Mao had attempted to 'liberalize' the party's methods of rule in the wake of destalinization and the Hungarian revolt, but the '100 flowers' experiment had blown up in his face. The unexpected torrent of bitter criticism of the party unleashed by his speeches had humiliated organization men like Liu Shao-ch'i, the CCP's senior Vice Chairman, who had shaped its structure and recruited its members. The party's counter-attack was a vigorous anti-rightist campaign—led by a five-man group under Peking 1st secretary P'eng Chen—which cowed the intellectuals. The striking achievements of the 1st FYP (1953–7) were insufficient to counter a growing mood of disenchantment with the Soviet model upon which it had been based. There was a feeling among many Chinese leaders that new methods were needed if China were to break out of its economic backwardness. The critical problem was a lagging agriculture which was unable to keep industry supplied and to feed the rapidly growing population. Surprisingly, this was a novel situation for China.[2]

In the six centuries between the founding of the Ming dynasty in 1368 and the People's Republic in 1949, the population of China appears to have risen from about 80 million to 580 million. From the fourteenth to the eighteenth centuries, despite grave epidemics in 1588 and 1642, the annual growth rate averaged ·4–·5 per cent, though it may have risen as high as 1 per cent during the stability of the eighteenth century. The Taiping rebellion and other political convulsions of the nineteenth century caused a large decline in the population. It began expanding again in the twentieth century at a rate of 1 per cent.

During those 600 years, China's grain output had kept roughly in step with the growth of population. The Chinese peasantry had expanded production by enlarging the cultivated acreage and by increasing yields. Most of the increases in productivity were accounted for by increased inputs of labour and organic fertilizer (both permitted by the rising population). Technical improvements, such as the introduction of the sweet potato from America, were responsible for only a small share of the rise in yields.

Despite the lack of major technical innovation during these six centuries and despite the population growth in the first half of the twentieth century, Chinese agriculture was providing an adequate subsistence diet. By the 1950s, Chinese rice yields were about double those of India at the same time and somewhat better than those in Meiji Japan at the start of that country's century of industrialization. It was this relatively favourable position that enabled the Chinese to siphon off a small surplus to pay for the industrialization programme of the 1st FYP.

But the relevant bench-mark for the Chinese was not Japan or India but the Soviet Union whose economic development methods they were attempting to emulate. Here the comparison was far less favourable. On the eve of their respective 1st FYPs, the per capita availability of grain was twice as large in the Soviet Union as in China. In 1932, after the shock of Stalin's collectivization programme, Soviet grain output was 25 per cent less than it had been just prior to World War I, but by the use of coercion the Soviet peasantry was compelled to market almost exactly the same amount. Even so, the net per capita availability of grain at the end of the traumatic Soviet 1st FYP in 1932 was over 60 per cent greater than the equivalent figure for China in 1957 at the end of a 1st FYP during which, by Soviet standards, the peasantry had been treated with kid gloves. In sum, the population/grain balance in the Soviet Union enabled Stalin to pursue an essentially extractive policy towards agriculture, siphoning off large quantities of grain to pay for machinery and to feed the growing number of urban workers, while virtually ignoring the development of agriculture. The Chinese, on the other hand, were compelled to develop agriculture along with industry and then only to obtain far smaller surpluses.

The restoration of peace and unity to the country in 1949, and subsequent expropriation of landlord property during land reform, gave Chinese agriculture an initial boost. During the course of the 1st FYP, gross agricultural output increased by about 3 per cent; grain output rose at an annual rate somewhere between ·92 per cent (the lowerst estimate by competent foreign analysts) to 3·78 per cent (the highest rate derivable from Chinese statistics). An increase in agricultural investment of 5 per cent a year, consisting mainly of more fertilizer and insecticide, contributed to the higher growth rate. But expansion in output depended mostly on traditional techniques: greater use of labour, more intensive use of land through double cropping, and more extensive irrigation.

In 1957, the last year of the 1st FYP, the increase in grain output was only 1·3 per cent according to the official figures, and the industrial growth rate—which was linked much more closely to the agricultural growth rate than in the Soviet Union—was the second lowest since the CCP had come to power. Moreover, peace, unity and public health measures had raised the annual rate of population growth from 1 per cent in the first half of the century to over 2 per cent in the 1950s. Under the dual burden of a doubled rate of population growth and a major industrialization programme, Chinese agriculture was loosing its ability to satisfy all the needs of the Chinese state. China's leaders almost certainly did not have the data to enable them to appreciate the historic nature of their dilemma; but the grain shortages of the late summer of 1957 must have indicated clearly enough that a fundamental reappraisal of their development strategy was essential.[3]

Two possibilities were open to them. They could have launched a major programme of agricultural modernization, diverting resources to industries directly promoting agricultural development—the strategy adopted in the late 1970s. The alternative was to attempt to expand agricultural output by exploiting traditional methods, particularly water conservancy, to the limits. It was the fateful decision to adopt this latter strategy that led to the great leap forward.

The hope of the Chinese leaders was to achieve an economic breakthrough that would put China on a path of self-sustaining growth. The overweening pretensions of Mao and his supporters in the face of nature and economics and their acts of impatient folly led to disaster. But the basic elements of the leap forward strategy were sound. The mass mobilization of the peasantry is seen by economists as a rational approach for developing countries seeking to convert surplus labour into capital. The initiation of small-scale, 'native'-style industrial projects, another feature of the leap, can be defined as the rational exploitation of dual technologies.[4]

Probably no such sophisticated analyses were offered at the CC's 3rd plenum in the autumn of 1957; indeed, no overall strategy was outlined. But the mood was clearly one of dissatisfaction and impatience; the reinstatement of elements of the 1956 production 'high tide' was symbolic. In his speech to the plenum, Mao called for speedy development, a more intensive agriculture and increased steel output. But, significantly, at this stage he envisaged only that China would produce 20 million tons of steel by 1967 or a little later; within a year he would be thinking in terms of 30 million tons by 1959 as a minimum. Mao was still in 1957 a firm advocate of family planning; the 'shortage of labour' which China's propagandists proclaimed during the leap was yet to be discovered. Mao's ambitions and frustrations were crystallized in one question which he posed: 'Can't we avoid the Soviet Union's detours and do things better and faster?' But it was still only a question. There was as yet no commitment to immediate leaps in output. No inspirational challenge was set to galvanize the nation into action.[5]

Curiously, it was the increasingly deprecated Russians who were to provide Mao with the idea for such a challenge. And it was in Moscow not Peking that Mao proclaimed the first of the impossible dreams that led to the catastrophes of the great leap forward.

PART ONE

CHARGE

1 MAO IN MOSCOW

In November 1957, the leaders of the world communist movement assembled in Moscow to celebrate the 40th anniversary of
the Bolshevik revolution.[1] It was an occasion to reaffirm unity
and restate principles after the trauma caused by Khrushchev's
secret speech and the Hungarian revolt. Mao Tse-tung led the
Chinese delegation and in conference aligned himself behind
Soviet leadership of international communism in the interests of
solidarity against imperialism. A joint declaration of all ruling
communist parties, Yugoslavia's excepted, enunciated agreed
positions on the world situation, the issues of peace and war, the
interrelationship of communist states, and the basic laws of
socialist revolution and construction. But behind the common
front lay serious Sino-Soviet differences over how to assess the
global balance of power and whether communist revolutions
should be peaceful or violent. In the light of these disagreements,
Mao had earlier warned his Chinese colleagues against maintaining 'illicit' relations with their Soviet opposite numbers.[2] Nevertheless, Mao's commitment to the cause of communist unity, coupled with Soviet promises of military and scientific collaboration,
led the Chairman to support Khrushchev and permitted compromises to be reached.

Strangely, the Stalin question, which had obsessed the Chinese
throughout 1956[3], seems not to have been at issue between the
Soviet and Chinese delegations to the Moscow summit. Sub-
sequent Chinese revelations about the meeting made no mention of
Mao upbraiding the Russians again on this topic.[4] Indeed, in his
speech to the Supreme Soviet on 6 November, Mao described the
CPSU's measures to overcome the cult of the individual as 'wise'.[5]
Perhaps the Russians were able to convince Mao while he was in
Moscow that the attack on Stalin in the secret speech had been
necessary and unavoidable; shortly after Mao's return home,
Khrushchev allegedly told China's Defence Minister P'eng Teh-
huai that the Chairman now understood the Soviet attack on the
personality cult and completely supported it.[6] More likely, Mao

felt that the damage had been done; that there was no need for further recrimination since Khrushchev himself was reversing destalinization[7]; and that the first priority was to exhibit solidarity to prevent more disasters.

'The chief subject of controversy' between the Chinese and Soviet delegations, according to the later Peking account, was how communist parties should achieve power, the question of the transition from capitalism to socialism.[8] In his official report to the CPSU's 20th Congress in February 1956, Khrushchev had argued that communists might come to power by parliamentary means.[9] Subsequently, the Chinese informed the Russians privately that they disagreed with Khrushchev's presentation of this issue and they were to claim retrospectively that Liu Shao-ch'i's discussion of the Chinese revolution in his speech to the CCP's 8th Congress was meant to indicate, by analogy, that peaceful transition to socialism was wrong and impracticable.[10]

In Moscow, Mao and his colleagues 'did a great deal of work', consulting and struggling with the Russians and liaising with the other delegations. According to the Chinese, the original Soviet draft of the declaration mentioned only peaceful transition.[11] Consequently, on 10 November the Chinese delegation submitted an 'Outline of views on the question of peaceful transition' to the Russians in which they accepted the tactical advantage of talking about peaceful transition, but insisted that violent revolution should also be mentioned because 'there is still not a single country where this possibility [of peaceful transition] is of any practical significance'.[12] During the 'repeated discussions' on this topic the Russians presented two draft declarations, the Chinese produced a revised draft and then the two of them submitted a joint draft to the other parties.[13] The final Declaration unquestionably gave pride of place to peaceful transition, but it added at the insistence of the Chinese that 'the possibility of non-peaceful transition to socialism should be borne in mind'.[14] It is not surprising that Mao felt that the Declaration, though improved, was still unsatisfactory. The later Chinese account of the occasion indicated that it was out of a comradely desire not to put the Russians on the spot that Mao did not press for excluding any reference to the theses advanced by Khrushchev at the 20th Congress.[15]

But however strongly the Chinese may have felt about 'peaceful transition', in the last analysis it was not an issue that affected them intimately. The process of revolution in non-communist countries would be determined by the communist parties of those countries. But another contentious issue which was linked with the new thesis on peace and war put forward by Khrushchev at the 20th Congress did concern the Chinese directly. This was the question of how to deal with imperialism, that is the United States. It was to be the focal point of the first public polemics of the Sino-Soviet dispute in 1960 and it was already agitating Chinese leaders. It seems strange, therefore, that the Chinese did not pursue this argument more forcefully in Moscow.

In his 20th Congress report, Khrushchev had admitted that according to Marxism–Leninism 'wars are inevitable as long as imperialism exists'.[16] But he had argued that the situation had changed since that theory had been formulated. The communist bloc, neutralist countries and the labour movement in the capitalist world were powerful forces working for peace; and so, though the economic basis for wars would exist so long as imperialism existed, 'war is not fatalistically inevitable'.[17]

At the time of the 20th Congress, the *People's Daily* had supported this 'profound' analysis and characterized it as a 'tremendously inspiring force for all who hold peace dear'.[18] Khrushchev's thesis fitted in with current Chinese ideas on peaceful coexistence and their belief that relaxation of tension was the key factor in the international situation.[19] But by the autumn of 1957, the failure of Peking's overtures to the Americans and the Chinese Nationalists had undermined whatever hopes Mao had placed in a friendlier policy towards the West.[20] Moreover, the newly demonstrated superiority of Soviet rocketry—the ICBM test in August and the launching of the first two sputniks in October and November—had convinced him that it was not merely desirable to adopt a harder line towards the United States, but also possible to do so from a position of strength.[21] On 18 November,[22] the Chairman gave the assembled leaders of the world communist movement an optimistic assessment of the global balance of power:

It is my opinion that the international situation has now reached a new turning point. There are two winds in the world today, the East Wind and the West Wind. There is a Chinese saying, 'Either the East Wind prevails over the West Wind or the West Wind prevails over the East Wind.' I believe it is characteristic of the situation today that the East Wind is prevailing over the West Wind. That is to say, the forces of socialism have become overwhelmingly superior to the forces of imperialism.[23]

Apart from citing the Soviet sputnik achievements—according to one participant[24] Mao derided the Americans for not yet putting even a potato into orbit—Mao listed ten major setbacks sustained by the West since World War II to justify his contention that 'a new turning point' in the international situation had been reached.[25] The Chinese have claimed that Mao proceeded to argue that this increased strength of the communist bloc meant that there was more chance of preventing world war.[26] But what apparently shocked many members of his audience was that he was also prepared to think about the unthinkable and coolly estimate the likely outcome of a nuclear war if one did occur. In public, to the Supreme Soviet on 6 November, he asserted only that the West would perish and the communist bloc would survive:

If the imperialist warriors are determined to start a third world war, they will bring about no other result than the end of the world capitalist system.[27]

In private, he spelled out his views in numerical terms:

Let us imagine, how many people will die if war should break out? Out of the world's population of 2,700 million, one third—or, if more, half—may be lost . . . if the worst came to the worst and half of mankind died, the other half would remain while imperialism would be razed to the ground and the whole world would become socialist; in a number of years there would be 2,700 million people again. . . .[28]

Twelve years later at another international communist conference in Moscow, Leonid Brezhnev was to remark: 'Many of the comrades here may remember Mao Tse-tung's speech in this hall during the 1957 meeting. With appalling airiness and cynicism he spoke of the possible destruction of half of mankind in the event of an atomic war.'[29] What evidently worried the Russians at the time was not Mao's alleged cynicism but his airiness, for they regarded his assertion of communist bloc superiority as unrealistic. The Russians did not claim that their achievements in rocketry had made the East 'predominant' overall, only that the East was now 'stronger' and the West weaker than before; nor did the Russians even claim that they had purely military superiority. They admitted that in a nuclear war the Soviet Union would suffer 'great damage',[30] and so would have been particularly alarmed at Mao's description of a nuclear-armed United States as a 'paper tiger'.[31] Khrushchev must have begun to wonder if Mao's support had been bought too dearly.

(i) The secret Sino-Soviet defence agreement

The most important reason why Mao refrained from flaying Khrushchev's policy towards the United States at the Moscow meeting was surely the Soviet leader's new-found willingness to help China acquire nuclear weapons. On 15 October, a secret agreement on 'new technology for national defence' was signed.[32] The very existence of this agreement was revealed only eight years later, and even now, after a quarter of a century, its precise nature and how it came to be signed remain mysteries. When the Chinese eventually attacked the Russians for 'unilaterally' tearing up the agreement they did not say which side proposed the agreement, what negotiations led up to its conclusion, or who signed it on behalf of the two sides. When the Russians replied to his charge, their only defence was that the 'facts' had been presented 'tendentiously, in a distorted light'. They effectively admitted that some such agreement existed by condemning China because 'disregarding its duty as an ally and abusing the relations of trust existing among the socialist countries, [it] has embarked upon the road of making public classified documents and information relating to the defences of the countries of the socialist community. . . .'[33] With such considerations in mind, the Russians were evidently less inclined than the Chinese to reveal any details of the agreement.

What seems certain is that it included some degree of assistance for a Chinese nuclear weapons programme; this may have covered the transfer of scientific know-how in relevant fields rather than direct collaboration on the manufacture of weapons. Help with missile technology was probably also included. The Chinese use of the word 'new' in describing the technology indicated that it concerned areas in which they had little expertise such as nuclear weapons and missiles. The Soviet Union had been assisting China in the field of nuclear physics since 1955 and the promise of a research reactor was fulfilled in 1958.[34] The secret agreement presumably extended such collaboration into the weapons area.

Mao had long been set upon having a Chinese bomb[35]; and Peking's militancy in the autumn of 1957 probably led the Chinese to put pressure on Moscow in the aftermath of the sputniks to share some of the new Soviet technology. For his part, Khrushchev must have been anxious for Mao's support: for himself in the aftermath of the purge of the 'anti-party group', and for the Soviet Union against the Poles and the Yugoslavs at the forthcoming communist summit. He could not bargain for that support with an offer of economic assistance; the Soviet economy was too stretched coping with the aftermath of turbulence in Eastern Europe.[36] But he surely knew of Mao's determination to get nuclear weapons, and the agreement on 'new technology for national defence may have seemed a convenient way to secure Chinese backing while at the same time keeping an eye on and possibly some control over Chinese nuclear weapons development.

Three days after the agreement was signed, a large, top-level scientific delegation arrived in the Soviet Union for three months of negotiation, eventually signing agreements on 18 January 1958. The overt objective of this delegation was to obtain Soviet overall assistance for China's 12-year science plan[37]; but later reports indicate that key fields envisaged for joint research were physics and the peaceful uses of atomic energy.[38] Probably the trip had been scheduled earlier, but in anticipation the Chinese may have pressured the Russians to sign some form of defence agreement covering advanced weapons.

Most analyses of the secret agreement have linked it not merely to the visit of the Chinese scientific delegation, but also to the arrival in Moscow on 6 November of a high-level Chinese military mission. But this does not explain the last-minute arrival of the latter group on the very eve of the anniversary celebrations. When Defence Minister P'eng Teh-huai left Peking on 2 November as a member of Mao's delegation to Moscow, there was no hint that within a few days he would assume the additional role of leader of a Chinese military delegation. The secret defence agreement was two weeks old and the names of the scientific mission had already been announced. There was no advance warning that generals, too, would be needed in Moscow, and of course nowhere is it normal for senior generals to be formed into a squad for a major foreign mission at short notice.

Moreover, statements by Chinese military leaders immediately prior to the dispatch of the mission gave no hint of what was to come. In a broadcast on 30 October, Marshal Yeh Chien-ying stated that the successful launch of the Soviet ICBM and the sputnik had enriched Marxist–Leninist military theory.[39] On 31 October, Marshal Liu Po-ch'eng wrote:

Today the Soviet army has become a highly modernised army, and possesses the most modern combat weapons including the inter-continental ballistic missiles. . . . As indicated by Chairman Mao Tse-tung, the Chinese Army, in its work of modernisation, will learn from all advanced Soviet experience.[40]

And on 4 November, Marshal P'eng Teh-huai wrote:

Since World War II, the Soviet armed forces have achieved fresh successes in the fields of military science and technology such as have shaken the world. The success in inter-continental ballistic missiles has demonstrated the indisputable scientific and technological superiority of the Soviet armed forces . . . [which] are the great example for the modernisation of the Chinese armed forces . . . [by learning from the armed forces of the Soviet Union and other socialist countries and with correct study methods] the modernisation of our army may thus be accomplished with a reduction of roundabout ways.[41]

The striking characteristic of these three statements is not the emphasis on learning from the Soviet Union, nor even the specific singling out of Soviet missile technology which had delighted the Chinese and convinced Mao of the bloc's superiority over the West. What is curious is that these three marshals did not allude anywhere in their statements to an even more important element in the development of Soviet military strength since World War II—the breaking of the US monopoly in the field of nuclear weapons.

The omission seems all the more extraordinary since the Chinese evidently did believe that even in the field of nuclear weapons the Soviet Union was ahead of the United States in some respects. This was revealed in another anniversary eulogy, but by a scientist not a soldier. The nuclear physicist Chien San-chiang, Deputy Secretary General of the Academy of Sciences, told a gathering of fellow scientists on 31 October that the Soviet Union was the first to produce a hydrogen bomb that could be delivered.[42] The fact that a distinguished Chinese scientist put Soviet H-bomb development first on a list of Soviet technological achievements may have reflected excitement in the Peking scientific community at prospective collaboration with Soviet colleagues in this field under the new agreement. The fact that the marshals did not make any such mention suggests that two weeks after that agreement was signed they did not foresee that it had any immediate relevance to themselves.

The presumption must surely be that the dispatch of the military mission was decided upon *after* Mao and P'eng Teh-huai had arrived in Moscow, as a result of their initial discussions there. We know from both Khrushchev's memoirs and Chinese polemics that at some point the Soviet leader agreed to give the Chinese a sample atomic bomb.[43] The Chinese allegations additionally indicate that the provision of the sample bomb was related to, but not part of, the secret agreement.[44] It seems likely, therefore, that at the first meeting between Mao and Khrushchev in Moscow, the Soviet leader offered to supply China with a sample atomic bomb *in addition to* the technical collaboration already envisaged under the defence agreement.

To greet a visiting statesman on arrival with a handsome offer he cannot refuse is of course a familiar diplomatic *démarche* designed to ensure the success of the ensuing exchanges. Khrushchev's need for Mao's support at the forthcoming summit has already been mentioned. Moreover, between the signing of the secret agreement and Mao's arrival in Moscow, Khrushchev had sacked Defence Minister Marshal Zhukov, his most important ally against the anti-party group during the summer. That move must have revived questions in Peking about the durability of Khrushchev's leadership if it needed to be sustained by frequent purges of his colleagues. An offer to supply a sample atomic bomb would have been a strong inducement to Mao to shelve his doubts about Khrushchev and his policies.

But while the Chinese high command was presumably pleased at the prospect of 'going nuclear', Khrushchev's generosity probably exacerbated the continuing disagreement between Mao and P'eng Teh-huai over the type of armed forces China should have. Basically, the disagreement sprang from two sources: differing views of China's role in the world and the shortness of funds for China's defence. Mao's view seems to have been that China ought to have nuclear weapons because with them China could play a major independent world role and also cut back on expenditure on up-to-date conventional weapons. P'eng, if forced to choose, evidently preferred to have modernized conventional forces and rely on the Soviet nuclear shield, presumably believing that China should play its world role as a member of the Soviet bloc.[45]

At the banquet that Marshal P'eng gave in Moscow for Soviet leaders on 27 November, on the eve of his military mission's departure for home, the Chinese Defence Minister again emphasized the importance he placed on having a modern army:

During our stay of over twenty days in the Soviet Union, the heroic Soviet army made a profound impression on us. The Soviet army is equipped with the latest modern weapons. It is in an excellent state of military preparedness and has been trained in a spirit of high patriotism and internationalism. . . . The Soviet army is also the best example for the People's Liberation Army in China. We shall certainly take away with us all that we have learned during our visit to the Soviet Union, shall carefully study it, and shall make use of it in practice in accordance with the specific conditions of the Chinese army.[46]

When he replied, Marshal Malinovsky, Zhukov's replacement, emphasized that the strength of communist armies depended more on their links with people and party than on modern weapons, a line that was hardly surprising in the immediate aftermath of the Zhukov affair and the reassertion of CPSU dominance over the Red Army[47]; after all, Malinovsky must have owed his new position in large part to an ostensible willingness to collaborate with Khrushchev on this policy. Perhaps more significant was Malinovsky's statement that the Russians were willing to transmit their 'experience' in army-building to the Chinese. This may have indicated that the Russians were not to be allowed to supply the Chinese with quantities of modern conventional weaponry; if so, the reason would have been Mao's opposition.

The Moscow visit was probably a turning point in the relations between Mao and P'eng Teh-huai. The speed and ease with which Khrushchev had got rid of Zhukov must surely have sent a psychological tremor through the already febrile comradeship between the Chinese party leader and his defence minister.[48] And Mao, reassured that he had Soviet assistance for the kind of defence effort he wanted, could turn his attention to reshaping the PLA on the lines he preferred. P'eng Teh-huai would have to submit or quit.

(ii) Khrushchev spurs Mao

However serious their differences on foreign policy and ideology, Mao and Khrushchev must have found their attitudes towards economics gratifyingly similar. Even before he came to Moscow, Mao could only have been delighted by Khrushchev's sweeping decentralization of the Soviet economy which added power to Mao's elbow in his own attempts to achieve a similar decentralization in China.[49] But even more important than their agreement on the ideal structural profile of a communist economy was the similarity of their attitudes towards the process of economic development.

Temperamentally both Mao and Khrushchev were bold optimists. In May 1957, Khrushchev had called for overtaking the United States in the per capita production of meat, butter and milk 'in the near future', evidently by 1961 at the latest; he derided cautious Soviet economists, who doubted this goal by pointing to spectacular increases in these products in a number of collective farms, and added, in the spirit if not the language of Mao: 'How can all this be reckoned in an arithmetical computation? This is a political phenomenon.'[50]

By the time Mao reached Moscow in November, Khrushchev was increasingly confident that the meat, butter and milk targets would be achieved,[51] and was prepared to proclaim an even more ambitious aim in the economic competition with the United States.[52] In his keynote address to the Supreme Soviet on 6 November, Khrushchev declared:

Comrades, the calculations of our planners show that within the next 15 years, the Soviet Union will be able not only to overtake but also to surpass the present volume of output of important products in the U.S.A.[53]

As he indicated in his speech, by 'important products' Khrushchev meant iron ore, pig iron, steel, coal, petroleum, electric power and cement as well as consumer products such as sugar, woollen textiles and leather footwear.[54] In his private conversations with Mao, Khrushchev may already have been prepared to indicate his belief that, on the basis of the recently announced Seven-Year Plan, the Soviet Union would overtake the United States in per capita as well as in total output of major industrial and agricultural products by 1970.[55]

Even before he heard Khrushchev's 6 November speech, Mao had secured the agreement of his colleagues to the launching of a new economic drive, symbolized by the revival, at short notice, of the unrealistic Twelve-Year Agricultural Programme and the slogan 'more, faster, better and more economically'.[56] At the CC's 3rd plenum in September–October, Mao had stated that there were two methods of doing things, 'one producing slower and

poorer results and the other faster and better ones'.[57] His preference clearly was for the faster method, and Liu Shao-ch'i would
elaborate this theme at the second session of the CCP's 8th Congress the following May, when the great leap was launched. In
the face of the joint determination of Mao and Liu to rescue China from a stagnating economic situation by going for growth, the
more cautious Politburo members such as Premier Chou En-lai
and the deputy premiers concerned with the economy—
Commerce Minister Ch'en Yun, the Chairman of the State Planning Commission Li Fu-ch'un and Finance Minister Li Hsien-
nien—had dropped their opposition to 'adventurism'.[58]

The importance of Mao's Moscow visit to the launching of the
'great leap forward' in 1958 was that the Chairman was able to return home, not merely personally excited by Khrushchev's grandiose plans—they would be called 'hare-brained schemes' after
the Soviet leader's fall in 1964—but also armed with the knowledge that the Soviet economic planners were now prepared to
launch the kind of industrial and agricultural drive that their
Chinese disciples had forced Mao to abandon the previous year.[59]
Khrushchev's adventurism undermined any hopes that Chou and
his colleagues may have had of moderating a new 'high tide', the
1956-style title still given at this stage to the proposed economic
drive.[60] While still in the Soviet Union, Mao revised a *People's
Daily* editorial on the slogan of the 1956 'leap'—'more, faster,
better and more economically',[61] and sent a letter to Peking
warning that the cautious officials of the Finance Ministry did not
have the support of the central leadership.[62] More importantly, in
front of the leaders of the international communist movement, he
committed China, presumably on his personal initiative, to overtaking the United Kingdom economically within 15 years.[63] On 2
December, within two weeks of Mao's return from Moscow, Liu
Shao-ch'i spelled out the Chairman's new economic goals publicly
to the congress of the All-China Federation of Trade Unions
(ACFTU):

In 15 years, the Soviet Union can catch up with and surpass the United
States in the output of the most important industrial and agricultural products. In the same period of time, we ought to catch up with and surpass
the United Kingdom in the output of iron, steel and other major industrial products.[64]

Five days later, Mao's new target was endorsed by the country's chief planner Li Fu-ch'un when he addressed the ACFTU congress on the FYPs. Li forecast that at the end of the 15-year period, China's steel output would be 40 million tons and vouchsafed his belief that the United Kingdom, currently producing something over 20 million tons, would not be able to equal that figure. He expressed his confidence that China would also surpass the United Kingdom in the output of coal, metal-cutting machine tools, cement and chemical fertilizers within the 15 years.[65]

Yet, though Li also admitted that the planners had paid insufficient attention to implementing the policy of 'more, faster, better and more economically' and undertook that they would do better in the future,[66] the new, 2nd FYP industrial targets he announced did not represent, with one exception, a major advance on those endorsed a year earlier at the CCP's 8th Congress: steel—12 million tons (Li) as compared with 10·5–12 million tons (8th Congress); coal—230 million tons as compared with 190–210 million tons; electricity—44,000 million kWh, as compared with 40,000–43,000 million kWh; cement—12·5 million tons, as compared with 12·5–14·5 millions tons a year earlier. The output of oil was to be lower than planned in 1956 due to extraction difficulties. The exception of this modest raising of targets was chemical fertilizer, presumably because of its importance in the Twelve-Year Agricultural Programme; Li raised the 1962 target from the 3–3·2 million tons endorsed at the 8th Congress to 7 million tons,[67] the upper level of the target (5–7 million tons) in the revised Twelve-Year Programme.[68]

Even more surprising than the industrial targets Li Fu-ch'un set for 1962 were his agricultural goals. At the 8th Congress, at a time when economic conservatism prevailed and 'impetuosity and adventurism' were under attack, the 2nd FYP proposals had included targets of 250 million metric tons of grain, 2·4 million metric tons of cotton and 250 million pigs.[69] Yet 14 months later, after the CC's 3rd plenum had heralded the defeat of economic conservatism, after the revival of the Twelve-Year Agricultural Programme and the reinstatement of the slogan 'more, faster, better and more economically', Li Fu-ch'un advanced new FYP targets that were *lower* than the previous ones: 240 million metric tons of grain, 2·15 million metric tons of cotton and 200 million pigs.[70]

Clearly, whatever the change of mood and attitude introduced by Mao and Liu Shao-ch'i at the 3rd plenum, it had not yet translated itself into hard figures at the Planning Commission. Mao later indicated that the only concrete decisions taken at the plenum concerned water conservancy and fertilizer accumulation.[71] The planners were presumably concerned then that the 2nd FYP was unattainable without a substantial new infusion of Soviet assistance, which could no longer be expected after Moscow's decision to bale out Eastern Europe to help avert further unrest there.[72] This made inevitable the mobilization of labour, China's only substantial surplus resource, if a high tide were to be achieved; and if across-the-board targets worthy of a high tide were to be set, Mao would have to do much of the work himself. This would require time and travel, and it was presumably for that reason that the second session of the 8th Congress, which only two months previously had been scheduled for the end of 1957,[73] was quietly postponed.

2 THE POLITBURO TOURS CHINA

Mao was always a great believer in the importance of grass roots inspection tours as a means of avoiding bureaucratism. At this time he was advocating that senior officials should spend four months of the year outside the capital in order to gather the raw data of political and economic life, for the central departments were merely processing factories. He said: 'When I stay in Peking too long I feel as if my mind's going blank; but once I get out of Peking I again feel as if I've got something (to work on).'[1]

By mid-December, Mao, Ch'en Yun, Teng Hsiao-p'ing (the party's General Secretary), P'eng Chen (1st secretary of the Peking municipal party and Teng's lieutenant on the central secretariat) and Po I-po (Chairman of the State Economic Commission) were out of Peking.[2] By the end of the month virtually all the other most important members of the Politburo had left the capital.[3] During the first four months of 1958, they were engaged in touring the country and conferring with each other, mainly in places other than Peking, though most of them returned to the capital from time to time. The objective was clearly to assess the economic and political situation at the grass roots and on the basis of their findings to draw up plans for the leap forward which was given a preliminary send-off at the annual NPC session at the beginning of February and then well and truly launched at the second session of the CCP's 8th Congress in May.

Mao himself probably travelled as much as if not more than any leader and his movements during the period will give an idea of the scope of the Politburo's inspection operation. He was in his beloved Hangchow, on the coast in the central province of Chekiang for about a month, probably from early December 1957 to early January 1958.[4] Here, in early January, Mao held the first of the series of conferences of top central and regional leaders.[5] On 6 January, Mao arrived by air in Nanning, the capital of the Kwangsi-Chuang Autonomous Region in the extreme south of the country. There he convened another conference, which he addressed on 11 and 12 January. Despite pressure of work and water temperature of only just over 60°F (17°C), he swam twice in the Yung River.[6] On 23 January he was in Canton,[7] and by the 28th he was back in Peking to summon the 14th session of the SSC and the annual session of the NPC.[8] Mao attended the final session of the NPC on 11 February, and by the 13th he was in the north-east and visiting the coal-mining centre of Fushun near Shenyang, the capital of Liaoning province.[9] Mao may well have spent much of the rest of the month in the north-east, since it is China's most important industrial region. But by 5 March he was in the south-west, in the country's most populous province, Szechwan, where he spent most of the month.[10] Much of the time he was at another top-level conference in the provincial capital Chengtu, which lasted at least from the 10th to the 22nd, but he found time for inspection trips both during and after the conference.[11] On the 28th, he got on a boat in Chungking and spent the next three days making the spectacular trip through the Yangtse River gorges, accompanied by the 1st secretaries of Szechwan (Li Ching-ch'üan) and Hupeh (Wang Jen-chung) provinces and Shanghai municipality (K'o Ch'ing-shih).[12] He ended his river trip in Wuhan, the capital of Hupeh, where he stayed until the 11th[13]; during his stay, on 6 April, he addressed a conference in Hankow, the most important of the three cities that make up the triple city of Wuhan.[14] On the 12th Mao was in Changsha, the capital of his native Hunan.[15] By 15 April he was in Canton, and the last report we have of him on tour is from the same city on 30 April.[16] The CC held its 4th plenum in Peking, presumably in early May, preparatory to the opening of the second session of the CCP's 8th Congress on 5 May.[17]

(i) The Hangchow conference and the campaign against the four pests

Virtually nothing has been disclosed about the Hangchow conference, which took place during the first ten days of January 1958.[18] However, it is clear that during this period Mao threw his personal prestige behind the national public health campaign which centred on the elimination of the four pests—rats, sparrows, flies, mosquitoes—singled out in a special article in the Twelve-Year Agricultural Programme.[19]

Mao had long stressed the importance of public health. As far back as December 1944, he had written:

Despots take advantage of the people's ignorance, while we take advantage of the people's wisdom. We must enable all the people to free themselves gradually from the state of ignorance and the unhygienic state. Government and Party organisations in various localities should place on their daily agenda the four items of cultural education work—newspapers, schools, arts, and health.

As recently as October 1957, he had informed the SSC of his particular interest in the provision for the elimination of the 'four pests' included in the Twelve-Year Agricultural Programme.[20] And indeed, the revival of that programme encouraged provincial authorities to launch campaigns against the four pests. In Szechwan, for instance, an editorial on the subject in the provincial paper on 30 November was followed up by an official 'notification' issued by the provincial party and government organs on 25 December.[21] Now, in early January, Mao visited a lane in Hangchow, known as a model health unit, and inquired about the prevalence of the four pests.[22] Then, behind the scenes at the Nanning conference in mid-January, Mao issued a directive:

A patriotic health campaign centring on the 'elimination of the four pests' should be unfolded. This year, a monthly examination should be conducted so as to lay the necessary groundwork. The various localities may, taking their own conditions into account, incorporate other objectives into the campaign other than the elimination of the 'four pests'.[23]

Within a few days, Peking city had launched an emulation campaign to spur the drive against the four pests,[24] and on 27 January the *Szechwan Jih-pao* published its first league table showing the numbers of pests killed in the various localities in the province. An earlier NCNA story from Chungking had revealed that, on average, almost half the city's two million people were engaged daily in fighting the four pests; since 24 December, they had killed over 230,000 rodents, dug out almost two tons of fly pupae and removed over 600 tons of garbage.[25]

More of the flavour of the campaign was conveyed by another NCNA story on the ingenuity of PLA units:

The officers and men of many units enthusiastically studied activity patterns of rats and sparrows. With such information on hand, they mapped out their tactics and operation programmes. The officers and men of a certain unit stationed in Shanghai found that the sparrows hid in the woods at night and were therefore difficult to trap. They then worked out a new method. They shook the trees to scare the sparrows from their nests, used flashlights to confuse the birds' vision, and finally with bamboos they hit the sparrows. The method was found effective. Deputy Platoon Leader Wang Shu-hua hit four sparrows with one stroke of his bamboo.[26]

Another technique for trapping the luckless sparrows were witnessed by a Soviet scientist, seconded as an adviser to China, who later recalled being

awakened in the early morning by a woman's bloodcurdling screams. Rushing to my window, I saw that a young woman was running to and fro on the roof of the building next door, frantically waving a bamboo pole with a large sheet tied to it. Suddenly, the woman stopped shouting, apparently to catch her breath, but a moment later, down below in the street, a drum started beating, and she resumed her frightful screams and the mad waving of her peculiar flag. . . . I realised that in all the upper stories of the hotel, white-clad females were waving sheets and towels that were supposed to keep the sparrows from alighting on the building.[27]

Of course, the government had concentrated on public health measures ever since its achievement of power, and with such success that one visiting British correspondent[28] had entitled his subsequent book *No Flies in China*. What marked out the 1958 campaign was its massiveness and the earnestness with which it was pursued. A Canadian scientist witnessed the following incident:

We crossed a railway line, said to be a spur leading to a coal mine, and saw a most astonishing sight. A teenage girl was running hither and thither along the railway tract in a most demented fashion, apparently beating the ground with a cloth. 'Oh she's chasing a fly to kill it', said Mr Tien. It was a most vivid illustration of the intensity of the effort that had been made in China to annihilate flies, bugs and sparrows. I never saw a single sparrow; I kept count of flies and saw one or more only fifteen times during nearly a month in China. In many of these instances the unfortunate fly was being pursued by a coursing Chinese. Only once did I see a swarm of flies, on a station platform near Sian, and they were buzzing around bamboo baskets, each of which held four small pigs awaiting shipment.[29]

Bizarre though such activities may have seemed to visiting foreigners, it was precisely the dedicated efforts of people in exterminating pests in late 1957 and early 1958 that encouraged the Chinese leaders to launch the public health campaign on a nationwide basis with good hopes of impressive results. On 29 January, the *People's Daily* published the news of Mao's health inspection in Hangchow to underline the Chairman's personal concern about the struggle against the four pests. This was followed on 12 February by the release of a joint CC-State Council directive officially launching the campaign. This directive, later attributed to Mao, revealed that 11 provinces and six major cities were planning to eliminate the four pests within five years; among these, Nanking was planning completion in 1958 and Peking in 1959.[30] While the campaign centred on the four pests, the aim was also to fight all major diseases. One of the most persistent of these was schistosomiasis or liver fluke (the Egyptian bilharzia) and the announcement, in June 1958,[31] that one *hsien* (county) in Kiangsi province had become the first to stamp out this dread disease so excited Mao that he could not sleep and instead wrote his only peom of the first year of the leap[32]:

The waters and hills displayed their green in vain
When the ablest physicians were baffled by these pests.
A thousand villages were overrun by brambles and men were feeble;
Ghosts sang their ballads in a myriad desolate houses.
Now, in a day, we have leapt round the earth
And inspected a thousand Milky Ways.
If the Cowherd asks about the god of plagues,
Tell him that with joy and sorrow he has been washed away
by the tide.[33]

During the cultural revolution it was suggested that 1958 was a year of 'Maoist' achievement on the health front. Apart from the mass campaign against the four pests, reforms in medical education were claimed as well as the increased study of native Chinese medicine.[34] In fact, it has been convincingly demonstrated that the reforms were far less spectacular and the political picture far more complex than was implied in retrospect.[35]

(ii)   The Nanning conference and the attack on the Finance Ministry

Although Mao issued his directive on public health at the Nanning conference, that was not his main preoccupation in the speeches he made there on 11 and 12 January. It is clear from those and from the Sixty Articles on Work Methods, which he signed on the 31st, that Mao's objectives at the beginning of what became the first year of the great leap forward were to change the mood within the party and the government, to mobilize official-dom for the projected production high tide and above all to re-assert political leadership over the bureaucracy. It was at Nanning that Mao first seized on the idea of a three-year period of all-out endeavour in order to achieve an economic breakthrough. The slogan 'Battle hard for three years to change the face of China' had originally been suggested by Anhwei province. Initially, Mao had had reservations about it, but the provincial leaders had con-vinced the Chairman by showing him their water-conservancy plans; however, with characteristic verbal caution, he had added the familiar adverb 'basically' to qualify the verb 'to change'.[36] Mao, himself, later commented on the Nanning and subsequent Chengtu meetings:

We tore into our problems, criticising those opposed to daring advances. We decided not to allow further opposition to daring advances. We proposed a general line for socialist construction. If there had been no Nanning meeting we could not have come up with a general line.[37]

So successful was Mao's onslaught, that it was later claimed that the Nanning conference, along with the earlier 3rd plenum, marked the rout of those who warned against adventurism.[38] Among those criticized by him were Premier Chou En-lai, Com-merce Minister Ch'en Yun, a PSC member and economic over-lord during the regime's early years, and Finance Minister Li Hsien-nien.[39] The Commerce Ministry, according to Mao, 'ex-ploited and deluded' the people.[40] But his main fire was directed against the stronghold of economic conservatism, the Finance Ministry.

There can be few countries in the world where the Finance Ministry does not act as the advocate of economic caution. In China, there were powerful additional reasons for such an atti-tude. Only a decade earlier, in the dying years of the Nationalist regime, China had experienced one of the worst inflations in modern history.[41] The Nationalists' failure to control prices had alienated the urban bourgeoisie, hitherto among their most loyal supporters. The Communists' restoration of price stability had been one of their earliest and most important successes.[42] It was an achievement that Finance Ministry officials would not have wanted to see thrown away as a result of adventurist economic policies, and it was they, at least in Mao's eyes, who had been principally responsible for halting the earlier leap in 1956.[43]

The role of the Finance Ministry appears to have been

discussed at Hangchow and at Chou En-lai's suggestion some of its senior officials were summoned to the Nanning meeting.[44] Here they were given a tongue-lashing by Mao, clearly *pour encourager les autres*, during the course of which he revealed that he had boycotted their documents ever since the halting of the 1956 leap. He explained that he had particularly resented what he considered to be the misuse of a quotation from himself—'using Mao Tse-tung's words to oppose Mao Tse-tung'—in the key *People's Daily* editorial justifying the halt.[45] But though clearly anger had been one reason why Mao had adopted this mode of behaviour, there was another that had more far-reaching implications. Mao attacked the bureaucracy in general for submitting a plethora of long-winded, pedantic and highly technical documents to the Politburo; the Finance Ministry had compounded this fault by submitting documents only at the last minute.[46] As a result the Politburo had become a 'rubber stamp', according to Mao, who compared it to 'Dulles's United Nations'.[47]

Part of Mao's solution to this problem was outlined later in the month in the Sixty Articles on Work Methods where, in articles 32 and 33, he talked about the submission of information and documents:

Once material and viewpoint are cut off from each other, there is no viewpoint when the material is explained and there is no material when the viewpoint is explained. . . . The method of putting forward only a big pile of material without advancing one's own viewpoint and explaining what one is for is even worse. . . . It is not necessary to have too much material so long as we are able to explain problems. It is sufficient to dissect one or a few sparrows, and it is not necessary to dissect too many . . . it is only necessary to produce some representative material at a meeting . . . holding a meeting is different from writing a long article.

Generally speaking, we must not make people accept within a few hours a big pile of material or viewpoints which these people are not given to at ordinary times . . . . It is necessary to have some drizzle, and it is undesirable to have a downpour which yields several hundred millimeters of precipitation in a few hours.[48]

Of course, the earlier submission of simpler documents could only be a subsidiary means of tackling the underlying problem indicated by Mao—how to ensure political control of the bureaucracy. There is perhaps a hint in the Sixty Articles that Mao blamed the bureaucrats more than he blamed those members of the Politburo, like Finance Minister Li Hsien-nien, who were their spokesmen. In article 33, it is laid down that 'a number of opportunities must be found every year to enable those people who normally seldom contact the functions of their lines to contact such functions'.[49] This is slightly obscure but it could well have applied to Li who is known to have spent most of his time in his State Council office[50] from where he supervised the Ministries of Food, Commerce and Foreign Trade, the People's Bank of China and the All-China Federation of Supply and Marketing Cooperatives, plus his Finance Ministry.[51] In his absence, the daily work of the Finance Ministry was in the charge of Deputy Minister Wu Po,[52] who had been a senior official of the ministry since the inception of the regime under three successive ministers.[53] Was it possible for Li Hsien-nien to impose a 'Politburo viewpoint' upon Wu Po and his ministry? Or was it more common for Li to act as the spokesman for his bureaucrats within the Politburo, believing that the standard-bearer of the mainsteam bureaucratic viewpoint would inevitably wield much power?

Similar questions can be asked about any government with a developed bureaucracy, and the questions are almost as difficult to answer even where the evidence is far more accessible than for China. For Mao, what was important was that the political leadership should be fed with information in the right way so that it could arrive at a collective view on how the economy should be developed and then impose it upon the bureaucracy. At the CC's 2nd plenum, in November 1956, he had suggested that there should be three rounds of discussions of the budget so that the non-experts would become familiar enough with financial matters to be able to offer informed judgements on the experts' proposals.[54] Now at Nanning, Mao indicated clearly that in order to achieve the requisite political dominance over the economic bureaucracy, he was prepared to commit his personal reputation to the forthcoming leap.

Referring to his preface to the book *Socialist Upsurge in China's Countryside*, Mao reminded his audience of the tremendous role it played in the launching of the 1956 leap. He indicated that he was not in the least troubled by possible allegations that the preface was part of the cult of his personality; the important thing was its impact.[55] The implication was that he would repeat the performance in 1958 if necessary.

At the SSC at the end of the month, Mao attempted to enlist the support of the bourgeois intellectuals for what he called the new war against nature.[56] The previous year's 'big blooming and contending' had everywhere unleashed the positive spirit. 'Things that we couldn't do in the past, we can now do; where in the past we had no means to do something, now we have the means.' China, Mao added in a phrase to become famous when published á few months later, was poor and blank; but because she was poor she wanted revolution and on a blank piece of paper one could write articles well.[57]

Mao adopted a placatory attitude towards the non-communists in his audience. He expressed his pleasure that not many senior officials of the democratic parties had emerged as rightists and only ten had done so among those who attended SSCs. The CCP had made its mistakes in line; the democratic parties were no wiser. Both the CCP and the democratic parties were products of the old society and so the CCP had produced its Kao Kang and Jao Shu-shih and the democratic parties their equivalents, evidently the rightists.[58]

Mao reiterated the CCP's continuing demand that the bourgeois intellectuals should reform and, using a phrase that had become current in recent months, he stressed the need for them to be both red and expert:

Red is politics; expert is one's job. To be only expert and not red is to be a white expert. If one pursues politics so that one is only red and not expert, doesn't know one's job and doesn't understand practical matters, then the redness is a false redness and one is an empty-headed politician. While grasping politics, one must be thoroughly familiar with one's job; grasping technique must start with redness. If we are to overtake Britain in 15 years, then we must mould millions upon millions of intellectuals whose loyalty is to the proletariat.[59]

An interesting aspect of this exhortation was that Mao seemed to have decided to try yet again to enlist the expertise of the bourgeois intellectuals. Six months earlier, he had been talking of the urgent need to train up a huge army of proletarian intellectuals, not just intellectuals who were loyal to the proletarian cause.[60] Possibly at this initial stage of the leap, in January 1958, with Mao's enthusiasm for the Soviet model temporarily restored as a result of Khrushchev's own predilection for leaping progress, not to mention the signing in mid-January of Sino-Soviet scientific cooperation agreements, the Chairman was toying with the idea of a re-run of the 1956 leap formula: pressuring the bureaucrats and bourgeois experts to get more steam out of the conventional

Stalinist development model. During the Hangchow conference, Mao had had three Shanghai intellectuals flown in for intensive discussions on China's science prospects.[61] It was not until a little later in the year that Mao grasped the possibility of short-circuiting this route by putting overwhelming emphasis on small-scale, indigenous technology which required little in the way of expertise.

In order to win over the intellectuals to the idea of rapid economic growth when the memory of the collapse of the 1956 leap was still fresh, Mao urged upon them the desirability of uninterrupted revolution, which he defined as striking while the iron is hot. He differentiated his views from those of Trotsky by suggesting that the latter wanted to anticipate the march of history, to undertake the socialist revolution before the completion of the democratic revolution.[62] Mao asserted:

Zeal should be bolstered, not dampened. Where there are deviations and mistakes, they should be rectified by the method of extensive contending and extensive blooming, not by pouring cold water on them . . . . The revolution has not yet been fully consummated. Our comrades are obligated to endeavour further.[63]

(iii) The Sixty Articles on Work Methods

There is no indication in Mao's speeches to the SSC that he unveiled the Sixty Articles on Work Methods on that occasion; moreover it seems clear that the Sixty Articles were envisaged from the start as an intra-party document.[64] Since it is also clear that the Sixty Articles were in the first instance presented to a conference of some sort,[65] one must envisage something like an expanded Politburo meeting, held probably in late January, or conceivably in early February.[66]

Most of the articles were written by Mao on the basis of what he had heard at the Hangchow and Nanning conferences; in some cases he simply recorded other people's views. One 'important' article on rules and regulations was drafted by Liu Shao-ch'i on the basis of consultations with local cadres. Not all the articles dealt with work methods, as Mao himself pointed out; some concerned work tasks, some embodied theories and principles. The document was circulated for comment with a view to revision before ratification by the Politburo.[67]

The Sixty Articles were Mao's attempt to provide a *vade mecum* for officialdom in the new 'production upsurge'[68] or 'great leap forward' as it was named for the first time in article 16, a term hitherto applied only to the water conservancy drive.[69] Without the guidelines of the Sixty Articles, there was the danger that cadres would again falter in the face of the inevitable difficulties that a new leap would engender.[70] Article 13 summed up the attitude and the method which Mao, following Anhwei province, wished to inculate and also confirmed the timetable of the leap:

The next ten years will be determined by the first three years. Efforts should be made to bring about the basic transformation of the look of most areas in the next three years. For other areas, a longer time may be called for. The slogan is to fight a hard battle in the next three years. The method is to rouse fully the masses and to test everything.[71]

The leap did indeed last from 1958 to 1960.

In the two longest articles (21, 22), Mao elaborated his views on uninterrupted revolution and 'red and expert', essential ingredients of the great leap philosophy.[72] A third ingredient— 'smashing those rules and regulations which restrict the development of productivity'—was spelled out in what was evidently Liu Shao-ch'i's 'important' article.[73] Interestingly, this article contained inner contradictions, for what sounded like an encouragement to administrative Luddism was in fact clearly envisaged as a carefully controlled process.[74] This perhaps reflected a certain ambivalence in Liu's attitude—enthusiasm for leaping progress in conflict with a predilection for order and organization—but the 'general rule' adumbrated in the article also indicated that the pro-leap leaders were not yet ready or able to ignore totally the caveats of Chou En-lai and his colleagues, for the 'more, faster . . .' slogan of the leap was modified by the 'proportionate development' beloved of the planners[75]:

Under the precondition of achieving more, faster, better and more economical results in the proportionate development of socialist undertakings according to plans and on the basis of raising mass awakening, the masses should be permitted and encouraged to make new creations for the purpose of smashing those rules and regulations which restrict the development of productivity.[76]

But as the year unfolded, this careful balancing of the divergent approaches to growth was to give way to the Maoist dictum, also inscribed in the Sixty Articles, that 'imbalance is constant and absolute, while equilibrium is temporary and relative'.[77]

Liu's article 23 contained the only substantial indication of the role of the government, as distinct from the party, in the leap: seconding the ratification of new rules and regulations by the CC. But at the local level it was the party that was accorded the initiative—the investigation and abolition of the old rules; and other articles indicated the interventionist role the party was supposed to play in running the economy from now on. Perhaps most significantly, article 2, in laying down the 14 items of industrial work which party committees had to grasp, stated that these items should provide the basis for a '40 point' general programme for industrial development.[78] Clearly the intention was to draw up a programme for industry to match the Twelve-Year Agricultural Programme with its 40 points. If such a programme had been produced it would have resulted in the supercession of the laboriously compiled FYPs of government ministries, even if at this stage the Sixty Articles were drawn up in terms of such plans.[79]

Although the FYP system was not thrust aside, article 9 of the Sixty Articles contained the seeds of the undermining of the basis of careful planning, the statistical system. Hitherto, the central authorities had been in the practice of setting a single set of national targets for the provinces in a given year.[80] In article 9, Mao introduced an insidious new system for three sets of production plans. The central authorities were to have two: one that *had* to be accomplished and was publicized, and a second one that would be *expected* to be accomplished but would not be made public. This second plan of the centre would be the first plan of the localities and *had* to be accomplished by them; then the localities would have a second plan (making three sets in all) which they *expected* to be accomplished.[81] In fact, this dual planning system was not restricted to the central and provincial authorities; it was extended downwards to the *hsien* level, thus adding a fourth set of production plans. The net effect of this system was a continuous raising of targets. In the first place, the national target would undergo successive upward revision as it percolated down to the villages; then, on receipt of the optimistic forecasts from the grass roots, the central authorities again raised their targets, which generated another wave of escalation, or as one scholar has put it a great leap—in targets.[82] This system of having public minimum and private maximum targets was maintained throughout the leap—as we shall see, even when public production forecasts seemed to be at their most optimistic, behind the scenes

Mao himself was setting even more euphoric targets—and led directly to the statistical fiasco of 1959.

Many of the key features of the great leap forward were prescribed in the Sixty Articles: a higher rate of accumulation (article 16); greater collectivism (17); experimental plots (18)[83]; the widespread popularization of advanced experience (19–20); the running of farms and factories by schools and colleges (48–50); the establishment of chemical fertilizer plants and farm implements research centres at the local level (52–53); popularization of high-yield seed varieties (54); the encouragement given to sweet potatoes (56). But the two most significant products of the great leap were not foreshadowed: the people's communes and the backyard steel furnaces.

In their absence the real shock of the Sixty Articles for those not in the know had nothing to do with the leap. It was Mao's formal if private announcement in the final article that he intended to retire from one of his two chairmanships, the post of head of state. He explained that this would give him more time to concentrate, as CCP Chairman, on party work; it would also be better for his health. The proposal had already been endorsed by the Politburo, and many cadres at the CC level and below had thought it a good idea. Now cadres at all levels should be informed and their views solicited; those who objected could be reassured that Mao could resume the state chairmanship in the event of a national emergency.[84]

I have argued in Volume I of this work that Mao's decision to retire from one of his posts was the first step in his retreat to what he called the 'second front' within the Politburo standing committee.[85] Mao had been appalled at the recent struggles for power in the Soviet Union and attributed them partly to the lack of prestige of Stalin's successors, notably his chosen heir-apparent, Malenkov. To prevent the same thing happening in China, Mao wished to build up his colleagues as credible national leaders in their own right, so that on his death they would have the standing to run the country. This he proposed to do by gradually handing over the reins of power while still alive, allowing the members of the 'first front' of the Politburo Standing Committee—Liu Shao-ch'i, Premier Chou En-lai, Ch'en Yun and Teng Hsiao-p'ing—to take more and more of the decisions. On further reflection, I believe one must also posit a canny desire by Mao to pre-empt comparisons of his role with Stalin's.

Mao's plan dated from 1956, and so the announcement of his impending retirement as head of state did not represent a self-criticism for the way in which the 1957 rectification campaign had gone off the rails. Nevertheless, some cadres may have speculated on this score, especially when, at the NPC within two weeks of Mao signing the Sixty Articles, the other leader held responsible for the bourgeois rightists' attacks on the CCP, Chou En-lai, also relinquished one of his posts, the Foreign Ministry.[86] I will examine the significance of Chou's move and show how Mao protected him in considering the second session of the CCP's 8th Congress.

(iv) The 1958 NPC session

The 1958 NPC was a watershed, the last major public occasion on which the Chinese leadership still seemed committed to relatively modest economic goals, albeit clothed in the language of the leap. The two main economic speakers, Finance Minister Li Hsien-nien and the Chairman of the State Economic Commission, Po I-po, both apologized for the conservatism of their departments in the winter of 1956–7.[87] But all that Li could say in praise of his new budget was that it 'opposes any tendency towards conservatism',[88] and the output targets for 1958 announced by Po were not extravagant: grain—196 million tons, 5·9 per cent up on 1957; cotton—1·75 million tons, 6·7 per cent up on 1957, both of which rates of increase Po could only characterize as 'fairly high' (*hsiang-tang kao*).[89] Nor were the industrial targets for 1958 any more exciting: steel—6,248,000 tons, 19·2 per cent up on 1957 as compared with a 17 per cent increase in 1957 over 1956; coal—150,724,000 tons, 17·2 per cent up on 1957 as compared with a 16·6 per cent increase in 1957 over 1956; and electric power—22,450 million kWh, 18 per cent up on 1957, as compared with the 14 per cent increase in 1957 over 1956.[90] Moreover, the higher rates of increase in steel and electric power could well have been forecast simply on the basis of the completion of a number of new plants the previous year rather than extra effort.[91]

Two significant figures did emerge, however, from the economic reports to the 1958 NPC. Li Hsien-nien announced that state aid to agriculture would increase considerably in 1958; in particular, state expenditure on agriculture (mainly on capital construction) would be 40·78 per cent up on 1957.[92] Almost a year after Mao had argued that 'as China is a great agricultural country, with over eighty per cent of its population in the villages, its industry and agriculture must be developed simultaneously',[93] the first steps were being taken to implement the policy.

Even more significant in influencing the course of developments during the rest of 1958 were the revelations about the success of the water conservancy drive since the publication of the joint CC–SC directive on the subject on 24 September 1957. The original plan for irrigation in the year October 1957 to September 1958 had been 43·9 million mou.[94] This had been raised in October 1957 to 61·8 million mou,[95] and then raised again to 92 million mou.[96] Po I-po was able to announce that the strenuous daily labours of 100 million men and women had resulted in the latest target being easily over-filled within four months; by 31 January 1958, 117 million mou had been irrigated.[97] It was later revealed that excessive emphasis on the storage of water during 1958 and 1959 resulted in a widespread increase in salinity and serious losses to agriculture in Hopei, Honan and Shantung.[98] But at the beginning of 1958 this impressive demonstration of what could be achieved by the massive use of disciplined battalions of peasant labour indicated that the 1958 'great leap forward'—the slogan proposed by Chou En-lai which emerged publicly as the national rallying cry at the end of the NPC[99]—could be organized on totally different principles from those of the leap of 1956. Armed with this knowledge, Mao set out again on his travels. By early March, when he arrived in Szechwan for the Chengtu conference, he was ready to demolish the remaining obstacles to an all-out production high tide.

3 THE CHENGTU CONFERENCE

Chengtu, the capital of Szechwan, stands in the middle of a vast plain known from time immemorial as the 'sea-on-land' because of the intricate irrigation system. Constructed by a provincial governor over 2,000 years ago, it transformed the plain into one of the most fertile and densely populated areas in the world.[1] The city reflected the prosperity of the surrounding countryside. Half a century earlier, the 'broad, clean streets, the gold-emblazoned shop signs, the myriad restaurants, wine and herb shops, or the great shops filled with precious Szechwan silks and foreign goods' of the Peking of the south-west had fired the imagination of the youthful Chu Teh.[2]

In the late 1950s, Chengtu had a population of just over a million, modest by Chinese standards.[3] But as the capital of the country's most populous province—over 72 million by this time—and the centre of one of the most important grain surplus areas, Chengtu's political weight was considerable.[4] It was increased by the high proportion of Szechwanese on the central committee and the calibre of the province's representation among the full members of the Politburo, where Chu Teh, Teng Hsiao-p'ing, Ch'en Yi and Liu Po-ch'eng made up the second biggest provincial group.[5] It had been Liu and Teng, as commander and political commissar of the communists' 2nd Field Army, who had played the major role in taking Szechwan from the Nationalists, though Chengtu itself had actually been liberated by the Hunanese Ho Lung.[6] These three men had stayed on during the early years of the communist regime and had run the whole of south-west China—Szechwan, Kweichow and Yunnan. Teng and Ho Lung maintained close links with Szechwan after they left, links that were later denounced as sinister by the Maoists of the cultural revolution.

In 1958, the key figure in Szechwan was the provincial party 1st secretary, Li Ching-ch'üan, a native of Kiangsi, who had fought in the armies of both Ho Lung and Liu Po-ch'eng and had been in Szechwan since its liberation.[7] The evidence suggests that during 1956–7 Li Ching-ch'üan had not been one of the supporters of Mao's experiment with liberalization[8]; but he had apparently responded more enthusiastically to Mao's attempts to launch a leap in 1956, when Szechwan had drawn up its own Twelve-Year Agricultural Programme after the national one was promulgated.[9] Despite allegations to the contrary during the cultural revolution, Li seems to have been an equally enthusiastic supporter of the 1958 leap.[10] Mao praised Li Ching-ch'üan at the Chengtu conference for his ability to keep cool under 'high tide' conditions,[11] and certainly seems to have singled out Li, along with the Shanghai party leader K'o Ch'ing-shih, the Chairman's loyal supporter during the previous year's rectification campaign, for favoured treatment.[12] During his visit to Szechwan, Mao made a number of inspection visits in town and country, usually escorted by Li and at least once by K'o as well[13]; and when on 28 March, after the end of the conference, the Chairman took ship in Chungking to make the three-day river trip through the Yangtse gorges to Wuhan, he was accompanied by Li, K'o and Wang Jen-chung, the Hupeh 1st secretary, another Mao favourite.[14] Clearly, if a leap was to be successful under conditions of decentralization, the keen support of provincial 1st secretaries was crucial; it was therefore not surprising that the most important of the pre-leap party conferences took place in one of the most important Chinese provinces and that Mao should display particular favour towards its leader.

(i) Mao v. parroting the Russians

In his three known speeches to the Chengtu conference,[15] Mao returned to the attack on the shackles that imprisoned the thinking of Chinese officials in an effort to liberate them so that they could boldly strive in the projected leap. His attack was on two fronts: against slavish adherence to the Soviet model and against excessive respect for experts. In his first speech on 10 March, Mao launched straight into the first topic:

Regulations and systems are a problem. Take, for example, the question of thinking methods: upholding principles and having a spirit of creativity. Internationally, we must be friends with the Soviet Union, all people's republics, the Communist parties and labour classes in various countries. That is a principle. In learning, however, there are two possibilities: one is concentrated copying, and the other is to have your own creative spirit. Learning should be coupled with creating; slavish copying of the Russian regulations and system lacks the spirit of creativity.[16]

Mao briefly reminded his audience of the unhappy history of the Chinese revolution during the period when it was led by dogmatists trained in or influenced by Moscow.[17] After the revolution, there had been a baneful Soviet influence in economic, cultural, educational and military affairs. Dogmatism in economics had been mainly in the spheres of heavy industry and planning, and also in banking and statistics; there had been less Soviet influence in commerce, light industry and agricultural collectivization and the socialist takeover of commerce and industry; this was due to the party centre's greater concern for and control over these areas.[18]

Mao explained that the Soviet Union had exerted this predominating influence 'because we knew nothing and were completely inexperienced, nobody could tell right from wrong. We were forced to copy others.' He recalled how for three years he had been forced not to eat eggs and chicken soup 'just because there was an article published in Russia saying that eggs and chicken soup were not good to eat. Later, they were said to be consumable. Whether the article was right or wrong, the Chinese all listened to it and followed its advice.' Even in education where the Chinese communists had their experience in the pre-1949 'liberated areas' to draw upon, the Soviet model was adhered to.[19] Mao could have added that many of his points merely echoed the criticisms of the 'bourgeois rightists' of the previous year.[20]

An additional problem had been that although China did have some experts in economics they belonged to the bourgeoisie and their influence had to be counteracted with Soviet advice. Furthermore, there had been 'no understanding of the overall economic situation, still less of the differences between the Russian and Chinese economic situation.'[21] However, Mao affirmed that a 'large proportion' of Soviet-style planning had been correct for China and now, moreover, Chinese could generally plan and construct big enterprises and had 'some understanding' of the differences between the two economies.[22]

If Mao wanted simply to erode excessive subservience towards the Soviet model, it would surely have been sufficient for him to have provided a series of examples similar to, if more serious than, the eggs and chicken soup story to demonstrate the dangers of blind copying; Chou En-lai, for instance, had warned the

Foreign Ministry some years earlier against copying the Soviet Union too closely in foreign affairs.[23] But Mao went further, for much of his speech was devoted to an analysis of Sino-Soviet policy differences since 1949. He had some interesting remarks to make on the Stalin personality cult: 'Chinese people used to be slaves and it appeared that they would continue that way. Whenever a Chinese artist painted a picture of me with Stalin, I was always shown shorter than Stalin.'[24] Mao distinguished between the 'correct' personality cult, which meant worshipping Marx, Engels, Lenin and Stalin for the truths they had propounded, and incorrect worshipping, which was simply blind obedience.[25]

In 1956, Stalin was criticised and repudiated. We felt glad on the one hand, worried on the other. To take off the cover, destroy blind obedience and liberate thoughts were completely necessary. To beat Stalin to death with a single stick was something however with which we don't agree. They don't hang his portrait, we hang it.[26]

Mao attacked Khrushchev for bringing pressure to bear on China with his sudden denunciation of Stalin, but though he asserted that most Chinese party members had resented this, he added, significantly, that some people had bowed to Soviet pressure and had wanted to pull down the personality cult. 'Some people are very interested in opposing personality cults.'[27] Here one senses Mao's resentment at the way in which some of his colleagues, notably Defence Minister P'eng Teh-huai, had taken advantage of de-stalinization to snipe at the Chairman's position.[28]

Mao's discussion of Khrushchev's mishandling of destalinization indicated his sensitivity at its repercussions within China, but it was in fact only one example he gave of Sino-Soviet disputes in the post-liberation period. Mao reminded his audience that the 'victory of the Chinese revolution was against Stalin's wishes'.[29] He told them that he had argued with Stalin for two months during his visit to Moscow immediately after the liberation and admitted that he had made important concessions on the mutual defence treaty and other matters:

Our attitudes were such that when he made a proposition which turned out to be unacceptable to me, then I would fight; and when he insisted on it, I would accept. It was so for the sake of socialism.[30]

The result was that China had been forced to accept 'colonies' in the north-east (formerly Manchuria) and Sinkiang (Chinese Tur-kestan). Only Chinese and Russians were allowed to live there.[31] Mao's frank acknowledgement that he had had to back down in the face of Soviet pressure must be remembered when considera-tion is given to charges that Liu Shao-ch'i and others colluded with Khrushchev at the 1960 Moscow conference of the world's communist parties.[32]

Despite the conclusion of the Moscow treaty, Stalin still con-sidered the Chinese revolution a 'fake' and did not change his mind until the Chinese showed their metal in the Korean war.[33] Even after that, Mao hinted, Stalin had flirted with Kao Kang—who was denounced within a year of Stalin's death.[34] Then came the disagreements over destalinization, and when Mao made his speech on internal contradictions in February 1957, the Russians apparently privately condemned it for 'promoting liberalism' and refused to accept the concept of contradictions between leaders and led in a communist country.[35]

While accepting Mao's penchant for historical reminiscing, it is difficult not to conclude from the length of his account of Sino-Soviet relations at Chengtu that he thought it necessary to put certain facts on the record for the benefit of senior members of the CCP. This is not to suggest that Mao already foresaw the bit-ter Sino-Soviet dispute of the 1960s; but in the light of relations between Moscow and Peking over the previous two years, Mao could understandably have felt that further conflict was conceiv-able, if not inevitable, and cadres should be mentally prepared for it. As part of this process, cultural collaboration with the Soviet Union was allegedly greatly reduced within weeks of the end of the Chengtu conference.[36]

But the immediate task was to emancipate China from the thralldom of the Soviet economic model. Mao dated the begin-ning of the process from his speech on ten great relationships of April 1956.[37] T'an Chen-lin, the agricultural overlord during the great leap forward, confirmed this indirectly in a speech at the end of 1958 when he stated that the destruction of the Stalin myth by Khrushchev (in February 1956) had also liberated people from superstitious reverence for the Soviet Union's experience in economic development.[38] The process of emancipation had con-tinued with Mao's speech on contradictions of February 1957 in which he had proposed 'the simultaneous development of industry and agriculture, the road to industrialisation, and the cooperativisation and birth control programs'.[39] Mao's reference to his advocacy of birth control—which had been excised from the official published text[40]—was striking because it suggested it was a policy innovation which he still stood by, whereas a key feature of the emerging great leap forward was to be a glorification of China's enormous population on the grounds that more people meant more production. As late as March, Mao seems still to have been groping for the strategy of the leap; but his attack on the Soviet model suggests that after three months of touring China his enthusiasm for Khrushchevian economics had worn thin. However much Khrushchev's attitudes towards development resembled Mao's, China's economic situation was totally different from the Soviet Union's and Mao would have been reminded of this everywhere he went. The Chinese, he must have concluded, had to go their own way.

(ii)   Mao denounces the experts

It was Mao's attack on his second target that was to be crucial to the evolution of the great leap strategy, for by diminishing respect for expertise he laid the foundations for exclusive reliance on the mass mobilization of labour. As recently as the end of January, Mao had been courting the bourgeois intellectuals. Even at Chengtu he suggested that more of the bourgeoisie supported the CCP as a result of rectification,[41] and at Hankow in April he advocated a 'cooling off' of the class struggle against them.[42] Other senior leaders—Teng Hsiao-p'ing, P'eng Chen, Ch'en Yi, K'o Ch'ing-shih—were deployed, even as late as July, to reassure the bourgeoisie about the new political atmosphere and their usefulness to the regime.[43] In return, the intellectuals 'gave their hearts' to the party, baring themselves in a new round of confessions.[44]

But despite this persisting ambivalence, the principal message that emerged from Chengtu was totally counter-productive to the effective employment of the bourgeoisie. In his final speech to the conference on 22 March, Mao launched a slashing attack on excessive respect for the 'professors':

Newcomers in big cities are always afraid of the professors. They are not despised, but just feared exceedingly. To see others with such enormous knowledge, one tends to think that he is good for nothing. Marxists are afraid of bourgeois intellectuals—not of imperialism but of professors— that's strange. I think this kind of mentality is also a remnant from the slave system of 'Thank God for his great blessings.' I don't think that one can stand it any longer.[45]

Mao pointed out that most of the world's intellectual innovators —Confucius, Jesus Christ, Buddha, Luther, Marx, Darwin, Sun Yat-sen—made their greatest contributions when quite young and without massive learning. The Chinese Communists, too, had started as youngsters in their twenties. 'As for knowledge, they had more; but as for truth, we had more.'[46]

Mao's message was that truth was more important than knowledge, redness superior to expertise. He did not say that truth or redness was sufficient by itself and as an educated dialectician in a position of leadership he has always been able to grasp both elements in a potential or actual contradiction. But the great majority of CCP members were short on knowledge, long on 'truth', and it was hardly surprising that with this sort of encouragement they should have given expertise short shift during the leap forward. In particular, criticism at Chengtu of dogmatism in statistical work undermined the position of the State Statistical Bureau, the watch-dog of economic realism, and paved the way for the grotesque exaggerations of the following three years.[47]

One practical method advocated by Mao for putting down the bourgeois intellectuals was the publication of magazines. He revealed that Ch'en Po-ta, his former political secretary and longtime confidant, most recently preoccupied with telling scientists to 'emphasise the present and down-play the past' (*hou chin po ku*),[48] had conquered his aversion to editing and agreed to run a new party theoretical journal; each province would be encouraged to put out a similar magazine of its own.[49] Mao left the organization of the provincial magazines to the provinces, asking only that they should submit half a dozen articles a year to the central journal. But he did provide one piece of intellectual stimulus: 'How about putting out some folk songs?'[50] Current poetry was unreadable; good new poetry, combining realism and romanticism, would have to be founded upon the folk song tradition.

Give everybody a few sheets of paper to write down some folk songs; get some people to write for labouring peasants who cannot write . . . . If we do it, we may obtain millions or tens of millions of folk songs. It won't consume much labour and makes one feel more comfortable than reading poems by Tu Fu and Li Po.[51]

Clearly Mao, as a poet, was appalled at the poetry produced in the name of socialist realism; but at the same time he wished to head off contemporary poets from emulating the classical styles he himself used.[52] Mao may also have intended swamping the professional poets and writers who had let him down during the 100 flowers period; certainly this was the effect of the tens of millions of folk songs which, as he had predicted, were collected or written during the great leap forward.[53]

(iii)   Honan points the way

Poetry aside, Mao did not launch the great leap forward at Chengtu; that was to be the function of the second session of the 8th Congress two months later. But his speech of 20 March formulated the general line of the great leap forward in its final form—'Go all out, aim high and achieve greater, faster, better and more economical results'[54]—and revealed that Honan province had already drawn up grandiose plans which other provinces felt compelled to emulate.

Honan's proposals were that certain of the principal goals of the Twelve-Year Agricultural Programme—the raising of grain yields by 100 per cent or more, a comprehensive water conservancy system, the elimination of the four pests and illiteracy[55]—should be achieved within one year. The four pests target alone illustrated the extent to which Honan's leaders, particularly the incoming 1st secretary Wu Chih-p'u, who had been Mao's student at the Peasant Movement Training Institute in Canton in the mid-1920s,[56] were in the grip of the mounting great leap fervour. Only a month earlier, the directive launching the nation-wide campaign against the four pests had contained a pledge that just five of Honan's cities and counties would eliminate them in 1958;[57] now the provincial leaders were prepared to aim for that target in every one of the well over 100 cities and counties for which they were responsible. All Honan's proposals were patently unrealizable and they placed Mao in a dilemma. He could not condemn them as 'impetuous and adventurist' for that risked damping enthusiasm for the leap, precisely the error for which he had blamed the planners who had halted the 1956 leap.[58] On the other hand, he was clearly reluctant to give provincial leaders *carte blanche*. He warned against publicizing targets and admonished other provinces not to aim as high as Honan.[59] If the Twelve-Year Programme took another eight or ten years to accomplish, this would not result in expulsion from the party. Mao foresaw that with this level of targets there was a strong possibility of 'very great shortcomings' in work and 'excessive tension' among the people.[60]

The speed of economic development is an objective thing. When something can be achieved, subjectively and objectively, then go all out, aim high and achieve greater, faster, better and more economical results; but if something can't be done then don't force it. Just now there's a puff of wind, a ten degrees typhoon. Don't obstruct it publicly. Get a clear picture of it in internal discussions. Compress the air a bit. Eliminate false reports and exaggerations. Don't vie for fame. Talk in concrete terms. It is not good if some targets are too high and can't be implemented. In sum, there must be concrete measures and one must talk in concrete terms. One must also discuss matters in terms of principles and politics, and revolutionary romanticism is good. But it's no use if there are no measures with which to implement things.[61]

Mao's cautionary words evidently had their effect. Honan's proposals would have meant aiming for a 100 per cent increase in grain production in 1958. But the Chengtu conference seems to have set guideline targets of a 10–20 per cent increase, and proposals of 18–27 per cent increases were apparently regarded as 'leftist'. Within three months, these latter proposals had begun to look middle-of-the-road, even 'rightist'.[62] Moreover, despite Mao's overt caution, he apparently encouraged intense competitiveness among provincial 1st secretaries by suggesting comparing provincial production increases after the autumn harvest.[63]

(iv)   The issue of agricultural mechanization

Even if doubts persisted after Chengtu as to the soundness of the targets proposed there, major increases in agricultural production were the order of the day, and the conference evidently discussed methods of achieving them. Mechanization was a key topic and a document entitled 'Opinions concerning the question of agricultural mechanisation' was drawn up and subsequently approved by the Politburo.[64] Since this question later provoked disagreements between Mao and some of his colleagues, it may be as well to sketch in the background.

Between the fifteenth and twentieth centuries, according to one scholar, China's farm implement technology was generally stagnant. 'On the north China plain, most tools used in the 20th century were well known as early as the Northern Wei Dynasty (fifth century AD) and perhaps the Han' (which fell in the third century AD).[65] This technological stagnation is unlikely to have been due to peasant conservatism; the most probable explanation is that progress was impossible without Diesel and electric engines.[66]

When the Chinese communists came to power, they had a naive belief that mechanization was a good thing in itself simply because it was widely used in the Soviet Union and the United States.[67] The only disagreement, between Mao and Liu Shao-ch'i, was whether or not mechanization had to precede collectivization as it had done in the Soviet Union. Liu accepted the Soviet model; Mao did not and proved his point with the successful, collectivization drive in the autumn of 1955.[68] Not that Mao scorned mechanization; on the contrary, in his collectivization speech of 31 July 1955, he stated:

If, in a period of roughly three five-year plans, we cannot fundamentally solve the problem of agricultural co-operation, if we cannot jump from small-scale farming with animal-drawn farm implements to large-scale farming with machinery . . . we shall fail to resolve the contradiction between the ever-increasing demand for marketable grain and industrial raw materials and the present generally poor yield of staple crops. In that case . . . we shall not be able to complete socialist industrialisation.[69]

Clearly Mao shared the fundamental Marxist error of believing agricultural productivity was inextricably linked with size[70]; hence his emphasis on mechanization. But by the mid-1950s some Chinese leaders were becoming aware of the importance of the difference in factor proportions, land and labour, between China and the Soviet Union. In 1956, Po I-po, the Chairman of the State Economic Commission, apparently stated that 'with such a large reservoir of manpower in the Chinese countryside and such complicated farming systems; it is impossible to introduce mechanisation . . . . If mechanisation is introduced, the problem of surplus labour power in the countryside will become so acute as to defy solution.'[71]

In the spring of 1957, a report, based it would seem on field research, was submitted to Mao and other leaders. It argued:

Judging by the condition of any state, the development of farm mechanisation is often the consequence of manpower shortage. The important role of farm mechanisation is to raise labour productivity, but its effect is insignificant where the raising of the per unit area output is concerned. . . .

Therefore, in view of the rich manpower and material resources of our country, the technical policy of farm mechanisation becomes debatable.[72]

This argument was endorsed by the Minister of Agriculture, Liao Lu-yen.[73]

But though superficially convincing, this thesis had weaknesses. Shortage of labour during the busiest periods of farm activity was a widespread phenomenon,[74] a fact which Mao doubtless remembered from his peasant youth.[75] Moreover the communists' encouragement of double cropping from 1956, after the advocacy of this means of increasing production in the Twelve-Year Agricultural Programme, increased the strain on the labour supply.[76] In 1955, Mao had expressed his belief that mechanization would not throw millions of peasants out of work in somewhat vague terms, but in the face of the arguments advanced by those who were cool towards mechanization he may have felt it necessary to commission a confirmed mechanizer, K'ang Sheng, an alternate member of the Politburo who emerged during the cultural revolution as one of his closest advisers, to do some research for him.[77]

The weight of Mao's arguments and prestige appear to have led to a compromise. Huang Ching, Chairman of the State Technological Commission, wrote in late 1957 that foreign farm machines were often unsuitable for the Chinese agricultural landscape and always consumers of scarce petroleum. But he criticized the 'biased' view that the objective of raising per unit yields was a direct contradiction to mechanization, and added:

Recently, we have organised a group of cadres and technicians and sent them to villages for field surveys. We have also talked with people in the agricultural and water conservation departments. We begin to understand the true conditions in the countryside, which are quite different from what we used to think. Chairman Mao's instructions concerning agricultural mechanisation have enabled us to understand this problem more clearly and to realise that our previous thought was erroneous.[78]

In this article and in another early in 1958, Huang Ching revealed that he was well aware that mechanization could help solve the problems of multiple cropping and the busy seasons.[79]

The essence of the compromise, codified in the Chengtu conference document 'Opinions concerning the question of agricultural mechanisation', was that the immediate task was the improvement of farm implements.[80] In his remarks on this subject at the conference, Mao said:

The mass movement to improve farming implements should be extended to all areas. The significance of it is tremendous—it is the start of a technical revolution, a great revolutionary movement. Hundreds of millions of people are working with their hands and feet. If we can get rid of shoulder-bearing labour, and implement this programme, we will be able to save many times on labour force. . . . *With this base further mechanization may be pursued*. China is such a big country that it is impossible to achieve complete mechanization.[81] (Emphasis added.)

The conference document completely endorsed this Maoist directive,[82] which, it is important to note, did not envisage any immediate leap into mechanization. The only concrete order contained in a directive issued by Mao in August was to discuss which tools could be fitted with ball-bearings.[83] And indeed, a pro-Maoist article on the mechanization question issued during the cultural revolution revealed that in September 1962 *and* in February 1966 the Chairman called for the 'basic' completion of agricultural mechanization in 25 years.[84] If the passage of three and a half years did not lead Mao to alter the length of his development programme, one must presume that he was thinking in loose terms when he referred to the quarter century.

In the absence of any further substantial remarks on mechanization by Mao at Chengtu, one must assume that other elements of what was later depicted as the Maoist strategy for mechanization were adumbrated in the conference document. These elements included reliance on APCs (Agricultural Producers' Cooperatives) for the development and management of mechanization and the decentralization of the manufacture of and research into agricultural machinery.

The possibility of relying on APCs to take charge of mechanization was apparently under investigation by K'ang Sheng as early as the summer of 1956,[85] a year in which the number of tractors in use went up by almost 150 per cent.[86] In that year, only about 11 per cent of the country's tractors were owned by APCs, nearly 37 per cent were owned by state farms, and over 50 per cent by agricultural machine stations modelled on the Soviet MTS (Machine Tractor Station).[87] For Stalin, the MTS's had been key elements in ensuring party control over the peasantry and the delivery of the harvest to the state.[88] But it is possible that K'ang was not as boldly innovative in wanting to break away from the Soviet model as cultural revolution sources have implied; quite probably the Soviet leadership was already privately debating the role of the MTS's when K'ang visited Eastern Europe in the spring of 1956.

As a result of K'ang's researches, experiments were initiated in 1957 in Heilungkiang and the Peking area. The Nanyuan agricultural machine station near Peking turned over its machines to APCs to manage while retaining ownership ('state ownership and cooperative management'), while the Paich'üan station in Heilungkiang turned its machines totally over to APCs ('cooperative ownership and management').[89] In January 1958, [90] the month in which Khrushchev announced that the MTS's would be abolished, the Chinese Ministry of Agriculture held a conference of heads of agricultural machine stations,[91] and a report on it approved the experiment. Liu Shao-ch'i, too, favoured the policy, apparently because he felt the tractor stations were not economic.[92] But the Chinese were far more circumspect than the Russians. The report reasserted that 'state-owned tractor stations remain the main form of agricultural mechanisation in our country at the present moment' and warned against the deviation of stations losing control or laying down the burden.[93] In March the Chengtu conference laid down that 'agricultural cooperatives must principally rely upon their own strength to realise agricultural mechanisation',[94] and when in May the 7th General Office of the State Council (supervising agricultural and related ministries) took formal note of the report on the January conference it stated that 'to place agricultural machinery under the management of APCs will facilitate the development of agricultural production'.[95] But the 7th General Office's comment was curiously ambivalent, for while it instructed the Ministry of Agriculture to investigate and report on the new problems that would result from the transfer of agricultural machinery to APCs it also agreed with the findings of the Ministry's report on the January conference which, as we have just seen, emphasized the continuing role of the agricultural machine stations. Consequently, although there was in 1958 a sevenfold expansion in the number of tractors owned by APCs (later the communes), this was evidently the result mainly of siphoning greatly increased imports to the collective sector; for in the same year the number of tractors in the possession of agricultural machine stations went down by less than 10 per cent.[96] This was in striking contrast to the Soviet Union where by the end of 1958 'most' of the MTS machinery had been transferred to the collective farms.[97] Khrushchev was far bolder than the Chinese.

The Chinese decision at Chengtu to assign the manufacture of farm tools and machinery to local industry was also cautiously phrased:

In regard to manufacture of farm machines (including machine-drawn farm implements, new-type animal-drawn farm implements and improved farm tools), *with the exception of large farm machines and those with relatively high technical standard, generally* the emphasis should be given to local industry. Arrangements may be made by the various localities or through the various coordinated working zones in the light of local conditions and needs. The relevant departments of the central government should help them with respect to techniques and exchange of experience. *In those places where the local industry is relatively weak in foundation, and where this problem cannot be solved by mutual readjustments between provinces in a coordinated working zone, the relevant departments of the central government should work out the readjustments.*[98] (Emphasis added.)

When one considers that in the Soviet Union in the previous year, Khrushchev had instituted a wholesale decentralization of the massive economic structure built up by Stalin over the course of decades, these Chinese measures in the field of agricultural machinery production, so loudly trumpeted in retrospect by the cultural revolutionaries, seem almost hesitant by comparison.[99]

In two other aspects of the new mechanizations strategy, Mao had already given a personal lead. In January 1958, he proposed that provincial authorities should set up research institutes to take 'exclusive responsibilities' for studying improved farm tools and medium and small farm machines.[100] Sensibly he did not suggest that research into advanced farm machinery should be conducted at provincial level. In the same month Mao also spearheaded a rehabilitation of the double-bladed, double-wheeled ploughs, the white elephant of the 1956 leap.[101] He visited the Chekiang Agricultural Research Institute and on 28 January the *People's Daily* published a picture of him being shown the use of a double-bladed, double-wheeled plough. Significantly, the venue was a province in the south where in 1956 these ploughs had proved difficult to use in wet paddy fields. Three days later the provincial newspaper published an editorial extolling the ploughs,[102] and at the end of February a conference was held (probably also in

Chekiang[103]) to exchange experience on the use of these ploughs in the south. The conference was addressed by the Minister of Agriculture, Liao Lu-yen,[104] allegedly one of the ministers who had decried the ploughs a year earlier as pretentious, describing them as the equivalent of 'planting onions in the pig's nose—to make the pig look like an elephant'.[105]

That description did not make Liao an anti-Maoist as later alleged; as recently as October 1957, Mao had told the SSC that the 6 million target for the ploughs in the original draft programme had been pure 'subjectivism' and had been eliminated.[106] But at any rate, by February 1958, Liao Lu-yen was concerned to 'restore the reputation' (hui-fu ming-yü) of these same ploughs.[107] It is possible that Mao insisted on this as a symbolic rehabilitation of the reputation of the 1956 leap. He is said to have told the Chengtu conference that in studying problems attention had to be paid to ideas, for some problems were ideological by nature; the double-bladed, double-wheeled ploughs which had been destined for the scrap heap were now in short supply and this was an ideological problem.[108]

But it is also possible that China's leaders agreed that if there were to be a major push on the agricultural front, the country could not afford to throw away the 800,000 ploughs that had been stockpiled in 1957,[109] especially if with modifications these tools could be used even in wet paddy fields, as a joint ministerial directive declared on 10 March.[110] But however many leaders were prepared to promote the use of the ploughs, caution prevailed here too. The ploughs had been singled out for mention in the January 1956 version of the Twelve-Year Agricultural Programme, but were dropped from the revised version presented to the CC's 3rd plenum in October 1957. The evidence suggests that they were not restored in the second revised version discussed at the second session of the CCP's 8th Congress in May 1958.[111]

But even if Mao and his senior colleagues were themselves as cautious about mechanization as they were on production targets, the atmosphere of the Chengtu conference was not calculated to restrain those provincial leaders who attended it.[112] By criticizing the Soviet model and the bourgeois experts, Mao undermined two important elements for caution in economic policy-making. By criticizing Chou En-lai and Ch'en Yun again at Chengtu, he had neutralized the two principal guardians of caution in economic policy-making.[113] Moreover, he even diminished the impact of his own words of warning by indicating that he had no objection to viewpoints contrary to his own, an attitude that was also spelled out by Teng Hsiao-p'ing at the conference.[114] The Chengtu conference thus played a crucial role in unshackling the thought of Chinese senior cadres—significantly, Teng told the conference Mao had been working for this ever since the Soviet 20th Congress[115]—and prepared them mentally to devise the extravagent plans and promises of the great leap forward.

4 THE LEAP IS LAUNCHED

The second session of the party's 8th Congress, which opened in Peking on 5 May, marked the culmination of the five-month period of mobilization which had started with Liu Shao-ch'i's public call to overtake Britain in 15 years.[1] During that period Mao and his colleagues had toured the country, held conferences, heard reports and issued exhortations. The time was now adjudged ripe to set the seal on this process by officially launching the great leap forward with the full panoply of a party congress.

The 1958 congress session represented the high point of the Mao-Liu alliance on development policy. Both men committed themselves, Liu publicly, Mao privately, to an all-out economic drive based primarily on the mass mobilization of China's 500 million peasants. Yet, even in this moment of greatest solidarity, the two men revealed plainly the gulf between their philosophies which does much to explain the final split between them during the cultural revolution.

(i) Liu: organized mobilization

Liu Shao-ch'i gave the main report to the congress on behalf of the CC. There was nothing surprising about this; he had performed the same role at the first session 18 months earlier. But in the context of 1958 Liu's role was politically more significant.

Although Liu's 1956 speech revealed important differences between him and Mao, it was essentially a *tour d'horizon*, a situation report on 11 years of revolution and rule.[2] Liu's 1958 speech, on the other hand, was specifically designed to launch a new campaign, and a comparison with the 1957 rectification campaign is revealing.

Then, Mao had to make the running, utilizing his position as head of state to deliver the keynote speeches to two SSCs. Liu apparently addressed neither of these sessions; nor did he speak at the party's national propaganda conference at which Mao delivered another important speech. Liu confined himself to addressing provincial party organizations, and on somewhat different lines from Mao, a clear indication that he was not prepared whole-heartedly to endorse the campaign.[3]

Now, Liu was aligning himself behind Mao, and this campaign could be launched publicly at a *party* occasion, not behind closed doors at a less important *state* occasion.[4] The Chairman could thus be confident that this time, unlike the previous year, he would have the great bulk of senior and middle-rank party officials supporting his policy.[5] For all his willingness boldly to strike out on his own, Mao was probably not unhappy to be going 'through channels'.

Moreover, Liu's exposition of the agreed policy embodies an attitude towards Mao that was in marked contrast to the tone of his report to the first session of the 8th Congress. In that 1956 speech, Liu mentioned Mao by name only in a few places and his objective seemed to be to downgrade the Chairman's role.[6] In his speech to the 1958 session, the tone of Liu's remarks about Mao reverted to the wholly laudatory one he had adopted when reporting to the party's 7th Congress in 1945.[7] He recalled approvingly all Mao's policy initiatives over the previous three years, even though he carefully distinguished between those that had and those that did not have formal CC backing at the time.[8] In particular, he praised Mao's attempts to push forwards economic development at a faster pace: his preface to *Socialist Upsurge in China's Countryside*,[9] his slogan 'more, faster, better, and more economically',[10] the Twelve-Year Agricultural Programme[11] and his speech on ten great relationships (now outlined in public for the first time in Liu's speech).[12] Liu summed up this review by asserting that 'These guiding lines and policies formulated by Comrade Mao Tse-tung have played a tremendous role in our work.'[13] And on the speed of economic development, Liu asserted that the CC and Mao had been as one since 1949; they had 'always taken a clear-cut stand, insisting that the method of working faster and better be adopted and the other method, of working slowly and not so well, be rejected.'[14]

According to Liu, the success of the rectification and anti-rightist campaign had led to a 'great revolutionary drive for socialist construction', and Mao's calls for faster economic development had 'quickly gripped the imagination of the huge army of hundreds of millions of working people and have been transformed into an immense material force'.[15]

As a result, the spring of 1958 had already witnessed the start of a leap forward on every front. Industrial output was 26 per cent higher in value in the first four months of 1958 as compared with 1957; the April increase was 42 per cent. Steel output in 1958 would be 7·1 million tons, coal would be 180 million tons. The rate of growth would be far higher than that set in the original plan and would surpass that of any year in the first plan.[16] On the agricultural front, the most striking leap had been in irrigation which had given proof of the masses' 'power to conquer nature'.[17]

After sketching surging progress in other fields, Liu summed up in a passage that conveyed the essence of the great leap forward:

The fact is that the growth of the social productive forces calls for a socialist revolution and the spiritual emancipation of the people; the victory of this revolution and emancipation in turn spurs a forward leap in the social productive forces; and this in turn impels a progressive change in the socialist relations of production and an advance in man's ideology. In their ceaseless struggle to transform nature, the people are continuously transforming society and themselves.[18]

Karl Marx prophesied that the proletarian revolution would usher us into a great epoch when 'twenty years are concentrated in a day'. If in past revolutionary struggles we experienced such great times, then is not our present socialist construction another great time again? Here one can see how the courageous and hard-working Chinese people, under the leadership of the great Chinese Communist Party and its leader Comrade Mao Tse-tung, have poured forth their history-making strength and wisdom in endless measure.[19]

In this passage one can see that Liu envisaged the leap being achieved by a combination of party leadership and the energies of the masses. In another passage he emphasized the importance of the human element in economic development:

It should be realised that machines are made and operated by men, and materials are produced only through the efforts of men. It is man that counts; the subjective initiative of the masses is a mighty driving force.[20]

Mao himself could hardly have expressed it better.

But a comparison of the two men's speeches to the congress does reveal a significant difference in their approach to the leap, even though it is to some extent disguised by their shared belief in the primacy of men over machines.

For Liu, it was essential that the energies of the masses be harnessed and organized. Party leadership was crucial; indeed one whole passage was devoted to it.[21] Elsewhere he talked of the need 'to mobilize' the biggest labour force in the world, the importance of the 'organized' revolutionary peasants of China for economic development.[22] Even when he stressed the significance of innovators who think, speak and act with daring, he went on to say that only by relying on such people 'can we *lead* the people of the whole country in making one forward leap after another' (emphasis added).[23]

(ii)   Mao: unleashed energy

While Mao would not have denied the need for party leadership, it is significant that in none of his five known speeches to the congress does he mention it. Apart from this negative evidence, there are also positive indications that for him the essence of the leap was *unleashing* more than *organizing* the energies of the masses. In a key passage in his first speech to the congress on 8 May, Mao stated:

The initiative and creativity of the labour people have always been abundant. In the past, they were held in restraint under the old system. Now they have been liberated and have begun to produce results. Our method is to lift the lid, break down superstition, *and let the initiative and creativity of the labouring people explode (pao-fa-ch'u-lai).*[24] (Emphasis added.)

In his second and third speeches, on 17 and 20 May, Mao attacked the Stalinist concept that 'cadres decide everything'. If that were the case, 'what about the masses?' he asked.[25] In his fourth speech on 23 May, the final day of the congress, Mao made his point even more explicit:

Take the problem of whom to follow. Whom should one follow first of all? First of all, one should learn from the people and follow them. The people have so much energy, [they are imbued with the spirit of] more, faster, better, and more economically, [they are the source of] many inventions and creations . . . . This is why we follow the people first, and afterwards the people follow us. Theory first comes from practice, and then it guides practice.[26]

In another revelatory passage, Mao discussed the suggestion by one congress delegate that one could not go wrong if one followed the Chairman:

This statement needs modification. One should follow and yet not follow. An individual is sometimes right and sometimes wrong. Follow him when he is right and do not follow him when he is wrong. One must not follow without discrimination. We follow Marx and Lenin, and we follow Stalin in some things. We follow whoever has the truth in his hands. *Even if he should be a manure carrier or a street sweeper, as long as he has the truth he should be followed.*[27] (Emphasis added.)

Suitably modest sentiments indeed; but what is glaringly absent from this statement is any hint of the orthodox view (to which Liu subscribed[28]) that the *party* rather than any *individual* might be the repository of truth!

It is striking also that in his strenuous efforts both at the Chengtu conference and at the congress to persuade cadres to cast off 'superstition', to convince them that they could accomplish anything provided they dared to think, talk and act, Mao adduced precedents that were almost exclusively examples of individual achievement.[29] All in all, it is difficult to escape the conclusion that Mao saw a successful leap as being the product of the efforts of 600 million individual Chinese united in boldness and purpose more than by the communist party.

Of course, if anyone had challenged Mao at the congress session, he would unquestionably have affirmed his belief in the role of party leadership; he could have cited remarks made by himself over a number of years to that effect.[30] But while Mao clearly appreciated the ability of the party to mobilize and organize the Chinese population, there can be little doubt from the quotations cited above that the Chairman envisaged the great leap as a voluntarist explosion of energy more than a supreme example of mass mobilization.

Clearly a party whose role was to unleash rather than to lead was not in the last analysis irreplaceable. But Mao was not to come to that realization for the better part of another decade. For the moment his differences with Liu were philosophical and subterranean and probably not fully appreciated by either. Both intended that the CCP should play a major role in the leap.

(iii) Mao protects the planners

Mao and Liu were probably more conscious of their differing attitudes towards the opponents of the leap, even though there is no indication that these differences caused major friction.

As early as November 1957, after the CC's 3rd plenum had endorsed a return to the high tide policies of early 1956, Liu took up and developed Mao's plenum characterization of the two approaches to economic policy, but underlined that they represented a split between people:

There are two ways to accomplish this task [economic construction]: one way is to do things quicker and better, and the other to do things slower and aim at lower standards. Which way should we adopt? The Central Committee of the Party considers that the former way should be adopted and the latter rejected. . . . The facts in the last two years have proved that vague doubt and rejection harboured by some people hinder the advance of our cause, damage the socialist initiative of the masses, and prevent the mobilisation of potentialities, and result not in the achievement of quantity and speed, nor in quality and economy, but in greater waste of manpower, money and resources.[31]

In his speech to the second session of the 8th Congress, Liu returned to this theme, this time associating Mao with the view that there were two methods of carrying on socialist construction. In particular he quoted Mao's preface to the book *Socialist Upsurge in China's Countryside*, published two year's earlier, in which the Chairman accused those who opposed speedier economic development of rightist conservatism.[32] It was at this point that Liu went into some detail about Mao's various proposals over the previous two years for speeding up economic development, giving them his full approval.[33] Liu concluded this passage with a reference to those who were less approving of leap-type policies:

Many of those comrades who expressed misgivings about the principle of building socialism by achieving 'greater, faster, better and more economical results', have learned a lesson from all this. But some of them have not learned anything. They say: 'We'll settle accounts with you after the autumn harvest'. Well, let them wait to settle accounts. They will lose out in the end![34]

The reference to the autumn harvest is not difficult to comprehend; the size of that harvest would indicate whether or not the leap had been a success in agriculture. Clearly the opponents of the leap anticipated that it would throw agriculture into confusion and so result in a smaller harvest.

Liu's systematic and detailed description of the debate unquestionably left the impression of a fundamental cleavage over what he described as the 'most important question' confronting the party since the victory of the socialist revolution.[35] Liu's objective was presumably to utilize his alliance with the Chairman to undermine the position of anyone in the SC who might challenge the party's handling of the leap, and in particular to consolidate his position *vis-à-vis* the one man he must have regarded as a serious threat to his prospects of taking over from Mao: Chou En-lai.

Mao, too, in his speeches to the congress session referred to post-harvest account-settlers; but he added the category of 'tide-watchers', apparently fence-sitters who did not either espouse or denounce the leap but would join the winning side when the 'accounts' were drawn up.[36] Moreover, while Liu prophesied defeat *tout court* for the account settlers, Mao argued that they must be struggled against in order 'to unite with them, not to exclude them from the revolution.'[37]

Mao's attitude, like that of Teng Hsiao-p'ing at Chengtu, seems consistently to have been that opposition to rapid economic growth was error—'rightist conservatism' he had dubbed it in the preface cited by Liu at the congress—but not a fundamental mistake in political line. This was important because a difference of line would have entailed a major intra-party struggle; the cultural revolution, for instance, was described as a struggle between two lines.

At the congress, Mao played down the seriousness of the transgressions of the 'tide-watchers' and 'account-settlers' by describing them as being in most cases guilty only to the extent of one finger in ten.[38] They had to be won over by repeated explanations of domestic developments.[39]

Mao's dilemma was that he wished to neutralize potential opposition to the leap from government bureaucrats but protect the bureaucrats' political masters, a group of men which included some of his oldest and most loyal associates. In 1956, the opponents of that year's leap had included Premier Chou En-lai, Ch'en Yun, the first ranking Deputy Premier, Li Hsien-nien, Deputy Premier and Finance Minister, whose department Mao regarded as particularly blameworthy, Teng Tzu-hui, Deputy Premier and Director of the SC office in charge of agriculture, and Po I-po, Deputy Premier and Chairman of the State Economic Commission.[40]

By 1958, most of these men had accepted that they could not resist a new leap. Chou En-lai had already criticized himself as the man principally responsible for opposition to the 1956 leap.[41] Li Fu-ch'un and Li Hsien-nien were drafted into the party secretariat after the second session of the 8th Congress. Po I-po, as a long-time associate of Liu Shao-ch'i, would not have found uncongenial the transfer of influence over economic policy to him from Chou En-lai.[42] If there were 'account-settlers' or 'tide-watchers' among the group, the most likely candidates were Teng Tzu-hui—who was denied effective control over agriculture during the leap as he had been during collectivization in 1955 for similar reasons[43]—and, to judge by his previous behaviour, Ch'en Yun. Significantly, the photograph chosen for publication in the *People's Daily* after the congress session included all PSC members except Ch'en Yun.[44]

But the crucial issue for Mao was that none of these men (with the possible exception of Po I-po) would push policy disagreements with him to the extent of a major political confrontation, whereas his ally on the leap, Liu Shao-ch'i, had revealed the previous year that he and his associates (like P'eng Chen) were prepared to do precisely that in the dispute over the rectification campaign.[45] Mao could not afford to abandon his more loyal supporters and allow himself to become dependent on allies less committed to or reliant upon him personally. Thus while Liu hinted that the difference over economic policy amounted to a difference on 'line'—without Mao's backing he could not say it explicitly—Mao was at pains to play down the seriousness of the disagreement. (Teng Hsiao-p'ing supported Mao on this point, only to be denounced for his attitude during the cultural revolution![46])

Most significantly, Mao went out of his way to defend Chou En-lai by praising his anti-rightist speech at the NPC in June 1957 and implying strongly that this was when Chou abandoned his opposition to leap-type policies.[47] The reason for this was presumably to establish that Chou had seen the light *before* the 3rd plenum in September 1957, which was probably the occasion of Chou's self-criticism,[48] and so dispel the image of the Premier as the leader of a faction that had lost out on a major policy issue on that occasion. Liu, on the other hand, never referred to any change of heart as taking place before the 3rd plenum, which even Mao had to admit was the occasion for the official change of policy.[49]

Mao also headed off attacks on Chou En-lai and his colleagues by painting in black colours the dangers that would ensue from a party split, an eventuality that he characterized in two speeches as a disaster to be ranked in the same category as a world war:

> If the party should split, there would be chaos for a time. If there are people who do not consider the overall situation, like X X X and Kao Kang, the party will split and imbalance will appear, though balance will return. . . . It is even more important for the members of the Central Committee to consider the overall situation. Whoever fails to do so will fail. . . . Did those disregarding the overall situation and clamouring for splits have a good ending?[50]
>
> We must prevent possible disasters, such as world war, or party splits.[51]

Whatever Liu's personal ambitions, Mao could expect to touch a responsive chord in him with this kind of appeal.[52]

(iv) The party asserts itself in relation to the government

If Mao was able to safeguard the leading members of the SC, he had no wish to defend the bureaucrats whom they led. His attack on the Finance Ministry at the Nanning conference had indicated his belief that the central bureaucracy was a conservative force that had to be made submissive to the more radical party leadership. Decentralization, which he had advocated since his speech on the ten great relationships in April 1956,[53] was the means by which he hoped to accomplish this, and the decrees which the SC finally produced in November 1957, after some prodding and 18 months gestation, transferred considerable powers over industry, commerce and finance downwards to the provincial authorities, effectively the provincial party committees.[54] The three main decrees, later supplemented by detailed reforms in the fields of taxation, price control, grain management, planning and materials distribution management, resulted in the handing over of 80 per cent of the central government's enterprises to provincial control by June 1959.[55] Among the effects of this accretion of provincial powers were that 'the share of the gross value of industrial output produced by enterprises under provincial and sub-provincial management increased from 54 per cent in 1957 to an estimated 73 per cent in 1958', while in the financial field the spending of the central government declined by 14 per cent in 1958 and the spending of the provinces increased by almost 150 per cent to comprise over half of total government spending.[56]

The recent revelation that the financial resources to be

transferred to the provinces over the course of three years were not to exceed 3–3·6 billion yuan, plus $45–50 million in foreign exchange, seems to confirm earlier analysis indicating that, despite the apparently wholesale transfer of power, Mao's *bête noir*, the Finance Ministry, was astute enough to ensure that it retained a great deal of its former leverage.[57] Ironically, Ch'en Yun, who masterminded the decentralization programme (with the assistance of Li Hsien-nien in the case of finance), was accused during the cultural revolution of having distorted Mao's ideas and of being 'leftist' in form but rightist in essence because the new dispensation deprived the state of vital revenue and had to be altered a year later. In fact, Ch'en had made it clear at the CC's 3rd plenum in September 1957 that the decentralization measures would be open to revision after a year in the light of developments. Ch'en anticipated the potential negative consequences of decentralization and had told the plenum that it had to be accompanied by reinforced efforts to achieve an overall national balance.[58] Thus, although the State Council and its ministries did lose much power—and the number of ministries was retrenched from the 1957 peak of 41 to 33 in 1958 and 30 in 1959—overall central supervision of the economy was not abandoned. The intention seems to have been to transfer it to the party secretariat whose links with provincial party committees placed that organ in a key position to play a supervisory role.

The projected task of the secretariat was indicated at the CC's post-Congress 5th plenum. Li Fu-ch'un, Chairman of the State Planning Commission, and Finance Minister Li Hsien-nien were inducted into the secretariat, presumably to enable them to exercise leadership through the party machine. Ch'en Yun, who had been in overall charge of the 1st FYP and the importation of industrial plants from the Soviet Union,[59] was not brought into the secretariat: that would have posed protocol problems since he formally outranked General Secretary Teng Hsiao-p'ing. From Mao's viewpoint, this was fortunate since the Chairman could legitimately have feared that Ch'en Yun's keenness on overall supervision would frustrate the effectiveness of decentralization; and indeed this may have been why Ch'en's speech to the 3rd plenum was not published. At the same time, the fourth-ranking member of the secretariat, T'an Chen-lin, who had been playing a major part in agricultural policy since the previous autumn, was made a full member of the party's Politburo. T'an's promotion enabled him to outrank Deputy Premier Teng Tzu-hui, and to assume the legitimacy the role of agricultural *supremo* during the leap.[60]

These moves did not merely enable the secretariat to play a key role in the economy; they also raised its status within the overall political scene. Previously only its two leading officials— General Secretary Teng Hsiao-p'ing and P'eng Chen—had been in the Politburo.[61] Now five out of nine secretariat officials were Politburo members: Teng, P'eng, the two Li's and T'an.

However, there was a significant difference between the CCP secretariat and that of the CPSU under Khrushchev at this time. The Soviet party leader had staffed the secretariat with his own supporters and when he defeated the anti-party group in the summer of 1957, he simply promoted secretariat members into the Presidium to replace those he had purged. The political allegiances of the five Politburo members in the CCP secretariat were too diverse for there to be any immediate prospect of that organ becoming a 'tightly-knit group of politically-motivated men' under Teng's leadership.[62] The links of Teng and T'an were directly with Mao.[63] P'eng Chen's first allegiance was to Liu Shao-ch'i.[64] Li Fu-ch'un and Li Hsien-nien probably remained loyal to Premier Chou En-lai despite their new concurrent appointments under Teng. Moreover, Chou took the precaution of sitting in on meetings of the secretariat, presumably to monitor its activities personally.[65]

If, therefore, it was unlikely that the CCP secretariat would achieve a dominant position on the Chinese political scene, there were plenty of indications of the party machine's powerful new role in 1958. Up till the end of 1957 it had been comparatively rare for the SC to issue decrees jointly with the party's CC. There was one joint decree in 1955, four in 1956 and seven in 1957. In 1958 the figure leapt to 17, the subjects dealt with being mainly agriculture and commerce. The number was to fall to 12 in 1959 and then, dramatically, to five in 1960, none in 1961, two in 1962 and none in 1963 as the SC reasserted its prime role in the direction of the economy.[66]

Another indication of the reduced role of the governmental machine was the drop in the number of plenary meetings of the SC. Whereas there had been 26 in 1957, there were only 16 in 1958, and the figure was to fall to nine in 1959.[67] There was a similar decline in the number of meetings of the standing committee of the NPC, from 37 in 1957 to 13 in 1958.[68] To a considerable extent, these figures also reflected the different, 'guerrilla-style' leadership practised during the leap forward. Senior party officials spent more time travelling the country, exhorting and instructing on the spot; there was less time and inclination for formal meetings back in the capital, with orders subsequently passed at deliberate pace down the hierarchy.

Two other promotions at the post-congress CC plenum provided further evidence of the enhanced role of the party machine after decentralization. The elevation to the Politburo of K'o Ch'ing-shih, the Shanghai 1st secretary, and Li Ching-ch'üan, the 1st secretary of Szechwan province and Teng Hsiao-p'ing's former subordinate there, underlined the new importance of the provincial-level party committees. Presumably these particular provincial leaders were chosen in large part because of the importance of their commands: Shanghai was the main source of funds for central government expenditure, accounting for 17·6 per cent during the 1st FYP and 33·2 per cent in 1958[69]; Szechwan was the country's most populous province and one of its richest granaries. But Mao's intervention may have been necessary in the case of K'o if, as seems likely, his support for the Chairman's rectification policies in 1957 had alienated many of his peers.[70] The significance of these two men's promotions was underlined by their inclusion, along with another provincial 1st secretary, Ulanfu of Inner Mongolia (already an alternate member of the Politburo), in the somewhat unusual photograph published at the end of the congress.[71]

But if the great leap was to represent a high-water mark in the power of provincial party officials, the congress also served to remind them of the penalties of failure in the months ahead. Purges of senior provincial leaders in 11 provinces were considered and agreed at the congress. Most of them were accused of, among other things, advocating the kind of conservative policies in the countryside that were anathema to the proponents of the leap.[72] Mao himself seems to have believed that the purges in fact represented no more than the culmination of provincial struggles for power.[73] But since they were certainly the product of his own attack on rightist party officials at the Tsingtao conference ten months earlier, the Chairman was in a poor position to criticize.[74] Indeed by the time of the congress he had accepted the conventional verdict and accused the purge victims of being splitters.[75] He could only try to temper the wind to some of the shorn lambs.[76]

(v) The party asserts itself in relation to the PLA

If the congress session and the subsequent CC plenum witnessed an accretion of power for the party *apparat* with regard to the government machine, the two-month meeting of the CC's Military Affairs Committee (MAC), which also followed hard upon the congress, represented an assertion of party supremacy over the military. More concretely, it marked the beginning of Mao's struggle to compel the PLA to eschew the Soviet model and return to its Yenan guerrilla traditions.

Mao's task should have been made easier by his achievement in getting Khrushchev to provide China with assistance in the field of nuclear weapons technology. The promise of a Chinese nuclear capability had been the basis on which, two years earlier, Mao had been able to win a majority of his colleagues over to the view that defence spending on modern conventional weapons could be cut back in favour of investment in economic growth.[77] That promise seemed capable of speedier fulfilment with Soviet aid and any demands of the generals for conventional weapons could be more readily brushed aside. As a result, Defence Minister Marshal P'eng Teh-huai, who had in the past argued that China should concentrate on modernizing its conventional forces, leaving the nuclear role to the Soviet Union,[78] seems to have conceded victory on this front to Mao by early 1958. In a speech on 22 January, P'eng endorsed the Maoist position that 'the modernisation of our army must be established on the basis of national industrialisation', thereby implicitly abandoning any hope of a short cut to military modernization by means of wholesale purchases from the Soviet Union.[79]

Instead, P'eng seems to have decided to concentrate his defences against any attempt to increase political work in, and controls over, the PLA. A new PLA training programme issued in January smacked of a placatory compromise. On the one hand, the object of training in the future should be 'to continue improving modern military techniques, and to learn the coordination of the various branches of the army in combat under the modern conditions of atom bombs, chemical warfare and guided missiles ... so that the army may be ready at all times to deal with any emergency'.[80]

But among the basic tasks of training, 'the two most important tasks listed are to increase the political consciousness of all personnel and to study Comrade Mao Tse-tung's writings on military matters'. The historical lessons of China's revolution had also to be learned, i.e. Yenan experience was still relevant and should not be discarded in favour of Soviet treatises on modern warfare.[81] These concessions were apparently insufficient, for the programme seems never to have been referred to again.[82]

On 22 February, P'eng Teh-huai made a long speech on the occasion of the 40th anniversary of Soviet Army Day during the course of which he both defended learning from the Soviets and absolved the PLA from falling down in its political tasks by arguing that the Soviet Red Army had handled correctly three crucial relationships—between the army and party, the army and civilians and officers and men—and the PLA had adapted this experience to Chinese conditions.[83] A further propitiatory gesture was his recommendation that the PLA should use rectification methods to improve these relationships further—an endorsement he had refrained from giving during the rectification campaign the previous year.[84] However, he did not apparently stress the need to study Mao's military writings.

To judge by subsequent developments, this speech also failed in its apparent objective, but one further aspect of it deserves mention. In discussing strategic problems, Marshal P'eng made the presence of fully armed imperialist forces with modern weapons on China's doorstep and the need to liberate Taiwan the justification for arguing that the Soviet and Chinese armies together must safeguard peace *in the Far East* and the world.[85] The *People's Daily* editorial the following day confined itself to the customary less specific and therefore more innocuous formula to the effect that the peoples and the armies of the two countries must struggle together to safeguard the communist bloc and world peace.[86] Was P'eng flying a kite for joint Sino-Soviet defence arrangements? And if so, had this idea been suggested to him by Malinovsky during his Moscow visit? We shall see that the Russians formally suggested certain joint defence arrangements in the second half of 1958 to which Mao reacted violently. If the Chinese Defence Minister were prepared to endorse the Soviet proposal, it would certainly have deepened the rift between him and the party Chairman.

Mao was doubtless aware that his attempt to increase political control over the PLA would be resisted, because of his increasing estrangement from P'eng Teh-huai in recent years, as well as for professional reasons. Moreover, if there were resistance, he had to assume that it could be powerful since there were seven marshals in the Politburo—a position of political pre-eminence deriving from the key role of the PLA in the Chinese communist victory and one never achieved by the Soviet military. Nor would Mao have forgotten that he had been disobeyed on occasion by P'eng and other generals, even though they had never questioned his party leadership.[87]

The Chairman's first act, therefore, was to raise up a potential rival to P'eng Teh-huai, and in the light of subsequent events the elevation of Marshal Lin Piao to membership of the Politburo Standing Committee was the most significant promotion at the post-congress plenum. The relatively young (51) but normally invisible and presumably ailing marshal thus became one of the seven top men in China. His political seniority to P'eng Teh-huai, which had been gradually built up since 1954, was now plainly visible. Less obvious, but presumably well-known to members of the Chinese leadership, was the long-standing antipathy between Lin and P'eng.[88] Although Mao could not have foreseen the setbacks to the great leap and P'eng's exploitation of them, it does seem likely that he was placing his acolyte Lin into a position from which to dominate the Defence Minister.[89]

The only practicable organizational method of asserting that dominance was through the MAC in which Mao had been supreme since 1935. The MAC had apparently been largely dormant since the communists came to power, possibly because Mao had been busy with the establishment of the new regime.[90] It seems that after P'eng Teh-huai returned from the Korean war and became Defence Minister, he was effectively left in charge of the MAC, possibly as senior Vice Chairman. But although he and his subordinates from the General Staff were probably able to control the MAC, P'eng allegedly resented the idea of party supervision and would have preferred to see the MAC abolished or replaced with a less prestigious body not directly responsible to the CC.[91] Lin Piao's promotion meant that the MAC could have a Vice Chairman politically senior to P'eng Teh-huai, with the requisite revolutionary prestige and professional knowledge to match P'eng's, and with the time to devote himself to the minutiae of PLA affairs which Mao had either lacked or grudged.

However, it does not seem that Mao took the provocative step of detailing Lin Piao to take over day-to-day control of the MAC from P'eng Teh-huai.[92] Instead Mao convened an enlarged session of the MAC which met from 27 May to 22 July. The over 1,000 senior officers who attended were addressed by nine of China's ten marshals, including P'eng who summed up at the end, and by two civilians, Mao and Teng Hsiao-p'ing. The fact that the Chairman and General Secretary were the only civilian party officials to speak could have been a diplomatic move on Mao's part; the officers might be expected to take the reassertion of party control better when put over by their professional superiors. But it is nevertheless a striking fact that, as far as can be ascertained, the MAC—the organ designed to maintain civilian party control over the military—has apparently always been almost entirely composed of soldiers with only one constant exception since 1935, Mao himself. In view of Mao's oft-quoted belief that 'political power grows out of the barrel of the gun', it seems reasonable to assume that the Chairman took steps to ensure that none of his senior civilian colleagues should have direct access to levers that controlled that power.[93]

The MAC session was to focus on the problem of how the PLA could be modern and yet loyal to its Yenan traditions and Mao's military ethos. It could have been no accident that four days before its commencement one of Lin Piao's oldest colleagues, who headed one of the PLA's most modern arms, Air Force Commander Liu Ya-lou, published an article in the *Chieh-fang Chün Pao* (Liberation Army News) entitled 'Seriously study Mao Tsetung's military thinking'. Here, he not only extolled the Chairman's writings, but also praised pilots of worker/peasant origin, sniped at foreign (i.e. Soviet) advisers (especially significant coming from a man who had studied in the Soviet Union), criticized the foreign practice of isolating soldiers from civilians through excessive security precautions and reaffirmed the importance of the party committee and the political commissar in a modernized army.[94] Perhaps most important of all, coming from the commander of a section of the PLA employing advanced weaponry, he subscribed to the Maoist doctrine that it is men not weapons that are decisive in war—the military equivalent of the great leap ethos that man could always conquer nature.

In view of Liu Ya-lou's article, it was not surprising that Mao singled him out for praise during the MAC conference. A full text of Mao's remarks is not available, but from what is known it is clear that the Chairman hoped that the session would result in a far more critical attitude towards the Soviet military model.[95] Liu Ya-lou's article and considerable other evidence indicates further areas of tension between party and army and the kind of measures on which Mao must have insisted at the MAC conference.[96] First and foremost, there was the controversy surrounding the role of the political commissar. As in the Soviet Union, Chinese commanders had sought to reduce the commissar's role and to minimize the importance of the party committee, arguing that political controls impeded military efficiency in modernized armed forces and under conditions of modern warfare. The enlarged MAC conference endeavoured to reverse this trend, laying particular stress on the need for studying Mao's military writings which some officers thought out of date.[97] The post-Zhukov reassertion of party control over the Red Army in the Soviet Union would have lent moral power to Mao's elbow.

Another important subject was relations between officers and men. With the regularization of the PLA since 1949 and the adoption of a more hierarchical, Soviet-style officer system, the intimate, comradely relationship between guerrilla commanders and their men had been dissipated. The introduction of conscription had been accompanied by the demobilization of many of the guerrilla veterans who had shared the experiences and often the background of their officers. Moreover, a new type of 'bourgeois' officer was recruited through the post-1949 military academies rather than through the ranks, and he was often status-conscious and contemptuous of peasant conscripts.[98]

Presumably the officers attending the conference were informed of and discussed the proposals of the party to remedy this situation. At any rate, two months after the conclusion of the conference, on 20 September, the PLA's General Political Department (GPD) issued a directive ordering all officers—except the aged, the infirm and the sick—to spend a month in the ranks annually as ordinary soldiers; younger officers who had not risen through the ranks as had many veterans had to spend six months of their first year as privates. By February 1959, some 150,000 officers, including 160 generals, had undergone this status-undermining process.[99]

Such post-MAC measures illustrate Mao's deep distaste for hierarchy, bureaucratism and inequality—an attitude that would later infuse the cultural revolution. The measures represented a genuine attempt to route the PLA back to its Yenan traditions, although clearly Mao must also have been concerned to prevent the growth of a cohesive Chinese officer class which might represent some sort of long-term threat to the party in view of the special place of the PLA in the Chinese revolution. Nor should one discount the element of Mao's displeasure at what the Chairman must have considered P'eng's antagonistic role during the events of 1956–7.[100] The combination of personal bitterness on both sides, together with critical differences of opinion on defence policy and the type of armed forces China needed, does much to explain why P'eng attacked Mao when he saw a chink in his armour at Lushan the following year, and why Mao gave no quarter when he counter-attacked.

In his struggle with P'eng, Mao was able to pray in aid both positive and negative aspects of the Sino-Soviet military relationship. The importance of Khrushchev's promise of assistance with nuclear weapons—the positive aspect—has already been mentioned. From early 1958, however, Soviet moves must have given Mao some cause to doubt how binding Khrushchev considered that commitment.

On 14 March in Kalinin, Khrushchev gave a hint that the Soviet Union might be about to announce a unilateral renunciation of nuclear testing.[101] Two weeks later, on 31 March, the Supreme Soviet passed a resolution to discontinue all nuclear tests,[102] and on 4 April Khrushchev followed this up with letters to the US President, the UK Prime Minister and other world leaders, including Premier Chou En-lai.

One passage that appeared in the letters, even in the one to Chou, must have given the Chinese leaders pause for thought:

Today only three powers so far—the U.S.S.R., the U.S.A., and Great Britain—possess nuclear weapons, and therefore an agreement on the discontinuance of nuclear weapons tests is comparatively easy to reach. However, if the tests are not now discontinued, then after some time other countries may become possessors of nuclear weapons and under such conditions it will of course be a more complicated matter to reach an agreement on the discontinuance of the tests.[103]

If the Soviet Premier—Khrushchev had replaced Bulganin at the Supreme Soviet and was now leader of both party and government—wished to achieve a test-ban agreement before the

Chinese had acquired nuclear weapons of their own, how genuine was his commitment to help them develop such weapons? Would Khrushchev's initiative be a failure, in which case, according to the Soviet Premier's letter, the Russians would feel free to resume their own testing?[104]

The initial Western response was cool, partly because the Americans were about to commence a new series of tests and Dulles clearly thought the Soviet move was designed to forestall or discredit it.[105] But the Americans could not reject the proposal out of hand and in his reply of 8 April, President Eisenhower suggested that US and Soviet technicians should get together to study methods of policing tests.[106] After an initial rejection of this suggestion in his reply of 22 April, Khrushchev 'surprisingly' agreed to it in a letter on 9 May.[107]

The public response of the Chinese to the original Khrushchev initiative had perforce been positive. In his letter of 13 April to the Soviet Premier, Chou En-lai promised him the Chinese government's full support, although, as one Western scholar has pointed out, he made no reference to the danger of more countries going nuclear.[108] By this time the Chinese had been able to study the American reaction and might understandably have concluded that Khrushchev's proposal would founder on the familiar East-West disagreement over policing. But the unexpected breakthrough represented by Khrushchev's concession on this issue in his letter on 9 May presented them with a new situation. The Chinese had to take on board the possibility that a test-ban agreement might be negotiated which would freeze them out of the nuclear club.[109]

We do not know if Moscow gave Peking any advance warning of the concession in Khrushchev's letter of 9 May. But by early May the Chinese could well have begun to suspect that his initiative was not designed simply to achieve a propaganda victory but represented a genuine desire to achieve a test ban. It would seem almost certain that it was such suspicions that led the Chinese for the first time to voice publicly their determination to obtain nuclear weapons. At any rate, on the morning of 10 May, Foreign Minister Marshal Ch'en Yi received two West German journalists and informed them that China would have its own nuclear weapons 'in the future' or 'in the near future'.[110] Two weeks later, in his article on the eve of the meeting of the MAC, Air Force Commander Liu Ya-lou served notice on the Soviet Union that China would make its own nuclear weapons in the 'not distant future', using its own workers and scientists.[111] The chairman of the Scientific Planning Commission, Deputy Premier Marshal Nieh Jung-chen, confirmed this later in the year.[112] Behind the scenes, Mao suggested that ten years would be sufficient to build Chinese nuclear weapons (for once the Chairman underestimated the speed of China's development), an indication that he was no longer counting on Soviet help.[113]

Liu Ya-lou's claim was not just a warning shot across Khrushchev's bows; it was also essential to preserve the credibility of Mao's plan for a Yenan-style army with a nuclear armoury that would permit it to eschew heavy investment in modern conventional weapons. Fortunately for Mao, although Khrushchev's recent diplomatic *démarches* undermined somewhat the significance of his promise of a sample atomic bomb, P'eng Teh-huai was in a poor position to make use of these developments. He had based his vision of the correct role for the PLA on a division of functions between it and the Soviet armed forces which in turn depended on close collaboration and trust between Moscow and Peking. To have exploited Khrushchev's test-ban proposal to suggest that the Russians were not serious about helping China acquire a nuclear capability and that the secret agreement was a fraud could only have contributed to destroy the confidence of the Chinese military that they could work with their Soviet opposite numbers. Indeed, although Mao must initially have been dismayed by Khrushchev's proposal, he unlike P'eng could exploit it to rub in the lesson that the PLA must go its own way, depending on China's own resources.

Articles published shortly after the conclusion of the MAC session in celebration of the 1 August PLA anniversary indicated that, whatever P'eng Teh-huai's attitude, some at least of his fellow marshals were prepared to go along with Mao. The grand old man of the PLA and Vice Chairman of the People's Republic, Chu Teh, affirmed the continuing relevance of Chinese revolutionary experience and Mao's military thought and advocated the selective study of Soviet experience on that basis.[114] Discussing the Nanchang uprising of 1927, whose anniversary the Chinese celebrate as their Army Day, Marshal Ho Lung avoided any mention of Soviet military doctrine or experience, simply asserting that for more than 30 years 'our armed forces have carried out Comrade Mao Tse-tung's line for armed forces building and principles of military operations'.[115] And though Mao's own views were not published, his sympathies were indicated by the appearance on 1 August, on the front page of the *People's Daily*, of a photograph of him at an Air Force base in the company of Liu Ya-lou.[116]

(vi) The party asserts itself in foreign affairs

Over and above its effect on the debate within the Chinese leadership on its military profile and doctrine, Khrushchev's test-ban offer must also have caused Mao to worry about the direction of Soviet foreign policy.[117] At the NPC session in February, Chou En-lai's posture in foreign affairs had been tougher than at any time since mid-1955. He reaffirmed Mao's analysis of the shift in global power from West to East, drew attention to economic and intra-alliance problems in the capitalist world and denounced US actions in East and Southeast Asia. Most importantly, he rejected 'two China' proposals that were being aired in diplomatic circles and reasserted China's determination to liberate Taiwan without making the normal qualification of the past two years that it would be done 'peacefully'.[118]

Nevertheless, Chou's speech still represented a moderate stance on one important issue—Yugoslavia. The Russians had already launched a campaign against revisionism to indicate their displeasure at Tito's refusal to attend the Moscow conference the previous November and rejoin the bloc, and at his continuing ideological independence. But Chou made a single vague reference to revisionism 'in various forms' when discussing the Hungarian revolt,[119] and his mentions of Yugoslavia were friendly. He described it as a socialist country and listed the visit of the Yugoslav Vice President to China together with those paid by other communist leaders such as Premiers Kadar of Hungary and Yugov of Bulgaria.[120]

It may have been Khrushchev's test-ban offer that led to a dramatic change in the Chinese attitude towards Yugoslavia in succeeding months. The offer represented a rejection of the militant, uncompromising posture advocated by Mao, and the Chinese had no direct means of compelling Khrushchev to adopt their point of view. The Yugoslav issue may have seemed a useful if roundabout method of affecting Soviet policy.

On 5 April, the Russians announced that they would not send a delegation to the forthcoming Yugoslav party congress. On 19

April, three days before the congress opened, the Soviet communist party journal *Kommunist* attacked the Yugoslavs' new draft party programme for its revisionist principles—its advocacy of non-alignment and neutrality for communist states, its suggestion that non-communist parties could represent progress in the non-communist world, and its assertion of the equality and autonomy of all communist parties. But although the Soviet denunciation was stern, it still recognized the Yugoslavs as friends on a state-to-state basis and as comrades on an inter-party basis.[121]

On 5 May, after the conclusion of the Yugoslav congress, the Chinese launched an attack on the Yugoslavs which contained no such courtesies. Tito and his colleagues were referred to simply as the 'leading group' of the Yugoslav party and it was implied that they had put forward their new 'out and out revisionist' programme at the request of the American imperialists.[122] Whereas the Soviet attacks had left open the possibility of compromise, the Chinese seemed only interested in capitulation. But, since it was unlikely that they expected to get that, the presumption must be that they were determined to cut out the cancer of Yugoslav revisionism because of their belief that 'the greater the solidarity... among the socialist countries, the more powerful we shall become'.[123] Even more importantly, a bloc propaganda offensive against Yugoslavia might be expected to foul the atmosphere of peaceful coexistence and so undermine Khrushchev's policy towards the United States.

But although the Chinese attack appears to have nudged Khrushchev into taking a harder line towards the Yugoslavs, the Soviet leaders did not endorse all the Chinese arguments and actions.[124] Moreover, at the first conference of bloc leaders after the Chinese attack—the meeting of the Warsaw Pact's Political Consultative Committee in late May—Khrushchev indicated he would not be diverted from his US policy. The chief Chinese observer, Ch'en Yun, echoed Mao and Chou in pointing to profound changes in the world balance of forces. He asserted that it was 'extremely erroneous and harmful' to overestimate the power of the West and asked why a superior socialist camp should fear imperialism. Khrushchev, by contrast, painted a dismal picture of the world-wide destruction that would accompany a new war and pointed hopefully to signs that some Western leaders recognized this danger and the consequent need for a new approach to international affairs. While Ch'en Yun urged that the Warsaw Pact should be strengthened, the Pact Declaration emphasized reductions in Pact forces and the evacuation of Soviet troops from Romania.[125]

What the Chinese did succeed in doing was in making it far more difficult for the Yugoslavs to contemplate compromise. On 15 June, Tito replied vigorously to his critics, especially the Chinese, but this only provoked a further broadside from Peking in which the Yugoslav leader was described as a 'traitor' whom it was necessary to drive to the side of imperialism.[126] The rupture was extended to state-to-state relations; in late June the Chinese boycotted the farewell reception of the Yugoslav ambassador and in September they recalled their own from Belgrade.

These latter developments were significant portents of the way in which Chinese ideology and foreign policy were to become increasingly interwoven in the months and years ahead as Peking sought to promote militant bloc solidarity *vis-à-vis* the imperialist camp. Premier Chou En-lai had given up his concurrent post as Foreign Minister to Marshal Ch'en Yi at the NPC in February, and while this move was probably a reflection of Chou's defeats in the two great policy debates of 1956–7,[127] it also symbolized the beginning of the end of the 'Bandung period' during which China, personified by its charming and supple Premier, seemed able to maintain friendly relations with most foreign countries despite ideological differences.

As ideology began to take precedence, important statements affecting foreign policy began to emanate from sources other than the Prime Minister and the new Foreign Minister. Ch'en Po-ta, for instance, authored one of the major attacks on Yugoslavia in the summer of 1958 in the first issue of the new party journal, *Red Flag*, which he edited.[128] Important commentaries on foreign affairs signed by Yü Chao-li were the product of a three-man team comprising two party propagandists and only one Foreign Ministry official.[129] This would suggest a greater role in the formulation of foreign policy for leaders outside Chou's immediate coteries in the SC and the Foreign Ministry, with the CC's international liaison department (charged with maintaining relations with other communist parties) increasingly involved in preparing policy statements.

It would be a mistake, however, to conclude further that the party machine usurped the functions of the SC or that Chou's influence over foreign affairs became negligible. Immediately after the NPC session, Chou left for North Korea with Ch'en Yi to negotiate the withdrawal of the Chinese force (Chinese People's Volunteers [CPV]) that had stayed on after the end of the Korean war. Chou had lost face, but not authority.

Nevertheless even Chou had to conform to Mao's tougher posture in foreign affairs, as his speech to the NPC had shown. For the time being this posture did not affect basic policies towards the neutralist countries of South and Southeast Asia, although already in 1958 some neutralists felt that China's attitude was changing from solicitude to truculence.[130] It was the United States' principal ally in Asia—Japan—which bore the first brunt of that truculence.

Substantial trade negotiations had been conducted in Peking by a Japanese delegation during the course of the autumn and winter of 1957–8. The Chinese had tried to insist that their flag should be flown over any trade mission they might establish in Japan, but in the face of Tokyo's intransigence on the issue they backed down and so enabled a trade agreement to be signed on 5 March 1958. However, when, on 2 May, a young Japanese took down and tore up a tiny Chinese flag which had been put on the roof of a building in Nagasaki housing a Chinese philatelic exhibition, the Chinese reacted strongly. Foreign Minister Ch'en Yi issued a statement in which he claimed that the incident showed that the Kishi government's hostile attitude towards China had become intolerable.[131] The following day, 10 May, the Japanese were informed by the Chinese trade delegation in Tokyo that all business would be suspended.

A number of reasons have been suggested for the over-reaction of the Chinese to the flag incident: anger at Kishi's stated policy that trade deals would have no effect on Japan's policy of non-recognition of the Peking government; Tokyo's reassuring messages to Chiang Kai-shek; the prospective negotiation of the Japanese defence treaty with the United States; possibly even a hope of helping to inflict a setback to Kishi in the forthcoming elections.[132] According to one scholar, 'it is generally accepted by well-informed Japanese that this decision was a purely political one, which Ch'en Yi personally formulated and presented to the Politburo for approval.'[133]

We cannot be sure whether or not 'well-informed Japanese' were in fact correct. But it is perhaps fair to say that China's new Foreign Minister was admirably suited by temperament to China's evolving new foreign policy. According to one authoritative biographical appraisal, 'most accounts indicate that [Ch'en Yi] is an outspoken man of considerable intelligence and wit. . . .'[134] In the years to come, Ch'en, one of the outstanding generals of the civil war and a poet to boot, was to give a number of examples of his outspokenness, both in foreign and domestic affairs: his bullying of the Indonesian Foreign Minister in October 1959[135]; his indignant outburst on the Sino-Indian border dispute at a press conference in Katmandu in April 1960[136]; his blunt negotiating style at the Geneva conference on Laos in 1961[137]; and his forthright self-defence when 'tried' by the Red Guards during the cultural revolution.[138]

The reasons for the choice of Marshal Ch'en as Foreign Minister, rather than other able and available men, are unclear. He had close early connections with four of China's principal leaders —Mao, Liu Shao-ch'i, Chou En-lai and Teng Hsiao-p'ing—and seems to have lacked driving political ambitions.[139] If he were a friend to all and enemy to none, he may have been chosen as a suitably neutral candidate for a post that could have provided sufficient prominence for exploitation for personal motives. As it was, Ch'en Yi seems to have been content to accept the continuing leadership of Chou En-lai in foreign affairs. But with Chou busy travelling the country during much of the great leap, Ch'en, left behind in Peking, was able in his contacts and utterances to provide Chinese foreign policy with the requisite more rugged profile. It was Ch'en's misfortune that when China, after the cultural revolution, took its seat in the UN and entered upon a period of friendlier relations with the West in general and the United States in particular, political setbacks and failing health prevented him from emerging to display the more convivial side to his character.

(vii) At the Ming Tombs Reservoir

The second session of the 8th Congress ended on 23 May and was followed on the 25th by the CC's 5th plenum at which Lin Piao and others formally received their promotions.[140] On the same day Mao led his most senior colleagues to the Ming Tombs Reservoir near the capital to help in construction work. The following month, Chou En-lai, leading a group of 500 CC and government officials, stayed five days, living in a nearby school and working from 3 pm to 11 pm.[141] His close associate Marshal Yeh

Chien-ying found time to write poetry.[142] Most importantly, the pictures that this expedition produced signalled Mao's determination to revive the Yenan style of hardships shared by leaders and men[143] and symbolized the importance to be placed on manual labour in the months ahead. The mobilization of that labour would be entrusted to a totally new type of rural organization: the people's commune.

5 THE COMING OF THE COMMUNES

Even today, the story of the emergence of the people's communes in rural China in the summer of 1958 remains obscure. Political exigencies seem to have led to a blurring of the record. A prime reason for this would appear to have been that Mao Tse-tung jumped the gun, pressing for the formation of communes without prior formal endorsement even by the Politburo. Besides, at one time it seemed advantageous to stress the suddenness with which the communes appeared in order to account for difficulties, while later it became essential to stress the gestation period in order to deflect criticisms that the communes had been set up without any objective basis.[1]

There seems little doubt that the seeds of the communes sprouted spontaneously during the water conservancy campaign of winter 1957–8, at a time when Mao still assumed that the successor organizations to the APCs would be state farms.[2] The massive inputs of labour required by the conservancy campaign required organization of manpower on a scale that far transcended the resources of the APCs, whose average size had fallen in 1957 to 164 families.[3] Despite the fact that the CC had promulgated directives as recently as September 1957 extolling small, decentralized APCs,[4] during the winter mergers of APCs took place to meet the demands of the water conservancy campaign.[5] These mergers were endorsed *ex post facto* at the Chengtu conference in March 1958 and the endorsement in turn encouraged further mergers.[6] Yet to judge by Mao's failure to mention the question in his lengthy speeches to the Chengtu conference, the mergers had not assumed the significance later attached to them; indeed, the merger in Honan of 27 APCs into one massive APC of 9,369 households, later pinpointed as the breakthrough, took place only in April.[7]

Moreover, the crucial problem is how and by whom it was decided to give the enlarged APCs a totally new dimension by calling them people's communes and designating them as the all-purpose basic units of Chinese society, embracing agriculture, industry, culture, commerce and military affairs; for during the intra-party crisis over the great leap and the communes a year later it was alleged that the latter had been devised by a few people in accordance with their subjective desires and that they were set up 'too soon and too fast . . .'.[8]

(i)   The role of Ch'en Po-ta

The term 'people's commune' (*jen-min kung-she*) does not appear in the Sixty Articles on Work Methods or in the available texts of the second session of the CCP's 8th Congress. Apparently neither Mao nor Liu thought the amalgamation of APCs sufficiently important to refer to in their speeches to the congress session. The omission from Mao's speeches is particularly significant; since they were not for publication he need not have had any inhibitions about mentioning the subject. One is forced to conclude that the prospective transmutation of enlarged APCs into communes was in May not yet under consideration by the Politburo.

Subsequent accounts stated that the enlarged APCs were given a variety of names in the earlier stages, but that in June the 'central committee and Comrade Mao Tse-tung selected the name "people's commune" as one that best expressed the essence of this form of organisation and would be most welcome to the masses'.[9]

In fact the first public mention of the term was by Ch'en Po-ta in an article in *Red Flag*, No. 3, published on 1 July. Ch'en was introducing two other articles on the achievements of an APC in Hupeh province, and he cited its transformation into an organizational unit which combined agriculture and industry as effectively making it into a 'people's commune'.[10]

On the same day as his article appeared, Ch'en made a speech at Peking University on the occasion of the CCP's 38th anniversary in which he quoted Mao as stating the need gradually and systematically to form a 'large commune' (*ta kung she*) combining 'agriculture, industry, commerce, culture and education, and militia, i.e. the whole people armed' and make it into the basic unit of the nation.[11]

This evidence suggests that Ch'en Po-ta conceived the idea of calling the enlarged APCs 'people's communes', and that Mao refined the concept by making it all-embracing and perhaps endorsed it as a model for the whole nation some time during the last week in June. Certainly Mao later disclaimed responsibility for inventing the communes, although not for approving them.[12]

However, it has been convincingly argued that the roots of the people's commune idea—not of its name which probably derives from the 1871 Paris commune,[13] but the emphasis on its 'largeness' (*ta*) and 'publicness' (*kung*)—can be traced to Mao's youthful enthusiasm for the political and social ideas of the scholar-statesman K'ang Yu-wei (1858–1927) as expounded in his book *Ta-t'ung Shu*.[14]

Questions remain. Why did Ch'en Po-ta, and subsequently T'an Chen-lin, when quoting from Mao, not include the word 'commune' in the quotation while indicating that he had used it? Was it because when Mao used the term *ta kung she* he was still only thinking of a 'large' and 'public' APC (i.e. *ta kung (nung-yeh sheng-ch'an ho-tso) she*) rather than a large (people's) commune (i.e. *ta (jen-min) kung-she*? Was it because Mao used the term 'large commune' rather than 'people's commune'? Was it because Mao did not want to go public in advocating communes before formally consulting his colleagues? Or was it because on the occasion cited by Ch'en and T'an—apparently a chat in late June with the director of the APC whose virtues Mao had extolled in the first issue of *Red Flag*[15]—Mao had really only been thinking aloud about the new concept and advocating experimentation by his auditor.[16]

What does seem certain is that the conception, development and adoption of the commune idea took place on the basis of limited evidence and in a surprisingly short period of time, especially in view of its ideological and intra-bloc implications which ought to have been clear to Mao and Ch'en from the start. The report on the APC which inspired Ch'en to call it a people's commune was dated 25 May 1958.[17] This would mean that in less than a month a report by a *hsien* committee filtered up through the bureaucracy to Ch'en, a decision was taken (by whom?) to interpret the report as a signal for a new form of rural organization, and an article was written (and cleared?) implementing that decision.

The APC whose success in combining industry and agriculture had inspired Ch'en to call it a commune had only been engaged in such operations for two months, hardly enough experience to enable it to bear so weighty an ideological crown.[18] Yet only two weeks after Ch'en's article appeared, an agricultural conference of North China provinces (including Honan) presided over by T'an Chen-lin concluded that it was necessary to investigate and prepare for 'the comparatively high-level commune-like form' of organization currently being experimented with because the management and distribution systems of the APC were now inadequate.[19]

Despite all his touring, Mao appears to have given his initial endorsement of the commune concept without the on-the-spot inspections which he himself regarded as so important. While he was presumably exposed to enlarged APCs on his various visits, there is no record of his having visited Honan province, the acknowledged crucible of the communes, until the movement was well under way and only awaiting the agreement of the Politburo.[20]

Finally, one must also take into account that during much of June, Mao's attention must have been principally directed towards military affairs in view of the critical meeting of the MAC that was in session under his chairmanship during the month. How much mature consideration could Mao have given the commune idea before giving it his initial endorsement?

It was not until after the conclusion of the lengthy MAC session on 22 July and the visit of Khrushchev to Peking from 31 July to 3 August that Mao was able to resume his touring and make his first on-the-spot appraisal of the communes. Between 4 and 13 August, he visited Hopei, Honan, Shantung, Tientsin and two APCs on the outskirts of the capital.[21] It was on this tour that he placed his imprimatur on the communes in advance of any formal agreement by the Politburo. On the evening of 4 August, immediately after an approving visit by Mao, a hitherto provisional commune at Taszukochuang in Hsushui *hsien*, Hopei, was formally inaugurated. Four days after his visit to Honan, the *People's Daily* reported that he had visited there the Ch'iliying people's commune which had been transformed from an APC according to the path laid down by Chairman Mao. The wording was perhaps deliberately imprecise, but presumably referred to his remark quoted by Ch'en Po-ta in *Red Flag*.

In an exchange with the Honan 1st secretary Wu Chih-p'u at Ch'iliying, Mao stated that he hoped that its production achievements could be duplicated throughout the province. Wu replied that if one had an organization (*she*) like this, it would not be a subject for gloom if one had still more. To which Mao replied: 'That's right. One should have many more organisations like this.' Again the wording was imprecise: the word *she* occurs in both agricultural producers' cooperative (*nung-yeh sheng-ch'an ho-tso she*) and people's commune (*jen-min kung-she*). Moreover, even if in context Mao was clearly referring to communes, he could still claim that he was promoting the universalization of the production achievements of Ch'iliying rather than its new organizational structure.[22]

However, on 9 August in Shantung, Mao placed on record his preference for communes. When provincial secretary T'an Ch'i-lung revealed that a certain area was proposing to set up a large-scale farm (*ta nung-ch'ang*), Mao told him: 'It would be better to set up a people's commune. Its advantage is that it combines industry, agriculture, commerce, education and military affairs and facilitates leadership.'[23] A year later, conscious that this was when he had jumped the gun, Mao excused himself by blaming the press, a politician's device more widely practised outside China.[24] As we shall see, Mao was not the only Chinese leader who regretted the eagerness with which correspondents reported his words during the high tide of the leap.

On 17 August, four days after Mao's approval of communes had been reported in the *People's Daily*, an expanded session of the Politburo opened in the Hopei coastal resort of Peitaiho. The following day, the *People Daily* announced the establishment of communes throughout Hsinyang special district in Honan province under the uncompromising banner headline 'People's communes are good'. The paper did not attribute the assertion to Mao, but by now most alert cadres must have been aware of the Chairman's attitude. The die was cast.[25]

Presumably the Chairman had by this time secured the backing of his principal colleagues although the Politburo did not officially adopt its resolution on the communes until 29 August. Certainly Liu Shao-ch'i had been talking of the need to combine industry, commerce, education and military affairs with agriculture as early as mid-July. In public he still talked of cooperatives[26]; but in private he already used the term commune. At Shihchingshan Liu argued that workers and peasants should exchange jobs for two months a year; this could not happen overnight, but over a period of five or ten years such a process would assist the introduction of communism. He went on: 'The factories are the villages, the villages are also the factories, what's yours is mine, what's mine is yours . . . . The young people of the villages can go to the factories, the sons and daughters of the workers can go to the villages to organise communist communes (*kung-ch'an kung-she*).'[27]

This evidence suggests that Mao and Ch'en Po-ta secured Liu's agreement to the creation of multi-purpose rural organizations at an early stage and that though Liu personally was careful not to be reported using the term 'commune' publicly prior to the Peitaiho Politburo session, he was too committed to the project to object to Mao doing so. It was therefore only in retrospect, in defending himself against people like P'eng Teh-huai, that Mao was forced to make excuses for his pre-empting enthusiasm.

(ii) The Peitaiho conference

The enlarged Politburo conference at Peitaiho from 17 to 30 August was the turning point in the leap. Up till that point, the leap was still basically a highly successful production drive, with a summer harvest 69 per cent up on 1957 already assured.[28] Commune and backyard steel plants were already in existence, but they could have been soft-pedalled. Over-ambitious production targets could have been sprinkled with cold water. In short, Peitaiho could have been the occasion for fine tuning of the economy to make sure the leap was on course. Instead, it was used as a spur to even greater production efforts and as a launching pad for an ideological leap towards communism. Before Peitaiho, China seemed sure to astonish the world by the manner in which its disciplined millions could achieve ever greater economic feats. As a result of Peitaiho, the genuine economic achievements of 1958 were obscured by the disastrously overweening pretensions of China's leadership.

The conference must have met in a mood of high optimism engendered by two carefully timed articles by T'an Chen-lin in which he painted a glowing picture of the agricultural prospects. Extrapolating from the bumper summer harvest, T'an predicted a per capita output for the year which implied that he believed that aggregate production of grain would reach at least 240 million tons and perhaps as much as 300 million tons.[29] The lower estimate represented almost a 25 per cent increase on the target announced at the NPC earlier in the year and was precisely the target for the end of the 2nd FYP set in December 1957; the higher estimate was over 50 per cent above that target.

T'an Chen-lin, a man proud of his close association with Mao from the late 1920s,[30] had effectively taken over the direction of agriculture the previous autumn from his one-time comrade-in-arms Teng Tzu-hui.[31] From October through December 1957, T'an Chen-lin made a number of visits to Honan to encourage and direct the province's ambitious water conservancy campaign, doubtlessly forging a good working relationship with the local rising star Wu Chih-p'u with whom he pioneered the commune project on the ground.[32]

Ironically, the 56-year-old Hunanese, a printer and bookbinder by trade, was one of the very few genuine representatives of the urban working class in the top ranks of the CCP.[33] After his early guerrilla experience under Mao in the Autumn Harvest Uprising and on Chingkangshan, T'an demonstrated outstanding abilities as both a military commander and a political commissar during the anti-Japanese and civil wars. After the communist victory in 1949, he worked for a time in East China and was by 1952 the third-ranking party secretary there, and often in charge due to the frequent absences of his superiors (Jao Shu-shih and Ch'en Yi). At this time, as governor of Kiangsu province, he was working in harness with K'o Ch'ing-shih, then the Kiangsu party secretary, who was elevated to the Politburo with him at the second session of the 8th Congress.[34] During the leap, the relationship between the two men became symbiotic, for while T'an spurred on the peasants to ever-greater agricultural achievements, it was K'o who, as we shall see, convinced Mao to press recklessly forwards on the steel front.

Few Westerners appear to have met T'an Chen-lin, even after his move to Peking and the CCP's central secretariat in the mid-1950s, but the leading historian of the Chinese communist military elite has described him (presumably on the basis of the evidence of Nationalist generals and communist defectors) as tough-minded and a master-organizer, 'stubborn, devious, sarcastic, coldly analytical, and ruthlessly "mission-oriented"'.[35] During the leap, T'an certainly revealed himself to be 'mission-oriented', but even Mao, wise after the event, had to suggest later that he had perhaps not been coldly analytical enough:

Boss T'an, you have had many big cannons, but they were not shot carefully and communization was too fast. He began to talk when he was in Honan, and the records of Kiangsi and Chekiang spread rapidly. He did not speak carefully, and since he was not too sure, it would be better to be more careful. It is to his credit that he was full of zest and was willing to assume responsibility. This was better than those who seemed to be so sad and dismal.[36]

T'an 's version of communism fitted him admirably for the task of propelling China towards plenty and suggests why he would have been full of zest during the leap. While all CCP leaders doubtless shared a desire to see their people prosperous, few can have expressed their vision of a communist cornucopia more graphically than T'an:

After all, what does communism mean? . . . First, taking good food and not merely eating one's fill. At each meal one enjoys a meat diet, eating chicken, pork, fish or eggs . . . . To be sure, delicacies like monkeys' heads, swallows' nests, white fungus are served to each according to his needs' . . . .

Second, clothing. Everything required is available. Clothing of various designs and styles, not a mass of black garments or a mass of blue garments. In future, ordinary cloth will be used for making working outfits. After working hours, people will wear silk, satin and woollen suits . . . . Foxes will multiply. When all people's communes raise foxes, there will be overcoats lined with fox furs . . . .

Third, housing. Housing is brought up to the standard of modern cities. What should be modernized? People's communes. Central heating is provided in the north and air conditioning in the south. All live in high buildings. Needless to say, there are electric light, telephone, piped water, receiving sets and TV . . . .

Fourth, communications. Except for those who take part in races, all travellers and commuters use transport. Air services are opened in all directions and every hsien has an airport . . . . The time is not remote when each will have an airplane . . . .

Fifth, higher education for everyone and education is popularized. Communism means these: food, clothing, housing, transportation, cultural entertainment, science institutes, and physical culture. The sum total of these means communism.[37]

This was 'goulash communism' with a vengeance, but there is no indication that T'an was out of joint with the times or with Mao. According to T'an, Mao depicted a happy life in terms of consumption, with short-range targets of 750 kg of grain, 50 kg of pork, 10 kg of vegetable oil and 10 kg of ginned cotton per capita per year.[38] Certainly during his visit to Hopei on 4 August, Mao suggested that if Hsushui *hsien* had grain surpluses which it could not sell then 'the cooperative members can eat more. They can certainly eat five meals a day if they like.'[39] During the cultural

revolution, T'an was criticized for permitting peasants to celebrate the bumper 1958 harvest with feasts; but Mao also sanctioned such celebrations at the time.[40]

During the cultural revolution Teng Hsiao-p'ing, too, was criticized for advocating goulash communism, which included a more
modest 30 kg of pork per capita per year, ·25 kg of apples per
capita per day, as well as 2 fluid oz of spirits. Teng's vision was in
general also more restrained than T'an's; where T'an talked glibly
of air transport, Teng proposed that China become a nation of
bicycles. The nearest that Teng approached controversy, speaking at a time when ascetism was increasingly overshadowing
abundance as the keynote of the leap, was in predicting that in
the future high-heeled shoes and lipstick would be permissible.[41]

In fact the image of the leap, both within China and abroad
was curiously contradictory. On the one hand, the escalating
claims of increases in agricultural production led propagandists to
depict China as entering into an era of plenty in which all would
eat well—and possibly for free—and have all their material
wants satisfied. On the other hand, the 'militarization' of labour,
the decrying of material incentives, and the apocalyptic assertions
that China was on the verge of entering the period of true communism conveyed an impression of ideological fervour and ascetism. The explanation of this contradiction lies in the grafting of
the communes on to what started as a supercharged production
drive. That graft was made at Peitaiho.

In keeping with the spirit of the leap, the Peitaiho conference
was enormously productive. A whole series of policies was
agreed—on communes, agriculture, industry, education, commerce, the militia and physical labour by cadres—and resolutions
or directives on most of these subjects were published in the ensuing weeks.[42] The key decisions were to develop communes
throughout the country and to raise the 1958 steel target to 10.7
million tons, double the 1957 output. China had already in the
first eight months of 1958 produced the same amount of steel as
in the whole of 1957[43]; but the new target meant that China now
had to produce again the same amount of steel as in 1957, but in
only four months. The major Peitaiho prediction was that grain
output would reach between 300 and 350 million tons, an escalation of up to another 25 per cent on the estimates T'an Chen-lin
had published only three weeks earlier.[44]

Regarded purely as a plan, the resolution on the communes

started modestly and moderately like all such CC documents. The formation of the communes was described as a 'natural trend', and a nation-wide high tide in their development was put no higher than 'quite possible', although it might then become 'irresistible'. The basis for the development was the success of the leap which had raised the political consciousness of the peasantry. Here hints of exaggeration crept in: the output of agricultural products was said to be increasing by 'one hundred per cent, several hundred per cent, over one thousand per cent, and several thousand per cent'—chastening reading for any rural cadres who might suspect that they could boast increases of less, perhaps far less, than 100 per cent.

The struggle for agricultural production had led to the breakdown of boundaries between APCs, even between *hsiang* and between *hsien*, to the militarization of organization and activities, to the collectivization of daily living and to the further raising of the 'communist' consciousness of the peasantry. Now prescription replaced description: the APCs were no longer suitable, and the development of all-embracing communes was 'a basic policy which must be adopted for the guidance of the peasants in the acceleration of socialist construction, the advanced building of socialism, and the gradual transition to communism.'[45]

The format laid down for a typical commune was one per *hsiang* (the basic rural unit originally consisting of a village but enlarged during collectivization to comprise two or more villages[46]), embracing about 2,000 households or roughly 10,000 people. Communes of 6,000 households were to be permitted where conditions were appropriate, and even communes of up to 20,000 households were not to be opposed. The preferred method of enlargement, however, was through federations of communes with the *hsien* (county) as the unit. The party and administrative organs of the *hsiang* and the commune were to be identical so that the commune would become the basic unit of state power in the countryside. The process of formation was in two stages; merger of small APCs into large APCs followed by transformation of the latter into communes. If the processes could be telescoped into one, well and good, but compulsion and commandism had to be prevented and the transformation should not harm production.[47] In the course of the transformation, the original small APCs could be turned into farming zones (*keng-tso ch'ü*) or production brigades (*sheng-ch'an tui*).[48]

Within the communes, a collectivist life-style was to be promoted through community mess halls, kindergartens, nurseries, tailoring teams, barber shops, public baths, 'happiness homes' for the aged, agricultural middle schools and schools for turning out red and expert personnel.[49] Private plots should 'generally' be transferred to the communes for collective operation, but some trees could continue to be privately owned. This was a critical decision, for although land retained for private cultivation was supposed nowhere to account for more than 5 per cent of collectively owned land it was of great importance to individual peasant families because, as one scholar has pointed out, it:

(1) provided the kind of foods needed for a balanced diet— green vegetables, fruit, pork, poultry;

(2) raised many families' standard of living from subsistence to a tolerable level;

(3) provided cash from sales of produce; and

(4) gave some security in contrast to the uncertainty of the level of income that would be forthcoming from the collective.[50]

The question of family shares in the old APCs should be shelved for a year or two when, with the development of production and the increase of income, and the elevation of popular consciousness, they would 'naturally' be converted into common ownership; presumably the regime did not want the fledgling communes to be saddled with an initial debt burden from buying out its members and hoped eventually to persuade the peasantry to donate their shares to the communes. For the moment the ownership system was collectivist, but the transition to ownership by the whole people was envisaged within three to six years in most places. The existing system of distribution should be retained, but a wage system could be introduced where conditions were ripe.[51] The final paragraph seemed cautious. The present task was the building of socialism, but it now appeared that 'the realisation of communism in our country is no longer a thing of the distant future. We should actively employ the form of the people's commune to produce a concrete path for transition to communism.'[52]

Experience indicates that the CC habitually set its targets low on the assumption that they could, should and would be overfulfilled, and this practice had been given formal endorsement in the Sixty Articles on Work Methods.[53] In this light, the passages just cited in the resolution on the communes must be seen as inflammatory, and designedly so. Subsequent allegations of excessive zeal at the lower levels notwithstanding, the resolution clearly foreshadowed a virtually overnight leap towards communism. Mao later claimed to have said that the transition from collective ownership to communist all-people's ownership might take over ten years, and up to 25 years, and that although he might have been crude he had been careful on this issue; but he did not attempt to suggest that the timetable in the Peitaiho resolution had been laid down over his objections.[54] Liu Shao-ch'i—who, like Mao, was later to bemoan the keenness with which journalists reported him during the leap[55]—had already been quoted in the *People's Daily* as urging people to 'go right ahead to realise communism. Now we must not think that communism will only be realised very slowly. So long as we work properly, it will be *very soon* when we shall realise communism' (emphasis added).[56]

Unfortunately, no texts of any speeches made at Peitaiho by Liu (or Mao for that matter) have come to light, but reports of his post-Peitaiho remarks give no indication of any retreat from this forecast. Indeed, the evidence provided by his provincial visits during 1958 suggests that Liu's prime interest was in 'the appearance of sprouts of communist life-style' and in encouraging their development.[57] Surprisingly, despite Mao's role in the formulation and encouragement of the commune concept, the party Chairman did not concentrate on such matters during his post-Peitaiho touring. He was in the grips of steel fever.

(iii)   Steel fever

Mao's obsession with steel production in the second half of 1958 is in some ways curious. His knowledge of industry was by his own admission slight.[58] It had been his early recognition of the overriding importance of the peasantry to the Chinese revolution that accounted in large measure for his rise to leadership of the CCP; and it had been his early recognition of the overriding importance of agriculture to the Chinese economy that led the CCP to seek a Chinese road to economic development. But by August 1958 Mao could have been forgiven for believing that the spread of the commune movement was an organizational task whose success could be assumed on the basis of the experience of collectivization in 1955–6, and that an autumn harvest of leap forward size could also be assumed on the basis of the record summer crop.[59] It was after all a feature of his political style to proclaim a victory in advance of its achievement and an aspect of his restless personality to want to fight the next battle, leaving subordinates to mop up after the previous one.[60] He told the SSC on 9 September in a revealingly brief reference to the communes that he anticipated basic completion of the framework of communization in that month, with contingent problems being dealt with during the winter and spring.[61]

There is thus no question but that in August Mao turned from the uncertainties of human behaviour and the vagaries of the weather to what in his ignorance he may have supposed to be the cold hard certainties of steel production. The Peitaiho communiqué reflected his new order of priorities:

The great victory on the agricultural front demanded that the industrial front should rapidly catch up with it, and also led to the possibility for party committees of the provincial level *to turn their major attention to industry*. For this reason the conference resolved that the first secretaries of party committees of all provinces and autonomous regions *must, from this date, give prior attention to leadership over industry*, though at the same time they must not relax leadership over agriculture . . . . The central issue in industry is iron and steel production and machine building, and the development of the machine-building industry is in turn decided by the development of iron and steel production. In accordance with the current demand for iron and steel . . . the leaping development of iron and steel production is both necessary and possible.[62] (Emphasis added.)

Steel production in 1957 had been 5·35 million tons. At the NPC in February, the 1958 target had been set at a modest 6.2 million tons. This had been increased by the Politburo at the end of May to between 8 and 8·5 million tons.[63] But in June—possibly when he examined the 2nd FYP targets on the 17th[64]—Mao decided that 10·7 million tons, a 100 per cent increase over 1957, could be achieved.[65] This target was endorsed at Peitaiho.[66]

After Mao's death, Chinese economists would point to the doubling of the steel target as the crucial error which threw the Chinese economy totally out of balance during the great leap forward.[67] Mao, who admitted that he had been the prime mover in the escalation of targets and that his adviser had been the Shanghai 1st secretary, K'o Ch'ing-shih,[68] explained a year later that he had not grasped that the nation-wide steel campaign would require massive movements of iron and coal to areas without them and that this process would overload China's rail network.[69] He blamed the State Planning Commission, headed by Li Fu-ch'un, for abdicating its responsibilities after Peitaiho and failing to cope with this problem.[70] Po I-po, Chairman of the State Economic Commission, was later said to have opposed the mass steel campaign in the Peitaiho discussions, but then to have fallen into line with such zeal that cultural revolutionaries felt justified in accusing him of excesses![71]

Behind the scenes, shortly after the Peitaiho conference, Mao revealed himself to be thinking in even more extravagant terms. In the course of three speeches to the SSC on 5, 8 and 9 September, he indicated that he envisaged that steel output in 1958 would actually reach 11 or 12 million tons. The fact that in one speech he mentioned both figures as possibilities underlines the airiness with which the Chairman juggled with increases of up to 24 per cent *additional to* the increase of 100 per cent already agreed at Peitaiho.[72]

The air of unreality was heightened by his projections for the future which even diligent excising of figures by friendly editors has not totally obscured. His expectation was that output in 1959 would reach 30 million tons,[73] an estimate that had been endorsed by the Peitaiho conference.[74] By 1960, China would be the world's third largest steel producer, catching up with the Soviet Union which would then be producing, Mao suggested, 60 million tons. By the end of the 2nd FYP in 1962, China would be catching up with or even overtaking the United States by attaining an output which Mao, allowing himself a wide margin of error, put at between 80 and 100 million tons.[75] Privately, he later admitted, his personal estimate for 1962 was even higher, 100–120 million tons.[76] The United States would be forced by economic constraints to hover around the 100 million ton mark, thus enabling China to pull away, reaching in a few more years an output of 150 million tons.[77] In 15 years or a little longer, that is by the mid-1970s, China would be producing *700 million tons of steel*, or twice the per capita output of the United Kingdom.[78]

Two years earlier, on the eve of the 1956 leap, Mao had envisaged overtaking the United States economically in 50–75 years.[79] In the euphoric summer of 1958,[80] he had clearly shortened his time-scale drastically.

6 HIGH TIDE

The two months that succeeded the Peitaiho conference in August 1958 were the high tide of the great leap forward, a period of superhuman endeavour in the field of production and exuberant experimentation with elements of a new society based on the communes. Mao, Liu Shao-ch'i and other leaders toured the country and gave encouragement. Thereafter, in November 1958, realism began to return and at the CC's 6th plenum in December a retreat was ordered.

Most of the enthusiasm during those euphoric two months was domestically generated by party cadres who had been encouraged by Mao to believe that China was on the verge of a millennial breakthrough. But it is impossible fully to comprehend the mood of those autumn days without a consideration of the international context.

The Chinese leaders were not responsible for the international crisis that developed in the summer of 1958. Indeed, just at its outset, General Secretary Teng Hsiao-p'ing was privately reassuring an audience that contained many non-party notables that there was no World War III in sight and that in general war could be avoided. China's strategy was economic competition, to increase its strength through economic development in order to impress the Americans, the Japanese and Tito. Certainly the Americans would continue to scorn a country with no atomic weapons and a minute steel output. China would also rely on the economic development of the neutralist world which would deny markets to the West and lead to revolution in the United States and United Kingdom.[1] But this cool, long-range perspective was overshadowed in the hectic weeks that followed, and Chinese actions exacerbated East–West tensions and helped to increase militancy within China. The divergent lines taken by Peking and Moscow at this time represented another milestone on the road towards the Sino-Soviet split.

(i) The Taiwan Strait crisis

It was the coup in Iraq on 13 July, which resulted in the overthrow of the pro-Western regime of King Faisal and Nuri es-Said, that precipitated the international crisis.[2] The Western reaction was to dispatch troops to other moderate, pro-Western Arab countries to forestall similar coups there; on 15 July President Eisenhower announced that US troops were being sent into the Lebanon, and UK troops arrived in Jordan on 17 July.

But Western concern was not confined to fears about the immediate future of Jordan and the Lebanon. The Iraqi coup undermined US 'containment' of the Soviet Union on its southern flank for it deprived the Baghdad Pact (later the Central Treaty Organization) of one of its key members. It also resulted in the abrupt dissolution of the moderate Arab Federation of Iraq and Jordan, which had been set up only five months earlier as a counterweight to the radical United Arab Republic of Egypt and Syria (and, later, the Yemen) proclaimed on 1 February 1958. It was therefore hardly surprising that Soviet leaders (perhaps remembering the early history of their own country) seem to have feared that the Anglo-US landings were the prelude to a counterrevolution in Iraq, either with the direct use of UK and US troops, or with Iraq's erstwhile partner Jordan used as a surrogate, with the possibility that such actions would precipitate a wider conflict in the area, that the Soviet Union would be dragged in and that the scene would then be set for a direct Soviet-US nuclear confrontation.

Consequently, on 19 July Khrushchev proposed a summit meeting, to comprise the Soviet Union, the United States, the United Kingdom, France, India and the UN Secretary General (although it would take place outside the ambit of the UN), 'in order that immediate steps may be taken to put an end to the conflict that has broken out.... The most important thing is to avoid delay.'[3] Despite this urgency, the UK and US replies were cool and only dispatched on 22 July, the day on which Khrushchev had hoped the summit conference would open, and they evinced a preference for the UN as the setting for any meeting that might be held. Khrushchev replied the next day, giving way on the context of the meeting and proposing that work should begin in the Security Council on 28 July. He reaffirmed the need to have Indian participation. This time the UK response welcomed the Soviet concession, but the Americans remained cool and stated that the 28th was too early; indeed, on the 28th and the 29th, Secretary of State Dulles was in London for a meeting of the Baghdad Pact powers. But by 28 July Khrushchev had anyway adopted a completely different tone, accusing the United States in a letter of that date of retreating from its original desire for a meeting within the Security Council, and indicating his willingness now to defer to the French preference for the meeting to take place in Europe. This change of tone was doubtless accounted for by a relieved realization in Moscow that the Western powers were not contemplating overthrowing the new Iraqi government; under those circumstances, Khrushchev presumably felt it advisable to pay heed to the views of his principal ally on the crisis and on the modalities for its resolution.

The Middle East crisis was the first to erupt since Mao had proclaimed that the East Wind was now prevailing over the West Wind and that the communist bloc should exploit this advantage by increased militancy. Khrushchev's hurried proposal of a summit conference must have appeared pusillanimous in Peking. While *Pravda* editorials called for calm and reasonableness on the grounds that both the United States and the Soviet Union possessed nuclear weapons, the *People's Daily* argued against any appeasement of US aggression and advocated the dispatch of volunteer armies, evidently from the communist bloc, to the Middle East. Peking editorials also expressed scepticism about using the UN machinery, hardly surprising in view of the Chinese Nationalist occupancy of China's seat in the Security Council, and behind the scenes there may have been resentment at Khrushchev's suggestion that India ought to attend the summit. Only on 22 July did the *People's Daily* finally endorse Khrushchev's appeal for an emergency summit meeting.[4] Nine days later, on the afternoon of 31 July Khrushchev arrived secretly in Peking accompanied by his Defence Minister Marshal Malinovsky.[5]

The communiqué issued at the end of Khrushchev's visit made it clear that the Middle East crisis was a major topic of discussion. Mao formally endorsed the Soviet leader's summit proposal, although the communiqué did not specify in what context the summit should occur.[6] Mao later stated that the question of whether or not there should be a four-power summit was not mentioned at the meeting.[7] This may mean that he did not choose to upbraid Khrushchev for a proposal arguably offensive to Chinese sensibilities, or that Khrushchev had already decided on a new course of action which he outlined to Mao, or both. At any rate, shortly after his return to Moscow, Khrushchev wrote again to Eisenhower in terms that Mao could not but have approved, dropping his summit proposal because the United States refused to consider 'the possibility of a meeting of the heads of government outside the procedure of the ordinary sessions of the Security Council', although 'it is well known that, under the existing state of affairs in the Security Council in which a majority of the members consists of states belonging to aggressive *blocs*, and the great Chinese People's Republic is not represented, this organ is not in a position to draw objective conclusions on the question of foreign armed intervention in the countries of the Arab East'.[8] He called instead for an extraordinary meeting of the General Assembly.

Even if the Soviet and Chinese diplomatic positions on the Middle East were now identical, Mao had had another taste of Khrushchev's lack of firmness in confronting the West. After Khrushchev's departure, the militant Maoist strategy of opposition to appeasement was reaffirmed in the strongest terms in an editorial on the summit in the *People's Daily*. 'The nonsensical idea that peace can be achieved only by currying favour and compromising with the aggressors' was roundly rejected. Ridicule was heaped on 'soft-hearted advocates of peace' who naively believed that in order to relax tension at all costs the enemy must not be provoked. In Moscow, on the other hand, *Pravda* editorials on the summit stressed 'the unshakeable determination of two great peoples to do everything possible to ease international tension and to prevent the disaster of a new war'.[9]

But Mao's suspicions of, and indeed anger at, the Soviet leader were evidently aroused far more by the latter's proposals for joint military arrangements which both men have indicated were the principal reason for their meeting.[10] According to Khrushchev, the Russians had requested the Chinese for permission to build a radio station on Chinese territory to permit communication with Soviet nuclear-powered submarines operating in the Pacific.[11] To their surprise, Mao reacted in fury, alleging an insult to China's national sovereignty[12]; the cable from Yudin, the Soviet ambassador in Peking, telling of his meeting with the Chairman 'was like a thunderbolt out of a clear blue sky—he [Yudin] was the first swallow bringing us tidings of the coming deterioration in our relations with China'.[13] This 'alarming' dispatch convinced the

Soviet leaders that Khrushchev and Malinovsky should fly secretly to Peking.[14]

The Mao-Khrushchev talks were apparently conducted most of the time beside a swimming pool, with the two leaders sunning themselves on their towels 'like seals on the warm sand'. Khrushchev claims to have apologized for the radio station proposal, insisting that there had been no intention of violating China's sovereignty. Mao, he says, made a counter-proposal: the Soviet Union would supply credits and China would build the radio station. Khrushchev accepted this suggestion, but claims that, although the deal was finalized, the Chinese never built the facility.[15]

With the radio station issue seemingly settled, Khrushchev made a further request: permission to refuel the Soviet submarines and send their sailors on short leave at ports along the Chinese coast. His own account suggests that he was in fact asking for a fully fledged base. Mao rejected this proposal out of hand as an encroachment on Chinese sovereignty and dealt similarly with a proposal for a reciprocal arrangement by which Chinese submarines would in exchange obtain access to Soviet Arctic Ocean ports.[16]

Mao's much shorter version of the meeting transmutes Khrushchev's request into an attempt 'to block the China sea-coast, to launch a joint fleet in China to dominate the coastal area, and to blockade us'.[17] The other Chinese account confirms that a request was also made for the reconstruction of a long-range navigational aid station on the Chinese mainland.[18]

It may be that Khrushchev was less than full and frank in his memoirs and that he did make a specific proposal for joint fleet operations; Defence Minister P'eng Teh-huai's speech on 22 February had contained a hint that he would welcome joint operations.[19] But what is important, and is confirmed by both sides, is that, whatever its aim, the proposal had a very deleterious effect on Sino-Soviet relations.

The communiqué issued at the end of the Sino-Soviet summit did not mention Taiwan, and according to Mao's account he and Khrushchev did not discuss the forthcoming Chinese bombardment of the Nationalist-held offshore islands.[20] Khrushchev does not specifically confirm this, but it is certainly the implication of his account of his dealings with the Chinese in 1958.[21] But Khrushchev does claim that at some time during that year, the

Chinese 'requested considerable military aid from us. They said they wanted it in order to stage a military operation against Chiang Kai-shek. They asked for aircraft, long-range artillery, and air force advisers.' He claims that the Russians gave the Chinese what they asked for, not seeking to restrain Peking because 'we thought they were absolutely right in trying to unify all the territories of China'. What this Soviet generosity amounted to is unclear. Western sources indicate that there was little change in the shape of the Chinese Air Force between mid-1957 and mid-1958 when it consisted mainly of Mig–15 and some Mig–17 fighters and IL–28 light bombers. By this time, the Mig–15, which had been the backbone of the Chinese Air Force during the Korean war, was 'almost obsolete'; the Mig–17 was becoming out of date in the Soviet Union.[22] Yet the only sign of any change in the Chinese Air Force during the Quemoy crisis was the replacement of Mig–15s by Mig–17s at forward bases opposite the offshore islands. However, the latter were superior to the Nationalists' F–84 Sabres.[23]

Khrushchev states that the Soviet side also offered to station its interceptor squadrons in China and professes surprise at the 'extremely odd', offended reaction of the Chinese at this display of 'fraternal solidarity'.[24] Despite his denials, it seems highly probable that both the offer to station interceptor planes in China and the requests for communications and naval facilities on the China coast were designed, in the event of hostilities in the Taiwan Strait, to give Moscow some leverage over an ally whose Chairman propounded what the Soviet leader considered to be alarmingly simplistic analyses of the effects of a nuclear war.[25] Certainly it is hardly surprising that these three, separate Soviet indications of a desire for military facilities in China should arouse Chinese suspicions—suspicions that may well account for Mao's failure to warn Khrushchev that the planned attack on the Nationalists would take place within three weeks of his departure from Peking.

Prior to the Mao-Khrushchev summit, just after the conclusion of the MAC session, there had been a 'sharp upsurge' in Chinese calls for the liberation of Taiwan, including at the mass rallies on the Middle East, but these had died down during Khrushchev's visit.[26] It is my hypothesis that after the summit Mao decided that it was essential to go it alone to prove to Khrushchev that his critique of 'appeasement' was correct by showing that the Americans would back down if confronted. The only place he could sensibly attempt this was in the Taiwan Strait, and according to his own account the bombardment of Quemoy was one of the three matters he concentrated on at the Peitaiho conference (the others being steel and the communes).[27] This suggests that the forthcoming operation was discussed at the conference.

A massive artillery barrage was initiated on 23 August while the conference was still in session.[28] Torpedo boats were also successfully used in the attempt to prevent reinforcements and supplies arriving in Quemoy. The evidence suggests that the Chinese objective was to force a Nationalist withdrawal rather than to soften up the islands for an attack.[29] However, from 27 August, the Chinese increased the pressure by beaming broadcasts at Quemoy from coastal radio stations threatening the garrison with an imminent landing and calling on it to surrender.[30] Significantly, these warnings were never repeated or mentioned by the national radio network and so most Chinese were kept in ignorance of the apparent seriousness of the crisis and thus could never have realized the riskiness of Mao's gamble and the extent of his failure.

The gamble failed because Mao's assessment of the US will was faulty. On the very day that the Chinese bombardment was commenced, Secretary of State Dulles in a comment on the previous build-up in the Chinese coastal area warned against the assumption that an attack on the offshore islands could be regarded as a limited operation.[31] As the Chinese blockade became increasingly effective, the Americans prepared to convoy Nationalist supply vessels.[32] Presumably in an attempt to deter such US support, the Chinese issued a claim to a 12-mile territorial sea on 4 September, which was promptly rejected by the Americans. On the same day Dulles indicated that the US government felt free to help defend the offshore islands.[33] The danger of a clash between Chinese and Americans now seemed imminent.

However, when the SSC met the next day, Mao reassured its members that the government was attempting to ameliorate the crisis because it would be better for the people of the world.[34] He had not anticipated the world-wide agitation that would ensue from the bombardment of the offshore islands, but he claimed that only South Korea and the Philippines (conditionally) supported the US position there. Moreover, a crisis was not a bad thing in that it activated the backward.[35] A little later he asserted that China, like the Soviet Union, did not want war and indeed opposed it. One reason was that nuclear weapons caused vast devastation and China did not have them—and, his audience were entitled to infer, could not depend on Soviet nuclear weapons. There would only be war if the other side attacked first. Nevertheless China did not fear war. He hinted that a China armed with grenades could not be oblivious to the losses that would accompany an atomic attack, but he attempted to persuade his audience, as he had the Moscow conference the previous year, that even if half the population of the world were wiped out this would not be a total disaster, and he informed them of a discussion he had had with Nehru on this point. The enemy might attack with atomic weapons whether the Chinese were afraid or not, but it was better for them not to be afraid for reasons of morale. That was why it was essential to train the militia on a large scale within the communes.[36]

Mao's speech on 5 September has even now not been officially published and it is not clear whether or not the Russians knew about it then. But by this time they were sufficiently anxious to dispatch Foreign Minister Gromyko secretly to Peking.[37] Gromyko allegedly sat in on a Chinese Politburo session on 6 September. His brief was apparently to ascertain Chinese objectives. Since the Russians had not been consulted about the Quemoy operation in advance, they were concerned to discover what their commitments might be. Up till this point, their propaganda had been extremely hesitant, indicating their considerable reluctance to get involved in a crisis with built-in risks of escalation for them because of the Sino-Soviet treaty.[38] Possibly Gromyko, alarmed to hear Mao at the Politburo meeting contemplating with equanimity a Soviet-US nuclear exchange because China could survive it, stated firmly Moscow's refusal to incur risks. At any rate it was presumably the combination of Khrushchev's excessive caution, as Mao later described it,[39] and Dulles' intransigence that forced the Chinese to act decisively to defuse the crisis. On 6 September, Premier Chou En-lai issued a statement agreeing to a resumption of Sino-US ambassadorial talks. It was only now, on 7 September, that Khrushchev risked writing a letter to Eisenhower pledging full-blooded support to Peking, asserting that an attack on China would be regarded as an attack on the Soviet Union.[40]

The following day, 8 September, Mao again addressed the

SSC, now in a clearly defensive mood. He hinted at disagreements within the US government over the conduct of the
Quemoy crisis and suggested that the Americans were considering the wisdom of a withdrawal of the 110,000 Nationalist troops
on the offshore islands. Even if they did not withdraw, China
would continue with its leap forward. Some members of his audience, he acknowledged, did not consider the crisis beneficial, but
he repeated his earlier analysis of how it had resulted in almost
universal obloquy for the United States with even the United
Kingdom wobbling in its support, while China was denounced
only in Washington, Taipei and Seoul. Most significantly,
although he was speaking within 24 hours of Khrushchev's letter
of support, Mao felt able only to claim that the Soviet leader was
'basically' united with the Chinese, adding: 'He agrees that
Taiwan should be returned to us, but hopes the matter can be solved
peacefully.'[41] Evidently Mao did not think that members of the
SSC would have been deceived by Khrushchev's bluster, and had
to try to make the best of the situation. At the time, he also felt
compelled to sign a letter from the Chinese CC which expressed
'sincere appreciation' for the Soviet undertaking in the event of
an attack on China.[42] But years later, the Chinese openly dismissed Soviet claims to have stood shoulder to shoulder with them
during the 1958 Quemoy crisis:

> The Soviet leaders expressed their support for China on September 7
> and 19 respectively. Athough at that time the situation in the Taiwan
> Straits was tense, there was no possibility that a nuclear war would break
> out and no need for the Soviet Union to support China with its nuclear
> weapons. It was only when they were clear that this was the situation
> that the Soviet leaders expressed their support for China. . . .[43]

The subsequent development of the Quemoy crisis witnessed
some dramatic moments but, as the above quotation underlines,
the main decisions had been taken by the principal protagonists
by the end of the first week in September.[44] The seeds of further
bitterness between Moscow and Peking had been sown. What is
of concern for the present narrative was the manner in which the
Chinese attempted to make the best of their setback and even to
utilize the crisis for the promotion of domestic policies.

In October, Peking published a collection of Mao dicta under
the heading *Imperialists and all Reactionaries are Paper Tigers*
implicitly designed to reassure Chinese that whatever temporary

setbacks they might experience in international affairs they would certainly be the ultimate victors. Despite Mao's assertion of Soviet support at the SSC, the quotations denounced communists who overestimated the enemy's strength, clearly a reference to Soviet behaviour during the recent crisis.[45] But behind the scenes, Mao was now less sanguine then the paper tiger theory implied. The Chinese Chargé d'Affaires in London evidently sent an optimistic dispatch to Peking in autumn 1958 depicting the Western alliance as disintegrating, on which Mao commented:

Huan Hsiang's theory is correct. The Western World is disintegrating. Currently it is in the process of breaking up, though not yet completely. But it is heading in that direction. Final disintegration is inevitable. *The transitional period may last quite a while: it will not happen overnight.*[46] (Emphasis added.)

On 25 October, Defence Minister Marshal P'eng Teh-huai announced that China's forces would only shell the offshore islands on alternate days from then on. This extraordinary arrangement, coupled with the earlier decision to issue an open-ended series of numbered 'serious warnings' about US violations of Chinese air space and territorial waters—warnings that, it soon became clear, were never going to result in retaliatory action—must have underlined the extent of the fiasco for politically aware Chinese. The crisis also sparked sharp clashes between China's political and military leaders. Allegedly, P'eng Teh-huai, disagreeing with Mao's orders on the bombardment, refused to cooperate, and Chou En-lai had to take charge. Chief-of-Staff Su Yü's dismissal on 12 October was possibly Mao's riposte, but General Su's return to favour a year later suggests that he was not held to blame for the failure of the bombardment to achieve its ends.[47]

In his speech to the SSC on 5 September, Mao had said that both the United States and China feared war; the question was, who feared whom most? He invited his audience to consider the question objectively and look at it again after a year or two. His own opinion was that Dulles feared China more than vice versa.[48] It is doubtful whether many of his audience could have been convinced of this by China's actions in the early autumn of 1958.

(ii) 'Everyone a soldier'

The one direct benefit that Mao was able to extract from this setback was the speedy formation of the militia, ostensibly to maintain morale and diminish fears of a nuclear attack.[49] Mao was able to press his views of the necessity for a militia on reluctant generals. In fact, the 'everyone a soldier' movement did not start on a nation-wide scale until after Chou En-lai had defused the international crisis, but its effect, and that of the massive anti-US rallies and propaganda, was to conceal China's retreat by suggesting the danger of war had been heightened not lessened.[50]

The militia movement facilitated the 'militarization of labour' within the communes and thus assisted cadres in arousing patriotic fervour and mobilizing peasants for even greater efforts during the high tide of the leap.

Within a month, tens of millions of Chinese had officially become militia members. There were 30 million in Szechwan alone, the country's most populous province, where in a Chengtu factory the workers spent two hours leisure time after the evening meal in military training, while in a rural *hsiang* three hours a day was the rule. In militia training the habit of 'unified rising, eating, sleeping, setting out to work, and returning from work' was fostered. 'This greatly strengthened the collectivization of life and organizational discipline, and nurtured the fighting style in production and work.'[51] Similarly the 25 million militiamen of Shantung province, in addition to stepping up military training, 'also actively played the role of a main force on the iron-steel and grain production fronts'.[52] The Peking militia had the motto: 'Training more when not busy in production, training less when busy, and not training when extremely busy'; this was published in the *People's Daily* presumably to restrain over-enthusiastic amateur drill sergeants.[53] Pace-setting Honan launched the first 'satellite' of militia training by achieving good results in rifle target practice[54]; each commune had its military department and militiamen sang their own song:

> With a hoe in the right hand and a rifle in the left,
> We consider the field the battleground where we use
> Our hoes to attain the 10,000-catty-per-mou target,
> And our rifles in training to guard the fatherland.
> Should the American imperialists dare to invade,
> We would definitely annihilate all of them.[55]

Despite all this activity, an Indian academic who visited four communes in November–December 1958 found one commune near Peking still only planning to have its own militia and reported that the reasons behind the decision to militarize the communes were not made clear to him, although he raised the question with the commune directors as well as with his otherwise well-informed interpreter:

As I went round the farms I saw a few rifles standing in a knot here and there on the fields. I saw groups of farmers drilling on lines of military formation with old fashioned rifles. I enquired how far the peasants had advanced in learning to fight with live ammunition. The Director didn't answer my question, but pointed out that the great Commune movement was in its *first* stage and I had come just when the whole country was becoming Commune-conscious and the fever was catching on.[56]

The director's evasiveness was understandable. With 220 million men and women recruited into the militia by January 1959, it was impracticable for them all to be given target practice with live ammunition even though Mao called at the SSC for the issuing of several million and eventually several tens of millions of rifles and for the manufacture of light weapons in every province.[57] While the ordinary militia consisted of all able-bodied citizens between 15 and 50, there was also a 'hard-core' militia recruited from those between 16 and 30 to give a lead in production as well as in military affairs. Of Honan's 20 million militiamen, only 200,000 had been trained as hard core by summer 1959, and only half of these had practised 'with the firing of loaded guns'.[58] But even the millions who did not practise with live ammunition were psychologically mobilized by the new use of martial terminology in relation to production tasks, terminology that transformed peasants into 'fighters' on the 'agricultural front', rural areas into 'battlefields' and the forces of nature into 'enemies' to be conquered.[59]

The mass organization of the militia in 1958 represented, as one scholar has pointed out, the rejection on the military front of conventional techniques and institutions characteristic of the leap.[60] For Mao, who called for the organization of militia divisions at the end of September, it represented a victory for his preferred defence against imperialist aggression, drowning the enemy in 'a sea formed by several hundred million militiamen' which was 'something that no modern weapon can destroy'.[61] It was also a reaffirmation of his principle that 'weapons are the main, but not the decisive, factor in a war; the decisive factor is men, not materials'.[62] But Mao's victory was undoubtedly resented by many professional officers.[63]

(iii) Collectivizing living

The collective life-style which militarization of labour encouraged rapidly became the basis of an attempted leap towards communism by inflamed cadres. One famous jingle, attributed to K'ang Sheng, ran:

> Communism is Paradise;
> The people's communes are the bridge [to it].

(*Kung-ch'an-chu-i shih t'ien-t'ang; Jen-min kung-she shih ch'iao-liang.*) Behind the rhetoric lay the need to satisfy an increasing demand for labour for the immense tasks of the leap by liberating women for production.

Public mess halls were one way of relieving women of domestic chores. The *People's Daily* quoted from Lenin in its editorial on mess halls on 25 October and cited the inevitable Honan to rub home the lesson: the provision of mess halls throughout the province meant that each commune member had three extra hours for work or study, labour productivity had been raised by about 30 per cent, and six million units of female labour power had been released from domestic chores. The paper recognized that collective eating 'involves the change of the habits, in existence for thousands of years, of all the peasants', but it argued that if the mess halls were properly run, the initial unfamiliarity and inconvenience would be overcome.[64] However, the paper had to devote a further editorial to the subject only two weeks later because a considerable number of mess halls were poorly run, many of them serving only rice and no vegetables. The editorial revealed that one corollary of the mess hall movement was the take-over of the peasants' private plots for unified operation by the commune.[65]

The practical advantages for the supply of labour of the mess hall system were buttressed by its ideological potentialities. On 1 October, the *People's Daily* had pointed out that many communes were operating a system of free grain rations or free meals, and even supplying basic necessities free of charge:

Some people's communes operate a system of 'seven guarantees' or 'ten guarantees', under which members are guaranteed meals, clothes, housing, schooling, medical attention, burial, haircuts, theatrical entertainment, money for heating in winter and money for weddings. Such a system, of course, is not tantamount to the communist system of 'to each according to his needs', but it has completely broken the barriers of 'pay according to labour'. It satisfies the requirement of further development and represents a step towards 'selflessness'. Therefore it belongs to the sphere of communism and is a germination of communism.[66]

Peasants were reported to be overjoyed that the age-old problem of ensuring the next meal had been overcome. Mao, touring Anhwei, said: 'Since one commune can put into practice the principle of eating rice without pay, other communes can do likewise. Since rice can be eaten without pay, clothing can also be had without pay in the future.'[67]

None of this had been advocated in the Politburo resolution on the communes, although the introduction of free meals had been suggested during the Peitaiho discussions, apparently by the Shanghai 1st secretary K'o Ch'ing-shih.[68] Indeed, Liu Shao-ch'i later admitted that the mess hall system had simply been imposed by the CC on 1 October.[69] Ideological advantages apart, the 'free supply' system appears to have been an attempt to solve the problems caused by the amalgamation in the communes of richer and poorer APCs, the disruption of the old work point system, the take-over of the private plots and the long hours of work during the leap. Some families with few consumers and many breadwinners objected that the system would diminish enthusiasm for work and increase the number of 'lazybones'. While such 'backward' thinking was rejected, an attempt was made to meet the argument in some communes by the institution of a system of half-free supply, half wages.[70] Liu Shao-ch'i acknowledged during an inspection tour in Kiangsu in September that idlers would only disappear completely under communism, but he gave his endorsement to the supply system:

Lenin once said that Communist labour was voluntary labour, irrespective of rates, labour performed without expectation of reward and without the condition of reward. The people always do more and better irrespective of how much the reward or whether there are rates of pay.[71]

Mao himself was very keen on the total free supply system and visited Hsushui commune in Hopei, accompanied by Ch'en Po-ta and a Shanghai propaganda official, Chang Ch'un-ch'iao, who was to rise rapidly to the highest ranks of the party during the cultural revolution, to finnd out how it could be instituted.[72] Even Finance Minister Li Hsien-nien, whose portfolio inclined him to the side of caution,[73] described the supply system as a 'great event without parallel in history.'[74]

Another device to free women for production was the development of boarding primary schools and even boarding kindergartens. Again, the institution was also seen as a means of promoting the collective life-style, the concept of 'one for all and all for one', at an early age. An article in the youth newspaper *Chung-kuo Ch'ing-nien Pao* described the socialization process in these terms:

Raised in nurseries where they eat, live, play, study and labour together, the children contract early the conception of 'ours' when referring to toys, candy, classrooms, nurses and governesses, teachers and even the sunflowers in the courtyard, and have little chance of saying 'mine' to indicate private ownership. Collective life which provides for mutual assistance helps foster the spirit of organisation, discipline and friendship.[75]

The boarding school movement apparently received its original impetus from Liu Shao-ch'i, demonstrating his interest in nurturing the sprouts of communism, who remarked during an inspection of Honan communes in September:

Full-time nurseries are better than day nurseries. Primary schools should develop in the direction of becoming boarding schools. Social education for children should be stepped up, and the emphasis should not be laid on home education though this is still necessary. Party organs should step up control over social and communist education . . . .'[76]

An Indian visitor who asked a teacher at a commune kindergarten if the children missed their parents was told: 'I don't think so, because we provide for all their needs. They have necessities and even comforts here, comforts they would never have had in their own homes, in the past I mean.' Nursing mothers and mothers of ailing children could visit the crèches and kindergartens, although in the latter case visits were not always considered necessary since the children were under the care of trained nurses as well as the teachers. Parents had to give up their bourgeois emotional attachments, stop worrying about their children and concentrate on work.[77] To ease their minds, child care in the nurseries had to be of the highest quality. General Secretary Teng Hsiao-p'ing asserted:

Taking care of babies will be the most important [kind of work in the future]. In the whole nation, 20 m. people are needed to do this job . . . . An important part of the work is to educate people and train child care personnel . . . .

They should be paid higher salaries than university professors.[78]

The new life-style demanded new forms of accommodation. Old people were no longer needed as child-minders; nor would there be anyone at home if they themselves needed care. Consequently Happiness Homes for the aged were set up.[79] This meant that the main need now was for residences only for couples. One foreign visitor was shown piles of bricks dumped in fields and was told that already the peasants were building the foundations of blocks of flats that were to replace their old individual cottages. Each family was to have a one- or two-room flat, but without a kitchen.[80] Another visitor met a commune director who had evidently been captivated by T'an Chen-lin's concept of all peasants living in high-rise buildings:

'You have seen the peasants' huts, the small uncomfortable houses scattered all over the villages without plan or purpose. But when this commune gets going, all these huts will be pulled down. In fact, we have already started demolishing them. And we shall have a few huge buildings of flats. In fact, eventually one skyscraper in this village will house all the villagers from this and all the neighbouring villages when they are brought under this Commune. In a few years our countryside will be dotted with self-contained skyscrapers with their own kitchens, dining halls, tailoring establishments, schools, gymnasiums etc.' He paused and let this vision of the skyscraper-studded Communes of the Chinese countryside-to-be sink into me.

'They tell me you have visited America often. Do they have skyscrapers in their villages?' he asked. 'No', I replied. 'I have no doubt we shall surpass them in this matter', he asserted with complete confidence.[81]

(iv) Promoting communist morality

A collectivist life-style had to be matched by a communist consciousness, each nourhsing the other. Writing in *Red Flag*, the propagandist Wang Li asserted that Mao attributed the achievements of the leap to the tremendous drive of the masses, the communist working spirit. Citing the examples of the mass water conservancy and iron and steel campaigns, Wang defined communist labour as 'voluntary labour, without set quotas, done without expectation of remuneration'. This voluntary labour had itself become a large-scale mass movement.[82] By this time the whole question of material incentives had become the topic of mass debate at the personal prompting of Mao.[83]

The Shanghai propagandist Chang Ch'un-ch'iao, presumably inspired by his visit to Hsushui with Mao and encouraged by the

Chairman, initiated the debate with an attack on the concept of 'bourgeois right' which he stated was the basis of the wage system; the latter he contrasted unfavourably with the 'supply system' of the liberated areas in the pre-1949 period under which food and other principal necessities were distributed free:

Although living standards differed because of work requirements, the difference was not great. . . . For this reason, workers, peasants, soldiers, students and traders were united as one like members of the same family; they fought hard against the enemy. Do you still remember how the big army corps fought during the period of the liberation war? To support the PLA, thousands upon thousands of militiamen followed the army in their march to the south. They led the same life of military communism as the army. They did not aim at becoming officials or getting rich. No idea of wages, let alone 'piece wages' entered their minds.[84]

This nostalgia for the Yenan 'way' was not untypical of much writing during the great leap forward, which many authors, like Chang, clearly saw as an opportunity to recapture the pure, revolutionary fire of the party's epic period in the wilderness. Citing the spirit of the long march, Chang scornfully rejected the idea that production enthusiasm could only be encouraged by a wage system, which he characterized as letting 'money instead of politics assume command'. He admitted that under socialism the principle of 'to each according to his work' had to be adopted; but he argued that Marx had never said that the system of bourgeois right and its hierarchy of inequality should be systematized and developed.[85] In all this, Chang was undoubtedly echoing the views of Mao, who regarded the wages system as a concession to the bourgeoisie and preferred to rely on the 'drumbeat of revolutionary spirit' rather than on material incentives.[86]

Chang Ch'un-ch'iao's article was reprinted in the *People's Daily*, with a brief, unsigned, generally approving but somewhat ambiguous introductory note by Mao,[87] at a time when press reports were describing the abandonment of piece wages in many factories in Shanghai and elsewhere.[88] One reason was doubtless the difficulty, and indeed superfluousness, of maintaining a satisfactory set of norms at a time of rapidly rising output. Another reason may have been the desire to avoid the cost and inflationary pressure that a greatly increased wage bill would have meant. Suffusing these practical considerations was the belief that material incentives could be minimized in the enthusiasm of the leap. At any rate, piece rates largely disappeared throughout the country during 1958, even though the hourly wage system was retained as still appropriate, as cautious critics of Chang Ch'un ch'iao argued.[89]

(v) Education for the new era

Fundamental to the inculcation of a new communist morality was to be a revamped educational system. The most important change was the systematic integration of manual labour with study.

The new system was given a push by Mao in the Sixty Articles on Work Methods, although in a far more tentative manner than cultural revolutionaries later implied. In articles 48–50, Mao advocated that 'wherever possible' secondary vocational and technical schools should 'experimentally' run factories and farms. Only for this category of student did he advocate part-work, part-study (pan-kung, pan-tu). Laboratories and workships attached to higher technical institutions should where possible engage in production, but the needs of teaching and research had to be protected. Agricultural schools could, and secondary and primary schools in rural areas should, contract for teachers and students to participate in labour in neighbouring APCs.[90] But in the cities, universities and middle schools could establish factories or workshops 'where conditions permit' (tsai k'o-neng t'iao-chien hsia), or could contract for work in neighbouring factories. City educational institutions with land ought to set up farms; those without land but near the outskirts could participate in labour in APCs.[91]

While Mao was groping towards increased participation of students in manual labour, Liu Shao-ch'i was approaching the problem from the other end, seeking to provide more education for youngsters in order to satisfy the great hunger for it which he had noted during his provincial tour in 1957.[92] Liu had discovered that in Shantung and Kiangsu provinces half of all school-age peasant children did not go to school, partly because there were no schools, partly because their parents could not afford to send them.[93] Nation-wide, the critical sector was probably the junior middle school age group (13–16) which included 37 million youngsters for whom there were only some 7 million places in regular middle schools.[94] As early as November 1957, Liu had suggested that the YCL should investigate the experience of US universities, where two-thirds of all students worked while studying, to see if it had any relevance for China.[95] Then, in May 1958, he again talked to the YCL, on the 7th, and addressed an enlarged meeting of the Politburo, specially summoned to discuss part-work, part-study, on the 30th.[96] At all stages of the educational ladder, Liu pointed out, students wanted to progress to the next stage[97]; junior middle school graduates who found themselves working in factories with no hope of further study experienced great frustration.[98] The only solution was to encourage the growth of locally run part-work, part-study schools which would satisfy the demand for a chance to study, without imposing a financial burden on the state, and in a very short period of time turn out a large number of educated technicians and university graduates.[99] In addition to educational deprivation, Liu stressed the need to turn out appropriately trained young people as a reason for part-work, part-study schools. Of the 1957 crop of almost 1·3 million middle school graduates, 800,000 were not able to continue their studies, but were also unfitted for work because they had no skills. A third reason he gave for the system was the need to break down the barrier between mental and physical labour.[100]

By the time Liu Shao-ch'i had put his imprimatur on part-work, part-study schools in May, there were already thousands of them in existence. The green light had been given in mid-March by Lu Ting-yi, Director of the CC's Propaganda Department and an alternate member of the Politburo, probably on the basis of discussions in the party secretariat on 7 March.[101] The main form of these 'schools run by the people' (*min-pan hsueh-hsiao*) was the agricultural middle school (*nung-yeh chung-hsueh*). These provided young people still too immature for a full day's work in the fields with some knowledge of scientific agricultural methods and a familiarity with the modern tools and machines the government was seeking gradually to introduce and popularize, as well as with instruction in language and mathematics.[102] Students divided their time equally between class work and manual labour and their wages helped pay for the running of the school, although some may have received pocket money.[103] By 1960, there were 30,000 of these schools with almost three million pupils.[104]

The development of a 'double-tracked' educational system consisting of both full-time and part-time schools was the responsibility of Liu Shao-ch'i, as the senior Politburo member charged with overseeing the whole field of culture, and Lu Ting-yi.[105] Mao did not foreshadow part-work, part-study schools in the Sixty Articles although he clearly appreciated the problem they were devised to deal with. He advocated that, where conditions permitted, secondary vocational and technical schools could enrol extra students, so long as additional state expenditure was not incurred, and agricultural schools should take in some suitable APC members.[106] These suggestions were hardly calcualted to deal with the problem of educational deprivation as effectively as Liu's proposals, and recognition of this and of Liu's path-breaking role may account for some of the bitterness with which the latter was denounced during the cultural revolution.[107]

Certainly there was no justification, on the basis of their own criteria, for cultural revolution critics to denounce the 'double-tracked' system as such. They apparently approved of the joint CC-SC directive on educational work prepared before, discussed at, and issued on 19 September after Peitaiho, and in it the operation of both full-time and part-time schools was specifically encouraged as part of a multi-pronged attack on the educational problem.[108] Only if Liu Shao-ch'i and Lu Ting-yi had resisted the introduction of manual labour into the curricula of full-time schools would there be any grounds for alleging a 'two-road struggle' over education in 1958, and the evidence does not support such a contention.[109] Rather, it would seem that Liu's views were if anything developed on more radical and certainly more systematic lines than Mao's. Moreover, Liu had focused on the political problem—demand for education, and Mao on the ideological ideal—manual labour for all.

At the beginning of 1958, Mao, Liu and other leaders were cautious about the introduction of manual labour and desirous of protecting the quality of the full-time schools.[110] From the spring and through the summer, part-work, part-study schools were pushed with a clear recognition that they would inevitably be inferior academically to full-time schools.[111] After Peitaiho, Mao, Liu and Lu Ting-yi all encouraged the development of manual labour in full-time institutions, with Liu making more detailed proposals than Mao.

Mao had been impressed during a visit to Tientsin on 13 August at the way some institutions of higher learning were running factories, and he praised this practice then and in a speech at Peitaiho, when he also ridiculed the siting of agricultural colleges in cities.[112] Then, on 9 September, addressing the SSC in private, Mao stated that the central problem of education was its integration with manual labour. Noting that the Russians were on the same tack, he went on:

If schools run factories, factories run schools, schools run farms, and communes run schools, if [people] work while studying, or do part-work part-study, then study and manual labour will be integrated. This will be a great revolution.[113]

Later in the month, during an inspection in Hupeh, Mao supported the demand of students for part-work, part-study and the widespread running of factories by schools.[114]

While touring in September, Liu Shao-ch'i elaborated in public the views he had expressed in an unreported speech at Shihching-shan in early July.[115] During his visit to Honan from 16 to 18 September, he pushed part-work, part-study for regular schools and universities:

New factories can set up schools and enroll a number of junior middle school students to study there. A factory is a senior middle school and the students there may study a few hours and work a few hours every day. Then factories become schools and schools factories. The method of part-work and part-study can be adopted for senior middle schools and also for unversities. A system must be established for the students to work six hours and study three hours a day, or work four hours and study four hours. The schedule must be relatively stable and last eight or ten years until the students graduate from the universities. In this way, the number of both students and workers will increase. At the end of the period, they will be both university graduates and skilled workers. *This is also a condition for the transition to Communism.*[116] (Emphasis added.)

During his visit to Kiangsu between 19 and 28 September, Liu went further, stating that one of the best ways to integrate education and manual labour was to merge factories and schools. In the past they had been run separately; in the future they could be gradually amalgamated. A new factory would also be a new school; workers would also be students and they would be enrolled jointly by the labour and education departments. After initial training, they would enter the part-work, part-study system, taking courses from junior middle school to university levels. Thus the differences between mental and manual labour would be more rapidly eliminated and true red and expert, proletarian intellectuals would be trained.[117] By this time, Liu's thinking seems to have moved on considerably, from an advocacy of a double-tracked educational system to a vision of a merger nor merely of the two education tracks but even of education and industry. Significantly, there appear to have been no cultural revolution quotations from or attacks on Liu's position on education in September 1958.

By this time Liu Shao-ch'i was clearly looking beyond the course charted by the CC-SC directive. Lu Ting-yi, as befitted a more junior official, only expanded upon the ideas in the directive in his article in *Red Flag* published on 1 September, and cultural revolution attempts to pin-point anti-Maoist sentiments in the article do not stand up when a comparison of the two is made.[118] Perhaps the most serious charge made against Lu and others was that they were determined to preserve quality, allegedly at the expense of proletarian politics.[119] Yet the directive underlined the vital importance of the preservation of quality education in the 'full-time' educational sector.[120] What might be said is that both the directive and Lu's article, drafted as they probably had been no later than July or early August, were outdated by the time they appeared with respect to Mao's and Liu's current thinking.

In educational institutions, the overt response to the new policy was predictably enthusiastic, though behind the scenes many teachers were concerned that it would be disastrous for education.[121] The teachers and students of the philosophy department of Wuhan University decamped to the countryside for ten months to the despair of the University president and, according to him, the peasants.[122] At Fukien Agricultural College, classes were suspended for eight months to permit students to perform manual labour.[123] An English visitor to a Kunming primary school, housed in what had apparently been an old Buddhist monastery, saw painted over an aged wooden doorway the slogan: 'We are pupils, but at the same time workers; these are our classrooms, but at the same time our workshops.'[124] At another primary school, in Chungking, he found that manual labour included grass-cutting, weeding of paths, cleaning of classrooms

or better still they went off to a local soda-water factory and were given odd jobs around the place to get them accustomed to factory conditions. I mentioned that it was a long time since seven-year-old children had worked in factories in England, but this headmistress, with her calm dismissal of everything that did not come under the General Line, was uninterested. 'The principle of education, she said, was to teach children to work, and the best way was to make them do it.'[125]

This visitor remarked on the universal enthusiasm among younger children for collecting scrap iron.[126] Official reports dilated upon the manner in which their elder brothers and sisters at middle schools and universities turned the scrap into pig iron and steel. By the end of August, 18 institutions of higher education in 11 cities were allegedly capable of refining almost 700,000 tons of steel. In Nanking and Canton there were 34 middle schools with various kinds of furnace. In Tsinan, the middle schools installed 77 furnaces during one week in July.[127] By October, Honan had moved into the van in this field too with the announcement that in Loyang 12 primary schools had combined to build an iron and steel plant which had produced 130 tons of 'high-quality' steel in its first month of operation and had now reached a productivity of 40 tons a day. Here again the seven- to nine-year-olds mainly collected material, for two hours a day, while much of the actual operation of the steel plant was in the hands of teachers and older teenagers. 'With a properly worked out rhythm of study, work and rest, the pupils became healthier and increased in weight.'[128] The Loyang enterprise was praised by no less than K'ang Sheng, an alternate member of the Politburo, and it may well have led to an escalation of the amount of manual labour expected of young children. Certainly by the following year Liu Shao-ch'i himself jibbed when his own nine-year-old son came home exhausted after an eight-hour stretch.[129]

(vi) The backyard steel drive

The schoolchildren and students of China were of course only emulating their elders. After Peitaiho, all China was plunged into an all-out steel drive in the effort to reach the new national target of 10·7 million tons. Chou En-lai, who had reportedly been full of vigour at Peitaiho[130] was assigned by Mao to take charge of the steel campaign,[131] an ironic decision in view of the earlier opposition of the Premier and his colleagues to 'blind advance', but a sensible one in view of his considerable energy and organizing ability. Chou became the head of the 'small leading group of the iron and steel great leap forward', regularly chaired SC iron and steel conferences and personally organized linking conferences (*hsieh-tso hui-i*) between ministries. He and eight Deputy Premiers divided the country into areas, each supervising and visiting the steel drive in one area. Chou also mobilized teams from specialist institutions to go to the 'front line' and help the masses with their steel-making.[132]

On 5 September, a *People's Daily* commentator instructed provincial papers that the focus of propaganda must be switched from agriculture to industry and especially to the steel drive.[133] The paper's editorials urged the population on to greater efforts.[134] Although Mao himself continued to talk of the need for a correct balance between agriculture and industry,[135] the effect of the propaganda was inevitable. By mid-September, over 20 million people were engaged in producing iron and steel[136]; at the height of the steel drive the figure rose to 90 million, according to Mao.[137] P'eng Teh-huai later alleged that 90 billion work days were expended on the campaign during the last four months of 1958.[138]

Liaoning province, the core of China's conventional steel industry, was given the task of producing over 44 per cent of the target,[139] and at the start of the campaign it was China's 18 major integrated iron and steel works that bore the principal responsibility for attaining the Peitaiho figure. Native-style operations were directed towards the production of iron. But on 4 October, presumably with the realization that the steel target might not be met by conventional means, the *People's Daily* called editorially for a mass steel-smelting campaign to match the iron one. As a result, whereas in September the output of native-style furnaces only accounted for 14 per cent of the month's steel output, in October the figure was 49 per cent.[140] Throughout the country, peasants, workers, clerks, housewives, students—Chou En-lai personally mobilized the Peking University campus[141]—even writers responded to the new call. The editors of *Peking Review* told it like it was:

In response to the government call for a nationwide effort to push forward steel production, we too turned to making steel in our own courtyard. Everybody lent a hand. In no time, some brought in broken pans, pots and kettles, others contributed old bricks and limestone, still others turned in all sorts of odds and ends. In a matter of hours a reverberatory puddling furnace, Chinese style, was built and trial production started within a day. The only person in the group who could claim some technical knowhow was a young man who had visited several office-run furnaces before our furnace went into operation. We failed in our first attempt with a 'crucible' type furnace, but have had smooth sailing with our reverberatory puddling furnace.

The editorial stated that the first heat of steel had been tested in the laboratory and been proved up to standard.[142]

Far from the capital, in the southernmost province of Yunnan among one of the minority nationalities, the steel drive was equally frenetic, as an English visitor reported:

We walked through the paddy to another village where four monstrous home-made blast furnaces had been rigged up. The place was a furious, seething, clattering scene of frenzy. People carried baskets of ore, people stoked, people goaded buffalo carts, people tipped cauldrons of white hot metal, people stood on rickety ladders and peered into furnaces, people wheeled barrows of crude metal—though to me the stuff that was being poured out at the bottom of the furnaces looked exactly like the stuff that was being poured in at the top.

When asked, the commune chairman stated that the peasants had learned to build a furnace and smelt the ore 'from the newspapers'. He then apparently burst into a 'torrent of passionate abuse', underlining in a revealing manner how, in the euphoric early autumn of 1958, the production drive was interwoven with the Taiwan Strait crisis in the minds of Chinese cadres:

But apart from learning new technical processes we also read in the papers about American aggression. While you imperialists are attacking the Arabs in the Middle East, we in China are carrying on our peaceful work. We love peace . . . but if the Americans attack us we will fight them. On this farm we have twelve hundred militiamen ready day and night to go to the front to fight America, waiting for their marching orders.[143]

That night at a Kunming theatre, sown on to the curtain, was the sentence: 'Without fail we shall liberate Taiwan.'[144]

In this overheated atmosphere of militancy and nationalism, no one dared to cast doubts on the steel campaign, as Ch'en Yi admitted five years later.[145] Even a down-to-earth leader like P'eng Chen praised the use of native methods in the iron and steel campaign,[146] though Teng Hsiao-p'ing, at least, may have been aware of the problems this form of manufacture raised.[147] Yet even in 1958, fervour was not enough, despite the propagandizing of Chang Ch'un-ch'iao. According to P'eng Teh-huai's later account, the long hours of extra toil had to be bought with 2 billion yuan of extra work-points paid by the central government and another 2 billion yuan of subsidies paid by provinces and municipalities, a sudden injection of additional purchasing power which dealt a 'violent shock' to markets.[148] The measures had their effect. With tens of millions of Chinese toiling fervently at their furnaces, the daily output figures for 'steel' rose sharply, and the 10·7 million ton target was achieved in mid-December.[149] But in the fields, bumper harvests of grain, cotton and other crops awaited collection. A massive tragedy was in the making.

PART TWO

RETREAT

7 WITHDRAWAL AT WUHAN

(i) More from less

The problem had been visible as early as the spring. In March 1958, two Soviet scientists seconded to the Chinese Academy of Sciences made a tour of central China by train. They remarked on the absence of peasants from the rice fields although it was the spring planting season. They concluded that the explanation was 'in the thousands of smoking chimneys we saw each day, and in the fires that were visible every night over half the horizon. The peasants were carrying out the orders of the Party, working night and day at the mines and at home-made blast furnaces to fulfil the "Drive to Produce Metals Locally"'.[1] Even before the peasants were flung into the mass steel campaign, the attempt to leap forward simultaneously in industry and agriculture had led to a 'tense situation of the rivalry between the cities and the countryside for labour power'.[2] By the end of the year the number of industrial workers had increased from just over 9 million in 1957 to well over 25 million in 1958,[3] the vast majority of these apparently employed on a temporary or 'contract' basis and thus ineligible for labour insurance or free medical care.[4] In Szechwan province alone the increase was over 2 million; in Honan it was 1 million.[5] As a result, 10 billion work-days, about one-third of the time normally devoted to the production of grain, were lost to agriculture in 1958, although it was claimed that about half of this loss was made up for by improved tools.[6]

One expedient adopted in an attempt to resolve the competiton for labour between agriculture and industry was the formation of reserve labour forces in the communes, apparently to be deployed on the industrial front where and when needed.[7] During the slack agricultural season, an estimated 40 per cent of the rural work force nation-wide was working on industrial tasks, particularly iron-smelting.[8] In Honan, the province that others tried to 'catch up with',[9] the figure seems to have been up to 50 per cent.[10] As the year of the leap drew to its frenetic close, 'shock brigades' were needed back in the fields to try to gather as

much of the bumper harvest as possible and to perform other vital rural tasks. On 22 October, the CC and the SC issued a joint
emergency directive ordering the shock collection and transportation of agricultural products.[11] Schools were closed, clerks and
shop assistants were drafted and less essential capital projects
were halted in the effort to provide more labour power.[12]
According to an official description, the peasants

work regardless of remuneration and time. They go wherever they are
needed; they work as long as it is necessary. Often they work day and
night. They eat and sleep where they work. Among them are both young
people and old people and both women and children.[13]

Sensible shock battalions worked only to midnight; the foolish-
ly over-zealous might work four or five days virtually non-stop.[14]
In a conversation in early July, Liu Shao-ch'i had advocated combining work with leisure lest people obtained 'everlasting rest',
but in context it appeared to be a far more perfunctory admonition than was alleged during the cultural revolution.[15] It was not
till 9 November that the *People's Daily* warned editorially: 'See
that peasants take rest'. It cited approvingly the practice of con-
fining shock work to not more than one week a month, with 20
days of normal working and three days for political, cultural and
personal activities; shock work periods should not last more than
48 hours at a time and there should normally be six hours sleep
during that period, with longer rest hours for young people, children and expectant mothers.[16] If that kind of timetable safe-
guarded peasants' rest, the rigours of an all-out shock campaign
can be readily imagined. Yet, Mao continued to defend the practice of shock work.[17]

Even with shock work, many areas failed to gather in all the
harvest, it was later admitted. In Shantung, the yield of crops was
'lower than originally planned as a result of crude autumn harvesting and consequent damage and waste'.[18] In Anhwei, 1st
secretary Tseng Hsi-sheng admitted that 'because we had to concentrate our efforts on big-scale steel production we did not do a
thorough and careful job in reaping our harvest. As a result, we
did a rough job and wasted some grain.'[19] In Szechwan, a bumper harvest was reaped, but 'ideological work and organisation
and management work did not catch up soon enough, resulting in
heavy waste of food grain'.[20] Po I-po, Chairman of the State Economic Commission, is reported to have commented bitterly in

private: 'Although there is an increase of 66 per cent in industrial output, yet when this is compared with the loss in agriculture through sending tens of millions of people to the mountains, how much has been gained and how much has been lost after all?'[21]

Such contemporary comments provide an important backdrop to P'eng Teh-huai's attack on the leap at the 1959 Lushan plenum. Even today, when frank public critiques of the leap are permissible in China,[22] no precise estimate of the loss of grain in 1958 is possible. In some areas, cadres who feared that they would not have enough food for the mess halls held back more than they admitted or needed, and consequently supplied the peasants with far more 'free' food than they might otherwise have expected.[23] The knowledge that there had been both wastage and under-reporting compounded the difficulty of assessing the size of the harvest, already made difficult by the undermining of the statistical services.[24] Since climatic conditions had undoubtedly been highly favourable, and output did genuinely reach record levels, the sketchiness of the data permitted politically motivated and intensely competitive party cadres to advance the most exaggerated claims and encouraged their wishful-thinking superior to believe much of them.[25] Even a hard-boiled pragmatist like Teng Hsiao-p'ing was moved to claim that per capita grain distribution would be 625 kg in 1958, 1,050 kg in 1959 and 2,500 kg in 1962, and to proclaim: 'We can have as much as we want.'[26]

In November–December, 1958, the Chinese leaders held three major conferences: at Chengchow in Honan from 2 to 10 November; at Wuchang in Hupeh from 21 to 27 November; and then the CC's 6th plenum from 28 November to 10 December, again in Wuchang although the meeting is often referred to as the Wuhan plenum after the 'triple' city of which Wuchang is part.[27] At none of these meetings, not even in private, does Mao seem to have indicated more than marginal doubts about the size of the 1958 grain harvest. On 30 November he referred to 'false reporting' as a major current problem, but in the next breath he asserted that the 1958 grain harvest was 375 million tons, 25 million tons higher than the top estimate made at Peitaiho[28] and over double the 1957 output; for safety's sake he advocated publishing a claim of only a 90 per cent increase—i.e. a total of 350 million tons—which would have represented a scaling down of 6 per cent of the estimated output. In his speech to the 6th plenum on 9 December, Mao again referred to cadres telling lies and making false reports about figures, but he now advocated publishing the 375 million ton figure (which was done) because within the space of ten days that figure had ceased to be the highest claimed output and instead represented a discounting of some 12 per cent of the newly claimed total output of *430 million tons* (of which a quarter was estimated to be sweet potatoes).[29] If such discounting seemed soberly sensible to Mao's audience, it was only because they were prepared to accept as realistic a scaled-down output claim which flew in the face to all agricultural experience, both Chinese and foreign.

The reason for their attitude was the success achieved in greatly expanding yields on a number of experimental fields in various parts of the country. Their mistake was to believe that such successes could be reproduced throughout the country. There were doubters who argued that high yields were obtainable on small areas but not over large ones. However, the *People's Daily* dismissed such caveats editorially, arguing that there was no 'celestial river' separating small from big; 'since we can do this [i.e. achieve outstanding results] on small areas, why can't we do it on large areas?'[30]

Behind the paper's confidence lay the conviction that during the leap the agricultural authorities had hammered out a formula for success. In the Twelve-Year Agricultural Programme, rehabilitated in October 1957 on the eve of the leap, twelve items had been listed as crucial to agricultural success.[31] In the Sixty Articles on Work Methods, finalized at the end of January 1958, the list was expanded and altered to 14 items.[32] Presenting the Twelve-Year Programme to the party congress in May 1958, T'an Chen-lin emphasized six points,[33] but the following month he listed seven.[34] Also in June, Agriculture Minister Liao Lu-yen mentioned six items in one section of an article in the *People's Daily* and eight in another section.[35] Multi-province agricultural conferences presided over by senior agricultural officials in the weeks before Peitaiho exhibited similar divergences.[36]

On the eve of Peitaiho, T'an Chen-lin attempted to codify the diverse prescriptions in his article in the *People's Daily* on 11 August, listing eight 'native methods' (*t'u pan-fa*) which accounted for the bumper summer harvest: water conservancy, fertilizer application, soil amelioration, popularization of better seed strains, reasonably close planting, prevention of insect pests and plant diseases, field management and the improvement of tools.[37]

These were to be the elements of the final formulation, but not quite in that order or with that emphasis, and not without further vicissitudes.

At Peitaiho, T'an's list was reduced to five items—water conservancy, fertilizer, soil, seed and close planting. Soil improvement took on a new significance, being defined as meaning principally deep ploughing which was now described as the 'central' (*chung-hsin*) technical device for increasing yields. A special directive on deep ploughing was one of five issued on rural matters after Peitaiho (the others covering socialist education, water conservancy, fertilizer and the campaign against the four pests).[38] The National Day editorial in the *People's Daily* on 1 October singled out the same five items in the same order, but a week later the paper printed an article by the 1st secretary of Kansu province, Chang Chung-liang, in which he cited five slightly different items: water conservancy, fertilizer, soil, close planting and field management.[39]

In mid-October, at the first of another round of multi-province agricultural conferences, T'an's eight-item formula, attributed now to Mao, re-emerged in its final order—water conservancy, fertilizer, soil improvement (i.e. deep ploughing), seed improvement, close planting, prevention of plant disease and pests, tool improvement and field management.[40] This Sian conference of northern and north-eastern provinces may have represented the apogee of T'an's influence during the 1958 leap, because the subsequent report listed him above his Politburo senior Li Hsiennien.[41] Thereafter, some time between 18 and 27 October, the eight-point programme was finally simplified to an eight-character formula—*shui, fei, t'u, chung, mi, hai, kung, kuan*—and the description adopted at Sian, 'the basic methods of agricultural production' (*nung-yeh sheng-ch'an-ti ken-pen fa*), altered to 'the agricultural "charter"' (*nung-yeh 'hsien-fa'*).[42]

This laborious gestation and ultimate sanctification of the eight-point charter illustrates admirably the manner in which the proponents of the leap groped towards a clear, simple formula for agricultural success which could be easily grasped, publicized and used by efficient and motivated cadres throughout the country as the motor of agricultural expansion. But while uniform policies and their mandatory fulfilment may suit the production lines of industry, they are counter-productive if applied to agriculture, especially in a vast country like China with its many greatly differing local environments. The charter merely listed eight general principles of agricultural production without specifying answers to such crucial subsidiary questions as how? how much? when? and where?[43] As such it was safe but useless. It became dangerous when Mao, T'an Chen-lin and their colleagues, aware of the weakness of a general *vade mecum*, attempted to infuse it with precise instructions for universal application.

Mao had become enthused with the idea of deep ploughing as a result of reading an article by the party secretary of Ch'ang-ko *hsien*, Honan, and he dilated upon it and close planting at some length on 17 May at the party congress. He argued that if Ch'ang-ko could achieve excellent results in this manner there was no reason other *hsien* could not copy it;[44] clearly the Chairman was one of the proponents of the view that advanced experience was infinitely transferable.[45] At the end of the congress Mao buttonholed T'an Chen-lin twice on this subject and urged him to publicize it; he also issued a directive that each province set up three model deep-ploughing areas.[46] As a result, deep ploughing was discussed and agreed upon at the pre-Peitaiho, multi-province agricultural conferences, and a CC directive, in which it was closely linked with close planting, was duly issued afterwards.[47]

Deep ploughing and close planting when practised on a large scale tend to exhaust the soil. In China, they also required additional labour power and financial resources. Consequently, it soon became apparent that they could not be carried out thoroughly on all China's farmland.[48] At Peitaiho, Mao put forward what came to be called the three-three system (*san-san chih*) according to which one-third of cultivatable land should be used for intensive grain-growing, one-third should be afforested and one-third should be left fallow.[49] Mao may have derived the idea from the development of what was described as the 'basic field system', which had been formulated in Shansi province earlier in the year as a device for coping with its labour shortage.[50] At the first post-Peitaiho, multi-province agricultural conference, consisting of northern and north-eastern provinces including Shansi, the matter was evidently thrashed out in detail because a week later the *People's Daily* carried reports and an editorial on the high-yield achievements of a number of counties and special regions in these provinces.[51] At this conference, despite the presence of Shansi, the new policy was called a 'sputnik field' movement, a term apparently coined in another northern province, Hopei, and it involved the intensive farming of 10 per cent of cultivated land.[52] A few days later the *People's Daily* was referring instead to 'high-yielding tracts', rich production fields or 'basic fields'; it emphasized that these innovations represented a major step towards the implementation of Mao's three-three system.[53] A subsequent conference of eastern provinces decided that between 10 and 30 per cent (Fukien, 50 per cent) of cultivated land should be allocated to sputnik *experimental* plots and high-yielding fields and that these should lead forward the ordinary fields.[54] This decision opened the way to the implementation of the policy of 'plant less, produce more, and harvest the most' according to the concrete conditions of each locality.[55] The north-western provinces talked at their conference in terms of a basic field system and of the allocation of 10–15 per cent of land for sputnik fields to promote the policy of higher production on smaller areas.[56] The southern and south-western provinces agreed on an allocation of 10 per cent of land for sputnik fields, seeing the measure like the other provinces as a step towards the 'plant less, produce more, and harvest the most' (*shao chung, kao ch'an, to shou*) policy.[57]

Later reports spelled out how individual provinces planned to carry out conference resolutions. Pioneering Shansi, where the 1958 sown acreage already represented a reduction on the 1957 figure, planned a further massive decrease by virtually one-third to 2·1 million hectares for 1959.[58] Other relatively sparsely populated and agriculturally less important northern and north-western provinces like Inner Mongolia and Tsinghai planned reductions of 21 per cent in cultivated acreage.[59] The heavily populated 'rice-bowl' province of Szechwan, on the other hand, planned a reduction of only just over 8 per cent; some 15 per cent of the grain acreage would be designated as high-yielding which would be expected to produce outputs in 1959 ten times as high as the average 1958 yield of 7·5 tons per hectare! Even the 'ordinary' grain fields were assigned outputs of between 22·5 and 37·5 tons per hectare.[60] In north-eastern Kirin similar targets were set but no acreage reduction was planned since the terrain favoured extensive farming.[61]

Due to the scattered nature of the statistics it is not possible to compare prognostication with implementation for each province, but later reports confirm the hint conveyed by Szechwan's plan figures that the densely populated heartland provinces did not take the risk of adopting Mao's three-three system lock, stock and barrel and attempt to feed their populations from one-third of their former cultivated acreage. In Anhwei, the acreage sown to wheat in 1959 was reduced by about 16 per cent. In Kwangtung, the cultivated acreage was reduced by only 7 per cent; in Liaoning by 8 per cent. In Heilungkiang, where extensive farming was the pattern, the cultivated acreage actually increased by 10 per cent. Figures from Hopei and Hunan indicate that there had been small reductions in cultivated acreage in 1958 and the cumulative effect of reductions over the two years 1958–9 may have been significant in such provinces. In Hopei, for instance, the reduction in cultivated acreage in 1959 was only 7 per cent, but it was only the latest in a series of reductions since 1956 which had reduced cultivated acreage over the three-year period by 1·3 million hectares, or almost 14·5 per cent. Even so, this figure too was considerably less than Mao's one-third. Moreover, one has to remember that reductions in *cultivated* acreage do not necessarily entail reductions in *sown* acreage if double cropping is introduced; in Shantung, the acreage under cultivation was reduced by over 10 per cent between 1957 and 1959, but the acreage sown to wheat which was reduced by 9 per cent in 1958 went up by 13 per cent in 1959, an increase that took the sown acreage for that crop over the 1957 figure. Similarly, cultivated acreage declined in Anhwei in 1958, but sown acreage increased.[62]

But despite the apparent caution of some provincial secretaries in implementing the 'plant less, produce more, and harvest the most' policy, acreage sown to grain declined by 6 million hectares in 1958 and a further 11·6 million hectares in 1959, a total reduction of 13 per cent over the two years.[63] Evidently few if any of the senior Chinese officials attending the various conferences of November–December 1958 could have had any conception of the magnitude of the statistical error upon which their optimistic forward planning was based. At the 6th plenum, Mao repeated his advocacy of the three-three system, indicating that he certainly saw no need to rein in the agricultural leap forward, even though he accepted that the agricultural 'charter' could not control sun or climate.[64] Indeed, misplaced confidence about grain output may well have accounted for the relative *sang froid* with which the plenum retreated on other fronts. As one outside observer later pointed out, party cadres tended to regard as bourgeois or petty the intricate interrelationships between such factors as irrigation, drainage, seepage, water table level, moisture retention ability, salinization, river flow, water pollution, flood control, etc. During the heady days of 1958 and 1959, it was easy for the Party to overlook the fact that nature is both ingenious and deliberate. To mobilize hundreds of millions of people to build in haste staggering amounts of earthworks may impress other people and nations—but not nature.[65]

As of the 6th plenum, Mao was certainly still impressed by the water conservancy achievements of the past year, and this helps to explain his continuing optimism about the agricultural leap.[66]

But rational if incorrect arguments are less important for the understanding of the frenzy that engulfed China in the second half of 1958 than voluntary gullibility, the willing suspension of disbelief of the country's leaders. In a recent speech by a former secretary of Liu Shao-ch'i, a speech too sensitive to be published even today, Teng Hsiao-p'ing is reported to have been deceived by a model peasant into thinking that he had produced 35 metric tons of rice on one-sixth of an acre of land[67]; the average output for the country claimed for 1958 even during the leap was only 0·2 tons.[68] A scientifically trained cadre of the CC's propaganda department persuaded Marshal Nieh Jung-chen, Chairman of the Scientific Planning Commission, to take him to Mao to relay a report that if an apple were inserted in a pumpkin it would grow with the pumpkin to a large size.[69] The Chairman's reaction is not recorded, but it seems unlikely that a junior official would have had the temerity to inveigle an interview with him if he had not anticipated an encouraging reception.

Mao's attitude fully justified T'an Chen-lin's continuing efforts to flay party secretaries into using new tools and achieving ever greater yields and outputs, efforts that were unfairly criticized as 'leftist' when cultural revolutionaries later attempted to exculpate the Chairman for the excesses of the leap.[70] All Mao did was rightly but mildly to rebuke the Sian conference, and thus indirectly T'an Chen-lin who had presided over it, for concentrating too much on grain production to the neglect of cash crops.[71] Liu Shao-ch'i, too, was accused a decade later, sometimes in the company of Teng Hsiao-p'ing, of responsibility for the policy of producing more grain from less acreage, whereas as we have seen Mao played a leading role in promoting it. If the proponents of the leap were to be blamed for the excesses of the second half of

1958, then the 'guilty men' should certainly include Liu and T'an and many others, but Mao would have to be the principal defendant.[72]

(ii)   Second thoughts on steel

In the same breath as he affirmed his belief in the most extravagant estimates for grain production in 1958, Mao implicitly admitted at the 6th plenum the total lack of realism that had characterized the steel campaign, and adjured his colleagues not to let 'foreigners' bragging' turn their heads! Of the 10·7 million tons produced, only 9 million were of good quality[73]; the following autumn the figure would be reduced further to 8 million tons. A little over two months after the launching of the backyard steel movement, Mao was thus prepared to acknowledge privately that it had been a mistake. The extent of his retreat was exhibited even more strikingly in his revised estimates for the future. Whereas in September he had thought in terms of China producing 30 million tons of steel in 1959, 60 million in 1960 and 80–120 million in 1962,[74] these targets he now felt were neither realistic nor possible and he talked instead of 18–23 million tons in 1959, 30–40 million by 1960–1 and 50–60 million by 1962.[75] He was still dealing in fantasies, but he was clearly trying to marry them with the real world. Earlier he admitted that 10 million tons of the former 30 million target for 1959 had been 'subjectivism', adding: 'One does not know the difficulties of a thing without experiencing it.'[76]

Mao's awakening on the steel question seems to have occurred after the Chengchow conference in the first ten days of November. He revealed that after he arrived in Wuchang (i.e. after 21 November) he had had second thoughts about the steel targets.[77] At the 6th plenum on 9 December, he announced that a 15-year economic plan that had been put forward as recently as Chengchow had now been laid aside until at least 1962 because there was no evidence on which to decide whether it was either necessary or possible. This had evidently caused some consternation among eager cadres who were not privy to all the reasons for the shelving of the plan.[78] What is unclear from Mao's account is why he had experienced his Damascene conversion on the steel question on the way to Wuhan. Perhaps by the time he arrived there he was in possession of realistic estimates of the worth of backyard steel. Perhaps in Wuhan, one of the country's principal steel-producing centres, plant officials had been emboldened to hint at the truth. Mao was almost certainly aware of the transportation crisis caused by the need to ship coal all over the country in order to fuel the steel drive.[79]

In Chengchow, Mao was possibly still under the spell of Honan's trail-blazing 1st secretary, Wu Chih-p'u; at any rate Chou En-lai was not there to advance the cause of realism.[80] But thereafter, the Premier—who had ordered at least one top-level investigation into the progress of the leap as early as August[81]—and his senior economic ministers were presumably able to put the facts to the Chairman. Wang Chia-hsiang, a CC member and onetime Politburo member with a special relationship to Mao,[82] was later said to have influenced his thinking in Wuhan.[83] At any rate, Mao there admitted his mistakes and defended the planners against probably opportunistic attacks by over-enthusiastic advocates of the leap. He specifically accused a recently dismissed Minister of Commerce, Yang Yi-ch'en, of attempting to take advantage of the occasion to knock down Chou and Deputy Premier Ch'en Yun, the other Commerce Minister, and he rejected attempts to pour cold water on the realistic plans of Li Fu-ch'un, Chairman of the State Planning Commission.[84] In return, Chou defended Mao's over-enthusiasm,[85] which the Chairman felt compelled to admit in a remarkable passage:

I made a mistake at the Peitaiho Conference. Concentrating on the 10·7 million tons of steel, the people's commune, and the bombardment of Quemoy, I did not think of other things. The Peitaiho Conference resolution must now be revised. I was enthusiastic at the time, and failed to combine revolutionary fervour and the practical spirit. The two were combined at the Wuchang Conference. The resolution must be revised. Walk on both legs, with Russia's revolutionary fervour and America's practical spirit.[86]

Most importantly, Mao now began to stress the favoured formulae of the planners—reliability, stable foundations, coordination, an overall viewpoint, arguing that the whole country must be taken as a chess board, a phrase which would be much repeated in the months ahead.[87] Moreover, he was apparently prepared to tolerate a request by the planners for Soviet advice on the steel drive.[88] Chou En-lai felt emboldened to order what was presumably (since he took the North Korean leader Kim Il Sung to see it) a show commune to stop making steel on the grounds that it lacked iron ore and fuel and had not grasped the techniques. This was an extraordinary step to take under the eyes of a foreign leader and suggests that the visit may have been highly embarrassing. However, Chou's directive was not publicized at the time.[89]

(iii) Ideological withdrawal on the communes

As early as the Chengcho conference, Mao had realized the need to restrain those more enthusiastic cadres who had been encouraged by the remarks of Liu Shao-ch'i and himself to believe that China could leap forward into communism through the communes, perhaps in as little as three to five years.[90] Mao warned that the party could 'only guide [the peasants] step by step to divorce themselves from relatively small collective ownership [i.e. APCs] and move toward the system of ownership by all the people [i.e. state farms] via the relatively large collective ownership [i.e. communes], but we cannot ask them to complete the process in one stroke. . . .'[91]

Mao elaborated on this theme in a further speech at Chengchow in which he admitted that '[s]ome comrades object to the dividing line between the two systems of ownership'.[92] The building of socialism meant the realization of a complete socialist system of ownership by all the people, including a changeover from collective to all-people ownership in the communes.[93] He rejected the idea that the communes already represented all-people ownership in the manner of the Anshan iron and steel works, and argued that if the distinction between the two types of ownership were ignored there would be no point to socialist construction, the objective of which was to increase the supply of products and thus facilitate the transition to the higher stage of ownership (i.e. by proving the success of the system). The commune was the best organizational form for the two transitions from the 'socialism of today to complete ownership by all the people, and from the latter to communism. When the transitions are completed in the future, the commune will serve as the basic level structure of the communist society.'[94]

One of the 'comrades' whom Mao had to rebuke at Chengchow for excessive enthusiasm was Ch'en Po-ta, who proposed the ending of commodity production and the abolition of currency. The curious aspect of this post-cultural revolution revelation is its failure to explain how Ch'en, who had been ideologically in step with Mao so far during the leap, moved ahead of him at Chengchow.[95] It is at least possible that Ch'en floated his proposals with the Chairman's tacit consent, but that the latter had to disavow them because the Chengchow discussions revealed that they would arouse opposition and cause confusion.

In his efforts to damp down ideological over-enthusiasm, Mao would have had the support of Liu Shao-ch'i. Liu's initial attitude to the leap and the communes had been one of great enthusiasm, and he had sent his children to work in a commune near Peking during the summer.[96] But as increasingly wild production claims were made he commented: 'We are being deceived.' When Hsushui commune announced it had entered communism, Liu, too, went personally to investigate. It was a reflection of the man and the times that although Liu found Hsushui's claims to be nonsense, he did not say so, apparently in order not to discourage the cadres.[97] Only when Mao had spoken would his colleagues move.

Mao's Chengchow speeches must have been available to the participants at the subsequent Wuhan plenum, because in his remarks there he felt no need to refer more than briefly to the 'two transitions on the way to communism'.[98] The plenum's 'Resolution on some questions concerning the people's communes' spelled these out as the transition from collective ownership to ownership by the whole people *in the countryside* and the transition from socialist to communist society. These two processes and the earlier transition from APCs to communes were interconnected but distinct. The move towards ownership by the whole people would mean the organization of federations of communes by counties. It would take three to six years, as laid down at Peitaiho. But even at this stage, pay would still be based on the socialist principle to each according to his work. Only when there was an abundance of social products would it be possible to adopt the communist principle to each according to his needs. To suggest that the communes would enter communism immediately was to vulgarize communism and to strengthen petty-bourgeois egalitarianism.[99] Mao, in private, was bold enough to suggest a time-scale for the entry into *communism*: 15–20 years or perhaps longer.[100] The resolution was far more restrained. It stated that 15–20 years or more would be required for the construction of an industrialized country with *socialist* ownership by the whole people.[101] After the death of Mao, this whole discussion would be ridiculed as 'transition in poverty' and blamed on Ch'en Po-ta.[102]

(iv) Mollifying Moscow

The moderate claims of the resolution were almost certainly designed to appease Moscow. Mao himself admitted to the plenum that the main spearhead (*feng-mang*) of the resolution on the communes was directed at international opinion which respected the enthusiasm of the commune movement but decried its haste and the claims made that it represented a rapid leap into communism.[103] Evidently, mounting Soviet pressure on this issue over previous months, culminating in Khrushchev's decision to summon a special party congress at which he could put Chinese ideological pretensions in their place, had finally had an effect. The Soviet carrot was the prospect of economic aid which the Chinese by now would have realized as vital if the pace of their industrial advance was to be maintained.[104]

Despite the public retreat of the Chinese CC, the issues raised by the commune movement were far too important in political and diplomatic terms as well as ideological ones for Khrushchev to call off his attack. But although he was almost certainly informed that in private Mao was still prepared to make claims for the communes that went far beyond the official line, Khrushchev was reasonably conciliatory at the CPSU's 21st Congress. He accepted, virtually in so many words, the Chinese proposition that there were no barriers between the stages of socialism and communism, although he insisted that the socialist phase could not be 'violated or bypassed at will'. On the question of speed of transition through socialism to communism, he asserted that while there could be no resting on laurels, 'there must be no undue haste, no hurried introduction of measures that have not yet matured'.

In a gesture towards Mao, Khrushchev reversed an ideological proposition advanced by a leading Soviet philosopher, T. A. Stepanyan, at the height of Soviet anger about the communes. Stepanyan had attempted to put down Chinese pretensions by asserting that the communist countries of Europe would enter the communist stage as a group, and well before Asian communist countries who would also enter as a group (i.e. with China waiting for North Korea and North Vietnam). Explaining the resolution on the communes, probably to the plenum, General Secretary Teng Hsiao-p'ing stated that even when China had prepared the material and spiritual conditions for entry into communism, it would be 'beneficial to the international communist movement' if the Soviet Union entered first; besides, the material conditions in the Soviet Union gave it the basis for entering communism first.[105] But a month later Khrushchev reversed Stepanyan by asserting that all communist countries would make the transition to communism 'more or less simultaneously'. This was the only proposition in Khrushchev's speech which the Chinese subsequently characterized as a 'creative' addition to Marxism-Leninism. There was a catch, however, as the Soviet Ambassador to China, Yudin, made clear in his speech to the congress: 'The more the economic plans of these [bloc] countries are coordinated and the more the developed countries help the less developed countries, the faster will all, in a single front, move towards Communism'. Yudin, more than most Soviet citizens, must have known that such an appeal for greater integration of the Chinese economy with the economies of the Soviet Union and Eastern Europe would fall on deaf ears.

Khrushchev could doubtless afford to be conciliatory on matters like the transition to communism because they were theoretical and hardly immediate, especially after the Chinese retreat at Wuhan. Moreover, Khrushchev may have hoped that Mao's decision to retire as head of state, finally ratified at the Wuhan plenum and announced thereafter, foreshadowed a declining role for the Chairman and his ideas which the Russians found so unpalatable.[106] But the communes were in existence and represented a concrete challenge to the traditional Soviet collective farm, and they had to be condemned, if not by name. Khrushchev asserted that collectives could 'go on serving for a long time the development of the productive forces of agriculture'. Premature introduction of the communist principle of distribution according to need would be 'levelling' which 'would mean not transition to communism, but the discrediting of communism'. Without material incentives, there could be no question of leading the millions forward to communism.[107]

The Chinese indicated their disagreement by implying that Khrushchev's proposition on collective farms was valid only for the Soviet Union.[108] They were not prepared to withdraw the proud opening words of the resolution on the communes. It had proclaimed lyrically: 'In 1958 a new social organisation appeared, fresh as the morning sun, above the broad horizon of East Asia',[109] and gone on to lay down that the commune was 'the basic unit of the socialist social structure of our country' as well as 'basic organisation of the socialist state power'.[110] All the resolution had been prepared to concede was the need for the period December 1958 to April 1959 to be spent on 'educational work, overhaul and consolidation, that is the work of checking up on the communes'.[111]

Moreover, despite his conciliatory attitude on the ideological implications of the communes, Mao at Chengchow had taken further steps to undermine the respect of Chinese cadres for the Soviet economic model in general and Stalin's economic views in particular. One of his speeches appears to have been devoted principally to a consideration of Stalin's last statement on economics, *Economic Problems of Socialism in the U.S.S.R*, which Mao advocated should be studied by provincial and local committees. But while he stated that many points in the first three chapters were accurate, Mao added that in places it was possible that 'Stalin himself was not clear'. Nor did Stalin coordinate current and long-range interests of the people well; mainly he 'was walking on one leg'. There was not enough emphasis on light industry and agriculture and there was too much stress on technology and technical cadres: 'he only stressed cadres, but ignored politics and the masses. This was walking on one leg.'[112] Stalin's rejection, in a reply to the economists Sanina and Venzher that was appended to the main text, of the suggestion that the means of production concentrated in the MTS's should be sold to the collective farms as a means of raising them to the stage of all-people ownership was criticized by Mao as 'almost completely wrong'. The reply showed that Stalin 'did not trust the peasants and did not want to let go of the farm machinery'. Stalin's arguments were only self-deception and he had failed to solve the problems of the two transitions in the countryside.[113] A few days later, P'eng Chen told Peking cadres that Khrushchev was more progressive than Stalin in transferring tractors to the collectives.[114]

Mao's remarks were logical developments of parts of his speech on the ten great relationships and his speeches at the Chengtu conference.[115] But whereas his criticisms of Soviet economic policies had hitherto been general rather than personalized, this direct and extensive attack on Stalin's economic ideas meant that the late Soviet leader was guilty of major errors, not just towards China, which he could perhaps be excused for misunderstanding, but even in this crucial domestic field. Indeed, Mao's speech at Chengchow represented something of an about turn from the public Chinese defence of Stalin in 'On the historical experience of the dictatorship of the proletariat'. There the late Soviet leader had been praised for defending 'Lenin's line on the industrialisation of the Soviet state and the collectivisation of agriculture' and thus bringing about the triumph of socialism in the Soviet Union and creating the conditions for victory in the war against Germany.[116] The change of line probably reflected Mao's newly acquired knowledge of Stalin's ideas; certainly the startling impression conveyed by Mao's Chengchow speech is that only very recently had he bothered seriously to study a treatise proclaimed on publication six years earlier to be the definitive Marxist analysis of contemporary economics, an impression which, if true, sheds interesting light on the relationship between Mao and the Soviet leadership. But even so, Mao's willingness to disseminate more of his uncomplimentary views on Stalin, at least within the party, and the decision to prepare a Chinese textbook on political economy embodying Mao's ideas probably owed much to the growing tension between Moscow and Peking.[117]

The compromise reached by Moscow and Peking in late 1958 and early 1959 was thus an uneasy one; it was no wonder that a proposal by Deputy Premier Marshal Ho Lung for a joint Sino-Soviet assult on Mt Everest was rejected by Chou En-lai.[118] The evidence suggests that the compromise was reached by a process of unilateral concessions by each side in response to moves by the other rather than by hard bargaining in private as at the Moscow conferences of 1957 and 1960. The Chinese would undoubtedly have been embittered by Khrushchev's unfraternal action in revealing to a leading 'imperialist', the US Senator Hubert Humphrey, his scorn for the commune idea,[119] and their resentment would not have been erased by the granting of a major new instalment of Soviet assistance for China's industrialization programme on the occasion of Chou En-lai's attendance at the CPSU's 21st congress in January–February 1959. But at least the Chou-Khrushchev economic agreement on the construction of 78 new enterprises worth 5 billion roubles, for which China would pay with exports, seemed to represent a joint commitment to renewed partnership.[120] And Mao's vision of the alliance as the rising East wind would have been reinforced by the launching of the first Soviet 'cosmic rocket' early in 1959, an event which was greeted jubilantly in China.[121] But within eight months the partnership would begin to fall apart.

8 MAO VEERS RIGHT

(i) Rectifying the communes

While the ideological retreat on the communes had its origins partly in the exigencies of intra-bloc politics, it also represented a response to concrete problems on the ground in China. It was these problems that the 'checking up on'[1] or rectification of the communes (*cheng she*)[2] ordained at Wuhan (and signposted by terminological changes discussed in Appendix 1, pp. 181–4) was supposed to solve. The five months designated for the rectification process, December 1958 to April 1959, were punctuated by important party conferences: in Peking on 27 January[3]; of provincial party secretaries in early February; an enlarged Politburo meeting—the 'second Chengchow conference'—from 27 February to 5 March; another enlarged Politburo meeting in Shanghai from 25 March to 1 April, leading to the 7th CC plenum in the same city from 2 to 5 April. Both the Wuhan plenum and the second Chengchow conference sparked meetings of provincial party officials and rural cadres throughout the country which evidently underlined sharp contradictions at the grass roots.[4] These contradictions were reflected in the discussions of the party leadership and led Mao to take what he himself described as a 'right opportunist' position.[5]

The rectification process started even before the publication of the Wuhan documents and was fuelled by official encouragement to the masses to 'bloom and contend' (*ta ming ta fang*) by putting up large character posters (*ta tzu pao*) in which they could air their views 'freely and frankly'.[6] But one important change was decided on at Wuhan without further consultation with the peasantry; a relaxation of the military-style discipline that had been promoted during the early days of the communes. The three changes or '–izations' (*san hua*) advocated by *Red Flag* in September—organization militarized, action martialized, life collectivized—were to be expanded into the four changes (*ssu hua*) with the addition of 'management democratized' (*kuan-li min-chu-hua*). When recommending the *san hua*, *Red Flag* had rejected the idea that they might lead to commandism.[7] But the Wuhan resolution indicated greater concern that the use of the militia system had impaired 'democratic life' in the communes.[8] The addition of the fourth '–ization' was designed to spur peasants to speak up against such a tendency.[9]

But despite its espousal of mass participation in the rectification process, the Wuhan resolution on the communes was couched in language too judicious and too balanced to encourage upheaval. In the accepted official style, it first emphasized the strong points of the communes and dealt with their defects as secondary matters, and this was the approach adopted by grass roots party committees.

Within a week of the conclusion of the Wuhan plenum, the first provincial party conference was summoned to discuss the CC's decisions. In Shantung, 3,000 cadres met under the leadership of 1st secretary Shu T'ung and spent nine days in conclave. One proposal was the creation of a commune rectification task force of up to 30,000 people.[10] Other provinces followed suit.[11] In line with Mao's new thinking on steel production, Shantung forbade the erection of any more backyard iron and steel plants, while other provinces ordered a changeover from native to foreign or modern methods of iron and steel production.[12] Characteristic of all the provincial press releases was an unshaken optimism that the achievements of 1959 would eclipse even those of 1958.[13]

However, underlying the press releases of even so pushful a province as Honan was a more realistic appraisal of the situation in the countryside. According to the Honan party committee's plan for overhauling the communes

opinions are at variance among the cadres and the masses regarding the people's communes. Some of the policies overlap, and certain nonsensical ideas still remain. Though order has been established in production, basically, a well-organised administrative system is still lacking. Though industrial production and agricultural production are attended to, the development of multiple economy has been somewhat neglected. Though the situation is one of big leaps forward, insufficient concern is shown over the masses' living conditions, and the simultaneous arrangements for production and living conditions are as yet inadequate.[14]

(ii) 'Departmentalism' in Kwangtung province

Far starker revelations about the situation in south China communes were reaching Chinese in Southeast Asia from their relatives in Kwangtung and Fukien provinces. They complained bitterly, for instance, about the confiscation of property. 'With the establishment of communes, all property has become State-owned; all houses and furniture have been turned into Government property. They merely do what they like. No one has any rights at all.'[15] 'Everything belongs to the commune now. There is no individual personal property or belongings.'[16] 'You know that sewing-machine of yours must be turned over to the commune for public use.... I have discussed the matter with Fifth Grand Uncle, Third Younger Sister and a few others. We finally decided we must sell the sewing machine as soon as we can. But the price of sewing-machines is too low because there are too many people selling their sewing-machines.'[17] 'Nowadays, everyone must give up things for "investment". No one seems to know just what "investment" really means. We are told we must give our things to the Government and that's "investment".'[18] 'All bank deposits are either used for investment or just taken over by the authorities. As to remittances from the South Seas [i.e. from relatives in Southeast Asia], only a small portion is paid to us, all the rest is taken as public money.'[19] Mao was to revert to this topic at the second Chengchow conference.

Another major cause of grief which was to become the prime concern at provincial and central level, and the focus of bitter disagreement within the CC, was the food problem. In a letter dated as early as 28 October, a teacher resident in the city of Amoy, in Fukien, foreshadowed the urban food supply crisis of the turn of the year in his complaint: 'For months we have not tasted a catty of meat or a single piece of fish. Everybody is in the same situation. Nothing edible is procurable.'[20] Commune mess halls supplied people with a basic diet of rice[21] or sweet potatoes[22]; but two pounds of rice a day was insufficient for an 18-hour working day,[23] and according to one letter writer: 'People fight each other to get to the rice barrels first, but there is never enough.'[24] Moreover few could afford or sometimes even find supplementary foodstuffs. 'Pork is priced at one yuan a *catty*. There is absolutely no fish from the open market. In the black market, the price is about 1·3 or 1·4 yuan a *catty*.'[25] 'Those who work will get two ration units worth of supplemental food. Actually it is impossible to buy supplemental food...shrimp sauce and other such items are not being sold.'[26] 'Nor are there vegetables available, not to mention fish and meat. Only sick people with certificates are permitted to buy. Eggs are selling for between 18 cents and 20 cents each and chicken between 3 yuan and 4 yuan each. This is the black market price.'[27] 'Take pork for instance. I have not been able to buy even one piece in the past month.'[28] 'Vegetables are much more expensive to buy. Not only that, they have become very difficult to buy.'[29] One letter summed up better than most what appeared to be a prevailing mood of despair: 'The present situation is frightening because there is nothing for sale; there is nothing to eat when we are hungry. People are afraid to die because they feel they will be unable to close their eyes after they are dead; and people hesitate to live on. Everybody is suffering. Everything is gone.'[30] Yet this was the best harvest year since the communists came to power and the Kwangtung 1st secretary, T'ao Chu, had advanced the disastrous slogan 'Eat three meals a day'.[31]

The likely impact of the letters on the overseas Chinese clearly alarmed the Kwangtung authorities. Remittances from Southeast Asia, a major source of foreign exchange, could dry up if it were generally believed that they were confiscated on arrival or shared out in the collectivist pool, or even on the strength of reports of harsh treatment of relatives. First Secretary T'ao Chu felt it worthwhile to answer questions on the communes put by visiting businessmen and pro-communist Chinese journalists from Hong Kong and Macao. The importance placed upon this public relations exercise was underlined by the re-publication of an abridged version of T'ao Chu's remarks in China's main organ for international propaganda, the *Peking Review*.

T'ao dealt principally with fears about the destruction of the family, the militarized discipline of the communes, the loss of freedom and overwork. On all these matters, T'ao defended policies stoutly and indeed often counter-attacked. Although he referred to the principle of 'democratic management' for the running of communes added by the Wuhan plenum, he gave no hint that this was the result of fears that military-style discipline had been carried too far; although he referred to the new emphasis on an eight-hour work day in the countryside, at no stage did he admit that this represented a realization by the Chinese leaders at Wuhan that they had been pushing the peasants too hard. Even more significantly, at no stage did T'ao deal with the problem of food shortages which was beginning seriously to worry him and his colleagues and which had already worried the letter writers of

Kwangtung. However, he did assert that bank deposits and over-seas Chinese remittances would be sacrosanct.[32]

Despite T'ao's bland reassurances, the Kwangtung party had been among those which began to modify the more extreme manifestations of the leap even before the conclusion of the Wuhan plenum. T'ao Chu's wife, Tseng Chih, published a short article in the *People's Daily* on 29 November stressing the need for adequate rest.[33] In a telephone conference on 3 December, one of the provincial party's most active secretaries and T'ao's 'faithful lieutenant', the 40-year-old Chao Tzu-yang, ordered a relaxation of work schedules, an improvement of mess halls and respect for private property like houses, clothes, furniture and savings.[34]

A month after his return from Wuhan, T'ao Chu led an inves-tigation team in a week-long analysis of the conditions of Humen commune, in Tungkuan *hsien*, near the mouth of the Pearl River; his findings were published in the *People's Daily* on 25 February.[35] At about the same time, mid-January, Chao Tzu-yang led another high-ranking team to Hsuwen *hsien* in the tip of the Luichow peninsula; his report appears to have been read by Mao and distributed widely.[36]

T'ao Chu's very detailed report on Humen—it occupied a full page of the *People's Daily*—was predictably upbeat in mood, but listed six major problems to be solved in Humen and in Kwang-tung communes generally.[37] Of these, the first was the conflict between centralization and unity on the one hand and depart-mentalism (*pen-wei-chu-i*) on the other. Departmentalism was prevalent among cadres to a 'comparatively remarkable' (*pi-chiao t'u-ch'u*) extent, and indeed some cadres had already become cor-rupt. If departmentalism were not corrected there was a danger that the commune might degenerate into an empty shell (*k'ung chia-tzu*).

Departmentalism meant the secreting and consumption of commune foodstuffs and financial resources by the commune's sub-units, the production brigades. In one case, the peasants had been relatively prosperous when their brigade, the Humenchai, had been an APC, but some families had suffered drops in in-come in the sharing out that resulted from its absorption in the commune. Their officials had attempted to make up by conceal-ing grain, money and supplementary foodstuffs that should have been assigned to the commune.[38] After a week-long meeting, some 5,588 metric tons of grain and 12,000 yuan were uncovered. Another grain-hoarding brigade explained that it had wanted to secure its food supplies in case the commune free supply system broke down and also to have a surplus that would permit it to concentrate on supplementary foodstuffs.[39] The hoarded funds represented almost a quarter of the commune's capital investments in October and November 1958; since the commune increased its investments 25 *times* in December as compared with the previous two months, perhaps the hoarding of cash was a hedge against all brigade resources being swallowed up in the commune's maw.[40]

Chao Tzu-yang's activities in Hsuwen *hsien* are known in detail only from a hostile account published during the cultural revolution[41]; but T'ao Chu's contemporary report and Mao's strictures on the two men at the second Chengchow conference permit one to extract an objectively bowdlerized version of what happened. The questions Chao sought to answer during his inspection were: 'Was there a bumper crop in autumn last year? If a bumper crop was harvested, why the grain shortage?'[42] After an inspection of fields in the *hsien*, Chao was convinced that there had been a bumper harvest, sufficient for there to be several tons of surplus grain.[43] A number of *hsien* officials reported that they had discovered hidden hoards of grain and a rally of 4,000 cadres was held on 23 January to launch an anti-concealment drive. Officials who owned up were promised that they would be allowed to keep the grain for their mess halls; those who did not would not be allowed home. No one spoke up and the conference had to be abruptly adjourned![44]

Individual investigations by *hsien* officials then uncovered seven brigade or team cadres who confessed (allegedly falsely and after coercion, according to the cultural revolution account) to have concealed grain.[45] Encouraged, Chao organized another, larger rally. Threats were used; the pressure was intensified. During the course of this anti-concealment drive, one team leader apparently committed suicide, another cadre attempted to, six were arrested of whom two were jailed and died in prison, and 109 were dismissed; altogether almost 50 per cent of the basic level cadres received some form of criticism.[46] Some 38,000 tons of concealed grain were uncovered.[47]

While still in Hsuwen, Chao held a province-wide telephone conference to announce his findings and to call for similar uncovering of hoarded grain elsewhere. He estimated that there might be over three million tons concealed in the whole of Kwangtung, or almost 10 per cent of the claimed output for 1958.[48] On 25 January he issued a directive indicating that he believed that the great majority of basic level cadres in the province were implicated in grain concealment activities, and he asserted that the food problem was 'the focus of the struggle between the two roads and two lines in the countryside at the present time', in short of great political importance.[49]

Three weeks later, at the Kwangtung provincial party congress, T'ao Chu placed the struggle against departmentalism firmly in the context of the policy enunciated by Mao at Wuhan of taking the whole country as a chess game. T'ao added that it was necessary to take the whole province as a chess game, and described this as 'a most important principle'. In particular, the people's communes should serve the unified national plan even more strictly, an implicit underlining of the importance of their grain deliveries to the state. He rejected the idea that departmentalism was simply an instance of revolutionary activism.[50]

The attitude of the Kwangtung party was endorsed by the Shansi 1st secretary T'ao Lu-chia in an article published in *Red Flag*.[51] There was clearly no doubt in T'ao Lu-chia's mind that departmentalism was the deviation that the chess game policy was designed to correct. In one of his concrete examples, he castigated a commune which had concealed how much grain, cotton and oil crops it had produced in 1958 and had only come clean after repeated investigations and a great debate—shades of Hsuwen—in which the commune's obligations to industry and city dwellers were stressed and the priority of interests was listed as state, collective, and individual.[52] T'ao buttressed his strong denunciation of departmentalism with a quotation from Mao (the provenance of which he did not give): 'The special mark of this kind of departmentalism is neglect of the big picture and complete indifference to other departments, other areas and other people.'[53]

(iii)   The chess game concept

To what extent did such provincial views coincide with the centre's definition of the chess game concept? The first *People's Daily* editorial on the chess game certainly indicated that departmentalism and dispersionism (*fen-san-chu-i*) must be opposed. Smaller interests must give way to larger, lower levels to higher levels, communes to counties, counties to provinces. Priority had to be accorded on a basis of urgency. It was impossible to accomplish all undertakings simultaneously; if one attempted to catch ten fleas at the same time, one might end up catching none. National arrangements had to be made in the selection of construction projects, the production of major items, the distribution of raw materials and in the procurement and allocation of the main products for production and for the people's livelihood.[54]

Unquestionably, the *People's Daily's* description of the chess game policy encompassed the delivery of surplus grain and other crops by brigades to communes, by communes to *hsien*, by *hsien* to provinces and by provinces to the central authorities. How else could the urban population be fed? How else could food processing and textile factories obtain their raw materials? But the main thrust of the editorial was to emphasize the importance of centralized leadership and unified arrangements and to convince provinces and lower levels of administration to restrain the helter-skelter, 'dispersionist' industrialization spawned by the 1958 leap with every locality going all out in all directions, in order that widespread bottlenecks could be reduced and major national enterprises, especially in heavy industry, should not be starved of raw materials. To underline the message the paper also printed a front page story recounting how Anhwei, Fukien, Chekiang, Kiangsi, and Honan were all passing their best iron to Shanghai in the spirit of the chess game policy.[55] Significantly, it had been the Shanghai 1st secretary K'o Ch'ing-shih who published the first major article on the chess game policy,[56] in which he stressed the dependence of the country's premier industrial city and largest urban conglomeration upon raw materials and food from elsewhere in the nation.[57]

Yet whatever the original motivation for the chess game policy, by the time K'o Ch'ing-shih and the *People's Daily* got round to adumbrating it, the grain concealment problem had resulted in it acquiring an additional meaning. The timing of the consequent attacks on departmentalism in the context of the chess game concept is important:

27 Jan.   Peking (Politburo?) meeting on the management of communes.
28 Jan.   T'ao Chu signs the report on Humen criticizing departmentalism.

16 Feb.   *Red Flag* published K'o Ch'ing-shih's article on the
             chess game policy.

17 Feb.   T'ao Chu addresses Kwangtung party congress, criti-
             cizing departmentalism in the context of the chess
             game policy.

21 Feb.   Mao defends departmentalism in the context of the
             chess game policy at Honan meeting.

24 Feb.   *People's Daily* editorial on the chess game policy.

25 Feb.   *People's Daily* publishes T'ao Chu's Humen report.

27 Feb.   Mao makes his first speech to the second Cheng-
             chow conference, defending departmentalism and
             grain concealment.

1 March   *Red Flag* publishes T'ao Lu-chia's article criticizing
             departmentalism in the context of the chess game
             policy.

2 March   *Nan-fang Jih-pao* publishes T'ao Chu's report to the
             Kwangtung party congress.

5 March   Mao refers critically to T'ao Chu and Chao Tzu-
             yang at the Chengchow conference.

In sum, by the time the Chengchow conference opened on 27
February,[58] there had been a substantial attack by Kwangtung
provincial leaders on the departmentalism of basic-level cadres as
the cause of the grain concealment problem and a call for its elimination under the rubric of the chess game policy; during the
early stages of the conference, *Red Flag* published a Shansi attack
on departmentalism couched in terms similar to Kwangtung's.
Mao disagreed profoundly with the stand adopted by these, and
probably other provinces, and his speeches to the second Chengchow conference were delivered with corresponding heat. It is to
Mao's thinking on the rural situation that we must now turn.

(iv) Mao rethinks

The Wuhan plenum had failed to appreciate that there was a food
problem. Only in the second half of December did Mao and other
central and provincial leaders begin to realize with growing
alarm, that, despite the bumper 1958 harvest, the state grain procurement targets were not being met and the cities were going
short.[59] According to Mao: 'Only when it was an ounce and
three quarters of vegetable per head in Peking was attention
aroused.'[60]

Mao's thinking on this and related problems concerning the

communes evolved after his return to Peking from Wuhan. He wrestled with them, eschewing sleep.[61] On 27 January he held a meeting at which the level of management within the commune was thrashed out.[62] On 2 February he addressed a meeting of provincial secretaries before setting out on a somewhat circuitous route to Chengchow[63]; he held discussions with the Hopei 1st secretary Liu Tzu-hou in Tientsin; in Shantung he met 2nd secretary T'an Ch'i-lung and visited the Aikuo commune led by a national model peasant, Lü Hung-pin[64]; and on 21 February he addressed a symposium of party committees from four districts in Honan province.[65]

At the meeting with provincial secretaries on 2 February, Mao was principally concerned to spur his audience to renewed efforts. There had been some relaxation, an 'air of cutting back', for two months; this was all right, but now 'we must exert efforts again'.[66] Agricultural work had started a little late and Mao was concerned about fertilizer accumulation.[67] The general line could not be changed. Most likely there would be a great leap forward every year.[68] The enthusiasm of cadres and working people must be protected. When mistakes were uncovered during the checking up on the communes, it must be remembered that defects were generally one finger among ten.[69]

Nevertheless Mao did warn against the subjectivism of attempting something which could not be done and called for further study of the problem of planned and proportionate development.[70] He listed current defects as 'tackling one side and overlooking another, causing waste in labour, the tense situation of supplementary foods, the still unsolved light industrial raw material problem . . . the lack of adjustment in transportation, undertaking too many projects in capital construction'. He went on to give the following characterization of Chinese leadership during the leap: 'Like a child playing with fire, without experience knowing pain only after getting burned. In economic construction, like a child without experience, we declared war on the earth, unfamiliar with the strategy and the tactics.'[71] Mao seemed prepared to shoulder the blame for the excessive work tempo during the leap, rejecting well-meaning attempts to excuse him which pointed to the fact that the combination of labour and leisure had been mentioned at the Chengtu conference; despite that reference, he noted that no concrete work timetable had been laid down.[72] But he reaffirmed that the party must still go all out to build socialism and to achieve greater, faster, better and more economical results.[73]

Within less than three weeks, by the time he spoke to Honan cadres on 21 February, Mao's perspective on the problems of the communes was totally altered. Evidently a key factor in his rethinking was the briefing he had received in Hopei, where, as he indicated to Honan cadres, the party had carried out an abrupt about-face.[74] Probably he had also received an advance copy of Chao Tzu-yang's report from Kwangtung, which was circulated at the second Chengchow conference a few days later.[75] He preferred Hopei's approach, as became clear at Chengchow.

Mao made six speeches to the second Chengchow conference, beginning with two on 27 February.[76] They are repetitious, suggesting that at least some were made at separate smaller sessions.[77] In them, themes adumbrated to the Honan cadres on the 21st are reaffirmed and developed, and all seven speeches can be considered together.

(v) Mao's Chengchow speeches

Mao still emphasized the primacy of success—nine fingers out of ten—and the need to rebut critics, and commended party committees which had adopted this approach while rectifying the communes[78]; after Mao's death, Po I-po would allege that the Chairman's desire to avoid discouraging activists hampered the work of correcting leftist mistakes.[79] But at least Mao realized that the Wuhan plenum had failed to resolve a number of major interrelated problems connected with the communes: accumulation and distribution; level of ownership[80] and level of management.[81] As a result, the first three months of rectification of the communes had been unimpressive: the public mess halls had been improved, people got more sleep, but nothing fundamental had been achieved.[82] Despite his lip-service to success, Mao's speeches contained little but criticism. There was none of the judiciousness of the Wuhan resolution. Mao probably calculated that he would only effect policy revisions with a sledgehammer attack.

Mao encapsulated his critique of the manner in which the party was implementing its rural programme in the phrase: 'one, egalitarianism; two [indiscriminate] transfer [of resources]; three, calling in of loans' (*i p'ing, erh tiao, san t'i-k'uan*).[83] According to Mao, this policy had caused 'considerable panic' (*hen ta k'ung-*

huang) among the peasants,[84] and could result in the 'collapse' (*k'ua-t'ai*) of the communes.[85] It represented a denial of the law of value, the exchange of equal values and payment according to labour,[86] and there was no possibility of calming the fears of commune cadres and defeating the tide-watchers, landlords and bad elements if it were persisted with.[87] It was a manifestation of 'adventurism committed by us in the upper ranks'.[88]

Mao described egalitarianism—along with excessive accumulation and corvée and the 'communization' of various products—as one of the elements of the 'communist wind' (*kung-ch'an feng*) of the previous autumn,[89] and stressed the importance of combating it.[90] When the lower levels accused the upper levels of egalitarianism, the latter retaliated with accusations of 'departmentalism'. Mao's advocacy of continued opposition to 'leftism' (*fan tso*) as the crucial point for the party indicated that his sympathies lay on the side of the departmentalists.[91] There should be no arbitrary transfer of wealth from rich to poor brigades within communes; this would be expropriation—even 'banditry, piracy'[92]—appropriate perhaps in the case of foreign holdings in China but a policy that had not been used even against native capitalists who had instead been bought out.[93] Expropriation in the present case represented a denial of the socialist principle of the more one worked the more one earned (*to lao, to te*).[94] Rather, poor brigades should attempt to emulate the rich ones, relying on their own efforts (*tzu-li keng-sheng*) in the manner of the Wang Kuo Fan APC, made famous by Mao during the collectivization movement in 1955–6.[95] According to Mao, the levelling of brigades—'cutting off the heads' of the rich brigades and handing them to the poor ones[96]—had by now been largely corrected, but 'heavy waves persisted [after the storm]' (*yü po*).[97]

In fact, the Peitaiho resolution had recognized that the merger of richer and poorer APCs in the communes could lead to problems and warned against egalitarianism, but it exuded an optimism that such issues were 'trifles' that would be ironed out in a year or two with the 'advance in the people's consciousness'.[98] No such advance took place. What actually happened was observed in southern Hopei by a sympathetic British couple resident in China. The leaders of Yangyi commune stated that very soon after its foundation they noticed that the tempo of work was slowing down. Members of a poorer brigade in the hills relaxed because they now felt they could depend on their more fortunate brethren; according to their party secretary: 'We're all a hundred per cent in favour of the merging of the co-ops into a commune. We've only got a mu [or mou: one sixth of an acre] of stoney soil per head up here. Now we can get help from the brigades down in the valley.' However, this attitude did not commend itself to the peasants in the valley brigades and they too began to slack off, clearly resentful either that the poorer brigades would climb to prosperity on their backs or that they would be dragged down to the level of the lowest common denominator. The situation was serious enough for the commune party secretary and his colleagues to conclude that the main contradiction in the commune was between the poor and the better-off brigades. They launched an education campaign to convince both rich and poor brigades that the commune benefited all and that everyone should make strenuous efforts in its interest and their own.[99] However, actions spoke louder than words. The leadership continued to think of the commune as a single unit and worked out average rates of pay and free supply of foodstuffs on that basis. This meant 'automatically raising pay in the poor brigades and lowering it in the better-off ones—regardless of work and conditions. That didn't call for the best efforts of either.'[100] Only after the Wuhan plenum and the second Chengchow conference did policies change. Yangyi commune also committed the second sin listed by Mao: indiscriminate transfer of properties. According to a commune party official a second mistake lay in

'transferring' property from the brigades to the commune or from one brigade to another without compensation. That is how the commune council came to take over 71 mule carts and 118 donkey carts from brigades along the highway; and how the sheep and goats were transferred from the mountain to the valley brigades—all without payment. This sort of mistake also dampened enthusiasm.[101]

The Yangyi account is significant not only as an illustration, but also because the cadre's analysis followed so closely upon Mao's categorization—one, egalitarianism; two, transfer—as to leave little doubt that the Chairman's intervention on these matters at the second Chengchow conference had been crucial. Mao listed two types of transferral: things and people.[102] 'Things' included not just the transfer of brigade assets,[103] but also private plots, privately owned pigs, poultry, houses and household goods— tables, chairs, stools, knives, cooking pots, bowls and chopsticks, mainly to the public mess halls. Mao accepted the reversion of private plots to the communes and acknowledged the necessity of the 'loan' of houses and household goods. But he criticized the transferral of animals without compensation.[104] This was 'daylight robbery' (*kung-k'ai ch'iang*).[105] The letter writers of Kwangtung and Fukien would have given him two cheers.

Mao argued that the peasants did not worry about the transfer of land because it could not physically be removed; this thought presumably lay behind his justification of the reversion of private plots to the communes. But goods and labour power could be taken away and this the peasants did fear.[106] He cited a commune in Hopei with a population of 70–80,000; out of a workforce of 20–30,000, over 10,000 had gone off because of the communization of pigs and poultry, some presumably 'blindly' to the cities.[107] He stated that even after commune ownership replaced brigade ownership as the principle form of public ownership, poultry and household animals, trees near houses, small agricultural implements and small tools, and—prior to the construction of public housing on a large scale—even houses would also remain in private hands.[108]

Mao's main strictures on the transfer of labour concerned the expansion of the industrial and service sectors of the economy, accompanied by a growth in the number of administrators, at the expense of agriculture.[109] From the central government to the commune there were five levels at which industry was run, and there was too much of it. It was essential to poor cold water on the enthusiasm for industry[110]—including, presumably, what Mao elsewhere described as the great turbulence of steel-making (*ta nao kang t'ieh*).[111] Mao stated that from the days of the Ch'ing dynasty statesman Chang Chih-tung (1837–1909), a prominent early advocate of modernization,[112] up to the communist victory in 1949 the industrial work force had risen to 4 million. A further 8 million had been added, at a rate of about a million a year, by the end of 1957. But as a result of the great leap, a further 26 million—Mao dismissed the official estimate of 10 million as unreal—had entered industry. To this had to be added a further 4 million transferred to industry from administrative and other jobs, making a total of 30 million new entrants in one year.[113]

Mao's estimates of the waste of labour in the three categories of industry, administration and services varied from 20 to 40 per cent, and he advocated a resolute reduction of numbers in these sectors; 20 per cent of industrial workers should return to the villages, to the five crucial rural activities—farming, forestry, animal husbandry, subsidiary occupations and fishing.[114] A Shansi commune had cut its industrial work force by 30 per cent at a stroke.[115] Service personnel should be greatly reduced; there were cases where one cook catered for only ten people.[116] Communes should not permit cultural work troupes and physical education teams, which tended to absorb young (and presumably vigorous) workers, to be divorced from production.[117] Administrative personnel should comprise no more than a fraction of 1 per cent of a commune's population.[118] Some large communes had thousands of work personnel who ate but did not labour.[119] Mao gave the specific example of a commune in southern Shansi where some 3,000 people did no manual labour or spent only 50 per cent of their time in manual labour; among these 3,000 was a cultural work troupe of over 180 persons—all divorced from production.[120] If this situation persisted, communes would certainly collapse, although even this eventuality, and the accompanying universal laughter, Mao professed to regard with equanimity—one would simply rebuild.[121]

Mao also criticized the excessive use of corvée for large-scale water conservancy projects, road and railway building and repairing.[122] 'Voluntary' labour had to be reduced[123]; the amount of work done for no reward was 'very great'.[124] Mao referred glowingly to the eleventh-century statesman Wang An-shih because he had substituted a tax that fell principally on the rich for corvée, and introduced wages for those employed on public projects.[125]

Mao's third major worry was the calling in of loans to communes by the Finance Ministry. This action on behalf of industry was leaving the communes unable to sustain themselves, and Mao advocated its reversal.[126] He suggested that the state banking system, which was not currently investing in agriculture, should extend long-term interest-free loans amounting to one billion yuan each year for the next decade, mainly to poor brigades.[127] Poor peasants had been granted four-year loans which did not reach their term until 1960; to call them in now meant that the People's Bank was disrupting agricultural production and disrupting the communes. Even loans that were due for repayment should be extended.[128]

At the NPC six weeks later, Finance Minister Li Hsien-nien

revealed that Mao's suggestion of massive investment in the communes had been accepted when he announced:

In 1959, *upon the instructions of* the Central Committee of the Party and Chairman Mao, 1000 million yuan as investment in the people's communes *is added to* the allocations for economic construction; this is a financial subsidy given to the people's communes by the state. This fund will be allocated mainly to those people's communes and their production brigades which have relatively poorer economic conditions, to help them expand production, and so enable them within a short period to catch up with the better off communes. (Emphasis added.)

But Li, like Mao, insisted that for the most part backward units would have to rely on their own efforts and resources like the Wang Kuo Fan APC.[129] Down in Yangyi commune, 'loans from state funds, amounting to 41,000 yuan were issued to the one-third or so poorest brigades'. At the same time, the latter were exhorted to 'work with a will' and catch up with the prosperous brigades, which in turn were urged to help their less fortunate brethren.[130]

To what extent the one billion yuan may have covered outstanding loans is not clear either from Mao or Li, or from the description of Yangyi commune, but Li was concerned to defend his ministry against criticisms from 'some well-meaning people' that the massive increase in state revenues in 1958 had meant that excessive burdens had been placed on the people.[131] Li had retreated but with flags flying, in the face of Mao's latest assult on Finance Ministry practices. Mao's objective was clear: by transferring the burden of supporting the poor brigades from the rich brigades to the state he was placating both rich and poor peasants, and their cadres, at the same time.

In his fulminations against current policies in and towards the communes, Mao from time to time conjured up the spectre of Stalin to underline the dangers of the situation. Stalin's fervour had been excessive and he had exploited the peasants thoroughly but unwisely; to quote Mao's graphic phrase literally, he had 'fished by emptying the water of the pond' (*chie tse erh yü*).[132] If the very great mistake of adventurism (*mao-chin-chu-i*) in evidence since September had not been corrected, there would have been a grave danger of committing Stalin's errors, including excessive accumulation, and agriculture could not have developed.[133] In 30 years, Stalin had failed to introduce true collective ownership; his was a system of exploitation exceeding that of landlords, involving the confiscation of 70 per cent of peasant produce.[134] Mao failed to point out that at one important period, when things were going wrong in the Russian countryside, it had been Stalin who had called a halt, blaming his officials for 'dizziness with success'[135] which was effectively what Mao was doing at the second Chengchow conference!

An outsider might consider Mao's comparison of the Chinese situation in early 1959 with that in the Soviet Union in the early 1930s somewhat melodramatic. But clearly his objective was to hammer home with every possible Soviet or Chinese historical analogy the urgency of a situation summed up by his rhetorical question at Chengchow: 'Who would have thought that a bumper harvest would produce a grain problem?'[136]

Food supplies are often tight in China during the period between the autumn harvest and the following year's early summer harvest, especially after the lunar new year holidays, which in 1959 fell at the end of the first week in February. After a bumper autumn harvest like that of 1958, the problem should have been minimal, but Mao stated that the tumult over food shortages—including grain, oil-bearing crops, pork and vegetables—was greater than during similar periods of crisis in 1953 and 1955 after bad harvests. The state purchasing targets for grain, cotton and oil-bearing crops had not been fulfilled even by this late date.[137] 'Last year's bumper harvest paralysed (ma-pi) us', Mao confessed.[138] Waste had been one cause, and Mao adjured his audience against ever entertaining complacent thoughts of having solved the food problem. When one set of needs had been satisfied, new needs would appear.[139]

However, the main cause of the widespread food shortages was not waste but peasant concealment of output and distribution of it among themselves (man ch'an, ssu fen).[140] In a dramatic phrase, Mao said that they had even buried their output deep and posted sentries to guard it (shen-ts'ang mi-chiao, chan-kang fang-shao).[141] To throw upper-level officials off the scent of the missing output, they also ate only turnips by day, but rice after dark.[142] Concealment of production was now universal; it was a kind of passive resistance (ho-p'ing-ti fan-k'ang).[143] Mao estimated that the concealed portion accounted for about 15 per cent of output and meant that peasants retained about 45 per cent of output[144] in total.[145] In some cases, old ladies blocked the way to prevent the grain from being taken away, as they had done in the first year of collectivization, 1956.[146]

Mao's attitude towards the concealment problem was evidently conditioned by its magnitude. How could one take on the combined opposition of 500 million peasants and anywhere between 10 and 30 million brigade and team cadres?[147] Ranged against them, and accusing them of 'departmentalism', were only the cadres of the six levels from the centre down to the commune and its management districts (*kuan-li-ch'ü*).[148] Moreover, if the people were unhappy, then the army was too,[149] composed as it was of peasant conscripts. This was a very important matter (*ta shih*).[150] Mao also criticized the communes for confiscating remittances sent by army officers to their peasant families.[151] In one speech he confessed: 'Our leadership does not have the support of the masses.'[152] In another, he warned chillingly against the peril of imitating two notorious dynasties—Ch'in and Sui—which had succeeded in uniting the country but had swiftly fallen due to the repressive measures of their rulers.[153]

These were strong words and clearly account for Mao's forthrightly and frequently declared rightism at Chengchow.[154] He stated that he opposed leftism, egalitarianism and excessively centralist thinking,[155] and supported conservativism and departmentalism.[156] He heartily endorsed the actions of teams and brigades that had hidden and guarded their grain as basically reasonable and lawful (*ho-li ho-fa-ti*),[157] and rejected allegations that his position represented appeasement of the peasantry.[158] The former order of precedence must be reversed; the individual's livelihood should take precedence over commune accumulation and state taxation.[159] With caustic rhetoric, he asked: 'They produced it, didn't they! Didn't Marx, a hundred years ago, talk about gaining more if one worked more! He understood a bit of Marxism and they are simply acting according to this principle.'[160] On one occasion Mao told his audience that if they wanted to be leftish, he would be rightist (*yu ch'ing*).[161] In the same speech he declared:

On behalf of the one million brigade-head-level cadres and the 500 million peasants, I say—firmly implement right opportunism, thoroughly and to the end. If you don't follow me then I'll do it on my own—even to the lengths of abandoning my party membership, and even to the extent of bringing a suit against Marx.[162]

(vi) Mao's solutions

Mao's overall prescription was in marked contrast to his exhortation to the provincial secretaries at the beginning of February. Now he argued that this year things should be done somewhat more slowly, people should be more relaxed. Fewer 'sputniks'—be they in physical culture, banking or poetry—should be released; indeed he punctured the basis of the mass poetry movement when he pointed out that not everyone could write poetry.[163]

Mao's more specific remedies for the problems of the communes were implicit in his criticisms. To prevent egalitarianism and transfers he called for the firm implementation of two policies: three levels of ownership with the brigade (the former higher-level APC) as the principal unit of ownership[164]; three levels of management and accounting with the brigade as the basic accounting unit.[165]

Mao argued that if the transition from mutual aid teams to higher APCs had taken four years it was understandable that the transition from basic ownership by the brigade to basic ownership by the commune should take anything between four and seven years.[166] Mao's time-scale for this process never exceeded seven years, but he sometimes shaved a year or two off the minimum and maximum length of time required, suggesting that it might be as little as three years and at most five or six.[167] Presumably he wished to dampen the enthusiasm of cadres as little as possible, and to this end he also projected that the further transition from socialist ownership by communes to communist ownership by the communes—effectively the entry of the great bulk of the Chinese people into the communist era—would be accomplished within 15 to 20 years.[168] Thus despite his disection of the problems of the communes he had not retreated from that optimistic forecast made at Wuhan.[169] And, as in the Wuhan resolution, Mao affirmed that the key prerequisite for the two transitions of ownership was the increase in the wealth of the communes via the expansion of commune-run enterprises.[170]

On the three levels of management and accounting, Mao stated that the communes exercised too many controls, at least ten.[171] Communes should devolve (*hsia-fang*) some of their powers[172]; one of the biggest bones of contention was commune seizure of labour power.[173] Excessive levels of commune accumulation, a feature of the communist wind[174] and a prime cause of concealment of grain,[175] should be reduced.[176] Down in Yangyi commune, some peasants said: 'We grow more grain, all right. But where does it go? The more we grow, the more they take.'[177] Clearly the views expressed by the letter writers of Kwangtung and Fukien were not confined to south China. Mao attacked Honan's practices, criticizing the province for exacting some 70 per cent of rural income in state taxes (7 per cent), commune accumulation (26 per cent), production expenses (20 per cent), management and welfare expenses (17 per cent), leaving only 30 per cent for consumption.[178] This was why peasants concealed an estimated 15 per cent of output to raise the share of consumption to 45 per cent. To discourage such behaviour and to calm the peasants, Mao advocated the publication of a statement reassuring then on the question of ownership[179] and on the division of output as between consumption and commune accumulation, with an undertaking that the latter would be reduced from 26 per cent to 18 per cent.[180]

In one speech Mao summed up his prescriptions in 14 phrases: unified leadership; the brigade as the basis; management divided by levels; devolution of powers; three levels of accounting; estimation of profit and loss at each level; appropriate accumulation; rational adjustments; distribution of income; decisions by communes; the more one works the more one earns; acknowledge differences; law of value; exchange of equal values.[181]

Mao wanted his prescriptions transmitted by means of six-level cadre conferences in each province at which policies would be clarified, name calling would be avoided and hearts would be united.[182]

(vii) Mao checks T'ao

On a number of occasions Mao had recourse to the chess game concept to bolster his argument. He asserted that the 500 million peasants must be the first and the major element in the national chess game.[183] At present it was only half a chess game because distribution was too small and ownership by the production brigade was not respected.[184] Truly to view the whole country as a chess game meant arranging the people's livelihood, commune accumulation and the needs of the state together.[185] In the past the concept of the chess game had only governed the upper levels, now it must embrace both upper and lower levels.[186]

Mao's line of argument on the chess game and departmentalism was diametrically opposed to that espoused by T'ao Chu, Chao Tzu-yang and the Kwangtung provincial committee. Lest there should be any doubt, Mao referred scathingly to T'ao and Chao in his last major speech to the second Chengchow conference. He had got hold of Chao and seized T'ao's 'pigtail'. He did not believe there was that much Marxism along the banks of the Pearl River (on which the Kwangtung capital Canton stands) or the Yangtse![187] Mao's mention of the Yangtse may be a reference to Anhwei where the provincial leadership apparently felt that the peasants had committed the error of departmentalism, but had taken the line of least resistance and decided against considering it an error. Similarly Honan had decided against disciplinary action on departmentalism.[188]

Surprisingly Mao made no reference to T'ao Lu-chia whose line on departmentalism in Shansi mirrored T'ao Chu's, but he did dilate upon the confrontation at model peasant Lü Hung-pin's 'cooperative' (sic) in Shantung where the masses had resisted grain collection and the leadership had ordered a search of their houses. The cadres had launched a war of nerves but then backed away.[189] Mao's most approving reference was to Liu Tzu-hou, whose Hopei party had adopted a 'communist' (i.e. leftist) line after Wuhan, but had reversed its policies five weeks later, on 13 February, when it realized the problems it confronted. However, even Hopei had not yet solved the ownership problem.[190]

The effect of Mao's remarks on T'ao Chu was decisive. At an enlarged conference of the Kwangtung party's standing committee, held in Swatow in April and May, T'ao used the theme of 'the general line and work methods' to sum up the lessons of the leap and acknowledge his own hotheadedness on a number of matters. Among these was opposing grain concealment. Related errors to which he apparently confessed were over-estimates of crop yields and excessive quotas for state purchases of grain; and he also acknowledged that there had been too much emphasis on close planting, over-enthusiasm for the mass steel campaign, and in general a 'communist wind' blowing in Kwangtung. According to Chao Tzu-yang's account two decades later, on all these matters T'ao took the initiative in accepting responsibility.[191]

Mao's fierce assault on the anti-departmentalists had achieved the desired effect. Pace-setting Kwangtung had backed off. The second Chengchow conference could have been the launching pad for a nation-wide drive against grain concealment, but Mao had nipped the campaign in the bud.

But in retrospect most participants at Chengchow surely felt that there had been an air of unreality about the Mao-T'ao confrontation. One must respect the on-the-spot findings of T'ao Chu, Chao Tzu-yang, T'ao Lu-chia and doubtless other senior provincial officials. Grain was being concealed, although it is doubtful if Mao was justified in extrapolating so widely from the scattered evidence at his disposal. But Mao and T'ao were both working on the assumption that the grain output figures issued for 1958 corresponded to reality. The answer to Chao Tzu-yang's first question in Hsuwen—'Was there a bumper crop in autumn last year?'—was not 'Yes'; the correct answer was 'Yes, but'—'Yes, but not that bumper!' Chao, T'ao and Mao were still trapped in the remorseless logic of the leap: if there had been a 100 per cent increase in grain output there had to be a massive grain surplus somewhere; they agreed that brigade and private storehouses were that 'somewhere', and disagreed only on what to do about this 'fact'. (It was to be some months before Mao was ready to acknowledge that '[b]y not paying for food we ate ourselves into a crisis in grains and nonstaple foods'.[192])

T'ao and his colleagues accepted the political soundness of Mao's prescription; and, if it would have been unwise to seize hidden brigade granaries, it would have been an error of Stalinist proportions to have flayed the peasants for hiding grain they actually had never possessed. The question remains, even today: did T'ao thereafter attempt to get some revenge by lashing out at Mao in an article entitled 'The radiance of the sun', written in mid-May and republished in the *People's Daily* on 3 June 1959?[193] One allegation is that T'ao emphasized the shortcomings of the leap far more than Mao by taking the 'nine fingers/one finger' simile and asserting that although it was correct it did not mean that the single affected finger did not hurt considerably.[194] This analysis does not hold up in the light of Mao's behaviour *at that time*; indeed it could be alleged, rather, that Mao's Chengchow speeches made a mockery of the 'nine fingers/one finger' formula since they contained nothing but criticism. Mao's stance changed under the impact of P'eng Teh-huai's attack at the Lushan plenum later in the year, but at this point T'ao was merely reinforcing Mao's Chengchow approach. Moreover, in the light of what took place in Kwangtung in early 1959, it would be wrong to suggest that T'ao drew back from the excesses of the leap sooner than Mao.[195]

In his latter-day defence of T'ao's article, Chao Tzu-yang claimed that it expressed the Kwangtung 1st secretary's attitude towards criticism and self-criticism. T'ao quoted from Mencius: 'The errors of the superior men of old were like eclipses of the sun and moon. All the people witnessed them, and when they had reformed them, all the people looked up to them *with their former admiration*.'[196] Chao underlined T'ao's point that party members must be able to exceed the 'superior men of old' since they worked within and not above the masses.[197]

Significantly, perhaps, Chao did not attempt to rebut the other, more important allegation made against T'ao's article during the cultural revolution by Yao Wen-yuan:

On the one hand, [T'ao] said that people used the words 'the east is red, the sun rises' to 'describe the vigour and vitality of our great cause' and that they 'eulogise our Party and leader by likening them to the sun'. On the other hand, he attacked the 'faults' of the sun openly and railed obliquely: 'In the depth of summer when the glaring sun is scorching the earth and making the people sweat, they grumble and say that the sun's light and heat are excessive. And as everyone knows, and has pointed out too, the sun itself has black spots on it'. . . . Is this not downright invective against our Party and great leader?[198]

Again, in the light of Mao's Chengchow speeches, the allegation that T'ao was making an extraordinary attack on the party does not hold water. By comparison with Mao, T'ao was metaphorical and moderate. But the allegation that T'ao was hinting that Mao too had made errors is more telling, especially as T'ao discreetly dropped the reference to the 'leader' when the article was republished in 1965, at a time when the cult of the Chairman was being built up on the eve of the cultural revolution.[199] It seems unlikely in the light of the retreat that Mao had forced upon T'ao that the latter could have been trying to blame the Chairman for all the faults of the leap.[200] It is more likely that T'ao, perhaps emboldened by Mao's own injunctions to party cadres to speak up fearlessly,[201] was attempting to offset his humiliation by indicating that Mao must shoulder some of the blame for the excesses of the leap and could not simply assign it to leftist party cadres.

If so, T'ao may have struck a sympathetic chord among other provincial leaders, resentful at the manner in which Mao had exacted compliance with his policies. While the reprimand levelled personally at T'ao Chu may have encouraged feelings of *Schadenfreude* on the part of his less dynamic and publicity-conscious colleagues,[202] they too were being attacked and, as loyal engineers of Mao's leap, must have felt betrayed when he took sides against them. None of them could threaten to leave the party, even in jest, without running a grave risk of accusations of adopting an anti-party stand, whereas Mao felt free to invoke this doomsday scenario in order to get his way. The 1958 leap had been a period when Mao reforged his links with party officials after the disagreements of the 1957 rectification campaign.[203] But the manner in which Mao executed his right wheel at Chengchow must surely have alienated provincial party officials, even if they supported his policies. But whether the mood of resentment symbolized by T'ao's article was sufficiently significant for P'eng Teh-huai, who was abroad when it was published, to sense it and decide to capitalize upon it at Lushan is far less certain, even with the benefit of hindsight.[204]

9 CHAIRMAN LIU

(i) A retreat from Chengchow

In the early hours of 9·March, four days after the Chengchow meeting ended, Mao signed a note to provincial-level 1st secretaries pressing in the first place for the speedy convocation of their six-level conferences—province, prefecture (*ti*), county, commune, management area and brigade—which he had advocated during his speeches at the conference.[1] These meetings were to last ten days and to discuss the administrative system of the communes and concrete policies. Honan, still trail-blazing, was already in the throes of its six-level meeting, which was due to end on 10 March. The documents it produced would be specially flown to other provinces by the 14th for reference purposes. But Mao indicated he did not want the 1st secretaries to sit around waiting for these papers to arrive, suggesting that meetings might start on the 11th as in the case of Hupeh. Thus the six-level meetings would conclude in time for 1st secreatries to report to Shanghai by the 25th for an enlarged meeting of the Politburo.

While provincial leaders were attending this session, their county officials would hold four-level conferences—county, commune, area, brigade,—comprising between one and two thousand people and lasting seven to ten days, concluding by the end of March. Communes, areas and brigades would then hold their own conferences, to end by 10 April. Mao dismissed suggestions that this would be too tight a schedule. Speed was essential to take the wind out of the sails of the critics of the communes and the great leap, the 'tide-watchers and account-reckoners'. At the end of this series of conferences, everyone would be able to return reinvigorated to production, to ensure a second leap forward in 1959.[2]

This multiplicity of meetings was evidently designed to eliminate 'the mass of confused thinking' on the communes,[3] to lay down the new line to cadres and to reassure the peasantry. But even Mao, despite his fondness for the mass meeting as a forum at which to thrash out problems, soon came to see that in this instance he had prescribed a plethora. On 17 March he told 1st secretaries in another note that the county meetings might embrace five levels—adding the production team (*hsiao tui/sheng-ch'an tsu/tso-yeh tsu*)—and up to 10,000 people. Communes and lower-level units could then dispense with their own special conferences, perhaps holding them later on an ad-hoc basis.[4]

But despite the lengthy deliberations at Chengchow, and the production of a draft document entitled 'Certain stipulations on the management system of the people's communes', even now the centre's line on the communes was not clear. From Chengchow in Honan, Mao moved south to Wuhan in Hupeh. There he studied carefully the reports from various provinces about their six-level meetings. He immediately detected that there was a difference in opinion as to which level within the commune should be the basic accounting unit. Honan had opted for the area/large brigade (*sheng-ch'an ta tui*), Hupeh for the brigade, i.e. APC (*sheng-ch'an tui*). Mao summoned the 1st secretary from neighbouring Hunan, Chou Hsiao-chou, to discuss the question with himself and the Hupeh 1st secretary, Wang Jen-chung. Chou preferred the Honan system, but after this discussion Mao received a report revealing that Kwangtung was adopting a line similar to Hupeh's. This was no mere debating point; it had given rise to fierce argument at the Hupeh six-level conference, where the higher-level cadres had preferred the higher-level organ (i.e. the large brigade) while the brigade cadres had wanted the brigade.

Mao's note on this topic indicated that the drafting of the minutes of the second Chengchow conference had been slipshod. They had said simply that the *tui* should be the basis (*tui wei chi-ch'u*) for accounting; in view of the confusion over the use of terminology (discussed in Appendix 1, pp. 181–4 below) the minutes should have spelled out just which *tui* was meant. But since the minutes were presumably based on Mao's original use of the phrase,[5] evidently the Chairman was too loose in his phraseology while speaking, and did not take the pains thereafter to ensure that the minutes spelled everything out accurately. Mao now emphasized that the *tui* in question had been the *sheng-ch'an tui* or former APC, now the production brigade, not the *sheng-ch'an ta tui* (the large brigade), alternatively known as the *kuan-li ch'ü* (administrative area).

The underlying issue was the one made familiar during the Chengchow debates: the degree of equality to be introduced into the countryside. The higher the level at which accounting was carried out, the greater the degree of egalitarianism; richer brigades would have to subsidize poorer brigades within the same area. Not surprisingly in view of his speeches at Chengchow, Mao's preference was for accounting at brigade level and thus less egalitarianism. But it does seem extraordinary that he was prepared, according to his note, to allow provinces to choose which system to adopt since he had just devoted considerable effort and eloquence to an attempt precisely to limit their choice to his preferred system.

One can only conclude that at this stage, half-way through most of the provincial six-level conferences, Mao felt it would be impracticable to attempt to direct the debates by long-distance lobbying in order to achieve what he had evidently failed to bring about by short-range shock tactics. Further, Mao was evidently made aware—for the first time?—during his discussions with Chou Hsiao-chou and Wang Jen-chung, and by reading the Kwangtung report, that areas and brigades varied in size, that in some cases the area was closer than the brigade to the old APC and that what might be appropriate in one province would not be in another. At any rate, while stressing yet again how crucial an issue this was for the peasantry and the 30 million basic-level cadres, Mao indicated that he was prepared to go along with the Honan pattern, provided Honan, and presumably other provinces, confirmed during the county four- or five-level conferences that it was acceptable to the grass roots.[6]

Another issue on which the Chengchow documents apparently left the conference participants confused was whether or not communes ought to pay compensation to brigades for expropriated property. It would seem that Shansi province had decided against compensation at its county five-level conferences, but when Mao read 1st secretary T'ao Lu-chia's report on this he immediately remonstrated, pointing out that if compensation could be paid by some communes it could certainly be paid by all.[7] Mao's views were endorsed by the enlarged Politburo conference in Shanghai.[8]

While Mao was following up the Chengchow conference with notes to 1st secretaries, Teng Hsiao-p'ing convened a meeting of the CC secretariat at which an instruction was issued to the NCNA to collect information about the problems of communes. That Teng felt it necessary to supplement party channels of communication about what was going on at the grass roots is an interesting indication of top-level distrust of the reports being received. From the sparse material available on the secretariat meeting, it would appear that party leaders were by now worried about production problems and exaggeration of output figures.[9]

(ii) Re-enter Ch'en Yun, stage right

In this atmosphere of mounting concern in the early months of 1959, China's leaders turned for counsel to their least assertive colleague, Ch'en Yun. Ch'en ranked fifth in the party—he was a Vice Chairman and a member of the Politburo Standing Committee—and he was the senior Vice Premier. Until the leap he had been in overall charge of the economy, but he appears to have accepted a back seat during 1958 without complaint. He turned up loyally to pull a handcart at the Ming Tombs Reservoir project,[10] but clearly had little influence on policy. Mao respected him for never having been a slavish adherent of the Soviet model,[11] but was not prepared to heed his level-headed wisdom during the heyday of the leap.

By the end of 1958, Mao probably felt the need for the muscular argumentation which he knew Ch'en could provide to justify his new-found anti-leftism to bewildered party officials.[12] More importantly, Ch'en was needed to help chart a course out of the morass into which Mao and more compliant colleagues had led the country.

Ch'en's first major, and only public, intervention in economic policy-making in 1959 took the form of an article on the principal problems facing the industrialization programme, which appeared in *Red Flag* on 1 March.[13] In it, he sought to re-assert the primacy of the nation over the provinces in the formulation of industrial development policy. He had long disapproved of the establishment of complete industrial systems in each province which his decentralization programme had permitted and Mao's self-help principle had encouraged.[14] Now he tried to repair the damage, using the chess game analogy, and contending that if China's limited resources were not marshalled from a national point of view, the development effort would be dissipated and—here a calculated appeasement of the speed fetishists of the leap—its pace slackened.[15]

The strategic issue was the location of industry. Ch'en Yun restated and developed the position which Li Fu-ch'un, Chairman of the State Planning Commission, had successfully argued against Mao in 1956: it was uneconomic to site new enterprises in already over-developed big cities, better to scatter them in small and medium-sized towns, closer to their raw materials amd markets. Mao's policy, as originally spelled out in his speech on the ten great relationships, would have been to the advantage of the great coastal industrial cities like Shanghai, and it would seem reasonable to assume that his back-stage prompter had been Shanghai 1st secretary, K'o Ch'ing-shih, who from all accounts (including the Chairman's) seems to have been one of the evil geniuses of the leap.[16] Early on in 1958, Shanghai had revealed that it had 698 industrial plants under construction or reconstruction, a programme unthinkable under the disciplines of the 1st FYP.[17] No wonder Ch'en Yun felt compelled to return to this topic.

Moving on from the strategic to what he called the tactical problems, Ch'en stressed the importance of establishing and adhering to an order of priorities in the construction programme to avoid delay on key projects. On the design of new plants, he argued that China had to cut its coat according to its very meagre cloth, installing small and medium enterprises where possible in preference to large ones. He insisted that the maintenance of quality was integral to all these issues.[18] Adjuring his colleagues to seek truth from facts (shih shih ch'iu shih)—a slogan emphasized by Mao in Yenan which Ch'en had always taken very seriously[19]—he sought additional support from the Marxist classics, recalling without attribution the dictum Engels had imbibed from Hegel: 'Freedom is necessity which has been recognized' (tzu-yu shih pei-jen-shih-le-ti pi-jan). In a striking instance of his willingness now to listen to Ch'en Yun rather than of respect for the founding fathers, Mao picked up this concept, modified the translation to accord more closely with the original and thus sound more positive—'Freedom is the recognition of necessity' (tzu-yu shih tui pi-jan-ti jen-shih)—and used it two months later to encourage greater realism among rural cadres.[20]

Ch'en Yun's next démarche took the form of a letter to the Central Finance and Economics Small Group (Chung-yang Ts'ai Ching Hsiao Tsu), the key body for the formulation of economic policy which he had previously chaired but apparently did not participate in at this time. The main topic of the letter was the tension in consumer markets. Its cause? 'After last year's summer and autumn harvests, we overestimated [grain] production and ate and used up too much.' Sales this year had increased—an extra 9 million tons would be needed—but reserves had fallen. No matter how much grain output rose in 1959, economy measures were vitally important. Contradicting the optimistic claims of the great leap propagandists, Ch'en averred that the country's grain problem had not yet been solved (*hai mei-yu kuo kuan*).

The supply to the markets of subsidiary foodstuffs such as pork, poultry, duck, fish, eggs and manufactured items was also tense; in financial terms the shortfall amounted to 4–5 billion yuan.[21] (Chou En-lai confirmed later in the year that in some cases this was not because the peasants produced less, but because they ate more.[22]) To remedy the deficiency even partially by, say, 1 billion yuan of additional supplies would require, Ch'en estimated, the rearing of 10 million pigs, 200 million chickens, 100,000 tons of eggs and several tens of thousands of tons of fish. As a start, he recommended 'walking on three legs', state, communes and households, pointing out that only the latter (squeezed out by commune takeovers in 1958) had sufficient experience of rearing livestock to increase supplies rapidly.[23] Ch'en also argued the need to encourage what would effectively be another form of private enterprise under the umbrella of the handicraft collectives in order to spur the output of consumer goods.[24] Turning to the demand side of the equation, he advocated sending industrial workers back to the countryside. This would ease the pressure on urban markets and simultaneously increase the number of rural producers of subsidiary foodstuffs.[25] To judge by Mao's pronouncements on the eve of the Lushan conference two months later, the Chairman bought Ch'en's ideas on the problems of the markets.[26] He acted even more swiftly to accept Ch'en Yun's recommendation to cut back the steel target.

(iii) Ch'en Yun and the 1959 steel target

According to his later recollection, Mao's proposal of a 30 million ton steel target for 1959 had been adopted at Peitaiho in August 1959; this had been reduced to 20 million tons at Wuhan in late 1958 and reduced again to 16·5 million tons at Shanghai in late March 1959.[27] The problem with this account is that the figure announced after the Wuhan plenum had been 18 million tons,[28] and this figure had been reaffirmed by the Shanghai plenum[29] and the subsequent NPC session.[30] Po I-po, who as Chairman of the

State Economic Commission was responsible for the annual plan, was said to have argued for a higher steel target at Shanghai with a view to undermining the leap.[31] If there is substance in this cultural revolution allegation, it probably means that Po insisted on sticking at least publicly to the 18 million ton target to avoid confusion and demoralization, an argument forcefully made at this time by the Ministry of the Metallurgical Industry, as we shall see. Within a month this position no longer appeared tenable. At a conference of the CC secretariat on 29–30 April, concern was expressed at the inevitability of a 20 per cent shortfall on the rolled steel target for the second quarter of the year which had been set only one month earlier; indeed the secretariat was probably already aware that only 3·36 million tons of steel (yielding 2·27 million tons of rolled steel) would be produced in the four months of 1959 just ending, leaving almost 15 million tons of the official target to be produced in the remaining eight months.[32] This crisis sparked three questions. First, should the 1959 steel target be divided into two, one dependable, the other a goal to be striven for? Secondly, should the distribution of rolled steel be planned only on the basis of the dependable figure? Thirdly, if the figures for rolled steel available for distribution were reduced, would it be necessary to slash (*hsueh-chien*) some construction projects? In a move which confirmed the crucial role played by the secretariat in the running of the economy during the leap, Teng Hsiao-p'ing and his colleagues commissioned the Central Finance and Economics Small Group to come up with answers.[33]

By this time, Ch'en Yun had been working for almost three months, apparently independently, on the problems of the steel industry.[34] Presumably for that reason, he was co-opted back on to the Small Group, joining Li Fu-ch'un, Po I-po and the less senior Chao Erh-lu, minister of the 1st Ministry of Machine Building, who must have been there to safeguard the interest of the defence industries for which his department was responsible. The four men held six hearings at which the Ministry of the Metallurgical Industry reported on general conditions in the steel industry, on iron ore, coke, refractory materials, steel smelting and varieties of rolled steel. After intensive subsequent discussions, Ch'en Yun detailed the Small Group's findings in a one-hour speech to the Politburo conference chaired by Liu Shao-ch'i in May.[35]

Ch'en's characteristically meticulous, sector-by-sector analysis was in stark contrast to the simplified documents advocated by Mao in the Sixty Articles on Work Methods.[36] Much of the detail would have been superfluous had the Politburo been familiar with the workings of the steel industry. The conclusion is inescapable that no such analysis was undertaken at Peitaiho prior to Mao's launching of the steel drive. Ch'en's speech provided devastating proof of the way in which that campaign had overloaded the system and of the confusion into which relevant ministries had been thrown. The Small Group was presented with the alternatives shown in Table 1[37]:

Table 1

(million tons)	Dependable steel targets		Steel targets to be striven for
Shanghai plenum	16·5 (unpublished)		18 (published)
Ministry of the Metallurgical Industry[a]		16[b] 15 14 13	
State Planning Commission's Heavy Industry Bureau	12·5–13		14
State Economic Commission's Metallurgy Bureau	13		15

[a] It was not specified which of these targets were dependable, and which not.
[b] 'The Ministry of the Metallurgical Industry also produced a figure of 16 m. tons, but it was not carefully explained.'!

It is not clear how officials who had presumably provided the advice on which the Shanghai targets were based could have been as far out in their estimates as these radical and rapid reductions indicate. One must assume that in the brief intervening weeks they had sniffed the whiff of realism in the air.

The Small Group opted for what it considered a dependable but still provisional target of 13 million tons (to yield 9 million tons of rolled steel), and refused to specify a target to be striven for until it had had further consultations with the Ministries of the Coal Industry, Machine Building and Railways. An output of 13 million tons would require cutbacks in capital construction, and the Small Group recommended special efforts to safeguard the petroleum and chemical industries. Even this target would not be easily achieved, Ch'en warned.[38] The tightness of iron ore supplies was one reason why, and Ch'en's discussion of this problem illustrates admirably the painstaking analysis that preceded the Small Group's recommendation.

To produce 13 million tons of steel required 20 million tons of pig iron which in turn required 70 million tons of ore. China had 14 large-scale mining enterprises with mechanical equipment and rail transport, which last year had extracted 34·6 million tons but this year could be pressed to extract 53 million tons. In addition there were 19 medium-scale enterprises, of which six were semi-mechanized and had rail transport, while 13 were unmechanized and without rail transport; altogether they produced 6·8 million tons last year and could be relied on for 8 million tons this year. Finally, there were 214 small-scale, pick-and-shovel-type units which could increase last year's output of 6·06 million tons to 10 million tons. This made a grand total of 71 million tons, of which only 70 million tons could be transported from the mines. Even 70 million tons could be guaranteed only with increased supplies of compressors, power shovels, explosives and so on.[39]

Assuming the iron ore could be delivered, the problem then was to turn it into pig iron of the requisite quality. Of the 20 million tons of pig iron needed, 9 million tons would have to be produced by small blast furnaces, 40–50 per cent of whose product contained unacceptably high levels of sulphur due to the use of impure coke. These impurities were the result of ineffective cleaning of coal, almost half of which had to be performed by the crudest possible methods, a process involving 600,000 men working on 20 million tons of coal over the course of 200 days, ideally with newly supplied pulverizers and other equipment. Ch'en Yun's figures gave ample indication of the wide margin for error and, if the impurities could not be removed, then up to 5 million tons of steel would be unsuitable for rolling.[40] But, provided these and other lesser hurdles which Ch'en outlined could be overcome, there was sufficient equipment to produce the recommended targets.[41] However, he cautioned that the overall assessment of the Small Group was based almost exclusively on conditions in the iron and steel industry. The recommendations would now have to be substantiated by further investigations of industries other than iron and steel. Ch'en Yun was doubtless well aware that during the leap various industrial ministers had blithely guaranteed the demands placed upon their departments without checking to ensure that they would get the necessary collaboration from their colleagues.[42] Ch'en said that further reports would be submitted to the Chairman, the Politburo and the secretariat, but not apparently to the SC, whose marginal role in the conduct of the economy at this time was thus again confirmed.

Despite Ch'en Yun's convincing analysis and the blue riband composition of the Central Finance and Economics Small Group, the Politburo conference could not reach a decision to adopt the recommended targets of 13 million tons of steel and 9 million tons of rolled steel. While Po I-po had apparently been weaned of leftism, the Ministry of the Metallurgical Industry still insisted that to drop the targets that low would cause doubt and demoralization, and many people in Peking and the provinces agreed. Liu Shao-ch'i, presumably chairing the conference in Mao's absence, rejected that judgement, arguing that it would be even more demoralizing to set the target too high and not reach it. But the ministry, emboldened perhaps by the diminution in Ch'en Yun's prestige as a result of his banishment from Mao's policy-making circle during the leap, held out for a 15 million ton target, probably calculating that Mao would inevitably support the higher figure.[43]

Even had the Politburo conference been unanimous in approving the 13 million ton figure, Mao's final consent would have been necessary, so closely linked was the Chairman with the steel campaign. But in view of the deadlock, the Politburo was unable to offer even a recommendation to Mao, and instead Ch'en Yun had to submit the report of the Small Group to the Chairman for decision. In a brief covering letter,[44] Ch'en pinpointed the iron produced by small blast furnaces as the weak link and the cleaning of coal as the critical factor in reaching the target. He freely admitted the differences of opinion over this figure and offered to bring the dissenting Minister of the Metallurgical Industry, Wang Ho-shou, along with the Small Group to see Mao to enable him to hear both sides of the argument.[45]

It is not clear whether or not Mao required the matter to be debated before him. But he later stated that a 13 million ton target was agreed in June and so he evidently opted for the Small Group's recommendation.[46] Five investigation teams were sent out by Chou En-lai and Teng Hsiao-p'ing to rectify iron and steel work: those small blast furnaces with equipment and prospects for development would be preserved, others closed down, with their labour force redeployed to agricultural production.[47]

One factor making Mao's decision on steel easier must have been the purely technical, totally apolitical nature of Ch'en's report. It contained no hint of recrimination—which Ch'en above all had a right to voice—even over the backyard furnaces. Consequently, acceptance of it by the Chairman did not imply self-criticism. A comparison of Ch'en Yun's reports during the first half of 1959 with P'eng Teh-huai's analysis of the great leap forward submitted at the Lushan conference in July[48] underlines why Mao readily endorsed the former but could not stomach the latter.

(iv) Rural realities

Within ten months of Peitaiho, Mao had accepted a reduction of over 56 per cent in the 1959 steel target set then, and Ch'en Yun's 13 million ton target was in fact attained, albeit at great cost.[49] Clearly the Chairman agreed with Ch'en's judgement that the need now was 'to steady the line and advance again' (wen-chu chen-ti tsai ch'ien-chin)[50] and even before he had tacitly acknowledged the unreality of the steel target he had become fully aware of the massive exaggerations in the claims and prognostications emanating from the countryside. On 29 April, the same day as the secretariat initiated reconsideration of the steel target, Mao wrote an intra-party letter for the widest possible distribution, right down to production team level. In it he insisted:

Fixing production targets must be based on realities. Just do not pay any attention to those stipulations made in the instructions from higher levels. Ignore them and simply concentrate on practical possibilities. For instance, if production per mou was actually only 300 catties last year, it will be very good indeed if production could be increased by 100 or 200 catties. Elevating it up to 800, 1000, or 1200 catties and even more is mere bragging and cannot be achieved at all. So what is the use of exaggerating?[51]

Mao went on to deal with some of the concrete measures by which T'an Chen-lin and his colleagues had sought rapid increases in output. He described the claim that 'the closer the planting, the better it will be' as 'incorrect', and ordered careful consultation with older peasants on the technique. The plan to obtain higher yields and output from a reduced acreage was correct, but its implementation would take well over a decade. The guideline for the next few years was the 'simultaneous implementation of extensive planting with low yields and less planting with richer harvests of high quota, high yield farmland'. Mechanization too would take at least a decade; improved farm tools and semi-mechanization were the main hopes for the immediate future.[52] Mao also emphasized the importance of economizing on food grains and concluded with a plea for candour: 'When you have exerted all efforts but failed to achieve something, do not force yourself to make false claims of success. State exactly how much you have harvested and refrain from making false statements which are contrary to facts. There must be honesty. ...'[53] Mao admitted that he was sounding low-key and even conservative—it was now that he quoted Ch'en Yun on freedom being the recognition of necessity—but if higher targets were achieved he would be very happy.[54]

It was around this time that Mao proposed adoption of the slogan 'Take agriculture as the basis' (*yi nung-yeh wei chi-ch'u*), though it would not come into use until 1960.[55] Chou En-lai suggested adding 'Take industry as the leading factor' (*yi kung-yeh wei chu-tao*). Ch'en Yun agreed with the dual formulation, but, typically, felt research was necessary to establish how best to implement such a policy. He went to investigate in the countryside, including, naturally, in path-breaking Honan. Here he found 1st secretary Wu Chih-p'u still arrogantly confident that Honan had doubled wheat production; the province no longer needed to import grain, it could actually begin exporting it. Ch'en Yun, apparently unimpressed, fired off a series of questions: What was the cultivated area? How much grain did it produce? What was the rural population? On the basis of current Honan standards, what was the bare minimum of grain needed per capita for survival in the rural areas? How much seed was needed? How much fodder? Taking all these into account, what was the minimum amount of grain to be left in the countryside? On the basis of such questions and a similar series relating to the urban demand for grain, Ch'en had hoped to establish an overall picture of the provincial food balance. If, as it would seem, the Honan cadres did not have these figures at their fingertips—Ch'en was said to have asked the questions repeatedly, implying he got no answers—the province was being mismanaged.

Unable to supply the facts, Wu Chih-p'u and his colleagues simply lied. They airily assured Ch'en that the cities were adequately fed when in fact minimum rations were only maintained by forcible exactions from the countryside on the grounds (as earlier in Kwangtung) that grain was being hidden and secretly distributed.[56] Mao's strictures at Chengchow were evidently being flouted, and at the outset of the Lushan conference he would appear ready to reassume the role of hammer of the utopian left.

(v)   The Shanghai work conference and the CC's 7th plenum

The results of the plethora of investigations unleashed from the spring onwards were not all in by the time the Politburo work conference assembled in Shanghai towards the end of March, to be followed by the CC's 7th plenum from 2 to 5 April. These sessions had probably been envisaged by Mao as bringing to a successful conclusion the process of commune rectification which he had relaunched in Chengchow in February. But, under the circumstances, more time was needed for China's leaders to become fully apprised of the state of the Chinese economy and these meetings decided on only 18 articles on the problems of the communes, and on what turned out to be the very interim 16·5 million ton steel target.[57] Mao confined himself to voicing a few thoughts on one of his perennial interests, work methods. Unlike in January 1958 when he laid down 60, this time he restricted himself to 16, mainly designed to encourage cadres to be flexible and to adapt their policies swiftly to changing circumstances.[58]

What seems extraordinary is that there is no record at either meeting of any major discussion of the subject which was to figure importantly at the NPC session in mid-April: the revolt which broke out in Tibet in mid-March. Possibly the material was too sensitive to be leaked even during the cultural revolution; possibly the main discussions were held within the CC's Military Affairs Committee. Nevertheless it is clearly significant that very little effort was made by cultural revolutionaries to utilize the gravest episode of internal disorder prior to the cultural revolution itself as a weapon against their political adversaries.[59] One must presume that the Tibetan revolt, which had so critical an impact on China's relations with India and, as a consequence, with the Soviet Union, provoked virtually no dissension within the

Chinese leadership. The further conclusion is that events in Tibet played no direct role in the origins of the cultural revolution. Consequently, the Tibetan revolt, the most important post-1949 episode in the age-old struggle of the Chinese to control the non-Han peoples along and within their inner-Asian frontiers,[60] is only dealt with in passing in these pages.

In the light of subsequent events, and indeed at the time, the main decision agreed at the 7th plenum was to put forward Liu Shao-ch'i to succeed Mao as head of state when the new (2nd) National People's Congress was convened shortly. After two and a half years of gestation, Mao's plan to retire to a 'second front' within the leadership was now to be realized.[61] Although he would retain for the present his more important chairmanship of the party's CC, from now on Mao intended that his senior colleagues, and Liu in particular, should take increasing responsibility for the conduct of affairs. The rationale for the plan was Mao's desire to nurture a well-established and self-confident leadership hierarchy to take over from him on his death in order to avert the kind of debilitating power struggle that took place in the Soviet Union after the death of Stalin.[62]

It was, understandably, not realistic for Mao simply to drop out immediately in the middle of the process of commune rectification, in which he had played so large a role; and later in the summer, as we shall see, he had to defend his position at the Lushan conference in the face of the criticisms of Defence Minister Marshal P'eng Teh-huai. But the swift diminution thereafter in the number and size of Mao's speeches and writings on current domestic policy issues suggest that for a few years he did genuinely retire to the second front. Teng Hsiao-p'ing's failure to report to him after 1959 is confirmatory evidence rather than the lèse majestè it was later implied by Mao to be.[63]

Certainly within Liu's family there was some domestic upheaval as a result of his elevation to the state chairmanship, with the children warned not to disturb their father who would now have no time for relaxation.[64] In fact, as Liu's children knew only too well, the new Chairman was already, and indeed always had been, a 'workaholic', regularly sitting ten hours a day at his desk, not uttering a word[65]; his wife Wang Kuang-mei once commented that his backside had been scraped away from sitting so long![66] Liu's total work day, including meetings, hearing reports and making investigations, was even longer, and it increased further, according to his secretaries, after he became head of state, reaching 17–18 hours a day.[67] He would normally read papers for a couple of hours after he had retired to bed.[68] He once stated that for a communist 'there is no suffering greater than not being able to work',[69] and he lived by that code. In 1956, preparing his political report to the CCP's 8th Congress, Liu worked for three days and nights, pausing only for a couple of hours of sleep a night.[70] During important conferences, he was often found going to bed when his staff were just rising.[71] In a very real sense, Liu had no interest in anything outside his work for the party.[72] This made his ultimate fate at the hands of Mao and the cultural revolutionaries even more tragic.

On Liu's bookshelves was the Soviet novel *How the Steel was Tempered*,[73] whose hero, according to a Western scholar, was 'less than human, a monolithic man who translates all experience in terms of the intolerant, ruthless moral code and political values of his personal faith in communism'.[74] Despite his dour humourlessness,[75] Liu did not come across as less than human, but he seems to have resembled that Stalinist fictional hero in attempting to live by a code of sea-green incorruptibility.[76] In 1959, Liu's party branch[77] found that after rent, water, electricity and the wages for the children's nurse were paid, not much was left out of the combined salaries of him and his wife. They decided to allot him an extra 1 yuan a day to which he was formally entitled because he worked after midnight. When Liu found this out three years later he insisted that the more than 1,000 yuan he had by then received in addition to his salary be repaid by regular deductions from his salary.[78] On inspection tours, he never accepted gifts, and even insisted on taking along his own tea and cheap brand of cigarettes.[79] On foreign trips, he would hand over his expenses entitlement to the local Chinese embassy.[80]

Liu was careful to ensure that his family got no special privileges. Around National Day 1959, he called a family conference in the small room in his house where the Politburo met when he was presiding over it. He took the time out of a busy schedule in order to disabuse his children and his relatives of any hopes they might entertain that his elevation to the state chairmanship would mean favours for them: a change of job from peasant to worker, a change of residence from countryside to city, and such like. Liu helped only one niece whose late father had worked for the revolution, not a common phenomenon in the head of state's family.[81] Liu adhered rigidly to the Politburo rule that official cars could only be used for official purposes. Liu's children walked or bicycled the long distance to school until he paid to have a special pedicab made for them. Wang Kuang-mei returned in a taxi from the hospital after having a baby. Liu set an example by walking to the theatre.[82]

Liu also took steps to ensure his children were not awarded privileges by others. At school, the Liu children were known by pseudonyms.[83] Their father indicated to the superiors of his grown-up children that they were to be treated like anyone else.[84] When one daughter was dispatched to a provincial job, her Peking friends were horrified: if she could be *hsia-fang*-ed (sent down), how could they escape![85] Although Liu was stern and serious, he rarely lost his temper; on the two occasions recalled by his staff it was because a child wanted to change an educational programme.[86] But the autobiography of his daughter by his earliest real marriage, Liu Ai-ch'in, reveals the unrelenting pressure he put upon his children to live up to his absolute standards.[87]

One of those standards was a thrifty life-style. The Liu household ate simply, often leftovers.[88] The children's clothes were hand-me-downs[89]; an expensive coat bought for one of them was sent back.[90] Liu himself dressed in a cotton shirt and trousers in summer, while in winter or on more formal occasions he had recourse to two old suits, a black one in wool and a grey one in gabardine 'for best'. His clothes were repeatedly repaired; an old pair of cloth shoes, his normal footwear, sent for recycling caused much merriment among his domestic staff who thought they belonged to one of his guards.[91] Face to face, Liu's staff apparently found him less droll, although he reportedly treated them with consideration partly because his wife Wang Kuang-mei was at his side to nudge him on such matters.[92]

Liu was not the only Chinese leader noted for frugality and hard work; Chou En-lai in particular was renowned for the same qualities. But Liu's remoter personality and bookish air helped to convey a more puritanical public persona. Even in private, the post-rehabilitation accounts indicate, Liu maintained no friendships—P'eng Chen is a possible exception—despite his wide range of organizational links. We do not find anything similar to the camaraderie of Chou's SC or the bonhomie of the marshals[93]; Liu's relationships to his colleagues seem to have been correct rather than close. He ensured that Chou En-lai—

who once in happier times credited Liu with having been always right on all critical historical problems[94]—received all documents on foreign affairs.[95] There is an intriguing hint of a less correct relationship in a later reminiscence of General Lo Jui-ch'ing, whose post as Minister of Public Security from the creation of the regime until 1959 should have given him access to a wide range of information, that Liu used to spread rumours and gossip about the Premier.[96]

Liu's relationship to Mao seems clearer. Liu saw it as his job to sift through matters of detail to ensure that the Chairman was free to concentrate on major issues.[97] More revealingly, Liu told his staff that if the Chairman called, he was to be notified immediately, no matter what the time of day or night; since Mao had developed the habit during the revolutionary years of working deep into the night, this often meant depriving Liu of his few hours of sleep.[98] Equally indicative of Liu's acceptance of a subordinate relationship is the fact that even a casual reference or quotation made by Mao could send him hurrying to the original text in an effort to plumb the Chairman's full meaning.[99] Mao, the self-confident leader, rarely criticized himself; Liu, who even as head of state probably still saw himself as a tool of the party, often made self-criticisms.[100] Yet it was apparently Liu who triggered some of Mao's most important policy initiatives, notably the analysis of the 'ten great relationships' in 1956.[101]

Now, in 1959, the long years of patient toil in the shadow of the leader had brought their reward. The self-effacing 60-year-old first lieutenant had finally come into his own, his potrait blazoned side by side, and equal in size, with Mao's in the official media. During the cultural revolution, it was revealed that the initiative for this significant new photographic formula came from the CC's Propaganda Department and was implemented by the head of the NCNA, Wu Leng-hsi. Chou En-lai's later version was that Liu was consulted by the NCNA and raised no objection, and that this made Mao reluctant to demur. Chou implied that when Liu saw the two portraits side by side for the first time he should have realized that he had overstepped the mark, but was not humble enough to order a change of policy.[102]

Whatever Mao's feelings of irritation at the propaganda consequences of his retreat, it was apparently the unanimous decision of himself and the CC that Liu should be his successor as head of state, according to a cultural revolution source not otherwise friendly to Liu.[103] Yet despite Liu's position as second-ranking party leader and thus the putative heir apparent, there is some evidence that, if not in Shanghai then earlier, the senior military veteran of the revolution Marshal Chu Teh, suggested that he could possibly step up from his post of deputy head of state. In a rare public display of sarcasm, Liu reportedly pointed out, with slight constitutional inexactitude, that it was not an urgent matter since anyone over 36 was eligible.[104] But, according to reports reaching Peking-based diplomats in the weeks after the first public intimation in December 1958 that Mao would be retiring, Chu Teh's possible candidacy was serious enough to be discussed by street committees.

The significance of Marshal Chu's thwarted ambitions is that they may help explain another somewhat obscure episode, Defence Minister P'eng Teh-huai's attack on Mao in Shanghai. Allegedly Marshal P'eng criticized Mao for 'personally taking command' (ch'in-tzu kua-shuai),[105] which he dated from the first rectification campaign in Yenan in 1942.[106] Mao later characterized critical remarks at Shanghai as mere 'mumbling',[107] but he replied in strong terms, even 'provocatively' (t'iao-po), according to P'eng himself.[108]

The curiousness of this incident is that Marshal P'eng should level this particular criticism at Mao just when the Chairman was about to give up one of his two posts and retire to the 'second front'. We know that P'eng had clashed with Mao on a number of occasions during their three decades of collaboration, and that it was P'eng who had proposed in 1956 that the reference to Mao's Thought should be excised from the new party constitution.[109] Did P'eng now doubt that Mao's retirement was genuine? Or did P'eng voice opposition to the system of one-man leadership not just because it undermined the authority of the Politburo standing committee,[110] but also because he objected to the choice of Liu as Mao's successor, especially since he might be expected to wield similar power?[111]

There had been hints of a conjunction of interests between Liu Shao-ch'i and P'eng Teh-huai in 1956.[112] But basically they belonged to the different wings of the party, the political/organizational and the military, whose fusion under Mao had been so potent an element in the revolutionary victory of 1949. In the early 1950s, Kao Kang had attempted to exploit lingering resentments felt by each wing for the other to his personal advantage when he angled for the support of the generals in his effort to supplant Liu and Chou En-lai in the succession to Mao.[113] At the time of the purge of Kao Kang, P'eng Teh-huai had made a self-criticism for collaborating with him. In the aftermath of the Lushan confrontation in the summer of 1959, a re-investigation allegedly established that the links between the two men had been even closer than hitherto admitted.[114]

If so, it can be inferred that P'eng resented the fact that the PLA had won China, but the organization men had inherited it.[115] According to Chou En-lai, at Lushan, seemingly in a flash of anger at an allegation by P'eng, Liu Shao-ch'i said: 'It is better for me than for you to usurp the party.'[116] P'eng himself later claimed that his attack at Lushan was directed against Liu not Mao.[117] Taken together, this fragmentary evidence suggests that at Shanghai, P'eng Teh-huai was voicing veiled resentment at the management of the succession, perhaps feeling that Chu Teh indeed deserved to be made head of state.[118]

Certainly, Liu's elevation and ultimate succession presaged a change in the way China would be led, from the 'guerrilla' style of unleashing individual energies to the organizational style of controlled mobilization, a difference that had emerged clearly in the speeches of Mao and Liu when they discussed the great leap at the second session of the party's 8th Congress.[119] For party officials who felt aggrieved by Mao's handling of the rectification campaign of 1957 and resentful at the Chairman's tongue-lashing at the second Chengchow conference for the excesses of the leap, the changeover promised a more predictable pattern of command. A municipal party secretary in Mao's home county in Hunan seemed to relish the prospect when he remarked: 'Chairman Mao is now advanced in years. After the demise of Chairman Mao, Comrade Shao-ch'i will be the lawful heir apparent. Liu Shao-ch'i is young and competent. A great theorist, his level is very high. . . .'[120]

Moreover Liu's long years of concentration on organizational matters probably gave him a larger circle of comrades-in-work than Mao himself. Cultural revolution sources tended to lump virtually every real or imagined opponent of Mao as a member of Liu's 'clique'.[121] But there are a number of names common to several sources who indeed had a record of close collaboration with Liu from the 1930s, originally in the Party's North China Bureau, and who were important figures in the party by 1959[122]:

P'eng Chen, Politburo member, second-ranking member of the CC secretariat and 1st secretary and Mayor of Peking; Po I-po, Politburo alternate member and Chairman of the State Economic Commission; Liu Lan-t'ao, CC member and alternate member of the CC secretariat; An Tzu-wen, CC member and head of the CC organization department; Yang Hsien-chen, CC member and President of the higher party school; Liao Lu-yen, CC alternate member and Minister of Agriculture.

Some of these men also had followings,[123] and doubtless Liu Shao-ch'i could have built on them if he had wished to hem Mao in with a ring of organizational steel. But Liu was no plotter, certainly no Stalin. He had achieved a leading role and he wished to get on with it.

Liu took over at a time when moderation was once more the watchword after the excesses of the 1958 leap. Mao had spearheaded the new approach, first at Wuhan and then more forcefully at the second Chengchow conference, with regard to the communes. But the new line had implications beyond the countryside. The return to a more orderly approach to economic development symbolized by the chess board slogan meant that the party had to restore expertise to near equality with redness. As early as September 1958, Mao, while visiting Wuhan University, had re-emphasized the importance of knowledge.[124] In a discussion with some actors immediately after the Wuhan plenum, Chou En-lai had advised them that the party secretary in their play should have expertise as well as redness.[125] Early in 1959, some restoration of pre-1958 educational ideas was initiated.[126] Addressing Peking middle school students in March, Foreign Minister Ch'en Yi underlined the importance of book-learning and deplored the recent tendency to slight studying in favour of productive labour; both had to be given their due weight.[127] In the wider cultural field, Chou En-lai encouraged writers and artists to vary their subject matter and to use both contemporary and historical themes.[128] Ch'en Po-ta, who advocated stressing the new and downgrading the old around the same time, seemed out of step.[129]

More immediately relevant to current economic concerns was the CCP's re-emphasis on the importance of the skills and experience of former businessmen and industrialists. P'eng Chen, who seems to have had overall supervision of united front work at this time,[130] praised capitalists for their response to the great leap and argued that they must be allowed to play their role in the nation's economic development.[131] This new line fitted well with Liu Shao-ch'i's vision of China's future. Liu revealed his aims later in the year in a letter to the venerable Huang Yen-p'ei, Chairman of the China Democratic National Construction Association, the non-communist political party drawn mainly from business circles and tolerated as part of China's united front. Liu told Huang that in the previous ten years the energies of China's leaders had been devoted primarily to the problems of socialist reform, i.e. the collectivization of agriculture and the nationalization of industry and commerce. Writing shortly after official revelations of economic exaggerations and scaling-down of targets, Liu admitted that the superiority of socialism 'has not been fully demonstrated'. He went on:

But in the next decade, things will be different. Now we have gained some necessary experience, and the work of preparing the ground for construction has been completed in the main. Although there are still old and new obstacles . . . we have nevertheless created the conditions which enable us and the broad masses of the people to devote our and their main energies to socialist construction. In this way, we shall be able to speed up socialist construction, and the results of construction in the next ten years will far surpass those of the last decade. . . .[132]

Unhappily for China, that prediction was not fulfilled. Otherwise perhaps Liu not Lin Piao would have risen as heir apparent to address the party's 9th Congress at the end of the ensuing decade.

APPENDIX 1

A RECTIFICATION OF NAMES: TERMINOLOGICAL TURBULENCE IN THE COMMUNES

In a famous passage in the Confucian *Analects*, the Master is quoted as saying: 'If language is incorrect, then what is said does not concord with what was meant; and if what is said does not concord with what was meant, what is to be done cannot be effected.'[1] Some scholars have doubted that Confucius ever said this[2]; but there is no disputing that his followers laid great emphasis on the correspondence of theory and reality, and the 'rectification of names' has been an important concept in Chinese political culture.[3]

Elsewhere in this study, the importance attached by Chinese communist leaders to precise terminology has been often indicated; perhaps the most famous example was to occur at the CC's 8th plenum at Lushan in the summer of 1959.[4] But on no occasion did the Chinese leaders strive harder to rectify names than during the rectification of the communes, and on no occasion was there greater semantic confusion. It would not have surprised the ancient Confucians to learn that this confusion, which affected Mao himself, corresponded to a shifting reality on the ground. The concrete issue was the locus of ownership and management within the communes; terminological problems arose because as that locus shifted upwards or downwards, so the names given to the different levels within the commune were changed. An additional confusion for foreign observers was that the changes in the Chinese terminology were not paralleled by changes in the official translations of that terminology.[5]

The semantic side of the commune story starts with the Peitaiho resolution, which proposed that when communes were formed out of the merger of APCs, the latter should be transformed into farming zones (*keng-tso ch'ü*) or production brigades (*sheng-ch'an tui*).[6] No name was suggested for a third layer of ownership or administration. This lacuna was remedied during the process of commune formation, but due to the latter's helter-skelter nature there was no nationwide consistency. Some communes were subdivided into large production brigades (*sheng-ch'an ta tui*) and production brigades (*sheng-ch'an tui*); others into targe brigades (*ta tui*) and small brigades (*hsiao tui*); or into large brigades and medium brigades (*chung tui*); or into work direction stations (*kung-tso chih-tao chan*) and production brigades; or work districts (*tso-yeh ch'ü*) and production brigades.[7]

At the Wuhan plenum, an attempt at standardization was begun. The two levels below the commune were called administrative district (*kuan-li ch'ü*) or large production brigade (*sheng-ch'an ta tui*) and production brigade (*sheng-ch'an tui*).[8] The official translation rendered the latter two terms 'production brigade' and 'production team' respectively and these became conventional both in China's English-language output ôn the communes and in most Western translations of Chinese materials thereafter.[9] But in Chinese, the new consistency of terms was undermined two months later. In his speeches to the second Chengchow conference, which have not been officially translated, Mao referred to three levels of ownership but four levels of management: commune, *shang-ch'an ta tui* or *kuan-li ch'ü*,[10] *sheng-ch'an tui*, and *sheng-ch'an hsiao tui*.[11]

In fact, Mao's reference to four levels was not an aberration; some large communes did interpose a management level between the commune and its component former APCs.[12] But unfortunately for his audiences, when Mao emphasized the importance of the *sheng-ch'an tui*,[13] he was referring, as he told them, to the level described as *sheng-ch'an ta tui* in the Wuhan resolution, i.e. the former APC.[14] Mao must have been made aware that confusion persisted despite his explanations because on 15 March 1959, shortly after the conclusion of the second Chengchow conference, he sent provincial and city 1st secretaries a circular indicating that where it was stated in the minutes of the conference that one should take the 'brigade as the basis' (*tui wei chi-ch'u*), the term 'brigade' (*tui*) referred to the *sheng-ch'an tui* or former APC and not to the *sheng-ch'an ta tui* or *kuan-li ch'ü*.[15] The reference to the former APCs should have clarified the position on the ground, but it would not have ended the linguistic confusion in those communes, possibly the majority, where the former APCs were referred to as *sheng-ch'an ta tui*![16]

Mao's four-level terminology was not used publicly, but the

three-level Wuhan nomenclature was changed after the Lushan plenum in the late summer of 1959, when the second level became *sheng-chan tui* and the third became *sheng-ch'an hsiao tui*. Finally, in April 1961, the Wuhan terminology was restored.[17] These changes in the official Chinese nomenclature for the commune's subdivisions from 1958 to 1961 can be summarized thus:

			Former APC	
Aug. 1958	Peitaiho conference		*sheng-ch'an tui* (*keng-tso ch'ü*)	
Dec. 1958	Wuhan plenum		*sheng-ch'an ta tui* (*kuan-li ch'ü*)	*sheng-ch'an tui*
Feb.–March 1959	2nd Chengchow conference (Mao)	*sheng-chan'an ta tui* (*kuan-li ch'ü*)	*sheng-ch'an tui*	*sheng-ch'an hsiao tui*
Aug. 1959	Lushan plenum		*sheng-ch'an tui*	*sheng-ch'an hsiao tui*
April 1961			*sheng-ch'an ta tui*	*sheng-ch'an tui*

A crucial point to note in the above scheme is which level is designated *sheng-ch'an tui*, unmodified by *ta* (big) or *hsiao* (small). This appears to have been the term with which the regime designated the most important level underneath the commune, with the Wuhan nomenclature being a possible exception.[18] At Peitaiho, the term was used for the single subordinate level of administration, the former APC, that was thought necessary at a time when everyone's attention was directed to the commune level. At Wuhan, the term was assigned to the third level, possibly an indication of the wish of party leaders to devolve some of the commune's management powers under a system of 'unified leadership as well as management at different levels' (*t'ung-i ling-tao, fen-chi kuan-li*).[19] At this point in time, the second level, the production brigade, now renamed *sheng-ch'an ta tui*, was to form a business accounting unit with its gains and losses pooled in the commune; it would 'manage industry, agriculture, trade, education, and military affairs in its area'. Both brigade and team should have 'necessary' powers over the organization of production and construction, finance and welfare under the leadership of the commune, but the production team was designated the basic unit of labour organization.[20] The significance of this latter assignment was the recognition of peasant dissatisfaction at the early commune practice of deploying rural labour for vast irrigation projects, 'fighting battles with large army corps' (*ta ping-t'uan tso chan*),[21] and for industrial and other non-agricultural tasks. Excessive corvée duties prevented peasants from ensuring the well-being of their crops, and insult was added to injury by the absence of payment for this kind of work. Peasant disgruntlement was reflected and legitimized by sympathetic references in Mao's speeches at the second Chengchow conference.[22] But it is unlikely that the use of the unmodified term at Wuhan signified that the team had become the most important level of commune administration.

However, there can be no doubt that Mao's espousal of a four level terminology and the brigade as the basis led to the later public alteration of terminology at Lushan, with the brigade becoming the *sheng-ch'an tui*. Indeed it was probably precisely because after Chengchow Mao had to spell out what he meant by *tui wei chi-ch'u* (brigade as the basis) that led the authorities now to decide it would be simpler to use the unmodified term for the crucial subdivision. Hence when the team replaced the brigade in this role in 1961, the unmodified term had to be transferred downwards so that *tui wei chi-ch'u* could still be an appropriate phrase, even if its English translation had to be altered to 'team as the basis'.

PART THREE

CLASH

10 HIGH NOON AT LUSHAN

(i) A sentimental journey

At 5.44 pm on the afternoon of 25 June 1959, Mao Tse-tung arrived in his home village, Shaoshan, for his first visit in 32 years.[1]
He had driven from Changsha, the capital of Hunan province,[2]
accompanied, as was often the case, by Lo Jui-ch'ing, the Minister of Public Security recently elevated to a vice premiership.[3]
His entourage included a secretary of the Hunan party, Hsu Ch'i-
wen, and also, curiously, the 1st secretary of neighbouring Hupeh
province, Wang Jen-chung,[4] while the presence of one of China's
leading Marxist novelists, Chou Li-po, seemed calculated to ensure that this historic moment would be captured for posterity in
deathless prose.[5]

On that first evening, the villagers turned out to greet Mao
with cheers, claps and laughter at the door of the Shaoshan reception centre.[6] He went indoors and obtained a briefing on production, water conservancy and the overall situation in the local
commune.[7] When he was taken to his sleeping quarters, where all
had been specially prepared, he revealed that he had brought his
own bedding roll.[8]

That night Mao worked late on documents and during a break
for a breath of fresh air he chatted with a young guard, Yang
Ming. Mao enquired about his education and, when told that
Yang had received schooling from the age of 9 until he was 15, he
exclaimed that his own experience had been exactly the same.
Yang's reply was tart, by implication if not in tone. He evidently
knew that Mao's father had been rich enough to employ hired
hands, for he replied: 'No, it's not the same, Chairman! My family had no labour power and I only studied in the winter and the
spring. I didn't learn much.' Mao defended himself by saying he
too had done manual labour when young.

He then asked Yang for his opinion of the communes, to which
Yang reportedly replied as honestly and as fully as he was able.
Evidently some of his comments must have been critical, for
although Mao is reported to have manifested satisfaction he felt

obliged to reassure Yang that after difficulties had been ironed out, the communes would be very good.[9]

The following morning at crack of dawn, wearing a 'snow-white' shirt and a pair of brown leather shoes, Mao set off up a hill road accompanied by Lo Jui-ch'ing, Hsu Ch'i-wen and others. He first dropped in on a couple of peasant homes, drank some tea and inquired about men who had followed him when he had first raised the revolutionary banner in the mid-1920s.[10] At the second cottage, the head of the family, Mao Hsia-sheng, had to be summoned filthy from the field, but he was delighted that his namesake the Chairman should have come to his house first before revisiting his own old home, close by across a small pond.[11] Mao Hsia-sheng did not later recall that the Chairman had scoffed at his claim to be producing 800 catties a mou and suggested the figure was likely to be nearer 500 catties. According to this version, Mao Tse-tung then utilized the occasion to lecture Mao Hsia-sheng on the need to avoid boastfulness and other manifestations of the 'five styles'.[12] To judge by this account, the Chairman was maintaining his 'rightist' posture on the eve of the fateful Lushan conference.

Mao's family home had been considerably damaged after confiscation by the Kuomintang, and its post-1949 restoration had been the particular concern of a rising young provincial official Hua Kuo-feng.[13] As Mao looked around in the central room, he reassured a questioner with a laugh: 'This is how it was.' Standing in his own room, gazing at portraits of his parents, he commented that nowadays illness would not have carried them off so young.[14] At no stage during his tour of the family farmhouse did Mao indicate any embarrassment or displeasure that it had been made into a shrine. He seemed to feel it was only natural and appropriate. Perhaps this was hardly surprising. The cult of his personality had been sedulously fostered from the party's 7th Congress in 1945; senior colleagues like Liu Shao-ch'i and Chou En-lai (who both recoiled in horror at any attempts to make their own home villages into tourist attractions) and even P'eng Teh-huai thought it fitting that Mao's birthplace should become a show place.[15]

Mao's next visit was to the school, sited in a field in which he had once tended cattle. The original village school house had been the Mao family school, where in 1925 Mao Tse-tung's first wife, Yang K'ai-hui, had started peasant night school classes. In 1953 a new school had been built and the Chairman had provided the inscription 'Shaoshan School' in his own calligraphy. At that time there were about a hundred or so students receiving only primary education, but a junior middle school had been added in 1958 and there were now over 700 students and 30 teachers.[16]

At 10 am, Mao left the school to have some breakfast and afterwards went to the fields to hear a report from the commune secretary. Again Mao was a model of moderation, carefully sifting out the facts and reassuring the local cadres that an increase of only 100–200 catties a mou in a year would be very good. He talked of the need to look after cattle in view of the shortage of tractors and emphasized the importance of forestry. There was also an enthusiastic discussion of water conservancy work, and Mao decided to take a look at the newly constructed local reservoir that afternoon.[17]

News of Mao's impending visit clearly spread fast. When he reached the reservoir at 3 pm, after a midday meal and a nap,[18] the banks were lined with cheering peasants. Mao conducted his inspection in the most down-to-water manner possible by taking a dip. He spent a couple of hours in the water, but it is not clear how much actual exercise he got since, as he explained to the young swimmers detailed to escort him, he could not do the breast, butterfly or crawl strokes. But the assembled masses, who resisted Mao's invitation to join him because they could not swim, were impressed enough with his ability to float motionlessly.[19]

It was probably en route to the reservoir that Mao paid a courtesy call on the widow of Mao Fu-hsuan, a revolutionary martyr who had been Shaoshan's first party branch secretary. Later that evening, she and the widow of another Mao martyr, along with four male members of the Mao clan,[20] joined other old folk, relatives of revolutionary martyrs and cadres at a reception given by the Chairman. Mao Tse-tung greeted the guests outside a single-storey grey-brick house surrounded by pine trees and bamboos, shaking hands with everyone and inviting them to take seats on the wooden benches provided. By 7 pm all had arrived and Mao asked them inside for the banquet laid out on four large, round dining tables. The Chairman went round the tables toasting everyone individually. One 70-year-old exclaimed: 'The Chairman toasting me—I don't deserve it'; to which Mao replied: 'One must toast the old and respect the worthy.'[21] In his speech, the Chairman called on the guests to voice their opinions and criticisms of party committees and officials and to write to him if they feared to speak up in public. Reportedly, a lively discussion ensued.[22]

When everyone had gone home, Mao returned to his quarters, apparently too keyed up with memories and emotions to think of sleeping. Instead he composed a poem:

> I curse the time that has flowed past
> Since the dimly-remembered dream of my departure
> From home, thirty-two years ago.
> With red pennons, the peasants lifted their lances;
> In their black hands, the rulers held up their whips.
> Lofty emotions were expressed in self-sacrifice:
> So the sun and moon were asked to give a new face to heaven.
> In delight I watch a thousand waves of growing rice and beans,
> And heroes everywhere going home in the smoky sunset.[23]

On the second morning of his visit, Mao set off up a nearby hill without explaining to Lo Jui-ch'ing and his other companions where they were going. At the top of the hill they discovered that they had arrived at the grave of Mao's parents. A quick-thinking youth improvised a wreath by binding together some pine branches with weeds and gave it to the Chairman. He quietly placed it on the grave and solemnly bowed. His companions followed suit.[24]

The experience moved Mao. Later, when Lo Jui-ch'ing came to fetch Mao after his noonday nap for the return journey to Changsha, the Chairman said to him as he was putting on his clothes: 'We communists are thorough-going materialists who don't believe in spirits. But one must acknowledge the parents who bore one and the party, the comrades, the old teachers, and friends who instructed one.' He added that he would revisit the grave when he returned again to Shaoshan.[25]

Huge crowds gathered to see the Chairman off that afternoon. On the drive back to Changsha, he stopped twice at places remembered from his youth. The delays meant that he did not reach the ferry quay in Changsha until midnight, but here again there were excited crowds to cheer him, and he brushed aside the guards in order to shake hands with people.[26]

(ii) The ascent of Lushan

It is not clear how Mao travelled from Changsha to the summer resort on the 5,000-foot-high Mt. Lu (Lushan) in neighboring

Kiangsi province where the CC was to hold its 8th plenum. But he evidently arrived in high good humour after his heart-warming experiences in Shaoshan. The beautiful scenery drew another poem out of him:

> Beside the Great River the mountain rises majestically.
> I ascend four hundred spirals to reach its verdant peaks. . . .[27]

A Western journalist who visited Lushan some years later described it as a place 'of special beauty where mountains or rock and evergreens rise abruptly from the flat Yangtse River plain . . .':

It is a place that evokes thoughts of eras past. Many centuries ago, poets and painters began coming here in search of inspiration. They stood in small pavilions built on the edge of precipices, gazing at the peaks they came to call the Five Old Men. They sat, as visitors can sit today, in the Cave of the Immortals. They drank from the Single Drop Spring and re-told the tale that drinking enough of this water will turn one into a spirit who lives forever.[28]

According to this correspondent, the resort boasted a 'huge chalet-like building' (possibly Chiang Kai-shek's summer retreat during the 1930s), 'dozens of summer homes built of stone' nest-ling among the treed slopes of the mountains, and two-bedroom cottages complete with live-in maids which seemed designed 'for some Chinese who are more equal than others'.

As the pre-plenum central work conference assembled in these pleasant surroundings, Mao had three sessions with his secretaries characterized by warmth and laughter. He had drawn up a list of 19 problems arising from the leftism of the leap that remained to be dealt with, but he and his staff evidently saw these as requiring a mopping-up operation more than another shock attack of the type he had felt obliged to mount at the second Cheng-chow conference four months earlier.[29]

As the Lushan conference got down to business, Mao issued several directives. He called on each county and commune to compile a book on 'good people and events', which would describe anecdotally people who in 1958 had upheld truth, not bent with the wind, done good work, not made false reports or exaggerated, and another book on 'bad people and events', which would tell of those who had lied, violated laws and discipline or committed serious blunders.[30] Some cadres destined for the black book may have felt that the Chairman was selling them down the

river when their only fault had been over-enthusiastic implementation of his directives. But Mao was no longer in favour of
exuberance; while excessive inactivity and activity were both to
be deplored, the current problem was excessive activity. In order
to restrain the 'semi-anarchism' produced by the excessive activity of lower-level cadres, Mao also advocated a recentralization,
the restoration of certain central powers devolved in 1958, and in-
veighed against egalitarianism.[31]

But the most striking evidence of Mao's 180° turnabout (not
untypical of him) was his espousal of the watchwords and arguments of the economic planners, the cautious prescriptions that had
been used by them to halt the little leap in 1956, to his great
annoyance then.[32] Comprehensiveness and balance were essential
to economic planning. 'One of the major lessons from the Great
Leap Forward is the lack of balance.' There had been excessive
concentration on production from backyard blast furnaces at the
expense of other forms of production; this would not do. Quantity and speed, effectively the shibboleths of the leap, were to be
played down. 'We prefer to produce less but of better quality and
greater variety.'[33]

Moreover, the traditional Soviet-type order of priorities—
heavy industry, light industry, agriculture—would have to be reversed, with heavy industry and agriculture changing places. And
in a noteworthy passage he paid tribute to the man whose advice
he had once more been taking so seriously over the previous few
months:

Comrade Ch'en Yun said: 'We should arrange the markets before we go
into capital construction'. Many comrades disagreed. But now we realise
that Comrade Ch'en Yun was right. We have to solve the problems of
clothing, food, housing, utilities and travel first for they concern the
stable life of 650 million people. . . . This will be advantageous to reconstruction and the state will be able to accumulate its resources.[34]

No wonder Mao's secretaries put up a proposal to the Chairman
that Ch'en Yun, who was not coming to Lushan,[35] should again
be entrusted with the direction of financial and economic work.
The Lushan conference, they felt, would be a conference of
immortals (shen-hsien hui), a brain-storming session at which
problems would be resolved in an intelligent and cooperative manner.[36] As Mao himself asserted, the prospects seemed
bright.[37]

(iii) Beating gongs with cucumbers

If the confrontation over the communes and great leap seemed unlikely to Mao and his staff as the Lushan conference got under way, Defence Minister P'eng Teh-huai was probably furthest from their minds as someone who might conceivably stir up trouble. He had no responsibility for economic affairs and had played no role in the disputes over the halting of the little leap of 1956 or the launching of the great leap in 1958. There were people who could have used the occasion to say 'I told you so', notably Ch'en Yun, or Li Fu-ch'un who had loyally suppressed his doubts when implementing the leap forward line at the State Planning Commission,[38] but P'eng Teh-huai was not among them.

Yet, although he did not bear the ministerial responsibility that might have made an attack on great leap policies institutionally logical, there were historical factors and personality traits that made P'eng's emergence as their principal critic less surprising.

Some of the historical factors have already been alluded to: major disputes over strategy during the anti-Japanese and Korean wars. More recently, Mao and P'eng had diverged on defence policy and the modernization of the armed forces and the gradual elevation of Marshal Lin Piao within the Politburo presaged problems for the Marshal.[39] But however bitter or apprehensive P'eng may justifiably have felt, he was not a man to submit without a fight, and this is crucial to an understanding of what happened at Lushan.

P'eng Teh-huai had a powerful constitution, combining the 'body of a bull and the face of a bulldog', according to one of his earliest comrades-in-arms. 'His character was strongly imbued with the conservative simplicity of the traditional Chinese peasant. He was hard-working and could endure hardships indefinitely along with his soldiers.'[40] Indeed, P'eng ate and dressed as simply as they—even in Peking he maintained a modest establishment[41]—and his ascetic image was emphasized by his shaven head, the traditional mark of the Buddhist monk.

P'eng hardiness derived from his origins, a peasant family down on its luck and drifting ever deeper into poverty. Born in 1898, P'eng had scraped only two years of schooling before becoming a cowherd and then, in his early teens, a coal-miner. Returning home, he worked in the fields, but during a famine in 1912 he helped organize resistance to local landlords pressing for the payment of rent and debts; when the revolt collapsed, Peng fled to the forest where for a couple of years he worked as a common labourer, carrying earth. Thereafter he became a soldier.[42]

P'eng was one of the earliest military recruits to Mao's banner, leading a few thousand men to join him and Chu Teh on Ching-kangshan in 1928.[43] Perhaps Mao was impressed by the bravery and loyalty of his fellow Hunanese, for though P'eng was never distinguished for his generalship, he was soon the second-ranking soldier, after Chu Teh, in his coterie. Indeed, on the Long March Mao dedicated a poem to P'eng:

> The mountains are high, the way long, the tunnels deep,
> But the great army sweeps all before it.
> Who dares gallop ahead, sword in hand,
> None other than our great General P'eng.[44]

P'eng more than reciprocated Mao's admiration. He was punctilious about attributing his victories to the Chairman, solicitous about his comfort and ready to drop everything instantly when summoned by him.[45] There was tension and ambivalence in the Mao-P'eng relationship, but mutual respect was certainly an important element.

As a commander, P'eng was notorious for bluntly dressing down his subordinate officers. As he himself admitted: 'I like to criticise others.' But according to his long-time comrade-in-arms, Huang K'o-ch'eng, who experienced his tongue-lashings, P'eng's criticisms were never resented because they were always fair and genuinely designed to improve performance.[46] Moreover, as his subordinates knew, and as Lushan was to confirm, P'eng was not afraid to stand up to his superiors. When the Soviet leader Anastas Mikoyan led the CPSU delegation to China to attend the CCP's 8th Congress in 1956, P'eng asked him face to face why it was only now that the Soviet party was criticizing Stalin. Mikoyan apparently replied: 'We did not dare advance our opinions at that time. To have done so would have meant death.' To which P'eng retorted: 'What kind of a communist is it who fears death?'

Even more apposite was an incident that occurred during the Korean war, when P'eng, evidently outraged by orders he had received, rushed back to China. He sought out Mao and brushing aside the remonstrations of the Chairman's guard dashed into the bedroom where he was resting and promptly started haranguing him. Mao not only gave way on the substantive issue, but also remarked admiringly: 'Only you, P'eng Teh-huai, would burst into someone's bedroom while they were sleeping in order to argue your case.'[47] And of course what Mao really meant was that no one else would have dared to dash into *his* bedroom.

P'eng's willingness to criticize Mao's method of leadership in Shanghai in the spring of 1959 is thus readily comprehensible. But a question remains as to why P'eng limited himself to this topic, for there is considerable justification for Mao's angry assertion that the Marshal did not utter a cheep about the leap or the communes prior to Lushan.[48] Moreover, the first-hand experience which originally fired P'eng on these questions was already over six months out of date by the time of the Lushan conference.

In October 1958, P'eng had revisited the north-western province of Kansu which he had liberated from Kuomintang forces almost a decade earlier.[49] According to P'eng's bodyguard, the marshal was enthusiastic about the backyard blast furnaces when he arrived, pointing to them from the window of the car and expatiating on their special qualities. P'eng was apparently sold on the official line that by this means the peasantry could use local materials to solve the steel shortage for agriculture. Looking to the future he foresaw a weapons spin-off with peasants manufacturing simple bombs and land mines.[50]

P'eng's complacency was first dented when he came upon a large pile of ripe crops lying on the ground, seemingly abandoned. After a lengthy search, an old peasant was finally located who explained that all able-bodied people were busy launching a steel sputnik (i.e. attempting to set a record). There was not enough manpower for all the tasks assigned by the higher levels and the order was that all the 'generals' should give way to 'Marshal Steel'.

P'eng exclaimed: 'Hasn't any one of you given a thought to what you will eat next year if you don't bring in the crops? You're never going to be able to eat steel!' The old peasant nodded vigorously in agreement, but added pointedly: 'True enough; who would disagree with that. But apart from when the centre sends down a high-ranking cadre [i.e. like you, who has the authority to enforce moderation], who can stand up against this wind?'

But P'eng's real shock probably came when he visited an infantry school and found that classes and training had come to a halt as the instructors laboured mightily at the blast furnaces, their clothes black as soot, their eyes red from lack of sleep. When P'eng arrived they rushed to greet him carrying 'steel' they had just smelted. He told them: 'I'm moved by your enthusiasm. But as for your leaders who don't treasure your enthusiasm and energy, I shall beat their buttocks.... If our army and military academies all carry on this way, our enemies will be ecstatic with joy, because we'll just collapse of our own accord without even waiting for them to attack!'[51]

Two of the staff at the school's reception centre, perhaps emboldened by P'eng's remarks, complained to him about domestic conditions locally. Some houses, as well as fruit trees, had been knocked down to provide wood to fuel the furnaces; iron cooking pots had been confiscated for use as raw material. That night P'eng had a heart-to-heart talk with a number of officers which gave him much food for thought. After they had left, he was writing long into the night.[52]

On the way back from Kansu, passing through the trail-blazing province of Honan at night, P'eng saw ⎽verywhere the flames of the backyard furnaces twinkling across the countryside. After a long, thoughtful silence, he turned to his bodyguard and asked: 'Tell me, do you think this method can lift our country out of poverty?' When the soldier remained discreetly silent, P'eng answered his own question: 'It won't work! Perhaps we can burn up our household goods this way! It's certainly not something we could have used our brains to devise!'[53]

Why did not P'eng Teh-huai voice these doubts about the backyard steel programme at the first Chengchow conference or the Wuchang conference and plenum in November–December 1958? According to P'eng's later account, he received notification of the Chengchow meeting too late to attend anything but the last day, when an evening meeting was held on a train (perhaps bound for Wuchang). Mao spoke, criticizing the 'communist wind', and since all agreed the session soon ended. In view of the Chairman's remarks, P'eng felt there was no need for him to intervene. At the Wuchang meetings, which he attended intermittently, P'eng did voice doubts in small group sessions about the wildest forecasts, which put likely grain output for 1958 at 500 million tons; when Mao opted for a published claim of 375 million tons, P'eng went along with it, albeit with lingering doubts.[54]

P'eng Teh-huai's post-Wuchang tour of Hunan, which included

visits to his home village Niaoshih, to Mao's home village Shaoshan in the same *hsien*, Hsiangt'an, to P'ingchiang, where 30 years earlier he had led an uprising (writ large in the annals of the revolution), and to Chuchou, must have been even more traumatic than his inspection tours in Kansu and elsewhere during 1958. As with Mao, this was P'eng's first trip home in three decades.[55] And like Mao, P'eng received a tremendous welcome.[56] But in contrast to the Chairman, P'eng was not allowed to see his old village through rose-tinted spectacles.

At a brigade iron and steel works, P'eng saw again smashed iron cooking vessels being used as raw material to produce simply more iron. Useless lumps of it were lying rusting on the ground. P'eng took aside the cadre in charge of the blast furnaces and patiently explained the uselessness of the whole operation, comparing it to beating a gong with a cucumber.[57]

P'eng also learned that the privately owned cooking pots had been confiscated with an additional objective in view—forcing the peasants to use new mess halls. At the Niaoshih Happiness Home, where aged peasants now lived collectively, P'eng found a number of old friends.[58] He was told that the mess halls had been readily accepted initially because the communist party had said that this system would guarantee their food supplies. Then they showed him the dish of vegetables with a few grains of rice which was their next meal. P'eng could tell from their physical condition the truth of their assertion that they could not be deceiving him about their dire straits since they had not known he was coming.[59]

One old man carrying a child told him: 'The youth can tighten their belts; the old can grit their teeth. But babies? They can only cry.'[60] Appalled at the conditions in the Happiness Home, P'eng commented sarcastically on its name,[61] suggesting that at best it could only be called a home for eliminating hunger.[62] He made a donation of 100 yuan to provide each inmate with a blanket to supplement the meagre bedding.[63]

The old folk indicated to P'eng that they could cope with natural disasters, but man-made ones were another matter. A key problem, P'eng clearly felt, was exaggeration, particularly of crop yields. He pointed out gently in his discussion at the Happiness Home that if claims for massive yields—10,000 catties a mou!—were false in the case of Niaoshih there was no point in hoping that nearby villages which reported even higher yields could help them out with their food problem. It was all 'deception' (*hung-kuei*). Some of his audience sighed, some wiped away tears.[64] Others reinforced his argument from their own experience, citing a proposal to set up a 10,000-head pig farm, when there was not even enough room for the ducks and chickens; it was like running a fever.[65] One of P'eng's meetings was with a county party secretary who openly admitted that only a very small number of high-yielding fields were producing, at the maximum, 800 catties a mou. P'eng praised him for his honesty and stated that he did not believe other areas which made claims for 8,000 catties a mou and upwards. The cadre explained that the false figures were produced as a result of pressure from above; if one did not launch a sputnik, be it for grain output, steel production or in eliminating payment for food, there was a danger of being dubbed rightist. P'eng lambasted such practices and averred that 'communism must be built, not boasted'.[66]

P'eng was soon to meet a boastful cadre, a brigade official who claimed yields of 3,000 catties a mou, with women and children doing the harvesting and the young men attending to steel production. When P'eng asked the peasants standing around if this were true they laughed, but probably nervously, because they did not dare to contradict the cadre. So P'eng dressed down the cadre in front of them, accusing him of boasting, asserting that from his personal observation of the fields it would be lucky if they were getting 300 catties a mou. This unleashed a torrent of peasant criticism of 'braggart sputniks' (*ch'ui-niu-p'i-ti wei-hsing*) and cadres's lies. Fears were expressed that next year people would go hungry. P'eng took the cadre aside and explained the importance of seeking the truth from facts; a great leap was desired, not a false leap. If commandism was used, the masses might rebel (*tsao-fan*).[67] P'eng had clearly taken to heart the warnings of his old revolutionary comrades.[68]

But cadre exaggeration was not the only source of peasant discontent. The old folk at the Happiness Home were fed up with collectivized eating and a militarized life-style.[69] Later that evening, pacing a moonlit courtyard with the provincial party 1st secretary, Chou Hsiao-chou, who was accompanying him on his tour, P'eng voiced his own doubts about the '–ization' of everything: militarization, collectivization, village-ization, water conservancy-ization, electrification. How was it all going to be done?[70]

And if anyone opposed any of it, he was automatically dubbed a capitalist.[71]

Here was the rub. The fear of punishment, heightened by the 1957 anti-rightist campaign, meant that it was difficult to report the truth to higher authority, as P'eng himself admitted at the Happiness Home.[72] A striking example of this fearfulness was given by Chou Hsiao-chou himself. P'eng asked him if the call for a mass steel campaign had been correct. Despite P'eng's demonstrated disapproval of the impact of the campaign, Chou did not feel able to criticize a Mao initiative and merely vouchsafed a non-committal 'It's difficult to say'. Only on the implementation of great leap policies would he agree that there had been and was still over-enthusiasm, lack of objectivity and a tendency to exaggerate.[73] If a provincial 1st secretary, an alternate CC member, felt thus constrained even in the presence of a sympathetic Politburo member, how much more terrifying must it have been for a lower-level official to report unpalatable facts to his superiors.

However, Chou did undertake to issue a provincial directive critical of the excesses of the leap. In return, P'eng promised him, as he had promised the peasants, that he would report to Mao.[74] But in giving that undertaking, P'eng had in a sense sold the pass, for he was implicitly confirming peasant assumptions that Mao's policies were being distorted and that the Chairman himself could not possibly know what was going on.[75]

It was of course politically unthinkable for P'eng Teh-huai even to have hinted at the grass roots that Mao was not merely aware of the problems deriving from the great leap and the communes but must in large measure take responsibility for them. Not only would he have been breaking party discipline; but in doing so he would also have been faced with the virtually insuperable obstacle of the Mao cult. Even P'eng, on his native heath and talking in some cases to friends of his youth, would have found it impossible to chip away single-handed at the myth of Maoist omniscience that had been built up since Liu Shao-ch'i had extolled the 'thought of Mao Tse-tung' at the party's 7th Congress in 1945.

Here was P'eng's dilemma in the months ahead, indeed the dilemma of all potential critics of Mao: how to separate man from myth, leader from legend? Perhaps that was why P'eng hesitated until Lushan. Certainly, when he left Hunan with a warning of peasant uprisings ringing in his ears, his intention was to speak out, as he declared in a poem composed on his final sleepless night:

> The millet is scattered all over the ground,
> The leaves of the sweet potatoes are withered.
> The young and the strong have gone to smelt iron,
> To harvest the grain there are children and old women.
> How shall we get through next year?
> I shall agitate and speak out on behalf of the people.[76]

And yet, despite subsequent visits to Kiangsi and Anhwei,[77] for six months P'eng did not really speak up on behalf of the people. At the end of his Hunan tour, he had run into Po I-po in Chuchou and voiced his disquiet about the grain purchase target of 60 million tons; his belief was that actual grain output was unlikely to allow of a figure higher than 45 million tons. Po suggested that P'eng cable Peking to that effect and, at the latter's request, drafted a telegram on his behalf which went off over the Marshal's name. But P'eng mentioned nothing of his disillusionment with the communes and the steel drive. Later, at the Shanghai plenum, P'eng was (he subsequently claimed) too preoccupied with master-minding military operations against the Tibetan rebels to take much part in the proceedings; yet as we have seen, this did not prevent him speaking up on methods of leadership. Even more strikingly, on his return from a goodwill visit to the Soviet Union, Eastern Europe and Mongolia that lasted from 24 April until 13 June, he asked his secretary to request permission to absent himself from the Lushan meeting because he felt so worn out. Ironically, it was a phone call from Mao that persuaded him to go.[78]

(iv)   P'eng Teh-huai's sighting shots

To be fair to P'eng, he may have felt constrained prior to the Lushan conference by his unfamiliarity with economic affairs. Besides, when the partial retreat had been ordered at the Wuhan plenum the previous December, there was no real sense of defeat among party leaders. Even after his December visit to Hunan, P'eng could only claim to have obtained a few bird's eye glimpses of grass-roots reality. But during his visit to Eastern Europe the situation changed rapidly.

Less than a week after P'eng's departure from Peking, Mao issued his directive in response to the first set of drastically revised output figures for 1958. By the time P'eng returned home, the further check-ups were virtually complete. Within the top ranks of the leadership there could be no disguising that the undoubted expansion in production in 1958 had been grotesquely exaggerated.

One of the topics scheduled for discussion at Lushan presumably was what to do about this realization. Had the prognostications for the 1959 harvest been good, even if not on a par with 1958, the party leadership could conceivably have decided not to publish revised figures for 1958; instead they could have deliberately underestimated the increases for 1959 over 1958 and gradually, over a course of years, synchronized actual and claimed output figures.

But even by the end of June, there were indications that 1959 would not be a good harvest year. In the north-east, a long dry spell, starting in many areas at the end of 1958 and not ending till June 1959, had caused setbacks to the early crops and meant problems with sowing later crops.[79] From May, flooding had affected a large number of provinces, particularly Kwangtung where 1st secretary T'ao Chu, ashen-faced and racked by fever, led the fight against the worst floods for a century.[80] Despite floods, reports of bumper summer wheat harvests were issued from a number of provinces in June,[81] but claims of production increases of 10–30 per cent over 1958 may not have seemed convincing to China's leaders, who by now were aware of the previous year's exaggerations.[82] In short, by the time the Lushan conference opened, the harvest prospects were sufficiently clouded—even though the drought that was to devastate the autumn harvest had only just begun[83]—to stiffen the resolve of someone who was unhappy about the great leap and the communes to speak out about them.

P'eng Teh-huai would not normally have seen all the reports on agricultural conditions which presumably daily reached the Ministries of Agriculture and Food. But his own Defence Ministry provided him with a unique access to grass roots opinion. The troops of the PLA tended to react with concern to letters complaining of hardships from their largely peasant families.[84] No information is available about what reports on this topic were reaching the Ministry of Defence from regional commands, but on his return from abroad P'eng was told by PLA Chief of Staff Huang K'och'eng that conditions in some areas of the country were grave, particularly in Kansu which he had visited the previous autumn. As recently as April, Kansu had proclaimed itself a grain surplus province; now it was admitting to a serious grain deficiency. Huang stated that any further diversion of military transport to grain shipment duties would endanger operations in Tibet and China's overall defence posture, but P'eng insisted that greater efforts should be made on behalf of grain deficit areas.[85]

Letters to overseas Chinese from their relatives in south China detailed the considerable distress in the countryside about which P'eng had been made aware through his own sources. Rations had been reduced[86]; grain allocations, it was claimed, varied from 2 to 4 oz a day for the elderly[87] to a maximum of 35 lb a month for the able-bodied in the countryside.[88] Sweet potatoes were expensive.[89] Edible oils were in short supply.[90]

P'eng Teh-huai took up this shortage of edible oils early on at Lushan.[91] During the opening days of the conference, the participants divided up into regional groups; P'eng caucused with the north-western group, presumably because this was the area of which he had been at least the nominal chief until the reorganization of the central government in 1954. On 9 July he told the group:

Suspending supplies of edible oil to rural villages for four months could not be done in fact. This was entirely subjectivism. As soon as I returned to the country and saw the telegram, I immediately put forward my opinion over the telephone.

Other participants commented that the central authorities had rescinded this order, but P'eng challenged them to say whether they had resisted it in the first place.[92] This typically outspoken slur on the courage of his colleagues probably cost P'eng dear when he needed allies in his confrontation with Mao in the weeks ahead.

During the period 3–10 July, P'eng Teh-huai made at least seven interventions in the discussions of the north-western group. His comments reflected the on-the-spot observations he had made in the latter months of 1958. He asserted that it had been against the interests of the people to smash their cooking pots and that the party had got away with it only because of its high prestige.[93] He questioned the value of the backyard steel campaign, but interestingly he did no more than question it—'Was the call for the whole people to make steel correct or not?'[94]—

and did not denounce it; perhaps he had learned some caution from Chou Hsiao-chou. He criticized the launching of the communes and the free food supply system without prior experimentation, and alleged that some communes, including trail-blazers in Hsushui, had collapsed.[95] P'eng complained of leftism and continuing exaggeration, summed up in his oft-used phrase 'fever in the brain'.[96]

In a very early intervention, apparently apropos of nothing, P'eng detailed four major mistakes he had made in his military career.[97] Possibly, he wished to undercut resentment at his forthright criticisms by displaying a readiness to criticize himself. In particular he may have been anticipating the reactions of Mao Tse-tung, whose share of the responsibility for the mistakes of 1958 he pinpointed in the same speech as his self-criticism.[98] But in fact P'eng had already committed far greater *lèse majesté*.

In his opening intervention on 3 July P'eng virtually accused the Chairman of lying. Reporting on his visit to Shaoshan, he said that although the commune there had raised production the increase had not been as great as touted:

I went there to find out the truth, which was an increase of only 16%. I also asked Comrade Chou Hsiao-chou. He told me that this commune had increased its production by only 14%, with much assistance and large loans from the state. The Chairman has also visited this commune. I asked the Chairman what was his finding. He said that he had not talked about the matter. In my opinion, he had.[99]

Since Mao had visited Shaoshan only just before coming to Lushan, this comment means that P'eng must have buttonholed the Chairman shortly after they had both arrived at the conference site. P'eng's tart remarks suggest that the Chairman blandly brushed him off, cavalier treatment which could well have triggered the Defence Minister's notoriously short temper and provoked his series of attacks on the leap to the north-western group.

On 10 July, the day after the last of those attacks, Mao felt compelled to reply, although in what precise forum is unclear. He acknowledged that a lack of consensus was undermining intraparty solidarity, but there was no hint of defensiveness in his allegation that the root of the problem was some comrades' inability to analyse the situation in a comprehensive manner. He rejected out of hand critics who said the general line was basically wrong—not P'eng, so far, it would seem. Drawbacks and errors must be admitted, but Mao, using a favourite simile, said these amounted to only one finger out of ten.[100]

(v)   The odd couple

Despite the pressure of work during the opening days of the conference, P'eng was very cheerful. Perhaps he was glad to be in action at last, speaking his mind after months of uncharacteristic restraint. He rose at dawn to look at the billowing clouds and watch the sun rise; at dusk he took strolls and sometimes visited historic sites. When he met one of his fellow marshals, they would chat and joke.

Abruptly this pattern changed. P'eng became morose and thoughtful. In the evenings, his bodyguard would draw his bath, but P'eng left the water unused. He stopped taking his habitual sleeping pill. He would lie down and then get up again and pace restlessly around. He never got to sleep until deep into the night.[101]

P'eng was probably disquieted by discussions with some of his colleagues. He had met the Hunan party secretary Chou Hsiao-chou on two occasions. At their first meeting, over a meal, Chou had waxed enthusiastic about the development of industry and water conservancy in his province as a result of the leap; on the second occasion, only two days later, Chou was in a very differ-ent mood, revealing that the Hunan grain figure had been ex-aggerated, and strongly criticizing commune mess halls. Chou had only had a brief opportunity to communicate his disquiet to the Chairman and expressed a hope that P'eng would speak to him.

More importantly, P'eng was by this time in regular consul-tation with a Politburo colleague, Chang Wen-t'ien, whose Lushan quarters were next door.[102] They were an odd couple. Whereas P'eng was genuinely a simple soldier, Chang was a cultured polyglot, a one-time literary translator and a party propagandist and historian.[103] In his twenties, he had worked in the United States and studied briefly in Japan and, for far longer, in the Soviet Union. He had returned from Moscow in 1930 as a leading member of that group of Soviet-trained young men, known col-lectively and derisively to their less-travelled but more experi-enced colleagues as the '28 Bolsheviks', who used Moscow's sponsorship to take over command of the Chinese communist party. However, unlike most members of this elite group, Chang found or placed himself often on Mao's side, and his vote was critically important in helping to bring about the crucial change of leadership on the Long March at the Tsunyi conference in January 1935. It was Chang, as the senior, who took over the post of General Secretary, while Mao had to be content with heading a three-man 'small group' in charge of military affairs. As General Secretary, Chang chaired the Politburo until he was accused by Moscow of Trotskyist connections; this provided Mao with the opportunity of relieving him of his office (subsequently transforming it into something far less important), although Chang continued to occupy prominent posts. After the communist victory in 1949, Chang had become exclusively concerned with foreign affairs, serving as ambassador to the Soviet Union and thereafter as Chou En-lai's principal deputy at the Foreign Ministry. He had retained his membership of Politburo, first achieved in 1931 and confirmed at the Mao-dominated 7th Congress in 1945. However, at the 8th Congress in 1956, Chang was demoted for no apparent reason to alternate membership, and at the NPC in 1958 he failed to obtain the succession to Chou En-lai when the latter relinquished the Foreign Ministry. Having lost face, Chang sought a back seat, arranging with the new Foreign Minister, Marshal Ch'en Yi, to give up day-to-day responsibilities in favour of analytical work on world affairs; ironically, an analysis he prepared on the contradictions within the Western alliance was praised by Mao and approved for distribution at Lushan. But Chang's relationship to Mao had always been ambiguous, a marriage of convenience that had lost much of its relevance after Chang gave up the Moscow embassy in 1955. Like P'eng Teh-huai, Chang Wen-t'ien had ample evidence that he was gradually being pushed aside, and their shared bitterness at Mao probably cemented their brief and ill-fated alliance.[104]

According to P'eng's own account, he and Chang had very few dealings prior to the spring of 1959. Coincidentally, they both flew to Eastern Europe within 24 hours of each other in late April, although on different missions, shortly after P'eng's attack on one-man rule at the Shanghai plenum. By this time, Chang's early enthusiasm for the leap had evaporated as a result of a tour of the south during which the impact of the food shortages had been brought home to him. He had raised this matter at Shanghai, albeit not in plenary session.[105] On 24 April, Chang and

P'eng flew together from Moscow to Warsaw, and met again in the Polish capital on 27 and 28 April.[106] But probably more important than any brief exchanges of jaundiced views on China's domestic situation that these encounters may have permitted, would have been the reinforcement of those views by evident Soviet disapproval of the communes and the leap of which both men were almost certainly made personally aware.

After P'eng's return on 13 June, Chang came to see him and specifically mentioned Mao's 29 April directive, commenting that it was very useful, but that it established an individualistic work style (*shu-li ko-jen tso-feng*). In other words, Mao's modification of great leap methods was welcome, but the manner in which he had personally issued the instructions was high-handed and reminiscent of the one-man rule criticized by P'eng in Shanghai. Predictably, P'eng agreed.[107]

From P'eng's account of his relationship with Chang, the inescapable conclusion is that the Defence Minister was manipulated by the politically more astute one-time General Secretary. Chang Wen-t'ien had no political base; indeed, his survival in the 7th and 8th CCs had been predicated upon his earlier abandonment of the only constituency he once had, the Soviet-educated 'Bolsheviks'.[108] In P'eng Teh-huai, Chang must have sensed an ideal ally: a soldier, highly esteemed as a leading revolutionary general and as the commander of the Chinese forces in the Korean war, widely respected for his ascetic life-style, and possessed of a very obvious constituency within the PLA and among his fellow marshals.

After the two men arrived at Lushan, their propinquity enabled them to meet often. They agreed that even the reduced targets for steel (13 million tons) and coal (340 million tons) were unattainable, and Chang put into P'eng's mind the idea that the losses attendant upon the backyard steel campaign had not been offset by the gains. They both bemoaned the atmosphere of mutual congratulation at Lushan which made it seem like bad manners to raise mistakes and shortcomings. There was no real discussion at Politburo meetings; effectively its members were only being briefed by Mao and other top leaders. Chang criticized Mao as brilliant but excessively tough in bringing people to heel. P'eng seemed to feel this was unsurprising in the founder of a new regime and compared Mao to the first emperors of the great Chinese dynasties.[109]

(vi) Hai Jui—red herring?

If Chang was attempting in his chats with P'eng to provoke the
Defence Minister into more radical action, he succeeded. But
Chang was not the only *provocateur*; Mao also played that role,
presumably unwittingly. Here it is necessary briefly to digress.

From time to time at Lushan, P'eng mused out loud in his
quarters about Mao's injunction at the Chengtu conference the
previous year to shatter superstitions, liberate one's thinking and
dare to think, speak and act.[110] More recently, at the Shanghai
work conference in late March 1959, Mao had enjoined his colleagues to emulate two Confucian bureaucrats of the imperial era
long extolled by Chinese historians as unbending moralists and
fearless remonstrators: Wei Cheng (AD 580–643) of the T'ang
dynasty and Hai Jui (AD 1515–87) of the Ming. As he had often
done in the past, Mao criticized the harmful work-style of fearing
to speak the truth.[111] Subsequently at the 7th plenum in early
April, Mao returned to this theme:

There ought to be created within the party an atmosphere of speaking
out and of correcting shortcomings. Criticising is sometimes rather pain-
ful, but so long as criticism results in correction it is all right. When people don't dare speak out it is for one of six reasons: fear of admonition,
fear of demotion, fear of loss of prestige, fear of dismissal from the party, fear of execution, fear of divorce. . . . Speaking out should involve no
penalty, and according to party regulations people are entitled to their
own opinions.[112]

Again Mao cited a figure from Chinese history to drive home his
point, this time the Sung general Yueh Fei (AD 1103–41). Since
Yueh was murdered in prison at the instance of the emperor, this
example must have seemed ambiguous to some of his audience,
especially since Mao stressed that it was precisely because he was
executed that Yueh achieved fame.[113]

Evidently acting on Mao's injunctions, the CC's propaganda
department issued instructions for Wei Cheng and Hai Jui an-
thologies to be prepared. In addition, Chou Yang, the department
deputy director in charge of the literary world, encouraged a
well-known Peking opera singer, Chou Hsin-fang, to produce a
play about Hai Jui and arranged for him to be supplied with relevant material. The commissioned play, written by Chou Hsin-
fang and two collaborators, was performed in Shanghai on the
eve of the tenth anniversary celebration on 1 October 1959. It was

entitled *Hai Jui sends a memorial*, a reference to the Ming bureaucrat's most famous act of criticizing the emperor directly.[114] A play about Yueh Fei was also written.[115]

Meanwhile, a 'leading comrade' had encouraged a prominent historian of the Ming dynasty, Wu Han, to respond to Mao's injunction.[116] Wu Han, by this time a deputy mayor of Peking, had emerged in the 1930s as one of China's most brilliant younger scholars. While still in his twenties, and a teaching assistant at Peking's Tsinghua University, he published a number of articles on the Ming period which became standard references. With the outbreak of the Sino-Japanese war in 1937, the staffs of Peking universities fled to south-west China and Wu Han spent the war years as a professor at the Southwest Associated University in Kunming. There he wrote a biography of the founder of the Ming dynasty, considered by many to be the 'best biography written by a modern Chinese'.

It was during this period that Wu Han began to take an interest in political matters. In articles for the press, he subtly satirized the KMT behind the cloak of historical allegory, 'reviling the locust tree while pointing at the mulberry' as he himself put it. In the post-war period, now a professor at Tsinghua, he became an active member of the political party of the liberal intellectuals, the China Democratic League, which sought a middle ground between the KMT and the CCP. But KMT persecution during the civil war forced him to flee to the communist-held areas where he began, at the age of 39, a gradual conversion to Marxism. In an early self-examination, he explained how he had come to terms with Mao's personality cult.[117]

As a prominent member of the post-1949 'united front' in Peking,[118] Wu Han found himself heavily involved in ceremonial and representational duties, devoting relatively little time to history.[119] His political role brought him closer to P'eng Chen, Peking's mayor and party 1st secretary, as well as a senior member of the Politburo. In 1957, the year Wu Han entered the CCP, P'eng Chen appears to have used the historian to deliver a veiled attack on Mao during the top-level controversy over 'blooming and contending' and the anti-rightist campaign.[120] In 1959, Wu Han emerged from his academically fallow period with a spate of short historical articles, primarily for popular consumption. One of his principal concerns was the evaluation of 'progressive' historical figures such as Ts'ao Ts'ao (died AD 220), Empress

Wu of the T'ang dynasty (AD c. 626–705)[121] and, most importantly, Hai Jui.

Wu Han's first reference to Hai Jui occurred in an article
attacking excessive verbiage which appeared in the *People's Daily*
on 15 June 1959, two days after P'eng Teh-huai's return from
Eastern Europe.[122] In the same paper on the following day, writing under an apparently meaningless pseudonym, Wu Han published his first article devoted exclusively to Hai Jui. It was entitled 'Hai Jui upbraids the emperor' and dealt with the Ming
bureaucrat's famous memorial. With the hindsight of cultural revolution attacks on Wu Han, it is possible to read much of this
article as a veiled but pointed denunciation of Mao.[123] But was
it?

Undoubtedly the credibility of later cultural revolution charges
against Wu Han revolved to a considerable extent around the
issues of timing and appropriateness. The historical Hai Jui had
been noted not just for his critical memorial to the emperor,
but also for being dismissed from office. P'eng Teh-huai, as will
soon appear, had implicitly criticized Mao in his 'letter of opinion' at Lushan and he was dismissed. The latter events occurred
in the late summer and early autumn of 1959 around the time Wu
Han was beginning to write about Hai Jui in earnest. Thus when
Mao later alleged that Hai Jui was meant to be P'eng Teh-huai[124]
it seemed to fit. Coincidence appeared inherently improbable.

But Mao and the cultural revolutionaries virtually never mentioned the crucial fact that the chairman himself had first brought
up the name of Hai Jui and encouraged attention to him and
other historical figures. Moreover, Mao, according to the
accounts available since his death, specifically drew attention to
men like Hai Jui because of their courageous willingness to risk
disgrace or even death by criticizing their superiors—in their case
the emperors of the day.[125]

The second fact barely mentioned in cultural revolution ver-
sions was that Wu Han did not spontaneously decided to write on
Hai Jui after learning about Mao's suggestion, but was actually
approached by a 'leading comrade' and specifically encouraged to
do so.[126] The questions then arise: who was this 'leading comrade' and why does his identity still have to remain veiled? Could
it have been someone who hoped to use Wu Han to attack Mao?

The obvious contender for such a role would be P'eng Chen,
who, as Peking party 1st secretary and mayor, was the most

important of Wu Han's direct superiors, and quite probably the man who briefed him on what had transpired at the Shanghai work conference.[127] P'eng had, after all, clashed head on with Mao only 18 months earlier.

Another possibility would be a senior CC propaganda department official like Chou Yang entrusted with encouraging implementation of Mao's suggestion. Conceivably it could have been a party leader like Chang Wen-t'ien who had the intellectual background to appreciate fully the way in which the Hai Jui story could be manipulated for political purposes. More dramatically, but more unlikely, it might have been P'eng Teh-huai himself.

But it seems inconceivable that any of these names would not have come out during the cultural revolution when such a revelation would have been a final nail in the coffin of the person concerned. This would apply equally to any other Chinese leader purged at that time.

Nor does it seem likely that the mysterious 'leading comrade' could have been anyone who, by the time this source was published in mid-1979, had been denounced or was under a cloud for his role in the cultural revolution. This would rule out men like Ch'en Po-ta or K'ang Sheng who concerned themselves with intellectual matters. If it had been one of them, by now he would surely have been condemned either for provocation in 1959 or hypocrisy during the cultural revolution or both.

Logically, therefore, the 'leading comrade' must have been someone who went through the cultural revolution virtually unscathed, but whose reputation had for some reason still to be protected in 1979. In this category, there were *prima facie* only two men who would have been involved enough in cultural affairs actually to have taken the concrete step of approaching Wu Han and encouraging him to write about Hai Jui. One was Chou En-lai; the other was Mao Tse-tung himself.

Chou is the more likely candidate. He had a special relationship with the intellectuals and had on occasion laid down policy in the cultural sphere on Mao's behalf.[128] Also, it is clear that Chou saw his role, at least in part, as Mao's *chef de cabinet*, whose job was to follow through on the Chairman's suggestions; one of the most extraordinary instances occurred in early 1958 when he took some senior leaders cruising on the Yangtse, en route for the Chengtu conference, to investigate how to put flesh on the proposal for a dam made two years earlier in Mao's poem

'Swimming'.[129] But Mao, too, relished his contacts with the intellectuals, perhaps finding in the obsequiousness of distinguished men of letters belated compensation for being ignored by academics in his youth.[130] Moreover, it was not unknown for Mao to single out intellectuals for special treatment, be it benevolent—as in his exchanges of poems with the President of the Academy of Sciences, Kuo Mo-jo[131]—or malevolent—as when he led the denunciation of the writer Hu Feng.[132] Indeed Wu Han himself had once been called in by the Chairman for a private chat about ·his biography of the founder of the Ming dynasty.[133]

If the 'leading comrade' who encouraged Wu Han to take up the study of Hai Jui was either Mao or Chou it is easy to see why this would have been impossible to reveal at the time of the cultural revolution and embarrassing to reveal now. Why, it might be asked, had he not spoken up in defence of Wu Han's motives in 1965? Furthermore, in the Chairman's case, the suspicion might arise that, knowing he was being blamed for the great leap, Mao deliberately promoted the portrayal of historical characters whose contemporary relevance would be easy to see in order to find out if anyone would take advantage of the device to criticize him.

The hypothesis that Wu Han was originally directed towards Hai Jui by either Mao or Chou would serve to explain the historian's otherwise uncharacteristically foolhardy conduct. He was not afraid to publish an article on Hai Jui which could be read as harshly critical of Mao[134] even *before* P'eng Teh-huai had given him a lead. After the Lushan plenum, at a time when P'eng was virtually isolated, with Liu Shao-ch'i and Chou En-lai standing shoulder to shoulder with Mao, Wu Han published another article on Hai Jui. This time the instigator was apparently Hu Ch'iao-mu, an alternate secretary of the CC secretariat and a senior propaganda official, who told Wu Han that when Hai Jui's name was mentioned at Lushan—by P'eng Teh-huai—many participants knew nothing about him; an explanatory article was therefore needed. Wu Han completed it on the very day P'eng Teh-Huai's dismissal was signed, 17 September, and it appeared in the *People's Daily* four days later. Wu Han included a disclaimer rejecting the pretensions of right opportunists who might see themselves in the role of the Ming bureaucrat. It must be remembered that it was about this time that Chou Hsin-fang's play *Hai Jui sends a memorial* was performed. Yet neither Chou nor Wu Han suffered, despite the mounting campaign against right opportunism. Moreover, Wu Han persisted with his studies of Hai Jui, producing a number of articles on the Ming official over the next few years leading up to the publication of a collection of Hai Jui's works in 1962 (the project that the propaganda department had promoted back in 1959).[135]

It seems inherently improbable that Wu Han would have decided in June 1959 to act as the lone conscience of the party, taking on the Chairman himself about the leap. However great his attainments academically, politically Wu Han was a creature of the Peking party apparatus and unlikely to stick his head above the parapet without a nudge from 1st secretary P'eng Chen. No allegations appear to have been made during the cultural revolution that P'eng Chen acted in such a manner at this time, and any such allegations would anyway have been barely credible. Top party apparatchiki were implicated as much as was Mao in the excesses of the leap. The divisions over it occurred later.[136]

It can of course be argued that in the early 1960s the groundswell of pro-P'eng Teh-huai opinion within the party was so pervasive that Wu Han's play *The dismissal of Hai Jui*, staged in Peking in February 1961, must be seen as a vindication of the former Defence Minister; this question will be dealt with in the final volume of this work. But Mao's promotion of the Hai Jui model, the specific encouragement given to Wu Han by the mysterious 'leading comrade', the historian's insouciant pursuit of his Hai Jui studies in the midst of the anti-right-opportunist campaign, the failure to punish any of the Hai Jui authors at this time,[137] all combine to suggest that at least in its origins the Hai Jui 'affair' was perfectly innocent and was seen as such by Mao.

(vii) P'eng Teh-huai's bombshell

One cannot be certain that P'eng Teh-huai read the first of Wu Han's major contributions on the Hai Jui theme at the time of its publication. But P'eng's 'unusual excitement' about Mao's injunctions to speak out is attested to by his bodyguard, and since he attended the Shanghai conference he presumably had heard Mao's original invocation of Hai Jui's name; and as we have seen, someone, perhaps P'eng, did raise the name of Hai Jui at Lushan. P'eng later stated that he was seized of the idea that despite the measures already taken, the Planning Commission had not brought blind expansionism under control. On the evening of 12 July he thought through what he wanted to say, but when he went to see Mao the following morning he found him still asleep.[138] Late on the night of 13 July,[139] the marshal told his bodyguard to brew him some stronger tea and then go to bed. In response to a suggestion that he too should get some rest to be in good shape for the following day's conference session, P'eng explained that the small group sessions had helped to clarify his thinking; now he was going to put together all that he had learned at the grass roots and report it in a letter to Mao. In front of him was a piece of paper on which he had written 'Chairman'. P'eng Teh-huai had begun his fateful 'letter of opinion' (*i-chien shu*). During the course of the evening Chang Wen-t'ien called on P'eng who read him part of his draft.[140]

Early the following morning, after performing *t'ai-chi-ch'üan*—the traditional Chinese setting-up exercises—P'eng summoned his aide-de-camp, handed him a completed draft, asked him to correct it and make a clean copy and later sent him with it to Mao's office. It was a moment of intense relief for P'eng as the nervousness of his gestures demonstrated, and there was a further release of tension when he ascertained from his aide that his letter had safely reached its destination. As P'eng explained: 'In the meetings there were some things I didn't want to say, or I didn't put accurately, but now I've written it all down in this [letter]. When I have something to say, I've just got to get it out and then once I've done so I feel like a new man.'[141] It was in almost exactly the same way that P'eng justified his letter of opinion in its opening paragraph,[142] but Mao was not to accept the explanation as sympathetically as P'eng's staff had.

P'eng commenced the substantive portion of his letter with an affirmation of the achievements of the great leap, even after the scaling-down of figures by the State Planning Commission. The value of the gross output of industry and agriculture had risen overall by 48·4 per cent, with industry going up 66·1 per cent and agriculture 25 per cent. Grain and cotton output had increased by at least 30 per cent. 'Such a rate of growth has never been achieved in other parts of the world ... the great leap forward has in the main proved the general line of achieving greater, faster, better and more economical results to be correct.'[143]

There had been excessive and hasty investment in some capital construction projects with consequent bottlenecks, and there had been a failure to correct this soon enough in 1959. However, the construction projects were needed and would in due course yield returns, and only where shortages of some items were further holding up production would capital construction projects have to be suspended.

The formation of the communes had been of great significance; they would enable the peasants to rid themselves of poverty and to speed up the construction of socialism and the transition to communism. Confusions regarding the system of ownership had mostly been corrected as a result of the meetings in Wuchang, Chengchow and Shanghai. Unemployment had been eliminated.[144]

Thus far P'eng, perhaps schooled by Chang Wen-t'ien, had been a model of tact. Although he had characterized himself as rough and without caution, the first part of his letter was in fact smooth and careful. It was a subtle presentation, particularly, as Mao later acknowledged,[145] in the final section of the first part which dealt with the backyard steel campaign:

[S]ome small and indigenous blast furnaces which were not necessary were built, with the consequence that some resources (material and financial) and manpower were wasted. This is of course a relatively big loss. But a preliminary geological survey on a huge scale was carried out throughout the country, and many technical personnel were trained. The broad masses of cadres have tempered and improved themselves in this movement. Although a tuition fee was spent (in the amount of 2 billion yuan), even in this respect there have been losses and gains.[146]

It was the reversal of the customary order, gains and losses, which, as Mao realized, gave bite to this passage, underlining the enormous financial cost of the backyard steel campaign and its insubstantial and unquantifiable benefits. Years later, P'eng claimed that he had used the customary order and that someone had copied it incorrectly, whether with malice aforethought he did not speculate. But it is curious that he did not apparently protest this point at the time, and that the version of his letter published with his 'autobiography' in 1981 as part of the effort to rehabilitate him reprinted the phrase as 'losses and gains'.[147]

It was in the second part of his letter, 'How to sum up the experiences and lessons in work'—additonal *lèse majesté*, since within the Politburo it was the Chairman's prerogative to sum up—

that P'eng really hit home, though even here he prefaced his remarks by asserting the need for a poor country to launch leaps to solve its massive economic problems. He acknowledged that inexperience made mistakes inevitable but added: 'We have not handled the problems of economic construction in so successful a way as we dealt with the problems of shelling Quemoy and quelling the revolt in Tibet', which seemed to imply that the PLA was more effective than the party and government.[148]

The first major problem, according to P'eng, was the universal habit of exaggeration, which he traced to the Peitaiho conference in August 1958, and the overestimate of likely grain production. This led to a feeling that the food problem had been solved and that attention could be turned to industry (a shift of focus directly attributable to Mao, though P'eng did not spell it out). However, the steel campaign had been based on superficial understanding:

We had not seriously considered such things as steel refining, steel rolling, stone-breaking equipment, coal and charcoal, mineral ores, coking equipment, supply of pitprops, the capacity of transport, the increase in manpower, the increase in purchasing power, and the arrangement of market supplies. In short, there were no plans for achieving balances that were necessary.[149]

The importance of this passage does not lie solely in the vision it conveys of the nation-wide chaos that the backyard steel campaign had created. One must recall that there was nothing in P'eng's training, experience or responsibility that could possibly have entitled him to make this kind of analysis *ex cathedra*. His presentation could only have been based on information he gathered at two meetings of the State Council which he attended at Lushan, on Ch'en Yun's earlier analysis of the steel industry, and on materials compiled by the State Planning and Economic Commissions and by the NCNA, as a direct result of Mao's own critique of the leap delivered at the second Chengchow conference earlier in the year, and distributed among Chinese leaders specifically to brief them for the Lushan conference.[150] In other words, there was nothing in P'eng's remarks that was original or could have sounded startling to Mao or anyone else at Lushan who had done his homework.

The same comment applies to P'eng's description of the mishandling of the autumn harvest and the dizzy feeling of some cadres that communism was round the corner.[151] Mao himself had sanctioned the squelching of utopianism at Wuchang the previous autumn.[152]

P'eng's real crime in Mao's eyes must have been that he had detailed all the disasters stemming from the great leap and the commune movement and then implicitly but unmistakably laid the blame where it ultimately belonged, at the door of the Chairman. P'eng referred to Mao's slogans—to combine sky-rocketing zeal with scientific analysis, to walk on two legs (for example, to make steel by both modern and backyard methods), to grow less, produce more and reap more and to overtake Britain in 15 years —and said that they had been misunderstood and misapplied. But everyone at Lushan knew that the slogans were the trigger and that the smoking gun was in Mao's hand; and P'eng, despite his later disclaimer, had to know that his letter amounted to an indictment of the Chairman. No wonder he was nervous when he dispatched it.[153]

Moreover, P'eng was insulting in a manner which Mao permitted himself to employ with regard to others but which had not been used against him for a quarter of a century. The Marshal attributed the 'leftist' mistakes of the previous 12 months to 'petty-bourgeois fanaticism' (*hsiao tzu-ch'an-chieh-chi-ti k'uang-je-hsing*),[154] a Marxist-type of condemnation with the flavour, perhaps, of Chang Wen-t'ien's erudition rather than P'eng Teh-huai's earthiness. The phrase clearly derives from Lenin's 'petty-bourgeois revolutionism, which smacks of anarchism' which the Soviet leader had employed when denouncing apostates in *Left-Wing Communism—An Infantile Disorder*.[155] This work was probably one of the few Marxist-Leninist classics P'eng had read. Ironically, he had originally been presented with a copy during the early days of the revolution by Mao himself, with a covering note which stated: 'If the Chinese revolution is to be victorious, this book must be read.'[156]

But whoever suggested the epithet which P'eng used at Lushan, nothing could have been more infuriating to the originator of the Thought of Mao Tse-tung, whose greatest intellectual accomplishment was the 'sinification' of Marxism, than effectively to be labelled a petty-bourgeois fanatic, and by an ideological novice.[157] As P'eng was shortly to discover, Mao had reached a stage when self-criticism was still possible, but criticism was difficult to accept and ridicule was quite intolerable.

(viii)   Mao's counter-attack

The precise sequence of events immediately following the dispatch of P'eng Teh-huai's letter is critical but confused. According to P'eng's confession during the cultural revolution, the letter was immediately printed and distributed to participants at the conference before Mao got down to reading it on 17 July. If so, it would have been the last straw for the Chairman. A private letter could have been finessed; a conference document, signed by a member of the Politburo, demanded a public rebuttal, especially when couched in the form of a letter to the Chairman. But the evidence suggests that P'eng's 'confession' was concocted by and dictated to him by his Red Guard captors in order to depict an even more aggressive challenge by the Marshal to the Chairman than had actually been offered. One collection of documents relevant to the P'eng Teh-huai affair, circulated to a restricted readership during the cultural revolution, includes alongside the 'letter of opinion' an authorization under Mao's name, dated 16 July, that it should be printed and distributed for colleagues to examine. P'eng himself, in his 'autobiography', asserted that the letter had not been meant for publication and that he was staggered when, on 17 July, the conference secretariat began distributing copies with the headline 'Comrade P'eng Teh-huai's letter of opinion'. At a small group meeting on 18 July, he requested in vain that it should be withdrawn.[158] All this indicates that Mao read the letter, intuited that P'eng, apart from intervening in group meetings, had probably not made much of a secret of his views, and decided he had to face the challenge head on.

But the Chairman did not make an immediate riposte. Possibly he was deliberately biding his time to see what support P'eng might get. Chou Hsiao-chou and Huang K'o-ch'eng, who reached Lushan on 18 or 19 July, spoke up on lines similar to P'eng's. On 20 July, Chang Wen-t'ien put forward some of the criticisms of the economy which he and P'eng had discussed in a speech to the conference, and then apparently returned to the attack with a three-hour speech on the 21st. On the second occasion, Chang had not warned P'eng in advance with the result that the Marshal did not even attend the session. When he learned what had transpired, he asked Chang to send over the text of his speech that night for him to read.[159] Chang's speeches were apparently not distributed to the conference.[160]

Without access to Chang's speeches, it is impossible to assess how bruising Mao found them. But the crucial point was not so much their substance as their source. That a politician as canny as Chang Wen-t'ien, a man with no obvious band of supporters, was bold enough to challenge Mao in public after long quiescent years on the periphery of the leadership, must surely have indicated a confidence that his comments would command widespread support. The danger for Mao was that the initiatives of P'eng and Chang might shame more formidable figures into speaking up.

Foreign Minister Ch'en Yi, whose duties had kept him in Peking, telephone Chang Wen-t'ien to congratulate and encourage him. Six years later, Ch'en Yi recalled the situation in 1959 in cataclysmic terms for a foreign delegation: 'The country was very tense. . . . There were very many chimneys from which no smoke came; factories didn't have machines; our money had gone.'[161] No wonder, therefore, that Ch'en wanted the matter thrashed out. Po I-po, the Chairman of the State Economic Commission, was preparing his own summation on the leap on the basis of analyses made by some of the country's leading economists, it was later alleged. But seeing the way the wind was blowing, Po discarded the speech drafted for him by Hsueh Mu-ch'iao, Director of the State Statistical Bureau and Vice Chairman of both the State Planning and State Economic Commissions, and Sun Yeh-fang, Director of the Institute of Economics at the Academy of Sciences. Instead, he spoke in support of the great leap. If he had delivered the original draft, with all the authority of his office, perhaps even more Chinese leaders would have shifted to the view that losses outweighed gains, that the leap and the communes had been ghastly mistakes.[162] Certainly Finance Minister Li Hsien-nien, even more senior than Po within the Politburo, was for a time swayed by P'eng Teh-huai.[163] According to Mao's own observation, 'some comrades are wavering'.[164] But the Chairman acted swiftly to prevent any further chain reaction. Two days after Chang Wen-t'ien's marathon speech, Mao counter-attacked.

Mao's speech to the Lushan conference on the morning of 23 July was a brilliant debating performance, designed to rally his supporters and frighten P'eng Teh-huai's sympathizers.[165] It combined obfuscation of the real issues with ridicule of real criticisms. The Chairman was disarmingly self-critical, but simultaneously diffused responsibility to indicate he would not 'take the rap' alone. This served to convince his collaborators of the need for self-defence, and to warn their potential opponents of the immensity of the task they faced. He appealed for unity and hinted darkly that, if isolated, he might bring down the whole communist structure, Samson-style.

Mao rallied his supporters by denouncing the criticisms as 'muddled' and explaining that he had remained silent for three weeks of the conference only because 'the more muddled they talked, the more one wanted to hear it. I have told comrades that we must stand it, stand it by stiffening our scalp, but for how long?... Some comrades would say "protracted war".' Mao agreed with this and added a further cheering note with an assertion that such comrades were the majority; China would not sink, the heavens would not fall.[166]

Early on, Mao likened the critics to leading 'bourgeois rightists' who had been excoriated two years earlier. The very first name he mentioned was that of Lo Lung-chi, a man with a personal link to P'eng Teh-huai. Later in his speech, he mentioned another bourgeois rightist to underline that this was a veiled threat, not an idle aside. If massive numbers of criticisms were published, then the people would rise up to overthrow the party. 'This would be a bourgeois nation and it would become the bourgeois Chang Po-chün's Political Planning Institute. Of course there is no one at this conference who will suggest this. I am merely exaggerating.'[167] Mao's heavy irony would not have deceived anyone; he was determined to make the criticisms into an issue of principle and P'eng's sympathizers should beware.

Mao then introduced a diversion, the campaign against the 'communist wind' earlier in the year. Mao, who repeatedly suggested that he himself was a middle-of-the-roader, was able to point out at some length that it had been the *hsien* and commune cadres who had been at fault and that the matter had been swiftly corrected.[168] He had no need to remind the conference that he had led that attack on leftism. More to the point, he had no need to discuss this episode at all since the gravamen of P'eng's charges was that the original decisions to set up the communes and launch the mass steel campaign were at fault. P'eng had said less about the the post-6th plenum tidying-up process of which he had no first-hand experience.[169]

There followed an even more clearcut warning to 'waverers' who might have jumped on to a P'eng Teh-huai bandwagon if it had shown signs of beginning to roll. This time Mao conjured up the spectre of past disputes within the party, an even more obvious hint that he projected labelling P'eng as the leader of another incorrect 'line'. First the stick, then the carrot—an appeal for solidarity, a convenient excuse which waverers could use to justify, to themselves and their colleagues, desertion of P'eng and a return to Mao's fold. And the Chairman reminded the economic planners, *prima facie* the men most likely to support P'eng on the basis of their knowledge and experience, how he had been magnanimous to them when their anti-adventurism had been criticized on the eve of the leap.[170] Now, he was calling in that debt.

Having prepared the ground, Mao then addressed himself to specific points, and first to the commune mess halls. Curiously this was a subject which did not figure in P'eng's letter of opinion, although he had briefly alluded to the smashing of individual cooking pots in one of his interventions in the north-western group.[171] Mao carefully avoided any reference to the use of such tough methods to force peasants to join the mess halls; he simply pronounced himself in favour of voluntary participation, and concentrated instead on their organizational problems, which possibly had been raised by Chang Wen-t'ien. He airily admitted the difficulties and expressed himself unperturbed if two-thirds of the mess halls had to be dissolved. However, he reaffirmed his faith in them and derided an investigation apparently undertaken under the auspices of the Academy of Sciences which had pinpointed shortages of pork and hairpins. 'Nobody can be without shortcomings; even Confucius had his mistakes. I have seen Lenin's own drafts that had been corrected pell-mell. If there were no errors, why should he correct them?'[172]

Finally, Mao reached the core issues: the formation of the communes, the mass steel campaign and the general line for the great leap forward. On all counts he admitted responsibility.

It was I who suggested and made the resolve for the smelting of 10,700,000 tons of steel, and the result was that 90 million people went ahead with it. . . . Next was the people's commune. I did not claim the right of inventing people's communes, but I had the right to suggest. In Shantung, a reporter asked me: 'Is the commune good?' I said, 'Good,' and he immediately published it in the newspaper. This might be due to some petty-bourgeois fervour. Hereafter, newspaper reporters should leave [me alone].[173]

As Mao's reference to the hapless journalist underlined, the Chairman was not prepared to accept sole blame for mistakes of 1958. In the case of steel, Mao accepted final responsibility but indicated clearly that the idea had been sold to him by his favourite provincial 1st secretary, K'o Ch'ing-shih of Shanghai.[174] The dislocation of production and transport caused by the steel campaign he attributed to ignorance on his own part, but also to the failure of Li Fu-ch'un and the State Planning Commission to do their job. T'an Chen-lin would have to accept some of the blame for the speed of communization, and for the high agricultural targets, along with the Minister of Agriculture, Liao Lu-yen.[175] In addition, by labelling a number of provinces 'leftist'— Honan, Szechwan, Hunan, Hupeh, Yunnan, Shanghai—Mao ensured that the local leaders there realized that they would have to line up with him or have their mistakes detailed.[176] 'Comrades', he said, 'you should analyse your own responsibility and your stomach will feel much more comfortable if you move your bowels and break wind.'[177]

Mao summed up in characteristically upbeat fashion. He reminded his audience that Marx, too, had been guilty of impetuousness, and a supporter chimed in from the audience that Lenin had committed the same error. Mao asserted that political movements could not be judged by economic accounting and he went on:

Will our present work be such a failure as in 1927 [when Chiang Kai-shek virtually wiped out the Communist party's urban organizations]? Will it be like the 25,000-li long march, when most of the bastions were lost and the Soviet area was reduced to one-tenth of its original size? No, we cannot put it this way. Haven't we failed now? All comrades who have come to this conference have gained something; we have not failed completely. Isn't this a failure by and large? No, it is only a partial failure. We have paid a price, blown some 'communist wind', and enabled the people of the entire nation to learn a lesson.[178]

In sum, Mao's view was that gains outweighed losses; P'eng's, whatever his actual phraseology, was that losses outweighed gains. Mao had admitted most of the mistakes so that the confrontation between him and the Marshal had been reduced to a question of judgement: how did one write the bottom line? Mao made it very clear to his colleagues that in deciding that question, they were choosing between P'eng and himself, and that their choice would have critical political consequences, possibly for themselves, certainly for the party. At one point Mao seemed ready to accept the consensus of the conference: 'If you have caught me in the wrong, you can punish me.'[179] But in another passage, he issued a not-too-oblique warning to P'eng's constituency, the Marshals and the generals: 'If you, the Liberation Army don't want to follow me, I will seek out a *Red* army; but I think the PLA will follow me' (emphasis added).[180] On another occasion during the conference, in a passage that P'eng could recall verbatim seven years later, Mao was even more threatening: 'If the Chinese People's Liberation Army should follow P'eng Teh-huai, I will go to fight guerrilla war.'[181] Mao's ultimatum underlined how seriously he took P'eng's challenge. It was here that Mao seemed ready to take on and bring down national institutions if need be, a course he finally took during the cultural revolution.

But there was no need for that now because Mao was of course right. Faced with a stark choice between Mao and even a revolutionary hero like P'eng Teh-huai, senior military men had no option but to choose the Chairman, particularly since it was evident that he had Liu Shao-ch'i and Premier Chou En-lai on his side.[182] The generals would have realized that rallying to P'eng meant taking on not just the father figure of the revolution but the whole civilian apparatus of party and government which they had been long schooled to obey. This was not a battle they were prepared to fight.

P'eng's misfortune lay in the form of *démarche* he had chosen to make. The pen was not his weapon; analytic overviews were not his forte. Had P'eng, not Chang Wen-t'ien, delivered a three-hour speech in plenary session, describing his personal findings on the great leap in simple language, the effect could have been dramatic. Waverers might have been swept along by his personal charisma; certainly the Chairman would have been put immediately on the defensive and deprived of the opportunity to prepare a carefully constructed response. Indeed, P'eng later claimed that he wrote rather than spoke precisely to avoid causing 'ideological confusion' (*ssu-hsiang hun-luan*).

As it was, Mao, as conference chairman, was able to ensure that P'eng had no effective right of reply.[183] The Marshal was understandably furious that Mao had refused to accept the legitimacy of criticism from one of his colleagues and had vengefully decided to have him consigned to the political outer darkness. But Mao said openly: 'In my days when I was a young man and later attained middle age, I used to get angry on hearing bad remarks against me. I never attack others if I am not attacked. If others attack me, I always attack back. Others attack me first, I attack them later. This principle I have never given up until this day.'[184] As it dawned on P'eng that Mao was delivering the last word, he exploded in earthy profanity: 'In Yenan you screwed my mother for 40 days. I have now screwed your mother for only 18 days in Lushan, and you have come forward to stop me. This won't do.'[185] But the show was being directed by a surer hand than P'eng's. The curtain did come down.[186] When it rose again, a new drama was being performed.

(ix)   The central committee's 8th plenum

The confrontation with Mao took its inevitable toll on P'eng's spirits. He lost his appetite and talked little. Lying on his bed, head in hands, he would stare moodily into space. His bodyguard failed to trace any connection between the letter of opinion and this behaviour, accepting the doctor's verdict that P'eng was ill. But the Marshal commented acidly: 'What are you examining me for? I'm not ill. If I've got a sickness, it's nothing that can be cured now.' When eventually, P'eng's aide-de-camp informed his bodyguard about what had happened, the latter was at a loss to understand why P'eng's political problems could not be solved by a self-criticism. Why not indeed.

Then the bodyguard was instructed that he could no longer enter the conference hall at will. Each successive day that P'eng attended the sessions, he seemed to drag his feet more and more and his normally ruddy complexion seemed to have paled. When he returned in the evenings, he stayed in his quarters, eschewing the cinema shows and even abandoning his customary evening stroll. Some of his fellow marshals would call, but now their voices no longer boomed out in mirth; they seemed laden with anxiety and after sitting for a short while they left again. P'eng's bodyguard finally realized just how serious the situation was.[187] The CC's 8th plenum was in session and P'eng Teh-huai's fate was in the balance.

Mao opened the 8th plenum on 2 August in the presence of 147 of the CC's 191 members. There were two items on the agenda: the revision of production targets and the 'problem of line' or what to do about P'eng and other dissidents.[188] Again, Mao framed his words artfully, emphasizing the weak points in the position of his opponents and skirting around those in his own.

His brief introduction to the question of revising targets emphasized that this was a matter that had been first discussed at the previous plenum four months earlier; the impression given was that the matter had been under continuous review. Mao thus played down the urgency of downward revisions now, after the shock of the new figures for 1958. At the Shanghai plenum some people had 'suggested that these targets be revised, although the majority disagreed'; in other words, Mao was certainly not solely responsible for clinging to wildly unrealistic targets any more than he had been for setting them at the 6th plenum in Wuhan the previous year! Mao described high targets like 'setting up a kind of Bodhisattva for one's own self to worship. Now we still have to break up those unrealistic targets, such as in steel, coal, grain, cotton, etc.' Nowhere was there any acknowledgement that the downward revision of the 1959 targets would have to be accompanied by a humiliating admission that the 1958 output claims had been ridiculously exaggerated. Yet it was precisely the habit of exaggeration bred by the leap forward atmosphere that had been a principal criticism in P'eng's letter of opinion.[189]

Turning to his critics, Mao remarked disingenuously that he did not understand what they meant by saying people dared not talk because of pressure. Had they not in fact used the Lushan conference to 'attack and sabotage the general line'? He accused them further of ignoring the anti-leftist measures which he had helped institute over the previous nine months; but he said nothing of their criticisms of the great leap itself. Finally, a renewed appeal for unity—'the solidarity of the Central Committee Plenum which involves the fate of Socialism in China'—was coupled with an implicit commitment to criticize strongly but deal gently with P'eng Teh-huai and Chang Wen-t'ien; '... we must be sympathetic with people, but not with errors that are poisonous and that must be dealt with drastically and severely.'[190]

In sharp contrast to this statesmanlike approach, Mao wrote the same day to Chang Wen-t'ien deriding his attacks, impugning his courage and coldly dismissing his appeal for an interview:

What did you do to have yourself entrapped in that Military Club? . . . What purpose do you have in mind this time? You have so assiduously and extensively searched out these dark materials that really are treasures! . . . However, after they have been exhibited, it showed that they were all fake. Two days after you spoke, you became so panicky and perturbed that you found it hard to free yourself. . . . Whom to blame? You deserved it. I think this was the relapse of your old sickness. . . . What can you do now? Now let me think for you. There are two words for you: 'Rectify painfully.' Since you [profess to] respect me, have phoned several times, and have wanted to come to my place for a talk, I am willing to talk to you. But I am busy these days. Please wait for some time. I am writing you this letter to express my sentiments.[191]

Here, rather than in his conference speeches, Mao revealed the implacable anger he felt at the challenge that P'eng and Chang had issued to his authority. For the public record,[192] Mao adopted a posture of reasonableness, to the extent of heartily congratulating a one-time minor official of the State Planning Commission, Li Chung-yun, for his courage in bypassing bureaucratic channels and sending directly to the CC a comprehensive and 'highly pertinent' indictment of planning work during the great leap.[193] But Li Chung-yun did not represent a threat. P'eng Teh-huai—who later claimed that he too had been basically attacking the planners—did.[194]

(x) A Soviet connection?

Mao was fortunate in the timing of his counter-attack. International events helped him to put P'eng in a false position. On 20 June, shortly after P'eng's return from his Eastern European tour, the Russians had reneged on their agreement to help China with nuclear weapons technology.[195] According to Khrushchev's memoirs, the Soviet leadership held a meeting just prior to the scheduled shipment of a prototype atomic bomb and decided that in view of a Chinese 'smear campaign' and 'all sorts of incredible territorial claims', it was necessary to disabuse them of the idea that 'we were their obedient slaves who would give them whatever they wanted, no matter how much they insulted us'.[196] It would seem that this anachronistic-sounding account reflected a telescoping in Khrushchev's mind of various later phases of the Sino-Soviet dispute. Fear of Chinese bellicosity, engendered by Mao's speeches in Moscow and the Taiwan Strait crisis, almost certainly played a role in the 1959 decision. More importantly, Khrushchev probably decided to sacrifice an already deteriorating relationship with the Chinese for the emerging possibilities of peaceful coexistence with the Americans.

Then on 23 July, the day on which Mao counter-attacked P'eng and Chang Wen-t'ien, Vice President Nixon hàd arrived in Moscow to open the first US exhibition in the Soviet capital. Despite the acrimony of the notorious 'kitchen debate' between Nixon and Khrushchev at the exhibition,[197] the visit represented a breakthrough in Soviet–US relations, consolidating trends towards détente already in evidence and foreshadowing Khrushchev's barnstorming tour of the United States two months later. The announcement of the latter visit, which had been proposed by President Eisenhower in mid-July, was made on 3 August just after the commencement of the Lushan plenum.[198]

These developments, coupled with the tumultuous reception given to Nixon when he visited Warsaw on 2 August on his way home from Moscow,[199] must have angered Mao and many of his colleagues. Khrushchev's policies represented a rejection of the Chinese views on the appropriate global policy for the communist bloc and, in the field of nuclear technology, had already resulted in a specific betrayal of Chinese interests. Undoubtedly these events weakened the position of someone like P'eng Teh-huai who had consistently placed great stress on military and diplomatic collaboration with the Soviet Union.

But Khrushchev made Mao's task of discrediting P'eng and Chang Wen-t'ien even easier and more credible. On 18 July, in the Polish town of Poznan, the Soviet leader delivered a sharp attack on the commune idea, stating that those who had flirted with it in Russia in the 1920s 'had a poor understanding of what Communism is and how it is to be built'. Clearly that condemnation was meant to apply also to the Chinese in the 1950s.

In the version of the speech released immediately by the Polish radio, the passage on the communes was omitted; then on 21 July, the Soviet and Polish media put out a new version containing the attack on the communes. Khrushchev's attack broke a six-month truce on the part of the Soviet leadership and media and the manner in which it was released sounded, according to one scholar, like a very carefully planned manoeuvre.[200]

Presumably the Chinese embassy in Moscow cabled home the text of Khrushchev's attack. Mao's reaction to this heaven-sent opportunity was to circulate on 29 July three documents dealing with the speech, giving pride of place to a report from New York by Taiwan's Central News Agency. Evidently he wished to illustrate the help and succour which critics of the communes were giving to the enemies of China. In a brief covering note, Mao jeered at the critics, implying that there were considerable differences between the Soviet and Chinese experiments with the communes.[201]

But Mao apparently felt that he would have to do better than that. The Chairman could count on Khrushchev's comments arousing a certain amount of nationalistic resentment, and the overall image of the Soviet Union in the eyes of CC members must have been damaged over the previous couple of years by his sniping, for instance at the Chengtu conference. Nevertheless, the Soviet Union was still the 'elder brother', the unquestioned leader of the communist bloc, not to mention China's principal military ally and trading partner. By Mao's own admision, some of the modifications of the communes introduced at the Wuhan plenum had been to placate the Russians.[202] Thus, a public condemnation of the communes, albeit indirect, by the Soviet leader who combined the posts of CPSU First Secretary and Soviet Prime Minister could not be lightly shrugged off.

Such considerations probably explain why on 1 August Mao sought the assistance of one of the CC's principal Soviet specialists, Wang Chia-hsiang, in his efforts to rebut Khrushchev.[203] Wang, like Chang Wen-t'ien, had been one of the '28 Bolsheviks' who had returned from training in the Soviet Union to take over control of the CCP in the early 1930s. A Politburo member at an early age, Wang's associations had cost him dearly. Although his switch to Mao's side had been an important element in the latter's victory at the Tsunyi conference and after—as the Chairman acknowledged many years later—at the first party congress controlled by Mao and his supporters, the 7th in 1945, Wang had been reduced to alternate membership of the CC. Despite this apparent lack of gratitude on the part of the Chairman, Wang performed an important personal service for him when he was in Moscow for medical treatment a year later. With Mao's agreement he arranged for the release of the Chairman's divorced wife Ho Tzu-ch'en from a mental asylum in Ivanovo and for the resettlement of her and her daughter in Harbin. Presumably it was the combination of his Soviet training and his services to Mao that led to Wang being appointed China's first ambassador to Moscow in 1949, by which time he had been restored to full membership of the CC.[204] By recruiting Wang to his side at Lushan, Mao effectively neutralized any attempt that might have been contemplated by Chang Wen-t'ien, another former envoy to the Soviet Union, to utilize Khrushchev's *démarche* in his defence.

In fact, the very precision of Khrushchev's timing was counter-productive. That his speech attacking the communes, which broke a six-month truce should be made just after P'eng Teh-huai's and just before Chang Wen-t'ien's must surely have seemed more than just a coincidence to the leaders gathered on Lushan. After all, P'eng and Chang's attacks came out of the blue too. Could there have been collusion between the three men? Did the Chinese members of the trio—or at least the notor-iously outspoken P'eng Teh-huai—disclose their unhappiness about the communes and the great leap to Khrushchev during their recent visits to the Soviet Union, and perhaps evince an incli-nation to speak up at an appropriate occasion? Was this why Soviet diplomats were trying desperately to find out what was happening on Lushan?[205] P'eng was almost certainly blameless; collusion with a foreigner on a Chinese domestic matter seems totally out of character. But it is conceivable that the Marshal may have re-tailed some of the criticisms of the communes made by Mao at the second Chengchow conference and indicated his agreement. Such information would have been meat and drink to Khrush-chev. Whatever the truth about P'eng's contacts with the Soviet leader, at Lushan there were reasonable grounds for suspicion, and the absence of proof may have been why nothing was said about this question in the resolution condemning P'eng and Chang.[206] But the surfacing during the cultural revolution of quotations designed to show that P'eng behaved with impropriety in his dealings with Khrushchev during his 1959 trip suggests that at the very least Mao was able to feed doubts and perhaps inspire rumours to discredit the Marshal.[207]

(xi) P'eng Teh-huai's isolation

The international ramifications of the criticism of the communes may provide one explanation for the discreditable and ultimately disastrous failure of P'eng Teh-huai's civilian Politburo colleagues to temper Mao's counter-attack. In the early stages of the Lushan conference, after P'eng had dispatched his letter but before Mao delivered his initial counter-attack on 23 July, Liu Shao-ch'i and Chou En-lai could surely have intervened with the Chairman, coupling an assurance of their personal support with a plea to avoid overkill in his rebuttal. P'eng doubtless had to be slapped down, but there was no need for him to be cast into outer darkness; his critique could simply be dismissed as blunt but belated and therefore irrelevant.

Of Mao's other most senior colleagues, the remaining members of the Politburo Standing Committee, two were absent. Ch'en Yun was resting in Dairen and did not attend; when he was informed after the conference about what had happened, his reaction was: 'Why did P'eng Teh-huai write the letter at such a time?' Evidently, he immediately realized the negative effect P'eng's intervention could have on his attempts to restore sanity to economic policy.[208] Teng Hsiao-p'ing broke his leg playing ping-pong at Lushan and had to leave.[209]

The remaining two members of the PSC were both marshals, but Lin Piao could not have been expected to speak up for P'eng. It must have been clear to Lin that Mao had him marked down as P'eng's eventual successor as Defence Minister and the letter of opinion was likely to speed up the succession process.[210] Besides, there had been a long-standing feud between Lin and P'eng even before the creation of the People's Republic.[211] That left Chu Teh, P'eng's friend and chess partner, who was the only member of the inner core of the Politburo to rally to his defence.[212] He urged: 'One shouldn't fear right or left. If someone's got something to say, let them say it. If people like us don't speak up, then who will dare to talk?' Chu, who was himself critical of the communes and their mess halls, failed to carry the day; but it was probably his opposition and that of most of his fellow Marshals that contributed towards securing a lighter punishment for P'eng than Mao might have wanted. When the CC resolution on P'eng and his 'clique' was passed, Chu intervened again: 'He's made mistakes; he's made a self-examination. That should be enough. We should now be able to unite with him.'[213] For his temerity, Chu Teh had to produce a self-criticism, a procedure that served to justify *ex post facto* Liu Shao-ch'i's right to the state chairmanship as one senior provincial official observed.[214]

What accounts for the failure of others to speak up in a similar vein?[215] In the first place one must posit a reluctance to cross Mao when his anger was aroused. The Chairman could summon up an awesome blend of sarcasm, ridicule and denunciation, couched in earthy language and spiced with barbed reminders of previous lapses from grace.[216] Why get in the way of this avenging fury for the sake of an awkward colleague who was obstinately beating a dead horse?[217]

To what extent that consideration may have played a part in the silence of any individual participant at the Lushan conference can only be a subject for speculation. More concrete concerns can, however, be hazarded to explain Liu Shao-ch'i's silence. P'eng Teh-huai's criticisms of Mao, earlier in Shanghai and now in Lushan, represented a threat also to Liu in both personal and institutional terms.

Liu had been a close supporter of Mao during the great leap forward. Indeed, his report to the second session of the party's 8th Congress in May 1958 was the keynote speech which launched it. In addition, Liu had acquiesced in the launching of the commune movement and played an enthusiastic role in exploring the possibilities of collective living. By the summer of 1959, Liu was as well aware as P'eng Teh-huai of the impact of the leap and the communes on the living standards of the people.[218] But any thorough post-mortem on responsibility for the events of 1958 which resulted in an assessment of 'more losses than gains' would inevitably have assigned a significant amount of blame to Liu. Indeed, Liu's consciousness of the extent to which he, like Mao, was responsible for the disastrous turn of events in the country may well explain why he, like Mao, attacked the press at Lushan for irresponsible reporting of the remarks of leaders during the high tide of the leap in 1958.[219] Liu may have feared pressure on him to cede his newly obtained state chairmanship to a more neutral figure, perhaps a party elder like Chu Teh or Tung Pi-wu, as a mark of self-criticism; after all, this would have been no more than Chou En-lai had been obliged to do 18 months earlier when he relinquished the Foreign Ministry.[220] Liu's party post too could conceivably have been at risk; P'eng is quoted as espousing at some stage a proposal to rotate the vice chairmen of the CC, the positions then held by Liu, Chou En-lai, Chu Teh, Ch'en Yun and Lin Piao.[221] All in all, it is perhaps hardly surprising, therefore, that in the afternoon of 23 July, following Mao's counter-attacking speech, Liu suggested collecting the conference documents and circulating them as an anti-right opportunist pamphlet.[222]

Even if Liu had not been obliged to resign as head of state, a successful challenge by P'eng Teh-huai could have posed serious institutional problems for him. In the first place, as Mao's presumed successor, Liu could hope in time to inherit the party Chairman's primacy in the field of policy formation, although his exercise of that prerogative would doubtless have been more disciplined. But had the Lushan plenum passed a negative resolution on, the leap and the communes, the decision-making process would surely have been opened up to a wider circle of leaders, certainly to the whole Politburo, with the possibility of the CC being brought into a more active role.

Secondly, a victory for P'eng Teh-huai would have posed a grave threat to the legitimacy of party leadership within the state structure and indeed to party cohesion. The Marshal and his subordinates within the PLA would implicitly have been recognized as being more closely in touch with the Chinese reality, as representing a more authentic voice of the Chinese people, because of their grass roots contacts through their conscript soldiers. There would have been a real chance of a factional split along the fault line mapped by Kao Kang: between the party of the Red areas, basically the PLA elite, and the party of the White areas, basically the civilians of the North China Bureau led by Liu Shao-ch'i, who had worked underground behind enemy lines, together with Chou En-lai and his group who had worked in Chungking during the war.[223]

Interestingly, the few remarks made by Liu Shao-ch'i at Lushan that were revealed by the Red Guards focused on these twin threats: the one was his angry affirmation that his right to take over the leadership of the party was greater than P'eng's; the other was his backing for Mao's emphasis on the Kao Kang affair as the essential background for understanding P'eng Teh-huai's activities at the Lushan conference. Mao asked rhetorically at Lushan: 'In the last analysis, was it a Kao-Jao[224] alliance or a Kao-P'eng alliance? Perhaps one should say it was a P'eng-Kao alliance.'[225] Although Liu had on occasion vouchsafed an extremely high appraisal of P'eng's strength of character, conscientiousness and lack of airs, at this juncture his view was that the Marshal was a 'left-over evil' (*yu-nieh*) of the Kao-Jao alliance. Indeed, on a later occasion Liu declared that there had been nothing wrong with P'eng's criticisms at Lushan, but as a participant in the Kao-Jao affair he had no right to talk.[226] How much real substance there was in the allegations of Mao and Liu is still uncertain.

Assured of his inheritance, Liu seems to have displayed no dismay at what happened at Lushan. During a recess from the conference, after Mao had counter-attacked P'eng, Liu made a trip down the mountain to revisit places he had been during the early years of his revolutionary career, three decades previously. He enjoyed himself enormously, and the Kiangsi party official who accompanied him noticed the difference: 'Normally Comrade Shao-ch'i didn't like to talk too much, but on this occasion he just prattled on.'[227] Contrast that with the behaviour of Mao's personal secretaries who used the recess to wander silently and disconsolately around the countryside, only too well aware of what their boss had perpetrated. During the walk, Mao's chief secretary, T'ien Chia-ying, who occupied the post once held by Ch'en Po-ta, composed a poem:

My eyes are pierced by the rivers and the mountains that encircle me;
The joys and the anxieties of the people penetrate my very heart.[228]

Although he had had disputes with the Defence Minister in the past, Chou En-lai had much less reason than Liu to fear criticism of the leap. However loyally he had participated in running it, Chou and his principal economic ministers had opposed 'reckless advance' in the past and could have been expected to profit politically from being proved right.[229] Chou would have been less than human if he had not viewed with equanimity a blow to Liu's position. But Mao's prestige was another matter. As the arguments grew more bitter at Lushan, Mao's opponents, their backs against the wall, directed their arguments ad hominem. Mao was accused of having 'come to Stalin's later years', of being 'despotic and dictatorial', 'vain and fond of credit, heeding and trusting only one side'. He was 'a bit like Tito'; no one was able to talk to him and only he was qualified to lead. He 'persisted in his errors till the bitter end and only then knew he had to make a turn; and when he made a turn it was 180 degrees'.[230]

As the Lushan conference progressed, siding with P'eng Teh-huai and his colleagues increasingly meant taking up arms against Mao personally. For Chou En-lai, whose whole career since the Tsunyi conference of 1935 had been characterized by personal commitment to Mao and his vision,[231] such a course was probably politically unthinkable and psychologically impossible. At any rate, at Lushan, Chou defended the steel campaign against P'eng Teh-huai's attacks.[232]

Thus Liu Shao-ch'i's ambition and Chou En-lai's loyalty permitted Mao to use his position and prestige to anathematize a major revolutionary figure, a comrade in arms of over 30 years standing, precisely in order to defend his position and prestige. Outraged by P'eng's temerity and its implications, Mao abandoned his preference for presiding over a unified leadership, justifying at least in part the very allegations of being despotic and dictatorial like Stalin that he resented. It was the first arbitrary use of personal power in such a context that Mao had indulged in.[233] By failing to check it, Liu and Chou helped pave the way for the similar abuse of power, albeit on a grander scale, that characterized the cultural revolution. The Lushan plenum cracked the Yenan 'Round Table'; the cultural revolution was to shatter it.

(xii) The fate of P'eng Teh-huai

But in 1959 there were still limits. Characteristically, P'eng's initial reaction had been to stick to his guns; in his naivety, he was particularly furious that Mao, after those long years of comradeship, had not simply called him in and explained what was wrong with the letter. But on the day after Mao's counter-attack, a couple of unnamed comrades spent two hours with him, underlining what he had also begun to realize, that the letter was no longer the issue and that he should take the overall situation into account. In other words, Mao's prestige was of greater importance to the revolution than P'eng's fate. Justice appears not to have been mentioned. P'eng was persuaded to go along with this analysis and to make a full, indeed exaggerated, self-criticism before the CC. After that it was not possible totally to humiliate him. His military colleagues and, to be fair, many of his party comrades would have found that difficult to stomach. Retribution was inevitable, however, and P'eng recognized that. He called his staff together and told them that he would not be able to carry on as Minister of Defence and that he wanted to give up his Politburo membership and his vice premiership in order to be able to return home and plant the earth. He went on: 'I have given the Chairman three guarantees; I will never become a counter-revolutionary; I won't commit suicide; I will support myself by the sweat of my brow.'[234] Of those three guarantees, the forswearing of suicide was the most important from Mao's point of view. A wave of indignation and disgust would have swept through the army and party had a popular military hero like P'eng Teh-huai felt compelled to take his life. The Marshal's suicide would have been a greater blow to Mao's reputation than a dozen letters of opinion.[235] P'eng's undertaking must have also been some consolation for his wife who had arrived at Lushan a few days earlier looking forward to a holiday only to be greeted with the devastating news that her husband's career was finished.[236]

Although the CC's 8th plenum passed a resolution describing the 'anti-party clique headed by P'eng Teh-huai' as a continuation and development of the Kao Kang–Jao Shu-shih 'anti-party alliance' and condemning it for activities over a longer period aimed at splitting the party, it was considered politic to deprive members of the clique only of their executive posts, not their party rankings. P'eng lost the Defence Ministry, but retained the titles of Politburo member and Vice Premier. Chang Wen-t'ien was dismissed as a Deputy Foreign Minister but remained an alternate member of the Politburo. The two other men grouped with P'eng and Chang in the anti-party clique, Huang K'o-ch'eng and Chou Hsiao-chou, lost their jobs as Chief of Staff and Hunan 1st secretary respectively, but stayed on the CC.[237] The conversations that Huang and Chou had had with P'eng made it possible to group them with him and Chang to provide the verisimilitude of a plot. Huang and Chou's real crimes were probably the supply of some of the information that informed P'eng's interventions at Lushan.

From Lushan, P'eng returned to Peking. The crisis over, he resumed his normal daily round. In the early morning he practised t'ai-chi-ch'üan; in the evenings he took walks. His eating and sleeping habits became regular. The only change noted by his bodyguard was that he started smoking again.

On 9 September, P'eng wrote a short letter to Mao, again acknowledging his mistakes and requesting permission either to study or to go to a commune to do physical labour. Mao was delighted with the tone of the letter which he ordered circulated to party organizations at all levels, but he rejected the proposal of a transfer to a commune on the grounds of P'eng's age. Study, interspersed with annual visits to factories and the countryside, would be P'eng's road back to grace.[238]

Finally, in October, P'eng was moved from his quarters in the Chungnanhai area of the Forbidden City, where Mao, Liu Shao-ch'i and other Politburo members lived, to a dilapidated house in the Wu Chia Hua Yuan (Wu Family Garden), a compound within the Yuan Ming Park on the northern outskirts of Peking. Here he was to spend the next six years. Before leaving, P'eng turned in his Marshal's uniforms, his fox-fur overcoat and the carpets and paintings that adorned his rooms; about all he took with him was books. Stating that he would live as simply as a peasant he also refused the offer of a nurse and general factotum, and from now on he swept the floors and washed and mended his own clothes. He retained only his bodyguard.[239]

Life appears to have been lonely at first. P'eng's wife, P'u An-hsiu, had a top-level job at Peking Normal University and only on Sundays was she able to visit him. His neighbours were a few peasant households whom the guard detachment refused to let in until P'eng threatened to write to Mao.[240] But P'eng himself discouraged the Politburo's doctor, Fu Lien-chang, from visiting him, saying: 'My present home is now a place of trouble. From now on, you should stop coming here. I appreciate your having come!' Puzzled, Fu later queried to Chou En-lai how the CCP's leaders had become so antagonistic. The Premier reportedly replied with tears in his eyes: 'History is history. History is ruthless, and will never flatter anyone. Please remember that the people have the highest sense of justice!' The politically naive Dr. Fu apparently remained bewildered.[241]

Meanwhile, P'eng threw himself into the task of setting up a mini experimental farm. He cut down the flowering shrubs, planted fruit trees, wheat, vegetables and melons, had the pond deepened and filled it with fish and lotuses, and bought pigs, ducks and chickens. He tested all the agro-techniques recommended in the newspapers and on the radio to see if the extravagant claims made for them had any substance. He questioned the local peasants so eagerly that before his identity was revealed one asked him if he was from an agricultural research station.

Once they knew who he was, P'eng's neighbours were in and out a great deal. One mother brought her sick child to see him, evidently believing that P'eng's laying-on of hands would help cure its illness. P'eng liked to entertain his peasant friends with films sent from Chungnanhai. He also distributed to them and the guards the many anonymous gifts of food he was sent during the 'three bitter years' (1959–61) of food shortages.[242]

But P'eng's main activity was study, a radical transformation of life-style for a man who had not hitherto been noted for being well-read.[243] He brought 20 boxes of books of all types from Chungnanhai, refusing to throw any away, and they littered the furniture in his new home. He got more from Yang Hsien-chen, the director of the Higher Party School, where he went to study from time to time. P'eng also perused carefully all major state documents which he continued to receive in his titular capacity as a Politburo member and Vice Premier. (Those rankings entitled him in addition to invitations to National Day and other formal celebrations, but he never accepted them.)[244]

As for Chang Wen-t'ien, he was a man more accustomed to intellectual activities than P'eng, but for some time he was not allowed to make use of his talents in a productive way. Before leaving Lushan on 18 August, Chang sent Mao a brief farewell note which indicated that the Chairman had not relented and seen him to tell him his fate. Mao welcomed the self-critical tone of the note and on the same day ordered it distributed to all those who had participated in the conference.[245] At a foreign affairs conference the following month, Ch'en Yi declared that Chang's attitude was better than P'eng Teh-huai's; perhaps Ch'en felt guilty at having egged Chang on.[246] But only after persistent lobbying by Chang was he finally permitted in October 1960 to join the Academy of Sciences' Economic Research Institute as a research worker. He concentrated on the analysis of theories of social science. His colleagues later commended his diligence, scholarship and lack of *amour propre*.[247]

The other civilian member of P'eng Teh-huai's supposed clique, Chou Hsiao-chou, the Hunan party 1st secretary, disappeared totally from sight and it was only in the late 1970s, after the purge of the 'gang of four', that his fate was revealed.[248] His successor was the 2nd secretary of neighbouring Hupeh province, Chang P'ing-hua, but the long-term beneficiary was a still obscure Hunanese official, Hua Kuo-feng. According to the later account of Chang P'ing-hua, issued in 1977 when Hua was at the apogee of his power and influence as both party Chairman and Premier, at Lushan Mao personally proposed that Hua be promoted to become a secretary of the provincial party secretariat.[249] If Mao was indeed concerned to occupy himself with the career of a relatively minor provincial official, one may speculate that Hua's elevation was connected with the P'eng Teh-huai affair; perhaps Hua had been helpful to the Chairman in providing him with material on the Marshal's activities at Shaoshan and his dealings with Chou Hsiao-chou. Mao was probably predisposed to favour Hua Kuo-feng on account of his earlier efforts to build up the Chairman's birthplace into a national shrine when he was the ranking party official of Hsiangt'an *hsien* in which Shaoshan is located[250]; but the specific ascription of his action to the time of the Lushan conference indicates that the promotion may have had something to do with the purge of P'eng Teh-huai.

At the time, however, the elevation of Hua Kuo-feng was a minor matter; there was no indication that a secretaryship in the Hunan party apparatus would provide this solid but unremarkable official with a launching pad from which he would rise to succeed both Mao Tse-tung and Chou En-lai.[251] For the moment, the key political issue after Lushan was the fallout on the PLA.

(xiii) The impact of Lushan on the PLA

The PLA had to be handled carefully. The disgrace of a revolutionary hero was no ordinary matter; indeed if P'eng Teh-huai's involvement in the Kao Kang affair had been as intimate as was now alleged, one probable reason why he had escaped serious censure then was that it would have been politically unthinkable to denounce the commander of the Chinese forces in the Korean war so soon after his triumphant return home.

Thus, before Liu Shao-ch'i, as head of state, signed the formal order replacing P'eng Teh-huai with Lin Piao as Minister of Defence on 17 September, Mao had to start explaining this and other changes in the high command to senior officers at an enlarged meeting of the CC's MAC which lasted from late August into October.[252] The question that Mao and his supporters had to answer to a probably sceptical and resentful officer corps was the one posed by Mao at Lushan and pursued by Ch'en Po-ta in an article he wrote a few weeks later justifying the sacking of the Defence Minister: 'Why has a man like P'eng Teh-huai, who only yesterday was a "hero" (*kung-ch'en*), today become a chief culprit (*huo shou*)?'[253]

Mao's answer, when he summed up at the MAC conference, was that P'eng had never been a true Marxist, but only a Marxist fellow traveller. He buttressed his allegation with quotations from P'eng's speeches and writings dating back to the 1930s, copies of which were distributed to his audience as evidence of the Marshal's bourgeois views. Mao pointed to P'eng's adherence to ideas of 'liberty, equality and fraternity' and his desire to avoid making distinctions between right and left in the anti-Japanese united front.[254] Mao even compared P'eng's revolutionary zeal unfavourably with that of Sun Yat-sen who had not even been a communist.[255] Of course, to maintain credibility Mao had also to demonstrate that he had not suddenly woken up to P'eng's ideological deviations at Lushan, and one of the documents distributed was a letter written by the Chairman in 1943 criticizing a talk the Marshal had given on democratic education.[256]

In sum, P'eng was an 'opportunist' who had infiltrated the party without changing his bourgeois world outlook[257]; or, as Ch'en Po-ta put it, he had entered the party organizationally, but not ideologically. This was the justification for the critical appellation applied to P'eng and his supporters: right opportunists. Interestingly, Ch'en also felt obliged to explain away Mao's lack of magnanimity towards P'eng, avowing that it was for the sake of the proletariat, the people and the revolution.[258]

As at Lushan, Mao attempted to deride concrete criticisms of the leap by emphasizing that the shortages complained of included such commodities as women's hairpins and umbrellas; and again he underlined P'eng's failure to speak up at conferences prior to Lushan.[259] In view of his audience, Mao put great emphasis on the need for 'iron discipline' to preserve the solidarity so vital if China were to be built into a powerful nation.[260] But Mao's bull point was again the Soviet 'connection', although in the available text of his speech he carefully hinted at much but specified little:

One should by no means betray one's own fatherland by conspiring with foreign countries . . . . We won't allow Chinese party members to sabotage the party organisations of foreign countries by encouraging one segment of the people to oppose another segment. Nor could we permit anyone to be lured by any foreign country behind the back of the Central Committee . . . .[261]

More important than any of these arguments, however, was probably the apparent submissiveness of P'eng Teh-huai himself after the battering he had received at Lushan. His contrite note

Inspecting

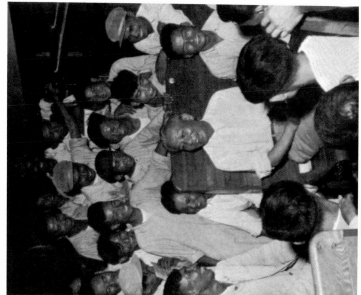

1 Mao Tse-tung with T'ao Chu, Kwangtung 1st secretary, in the countryside near Canton, April 1958

2 Liu Shao-ch'i chatting with passengers on the train to Tsinan, July 1958

Meeting

3 Mao and Politburo colleagues at the CCP's 8th Congress (2nd session) in May 1958; from the left: Finance Minister Li Hsien-nien, Defence Minister P'eng Teh-huai, Foreign Minister Ch'en Yi, and, behind Mao, CCP General Secretary Teng Hsiao-p'ing

4 Liu Shao-ch'i voting at the 1959 NPC session at which he was elected to replace Mao as head of state

Setting an example

6

5

Mao Tse-tung (5) and Premier Chou En-lai (6) working at the Ming Tombs Reservoir project outside Peking, May 1958

7 Peasants working all hours in the fields, autumn 1958

8 Women toiling during the 'backyard' steel campaign, autumn 1958

9 Combining education with productive labour; students at a construction project, autumn 1958

10 Everyone a soldier; peasant militia men after the Taiwan Strait crisis, autumn 1958

Problems

11 P'eng Teh-huai listening to old peasants on an inspection tour in late 1958

12 The sacrifice of household pots and pans to the steel campaign; one of the complaints made to P'eng Teh-huai

13 The meeting place of the Lushan conference, July–Aug. 1958

14 P'eng Teh-huai's residence at Lushan

Leap leaders

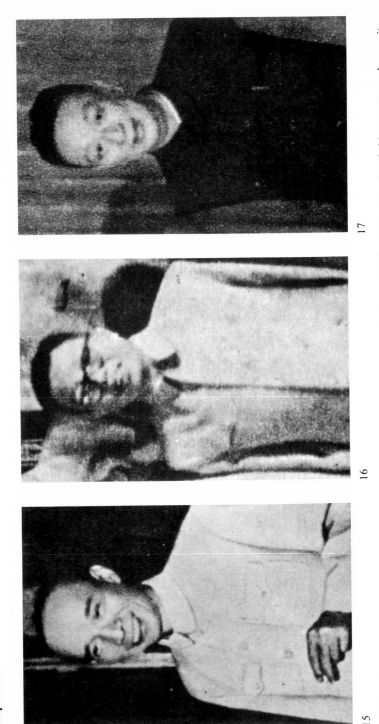

15   16   17

Li Fu-ch'un, Chairman of the State Planning Commission (15); T'an Chen-lin, agricultural supremo (16); K'o Ch'ing-shih, Shanghai 1st secretary and progenitor of the steel drive (17).

of 9 September has already been cited. Mao had it distributed to the conferees with his own seemingly magnanimous comment that if P'eng continued to be sincere and avoided any further major vacillations, then 'he will "instantly become a Buddha", or rather a Marxist'. There was only one issue on which P'eng refused to play ball. He resolutely denied the existence of any 'military club'—the phrase appears to have originated in Mao's letter to Chang Wen-t'en—that had plotted to undermine Mao and 'usurp' the party. The pressure on P'eng to admit just that amounted, according to his later account, to an attempt to extort a confession. But when some participants at the MAC conference, presumably inspired by Lin Piao, jeered at his stubbornness—'Don't keep deceiving us'—he lost his temper and fired back: 'Take away my party credentials, take me away and shoot me. But whichever of you is a member of this military club will have to give his own name.'[262]

Despite his confession, P'eng Teh-huai was still convinced that the analysis he had presented at Lushan was correct, as is revealed by some notes he made after reading a letter from Ch'en Po-ta to Mao and three economic articles published in an internal publication of the party, Nei-pu Ts'an-k'ao (Internal Reference), in September. Writing on 10 October, P'eng derided the attempts to manipulate figures from the State Statistical Bureau to prove that the leap had not distorted the proportions or balance of the national economy, commenting:

I believe that those comrade experts and Comrade Ch'en Po-ta had pure and fine motives, but with open eyes stubbornly refusing to see the realities, willfully starting out by relying on subjective imagination, looking with a magnifying glass for material that would conform to one's own subjective desires, always thinking that the objective world would reflect their subjective desires; however, the objective world will not conform and will not move and develop except according to its own laws.

Unconstrained now by any need to put his comments diplomatically, P'eng was even more scathing than he had been at Lushan. The egalitarian communist wind of the commune movement had led to widespread slaughter of farm animals. 'Work enthusiasm on the farms immediately fell, and there was unchecked flight of farm population from the land. It created a period of social chaos....' Some had said the communes had been premature, 'and in my opinion they are not altogether wrong'.

The failure to harvest all the crops as a result of the mass iron and steel campaign had led to destruction and loss that was 'beyond calculation'. As for the campaign itself: 'This iron-smelting by the entire people was actually one big widespread destruction. A destruction that damages the people's vigour and vitality can be made good only over a period of years, or even decades...'[263]

Those comments were to remain private for over two decades. But even with P'eng's publicly complaisant attitude, Mao seems not to have been able to drum up much support from the other marshals. For example, Ho Lung, who later was deputed to chair a committee of enquiry into P'eng Teh-huai's case, failed to comply with a CC instruction to produce an anti-P'eng speech until he was rebuked by Chou En-lai.[264] At least one regional military commander publicly expressed disquiet over P'eng's dismissal.[265] In his speech, Mao was able to quote only one Marshal, Liu Po-ch'eng, who had apparently averred that it was necessary 'to change one's bones and be reborn'; presumably this was advice to P'eng.[266]

The dismissal of P'eng Teh-huai was not, however, the generals' only cause for resentment. Like their old chief, they appear to have disapproved of Liu Shao-ch'i's promotion, his projected 'usurpation' of the party leadership. This would seem to be the logical explanation for the highly defensive tone of some of Liu's remarks in his speech to the MAC conference. He justified the changes of policy that had taken place in the recent past by saying that there was no leadership which was absolutely correct and had never deviated either to right or to left.[267] Indeed policy-making was something like flying a plane to Moscow; one turned first one way, then the other.[268] It was quite possibly on this occasion that Liu defended Mao's leadership (and by extension his own) during the leap:

In the past, successive revolutionary movements were led personally by Chairman Mao. Yet the movements he led were not without some defects. Could it be possible that if those movements were led by someone else, there would be more shortcomings and mistakes? I think so myself. Even with Chairman Mao's leadership, some shortcomings have occurred. Isn't it possible for more shortcomings to appear without Chairman Mao?[269]

Liu appeared concerned to defend not merely Mao's actions but also his cult. He argued that for a long time, 'proletarian' prestige had not been as high as 'bourgeois' prestige; the prestige of the CCP's first leader, Ch'en Tu-hsiu, had not equalled Sun Yat-sen's, and even Mao's had not approached Chiang Kai-shek's.[270] The implication was that it had been politically necessary for Liu and others to build up Mao's personality cult in the 1940s, precisely the point made by the party's organization chief, An Tzu-wen, three years earlier. An had gone on to argue that there was no longer a need for any artificial boosting of Mao's prestige,[271] and Liu seemed to be making the same point when he suggested at Lushan that the time had come for dispensing with shouting 'long live' (*wan sui*) and singing the 'East Is Red'.[272]

But the contexts of the men's remarks were very different. An Tzu-wen, speaking at the time of the party's 8th Congress, was trying to explain away the dropping of Mao's thought from the party constitution; that had been part of a controlled Chinese accommodation to destalinization in the Soviet bloc. The diminution of Mao's prestige may have given Liu Shao-ch'i some satisfaction in 1956,[273] but in 1959 he had different preoccupations. He had to reassure the military that he would not foster his own personality cult. This he sought to do by telling the MAC conference that whereas in the past he had backed the cult of Mao, now he was in favour of the cult of Chou En-lai, Teng Hsiao-p'ing and P'eng Teh-huai's successor Lin Piao.[274] In other words, Liu undertook to promote collective leadership. Implicitly, too, he committed himself to a less autocratic style of leadership by stating that anyone could be opposed if they were wrong, be it Mao, Liu himself or Lin Piao.[275]

But Liu was not totally defensive. He rebutted apparent insinuations that he was just an urban intellectual, a suggestion that had the flavour of the Kao Kang heresy. Mao, too, was an urban intellectual, he retorted, and so too were Castro and the then-leader of the Algerian liberation struggle, Ben Bella. Even his audience of officers were part of the urban intelligentsia, he alleged. And in that company he was prepared to assert his right of succession:

In the event Chairman Mao has some other things to do or becomes sick, the central committee has resolved to ask me to act for him. I too believe that I can act for him Moreover, I see no reason why I should not be able to act for him as satisfactorily as others. At such a time, I will not decline.[276]

Liu's audience may not have been won over, but fortunately for him he had Mao and Lin Piao on his side, and the crucial issue was no longer Liu's promotion, but P'eng's demotion. It was Lin Piao who had to play the main supporting role to Mao in this group, wielding the big stick in the PLA and justifying *his* promotion. Addressing the MAC conference on 11 September,[277] Lin Piao stoutly defended Mao's tough handling of P'eng Teh-huai:

Our Communist Party follows one principle, that is, a contradiction can only be solved through struggle . . . . This is the reason [our party] has the vernal spirit of youth and is uncorrupt—the philosophy of struggle . . . .[278]

Lin accused P'eng of making five mistakes of line, swinging wildly from right to left and back, driven solely by ambition. (Not for P'eng the luxury of a flight to Moscow!) Addressing P'eng directly, Lin admonished him: 'Discredit must be brought on your name, otherwise nothing can be done. This will do both you and the party good. This will make it possible to mend your way.' One justification Lin Piao cited for this harsh judgement was that if the Marshal's right opportunism were not crushed and Mao were to die, 'a still bigger problem will crop up'. This somewhat obscure argument had apparently weighed heavily at Lushan.[279] What it seemed to imply was that if P'eng were not totally discredited, he could be a serious challenger for the leadership, or at least a rallying point for those opposed to Liu Shao-ch'i. Circumstances had made allies of Liu and Lin.

In view of the PLA's lack of enthusiasm for the Lushan decisions, it is perhaps not surprising that Mao and Lin Piao felt it necessary not merely to replace Chief of Staff General Huang K'o-ch'eng (allegedly P'eng's principal co-conspirator) with someone from outside the existing military hierarchy, but also to sack a number of other generals whose ties to the departing Defence Minister might make suspect their loyalty to the incoming one.[280]

The new Chief of Staff, Lo Jui-ch'ing, had a number of advantages. His relationship with P'eng Teh-huai had been an ambivalent one; despite spells of collaboration during the revolutionary period, Lo had criticized P'eng at the time of the Yenan rectification campaign.[281] Lo had worked closely with Mao for some years.[282] Although he had been a senior political commissar in the PLA during the revolutionary period, he had developed a separate institutional base as Minister of Public Security since 1949. Yet at the same time he had held the concurrent posts of Commander arid Commissar of the PLA's Public Security Forces which presumably gave him the knowledge and authority to deal with potential disaffection among the military. Finally, his career pattern held out the promise that he would be an ideal man to inject greater political consciousness and control into a body that P'eng had been trying to make professional[283]

The other top military men removed or moved were: Generals Hung Hsueh-chih, Li Ta, Hsiao K'o and Teng Hua. General Hung, commanding the PLA's General Logistics Department, was dismissed on 14 October; he had performed the same role for P'eng Teh-huai in the Korean war, and had been Deputy Commander of General Logistics under Huang K'o-ch'eng before taking over from him.[284] Generals Li Ta and Hsiao K'o, both Deputy Defence Ministers, were demoted to far less important posts; Li became Vice Chairman of the Physical Culture and Sports Commission under one of his principal former commanders, Marshal Ho Lung, while Hsiao K'o became Deputy Minister of State Farms and Land Reclamation under his old comrade of Long March days, Wang Chen. Li Ta had been Chief of Staff of the Chinese People's Volunteers (CPV) for part of the Korean war; Hsiao K'o probably suffered because as Director of the PLA's General Training Department he was one of P'eng Teh-huai's principal agents in the professionalization of the armed forces.[285] General Teng Hua, the Commander of the Shenyang Military Region, one of P'eng's two Deputy Commanders in Korea, was transferred to a far less important post in Szechwan province.[286] Ironically, Generals Teng, Hung and Hsiao had career connections also with Lin Piao, the first two because the principal component of the CPV commanded by P'eng Teh-huai in Korea had been Lin Piao's Fourth Field Army.

One must assume that the replacements for these men were chosen with care. Four new Deputy Defence Ministers were appointed in September 1959. Ch'en Keng had been the other deputy commander in Korea, a promotion calculated to appease veterans of that war, unhappy at the purge of P'eng and Teng Hua. Liu Ya-lou, who was already the Air Force Commander, had been a close associate of Lin Piao's since the late 1920s; perhaps it was no accident that Lin Piao's son attained high rank in the air force. Hsu Shih-yu, the Nanking Military Region Commander, had no obvious connections with Lin although he did originate from the same province, Hupeh. The fourth, Su Yü, had been Chief of Staff until replaced by Huang K'o-ch'eng after the Taiwan Strait crisis of 1958; this may have been an attempt to earn the gratitude of an important and brilliant officer by suggesting that his fall had been due to the machinations of P'eng and Huang. Details of the early career of the new Commander of the General Logistics Department, Ch'iu Hui-tso, are few and far between, but he does appear to have worked in Lin Piao's Fourth Field Army in the early years of the communist regime. Ch'en Hsi-lien, the new Shenyang Commander, was another Hupeh man, but he had no other obvious links to Lin Piao.[287]

Ch'en Keng died in 1961 and Liu Ya-lou in 1965, a few months before the start of the cultural revolution, but three of the others rose to the Politburo at the party's 9th Congress in 1969 as a result of that upheaval: Ch'en Hsi-lien, Ch'iu Hui-tso and Hsu Shih-yu. Ch'iu Hui-tso fell with Lin Piao in 1971; Ch'en Hsi-lien fell in 1980 as a result of his previous connections with the 'gang of four' and the role he played at the time of the second disgrace of Teng Hsiao-p'ing in 1976; Hsu Shih-yu, who helped to protect Teng thereafter, retains his Politburo membership as this is written. Despite his new title, Su Yü played a minor role during the early 1960s, which perhaps explains his survival as a respected military figure and CC member during and after the cultural revolution.

Thus P'eng's attack on the great leap had provided Mao with the opportunity to carry out what he had almost certainly long been planning, the transfer of responsibility for military affairs to Lin Piao.[288] At the same time, the campaign against P'eng's anti-party group, together with the canard about the 'military club', provided a justification for Lin Piao to reorganize the top military hierarchy more to his liking. Additionally, P'eng having initiated the confrontation and with Mao spearheading the attack at Lushan, Lin Piao presumably incurred less odium among his brother officers for supplanting his fellow Marshal.

(xiv) The new Defence Minister

Most important for the smoothness of the transition, the new Defence Minister was a genuine hero of the revolutionary wars, probably the greatest tactical genius the communist armies had produced. The son of a small landlord in the central Chinese province of Hupeh, Lin had a more thorough education than many of his senior colleagues. Fired by demonstrations against imperialism, Lin had joined the Young Communist League in 1925. This proved to be a stepping stone to the Whampoa Military Academy near Canton where Chiang Kai-shek, with Soviet assistance and CCP backing, was training officers for the armies that were to reunite much of China under the Kuomintang banner. By the age of 20, Lin was commanding a battalion on Chiang's Northern Expedition. After the break between the Communists and the Nationalists in 1927, Lin's troops were part of the force led by Chu Teh which joined up with Mao on the Chingkang Mountains, and he soon became a member of the future Chairman's inner coterie.[289]

According to the principal Western expert on Lin Piao, writing before Lin's death, he was universally described as

quiet, reserved, non-talkative, calm, unemotional and deliberate, and astute. He drives himself very hard, sometimes losing much sleep in the process, and is willing to learn, indirectly through books, directly through field experience, and from his own and others' mistakes. He likes to bury himself in the details of his work and to pursue a matter, once begun, to its conclusion. At the same time, he is obviously not a 'public figure' in the sense of enjoying the public admiration of those around him. He prefers to work behind the scenes, for the most part, issuing instructions by telephone and handwritten orders and by calling officials to his residence instead of attending meetings.[290]

Undoubtedly, one other reason for Lin's lack of visibility over the years was poor health. The rigours of the Long March took their toll. Also, in the spring of 1938, a few months after he had scored his most famous victory against the Japanese at the P'inghsing Pass near the Great Wall in Shansi province, Lin was wounded and had to leave active service. Although reported as having recovered later that year, he left for Moscow for medical treatment and spent three years in the Soviet Union. After his return in 1942, he was engaged either in training activities or high-level diplomacy, alongside Chou En-lai, with the Chinese Nationalists. However, when the civil war began, Lin Piao was again on active service. He commanded what was later called the Fourth Field Army which fought its way from the north-east all the way to the far south. Evidently this strenuous campaign proved too much for his fragile constitution. He did not accompany his troops to Korea in 1950; by the end of 1951 he was

clearly unwell again—reportedly with tuberculosis and an ul-
cer—and he did not make another public appearance until the
party's 8th Congress in 1956.[291]

Despite this record of feeble health, Mao chose Lin Piao to
take control of the PLA, although, interestingly, the Chairman
had taken the precaution of having Lin's health thoroughly
checked in 1953 before the young Marshal began his meteoric
post-1949 political rise.[292] Two conclusions seem inescapable.
First, there was no one else of comparable stature whom Mao
trusted in that role, or, to put it more positively, Mao felt that
Lin Piao would restore to the PLA the requisite degree of political control and orientation. This Lin Piao tackled immediately. At
the conference, he advised his colleagues to study Mao: 'How
should we study Marxism-Leninism? I suggest, comrades, that
the principal way is to study Comrade Mao Tse-tung's works.
That is the shortcut to studying Marxism-Leninism.'[293] The following month, in his article on the occasion of the 10th anniversary of the communist victory, Lin Piao affirmed that

political and ideological work in the army is very important and must
never be slackened. 'Political work is the life-blood of our army'—this is
a truth which has been proved by decades of revolutionary practice of
our army. . . . Our army is an army to serve political interests . . . if political and ideological work is not done well, everything else is out of the
question.[294]

Secondly, Mao presumably felt that this task was so critical that
he was prepared to take a chance on a man with a past record of
chronic bad health in order to ensure it was tackled appropriately. As is well known, Mao, from very early on in his revolutionary career, had stressed the importance of political control of
the armed forces.[295] More importantly, he dated his own succession to party leadership to his assumption of the leadership of the
CCP forces in January 1935, from which vantage point he eventually out-manoeuvred his nominal superior the then-party
General Secretary Chang Wen-t'ien. In that task he was assisted
by having a loyal deputy, Chou En-lai, who attended to the detailed work which ensured that nominal control became real
control.[296] Since his return from Korea, P'eng Teh-huai, by vir-
tue of his position, had been in charge of the day-to-day work of
the MAC; in view of the relationship between P'eng and Mao,
this meant that the party Chairman no longer felt he had any real

control over that body. Indeed, it was later alleged that P'eng wanted to abolish the MAC.[297] With Lin's displacement of P'eng, Mao evidently felt he would be back in the saddle.

(xv) The leap revived

The disgrace of P'eng Teh-huai and the shuffling of the PLA leadership did not solve the economic problems brought on by the great leap forward which had provoked the Marshal to speak out. On the contrary, the purge was the direct cause of further economic disruption. Instead of proceeding with the programme of retrenchment, the regime felt obliged to reassert the correctness of the policies of 1958 to justify the disciplinary measures which it had taken, and this despite the public admission of massive statistical exaggeration stemming from those policies which now had to be made. The grain output figure for 1958 was reduced from 375 million tons to 250 million tons, the cotton figure from 3.35 million tons to 2.1 million tons, the steel figure from 11.08 million tons to 8 million tons (with an estimated 3.08 million tons produced in backyard furnaces now disregarded as being below quality). These reductions, published in the 8th plenum communiqué, forced corresponding reductions in the 1959 targets: grain down from 525 to 275 million tons, cotton down from 5 to 2.31 million tons, steel down from 18 to 12 million tons.[298]

The extraordinary extent of this statistical retreat probably accounted for much of the stridency with which the press now called for a renewal of leaping progress, making recourse to the methods of 1958 almost inevitable.[299] And the chorus of denunciation of 'right opportunism' which was unleashed in the press following Lushan would anyway have frightened off cadres from pursuing the reforms initiated during the previous nine months, even though the Lushan resolution formally endorsed them.

The process of revindication was initiated by Mao himself at Lushan. In a comment on the restoration of mess halls in a commune in Hunan, he wrote:

The moral is that one must not capitulate in the face of difficulties. Things like people's communes and collective mess halls have deep economic roots. They should not nor can they be blown away by a gust of wind. . . . Sun Yat-sen said: 'Where it is in keeping with the reasons of heaven, commensurate with the sentiments of man, adapted to the tide of the world, and geared to the needs of human emotions, and where it is done resolutely by men of foresight and vision, it will surely succeed.'

This appraisal is a correct one. Our great leap forward and the people's communes belong to this category.[300]

A few days later in another comment on a document, Mao described as 'right opportunist' an Anhwei provincial secretary, Chang K'ai-fan, who had ordered the dissolution of mess halls in a certain *hsien*[301]; in yet another comment, he praised Liaoning province for the speed with which it had acted 'to oppose the rightist tendency and bolster the zeal for endeavour' (i.e. the leap forward spirit) and called on other provinces to emulate it.[302] Just before the conclusion of the plenum, he ordered the distribution of an article entitled 'Empiricism or Marxism-Leninism', and in his foreword he wrote: 'We must now engage in combat in order to defeat the anti-party and anti-Marxist-Leninist ideological tide from three aspects: ideologically, politically, and *economically*' (emphasis added).[303] In obedience to Mao's directive, battle was joined in the weeks that followed, at provincial conferences throughout the country, and 'quite a number of senior cadres who were rightist opportunists' were exposed.[304]

The public onslaught began in a low key with an editorial in the *People's Daily* on 6 August which criticized rightist ideas that undermined the production drive, quoting from a statement made by Mao in 1955.[305] The paper returned to the theme editorially the following day, arguing that a failure to criticize rightist sentiments would make it impossible to arouse mass enthusiasm for the struggle against natural calamities and for a bumper harvest.

A small number of cadres, having overcome subjectivism and commandism, have gone to another extreme. They do not make efforts to popularise those working methods and technical methods for raising production in keeping with the mass line which have proven effective in the course of the great leap forward. . . .[306]

At this stage, alert cadres who remembered the context of Mao's 1955 statement would have realized only that a new economic push was in the making.[307] It was not until 26 August, when the *People's Daily* published the Lushan resolution and the report of a speech made by Chou En-lai to the NPC standing committee, that the Chinese people were publicly informed about the dangers of right opportunism, a term which would have signalled at least to party members that the problem was not simply demoralization but serious political error.[308] This of course meant that failure to respond to the new production imperatives could seriously jeopardize a cadre's political future, as the bare announcement of the dismissal of P'eng Teh-huai and his fellows on 17 September would have underlined; public denunciation of them as right opportunists, which did not take place until the cultural revolution, was unnecessary.

Next, the counter-attack took the form of reaffirmation of the major features of the great leap year. On 29 August, the *People's Daily* published a long editorial entitled 'Long live the people's communes' which ended on a defiant note that boded ill for anyone who now questioned that form of organization:

However much abuse and damage have come from the hostile forces within the country and abroad, however much the right opportunists within the party have condemned and opposed, and however great the onslaught of natural calamities, the people's communes have not collapsed. We have therefore, the right to say that the people's communes will never collapse. . . .[309]

Three days later it was the turn of the mass iron and steel campaign to receive an editorial accolade from the *People's Daily*, which declared poetically: 'Now every province in the whole country is dotted everywhere with iron and steel plants of different sizes and iron-smelting bases. Molten iron flows like water; the sparks of steel splash all around.'[310] In mid-September, the paper refuted the 'absurd view' that the balance of the economy had been upset, and a few days later asserted that commune mess halls, probably the innovation that had most angered P'eng Teh-huai, had a 'boundless future'.[311]

But behind the recycled rhetoric, some realism prevailed. The CC's Lushan resolution admitted that rural steel-making had hampered harvesting, and recognized that the labour shortage could not be ignored in a year which did not promise a bumper harvest. It suggested that the production of steel by 'local, simple methods be determined in the future by the local authorities in accordance with local conditions and for local use; it will no longer be included in the state plan'.[312] Ch'en Yun's work had not been totally in vain.

The journalistic chorus was swelled and given added strength by attacks on right opportunism contained in articles written by China's leaders in commemoration of the regime's tenth anniversary on 1 October 1959. While the most senior leaders like Liu Shao-ch'i, Chou En-lai and Teng Hsiao-p'ing looked at the issues from a somewhat Olympian perspective,[313] the two provincial 1st secretaries who were also members of the Politburo took up the cudgels on behalf of the mass movement in industry and the communes. The Shanghai leader, K'o Ch'ing-shih, whom Mao had credited with the idea of the mass steel campaign, rejected the 'preposterous' arguments that would lead industrial production away from party leadership, from politics and from the masses. The error of those with right opportunist ideas lay in their refusal to acknowledge the enthusiasm and initiative of the people in the work of construction. He went on to warn that at bottom the right opportunists opposed the party's general line since its starting point was to rely on the inexhaustible energies of the people.[314]

The Szechwan leader Li Ching-ch'üan, who had criticized P'eng Teh-huai at Lushan, was, if anything, even more categorical in his defence of the communes: the allegations of the right opportunists that the communes were set up prematurely ran 'completely counter to the principles of Marxism-Leninism and to the facts'[315]; proposals to dissolve community dining rooms were 'absolutely wrong'[316]; in the light of the CC decision taken at the Peitaiho conference in 1958,

'we have every reason to believe that in three or four, five or six years, or a little longer, it will be possible for the people's communes in most areas to switch from the collective ownership of the means of production to ownership by the whole people. After this is accomplished, the people's communes will assume their further historic task—the gradual transition from socialism to communism'.[317]

The result of such clarion calls: land returned to private use in the spring was recollectivized in the autumn.

But it was left to the Kwangtung 1st secretary, T'ao Chu, to inject the relaunching of the leap with some of the eloquence that was necessary if jaded cadres and peasants were to react with any genuine enthusiasm. T'ao explained the need for 'revolutionary resoluteness' of the type displayed during the revolutionary period, arguing that although there were no bloody struggles involved, the transition from capitalism to socialism was more profound, extensive and protracted. The opposite of revolutionary resoluteness was vacillation, found in those who lacked confidence in socialist construction. He derided them as advocates of the 'safe and steady line'; they could not stand any tension. They took a 'mandarin' attitude towards the revolutionary mass movement and did not tolerate any slight error in the process of freely mobilizing the masses. They had a little desire to build socialism, but were not prepared to pay a little price. When they ran into certain difficulties, they heaved a sigh and stopped their advance. When they were temporarily unable to obtain a catty of pork or a cake of soap, they closed their eyes to the might of socialism. T'ao concluded with a stirring coda:

As revolutionaries of the proletariat we must be firm like a rock. Think of rocks on the coast! See how they stand firm, crouch, point to the sky and face the sea. . . . How many times nave they been attacked by storms and struck by surging tides? Yet they do not waver!. . . When the storm is over and the tides recede, they still stand firm on the coast, pointing to the sky and facing the sea. . . . We should emulate the firmness of the rocks.[318]

And the party did stand firm in the face of natural and man-made calamities. The leap was resumed, the problems were compounded and disaster was the result.

PART FOUR

DEFEAT

11 THE SINO-SOVIET SPLIT EMERGES

(i) The Sino-Indian border issue

The purge of P'eng Teh-huai in September 1959 was one important staging post on the road to cultural revolution. The visit of Nikita Khrushchev to China later the same month was another.

The Soviet Premier arrived at Peking airport for China's tenth anniversary celebrations on 30 September, 'immediately after my return to Moscow from my visit to the United States of America, literally speaking, by changing from one plane to another', as he told the Chinese leaders grimly gathered to greet him.[1] Khrushchev was throwing his policy of peaceful coexistence, just climaxed by a Camp David summit, in the faces of his Chinese hosts. But he probably considered he had little to lose. Years later he recalled:

I have to admit I wasn't at all enthusiastic about flying to Peking when hostilities broke out between China and India in 1959. I knew my official welcome would be laid on according to form, but I didn't expect to be greeted with the same fraternal good will I'd encountered in 1954, on my first trip to Peking. The warmth had gone out of our relations with China, and it had been replaced by a chill that I could sense as soon as I arrived.[2]

Khrushchev was right to pinpoint the Sino-Indian border dispute. The Chinese were increasingly alarmed at the overall direction taken by Soviet global strategy, as they would reveal publicly the following year. But the Soviet attitude on the escalating quarrel between Peking and New Delhi was a concrete manifestation of this strategy which deeply offended Chinese nationalist sentiments.

For much of the 1950s, Sino-Indian relations had been warm. The two countries' Prime Ministers, Jawaharlal Nehru and Chou En-lai, had exchanged visits, the latter being greeted in New Delhi with shouts proclaiming the brotherhood of Indians and Chinese. A treaty embodying the 'five principles of peaceful coexistence' had been signed in 1954 to clear away problems associated with the trading and other rights in Tibet which the Indians had inherited from the British. Unfortunately, as it turned out, neither side took the opportunity to press for a precise demarcation of the Indo-Tibetan border.[3]

In the eastern sector, the boundary was controversial, but essentially the problem was manageable. The Indians maintained that the frontier was defined by the McMahon Line which they had inherited from the British. According to Peking, the McMahon Line was an imperialist hangover which had never been accepted by any central Chinese government, but Chou En-lai indicated that China was prepared to acknowledge reality and accept the status quo. Implicit in his position was the assumption that the precise boundary line would have to be negotiated and formalized in a treaty, but he did not spell this out. For his part, Nehru appears to have preferred to let sleeping frontiers lie, on the assumption that if Chou did not press the matter, it could legitimately be concluded that the Chinese accepted the Indian demarcation.

Chou's failure, during his visit to New Delhi late in 1956, to propose boundary talks leading to the signature of a boundary treaty may be explicable in precisely the same way as Nehru's reticence on this issue. The McMahon Line section of the frontier would probably have been easily settled, but Chou may have anticipated difficulties in the western sector where the maps of the two countries indicated disagreement over the ownership of a large segment of territory. At this time, the Chinese were about half-way through building a road from Sinkiang into western Tibet, and over 100 miles of it lay across the Indian-claimed Aksai Chin. This road was of critical importance to the Chinese for communications with Tibet, partly because the route from Szechwan across the mountains into eastern Tibet was a difficult one anyway, more importantly because the first rumblings of the Khampa revolt carried the threat that the latter route would be cut. A frank admission by Chou of the road-building activities and China's need of the disputed Aksai Chin might have prompted Nehru to sign away a barren wilderness into which Indian patrols had never penetrated and in which India had, at bottom, only a cartographic interest. But Chou, like Nehru, possibly felt that there was no point in stirring up a problem which was not thought to exist by the other side. Had Nehru raised objections and started to assert Indian rights by the dispatch of troops, it could have proved embarrassing to the Chinese at that stage of the construction of the road. As it was, the Indian government only learned about the road's existence when concern over Chinese maps finally prompted it to send patrols into the area in July 1958. The mode of this discovery made success in the subsequent border discussions problematical, but clashes between Indian and Chinese troops in which both sides suffered casualties probably dictated failure.

The shock of the discovery of the road prompted Nehru to adopt a more assertive policy, pushing patrols forward along the whole border. He was strengthened in his resolve by the impact on Indian public opinion of the revolt in Tibet in the spring of 1959 and the subsequent flight of the Dalai Lama to India. At the same time, too, Chinese troops pressed closer to the border, in order to cut off Tibetan fugitives and rebels. Shots were exchanged between troops of the two sides on 25 August when an Indian patrol set up a post just on the Chinese side of the McMahon Line at Longju; one Indian soldier was killed, another wounded. It was this incident that finally brought the border dispute into the open for the first time and forced the Soviet Union to take a public stand upon it.[4]

(ii) The Tass statement

According to the Chinese, the Soviet Chargé d'Affaires in Peking was briefed on the details of the incident on 6 September. *Prima facie* there was no reason why the Russians should not have accepted the Chinese account, though it was evidently packaged in an assessment of India's policy which did not accord with current Soviet thinking about that country. The Chinese alleged that the Indian government had provoked the incident in order to oppose communism and China, and they warned the Russians not to be taken in by Nehru 'who was striving to put pressure on China by utilizing the Soviet Union'.

On the morning of 9 September, the Soviet Chargé gave the Chinese a copy of a Tass statement on the border clash which was due to be issued the following day.[5] This presumably was the occasion that Soviet writers had in mind when they later referred to Moscow's resort to 'diplomatic and other channels in order to give *timely* notification of its position'.[6] The statement described the incident as 'deplorable', pointed out that the Soviet Union maintained friendly relations with both China ('based on the great principles of socialist internationalism') and India ('in keeping with the ideas of peaceful co-existence'), and reported that Soviet leading circles expressed their confidence that 'the two governments will settle the misunderstandings that have arisen. . . .'[7]

The Tass statement was very clearly neutral and the principal reason for this balanced attitude was patently obvious. The first half of the statement was in fact devoted not to the incident itself but to its impact in the West. In particular, the statement alleged that the incident had been seized upon, especially in the United States, by those who sought to 'obstruct a relaxation of tension and to complicate the situation' on the eve of Khrushchev's visit to that country.[8] Four years later, the Russians were to accuse the Chinese of having got involved in an armed clash with India in 1959 with the aim of torpedoing peaceful coexistence.[9]

The late Soviet leader's memoirs make it clear that he was looking forward to his trip to America with a mixture of eagerness and nervousness.[10] Soviet press coverage at the time indicates that Khrushchev saw it as a turning point in Soviet history and international diplomacy, the visible recognition that the Soviet Union now ranked with the United States as a super power, and as joint arbiter of world affairs.[11] In addition, he was clearly seized of the importance of avoiding nuclear war between the Soviet Union and the United States. As he told a group of US state governors and later a Soviet audience in the summer of 1959:

Our country and the United States are the two most mighty Powers in the world. If other countries fight among themselves they can be separated; but if war breaks out between America and our country, no one will be able to stop it. It will be a catastrophe on a colossal scale.[12]

The last thing the Soviet leader would have wanted was for a totally extraneous factor like the Sino-Indian border dispute to undermine his American tour. Yet if Moscow issued a pro-Chinese statement, he could anticipate considerable coolness from a US administration hostile to China; if Moscow issued no statement, Khrushchev would have been intensively questioned at every opportunity about his attitude to the dispute. Hence the need for a neutral statement with which he could hope to put the matter into cold storage at least for the purposes of his US tour.[13]

Some such reasoning must be adduced to explain the Russians' insistence on publishing the Tass statement despite desperate efforts by the Chinese to dissuade them. According to the Chinese—the Russians have never published a detailed account of this episode—immediately on seeing the Tass statement on the morning of the 9th they indicated that they would prefer Moscow not to issue any comment on the border issue. That afternoon, in a further effort to deflect the Russians, the Chinese showed the Soviet Chargé a copy of the latest letter from Chou En-lai to Nehru, dated the previous day. That same evening, the Chinese informed the Soviet Chargé that they had now published the letter and urged that, in the light of the position outlined by Chou, the Soviet government should refrain from issuing the Tass statement.[14]

The timing of the Chou letter was probably explained by the publication on 7 September of an Indian White Paper on the border dispute. The correspondence between the two premiers had been initiated by Nehru in December 1958; Chou had replied and Nehru had then written again on 22 March 1959. The Indian White Paper, revealing these details, underlined the fact that six months had gone by without Chou replying, six months during which the eruption of the Tibetan revolt and the flight to India of the Dalai Lama might have seemed a justification for a further communication from the Chinese premier. Instead the *People's Daily* had commented critically on 'the revolution in Tibet and Nehru's philosophy' and Chou had remained silent.[15] Now, however, appearances demanded a reply. China must be seen to be treating the border clash as seriously as India; hence Chou's letter and the summoning of a session of the standing committee of the NPC to discuss the dispute on 11 September. But it may well be that the Chinese got wind that the Soviet government was considering issuing a statement and hoped also to prevent this by Chou's long-delayed reply.

Whatever the motivation, neither Chou's letter nor its immediate publication had the desired effect. Instead of holding up the Tass statement to give time for consideration of the latest Chinese *démarche*, the Russians advanced its publication, issuing it on the night of the 9th, less than six hours after the Chinese broadcast of the Chou letter, instead of waiting for the 10th.[16] Presumably they wished to pre-empt any higher level diplomatic exchanges between Peking and Moscow about the Tass statement which could have made Soviet motivation embarrassingly transparent. Under the circumstances all the Chinese could do was to send a note to Moscow on 13 September alleging that 'the Tass declaration revealed to all the world the divergence of views of China and the Soviet Union with respect to the incident on the Chinese-Indian border, about which the Indian bourgeoisie, and the American and English imperialism, literally rejoice and are exultant'.[17]

Khrushchev's manoeuvre did not work. On his US trip, he was unable to avoid questioning, for instance by senators, on China's policies,[18] and Eisenhower publicly denied the Soviet Premier's excuse that the two heads of government had agreed not to discuss third countries.[19] However, it is clear that in the Camp David discussions, Khrushchev simply stonewalled on China.[20] Even this did not help him, for shortly after the visit to the United States, Secretary of State Herter stated that if the Soviet Union claimed leadership of the communist bloc it had to accept some responsibility for China's actions,[21] a suggestion which Khrushchev indignantly rejected at a meeting of the Supreme Soviet at the end of October.[22] His anger at Herter was doubtless fuelled by the memory of his clash with the Chinese on the Sino-Indian border issue during his visit to Peking, which must have convinced him that he had no power to influence the Chinese, let alone restrain them as the Secretary of State had implied he could.

(iii)   Khrushchev in Peking

Characteristically, Khrushchev had not minced his words in Peking, despite his forebodings. At the gala banquet on the night of his arrival, he told his hosts three things: that he believed Eisenhower wanted to relax East–West tension; that peaceful coexistence had been approved by Lenin; and that strong though the communist bloc was, it must not test the stability of the capitalist system by force[23]—'[t]his would be wrong: the peoples would never understand and would never support those who took it into their heads to act in this way.'[24] Mao made no public reply, a remarkable phenomenon in the light of the importance of the occasion and his guest. Indeed he played a relatively minor role even in the subsequent private discussions, according to Khrushchev. The major protagonist on the Chinese side was Foreign Minister Ch'en Yi,[25] who had presumably been in operational control on the Sino-Indian border issue during the crucial month of August, while his Politburo colleagues were closeted in Lushan, and who was therefore best briefed on the subject.

The confrontation took place on 2 October.[26] The Chinese fielded a formidable team consisting of Mao, Liu Shao-ch'i, Premier Chou En-lai, Marshal Chu Teh (Chairman of the NPC), Defence Minister Marshal Lin Piao, P'eng Chen, the Peking party 1st secretary and the second-ranking member of the CC secretariat, Ch'en Yi, and the 'Soviet expert' in the secretariat, Wang Chia-hsiang. Khrushchev was flanked by the leading Soviet theoretician Suslov and Foreign Minister Gromyko, with the Soviet Chargé in attendance.[27] According to the terse account issued by the People's Daily four years later, the Chinese side gave their version of the border clash, accusing the Indians of provocation and arguing that 'it would not do to yield to the Indian reactionaries all the time'. Khrushchev allegedly brushed aside the detailed explanation, insisting only that 'it was wrong to shoot people dead'.[28]

The Soviet Premier's memory of the occasion was altogether more vivid:

In this case, the Chinese side decided to unleash Ch'en Yi on me. The talks immediately became agitated and tense. Ch'en Yi was downright rude. I don't know whether his rudeness was a calculated political move or whether it was a character trait.[29]

Perhaps Ch'en Yi's colleagues had also chosen him as spokesman because of all of them, he most resembled Khrushchev, being impetuously outspoken by temperament and therefore best adapted to match the Soviet Premier's pugnacious debating style.[30]

Ch'en Yi, in Khrushchev's version of their clash, 'blurted out': 'How could you make such a statement?'—an indication of the anger caused in Peking by Moscow's publicly neutral stance in the border dispute. Ch'en argued that Nehru was an agent of US imperialism and that as a communist country the Soviet Union was obligated to support China. Khrushchev replied that Nehru was progressive and anti-imperialist and that border disputes were anyway not worth fighting over, especially when as in this case the frontier had been settled decades earlier, an assertion which prompted Ch'en to counter that the territory was rightfully China's although it had been seized by Britain during the raj—and that China needed it (evidently for the road).[31] Khrushchev again took India's part, asking the Chinese to put themselves in

Nehru's shoes and see why he could legitimately consider a Chinese-held Tibet a possible threat, a line of argument hardly calculated to appeal to his interlocutors. At bottom, Khrushchev simply did not believe the Chinese version of the border clash itself[32]; as he was to tell P'eng Chen in Bucharest nine months later, after further bloodshed on the border: 'I know what war is. Since Indians were killed, this meant that China attacked India.'[33]

Chen Yi's expostulations were followed up with a series of protest notes about Soviet neutralism in the dispute, six being handed to the Soviet Ambassador Chervonenko between 10 December 1959 and 30 January 1960. In a reply dated 6 February, the Russians accused the Chinese of being 'narrowly nationalistic' in their attitude on India.[34]

Reflecting on the dispute in retirement years later, Khrushchev stated: 'I think Mao created the Sino-Indian conflict precisely in order to draw the Soviet Union into it. He wanted to put us in the position of having no choice but to support him. He wanted to be the one who decided what we should do.'[35] The evidence does not in fact indicate so Machiavellian an explanation of Chinese conduct during the autumn of 1959, but Khrushchev's musings do illustrate the mixture of ignorance and suspicion which by then coloured the relationship between the leaders of China and the Soviet Union. The cancer of mistrust was already eating away at the Sino-Soviet alliance.

For his part, Khrushchev pointed to Chinese bellicosity,[36] duplicity[37] and nationalism.[38] He professed himself unable to understand the logic of many Chinese domestic policies like the 'hundred flowers' and the great leap forward.[39] He must have been even more concerned to find such policies arousing sympathetic echoes in Eastern Europe, and indeed later recalled his efforts to pull the normally ultra-loyal Bulgarian party back from the brink of their own leap forward.[40]

On the Chinese side, the suspicion was that Khrushchev was selling them down the river, sacrificing China's national interests to the Soviet Union's. The Sino-Indian border was not the only issue. The Soviet stance on Taiwan also angered the Chinese. In the United States, Khrushchev had failed to exclude the island from an agreement on the renunciation of force.[41] When he was in Peking, the Soviet Premier argued privately that the Taiwan issue could be solved by peaceful means as well as by military ones. Moscow later claimed that he was advocating no more than the Chinese themselves had done when they had indicated a willingness (1956–7) to form another united front government with the Nationalists, giving Chiang Kai-shek a high post in it.[42]

This somewhat disingenuous explanation glossed over the change of Chinese policy on Taiwan since 1957[43] of which the Russians were well aware. Khrushchev was clearly concerned to avert any further crises in the Taiwan Strait which would inevitably have an impact on Soviet-US relations in view of Washington's insistence on Moscow's partial responsibility for Peking's actions. According to the fuller Chinese account of the private discussions—Khrushchev's memoirs are silent on this point—the Soviet Premier said that

the question of Taiwan was an incendiary factor in the international situation and that because the United States supported China, there resulted the atmosphere of an imminent great war; but what the Soviet Union stood for was the creation of all conditions to ease international tension and eliminate war.[44]

China's response was firm and unequivocal; indeed it had already been delivered. At the 1 October National Day parade, the day before the confrontation between Khrushchev and Ch'en Yi, Defence Minister Lin Piao stated:

The integrity of the sovereign rights of the sacred soil, territorial air and territorial sea of the People's Republic of China must be respected. The aspiration of the Chinese people to liberate their own territory of Taiwan and the coastal islands *by one method or another* and so completely unite our great motherland will definitely be realised. Foreign countries must not interfere.[45] (Emphasis added.)

The Chinese were not prepared to compromise on issues of territorial integrity. If force were necessary, it would be employed, Moscow's pleas notwithstanding.

Underlying China's national concerns was an apparently incredulous anger at the extent to which Khrushchev was prepared in the 'spirit of Camp David' to 'endorse' the leader of the world's leading imperialist power. A year later, Teng Hsiao-p'ing told the Moscow summit conference of communist leaders:

No considerations of diplomatic protocol can explain away, or excuse, Khrushchev's tactless eulogy of Eisenhower and other imperialists, when he said in public that Eisenhower enjoyed the complete support of the American people.[46]

After his US trip, Khrushchev's loyalty to Leninism in world affairs was suspect in Chinese eyes.

(iv) Peking's agonizing reappraisal

Over the course of the next six months, the Chinese leaders proceeded to work out the implications for the communist bloc and China's national interests of the positions taken by Khrushchev on peaceful coexistence in his private discussions with them in Peking. The Chinese analysis was developed in a series of commentaries in the remaining months of 1959, and then argued out in early 1960 at a series of top-level meetings—at Shanghai in January, Canton in February, Hangchow in March[47]—before Peking's major polemical outburst in April on the occasion of the 90th anniversary of Lenin's birth.

Chinese press comment in the latter months of 1959 emphasized increased US military activity and capability in the East Asian region, and the importance of the US position in Laos and the Seato area. Peking's analyses of US strategy argued that any peaceful gestures made by Washington were contradicted by its acts and were indeed a 'smokescreen for war' or a 'camouflage for an aggressive policy'; Washington's real aims were to reduce the missile gap, to consolidate its world-wide system of military alliances and bases, and to increase its capability of waging limited wars. A western analyst commented that the Chinese press output seemed deliberately to have overdrawn the menace to China, implying that the Soviet bloc's position of strength, stemming from the launch of the sputnik and the favourable situation in the Third World, could be lost through imprudence.[48]

Two critical theses emerged from the Chinese analysis, the first being the irreconcilable hostility of the imperialists to the socialist camp: 'In a word, one can see from these hard facts that although there are certain tactical changes in United States foreign policy, the fundamental policy of the United States still rests on two sets of tactics (one set is to prepare actively for war and the other is to hang out a peace signboard), both having a single objective—to destroy socialism'. The second thesis was that, contrary to what Khrushchev had argued, the majority of US leaders opposed rather than accepted peaceful coexistence.[49] More colourfully, the Chinese quoted repeatedly Mao's assessment of imperialism:

'Imperialism is very vicious'. That is to say that its fundamental nature cannot be changed. Till their doom, the imperialist elements will never lay down their butcher's knife, nor will they ever become Buddhas.[50]

If the Chinese had entertained any hopes of deflecting the course of Soviet foreign policy, they were soon disabused by Khrushchev's forceful restatement of his peaceful coexistence policy when he formally reported to the Supreme Soviet on 31 October. The Soviet Premier reiterated his assessment that the prevalent view in the West was that the balance of forces meant that war must now be ruled out. Arguing in favour of 'mutual concessions in the interests of peace', he claimed that this was no abdication of principle, but merely an emulation of Lenin's flexibility at the time of the treaty of Brest-Litovsk with Germany in 1918; and by alluding to Trotsky's 'adventurist' opposition to the treaty, he appeared to be hinting that Mao should be classified with that heretic. The Soviet Premier followed up with his evidence of a genuine thaw in international affairs, clearly intending to rebut Chinese allegations about imperialist 'smokescreens'. More immediately relevant to Peking, Khrushchev indicated the Soviet Union's continuing insistence on remaining neutral on the Sino-Indian border dispute[51] which had claimed further lives since his visit to China.[52] More surprisingly, he also made a volte-face on the Algerian liberation struggle, pronouncing himself in support of President de Gaulle's ceasefire proposals. His motive was evidently to improve the climate of Franco-Soviet relations prior to his visit to France the following spring.[53] But to the Chinese, who continued vigorously to denounce the de Gaulle plan,[54] this was yet more evidence that Khrushchev was prepared to betray his friends and allies in order to appease the West.

A month later, in a speech to the Hungarian party congress on 1 December, Khrushchev made a more direct if still veiled attack on Mao and the CCP. 'If we become conceited, if we commit mistakes in our leadership, if we distort the teaching of Marxism-Leninism on the building of socialism and Communism, these mistakes can be exploited by the enemies of Communism as was done in 1956. . . .' This was clearly another dig at the communes and the great leap forward. On international affairs, Khrushchev insisted on the need for unity—'We must, figuratively speaking, synchronize our watches'—in the spirit of proletarian internationalism, evidently a demand that bloc foreign policy should be consistent and decided in Moscow.[55] Behind the scenes at the congress, Khrushchev was apparently even more vehement in his criticisms of the Chinese.[56]

Khrushchev's call for unity was ignored in Peking. Ch'en Yi was prepared to concede only that imperialism might step down peacefully once the communist bloc was dominant economically, clearly a long way off.[57] Speaking at the same cultural work conference in December, Teng Hsiao-p'ing called for continual criticism of the Soviet Union rather than one general attack.[58] Chinese public assessments of world affairs now differed even more obviously from Moscow's, notably in reaction to Eisenhower's State of the Union Message in January 1960.[59] Moreover, the Chinese indicated that they had no intention of putting their foreign policy in pawn to the Russians. Officially, they welcomed Khrushchev's comprehensive disarmament proposal enunciated on 14 January as proof of the Soviet Union's desire for peace and its confidence in its military strength. But less than a week later, on 21 January, after hearing a speech on the subject by Foreign Minister Ch'en Yi, the NPC standing committee passed a resolution which stated flatly that 'any international disarmament agreement which is arrived at without the formal participation of the Chinese People's Republic and the signature of its delegate cannot, of course, have any binding force on China.'[60]

Perhaps even more alarming from the Soviet point of view, the Chinese began in January 1960 to lobby for their point of view within international communist front organizations, in this case the World Peace Council and the International Union of Students.[61] At this time, Liu Shao-ch'i was privately expressing concern at what he saw as Western attempts to drive a wedge between China and Russia by describing the former as a revolutionary Marxist-Leninist power and the latter as a conservative one[62]; but it would be Chinese actions and polemics rather than Western articles that would have that effect. In January, too, the CC summoned a work conference in Shanghai to discuss foreign affairs, presumably the occasion when the Chinese leaders hammered out the position later enunciated at the first major Sino-Soviet confrontation since Khrushchev's visit to Peking.

(v) The Warsaw Pact conference

To this day, the circumstances surrounding the top-level meeting of the Warsaw Pact powers in Moscow on 4 February are shrouded in mystery.[63] The evidence suggests that the Russians hoped to prevent the Chinese from coming by not announcing the meeting until just before it was due to take place; in the meanwhile East European leaders were brought to Moscow under the pretext of attending an agricultural conference. Whatever the Soviet plan, the Chinese learned of the meeting, perhaps from the Albanians who would soon emerge as their ideological allies, and decided to exercise their right to attend in their capacity as 'observers'; there is no indication that they were formally invited.[64] They chose a delegation consisting of 'old Soviet hands': K'ang Sheng, alternate member of the Politburo, and CC member Wu Hsiu-ch'üan had both spent some years in the Soviet Union; the third member of the delegation was the current Chinese ambassador in Moscow, Liu Hsiao.[65]

They were an experienced trio, capable of handling themselves well under the inauspicious circumstances which could be anticipated.[66]

The purpose of the Warsaw Pact meeting was to endorse Khrushchev's peaceful coexistence policy and disarmament proposals in anticipation of a series of important meetings he would be having with western statesmen in the months ahead, notably a 'big four' summit in Paris in the spring and Eisenhower's return visit to the Soviet Union in the summer. The conference participants agreed that it was their 'common and wholehearted desire' that the US president's visit 'should lead to a further development of the relations between the U.S.S.R. and the United States towards friendship and co-operation, which would be an important guarantee of the inviolability of peace throughout the world'.[67]

The purpose of the Chinese in sending their observer delegation was to spell out their views in this important forum, their first opportunity to do so before Moscow's Eastern European allies. The contrast between K'ang Sheng's speech to the conference (which was not even mentioned let alone published in the Warsaw Pact countries) and the declaration of the Warsaw Pact powers (which *was* published in China) was particularly marked because both statements dealt with the same concrete events, whereas the polemics later in the year were couched in more ideological terms.

The tone of the declaration was relatively mild and optimistic, while that of K'ang Sheng's speech was tough and pessimistic.[68]

The declaration did not mention 'American imperialism'; the speech mentioned it repeatedly. The former referred to Nato's strengthening of German 'militarism', but added that the conferees 'express confidence that the plans of the West German revenge-seekers will not be supported by the present allies of the Federal Republic of Germany either'; by comparison, K'ang Sheng's speech stated that the 'speeded-up revival of West German militarism' was 'an important component part of the U.S. imperialist policy of war and aggression'. Where K'ang condemned, the declaration reproved, more in sorrow than in anger.

The declaration cited four pieces of evidence to justify its optimistic tone; K'ang Sheng's speech ignored three of them and explained away the fourth—Khrushchev's US tour—as a meaningless gesture which Washington had been compelled to make.[69] While K'ang admitted some signs of relaxed tension, he attributed this to the struggles of a strong and united communist bloc, backed by 'forces of peace and democracy' and, most significantly, national liberation movements.

The major policy theme underlying the declaration was that which informed Khrushchev's whole policy of peaceful coexistence: the certainty that nuclear war would result in massive obliteration on both sides, not just of the imperialists. The key passage in K'ang's speech was his reference to the United States' 'discriminatory attitude against our country in international affairs' which was his justification for China's refusal to adhere to any international agreement which it had not helped to draw up. Washington's willingness to deal with Moscow while ostracizing Peking other than at the continuing ambassadorial talks was a differentiated policy towards the various components of the communist bloc greatly resented by the Chinese. Khrushchev's readiness to fall in with this approach was a major reason for his unpopularity in the Chinese capital.

Another was his increasing tendency to deride Mao in public. At the banquet at the end of the Warsaw Pact session, he reportedly depicted the Chairman as 'an elderly, crotchety person, rather like an old shoe, which is just good enough to put in a corner to be admired'.[70]

Both Moscow and Peking were now on the record with diametrically opposed analyses of world affairs and prescriptions for bloc policies. The policy dispute was increasingly serious. Yet only ten days after the Warsaw Pact meeting the tenth anniversary of the Sino-Soviet treaty of 'friendship, alliance and mutual assistance' was celebrated with great ceremony in both capitals, almost as if nothing had happened.[71] At a banquet at the Soviet embassy in Peking, Liu Shao-ch'i toasted the 'great eternal and indestructible close friendship' of the peoples of the two countries and Chu Teh expressed China's 'heartfelt gratitude' to the Soviet Union for the assistance given to his nation's economic development programme. However, a hint of the underlying problems was conveyed by Chu Teh's reference to the Moscow declaration of 1957 as the basis of bloc unity, while Soviet ambassador Chervonenko stressed the inseparability of socialism and peace and the importance of the recent Warsaw Pact declaration in the search for peaceful coexistence.[72]

Perhaps Chu Teh was restrained because he was a guest at the Soviet embassy. Certainly Foreign Minister Ch'en Yi had no inhibitions about restating his country's grim analysis of the global situation at the Chinese banquet to mark the occasion,[73] even though behind the scenes he seems to have been more reasonable, hinting that if China got nuclear weapons it might be possible to secure an agreement not to use them.[74]

(vi) China's isolation

It appears to have been immediately after these anniversary celebrations that the Chinese CC held another work conference on foreign affairs, this time in Canton, presumably to discuss the Warsaw Pact meeting and decide how best to proceed.[75] The following month, a third conference was held, in Hangchow, at which it must be assumed the Chinese leaders agreed the drafts or texts of the polemics to be published in April.

Despite the self-confident tone that would characterize those polemics, Mao's speech at the Hangchow meeting indicated that at least some of his colleagues were concerned at China's increasing isolation.[76] Mao's remarks 'On the anti-China question' contained a characteristic reassurance based on statistics pulled out of the air. China's enemies consisted of imperialists in the West, reactionaries and semi-reactionaries in other countries (presumably the Third World), and revisionists and semi-revisionists in the world communist movement:

The above three categories of people are estimated to constitute a small percentage, say 5%, of mankind. At the most, it cannot be more than 10%. Let us assume that 10 out of every 100 people are against us. Of the world's population of 2·7 billion, no more than 270 million oppose us. The rest, and there are 2·43 billion, either support us, or are not against us, or are temporarily deceived by our enemies into suspecting us.[77]

Mao went on to state that currently there was brief pause in anti-Chinese activities and that this pause would be lengthened if China performed well economically. He cited the Russian example in somewhat surprising language: 'We have the advanced experience of the Soviet Union to go by. In the past several decades, no one has opposed the Soviet Union with good results.'[78] And yet despite that lesson from history, Mao was about to lead the CCP into opposition to the Soviet Union!

Mao's remarks—and Liu held similar views[79]—were pegged to the opening of a Chinese exhibition in Pakistan,[80] and of course anti-China feelings existed principally in Asia as a result of current Chinese disputes with neighbours and near-neighbours. The pause to which Mao referred to was the result of steps taken by Peking to defuse these disputes.

In the case of India, Premier Chou had proposed a summit conference to Prime Minister Nehru as far back as 7 November, in a letter that had been considerably friendlier in tone than earlier Chinese communications.[81] After initial refusals, Nehru finally agreed to a summit and asked Chou to come to New Delhi, an invitation which the Chinese Premier accepted on 26 February. The dates for the visit were later fixed for mid-April.[82]

In the meanwhile, the Chinese acted swiftly to eliminate some of their other border problems. Peking played host to the Burmese Prime Minister, General Ne Win, in January, and to the Nepalese Prime Minister, Mr Koirala, in March. Both visits resulted in border agreements, though in the Burmese case final delimitation was left to the findings of joint commissions. The Chinese and Burmese also signed a treaty of friendship and mutual non-aggression; to the Nepalese, the Chinese extended a grant of 100 million rupees. After the Burmese agreement was signed, the Chinese media queried, in an obvious reference to India: 'Why cannot things which have happened between China and Burma also take place between China and other Asian countries?'[83]

China's other major Asian dispute was with Indonesia and arose from the Jakarta government's decision in May 1959 to end rural trading by overseas Chinese. A visit to Peking in October by Foreign Minister Subandrio failed to resolve matters.[84] Leaks emanating from Indonesian sources at the time suggest that Sub-andrio's discussions with Ch'en Yi were as acrimonious as those between the Chinese Foreign Minister and Khrushchev, even though there is evidence to suggest that Ch'en did appreciate the historical dimensions to the overseas Chinese problem and the need for adaptation to the realities of post-colonial Southeast Asia.[85] At any rate, the following month Chinese were evicted from homes and shops. Goods were confiscated. Some Chinese were beaten, others jailed.[86] Renewed diplomatic activity resulted in Peking's agreement in December at last to ratify the 1955 dual-nationality treaty. Simultaneously, China offered to provide asylum to Chinese who no longer wished to remain in Indonesia; over 100,000 people accepted the offer and were evacuated in Chinese ships.[87]

China's Asian disputes cannot be explained simply as the product of Chinese truculence, as the record shows. Nevertheless, China's diplomatic behaviour had been characterized by a greater toughness reflecting the generally more militant mood that accompanied the launching of the great leap forward. In addition, Chinese polemics against Yugoslav revisionism had not improved their image among non-aligned countries, with many of whose leaders Marshal Tito had developed close ties. Peking's more accommodating manner in late 1959 and early 1960 indicated an awareness that the gains achieved by Chou En-lai's skilful Asian diplomacy since the Bandung conference were being squandered at a time when China might need friends in its forthcoming confrontation with the Soviet Union and its continuing confrontation with the United States. Eisenhower's visit to India in December 1959 and Khrushchev's visits to India and Indonesia in February 1960 may have seemed to the Chinese as foreshadowing a forging of links between the anti-China forces. Any such development had to be prevented.[88]

One method was for China to develop its own ties with the outside world. It could hardly have been coincidental that on 19 March a mass rally in Peking celebrated the creation of a China-Latin America Friendship Association, and that less than a month later, on 12 April, a Sino-African People's Friendship Association was formed with a leading Chinese trade union official, Liu Ch'ang-sheng, as its Chairman.[89] In May, in the aftermath of Chou En-lai's unsuccessful border negotiations with Nehru,[90] Mao would make his contribution to fence-building with the Third World by receiving delegations from Africa, Latin America and the Middle East at a series of four meetings. The Chairman stressed to his various groups of guests that the common enemy was US imperialism and that it could only be defeated by unity and struggle.[91]

Lest China's fruitless but nevertheless continuing ambassadorial talks with the United States should prompt queries in the Third World, or jibes in Moscow, about Peking's commitment to the struggle with imperialism, the Chinese government threw a spanner in its own works. In mid-March, about two weeks after the Chinese CC had assessed the implications of the Warsaw Pact conference at its Canton meeting, two Catholic bishops, one American, one Chinese, were suddenly brought to trial in Shanghai. The Chinese, Kung P'ing-mei, was convicted of high treason and sentenced to life imprisonment and 13 other Chinese Catholics were also tried and sentenced to terms ranging from 5 to 20 years, while the American James Edward Walsh (who had refused repatriation after the communist revolution), accused of directing Kung's 'traitorous counter-revolutionary clique', was awarded 20 years.[92] Both Walsh and Kung had been in prison for years and the decision to try and sentence them at this particular time seems explicable only in terms of China's desire to make an anti-American gesture on the eve of its first polemics against Khrushchev's peaceful coexistence policy. The gesture was certainly effective. According to a historian of the talks: 'Washington was profoundly provoked and the Ambassadorial Talks were severely jolted. The incident raised the question for Washington whether there was really any usefulness in continuing the talks.'[93]

(vii) The Lenin anniversary polemics

The 90th anniversary of the birth of Lenin on 22 April 1960 was used by the Chinese as the occasion for a major denunciation of Soviet foreign policy. There were four polemics in all[94] including a *People's Daily* editorial which listed 37 recent events to prove that 'even after the Camp David talks and even on the eve of the East–West summit conference, we see no change at all in substance in U.S. imperialist war policy, in the policy carried out by the U.S. Government and by Eisenhower personally'.[95] But unquestionably the main polemic was a long, unsigned article carried by *Red Flag* entitled 'Long live Leninism!' because it raised the level of the argument from the details of policy to the principles of ideology.[96]

Here finally, the Chinese presented their rebuttal of the doctrinal innovations introduced by Khrushchev at the CPSU's 20th congress; now at last the Chinese felt able to set aside the compromises Mao had agreed to in the 1957 Moscow Declaration in order not to rock the boat.[97] The issues were war and peace, revolution or reformism.

The article—surely finalized by Mao[98]—argued that Lenin's theses on these issues were still true and relevant. Neither the imperialists in the West nor the bourgeoisie in the Third World had changed their spots; and the nature of the global struggle had not been fundamentally modified by the existence of such 'specific details of technological progress' as nuclear weapons.[99] War was still 'an inevitable outcome of systems of exploitation, and the source of modern wars is the imperialist system. Until the imperialist system and the exploiting classes come to an end, wars of one kind or another will always occur.'[100]

From Lenin on, communists had advocated peaceful coexistence. But experience demonstrated that eventually imperialism would abandon peace for war. The correct response was a combination of two tactics: 'thoroughly exposing the imperialist peace fraud', and 'preparing for a just war to end the imperialist unjust war when and if the imperialists should unleash it'.[101]

Peaceful coexistence applied only to international relations, not to the relations between the proletariat and the bourgeoisie within capitalist countries. Communists should take part in parliamentary struggles but should have no illusions about the parliamentary system which was merely an adornment of bourgeois dictatorship. As Lenin had pointed out, no ruling class had ever given way without a struggle, and not a single great revolution in history had ever been carried out without a civil war. The Bolshevik and Chinese revolutions were clear proof of these propositions. 'Let us, in the light of bloody facts both of the historical past and of the modern capitalist world examine all this nonsense about the "peaceful growth of capitalism into socialism" put out by the old revisionists and their modern counterparts.' 'Peaceful transition', as Lenin had argued, was an 'extraordinarily rare opportunity.'[102]

Interspersing the copious quotations from Lenin were jibes at Tito, a target in his own right but more importantly a codename for Khrushchev. The Yugoslavs were denounced for 'shamelessly' calling the US 'imperialist chieftain Eisenhower the man who laid the cornerstone for eliminating the cold war and establishing lasting peace with peaceful competition between different political systems'; Khrushchev had laid out a similar proposition during his visit to Peking.[103]

Moscow and Peking's antagonistic positions on India were also implicit. 'Socialist countries never permit themselves to send, never should and never will send their troops across their borders unless they are subjected to aggression from a foreign enemy.'[104] In non-communist states, it was always possible for the bourgeoisie 'either to dissolve parliament when necessary, or to use various open and underhanded tricks to turn a working-class party which is the biggest party in parliament into a minority, or to reduce its seats in parliament, even when it has polled more votes in an election ... the experiences in various European and Asian countries after the Second World War provide additional proof...'.[105] Here the Chinese clearly had in mind Nehru's dissolution of the first significant communist government to be elected anywhere in the world, that of the state of Kerala.[106]

It was the concrete allusions to Sino-Soviet foreign policy disagreements over recent years which fuelled the passion which infused 'Long live Leninism!' But it was the theoretical framework that was of more fundamental importance and lasting significance. For the first time, the Chinese were asserting their right to lay down the law for the communist bloc. Hitherto, Chinese theoretical analyses could be explained away either as contributions to a discussion within the world communist movement (as in the case with their two articles on the Stalin issue in 1956) or as relevant only to China (as in the case of Mao's contradictions speech in 1957). But now the Chinese were undertaking the most basic ideological task of analysing the nature of the epoch and drawing conclusions for class struggle on a global basis. If unchallenged, Peking would take over from Moscow as the locus of doctrinal orthodoxy, the Rome of the world communist movement. It was a gauntlet which Khrushchev had to take up.

(viii) Lobbying in Peking, bullying at Bucharest

Unfortunately for Khrushchev, he possessed neither the personal prestige nor the intellectual authority to enable him credibly to challenge the doctrinal orthodoxy of Marx and Lenin as adumbrated by Mao. The public Soviet ideological response to 'Long live Leninism' was feeble, and probably for that reason was shuffled off on to a lesser figure in the Soviet leadership whose only claim to give the speech at the anniversary meeting was that he was a veteran of Lenin's generation. Otto Kuusinen could appeal only to a few quotations from Lenin's works—all of which could equally well have been used by the Chinese—and to Lenin's widow's recollection that the great revolutionary had foreseen that 'the time will come when war will become so destructive as to be impossible'.[107] Soviet insistence on the disastrous consequences of a nuclear war gave Kuusinen's speech a moral appeal lacking in the chilling logic of Peking; but Soviet dialecticians had failed to provide him with the intellectual infrastructure to transmute sentiment into dogma.[108] Consequently, most of Kuusinen's speech was a pragmatic justification of Soviet policies, with particular reference to non-communist Afro-Asian countries. To the poverty of Soviet theory was now added a severe blow to Khrushchev's foreign policy: in the wake of the shooting down of an American U-2 spy plane over the Soviet Union, Khrushchev was compelled to abort the four-power Paris summit. In Peking, Teng Hsiao-p'ing applauded his action.[109] The Chinese must have been delighted that Eisenhower's assumption of personal responsibility for the U-2 flight lent credibility to their image of the US president rather than the Soviet one. In May 1960, Khrushchev appeared to have lost both the theoretical and the practical arguments.

The Chinese seized the initiative. At a plenary session of the general council of the communist-controlled World Federation of Trade Unions (WFTU) in Peking from 5 to 9 June, the Chinese lobbied for their viewpoint with a violence that amazed other communist delegates. The Chinese WFTU Vice President, Liu Ch'ang-sheng, denounced as fantasy Khrushchev's position at the CPSU's 21st congress that war could be eliminated even while imperialism remained in existence.[110] The Chinese delegation convened a special session of the communist delegates to the WFTU meeting with the object of changing WFTU policy. At this session, the Chairman of the All-China Trade Union Federation, Liu Ning-yi, denounced modern revisionism in terms that made it crystal clear that his target was Khrushchev.[111] It may well have been the behaviour of the Chinese on this occasion, coming on the heels of the Lenin anniversary articles, that lost them the sympathy of Kremlin hawks who agreed with their criticisms of Khrushchev's foreign policy, but were not prepared to concede Soviet leadership of the world communist movement.[112]

Within a few days of the conclusion of the WFTU meeting, the Chinese could claim another triumphant vindication of their theses. Violent street demonstrations by the Japanese Communist and Socialist parties, backed by militant students, against the renewal of the US-Japan security treaty forced the Japanese government to request a postponement of the imminent visit of President Eisenhower. Although the new pact was ratified by the diet, Premier Kishi felt obliged to resign immediately thereafter. There could have been no more convincing evidence of the effectiveness of revolutionary struggle as compared with parliamentary manoeuvring.[113] In the light of such events, Soviet attempts to utilize the 40th anniversary of the publication of Lenin's *Left-wing Communism—An Infantile Disorder* as an opportunity to level veiled attacks on Chinese extremism lacked bite.[114] At bay, Khrushchev counter-attacked ferociously.

On 12 May, on the eve of what they knew would be a debacle at the Paris summit, the Soviet leaders had invited Mao to Moscow. Mao had refused.[115] Then, early in June, the CPSU CC had proposed that the Romanian communist party's 3rd Congress scheduled to open on the 20th of that month, should be used as an opportunity for ruling communist parties to exchange views on the international situation in the aftermath of the abortive summit. The Chinese objected both to the hastiness of the meeting and to the exclusion of non-ruling parties. The two CCs agreed that a conference of all communist parties should be held (it met in Moscow in November) and that the Bucharest meeting could be the occasion for preliminary discussions.[116]

During the public sessions of the Romanian party Congress, Khrushchev and the chief Chinese fraternal delegate P'eng Chen, rehearsed again the familiar Soviet and Chinese arguments on peace, war and revolution.[117] Behind the scenes a bitter confrontation was brewing. Soviet delegates were systematically briefing fraternal parties on the Sino-Soviet quarrel and distributing copies of an 80-page 'letter of information', dated 21 June, condemning China's ideological errors and uncomradely activities (most recently in publishing the Lenin anniversary articles and lobbying against the Russians at the WFTU meeting). For the first time, the Russians were attempting to reassert their doctrinal pre-eminence, but how authoritatively cannot be assessed since a text of the document has never been published.[118]

The secret sessions at the Bucharest congress started on 24 June and lasted until the 26th.[119] P'eng Chen was reportedly taken aback at the succession of anti-Chinese speeches that Soviet lobbying produced, but he was calm and reasoned in his reply. More effectively, he had taken the precaution of distributing to delegates another 80-page Soviet letter, this one a private communication from the CPSU to the CCP. Its 'hectoring and bitter' tone contrasted sharply with the reasoned argumentation of the letter of information and undermined the statesmanlike image the latter projected.

Incensed by the dextrous step taken by the Chinese to remind other communists of the realities of CPSU dealings with fraternal parties, Khrushchev took the floor. In his speech, he 'abandoned reasoned argument and, indeed, all pretence of judicious analysis of differences and embarked on a violent tirade couched in purely personal terms...'.[120] According to the Chinese account, the Soviet party leader 'wantonly vilified the Chinese Communist Party as "madmen", "wanting to unleash war", "picking up the banner of the imperialist monopoly capitalists", being "pure nationalist" on the Sino-Indian boundary question and employing "Trotskyite ways" against the CPSU' (at the WFTU meeting according to another version.)[121] The Chinese did not mention Khrushchev's attack on Mao by name in which he described the Chairman as in effect another Stalin 'oblivious of any interests other than his own, spinning theories detached from the realities of the modern world'; the Chinese leader had become 'an ultra Leftist, an ultra dogmatist, indeed a left revisionist'.[122] Khrushchev also referred to the case of P'eng Teh-huai, apparently suggesting that he had been dismissed for giving his views on the leap to the Russians.[123] P'eng was a 'good friend' and he, Khrushchev, would like to hang up his portrait.[124]

Khrushchev's bullying manner apparently did not intimidate P'eng Chen who reportedly replied 'with far more elegance and real bite' than the Soviet leader had displayed. In the light of Khrushchev's sharply contrasted behaviour after Camp David and at the Paris summit, P'eng was able to accuse him of blowing now hot now cold towards the imperialist powers.[125] More importantly, P'eng was authorized to issue a statement on behalf of the CCP CC accusing the CPSU 1st secretary of 'an extremely crude act of imposing one's own will on other people' and adopting a 'patriarchal, arbitrary and tyrannical' attitude.

> He has in fact treated the relationship between the great Communist Party of the Soviet Union and our Party not as one between brothers, but as one between patriarchal father and son. At this meeting he has exerted pressure in an attempt to make our party submit to his non-Marxist-Leninist views.[126]

The Chinese statement objected to portions of the proposed communiqué of the meeting, but since it also protested a desire for communist unity,[127] P'eng Chen signed it, 'for the sake of the larger interest' as the Chinese later declared.[128]

(ix) The Russians are going, the Russians are going

The larger interest was driven from Khrushchev's mind after his confrontation with P'eng Chen in Bucharest. When the CPSU's CC met from 13 to 16 July, it heard on its final day a report on the Bucharest meeting. The rapporteur was Frol Kozlov, even though this senior Soviet leader had not been there. The motive was presumably to demonstrate to the Chinese that the Soviet leadership was united against them—Kozlov being something of an anti-Western hawk in the CPSU Presidium[129]—and the CC duly 'completely approved the political line of the activity of the CPSU delegation headed by Comrade Khrushchev'.[130] Reporting on the plenum later in the month the leading Soviet ideologist Suslov apparently told CPSU members in Moscow and Leningrad that because of Chinese bellicosity, relations henceforth would be conducted solely on a state-to-state basis, and that if a world party conference later in the year could not resolve the dispute, an open breach would be announced.[131] More immediately, the Soviet CC plenum evidently also endorsed a Presidium decision to withdraw all Soviet advisers from China. The Chinese Foreign Ministry received a note to that effect on 16 July (according to both Soviet[132] and Chinese[133] sources). Action was immediately taken: the Stalin Prize-winning chemist Mikhail Klochko (then attached to the Institute of Metallurgy and Ceramics in remote Kunming) later reported that his recall telegram arrived on 16 July.[134]

The recall decision was never published by the Russians, but the Chinese showed all departing Soviet advisers the text of the Soviet note to Peking explaining it. The main reasons given were that: the Chinese did not follow Soviet technical advice and often demonstrated their scorn for it; the Chinese had created intolerable conditions for Soviet advisers, spying on them, searching their belongings, opening their mail; in some cases, Soviet specialists had been molested and even attacked. Consequently, all Soviet advisers would be withdrawn during July and August.[135] The Chinese reply was received by the Soviet embassy in Peking on 31 July.[136] It denied the Soviet accusations point by point, describing them as 'a strange and futile exercise, just like trying to catch the wind out in the fields'.[137]

The Soviet decision appears to have taken the advisers themselves as well as their Chinese hosts totally by surprise. Klochko's recall telegram arrived from the Chinese Academy of Sciences stating he was urgently needed back at his Moscow institute. The news puzzled Klochko, not yet privy to the background, because he had been informed as recently as the third week in June that he could stay until December. Klochko knew, too, that it was currently the 'dead season' at the Soviet Academy of Sciences and that 'not a research scientist was to be found in all of Moscow until September, even if you hunted for him with a candle'.[138]

Klochko had been aware from the moment of his arrival in March that a tension existed between the Chinese and their Soviet advisers which had not been there during his previous secondment in 1958.[139] A month later, he and other foreign specialists attended a meeting at which a senior provincial party official lectured other cadres on 'Long live Leninism!'. After the speech, of which Klochko understood virtually nothing, each Soviet specialist was presented with the text of the article in Russian. Subsequently every Soviet adviser in China was questioned by his embassy about whether or not he had ever had a copy of this heretical document in his hands. Klochko attributed this diplomatic agitation not to the contents of the article, 'which could easily be dismissed as foolish, but to the fact that it represented the first open attempt by the Chinese government to advocate its own views in contrast to those of the Soviet Union.'[140] Yet May Day was celebrated with the customary courtesies.[141]

Despite the telegram, Klochko conscientiously wished to finish his current work before leaving and as a result was witness to the considerable pressure upon Soviet diplomats to effectuate a rapid withdrawal of Soviet advisory personnel in China. After successive telephone conversations with his embassy in Peking and repeated and peremptory orders to pack up and leave, Klochko felt he could procrastinate no longer and flew to Peking on 28 July after a touching farewell party given by his Chinese colleagues.[142]

In the Chinese capital, Klochko was informed by a Soviet diplomat that the Soviet government had arranged for two additional trains a week on the Peking–Moscow service. About 1,500 advisers and 2,500 dependants still remained in China and they had all to be evacuated by the end of August. Klochko himself was required to leave by 4 or 5 August. Again he managed to procrastinate in order to write a general report on Chinese science for his hosts and did not actually depart until 13 August.[143]

During his final days in Peking, Klochko heard an explanation of the evacuation given to party members among the advisers by the Soviet ambassador Chervonenko. The latter criticized the Chinese for their domestic policies—the 100 flowers, the communes—but reserved his principal fire for their foreign policies—the folly of Chinese aggression against India; responsibility for worsening relations with Indonesia 'for the sake of a few petty merchants'; needless exacerbation of relations with Yugoslavia and excessive friendship with Albania; anti-Soviet lobbying among Third World citizens; the contradictions in Chinese analyses of the US threat. He was especially violent over Chinese behaviour at the WFTU meeting. More generally, China was attempting to take over the leadership of the world revolution despite its lack of proficiency in Marxism or revolution. The Soviet withdrawal was designed to force the Chinese to reconsider their actions and perhaps change their ways.[144]

The Chinese showed no sign of a sudden change of heart, but they remained courteous to the last. Klochko reported that his Chinese colleagues displayed even greater warmth than before,[145] and that Foreign Minister Ch'en Yi gave a banquet for the departing advisers. On this occasion, Ch'en thanked the advisers for their immense services and wished them good health and successful work back at home. Chervonenko reminded the Chinese of the 6 billion roubles Moscow had given China and the 10,000 advisers who had been seconded. A Soviet delegate then spoke broadly on the theme: 'We've done so much for you, and you are not content.'[146]

That sentiment, according to Klochko's testimony, was not echoed by the vast majority of Soviet advisers or Soviet scientists at home. In such circles at least, the withdrawal was seen as harmful to Soviet interests.[147] It is easy to understand why. At that time there were 1,390 Soviet advisers working in China. In addition to pulling them out, the Russians also 'tore up 343 contracts and supplementary contracts concerning experts, and scrapped 257 projects of scientific and technical cooperation'.[148] As a result of the evacuation, many of China's 'important designing and scientific research projects had to be suspended, and some of the construction projects in progress had to be suspended, and some of the factories and mines which were conducting trial production could not go into production according to schedule'.[149] Chou En-lai called a meeting to discuss the implications of the withdrawal of Soviet advisers on naval construction.[150] According to the later, bitter Chinese account, the Soviet action inflicted 'enormous losses' on China's development.[151] Liu Shao-ch'i was probably not the only Chinese leader to express concern at the withdrawal and advocate turning to the West to make good the damage.[152] Not until after Liu's disgrace and death would that advice be followed.

Quite apart from the economic and political impact on the Chinese, if the Russians believed their own predictions about the disasters which Chinese policy would entail, they should surely have kept their advisers in place to help pick up the pieces when the day of reckoning arrived. At that stage, Soviet advisers would have been in a very strong position. Instead, the Chinese were able to blame their economic difficulties partly on the Soviet withdrawal.

In the meanwhile, even if Soviet allegations about Chinese mistreatment of their advisers were partially true—and Klochko indicates that they were[153]—these thousands of Soviet citizens represented a unique source of information for their government, information about policies in ministries, conditions in factories, living standards in remoter areas, the status of science, about life in China generally. By withdrawing their advisers, the Russians reduced their access to information to the level enjoyed by any other diplomatic mission, and precisely at a time when their alarm about Chinese behaviour should have made them desirous of increasing rather than decreasing their knowledge about their large neighbour.

But the withdrawal had a deeper emotional and symbolic significance. However imperfectly the collaborative relationship had worked, those 10,000 Soviet advisers had represented over the years a massive commitment of human resources to the Chinese development effort. China's debt to the Soviet Union was enormous; Ch'en Yi's expression of gratitude at the last supper he gave for the advisers was genuine. But the debt was wiped out, the gratitude negated by the manner in which the relationship was ended.

Perhaps as significantly, if less tangibly, the Soviet move destroyed the innumerable human ties between the middle ranks of the governmental, industrial and intellectual elites of the two countries that had been developed through working together, ties that would have greatly assisted fence-building in the future. Moreover, the Russians had undermined the position of their principal constituency within the Chinese elite: the Soviet-trained planners, scientists and engineers. Their special relationship with Russians would no longer be a source of status, but increasingly grounds for suspicion. Many would retool in English.

If the Soviet leadership had decided as of mid-July 1960 that a total break with China was inevitable and perhaps desirable, then the withdrawal of the advisers had to come sooner or later. But if the Soviet action was taken in a mood of fury at Chinese behaviour, Bucharest being the last straw, with the intention of bringing Peking to its senses, then the Russians totally misjudged Chinese psychology. The effect of the withdrawal was clearly to inflame Chinese nationalist sentiments, to stiffen Mao's determination to go his own way, and to rally to his banner any members of the Chinese leadership who may have felt he had been pressing the Russians too hard. At a CC work conference in August Teng Hsiao-p'ing characterized the Soviet position as insisting on a total disavowal by the Chinese of their domestic policies.[154] Few native opponents of the leap would have agreed to such humiliating terms.

Seen in this light, the withdrawal of the experts assumes a significance perhaps greater than the disputes over policy towards the United States and India. Policies could be changed, compromises might be made, especially after the collapse of the Paris summit; but the human dimension to the alliance could never be replaced. Thus the key developments in 1960 that transformed a major policy dispute into an inexorably widening rift were the Chinese challenge to the CPSU's ideological supremacy with the publication of 'Long live Leninism!' and the Soviet withdrawal of experts which destroyed a close working relationship at the state level.

Yet for the moment the Chinese preserved their sense of proportion and priorities; US imperialism, not revisionism, was still the main enemy, Ch'en Yi told a foreign affairs conference on 1 August.[155] It was perhaps on this occasion that Ch'en acknowledged in private what the Chinese never accepted publicly during the 1960 debate with Moscow, that some US leaders recognized the need to relax tension.[156] Ch'en's attitude was that of course China wanted peaceful coexistence, but to utilize it to eliminate imperialism, just as imperialism wished to use it to eliminate socialism.[157]

(x) The Moscow conference

On 10 September, the CCP replied formally to the CPSU's letter of information distributed at the Bucharest congress. The Chinese letter contained five proposals for the resolution of difficulties: the ideological foundations of unity between the CPSU and the CCP should be the fundamental theories of Marxism–Leninism and the 1957 Moscow Declaration; relations between communist parties and countries should be on the basis of equality, comradeship and internationalism; the CCP and the CPSU should have 'full consultations and unhurried discussions' on all matters in dispute and 'when necessary' these views should be presented to other parties; statements and actions likely to undermine unity and aid the enemy should be eschewed; on the basis of these principles communist parties should consult together in order to produce at the November Moscow meeting a document that would serve them all as a programme.[158] The Chinese rejected the suggestion allegedly made by the Russians that democratic centralism applied between communist parties as it did within communist parties:

...where the fundamental principles of Marxism-Leninism are concerned, the problem of exactly who is right and who is wrong cannot in every case be judged by who has the majority. After all, truth is truth. Error cannot be turned into truth because of a temporary majority, nor will truth be turned into error because of a temporary minority.[159]

It was in this long letter, according to other accounts, that the Chinese first traced the dispute back to the CPSU's 20th Congress, when the Russians had ignored Stalin's positive role and put forward the theory of peaceful transition, both without consultation. The Chinese also took this opportunity to reveal that in 1956 they had advised the Russians against using force in Poland and in favour of using force in Hungary. The letter reminded the Russians of differences at the 1957 Moscow conference and of the revisions on which Mao had insisted before signing the Declaration. For the most part, the letter was an attempt to restore the argument to the level of ideological fundamentals initiated by 'Long live Leninism!' but there was 'one moment of light relief'. Khrushchev had poked fun at Mao's depiction of the USA as a 'paper tiger'; but, the Chinese letter pointed out, Lenin himself had said 'Anglo-French imperialism has feet of clay'. (This debating point proved so regularly effective that finally in December 1962, *Pravda* felt compelled to define the differences between paper tigers and feet of clay![160]

This letter was the brief of a CCP delegation to Moscow, headed by Teng Hsiao-p'ing, which engaged in bitter and unproductive discussions from 10 to 22 September with a CPSU team led by Suslov, the top Soviet ideologue.[161] Probably an additional factor contributing to Chinese intransigence was the knowledge that during August Khrushchev had attempted to suborn the Albanians into the anti-Chinese bloc.[162] Thereafter, the Chinese apparently went home, returning again for the opening on 1 October of a meeting of 26 parties whose task was to draft a statement for the world communist conference that would coincide with the anniversay celebrations of the Bolshevik revolution in November.

This preparatory commission met until 20 October.[163] Agreement was reached on a number of points for a draft statement, but some major issues remained unsettled.[164] The Chinese were supported by the Albanian and Indonesian parties in objecting to the Soviet formulation on the 'cult of personality' which clearly could be used as a weapon against Mao as well as its original target, Stalin. The Chinese were supported by an even larger number of parties—the Japanese, North Korean, Indonesian, Vietnamese and Australian—in objecting to any attack on 'fractional' activities (by which the Russian clearly meant Chinese lobbying for their own point of view as at the WFTU meeting) in a final document.[165]

Even this limited accord was disrupted when Khrushchev, on his return from the UN General Assembly session in New York, insisted on scrapping some of the agreements that had been hammered out[166]; and the atmosphere was further soured when the Soviet leader got himself involved in a heated exchange with the Chinese General Secretary at a banquet concluding the preparatory sessions.[167] Thus when the leaders of 81 of the world communist movement's 87 parties convened in Moscow the following month they were faced with the formidable task of producing a consensus document which the two earlier and more conveniently sized meetings had failed to agree on.

The Chinese delegation was high-powered. Mao evidently preferred discretion in a situation in which he might lose face[168] but Liu Shao-ch'i went as leader, despite considerable family problems connected with the Soviet Union. A brother-in-law defected to the Soviet Union in October 1960.[169] A son, Liu Yun-pin, divorced his Russian wife in 1960.[170] Another son Liu Yun-jo, returned from studies in the Soviet Union in June 1960, expressed dissatisfaction with Chinese conditions, stated he was in love with a Russian girl and wanted to visit her, and even demanded to go to Moscow with his father on the latter's official mission. To avoid any embarrassing incident at the airport, Liu forbade any of his family from seeing him off to Moscow.[171]

Liu was accompanied by most of the men who had carried China's ideological banner at previous confrontations earlier in the year: Teng Hsiao-p'ing, P'eng Chen, K'ang Sheng. The Szechwan party 1st secretary, Li Ching-ch'üan, was an unexpected delegation member; not so propaganda chief Lu Ting-yi. The inclusion of Liao Ch'eng-chih, Chairman of the Chinese Afro-Asian Solidarity Committee and one of Peking's principal 'Japan experts', and Liu Ning-yi, the Chinese trade union Chairman, both of whom had done much work in international front organizations, indicated Peking's realization of the need there would be in Moscow to lobby non-ruling communist parties, particularly those from the Third World. In all, the delegation consisted of four full and two alternate members of the CCP Politburo, together with five other members of the CCP CC.[172]

The Chinese was one of only five delegations not headed by its top leader. Yet despite the seniority of the communists assembled from the four corners of the globe, the delegations were for the most part treated with suspicion by the Russians, effectively confined to their quarters when not actually in session, evidently to prevent third party discussions of the Moscow-Peking dispute. As at Bucharest, the CPSU emissaries lobbied fraternal delegates intensively on a bilateral basis.[173]

All delegations received from the Russians a copy of a draft declaration, representing the extent of agreement at the preparatory conference, accompanied by a commentary by the leading Soviet ideologist Suslov which outlined the main points of difference on doctrinal matters, particularly as they related to peace and war, peaceful transition and the cult of personality. Then, a few days before the conference opened, the CPSU circulated a 127-page letter, dated 5 November, replying to the CCP letter of 10 September. In this, the Russians sought to rebut the concrete attacks made by the Chinese on their foreign policy in general and Khrushchev in particular.[174]

The conference met in the Kremlin's St George's Hall from 25 November with breaks only on Sundays. The morning session lasted from 10 am till 2 pm; after a two-hour recess, the conference reconvened and continued in session till late in the evening. Much of the time was occupied by the not always relevant speeches of the leaders of small communist parties from small countries who were determined to have their moment in the spotlight in front of the great figures of the world communist movement[175]; in all, 108 delegates spoke at the 33 sessions.[176]

Khrushchev formally opened the proceedings and restated the Soviet case in a restrained manner. Then Suslov introduced the draft declaration, stating that its adoption merely as a basis for discussion was an achievement. But this atmosphere of rational debate was unreal and was soon shattered by attacks on the CCP's position by a large number of non-ruling parties, many of them from the Third World to the apparent discomfiture of the Chinese who looked to such delegations as their natural constituency.[177]

According to the French communist leader, Maurice Thorez, the main topics of discussion at the conference were the nature of the present epoch; the problem of war and peace; the paths for the transition to socialism; and the conduct of the international communist movement.[178] On 14 November, Teng Hsiao-p'ing, who emerged as the principal Chinese protagonist during the conference, replied in strong terms to criticisms of his party's position. On the issue of war and peace, he stated that the Chinese had never argued that world war or indeed any war was inevitable, only that the existence of imperialism made it only too likely; and if war were launched by the imperialists, even nuclear war, it would be the duty of communists to resist. Thus talk of disarmament was misleading; and peaceful coexistence could only be one aspect of the foreign policy of communist countries.[179]

Turning to the question of peaceful transition to socialism, Teng reasserted the Chinese view that this was virtually impossible. Citing the Indian example, he argued that it showed how bourgeois leaders tended to move to the right and closer to imperialism.[180] However, Teng made it clear that the CCP did not totally reject everything about the CPSU's 20th Congress.[181] It was on the conduct of the international communist movement that Teng posed again the challenge implicit in the publication of 'Long live Leninism!': the CPSU had no right to lay down the law for the world communist movement. Teng asked:

On what supra-Party constitution does the Central Committee of the CPSU base itself in advancing such an organisational principle [that the minority should submit to the majority]? When and where did the Communist and Workers' Parties of all countries ever adopt such a supra-Party constitution?[182]

And yet despite his fierce defence of the CCP's right to lobby for its point of view, the Chinese delegation also argued strongly in favour of maintaining a leading party within the movement which they said had to be the CPSU. The Russians, who had agreed to retain this role at the 1957 Moscow conference at Mao's insistence, discarded it at the 1960 conference, perhaps anticipating that the Chinese hoped one day to take it over from them.[183]

On the day following Teng's speech, the French party chief, Thorez, attempted to take up this challenge on fractionalism, stating unequivocally that 'there would no longer be a unitary international Communist movement if groups could form or factions crystallize'.[184] The Chinese had confused 'the right to their own opinion on the problems being discussed with the "right" to spread their erroneous ideas after the majority of parties has rejected them'.[185] Thorez faced head on the problem posed for supporters of the CPSU caused by the accuracy with which the CCP had quoted Lenin to define the nature of the epoch. He asked: 'Is our world still the one which Lenin saw before him when he wrote his masterful book on imperialism?' His answer was a decisive 'no' on the grounds that in Lenin's time there were no communist countries; that today imperialism was challenged not merely by a well-developed Soviet Union and a powerful communist bloc, but also by the ex-colonial Third World, an international workers' movement and a world peace movement. The present epoch was not that of imperialism but of the 'breakup of imperialism, the era of the transition from capitalism to socialism, the era of the formation and reinforcement of the world socialist system . . .':

To pass by without seeing the profound changes in the world, to hold on to Lenin's half-a-century-old definition and continue to consider imperialism as the determining force, is to lose the sense of reality, to lack the creative spirit of Marxism.[186]

Thorez' tone carried the magisterial certainty of one who knows he can challenge a more prestigious opponent because he is on the winning side. Yet he refrained from abuse. But after an anti-Soviet diatribe from the Albanian party leader Enver Hoxha on 16 November, Soviet supporters were presented with a proxy target on which they could vent the fury they almost certainly felt also against the Chinese. Hoxha, who had repulsed a last Soviet effort to win him back just after the start of the conference,[187] made a bitter attack on Khrushchev, accusing him of trickery and stupidity. Denouncing Soviet attempts to exploit Albanian natural disasters in order to bring the Albanian party to heel, Hoxha proclaimed that the 'Soviet rats had been able to feed while the Albanian people were starving. And for the little they gave they demanded payment in gold'.[188] Hoxha's speech was described by the Polish 1st secretary Gomulka as a 'disgusting, shameful, gangsterish, irresponsible attack'.[189] The leader of the Italian party delegation, Luigi Longo, claimed that 'words fail us for proper denunciation' of Hoxha's allegations and criticisms, but nevertheless managed to condemn the Albanian at some length. Hoxha's efforts were 'beneath contempt'. He had employed 'duplicity'. 'The action of the Albanian delegate appears to us all the more offensive the more it is masked behind oily assurances of friendship and fraternity, with epithets and turns of expression that one can conceive of addressing only to a class enemy.'[190]

But Longo's principal concern was probably to defend Khrushchev's thesis on the possibility of a peaceful transition to socialism because this was the centrepiece of PCI policy:

Our Chinese comrades ask us to show them what country is making progress by this means. We answer, with firm confidence, that our own

PCI has long acted on this belief, which best fits the Italian situation, and that so far it has had undoubtedly significant successes. At our last two congresses . . . we defined exactly what we mean by the democratic way, the Italian way to socialism . . . a way of mass democratic struggle, directed at changing the balance of power in Parliament and the political leadership of the country, by changing the real relationship among political and social forces. . . .[191]

Longo's spirited defence of the PCI line illustrated the problem the CCP delegation faced in Moscow. Some, perhaps many, of the fraternal delegations must surely have relished the CCP's defiance of the CPSU's leadership, precisely because it was a luxury they themselves could not afford. But most of the non-ruling parties were locked into domestic situations that conformed more to Khrushchev's analysis than Mao's prescriptions. To subscribe to the CCP position, with its aura of insouciant bellicosity which Khrushchev had skilfully fostered, would mean political suicide back home. The Chinese could not hope to win allies under such circumstances, however purist the quality of their Marxist-Leninist reasoning.

Perhaps it was his recognition of the futility of argument that led Teng to include bitter personal attacks on Khrushchev and Gomulka in his second speech on 24 November. According to Teng, a large part of the Soviet 1st secretary's speech had been an indirect attack on Mao, and 'Khrushchev had evidently been talking without knowing what he was saying, as he did all too frequently'.[192] Teng presumably felt no need again to defend the Chairman fulsomely and at length as he had done in his first speech.[193] As for Gomulka—who had implicitly characterized the Chinese as dogmatists, revisionists, frationalists, sectarians, Trotskyites, and schismatics[194]—he had 'insulted Albania by his filthy attack', Teng stated.[195]

The Chinese General Secretary's second speech was the last major event of the conference sessions which ended the following day. There had been moments of high drama and unintended humour[196] interspersing the long hours of tedium. But the conference had resolved nothing, for neither the CPSU nor the CCP had given way on any vital points. The question now was: could a compromise document be patched together if only to maintain a public façade of unity?

There may have been a disagreement over tactics at this stage between the CCP delegation in Moscow and Mao and other colleagues in Peking. When the delegation caucused to discuss what to do if the CPSU refused to remove the points offensive to the Chinese, Liu Shao-ch'i apparently suggested signing the final Statement but simultaneously issuing an explanatory declaration. Mao cabled the delegation ordering a fight to the very brink of a breach in an effort to remove the offending items.[197] However, not even biased cultural revolutionaries said that the delegation was prepared to capitulate to the CPSU or that Mao would have preferred a breach to signing the Statement.

Despite their overt obduracy, the Chinese, Mao included, evidently decided that it would be counter-productive for their cause to incur at this stage the odium attached to schismatics down the centuries. Tallies differ, but the CCP was certainly in a very small minority, with only a few parties giving them overall support.[198] Considerable pressure was put on Liu and his colleagues by other delegations, especially the Indian, to accept a compromise. The Chinese, therefore, agreed to sign a conference Statement hammered out after the conclusion of the conference sessions, once certain concessions—notably, the omission of a condemnation of fractionalism—had been made to their views in what was basically a Soviet document. But when signing, Liu Shao-ch'i stated that he disagreed still with some of the Statement's provisions, the tactic he had originally suggested.[199] From a later Chinese account it would appear that the CCP delegation had felt obliged to make the same concessions as Mao had done three years earlier: on the estimation of the CPSU's 20th Congress (at which the doctrine on peace and war had been revised and the attack on the cult of personality spurred[200]) and on the question of peaceful transition to socialism.[201] The principal difference was that the CPSU delegation was adamant that the 1960 statement should have a specific, positive reference to the attack on the cult of personality, which had not been in the 1957 Declaration.[202] P'eng Chen, apparently the chief Chinese delegate on the drafting committee, was finally instructed to accept this item, a fact that was held against him as well as Liu Shao-ch'i and Teng Hsiao-p'ing during the cultural revolution.[203] But while the Russians probably insisted on this inclusion as a dig at Mao, it seems highly improbable that the CCP delegation would have acceded to this demand without authorization from the Chairman, and highly unlikely that the latter would have taken the unprecedented step of turning up at the airport to welcome home

Liu and the returning delegation if he had blamed them for making a concession which affected him so closely.[204]

On all the other major issues debated during the two long weeks within the Kremlin, every Soviet formulation was supplemented by a Chinese codicil which meant that the Statement could be interpreted by either side for its own purposes with perfect propriety.[205] Doctrinal consistency and a programme for united action had been sacrificed for a cosmetic truce. It lasted less than a year.

But for the moment the amenities were preserved. The leaders of the Soviet and Chinese delegations allowed themselves to be photographed in a convivial huddle, the Russians smiling, the Chinese more non-committal, although only the Chinese proved willing to allow their people to view this 'evidence' of fraternal harmony.[206]

After the signing of the statement, Liu Shao-ch'i made a brief goodwill tour, visiting Minsk and Kiev. Ch'en Yi informed a national propaganda work conference on 14 December that the emphasis must now be on struggling against the United States and not on planning for a split with Russia. The prestige of the CPSU's CC must be supported.[207] Having pressed the dispute to the brink of a rift, the Chinese appeared keen to illustrate a commitment to Sino-Soviet friendship. If Peking were to hope to gain more allies in the dispute in the future, it was important for the CCP to be seen as sincerely in favour of friendship with the CPSU, but forced reluctantly into opposition by Soviet errors and onslaughts.

Looking back over the period from the early autumn of 1959, it is possible to discern most of the major elements that transformed the Sino-Soviet dispute into a total rupture. Chinese nationalism had been inflamed by the Soviet attitude on the Sino-Indian border dispute and Moscow's peaceful coexistence policy towards the United States which appeared to ignore China's interests. The Soviet leadership had been incensed by the Chinese challenge to the CPSU's right to lay down the law for the world communist movement. Both sides felt they had been betrayed, the Russians as a result of Chinese behaviour at the WFTU meeting, the Chinese by the withdrawal of Soviet advisers.

Two elements of the dispute in 1959–60 must be singled out because of their profound impact on Chinese domestic developments in the years leading up to the cultural revolution. The first is the role of Khrushchev. His Soviet colleagues appear to have allowed him a free hand much of the time,[208] and consequently the CPSU 1st secretary's aggressive manner and insulting remarks came to symbolize the whole Soviet attitude towards China, and towards Mao personally, and thus to exacerbate the quarrel at key moments—in Peking in September–October 1959, in Bucharest in June 1960 and in Moscow in November 1960.

Increasingly, the Chinese appeared to feel that this one man—his policies, his attitudes, his actions—was the fundamental cause of the dispute. Reportedly, Liu Shao-ch'i even suggested to Khrushchev when they met at the end of the 81-party conference that the Soviet leader should retreat from the front line in Sino-Soviet matters in order to allow room for improvement of relations.[209] This helps to explain why, when Khrushchev fell in 1964, the Chinese would make one last effort to see if the Sino-Soviet relationship could be salvaged, even though Peking polemics had by that time anathematized the whole Soviet system. More importantly, Khrushchev's role helps to account for the growing obsession of Mao Tse-tung in the early 1960s with the nature of leadership in communist societies and the importance of rearing revolutionary successors, an obsession which, as we shall see,[210] was an important ingredient of the cultural revolution.

The second element is the elevation of the dispute to the ideological plane by the Chinese. This of course raised the stakes and made agreement between Moscow and Peking more difficult, as already argued. It also made it logical, almost inevitable, that as the dispute worsened the Chinese should extend their ideological analysis from the *nature* of the Soviet foreign policy mistakes to the *origins* of those mistakes. Those origins the Chinese traced to the degeneration of Soviet society,[211] and this led Mao to ponder the implications for China. The cultural revolution would be his response.

12 THE END OF THE LEAP

(i) Liu's Hainan seminar

Preoccupation with the Sino-Soviet dispute prevented the Chinese leadership from paying adequate attention to internal affairs during 1960, Mao admitted early the following year.[1] Important domestic matters were shelved by senior leaders and party propagandists preparing for the next round with the Russians.[2] Foreign affairs were the focus of six CC conferences in 1960 and probably a major topic of discussion at other central meetings.[3] The two leading officials of the party secretariat, Teng Hsiao-p'ing and P'eng Chen, spent much of the period from June till early December abroad at international communist meetings, and presumably spent the intervals back in Peking consulting with colleagues on the dispute. One-quarter of all Politburo members in good standing were tied up in Moscow for the month-long 81-party conference.[4]

Yet in the aftermath of the confrontation at Lushan, inattention to the home front seemed unlikely to be a problem. On their mettle as a result of P'eng Teh-huai's criticisms of the leap, Mao, Liu and other leaders appear to have devoted particular attention in late 1959 and early 1960 to acquiring a deeper understanding of economics. Unfortunately, the need to prove P'eng Teh-huai wrong prevented their inquiries from producing more sensible policies, as Mao, Liu and the Kwangtung 1st secretary, T'ao Chu, later acknowledged.[5]

In November 1959, Liu went to Hainan for a month's sick leave in the hope of relieving the agonizing pain of an inflamed shoulder and elbow which had first begun to trouble him during the revolutionary years.[6] Mao had enjoined his colleagues to study economics in order to equip themselves to cope with the problems of the great leap, and so Liu took with him several volumes of the third edition of a Soviet *Text-book on Political Economy* which the Chariman was also reading at about this time.[7] Liu decided to take advantage of his enforced idleness to hold an economics seminar. The participants, along with him and his wife, Wang Kuang-mei, included his secretaries, his doctor, his nurse and his guards, as well as T'ao Chu and other leading Kwangtung provincial officials.[8]

As 'professors', Liu invited along Wang Hsueh-wen, the translator of *Das Kapital*,[9] and Hsueh Mu-ch'iao, Vice Chairman of the State Economic Commission who had recently been relieved of his concurrent posts as Vice Chairman of the State Planning Commission and Director of the State Statistical Bureau.[10] Hsueh's inclusion is striking since his loss of those two jobs has usually been assumed to have signified punishment for defending professionalism in statistical work during the leap,[11] and perhaps for drawing up a catalogue of economics shortcomings and errors for Po I-po to talk about at Lushan.[12] Cultural revolution attacks on Hsueh did not explain his dismissal in that way, but after the death of Mao it was revealed that he had been criticized for circulating an article (perhaps his report to Po) among 'inner circles' on the lessons of the leap. It seems likely that Hsueh's views mirrored Ch'en Yun's, but perhaps they were couched more incautiously.[13] Hsueh probably also had to resign as a result of the humiliating statistical retreat announced after Lushan, to take responsibility, however unjustly, for the State Statistical Bureau's imprimatur on the exaggerated output figures issued for 1958.[14] Hsueh had clearly been reprimanded, but it is inconceivable that Liu would have invited him to Hainan if his errors had been political ones connected with 'right opportunism'. Even less credible are cultural revolution allegations that Liu and Hsueh were deliberately concocting an anti-Mao economic programme at a time when Liu had every reason to wish to retain the Chairman's support for his newly won eminence.[15] But it is likely that imbibing Hsueh's views for a month made Liu readier to change direction later as the post-leap economic crisis deepened.

The seminar began on 10 November.[16] Liu took it very seriously. He was apt to compare studying to a 'boat sailing against the current which must forge ahead or it will be driven back',[17] and in Hainan he used to work into the early hours of the morning. When he found that his nurse was waiting up to give him the treatment he was supposed to have before going to bed, he suggested that she retire at her normal time and allow the guard to waken her when he was ready to put away his books. Yet even during treatment he would keep reading.[18]

Regrettably, the available accounts of the Hainan seminar tell us more about Liu's moral fibre than his intellectual development. We learn that he indignantly refused special food and a cake on his 61st birthday, 24 November,[19] because the party centre had decided against the celebration of the birthdays of Politburo members[20]; but about all that is vouchsafed about his interventions in the seminar is that he expressed disapproval of some of the absurdities thrown up by the system of paying cadres partly in kind which the CCP retained in the cities in the early years after the revolution.[21] (Mao, on the other hand, still hankered after this 'free supply system' as a means of eradicating bourgeois concern for status and moving towards communism.[22])

Allegedly, Hsueh Mu-ch'iao distributed the minutes of the seminar to Sun Yeh-fang and other economists, but an attempt to compile a volume entitled 'On socialist economy', apparently based on the Hainan meetings, came to naught,[23] probably because Mao was issuing his own reading notes on the Soviet volume. At any rate, post-cultural revolution accounts by economists date Liu's emphasis on economic realism from this period,[24] perhaps because he consulted those economists regularly from this time on![25]

It was during his stay in Hainan that Liu must have written to Huang Yen-p'ei explaining that economic development would be the watchword for the 1960s, now that socialist transformation had been largely completed.[26] But even here he did not explain how development would be achieved, except that he clearly anticipated that industrialists and businessmen from the former private sector would play an important role.[27]

(ii) Mao's economic studies

At about the time Liu was holding his seminar down in Hainan, Mao was making his own study of the same Soviet textbook on political economy.[28] His reading notes are peppered with the kind of criticisms of the current Soviet position on revolutionary violence, peaceful transition and war which were to be formally outlined in the Lenin anniversary polemics.[29] But for the most part Mao seemed concerned to bounce his own economic ideas off this manual of Soviet orthodoxy in order to guide his colleagues along the Chinese road which they were painfully hacking out together.

Dissatisfaction with and differences from the Soviet model are stressed: 'In the early stages of Liberation we had no experience of managing the economy of the entire nation. So in the period of the first five-year plan we could do no more than copy the Soviet Union's methods, although we never felt altogether satisfied about it.'[30]

To the Soviet concept of rigidly determined economic stages, each coming to a clear-cut, easily definable end, Mao counterposed his own vision of a world permanently in flux:

'... fully consolidated the collective farm system' it says on page 407. *'Full consolidation'—a phrase to make one uneasy.* The consolidation of anything is relative.... In the universe, on our globe, all things come into being, develop, and pass away ceaselessly. None of them is ever 'fully consolidated'.... It is quite possible that communism will have to pass through a number of different stages. How can we say that once communism has been reached nothing will change, that everything will continue 'fully consolidated'....[31] (Emphasis added.)

Relating this overall concept of flux to economic development, Mao commented that the text 'seems to be unacquainted with the wavelike advances of the development of socialist production and speaks of the development of socialist economy as perfectly linear, free of dips. This is unthinkable. No line of development is straight; it is wave or spiral shaped.'[32] Returning to a favourite theme, he argued that while planned, proportional development was possible in a socialist economy, imbalance never went away:

Balance is relative, imbalance absolute. This is a universal law which I am convinced apples to socialist society. Contradiction and struggle are absolutes; unity, unanimity, and solidarity are transitional, hence relative. The various balances attained in planning are temporary, transitional, and conditional, hence relative.[33]

This was of course the philosophical underpinning of the sangfroid with which Mao had reacted to the ups and downs of the great leap forward, and as one might expect many of the comments in his reading notes reflect post-Lushan, pro-leap revivalism rather than the more conservative views the Chairman had been espousing in the first half of 1959. China's industrialization could be very rapid.[34] Although at one point Mao seemed to express puzzlement as to how this could be achieved,[35] in another passage he asserted firmly that crash programmes were necessary if the advanced industrial nations were to be overtaken.[36] The communes had been created by the people,[37] and should be enlarged.[38] Enthusiasm and the mass movement—'it is for people to act'[39]—were critical; material incentives must not be over-stressed or capitalism would be 'unbeatable!'[40]:

Hard bitter struggle, expanding reproduction, the future prospects of communism—these are what have to be emphasised, not individual material interest. The goal to lead people toward is not 'one spouse, one country house, one automobile, one piano, one television.' This is the road of serving the self, not the society. A 'ten-thousand league journey begins where you are standing.' But if one looks only at the feet without giving thought to the future, then the question is: *What is left of revolutionary excitement and ardor?*[41] (Emphasis added.)

There was but one echo of the caution Mao had displayed in the spring of 1959 when he reiterated the phrase he had borrowed from Ch'en Yun at that time, 'freedom is the recognition of necessity'.[42] However, on this occasion, unlike in April 1959, he added a qualification which greatly diminished the force of the original phrase—'but necessity is not perceived in a glance'.[43]

Unsurprisingly, Mao faulted the Soviet textbook on ideological grounds for its failure to stress the role of the superstructure in the promotion of economic and social change.[44] More interestingly, in a discussion of the law of value, Mao effectively conceded that P'eng Teh-huai's criticisms of the mass steel campaign had been correct—that the losses had outweighed the gains—and that even the leap overall would have to be judged not worth the candle from a narrow, short-term economic viewpoint; 'but the overall long-term view is that there was great value to the (steel) campaign because it opened wide a whole economic construction phase. . . . This enabled us to step up our pace greatly'.[45]

On current and future policies, Mao had disappointingly little to say, but he did reaffirm that 'industry and agriculture should be developed together with priority given to developing heavy industry' in contrast to the flat insistence in the Soviet textbook on priority development for industry. Mao estimated that 90 per cent of steel products in 1960 would be used for heavy industry, 10 per cent for agriculture.[46] Mao also stressed self-reliance, down to the provincial level, as far as possible.[47]

The one major policy issue which Mao appeared anxious to open up for debate was how to handle the population problem—not how to bring the rate of increase under control, but how to deal with an excessively high percentage living in the countryside, 80 per cent in China as compared with 13 per cent in the United

States. Industry would have to be brought to the countryside—this was of course a key element in the great leap—to avoid urban overcrowding. The policy question was: '(D)o we want to keep rural living conditions from falling below that in the cities, keep the two roughly the same, or keep the rural slightly higher than the urban?'[48] (Only the venerable President of Peking University, the economist Ma Yin-ch'u, had the courage, in the face of friendly warnings from Chou En-lai, to reassert publicly at this time that China's population size ought to be controlled[49]; he was roundly criticized for his pains,[50] and dismissed from his university post.[51]

Whatever the growth rate of China's population, Mao gave clear evidence in his speech to the Hangchow conference in March 1960 that he retained some of his fantasies about the level of economic development that the country could achieve, albeit he now projected his vision somewhat further and therefore more safely into the future. By the end of the century, he predicted, China could expect to be producing one ton of steel per capita; even allowing for no increase in population at all between 1960 and 2000, this would have meant a steel output of 650 million tons, a totally unrealistic figure. By 2000, he also anticipated China would be producing anywhere between one and two metric tons of grain per capita; again, even on the impossible assumption that there would be no population increase whatsoever in the interim, this would have meant a grain output of between 650 million and 1,300 million tons, figures barely comprehensible in the light of the forced scaling-down of the output claims for 1958 and 1959.[52]

It was perhaps fortunate, therefore, that the exigencies of the Sino-Soviet dispute prevented the Chairman from taking a day-to-day interest in the economy at this time. The only detailed directive on rural policy he appears to have issued in the 12 months following Khrushchev's visit to Peking was a letter on pig-breeding, dated 11 October 1959.[53] However Mao had already adumbrated an overall policy which was to guide the party in the post-Lushan period.

(iii)   Agriculture as the foundation

As early as the Chengtu conference in March 1958, Mao had pressed for the mechanization of agriculture. Then in April 1959 he had declared that the 'fundamental way out for agriculture lies in mechanisation. Ten years will be needed to achieve this. There will be minor solutions in four years, intermediate ones in seven, and major solutions in ten.' From 1959 to 1962, the 2nd FYP period, China would have to rely mainly on improved farm tools and semi-mechanized implements. Each province, district and county should establish farm tools research stations to devise and try out new implements.[54] Then at the Lushan plenum, Mao laid down that agriculture should be taken as the foundation of the economy when evolving priorities; and he pressed for the creation of a Ministry of Agricultural Machinery.[55] This ministry was in fact set up immediately, and one of Mao's most trusted subordinates, Ch'en Cheng-jen, was put in charge.[56]

In October, the Chairman of the State Economic Commission, Po I-po, justified a drive for the technical transformation of agriculture partly on the ground that more grain and cotton were needed, but more importantly because the great leap had transformed China from a labour-surplus country to a labour-deficit one. Po cited the example of a Hopei commune which had boasted a labour force of 18,958 in 1958, but which in the autumn of that year had lost 2,000 peasants who had gone off to swell the urban industrial work force and another 2,000 who had been reassigned from agricultural tasks to commune-run industry. Some of the latter 2,000 had returned in the spring of 1959—presumably a reflection of the tapering off of the rural steel campaign in the countryside—but the commune was still short of its labour requirements.[57] This was of course but a single example of the massive flow of labour from the countryside to the cities which had led to an increase in the urban labour force from just over 9 million in 1957 to well over 25 million in 1958 and over 28·5 million in 1959.[58]

Another way of looking at the same problem was elaborated later by T'an Chen-lin, who had evidently retained his overseeing role for agriculture. The total rural labour force, full-time and part-time, was over 230 million, the equivalent of something over 200 million full-time working peasants. With a total cultivated acreage of 1,600 million mou, this gave a perfectly adequate ratio of eight mou per peasant. But 20 per cent of the work force could be diverted to water conservancy operations; in the winter of 1959 and spring of 1960, some 70 million people had been involved in such work. Further, T'an estimated that rural subsidiary occupations took away 30 million people, commune industry another 5 million and welfare activities yet another 15 million. Thus the labour force actually engaged in main-line agricultural production was little more than 50 per cent of the total, about 100 million, each peasant on average having responsibility for 15 mou. If one then factored into the equation the information that each peasant worked only 300 days on average, this gave a ratio of 20 work days per cultivated mou and only 14–15 work days per sown mou, a quite inadequate figure if all the injunctions of the 'eight character constitution' were to be implemented.[59] Mechanization was the only answer to the problem, T'an indicated, and he reaffirmed Mao's four/seven/ten year programme.[60]

The precise tasks for those three periods were spelled out by the new minister, Ch'en Cheng-jen. Revealing that machinery was used on only 5 per cent of the cultivated acreage, he stated that the four-year minor solution would encompass a small degree of mechanization of farming and animal husbandry and 'basic' mechanization of irrigation and drainage. With the growth of the agricultural machinery industry, within seven years mechanization might be achieved for half the country's cultivated land. In approximately ten years, the whole countryside would be basically mechanized and would have achieved a certain level of electrification.[61]

But while the agricultural mechanization policy was elaborated and acted upon immediately after Lushan and in the months that ensued, the more general policy of 'taking agriculture as the foundation and coordinating the task of giving priority to the development of heavy industry and the task of rapidly developing agriculture' was not announced until Li Fu-ch'un, the Chairman of the State Planning Commission, summed up the economic achievements of 1959 and set the tasks for 1960 in a New Year article in the *People's Daily*. One reason for the delay may have been a wish to avoid saddling cadres with a brand-new policy at a time when their principal preoccupation was supposed to be attacking right opportunism; however, that campaign appears to have been wound up at the end of 1959, perhaps because the leadership felt that a 1960 leap would be better served by a positive campaign in its favour than a negative one against dissidents which only recalled problems. In addition, the leadership may have thought it advisable to give cadres a breathing space to get over the shock of the statistical exaggerations before launching a new economic policy.[62]

Be that as it may, Li described taking agriculture as the foundation as a 'conspicuously' new policy,[63] and revealed that its novelty was not pleasing to 'some comrades' who saw rapid agricultural development undermining the priority hitherto accorded heavy industry. Li went to some lengths to argue the complementarity of agricultural and industrial growth in an effort to dispel the gloom of such orthodox Stalin-style industrializers.[64]

In his article, Li announced that the targets of the 2nd FYP, first outlined at the party's 8th Congress in 1956, had been fulfilled or over-fulfilled in the first two years of the plan, 1958–9. New targets could therefore be set for the final three years of the plan 'at considerably higher levels', although Li was not bold enough to suggest what these should be. Li also claimed that the industrial targets set at the 8th plenum in August had been achieved—steel production for instance had reached 13 million tons compared with the 12 million ton target—but he made no such claim for agriculture which had suffered 'such serious natural calamities as had rarely been seen in the past several decades', with over one-third of the cultivated land affected. From the way he phrased himself, Li seemed to be indicating that the 1959 grain output was around the 2nd FYP target of 250 million tons rather than the 8th plenum target of 275 million tons but when the official figure—270·05 million tons—was issued three weeks later, it was not far short of the latter target.[65] None of these figures remotely corresponded to reality, it would be revealed years later.

Characteristically,[66] Li stressed that the 1960 leap should be achieved in a proportionate manner as well as at a high speed.[67] But the title—'Greeting the new forward leap in 1960'—and the general tenor of his article could only have encouraged cadres to believe that the Lushan reassertion of great leap attitudes and methods was to persist in the new year. Li underlined the importance of mass movements 'on a large scale', called on all heavy industry departments to carry out capital construction 'on a gigantic scale', and demanded a continuing struggle against rightism in all enterprises.[68]

The renewal of the leap articulated by Li Fu-ch'un was reflected in literature. In a short story entitled 'Try and catch me', published in 1960, the veteran author Sha T'ing described the keen competition between production brigades to win the monthly accolade of launching a 'satellite', or sputnik, precisely the system of emulation which led to exaggeration and about which peasants had protested to P'eng Teh-huai:

Since the competition began, people had gotten more and more excited by it; the desire to win glory had grown more powerful. In these relatively large-scale end-of-month competitions, if one administrative district suffered a demotion, there were always some people who did not take the verdict well. Last spring, when Shih-men dropped from 'airplane' to 'oxcart' in the competition, Old Lady Teng had broken into sobs. But Lung Wei-ling had encouraged her, full of confidence, saying 'Why cry? We can get up and try again!'[69]

The language of the party branch secretary, Lung Wei-ling, of the pace-setting Shih-men brigade was redolent of the high tide of 1958:

As he walked he discussed strategy with his comrades in a loud, clear voice. His words were military: 'strategic point', 'battle front', 'concentrate our firepower', and so on. He had never been to war, but he understood nonetheless that they were engaged in struggle with Nature itself. Ever since the Great Leap Forward, just about all rural cadres had talked about crop production this way.[70]

Real-life Lung Wei-lings were encouraged by the more left-wing provincial 1st secretaries, like Wu Chih-p'u of path-breaking Honan, to revive their faith in the communes as being much more powerful than the old APCs and thus able 'more effectively (to) fight natural calamities and transform and conquer nature'.[71] Wu's reappearance as a contributor to *Red Flag* was in itself a sign of the times. Probably the most headstrong of all the provincial leaders during the high tide of the leap, he had discreetly refrained from writing for the party journal during 1959—or had been sidelined by editor Ch'en Po-ta—only to reappear twice in its pages in 1960. Those were to be his final contributions, for the mood of the post-leap years was not sympathetic to men of Wu's stamp, and indeed Wu himself was replaced as Honan 1st secretary. But on 1 January 1960, Wu was still able to extol the collectivist achievements of Honan: 29·8 per cent of all production brigades practising the free food supply system; 46·9 per cent practising the free food grain supply system; 19·1 per cent practising the free basic food grain supply system or the free partial food grain supply system; 4·2 per cent practising the wage plus free supply system. In all, free supply accounted for 40 per cent of total distribution to commune members.[72] The extent to which Wu

Chih-p'u was again striving to make Honan into a sputnik province is illustrated by the fact that over the whole country, the average amount distributed as free supply accounted for only 20–30 per cent of the total income of commune members.[73]

Illustrative of how men like Wu had been on the defensive during the earlier part of 1959 was his account of a 'very typical example' of the 'struggle between the two roads' in which a production brigade had assigned individual families full responsibility for the provision of labour and for production.[74] The writer Wang Wen-shih described the identical situation far more graphically in a story about the post-Lushan struggle in a village in the autumn of 1959:

In production, they pushed the individual contract system against the collectivisation movement, which led many commune members to revert to their capitalist frame of mind, all bent on doing some market speculating to get rich quick. Nobody bothered about the collectivised fields, even when the weeds there had grown taller than the planted crop. Yen Tzu-yü and his gang didn't stop at that; they further planned to assign the draft animals and tools permanently to the members' households, thus virtually splitting up the commune.[75]

It was at the point that the hero of the story began his successful counter-attack.

The real-life counter-attack in Honan went overboard, even according to cultural revolution accounts which naturally applauded attacks upon P'eng Teh-huai and right opportunism. Such accounts admitted that in Honan during the autumn of 1959 good cadres had been wrongly branded as 'guilty of serious rightist deviation'. Wu Chih-p'u's successor as Honan 1st secretary, Liu Chien-hsun, was far more condemnatory, describing the movement against the right opportunists as a 'brutal struggle and a ruthless blow', in which 'each and everybody were in a state of danger and fathers and mothers and husbands and wives dared not speak to each other'.[76] According to one post-cultural revolution account, the movement caused the people of the province to suffer 'even more serious difficulties'. Another such account refers to a serious incident taking place in Hsinyang district in 1960 as a result of excessive purchases of grain.[77] During his visit to Honan in April 1960, Liu Shao-ch'i attempted to inject realism into Wu Chih-p'u and his colleagues. He warned against underestimating difficulties and excessive egalitarianism.[78] But in view of Honan's later problems, it is questionable how effective he was. Recalling this period in late 1961, T'ao Chu remarked:

It was not till March 1959 that the Chairman discovered that we could not have a 'gust of communist wind', but should operate on a system of three-level ownership. *If we had done that*, things would have been different today, the time for acquiring experience would have been shortened, and the price we paid would have been smaller. Why didn't we carry on that way? Because of the appearance of Marshal P'eng Teh-huai at the Lushan conference. After that the campaign against the 'left' became one against the right.[79] (Emphasis added.)

Yet by the early months of 1960, despite the militant and militaristic bravado of the renewed leap, it was already apparent that the food situation was not improving. By May, the sympathetic but not uncritical Soviet scientific adviser Mikhail Klochko observed that

it was well known that the monthly ration of meat per adult was only four ounces, and that the authorities invited people voluntarily to renounce these miserable portions so that they could be allotted to workers engaged in particularly strenuous physical labour. It was also common knowledge that flour and rice rations had been reduced and that, in some parts of the south, the rice ration was partly or entirely replaced by corn. Candy and gingerbread, sold freely in the Peking markets in 1958, could be purchased only in the lobbies of deluxe hotels. The easy availability of fruits and vegetables was only a dream and the allowances for cotton goods had been cut by almost 50%.[80]

It was such conditions that led some provincial officials to send gifts of food to central leaders. Chou En-lai, for instance, was sent some fish, but ordered his general office to telephone the solicitous officials of criticize them for an action which suggested that a man in his position should be given special status and privileges.[81] Liu Shao-ch'i reportedly was a stickler for observing the rates for living expenses laid down by the CC general office.[82] At this time the daily food allowance for top leaders was set at 2·40 yuan.[83] The only supplement permitted was from homegrown produce. Liu's secretaries planted vegetables beside his office in his house in the Chungnanhai; Liu himself planted kidney beans with his guards. Chu Teh and his wife, who lived nearby, were noted among other things for their pumpkins.[84]

Despite this personal acquaintance with the hardships of daily life, the Chinese leadership was not deflected from its goal of a third year of leaping progress. Perhaps in the spring it was felt that the shortages were a legacy of the bad weather of 1959 and that better luck in 1960 would restore the brief abundance of late 1958. At any rate, the annual session of the NPC which opened on 29 March called for 10 per cent increases in grain and cotton output and a 35 per cent increase in the number of pigs, possibly a reflection of the interest expressed by Mao the previous autumn.[85]

Moreover, the Twelve-Year Agricultural Programme was dusted off, reaffirmed and solemnly adopted by the NPC. It contained only one significant change from the previous draft, the substitution of bed bugs for sparrows among the four pests to be eliminated; this was to rectify the disastrous error of sparrow-cide committed in 1958 which had permitted the insect pests normally eaten by sparrows to flourish. Even the major change-over in the countryside from APCs to communes was not reflected in this final version, so that the document had a somewhat shop-worn air. It was as if the Politburo had decided that some banner had to wave over the third leap year, but no one had the patience to revise the programme in the light of the production and organizational achievements claimed for 1958–9, because faith in the latter had been so badly shaken.[86]

(iv) Urban communes

In the cities, the main symbol of the revived leap was the urban commune. There had been some experiments with communes in the cities in 1958, but they had been shelved at the CC's 6th plenum at the end of that year. Popular opposition among city dwellers to the innovation was clearly a factor. In the aftermath of Lushan, that opposition was set aside.

Urban communes developed on three patterns, according to their focus: around factories, around government organizations or schools, or around residential areas. Size varied, but 20,000–30,000 people appeared to be an average population. As in the case of the rural communes, propagandists argued that a principal advantage of the new organization was the rational mobilization of new labour power, particularly women freed by communal mess halls and kindergartens, to work in small 'factories' using discarded materials to supply parts to regular factories or to produce articles for daily use. Commune concerns included a wide range of welfare and service activities. Wages could comprise free supply. Unlike in the countryside, commune boundaries often cut across urban administrative divisions, which might have caused a problem had the urban experiment continued long.[87]

In one respect the urban communes duplicated the rural ones: they were depicted in lyrical terms as the solution to the economic, social and personal problems of their members. Even the traditional tension between mother-in-law and daughter-in-law could evaporate. In one of the earliest urban communes, originally set up in 1958, almost inevitably in the capital of Honan province, Chengchow, 30,000 paeans of praise were written to the new organization. One of them read:

> The people's commune is a flower in full bloom;
> Its fragrance is wafted to ten thousand homes.
> Working together we laugh, carefree;
> Again and again we say:
> The Party leads well. The commune has great strength.[88]

(v) The Anshan charter

Urban leftism was not confined to communes. It permeated industry, and must be directly attributed to Mao. During the Lushan conference, officials of Anshan, China's principal steel centre, located in the north-eastern industrial province of Liaoning, submitted a report opposing rightism, advocating a great leap forward, and submitting a high but feasible target. Mao later recalled that the CC 'was extremely happy when it read this report'. The chairman himself must have been particularly pleased to have had this authoritative backing for the leap shortly after P'eng Teh-huai's slashing attack on it. The report was immediately telephoned to various parts of the country to assist in the anti-right opportunist struggle and Mao instructed Anshan: 'Oppose the rightist deviation; go all out. Now is the hour; do not lose the opportunity, it may not occur again'.[89] Later at the same conference he strongly commended the speed with which Liaoning had responded to this directive.[90]

One of the most enthusiastic implementers of the new line for industry was apparently Po I-po, perhaps over-compensating for almost committing the right opportunist sin of denouncing the great leap. After Lushan, 'he set high targets, blindly issued directives and resorted to exaggeration in a big way'. As part of this effort, he issued the slogan for 1960: 'Let the beginning of the year be crowned with achievements' (literally, 'Let the gates open up to redness').[91] He capped this by calling for 'sharp rises' in production to crown every day and every month with achievements. Allegedly, the coal industry suffered severely as a result of these policies and output declined considerably in the second half of 1960, 'thus bringing serious losses to the national economy and the livelihood of the people'.[92]

But the flagship was still iron and steel. Backyard steel had basically been abandoned, but the plan was still to increase steel production by over 37 per cent. The method was to transform 'small, native, and mass-(run)' iron and steel plants into 'small, modern/foreign, and mass-(run)' ones; in other words to consolidate and upgrade backyard furnaces where possible or to substitute more modern equipment where not. This process, according to the speech of the Minister of the Metallurgical Industry, Wang Ho-shou, at the 1960 NPC on 10 April, was 'like a rising sun in the east, full of energy and with a bright future'. According to his statistics, the two types of small plants between them had produced half of the country's iron ore in 1959. The small, modern plants had supplied 4 million tons of pig iron, steel and steel products to the rural areas, in addition to supplying the larger plants with pig iron. The steel from one such plant cited by Wang had apparently been good enough to be used in the manufacture of sowing and sawing machines and 'native lathes', as well as barrows, picks, hammers, spades, ploughs and harrows.[93]

Wang admitted inefficiencies, such as an excessive use of manual labour, but rejected the criticism that small plants could only be a short-term solution. The 'hundreds of thousands' of small modern plants were still too few and it was necessary in the next few years to mobilize the masses continually, to set up more, both modern *and native*.[94] Unlikely as it might seem in the light of the 1958 experience and the Lushan decision, the minister appeared to be contemplating another mass steel drive. In the event, no such drive took place, but Wang was clearly exploiting the new atmosphere to restore some of the face he had lost as a result of his defeat at the hands of Ch'en Yun the previous summer.

Wang Ho-shou did not confine his advocacy of the mass movement to small iron and steel plants. He talked also of the 'large, modern, and mass' principle in the iron and steel industry. In order for the major steel plants to operate in line with the policy of 'more, faster, better, and more economically', it was necessary

for them to strive for them to strive harder 'to abolish all superstitions, emancipate their ideology, and vigorously carry out
the mass movement'.[95]

Wang's admonitions would seem to have been directly inspired
by comments made by Mao three weeks earlier concerning further developments at Anshan. The municipal committee there had
now submitted a report on technical innovation and technological
revolution in industry. It would appear that part of this report
consisted of proposals for a system of management radically different from Anshan's current, conventional one, which was modelled on the Magnitogorsk iron and steel plant in the Soviet
Union.[96] The basic principles of the new system were: strengthening party leadership, placing politics in command; launching
mass movements; 'participating in two, transforming one, and
combining three' or functionaries taking part in productive
labour and workers taking part in management, revising irration-
al and outdated rules and regulations, and functionaries, workers
and technicians working in close cooperation; a vigorous technological revolution.[97] Commenting on this on 22 March,[98]
Mao dubbed the new system the 'Charter of the Anshan Iron and
Steel Company' (*An Kang Hsien-fa*), which had 'emerged in the
Far East, in China'.[99] Elsewhere he wrote about striking down the
'superstitions' connected with the Magnitogorsk constitution.[100]

During the cultural revolution, considerable criticism was levelled at 'capitalist-roaders', particularly Po I-po, for suppressing the
Anshan charter and substituting the 70 Articles on Industry
(promulgated in late 1961).[101] The truth appears to have been
less sinister, and to have reflected precisely that overcommit-
ment to the conduct of the Sino-Soviet dispute which Mao himself later admitted led to a neglect of domestic affairs.

After Mao's favourable comments on the Anshan charter, the
People's Daily prepared some commentaries in order to publicize
its principles. The paper's editor-in-chief, Wu Leng-hsi, was busy
working on the drafts of the Lenin anniversary polemics against
Moscow and did not get around to approving them for publication. In June, at a conference on the machine industry in
Shanghai, Wu asked Teng Hsiao-p'ing for instructions on how to
propagate the Anshan charter. Teng stated that there was no
urgency about the matter since everyone was concentrating on the
struggle against Soviet revisionism. He apparently added that, anyway, there were problems connected with the charter.[102] There is

no evidence as to what problems Teng had in mind, but if, for instance, he had voiced opposition to the mass movement in industry, Wu would certainly have had to reveal as much in his cultural revolution confession. Moreover, the evidence suggests that even without the universalization of the Anshan 'model', party officials were well aware of the importance of encouraging its basic principles elsewhere.

T'ao Chu lauded a photochemical plant in Swatow, whose success he attributed in large measure to the raising of the workers' political consciousness and an avoidance of a one-sided stress on material incentives. He emphasized that its outstanding results had been achieved without the assistance of experts; the 'heaven-storming zeal' of the workers and staff had enabled them to make successive technological breakthroughs.[103] The party secretary of the steel plant at Paotow, one of China's principal steel centres, emphasized the importance of politics taking command and unleashing the mass movement.[104] At some point, Chou En-lai praised the Ta Ch'ing oil-field for putting Anshan principles into practice.[105]

But the abrupt withdrawal of Soviet experts in July–August, and the setbacks to the 1960 leap, forced China's leaders to reappraise industrial policy. The Anshan charter was evidently a casualty of that process; and no cultural revolution source has ever suggested that Mao fought for its retention in the dark days of 1961.

(vi) Trusts

Another policy proposal which appears to have foundered in the wake of the Soviet withdrawal was made by Liu Shao-ch'i on 10 June at the Shanghai on-the-spot conference on the machine industry.[106] He called for the formation of industrial trusts (*t'o-la-ssu*), but nothing appears to have come of this suggestion until 1963–4.[107]

During the cultural revolution, Liu came under fire for this idea, but it is not clear that the original proposal was seriously out of line with Mao's own thinking at the time. Liu's words were: 'One must organise trusts, multiple-product factories (*tsung-ho-hsing kung-ch'ang*) and integrated complexes (*lien-ho ch'i-yeh*). This is also a reform in production relations.'[108] At the height of the great leap in September 1958, Mao had stated in Wuhan that large enterprises like the steel plant in that city 'could gradually be transformed into multiple-product integrated complexes' (*tsung-ho-hsing-ti lien-ho ch'i-yeh*). In the case of the Wuhan plant, Mao felt that apart from iron and steel it could manufacture machines and chemicals, and go in for construction. Evidently with the rural communes as a model, he added that such plants could also embrace agriculture, commerce, education and military affairs (presumably a militia).[109]

The seriousness with which this directive was taken and followed through is illustrated by the already cited article by the party secretary of the Paotow steel plant. While he was up-to-date in his stress on the importance of the mass movement in large, modern enterprises, his main purpose was to demonstrate how faithfully Paotow had implemented Mao's earlier instructions.[110]

The difference between the multiple-product companies which both Mao and Liu mentioned and the trusts which are attributed only to Liu is that the former are examples of horizontal integration—Mao-style conglomerates—the latter of vertical integration. As developed later in the 1960s, trusts involved bringing whole industries or trades under unified management.[111] But there was no a priori reason why vertical integration should not embrace the out-reach aspects of the multi-purpose enterprises which Mao had advocated in September 1958; a steel plant could run the coal mine which supplied it with raw material. Nor is there any a priori reason why horizontal integration should be more proletarian than vertical integration. Finally, there is no evidence from cultural revolution sources or elsewhere that Mao criticized the trust proposal when Liu articulated it first in 1960. The chairman may well have supported it. Whether he still felt the same way later in the 1960s will be examined in the projected final volume of this study.

(vii) Cultivating the capitalists

Despite the general leftward drift in CCP urban and industrial policy in late 1959 and early 1960, in one important respect the party manifested a realism which could have been, and was subsequently, described as rightist. This was in its policy towards the merchants and industrialists who had been bought out in 1956, their firms transformed into joint state-private companies.[112] There are clear hints in cultural revolution sources that Mao himself approved of and perhaps initiated the new line, but Liu Shao-ch'i was the principal articulator and was in due course blamed for it.[113]

Liu Shao-ch'i was an appropriate man for the job. His ambivalence towards Mao's liberalizing line in 1957 would have been remembered, as well as the role he played, along with P'eng Chen, in bringing that experiment to a close and launching the anti-rightist campaign.[114] Whereas Mao and Chou En-lai were viewed by the bourgeoisie as national leaders who attempted to bridge the gap between party and non-party personnel, Liu Shao-ch'i was probably seen more as the archetypical high functionary of the party whose principal concern was to preserve the purity of its ideology and to protect the interests of its members. Sadly for Liu, even after he became head of state his natural reserve suggested aloofness, and his fall, when it occurred in 1966, would be accepted as a matter of party rather than national concern. But precisely because he was distanced from non-party people, his reassurances to them in early 1960 must have seemed more important than if they had been delivered by, say, Chou En-lai.

The Chinese bourgeoisie were troubled and anxious at this time as a result of the experiences they had undergone in recent years. In 1957, they had responded to Mao's call to criticize the party and been denounced as rightists. In 1958, they had effectively been shunted aside as the CCP turned to mobilization of the masses as the key to economic development. In 1959, they witnessed the attack on the right opportunists and the right deviation in economic work with mounting concern. According to the later account of the party official most closely in touch with them—Li Wei-han, then head of the CC's United Front Work Department (UFWD)—'(i)deologically disturbed, they doubted the superiority of the socialist system and particularly feared that the inner-party rectification and anti-rightist struggle might spread outside the party and that the counter-attack in 1957 against the bourgeois rightists would be repeated'.[115]

Liu's first post-Lushan attempt to set at ease the minds of the bourgeoisie had been the summoning of an SSC. The SSC was the body created under the constitution for the head of state to call together both communists and non-communists for the discussion of major policy issues; it had been used by Mao as a means of informing non-party people of what had been decided by the CC and thus to alert them to forthcoming policy changes. Liu's first SSC was held on 24 August 1959. Chou En-lai briefed the audience on the revisions in the economic plan and on the need to oppose the right deviation. Liu himself spoke generally on the domestic and international situation.[116] But it was a measure of the uncertainty with which Liu was still regarded in non-communist circles, as well as the preponderant prestige of Mao, that only three weeks later the Chairman had to call an ad hoc meeting of the same kind of people to exchange views on essentially the same topics.[117]

Liu's next effort at reassurance was his letter of 29 November to Huang Yen-p'ei, Chairman of the China Democratic National Construction Association (CDNCA), one of the two major organizations in which businessmen were grouped. Apart from stating his personal commitment to economic growth rather than ideological change in the decade ahead, Liu expressed the conviction that the overwhelming majority of businessmen would be able to transform their thinking provided 'they adopt the honest attitude of acknowledging facts' and 'they make subjective efforts and seriously study Marxism-Leninism'.[118]

The CCP could not afford an uneasy 'business community'. Led by Mao, the CCP was now putting great stress on technical innovation and technological revolution.[119] The essential feature of the revived leap was the change of commitment from 'native'-type industry to modern industry, albeit mobilized on 'mass' lines. Critical to the success of that shift of emphasis was the assistance of bourgeois industrialists and technicians. They had to be calmed and enlisted. So, two weeks after Liu's letter, presumably at the instigation of Li Wei-han, the CDNCA and the other major businessmen's organization, the All-China Federation of Industry and Commerce (ACFIC), held congresses in Peking. They lasted a full two months, starting on 16 December 1959, and concluding with formal sessions from 19 to 21 February 1960, at which a document drawn up on the basis of earlier discussions was passed.[120]

At first all had not gone well. 'Being nervous, many representatives put the texts of their speeches in their pockets and were ready to show their support and make self-criticisms at the congresses so that they would be able to pass the test.' Li Wei-han, it would seem, then suggested that the two congresses should be held jointly and practise the principles of the 'three selfs' and the 'three nots': raise questions by oneself, analyse problems by oneself and solve problems by oneself; not seizing on others' faults, not putting labels on people, and not using big sticks. But in view of the 'ideological misgivings of people in industrial and commercial circles', Liu Shao-ch'i was brought in to reinforce the reassuring message which Li Wei-han and the UFWD were trying to convey.[121]

On 11 February, Liu instructed a Politburo conference to adopt a positive attitude towards the work and development of the bourgeoisie: 'We still have three years before we do away with fixed interest in 1962. Within those three years, we must do a good job, adopt a positive attitude and some positive measures.'[122] According to another account, he said that since the bourgeoisie was 'drawing closer' (*k'ao-lung*) to the party, the party should draw a bit closer to them.[123]

The following day, Liu received members of the standing committees of the CDNCA and ACFIC.[124] From Li Wei-han's later account it would appear that the essence of the speech Liu made on this occasion was the offer of a trade-off: businessmen should 'pay attention to remoulding themselves and serving the people' while the state should 'satisfy the industrial and commercial circles with material benefits'.[125] But in fact Liu's speech contained few concrete promises on this score.

When the businessmen had been hustled into joint state-private firms in 1956, the sweetener had been that they would be bought out with the payment of 'dividends' over the course of seven years, 1956–62. During the 1957 rectification campaign, some bold souls had suggested that the payments should be extended to 12 years but they were denounced.[126] The brief report available of Liu's remarks to the Politburo indicates that there was no room for manoeuvre on this question. He indicated as much to the businessmen, but yet contrived to hint at rethinking:

What will result from the abolition of dividends? We haven't thought of that, but you industrialists and businessmen have . . . . (O)n this question Chairman Mao himself has directed that dividends . . . . should be abolished in 1962. But at the present time they have not been abolished, and if necessary, changes may be made. We haven't studied this, but you may think about it. There is still time for changes to be made. . . . It may be difficult to settle this, but settled it must be.[127]

Linked to the dividends issue was the question of the high salaries received by businessmen. From Liu's remarks, it is clear that some of his audience entertained hopes that their salaries would be raised to compensate for the loss of dividends. Liu disabused them: 'The high salaries which some are receiving will not be reduced but, I am afraid, they will not be increased either.' All he would promise was that any reductions in salary caused by job transfers would be made good. On retirement benefits, for which there was no official provision, Liu pledged that the state would take care of all collaborative businessmen. The current 'temporary' arrangements under which businessmen who could no longer work simply took leave while continuing to draw the same salaries would remain in force for the moment.[128]

Basically Liu was asking businessmen to take the party's intentions on trust: 'The state will be responsible for you whether you are old or sick or have other problems. On this point, you may set your minds at rest. Concrete measures will be devised; and in the last resort you will be taken care of. There is no need to worry.'[129]

The desired quid pro quo was a continuing change in the world view of businessmen, achieved by gentle means, so that they could accept socialism gladly. It was necessary for them to subordinate their personal interests to the collective interest; 'subordinating everything to the greatest interest of the greatest number—this is the fundamental requirement', was Liu's Utilitarian dictum.[130] Voicing a deeply held personal conviction, Liu argued that it was precisely by taking care of the larger interest that one's personal interests would be best served in the long run.[131]

Since there was no real indication from the content of Liu's speech that the CCP had adopted a new line towards businessmen, one can only assume that the friendly attitude adopted by him and Li Wei-han unmistakably conveyed reassurance that they were not to become targets of the campaign against rightism. And though there was no promise of a maintenance of dividends after 1962, Li Wei-han may have indicated privately that the ending of those payments would at least result in the removal of businessmen's capitalist label; certainly during the cultural revolution it was alleged that Liu had instructed Li in 1960 to draw up a plan for eliminating the capitalist class by 1962.[132] What Liu was apparently not prepared to contemplate was the large-scale induction of reformed businessmen into the CCP; that, he told his brother-in-law, a businessmen, would undermine their influence with foreigners.[133] Presumably Liu meant that the image of China as a state in which communists and capitalists collaborated with profit both to themselves and their country was more appealing abroad than the more monolithic image of the one-party state presented by the Soviet Union.

But even without the prospect of party membership dangling before them, businessmen had received sufficient encouragement to galvanize them into a frenzy of planning at national and local level as to how best to fulfil their side of the political bargain.[134] And the leaders of the CDNCA and the ACFIC were inspired to send a message to Mao in language that smacked of the Lord's Prayer:

For our mistakes and shortcomings, we have been given firm guidance and earnest help, so that we can continually increase our awareness and confidence, destroy bourgeois [thought] and establish socialist thought [instead], and so that we can continue to go onward. Dear Chairman Mao, the party and you are like parents in your affection for us. The party and you are like teachers to us. We cannot find the appropriate words to express our gratitude to you and love for the party and you . . . . We shout with joy for the dazzling future of socialism and communism in the great motherland. We feel that we are fortunate indeed to be able to enjoy with the people of the nation a happy existence under socialism and communism which is improving day by day. We are proud to be living in the era of Mao Tse-tung.[135]

The sycophancy of this message was presumably a measure of the relief of the men who composed it; and it was as well that chairman and party earned their gratitude early in 1960. After the withdrawal of the Soviet technicians, the expertise of China's one-time capitalists would become even more crucial. But if the CCP had made its overtures to them only then, the impact would have been greatly diminished.

(viii) Educational reform

The contrast between the anxieties of China's businessmen and the relatively understanding manner in which the CCP was able to deal with them points up the schizophrenia of Chinese political life in the final year of the leap. The recycled euphoria of 1958 mingled with a persisting realism from the first half of 1959. The mixture made for complexity and confusion in 1960. This was noticeable in the cultural sphere as well as the economic.

In education, the swing to the right in early 1959 had meant a re-emphasis on quality. At a long-drawn-out national education work conference which began in January of that year, propaganda chief Lu Ting-yi admitted that there had been mistakes in the 'great' educational developments of 1958 due to 'feverish headiness and inept ideological methods': 'What has happened to cultural and educational work in the great leap forward? Speaking on the whole it was a great leap; speaking specifically, some have leapt, others not, and still others retrogressed.'[136] He stressed educational improvement (*kai-liang*) rather than reform (*kai-ko*),[137] levelling up rather than down,[138] and the cultivation of centres of excellence.[139] Education Minister Yang Hsiu-feng told the 1959 NPC that middle and primary schools had to concentrate their 'utmost efforts to enhance the quality of the teaching of basic disciplines in order to lay a firm foundation for cultural and scientific knowledge';[140] and later in the year, Lu Ting-yi told provincial cultural and education officials that in some place it would be preferable not to set up a primary school than to have a rough and ready one.[141]

The January–March 1959 education conference evidently prompted much re-thinking in pedagogical circles which in turn gave birth to the 1960 educational reform proposals.[142] Despite Lushan and the revival of leap forward attitudes, quality was still stressed. Explaining the proposals to the 1960 NPC, both Lu Ting-yi and Yang Hsiu-feng admitted that standards of instruction in mathematics and foreign languages had fallen since 1949; indeed 'much of the mathematics, physics, and chemistry now taught in middle schools, in particular, is old stuff from the nineteenth century which in no way represents the science and technology of today'.[143] Methods of improving the situation were proposed.

But despite the stress on quality in the speeches of their proponents, the reforms themselves seemed likely to produce the opposite result. The principal element in the proposals was to reduce the current 12-year primary-secondary educational cycle to ten years. Already experiments had been conducted into various ways of achieving this, and Peking Normal (Teachers) University had even suggested that a nine-year cycle was possible. Yet despite a reduction of two to three years in the period of schooling, Lu Ting-yi averred that it would be possible to raise the standard of high-school graduates to the level currently achieved at the end of the first year of university.

The motivation behind the proposals reflected the lopsided economics of the leap. The massive expansion of small-scale industry and the haemorrhage of peasants to the cities continued to confront Chinese economic planners with the problem of a shortage of labour. The education reforms were designed to speed up the entry of Chinese school children into the labour market. Lu Ting-yi explained the situation bluntly:

Why do we advocate 'approximately ten years'? Because it takes ten years for children who start schooling at six or seven years of age to grow to the age of sixteen or seventeen, when they will be considered as full manpower units.... (A)ll students in our present senior middle schools now are full manpower units. For this reason we cannot afford to extend our present senior middle school education to too many persons.... Should we try to increase we would take away too much manpower from production.[144]

But if the economy demanded earlier entry of school-leavers into the labour market, logic would have seemed to dictate that a higher proportion of the shortened schooling cycle would be devoted to class work. This would have meant a reduction in the hours devoted to physical labour as a result of the 1958 reforms. In early 1959, on average primary school children were spending four hours a week doing manual jobs, junior middle school children six hours and senior middle school children eight. In the aftermath of the retreat at the Wuhan plenum, officials were prepared to entertain the idea that the introduction of physical labour might have affected the quality of teaching and learning; students and teachers were reminded that the main purpose of schools was study.[145]

But in the aftermath of the revival initiated at the Lushan plenum, those warnings were forgotten, and Chinese leaders reaffirmed their commitment to leap forward values. In October 1959, Liu Shao-ch'i looked forward to a time when education and manual labour would be meshed, when factories would turn out university students, teachers, engineers and cadres.[146] Lu Ting-yi spoke in February 1960 of the withering away of the agricultural middle schools spawned by the leap, but he saw them being replaced by full-time junior middle schools in which education and labour were inextricably linked.[147] And Lu and Yang Hsiu-feng informed the 1960 NPC that more manual labour was needed in schools not less. The reduction in class hours would have to be made up by extra homework.[148]

Post-Lushan revivalism had other effects in the educational sphere. It gave a boost to the enrolment of the children of workers and peasants in universities. In the class of 1960 at Peking University, the proportion was 61 per cent.[149] The Soviet chemist Klochko came across a 16-year-old former cleaner from the Kunming Academy of Sciences who had been made a research worker at the city's Institute of Metallurgy and Ceramics; she spent most of her time playing ball games with men.[150] At a local teacher training college, he saw a beginners' class in organic chemistry writing their own textbook as they went along.[151]

Mao attempted to ensure that the professors of such students should not adopt airs and graces by ordering that there should be no academic prizes or doctorates.[152] Klochko's observations in the first half of 1960 suggest that there was little danger of that. A senior Chinese colleague at the Academy of Sciences in Peking was kept busy as foreman in charge of the 40 members of his institute's staff who ran its pigsties.[153] Although more scientists were working in the laboratory or at their desks than in 1958, 'it was still by and large true that the higher a man's training and the more responsible his position, the more time he was forced to waste at meetings'.[154] At Peking's Geological Institute, Klochko found laboratory staff engaged in political discussion in the middle of a Mondy morning, whereas hitherto that activity had been confined to the end of the week; one reason may have been their lack of understanding of the equipment which was standing idle.[155] Klochko's overall assessment was that the state of Chinese science was lamentable.[156] But the cultural revolutionaries, praising the surge of technological revolution and technical innovation in 1960, later referred to the whole of the three-year period of the leap as the 'great educational revolution'.[157]

(ix) Ideological cross-currents

In the more strictly ideological realm as well, the post-Lushan period appears to have been a time of confusion. In this case it was not that one official was attempting to combine irreconcilable objectives into a single policy (as with Lu Ting-yi in education), but rather that different leaders were pursuing contradictory policies. There do not seem to have been any major confrontations, but it was now that the later commanders of the cultural revolution began to take up positions. The point of divergence was attitude towards Mao's thought and works.

The agreed position adopted by the Politburo at the time of the CCP's 8th Congress was that reference to the Thought of

Mao Tse-tung should be dropped from the party constitution. Party propagandists were told instead to refer to Comrade Mao Tse-tung's works.[158] The question arose again in the context of a post-Lushan decision to push the study of Mao's writings, presumably to counter the impact of P'eng Teh-huai and in anticipation of the publication of the fourth volume of his *Selected Works* in the autumn. The 1956 position was maintained by the CC's propaganda department when in January 1960 it approved a YCL document, apparently also passed by Liu Shao-ch'i and Teng Hsiao-p'ing, on the study of Mao's writings.[159] The position of the YCL 1st secretary, Hu Yao-pang, was that the use of the term 'Mao's thought' was inevitable, but that it should not appear all the time.[160] In fact, the study of Mao's works was hampered at this time by a shortage of copies due to paper rationing; priority was accorded to school texts.[161]

Two months later, a propaganda department report on this topic warned against the vulgarization of Mao's works; an example cited appears to have had to do with the attribution to them of achievements in health work.[162] An article by a table tennis player on how the study of Mao's works could help one win games was criticized on similar grounds, among others by T'an Chen-lin[163] (and was consequently acclaimed during the cultural revolution).[164]

Liu Shao-ch'i warned against the attribution of everything to Mao's works and also ordered that the phrase the 'Thought of Mao Tse-tung' should not be used in propaganda abroad.[165] P'eng Chen adopted a similarly deflationary attitude when enthusiasts in his local party hailed Mao as the greatest Marxist-Leninist theorist of the age and the teacher of world revolution, and he suggested that after Marx and Lenin there was no need for further discussion of political economy and the theory of imperialism.[166] Lu Ting-yi explained why Mao's thought could not be said to surpass Marxism-Leninism.[167]

One counter-current was provided by K'ang Sheng, who appears to have taken over supervision of the higher party school from Liu Shao-ch'i around 1957.[168] In the post-Lushan period, apart from encouraging the school to produce anti-P'eng Teh-huai articles, he also forced on it an increasing emphasis on the study of Mao's works at the expense of the study of the Marxist-Leninist classics.[169] K'ang, who in the summer of 1958 had described Mao's thought as the summit of Marxism, appears to have been in a strong position, because the head of the school, Yang Hsien-chen, was currently under a cloud for doubts he had expressed about the great leap.[170]

The other major promoter of the Thought of Mao Tse-tung was Defence Minister Lin Piao. In mid-1960, he issued a series of directives stressing the importance of political and ideological work.[171] He pushed Mao's 'three-eight' military style, allegedly meeting opposition within the PLA's general political department,[172] and spoke up strongly in favour of the militia in a manner it would have been hard to associate with his predecessor.[173]

But Lin Piao's most important activities in this arena took place in September and October when he summoned an enlarged meeting of the CC's MAC—of whose work he was now in charge[174]—and published the principal article hailing the publication of the fourth volume of Mao's *Selected Works*.

The MAC conference, which lasted from 14 September to 20 October, took place after what had been in effect a year-long reconnaissance of Lin's newly won empire. At it, he laid down the principles on which he would seek to build a new model army, a process which will be examined in the concluding volume of this study. In the context of 1960, it is sufficient to examine his main principles.

Underlying everything was political work, 'the supreme commander, the soul and guarantor of all work'. It was, as Mao had stated, the 'life line of the PLA'. Interrelated with political work were four key relationships. The first was the relationship between men and weapons, on which Lin said:

We handle both weapons and men, but attach greater importance to man's role. The atom bomb of spirit is much more powerful and more useful than the material atom bomb. Only we can possess this. Our enemy cannot have it. It is therefore exclusively ours. Imperialism has nothing with which to compete with us in this respect.

Then there were the relationship between political and other work—when political work was done well, everything else could be done well, political work being the 'link that solved everything'; the relationship between ideological and other aspects of political work—here ideological work was the key; and the relationship between ideas from books and living ideas—the former were necessary, but living ideas were what was important.[175]

There was no indication in the contemporary report·of Lin's remarks at the MAC conference that he singled out Mao Tse-tung's thought for high praise, but a cultural revolution source disclosed that at the conference it was proclaimed as the 'pinnacle of Marxism-Leninism of the present era'.[176] Lu Ting-yi ordered propagandists not to use the accolade and it did not surface at the time.[177] But even then it could be inferred that if ideological work was to be stressed in the PLA, only Mao's writings would be seriously studied since Marx, Engels, Lenin and Stalin had had little to say on military affairs. Any doubt on this score would have been dispelled by Lin's review of Mao's fourth volume, which included the chairman's writings from the late 1940s, dealing with the final round of the civil war with the KMT.

The article's title underlined the major theme: 'The victory of the Chinese people's revolutionary war is the victory of the thought of Mao Tse-tung.'[178] Tracing the course of the civil war and indicating how Mao's strategy and tactics had been appropriate at every turn—and hinting broadly to the Russians that only by revolutionary violence could communists come to power—Lin offered the assessment that the book's publication was a 'great event in the international working class movement because this work is a reflection of the victory of Marxism-Leninism in a big and the most populous country in the world'. He concluded, surely as much for the benefit of his senior colleagues as for Russians and other communists abroad: 'It is our present important fighting task to arm our minds with Mao Tse-tung's thought, to defend the purity of Marxism-Leninism and combat every form of ideological trend of modern revisionism.'[179]

Interestingly, in Peking's English-language version of Lin's article the word 'thought' in that concluding sentence was not capitalized as it would be during the cultural revolution, perhaps because of Liu Shao-ch'i's instruction not to use the term abroad. But Lin had raised the banner of Mao's thought nevertheless, causing confusion among other commentators on Mao's fourth volume, some of whom only referred to the chairman's works, others to his thought as well.[180] Lin had thus thrust aside the agreement reached in 1956 and reaffirmed earlier in the year, serving notice on his colleagues that he would be pinning his fortunes to Mao's star. And the marshal evidently won the chairman's approbation for his performance:

The 'four firsts' [i.e. the four relationships] is a creation. After Comrade

Lin Piao proposed the four firsts and the three-eight working style, the PLA's ideological political work and military work have attained greater development than before, become more concrete and reached a new theoretical height.[181]

The forging of the Mao-Lin alliance was in process.

(x) Agricultural disaster

By the autumn of 1960, however, there were far more urgent matters than Lin Piao's ambitions and the correct appellation for Mao's writings to worry China's leaders. The country was in the throes of the worst agricultural disaster in a century, far worse than in 1959, and worse still because of 1959. By the end of the year, 900 million mou or well over half the cultivated acreage had been devastated, sometimes repreatedly.

The catastrophe had been emerging for some months. The most serious problem in 1960 was drought which in the spring and summer affected 600 million mou in every province of China, apart from Tibet and Sinkiang; 13 provinces were affected in both seasons. The worst devastation was centred round the north China provinces of Hopei, Honan, Shantung and Shansi, where 60 per cent of the cultivated acreage was affected over a period of six to seven months. At the worst period in Shantung, eight of the province's 12 rivers had no water in them; for 40 days in March and June, it was possible to wade across the lower reaches of the Yellow River.

Shantung had also been battered by typhoons and floods that affected 12 provinces in all. Apart from Shantung, the most seriously hit were the three in the north-east, and other coastal provinces like Kwangtung, Fukien and Kiangsu. The floods in east Liaoning were the worst since records had been kept.

Not suprisingly in view of the drought, most of the flooding had been due to the typhoons, more of which had hit the Chinese mainland than in any of the previous 50 years, 11 between June and October; and each typhoon had lasted longer than usual, averaging ten hours, the longest stretching to 20.

Moreover, nature had played an additional trick. The typhoons did not strike north-westwards as usual, but northwards. This added to their impact because it meant there were no high mountains to ward them off, and that less rain reached the west of the country. In the aftermath of the drought and the floods came insect pests and plant diseases.[182]

In July, China's leaders met for their annual summer work conference, not in ill-starred Lushan, but in Peitaiho as in 1959. But the mood was very different from two years earlier, and retrenchment not expansion was in the air. It was now that the Chairman of the State Planning Commission, Li Fu-ch'un, made the first proposal that would effectively have brought the revived leap to an end, advocating a policy of 'adjustment, consolidation, and improvement' (*t'iao-cheng, kung-ku, t'i-kao*). No action appears to have been taken on this suggestion at Peitaiho; perhaps Mao was not yet ready to face another retreat, or perhaps the leadership had little time left over from consideration of the Sino-Soviet dispute to take decisions on the economy. However, Li raised the matter again when reporting to Chou En-lai at the end of August. The Premier approved it, adding an additional phrase 'filling out' (*ch'ung-shih*).[183]

In the autumn, Chou held a small conference in an SC auditorium at which Ch'en Yun reportedly gave a masterful analysis of the country's economic plight with which the Premier entirely agreed.[184] It may have been on this occasion that Li Hsien-nien vouchsafed his preference for Ch'en's analysis over Mao's.[185] It was probably around this time that Po I-po abandoned leftism for his more familiar moderation.[186] But even with all the economic planners in accord, the retrenchment package still had to be sold to Mao and those who thought like him. This was done by Chou and Li Fu-ch'un, not without difficulty. Then, with Mao, Liu, and Teng Hsiao-p'ing preoccupied with the Moscow conference, Chou and the planners regained operational control of the economy; Li Fu-ch'un chaired the secretariat while Teng and P'eng Chen were away.[187] Since Chou En-lai had made a practice of sitting in on the meetings of the secretariat and Li Hsien-nien was a member, the secretariat took on the flavour of the SC.

Mao had no option but to concur. As in the spring of 1959, he suddenly executed a 180 degree turn in a desperate attempt to prevent the follies of the leap from immeasurably worsening the disasters imposed by nature. On 27 October, he signified his approval of the measures taken by Shansi, one of the worst-hit provinces, to mobilize all possible manpower for the rehabilitation of its farm land by redeploying 1·1 million people from industry back to agriculture. As Mao acknowledged:

If we don't immediately change the current situation on the agricultural front of a labour force which is too small and too weak, then the so-called 'national economy with agriculture as the foundation' and 'grain as the foundation of that foundation' will become empty talk. Man must eat every day whether engaged in industry, communications, education capital construction, or any other enterprise. Noone can do without grain. No member of the communist party ought to forget this very simple and absolutely true and correct principle.

Then came the crucial order: 'On the basis of your actual conditions, adopt all effective measures, squeeze out all of the labour force that can be squeezed out, strengthen the first line of agricultural production, and speedily change the grave situation of the present insufficiency of labour force'.[188] An interesting aspect of this directive, which went to all provincial parties, is that it sanctioned a policy that Shansi had been carrying out for *three months*. Presumably this was an example of how preoccupation with the Sino-Soviet dispute prevented Mao from focusing on desperately urgent domestic matters. But it also raises the question as to how many other provinces had taken matters into their own hands; it is possible that Mao's circular was less a directive than *ex post facto* approval.

The next step was to restore incentives to the peasantry. Once again the tide of commune-run collectivism had to be rolled back. Although Mao himself had argued against egalitarianism at the second Chengchow conference, and the Shanghai and Lushan plenums had ratified basic ownership by the production brigade, the post-Lushan campaign against the right deviation had encouraged men like Wu Chih-p'u to retake surrendered positions, reinforcing the rights and prerogatives of the communes as against the production brigades and teams. No less an authority than T'an Chen-lin admitted, too, the reappearance of the 'five styles' —egalitarianism, commandism, blind leadership, pomposity, superior attitude[189]—had caused enormous losses to the communes.[190]

In September, Mao sent a memorandum to his colleagues on the Politburo standing committee reaffirming his original Chengchow position that the brigade, not the area, should be the basic unit of ownership and accounting.[191] This gave the go-ahead for the CC's 12-point urgent directive on rural work, issued on 3 November, which also appeared to do no more than reaffirm what had been agreed in the tidying up of the communes in 1959, but clearly would not have been needed if the 1959 situation had actually prevailed. The CC enjoined resolute opposition to egalitarianism and the transfer of men and equipment, the battle-cry of Mao at Chengchow 18 months earlier. Following Mao's memorandum, and probably because of the critical agrarian situation in 1960, while, basic ownership of land went to the production brigade, some was assigned to the team. A higher percentage of collective income should be distributed to the peasants, who were also to be allowed to cultivate private plots and engage in sideline occupations for their own profit. A resuscitation of rural markets was sanctioned to give them somewhere to sell their produce. The right combination of work and leisure was once again to be a focus of cadre concern; men were to have four days off a month, women six.[192]

The leap officially ended with the year 1960. A long march backwards to economic recovery began. Along the way there would be many more setbacks, both natural and man-made. The destination, restoration of the economy to a condition permitting the launching of a 3rd FYP, would be reached on the eve of the cultural revolution. At that point, the spirit and methods of the great leap would be only memories. Mao's second bold experiment was over.

CONCLUSIONS

(i) Balance sheet of the leap

The great leap forward ended not with a bang but a whimper.[1] No rallies were held. No speeches were made. No pamphlets were issued. Indeed no announcement was ever made that the leap was over. It had to be inferred from the 1961 New Year editorial in *Red Flag* which referred to 1958–60 as the three years of great leap achievement. The magazine called now not for a new leap forward, but for a brave advance under the three banners of the general line, the greap leap forward and the people's communes—a semantic shift only, but one of great significance.[2]

No government likes to admit failure. When a totally new policy is adopted, it is often smoke-screened by claims for the success of the policy that is being abandoned. The CCP was no exception to the rule. When it held its 9th plenum in January 1961, the final communiqué listed a series of achievements, mainly in the industrial sector: China had risen from ninth place to sixth in the world league table for steel output, from fifth to second for coal; the material and technical base of industry had been 'enormously strengthened'; the stock of machine tools was more than double that of 1957; the number of engineers and technicians had also more than doubled; the gross value of industrial output had increased at an average annual rate of over 40 per cent, more than twice the rate achieved during the 1st FYP[3]; or so it was claimed.

A more objective appraisal of the leap by Chinese only became publishable two decades later—after the death of Mao, after the purge of the last of the cultural revolutionaries, after the third coming of Teng Hsiao-p'ing and after the adoption of the watchword 'Seek truth from facts'.

Rapid industrial growth did occur during the leap, but at enormous cost. According to the official record, heavy industry grew by 230 per cent between 1958 and 1960. In 1958 alone, as a result of the steel drive, investment in the metallurgical industry almost trebled, and investment in heavy industry as a whole more than doubled. The value of heavy industry's output apparently rose 78·8 per cent as a result of the rate of capital accumulation having been raised from 24·9 per cent in 1957 to 33·9 per cent in 1958. The consequence of the high investment in heavy industry was less investment for light industry and agriculture. The consequence of high investment generally was declining consumption. The 1958 pattern was repeated in 1959 despite the fall in agricultural output, and capital accumulation reached the 'disastrous' level of 43·8 per cent. The imbalances in the economy were further aggravated in 1960 as the leadership sought to fulfil the steel target 'by every artificial means'.[4] The rate of investment, 39·6 per cent,[5] again exceeded 1958. The distortions in investment policy are shown in Table 1.[6]

Table 1: Proportions of investment in agriculture, light industry and heavy industry within the total investment in capital construction (%)

Sector	1st FYP, 1953–7 (annual average)	1958	1959	1960
Agriculture	7·8	10·5	10·5	13·0
Light industry	5·9	7·3	5·2	4·0
Heavy industry	46·5	57·0	56·7	55·3
Portion attributable to metallurgical industry	10·14	17·68	16·13	13·16

The principal beneficiary was the steel industry, which rose from an output of 5·35 million tons in 1957 to 18 million tons in 1960 at the end of the leap. According to one Chinese analysis, the high targets for industry were achieved by means of 'intensified mining' (coal production rose from 130 million tons in 1957 to 390 million tons in 1960[7]), 'overloading operations and manufacturing in a rough and slipshod way'.[8] A large part of the steel produced throughout the three years of the leap came from 'native'-type plants and small blast furnaces and had to be smelted again in 'big foreign furnaces'. 'The cost was so high and quality so poor that this unreal "peak" did not last very long. Consequently, production had to be cut back, a severe blow to the machine making industry and many capital construction projects which use steel as raw material.'[9] At the end of the 2nd FYP, steel production was down to 7 million tons.[10] Labour productivity in state enterprises, up during the 1st FYP by 8·7 per cent, declined by 5·4 per cent during the 2nd FYP.[11] Light industry, starved for funds, slumped for three years from 1960.[12] The human implications of those investment figures were staggering (Table 2).[13]

Table 2

(in millions)	1957	1958	1959	1960
Workers in heavy industry[a]	4·5	17·5	14·18	15·72
Heavy industrial workers[a]	5·57	35·5		
Non-agricultural population	106·18	122·1		
Urban population	99·49	107·21		
Agricultural labour force	192·0	151·0		192·0[b]

[a] Presumably workers in heavy industry are in modern industrial plants, while heavy industrial workers includes those making backyard steel.

[b] T'an Chen-lin used a figure of 200 million in early 1960; see above p. 299.

A colossal shift of labour had taken place from countryside to town and city, from agriculture to industry. The movement seemed less important in 1958 when the weather was favourable and agricultural output increased. But even in that year, as a result of the exaggerated notions of the harvest and the institution of mess halls providing 'free food' there was a 'consumption spree' which ate into the reserves accumulated over the previous two to three years. Moreover, those who made steel got extra rations. When nature turned nasty in 1959, an agricultural labour force reduced by over 20 per cent in 1958 was in no position to cope. On average, a peasant who had to look after 8·8 mou in 1957 now had to cultivate 11 mou; and since the number of draft animals had dropped sharply—presumably slaughtered at the time of the formation of the communes in fear of confiscation—the work was even harder. Although heavy industry did supply twice as much of the means of production (tractors, fertilizer, etc.) during the leap, it could not make up for the decline in the labour force because of its 'poor quality, unsuitability or general ineffectiveness'.[14]

It was hardly surprising that the combination of natural calamities and labour shortages should have had a profound impact on agricultural production, with 'famine' conditions prevailing in the winter of 1959 and especially in 1960–1.[15] The grain figures for

Table 3:   Grain output (million tons)

	1957	1958	1959	1960
Claimed (without soya beans)	185·0	250·0	270·5	n.a.
Actual (without soya beans)	185·0	n.a.	n.a.	136·2
Claimed (with soya beans)	195·05	260·05	281·55	n.a.
Actual (with soya beans)	195·05	200·0	170·0	143·5

all of the leap years have now been revealed and in Table 3 are compared with the contemporary claims. What has also been revealed by Chinese sources is when the 200 million ton figure for 1958 was arrived at. It was apparently 'verified' in 1961, that is some two years after the grain had been eaten, according to economist Hsueh Mu-ch'iao.[16]

What is clear is that the living standards achieved by 1956–7 declined thereafter and only regained the pre-leap level in 1965.[17] The grain ration figures for the leap are shown in Table 4[18].

Table 4

Grain ration	1957	1958	1959	1960
Kg per head	203·0	198·0	186·5	163·5

The peasantry suffered particularly severely. Government procurement of grain to feed the swollen urban population was based on claims not actuality. Although marketable farm produce represented about 15–20 per cent of total agricultural output, state procurement amounted to more than 20 percent in many years, over 25 per cent in a few years, and was as high as 28 per cent in 1959, a year in which output declined drastically. In the countryside, despite the heavy nature of the work, the ration was about 200 kg in many areas and went as low as 150 kg in a few. 'How could the tillers bring their initiative into play when they were working in a state of semi-starvation?'[19]

The plight of the peasants surfaced in 1960 in the angry comments of their sons and brothers serving in the PLA[20]:

At present what the peasants eat in the villages is even worse than what dogs ate in the past. At that time dogs ate chaff and grain. Now the people are too hungry to work and pigs are too hungry to stand up. Commune members ask: 'Is Chairman Mao going to allow us to starve to death?'

Chairman Mao lives in Peking. Does he know about the everyday living of the peasant? So much grain was harvested. Where has it gone?

Is it the order of Chairman Mao that people should eat vegetables? The workers repairing the Chungnanhai [where Mao and other central leaders lived] have a ration of 60 catties of grain a month [i.e. 360 kg a year]. Still they complain that they have no strength to do the work. The peasants eat only vegetables and sweet potatoes and have no grain.

In the city there is enough grain, and the grain supplied is fine grain, but in the villages the grain supplied is coarse. . . . Even the sick people at home have to eat sweet potatoes. The workers eat rice and flour. Why is life in the villages so bad?

What these comments meant for one *hsien* in Kwangtung province was revealed during the cultural revolution: 20,000 people starved to death.[21] Nationwide, the mortality rate doubled from 1·08 per cent in 1957 to 2·54 per cent in 1960. In that year the population actually *declined* by 4·5 per cent. Anywhere from 16·4 to 29·5 million extra people died during the leap, because of the leap.[22]

Looking back on those grim days, Chinese economists are harsh in their condemnation. Hsueh Mu-ch'iao, now the doyen of his profession, has talked about the 'colossal waste and disproportion'.[23] Sun Yeh-fang described the leap as a 'disruption of socialism'.[24] Lo Keng-mo, once a Vice Chairman of the State Planning Commission, has said 'the great leap forward became a great leap backward'.[25]

The figures confirm that judgement. Between 1960 and 1965, 100,000 enterprises were closed down. Some 20 million people— 10 million by spring 1961[26]—were withdrawn from the urban areas to help salvage something from the agricultural disaster.[27] The total loss to the national economy as a result of the leap is now estimated at 100 billion yuan, almost twice the total investment in capital construction during the 1st FYP (55 billion yuan). A comparison of the 1st and 2nd FYPs shows the broader picture (Table 5)[28]:

Table 5:   Average annual growth rate (%)

	1st FYP (1953–7)	2nd FYP (1958–62)
National income	8·9	−3·1
Industrial production (value)	18·0	3·8
Agricultural production (value)	4·5	−4·3
Industry and agriculture (value)	10·9	0·6

(ii)   Why did it happen?

The resolution 'On questions of party history' adopted by the CC on 27 June 1981, explained the leap in measured language[29]: the general line agreed at the second session of the CCP's 8th Congress was fundamentally correct; its shortcoming was 'that it overlooked the objective economic laws'. Enthusiasm produced some achievements.

However, 'Left' errors, characterised by excessive targets, the issuing of arbitrary directions, boastfulness and the stirring up of a 'communist wind', spread unchecked throughout the country. This was due to our lack of experience in socialist construction and inadequate understanding of the laws of economic development and of the basic economic conditions in China. More important, it was due to the fact that Comrade Mao Tse-tung and many leading comrades, both at the centre and in the localities, had become smug about their successes, were impatient for quick results and overestimated the role of man's subjective will and efforts. After the general line was formulated, the great leap forward and the movement for rural people's communes were initiated without careful investigation and study and without prior experimentation.

T'an Chen-lin, one of those leading comrades who backed Mao during the leap, has said that after the achievement of socialist transformation in 1956, 'we began to be proud and careless'; there was 'endless fuss' about the transformation of the relations of production, presumably referring to the formation of the communes; an 'infatuated' concern for the predominance of the socialist economy; failure to reform management and perfect distribution according to work.[30]

Po I-po, perhaps a reluctant leftist during the leap, has also told how Mao and other central and local officials, 'including myself', became 'careless and arrogant and over-eager for quick results'. After Mao had suggested the formation of the communes at Peitaiho, '[a]s a result of his incorrect estimate of the situation, and overestimation of the role of man's subjective will and efforts, a great rash advance occurred. This tendency, characterized by excessive targets, the issuing of arbitrary directions, boastfulness and the stirring up of a 'communist wind', spread unchecked throughout the country. . . . To be fair, it was Comrade Mao Tse-tung who first called for correcting the leftist mistakes made in 1958'; but then came Lushan.[31]

The 1981 resolution on party history said that all went well at first.

However, in the later part of the meeting, [Mao] erred in initiating criticism of Comrade P'eng Teh-huai and then in launching a party-wide struggle against 'Right opportunism'. The resolution . . . concerning the so-called anti-Party group of P'eng Teh-huai, Huang K'o-ch'eng, Chang Wen-t'ien and Chou Hsiao-chou was entirely wrong. Politically, this struggle gravely undermined inner-party democracy from the central level down to the grass roots; economically, it cut short the process of the rectification of 'Left' errors, thus prolonging their influence. It was mainly due to the errors of the great leap forward and of the struggle against 'Right opportunism' together with a succession of natural calamities and the perfidious scrapping of contracts by the Soviet Government that our economy encountered serious difficulties between 1959 and 1961, which caused serious losses to our country and people.[32]

Lo Keng-mo blamed the anti-rightist drives of 1957 and 1959 for making people within and without the party frightened to report anything but good news—'all statistical data and investigation reports have lost their credibility as they covered up and white-washed food shortages in the villages'. People argued at that time whether it was the communes and their impact on productivity and peasant enthusiasm or the natural calamities which were the principal reason for the 'setback'. 'If we were to draw a conclusion now we would say "human factors" played a more decisive role than "forces of nature".'[33]

And why did the Chinese leadership tilt the economy so disastrously in the direction of heavy industry? Had not Mao himself underlined the crucial importance of agriculture and light industry as early as 1956 in his speech on the ten great relationships and advocated more investment in them? Had not the party proclaimed the policy of taking agriculture as the foundation in 1960? What went wrong? Po I-po now acknowledges that 'we who were engaged in heavy industry were so zealous that we brought pressure to bear on others',[34] effectively an admission of the truth of the cultural revolution accusation that he pushed heavy industry too hard in 1959–60. According to two Chinese economists: 'The trouble is that giving undue prominence to heavy industry has become a habit, a habit far stronger than the party's guidelines and policies.'[35] And although supposed to serve the other sectors, heavy industry thought only of itself.[36] Possibly Mao never fully accepted the economic ideas he had enunciated in the ten great relationships; they appear not to have been his own.[37]

(iii) The Mao factor

All the retrospective Chinese assessments are valid. They reflect a bitter truth experienced personally by men who lived and led during those grim years. But in June 1981, it was not possible for the Chinese leadership to be totally frank about one dimension of the leap, the Mao factor. Even those most critical of the late Chairman would not have wanted to repeat what has always been seen in Peking as Khrushchev's mistake in destalinization: stripping so many veils from the dead leader that the party and the cause are threatened. Besides, factional politics in the CCP's upper ranks dictated compromise.

To be sure, Mao's ultimate responsibility is stated, but if one were to go by the June resolution, he was merely primus inter pares in the launching of the leap. Yet anyone who is not hamstrung by the exigencies of Peking politics must conclude from the record that without Mao there would have been no leap, without Mao there would have been no communes, without Mao there would have been no mass steel campaign and without Mao there would have been no revival of the leap.

Mao may have advocated attention to objective conditions, but it was his demonic desire for earth-shaking progress that demanded exaggerated claims of success. Mao may have warned against skipping stages of socialism, but it was his burning ambition to reshape society instantly that led to the communist five styles and the ultra-leftism of the early communes. Mao may have paid lip-service to agriculture, but it was his dream of overtaking the Soviet Union and the United States that hurtled China into its massive industrial drive spearheaded by steel, still an international virility symbol in the 1950s. While Mao perennially preached treating the disease to save the patient, it was his butchery of P'eng Teh-huai at Lushan that re-launched the leap on its erratic course towards disaster—that, the resolution on party history did acknowledge. Liu Shao-ch'i, T'an Chen-lin, Po I-po and many others were accessories to all that, but accessories after the fact.

There was a positive side to the leap. In any developing country, it is critical that the people should be seized of the idea that they do not have to sit submissively under the yoke of nature. Mao hammered home that point insistently. Like a sergeant major inducting raw recruits into their new world by bawling his squad into life, Mao galvanized his people. While many peasants must have received the targets suggested to them by fired-up, basic-level cadres with scepticism born of experience, doubtless many others were enthused by the notion that with one supreme effort they might burst the bonds of poverty.[38] But the excesses of the leap and its ultimate collapse could have stunned a less resilient people into apathy about economic development.

Mao's colleagues seem to have been swept along by his vision. They had made a revolution in order to remake China. The man who had led them on the long march to victory now offered them a short sprint to Utopia; not some misty Marxist nirvana beyond the horizon, but a new nation—socially pure, economically strong, internationally respected—here and now in the fields and factories of China. Lo Keng-mo has admitted frankly how even he, an economist, was carried away:

[M]any comrades were quite concerned about the rapid increase of grain production. Believing that if the grain were not exported we would not be able to build storages fast enough to meet the need, they proposed to cut back the grain acreage to make room for economic crops and afforestation. At that time I myself was fascinated by this beautiful picture in the country's future, which I realise now represents nothing but wishful thinking.[39]

But at the time who would remind Prometheus that nature can be tamed but not trampled on, that men can move mountains, but cannot work miracles, that a political revolution can succeed in a decade or even a day, but a spiritual revolution demands centuries. Given Mao's sheer personal dominance in his colleagues, demonstrated so fearsomely at Lushan, who would say him nay—Chou En-lai, possibly; Ch'en Yun, certainly; P'eng Teh-huai, only after the event; very few.

And what of Liu Shao-ch'i? Cautious and painstaking, he should have found the headlong rush totally alien. Wedded to Marxist materialism he should have spurned Maoist voluntarism. The image of sea-green incorruptibility, he should have shrunk from the leap's exaggeration and boastfulness. But Liu shared Mao's goals; the instrument, the party, he had helped shape; and the method, mass mobilization, he understood. And what a way to launch his gradual assumption of power: jointly presiding over an 'economic breakthrough. What better way for the party to restore its prestige after the criticism it had taken during the 1957 rectification movement. When he or any of Mao's colleagues had doubts, probably most of them took comfort from the fact that the Chairman had been right when it had mattered most; maybe he was right again. If non-Chinese under no compulsion to believe, including economists who should have known better, could be swept along with the euphoria of the leap,[40] why not Chinese with the heady prospect of implementing it?

A few may have remembered Marx and Engels who had argued that the economic base shaped the social superstructure. But they were essentially armchair theoreticians, foreigners who had never imagined that China would have a revolution ahead of their native Germany. Above all, they were dead, while Mao was here and now and exuding the very willpower which he promised would transform the economic base (and turn Marxism on its head).

There were, of course, the Soviet advisers; they did say nay. But they, too, were foreign, and uncouth and arrogant in Chinese eyes. They had launched a sputnik, but they had killed their peasants and crippled their agriculture, and their model of industrial management confirmed that they knew nothing about mobilizing the masses.[41] Besides if China went the Soviet road, it was almost inevitably condemned to be always the follower, never the leader. That surely did not fit any Chinese leader's picture of a desirable future, especially at a time when Soviet foreign policy was inimical to Chinese interests.

And what of Mao himself: was he, too, swept along by his own vision? In one sense the question is absurd; as already indicated Mao was gripped by the idea of instant, earthshaking progress. Unlike Liu, he revelled in upheaval, in *luan*[42]; a sentence quoted earlier from his critique of Soviet economics epitomizes his personality—'"full consolidation"—a phrase to make one uneasy'. And he seems to have been exhilarated by the power to be wielded; Po I-po has reported that when Mao learned that 20 million had been sent back to the countryside, he exclaimed, more than once: 'We have 20 m. people at our beck and call. What political party other than the ruling CCP could have done it?'[43]

Yet although Mao dreamed dreams, he had acute political antennae. That was one reason why he initiated the retreat in the autumn of 1958, as the resolution on party history confirms. (There was another likely reason: only Mao dared initiate a retreat.) In the spring of 1959, he scented danger and ordered a further pull-back.

If he was reluctant to give up the leap, as Po I-po indicates,[44] it was probably because he did not want to acknowledge that P'eng Teh-huai had been right. Mao had, however, already prepared his defence. In June 1960, summing up ten years of rule, he wrote:

It is impossible not to commit errors. As Lenin said, there has never been a man who did not commit errors. . . . Our party's general line is correct, and actual work has basically been carried out well. There are some errors which are difficult to avoid. Where is the so-called saint who never commits errors and who at once carries out truth to completion? . . . Freedom is the recognition of necessity; the leap from the kingdom of necessity to the kingdom of freedom is gradually achieved in a long-term process of recognition.[45]

In the end, Mao conceded gracefully. The great leap was the greatest trauma experienced by the CCP before the cultural revolution. Yet in 1960, at the conclusion of the leap, there was no confrontation between Mao and colleagues as there had been between him and Liu and P'eng Chen in 1957 at the end of his experiment with liberalization.[46] Probably it was because the men who could have made political capital about the failure of the leap—Chou En-lai, Ch'en Yun, Li Fu-ch'un—had never shown any disposition to challenge his personal position or authority.

So Mao retreated to the 'second front' to lick his wounds—he appears to have said very little in 1961 after the 9th plenum in January—leaving Liu and other colleagues to pick up the pieces.[47] To party members, it must have seemed that one era was ending and another was beginning, less exhilarating but more predictable, duller but safer.

In the event, Mao's unhappiness at the way in which his colleagues chose to hack their way out of the post-leap depression, his anger at his own diminished prestige and authority, and, most importantly, his growing obsession with the problem of revolutionary degeneration as the Sino-Soviet dispute worsened, brought him back into the political arena with a vengeance—literally and metaphorically. The coming of the cataclysm will be the subject of the final volume of this study.

Abbreviations used in notes

BDRC	*Biographical Dictionary of Republican China*
CB	Current Background
CLG	*Chinese Law and Government*
CQ	*The China Quarterly*
CYWK	*Ch'en Yun T'ung-chih Wen-kao Hsuan-pien* (A Selection of Comrade Ch'en Yun's Manuscripts)
ECMM	Extracts from China Mainland Magazines
8th National Congress	*Eighth National Congress of the Communist Party of China*
FBIS	Foreign Broadcast Information Service
Gold Chou ('gold' refers to the colour of the book's binding)	*Chou En-lai Tsung-li Pa-shih Tan-ch'en Chi-nien Shih Wen-hsuan*
Green Chou	*Jen-min-ti Hao Tsung-li* (1977)
Grey Chou	*Jen-min-ti Hao Tsung-li*, II (1978), III (1979)
Halpern MS	A. M. Halpern, *The People's Republic of China in the Post-war World*
HC	*Hung Ch'i (Red Flag)*
HCPP	*Hung Ch'i P'iao-p'iao* (Red Flags Fluttering)
HHPYK	*Hsin Hua Pan-yueh-k'an* (New China Semi-Monthly)
HHWC	*Hsin Hua Wen-chai* (New China Digest) (This was the title given to HHYP—WCP from Jan. 1981)
HHYP	*Hsin Hua Yueh-pao* (New China Monthly)
HHYP—WCP	*Hsin Hua Yueh-pao Wen-chai-pan* (New China Monthly Digest)
IIR, *Who's Who*	Institute of International Relations, *Chinese Communist Who's Who*
JMJP	*Jen-min Jih-pao (People's Daily)*
JMST	*Jen-min Shou-ts'e (People's Handbook)*
JPRS	Joint Publications Research Service
Lieberthal	Lieberthal, *Research Guide to Central Meetings in China*
Mao, *HC*	Mao, *Hsuan Chi* (Selected Works)
Mao, *Miscellany*	*Miscellany of Mao-Tse tung Thought (1949–1968)*
Mao, *Pa-shih-wu Tan-ch'en*	*Mao Tse-tung T'ung-chih Pa-shih-wu Tan-ch'en Chi-nien Wen-hsuan*
Mao, *Critique*	Mao Tse-tung, *A Critique of Soviet Economics*
Mao, *SW*	Mao, *Selected Works*
NYT	*New York Times*
Oksenberg MS	Oksenberg, *Policy Formulation in Communist China*

Pol. Docs	*Communist China, 1955–9: Policy documents with analysis*
PR	*Peking Review*
SCMM & SCMM(S)	Selections from China Mainland Magazines and ditto (Supplement)
SCMP & SCMP(S)	Survey of the China Mainland Press and ditto (Supplement)
Shaoshan Hung Jih	*Shaoshan Hung Jih Chao Ch'ien Ch'iu*
SSC	Supreme State Conference
SSIC	*Social Sciences in China*
SWB/FE & SWB/FE/ES	BBC, Summary of World Broadcasts, Part V, The Far East and ditto Economic Supplement
Ta Hai	*Ta hai hang-hsing k'ao to-shou*
The Polemic	*The Polemic on the General Line of the International Communist Movement*
The Sino-Soviet Dispute	Hudson, Lowenthal & MacFarquhar, *The Sino-Soviet Dispute*
TLC	Teng Li-ch'ün, *Hsiang Ch'en Yun T'ung-chih Hsueh-hsi Tso Ching-chi Kung-tso* (Study Comrade Ch'en Yun's Way of Doing Economic Work)
Tsai Mao . . . Shen-pien	*Wo-men Tsai Mao Chu-hsi Shen-pien*
URI, *Who's Who*	Union Research Institute, *Who's Who in Communist China*
White Chou	*Ching-ai-ti Chou Tsung-li Wo-men Yung-yuan Huai-nien Ni*
WHP	*Wen-hui Pao*
WWAR	*We Will Always Remember Premier Chou En-lai*

NOTES

INTRODUCTION

[1] For typical Chinese analyses of the impact of the great leap forward, see Conclusions. For a contemporary Chinese view of the vicissitudes of the country's population policies, see Liu Zheng et al., *China's Population: Problems and Prospects*, especially pp. 58–65. For a proposal to abolish the communes, see Lin Tien, 'Inquiry into the question of the system of people's communes', *Ching-chi Kuan-li* (Economic Management), No. 1, 1981, trans. in FBIS-CHI-81-046, p. L25.

[2] For an analysis of the mood of the Chinese leadership in the autumn of 1957 and what shaped it, see *Origins*, I, especially Conclusions.

[3] The above analysis is based heavily on Perkins, *Agricultural Development in China, 1368–1968*, especially pp. 13–78.; Anthony M. Tang, 'Policy and performance in agriculture', in Eckstein et al. (eds.), *Economic Trends in Communist China*, especially pp. 466–8, 491–7; Kang Chao, *Agricultural Production in Communist China*, p. 227; Elvin, *The Pattern of the Chinese Past*, especially pp. 285–316; Lippit, *Land Reform and Economic Development in China*, passim.

[4] See Eckstein, *China's Economic Revolution*, especially pp. 54–9; Tang, 'Policy and performance', pp. 503–5.

[5] For Mao's speech to the 3rd plenum, see Mao, *SW*, pp. 483–97.

PART ONE: CHARGE

Chapter 1.   Mao in Moscow

[1] The 1957 Moscow conference has been the object of much study and I have not thought it necessary to cover the ground again in great detail. In addition to the sources cited in subsequent footnotes, I have derived profit from Brzezinski, *The Soviet Bloc*, Crankshaw, *The New Cold War*, Floyd, *Mao against Khrushchev*, and Halpern MS.

[2] Mao, *SW*, V, pp. 340–1.

[3] See *Origins*, I, pp. 332–3 (notes 16, 17).

[4] See *The Polemic*, pp. 70–4.

[5] *People's China*, No. 23 (Dec. 1957), p. 5. See also the disgusted comments of the Albanian Communist leader on Mao's line on this issue in Enver Hoxha, *Reflections on China*, pp. 85–6.

[6] See 'The ten great crimes of bandit P'eng in foreign affairs', *Lien Ho Pan*, 11 Aug. 1967, p. 4, col. 4.

[7] Khrushchev had launched a counter-attack on Soviet writers in May 1957; for an assessment of the effect of this Soviet move on Mao, see *Origins*, I, p. 298.

[8] *The Polemic*, p. 71.

[9] The relevant portion of his report is to be found in *The Sino-Soviet Dispute*, pp. 44–6.

[10] *The Polemic*, pp. 65–6.

[11] Ibid., p. 71.

[12] Ibid., p. 106.

[13] Ibid., p. 72. These were presumably the four drafts referred to by Mao in his 18 Nov. speech; Mao, *SW*, V, p. 514.

[14] *The Sino-Soviet Dispute*, p. 54.

[15] *The Polemic*, pp. 72, 74.

[16] *The Sino-Soviet Dispute*, p. 43.

[17] Ibid., p. 44.

[18] SCMP 1239, p. 30, quoted in *Origins*, I, p. 41.

[19] *Origins*, I, p. 42.

[20] Ibid., pp. 299–301, 316–17.

[21] See Hsieh, *Communist China's Strategy in the Nuclear Era*, pp. 76–83.

[22] There were two formal conferences during the Moscow celebrations: a conference of ruling Communist parties (without Yugoslavia) which took place from 14 to 16 November and produced a Declaration; and a conference of all 64 parties represented in Moscow (including Yugoslavia) which met from 16 to 19 November and issued a Peace Manifesto.

[23] *Quotations from Chairman Mao Tse-tung*, pp. 80–1. According to Mao, the East Wind/West Wind formulation was derived from a character in a Chinese classical novel; see Mao, *SW*, V, p. 340, and *Mao Tse-tung ssu-hsiang wan sui* (1969), p. 212.

[24] The British communist leader John Gollan, quoted in Gittings, *Survey of the Sino-Soviet Dispute*, p. 80.

[25] Ibid., pp. 79–80, 80–1.

[26] Quoted ibid., p. 82.

27 *People's China*, No. 23 (Dec. 1957), p. 6.

28 Gittings, *Sino-Soviet Dispute*, p. 82. For the Soviet version of what he said, see ibid., p. 83; for a French communist version, see Fetjö, *Chine-URSS, La Fin d'une Hégémonie*, p. 199. Mao put the same argument equally positively to the second session of the CCP's 8th Congress seven months later (when he revised his estimate of the world's population to 2,900 million); see *Mao Tse-tung ssu-hsiang wan sui* (1969), p. 208.

29 *Soviet News* (London: Soviet Embassy), No. 5493 (10 June 1969), p. 128.

30 This analysis of the Russians' views is based on Zagoria, *The Sino-Soviet Conflict, 1956–1961*, pp. 155–60.

31 Gittings, *Sino-Soviet Dispute*, pp. 83–4.

32 See the Chinese government statement of 15 Aug. 1963 quoted in Gittings, *Sino-Soviet Dispute*, p. 105.

33 Ibid. According to Mackintosh, to the Russians the phrase 'new technology' would mean atomic weapons, missiles and electronic means of warfare; see Malcolm Mackintosh, 'The Soviet attitude [in a US-China crisis]', in Halperin (ed.), *Sino-Soviet Relations and Arms Control*, p. 206.

34 Halperin, *China and the Bomb*, pp. 75–82.

35 The decision was contained in Mao's speech on ten great relationships made in April 1956, unpublished at the time but almost certainly known in some detail by the Russians; see *Origins*, I, pp. 68–9.

36 Ibid., pp. 313–14.

37 SCMP 1696, pp. 34–5.

38 Clemens, *The Arms Race and Sino-Soviet Relations*, p. 17.

39 SCMP 1644, p. 27.

40 SCMP 1647, p. 30. The NCNA issued the article on 30 Oct. but it appeared in *JMJP* on 31 Oct.

41 SCMP 1649, pp. 29–30.

42 SCMP 1645, p. 27.

43 *Khrushchev Remembers: The Last Testament*, p. 269; Gittings, *Sino-Soviet Dispute*, p. 105.

44 Gittings, ibid.

45 See *Origins*, I, pp. 68–9.

46 Quoted in Hsieh, *Communist China's Strategy*, p. 102; see also SCMP 1663, p. 48.

47 See Kolkowicz, *The Soviet Military and the Communist Party*, pp. 130–42; Leonhard, *The Kremlin since Stalin*, pp. 253–60.

48 For an account of earlier tensions between the two men, see *Origins*, I, p. 147.

49 Ibid., pp. 67–8, 315.

50 See Schwartz, *The Soviet Economy since Stalin*, pp. 109–10. Schwartz comments: 'This was a sort of Khrushchevian precursor of what the Chinese soon afterward called the "great leap forward".'

51 Khrushchev, *Report to a Joint Session of the Supreme Soviet of the U.S.S.R.*, 6 November 1957, p. 12.

52 When issuing his call to overtake the United States in the production of livestock produce Khrushchev said: 'We do not intend to blow up the capitalist world with bombs. If we catch up to the United States level of meat, milk and butter we shall have shot a highly powerful torpedo at the underpinnings of capitalism.... We have dared to challenge America to peaceful competition in a most important economic field...' (quoted in Schwartz, *Soviet Economy*, p. 111).

53 Khrushchev, *Report*, p. 24.

54 See ibid., p. 22, where Khrushchev compared the 1956 US outputs of these products with the actual 1956 and estimated 1972 Soviet output figures.

[55] Khrushchev did not spell this out publicly until Nov. 1958, when he issued the theses of his report on the Seven-Year Plan to the forthcoming 21st CPSU Congress; see *Soviet News*, No. 3957 (24 Nov. 1958), p. 167.

[56] For the genesis of the Programme and the slogan, see *Origins*, I, pp. 27–32. In Jan. 1958, Mao mentioned, along with these two items, 'committees for promoting progress' (*ts'u-chin wei-yuan-hui*) as a third thing that was blown away by the campaign against adventurism in 1956 (*Mao Tse-tung ssu-hsiang was sui* (1969), p. 147). To judge from Mao's speech to the 3rd plenum, this was not a reference to some special body/bodies set up to mastermind the 1956 little leap, but rather expressed the view that all party and governmental committees should be by definition committees for promoting progress rather than retrogression; Mao, *SW*, V, p. 492, and Mao, *HC*, V, p. 474. Indeed, in the Chinese edition of Mao's works, his speech to the 3rd plenum is entitled 'Be a revolutionary clique for promoting progress' (*Tso ko-ming-ti ts'u-chin p'ai*). For further references by Mao to the clique (at the Chengtu conference) and the committee (at the second session of the 8th Congress), see *Mao Chu-hsi Wen-hsuan*, p. 83, and *Mao Tse-tung ssu-hsiang wan sui* (1969), p. 220. I infer that the Twelve-Year Agricultural Programme was revised at short notice because of the failure to adjust the article on water consevancy to fit current policy as elaborated in a recent CC-SC directive; see Oksenberg MS, ch. 11. For a discussion of the fallacious basis of the Programme, see Klatt, *The Chinese Model*, p. 104.

[57] Mao, *SW*, V, p. 490.

[58] See *Origins*, I, pp. 312–15. It was presumably the uncertainty engendered by the plenum that was among the reasons why it was difficult to finalize the 2nd FYP. A British politician who visited China in Oct. 1957 and interviewed Po I-po reported that the targets put forward by Chou En-lai a year earlier at the 8th Congress were still being discussed in detail. It was clearly his impression that any revisions would be downwards; see Donnelly, *The March Wind*, p. 241.

[59] See *Origins*, I, ch. 7.

[60] *JMJP* editorials of 13 and 29 Nov. called for 'high tides' in agriculture and industry respectively; the term 'great leap forward' appears to have been first used in the Sixty Articles on Work Methods (art. 16) (CB 892, p. 4), signed by Mao on 31 Jan. 1958 but never officially published, and first publicized in the *JMJP* editorial on the annual session of the NPC, 12 Feb. 1958.

[61] *Mao, Miscellany*, II, p. 310.

[62] *Mao Tse-tung ssu-hsiang wan sui* (1969), p. 150. Mao was clearly not in a good position to consult his colleagues in the central leadership while he was in Moscow, and so presumably his assertion was based on the outcome of the 3rd plenum. Why Mao wrote this warning is unclear; perhaps an unpalatable Finance Ministry document had been forwarded to him in Moscow for his approval.

[63] According to Po I-po's later account; see FBIS-CHI-81-145, p. K33.

[64] *HHPYK*, No. 1 (1958), p. 2. Liu was addressing the ACFTU congress on behalf of the CCP's CC, but, significantly, in his speech to the second session of the CCP's 8th Congress five months later, he attributed the 'militant call' to overtake Britain to Mao personally (*Pol. Docs*, p. 427). But there was no indication that Liu disapproved of Mao's initiative, though he may have had private reservations about the unilateral manner in which it was launched.

One must assume that Mao's senior colleagues endorsed his initiative only very shortly before the ACFTU congress and that the propaganda authorities were alerted to it at the last minute. Otherwise it is difficult to account for the failure of *JMJP* to emphasize this important new target when reproducing Liu Shao-ch'i's message on 3 Dec.; it only received headline treatment when it was taken up again by Li Fu-ch'un (*JMJP*, 8 Dec. 1957).

[65] CB 483, p. 6. The following month Mao told a closed sesion of the SSC that the 15-year target for coal was 500 million tons (four times the current output) and for electric power 450,000 million kWh capacity (which was, according to Mao, ten times the current figure, but in reality over 20 times that figure); see *CLG*, I, No. 4, p. 12.

[66] CB 483, p. 5.

[67] Li's targets are ibid., p. 10; the targets endorsed by the 8th Congress are in *8th National Congress*, I, p. 236.

[68] Art. 6; *JMJP*, 26 Oct. 1957.

[69] *8th National Congress*, I, pp. 240–1. The figures there are in Chinese measures: 500 billion catties of grain and 48·8 million tan of cotton (1 catty = about 0·67 kg; 1 tan = 0·0492 ton).

[70] CB 483, p. 11; the original Chinese measures were 480 billion catties of grain and 43 million tan of cotton (*JMST*, 1958, p. 26).

[71] *Mao Tse-tung ssu-hsiang wan sui* (1969), p. 155.

[72] See Werner Klatt's contribution in *The Sino-Soviet Dispute*, p. 37.

[73] See *Origins*, I, pp. 315, 405 (note 14).

Chapter 2.   The Politburo Tours China

[1] *Mao Tse-tung ssu-hsiang wan sui* (1969), p. 156.

[2] None of these men were present when Liu Shao-ch'i, Chou En-lai and other Politburo members received the delegates to the ACFTU congress on 12 Dec. (*JMJP*, 13 Dec. 1957).

[3] On 14 Dec., Chou En-lai escorted some Burmese dignitaries to Hangchow (*JMJP*, 15 Dec.); on 17 Dec., *JMJP* carried a report that Mao had received the Burmese 'in the south', presumably in Hangchow. By 22 Dec., Chou was in Shanghai with the head of the CC's propaganda department, Lu Ting-yi (an alternate member of the Politburo), and Li Hsueh-feng, a member of the central secretariat. He inspected the Shanghai suburbs with the 1st secretary, K'o Ch'ing-shih (*Chou Tsung-li-ti Ku-shih*, pp. 55–8). In Jan., he was in Anhwei (Grey Chou, II, pp. 347–8). Liu Shao-ch'i was still in Peking on 20 Dec., when, accompanied only by an alternate member of the secretariat, Yang Shang-k'un, he received Indonesian and Canadian party leaders (*JMJP*, 21 Dec.).

One result of the mass exodus of leaders was that instructions to important agricultural and financial conferences had to be given by the prestigious but unlikely figure of Marshal Chu Teh, Mao's deputy as head of state (see *JMJP*, 28 and 29 Dec. 1957). Apart from Chu Teh, the active Politburo members who probably did not do much touring were three other Marshals: Ch'en Yi (presumably busy learning the ropes at the Foreign Ministry which he was to take over from Chou En-lai at the NPC in Feb. 1958), P'eng Teh-huai, the Defence Minister, and Ho Lung.

[4] Mao's last official appearance in Peking seems to have been at the ACFTU congress on 2 Dec. (*JMJP*, 3 Dec. 1957). Mao did not receive the Burmese Vice Premier U Kyaw Nyein after his arrival in Peking on 4 Dec., and so he may have left Peking by then. Mao met a Czech military delegation at an undisclosed site on 7 Dec.; the somewhat untypical photograph taken of the meeting suggests it did not take place in Peking (*JMJP*, 8 Dec. 1957). Mao's first appearance in Hangchow (see note 3 above) was when he received U Kyaw Nyein and his colleague U Ba Swe in mid-Dec. Mao was again reported to be in Hangchow in 1 Jan. (*JMJP*, 29 Jan. 1958) and on 3 Jan. where he received the Yemeni crown prince in the company of Chou En-lai (*JMJP*, 4 Jan.

1958). He was still in the area on 5 Jan. (*Shen-ch'ieh Huai-nien Lo Jui-ch'ing T'ung-chih*, p. 121).

5 CB 892, p. 1.

6 SCMP 1946, pp. 2-3; for Mao's speeches at the conference, see *Mao Tse-tung ssu-hsiang wan sui* (1969), pp. 145-54.

7 Mao received the Indian ambassador in Canton on the 23rd; SCMP 1701, p. 29.

8 Mao addressed the SSC on 28 and 30 Jan.; see *Mao Tse-tung ssu-hsiang wan sui* (1969), pp. 154-9. Mao was at least at the opening (1 Feb.) and closing (11 Feb.) sessions of the NPC; see *JMJP*, 2 and 12 Feb. 1958.

9 SCMP 1761, p. 4; SCMP 1766, pp. 1-3.

10 On 5 March, Mao visited a factory in Chengtu; see *Szechwan Jih-pao*, 7 April 1958, and *JMJP*, 11 April 1958.

11 Mao addressed the Chengtu conference on 10, 20 and 22 March; *Mao Tse-tung ssu-hsiang wan sui* (1969), pp. 159-80. For reports of his inspection visits see *Szechwan Jih-pao*, 7 April 1958, *JMJP*, 27 April 1958, SCMP 1766, p. 3 ff.

12 *JMJP*, 15 April 1958.

13 Mao received some Polish dignitaries in Wuhan on the evening of 2 April (*JMJP*, 4 April 1958); on 3 April he visited a Wuhan restaurant (SCMP 1779, pp. 1-4). A report of Mao's activities in the city on 11 April is in *JMJP*, 15 April 1958.

14 *Mao Tse-tung ssu-hsiang wan sui* (1969), pp. 180-6.

15 *JMJP*, 22 April 1958. See also *Shao-shan Hung Jih Chao Ch'ien Ch'iu*, pp. 240, 251-3.

16 *HC*, No. 1, 1958, p. 4; *JMJP*, 1 May 1958; SCMP 1779, pp. 6-10. Mao saw an agricultural tools exhibition on 30 April; Liu Shao-ch'i, Teng Hsiao-p'ing, K'ang Sheng and Lu Ting-yi visited the same exhibition in the last ten days of April (*JMJP*, 4 May 1958).

17 *JMST* 1959, p. 32.

18 We know the approximate date of this conference because Mao tells us that it took place in January before the Nanning conference (CB 892, p. 1), and because we know from *Chung-kuo Pai-k'o Nien-chien* (China Encyclopedic Yearbook) *1981*, p. 562, that the latter conference lasted from 11 to 22 Jan. Mao stated that the discussions at Hangchow, like those at Nanning, formed part of the basis of the Sixty Articles on Work Methods which he drew up at the end of the month (CB 892, p. 1).

19 *JMJP*, 26 Oct. 1957. The article in this revised draft of the programme differed from the original article (*Pol. Docs*, p. 125); only grain-eating sparrows were now declared a threat, those in towns and forests being excused execution.

20 The editorial Mao wrote for the *Chieh-fang Jih-pao*, 16 Dec. 1944, is quoted in 'Chairman Mao's instructions on health work—1928-1966', reprinted by *Hsin Jen Wei* (New People's Health) (People's Health Press, June 1967), trans. in SCMM(S) 22, p. 5. Mao's speech to the SSC on 13 Oct. 1957 is in Mao, *SW*, V; see p. 512.

21 See *Szechwan Jih-pao*, 30 Nov. 1957, and ibid., 26 Dec. 1957.

22 SCMP 1707, pp. 10-12. The news of Mao's visit was not published in *JMJP* until 29 Jan. 1958.

23 SCMM(S) 22, p. 11.

24 *JMJP*, 16 Jan. 1958.

25 SCMP 1722, pp. 26-7.

26 Ibid., p. 14.

27 Klochko, *Soviet Scientist in Red China*, p. 68.

28 George Gale, who accompanied the British Labour Party delegation in 1954.

29 Wilson, *One Chinese Moon*, p. 207.

[30] SCMP 1722, p. 1. For the attribution to Mao of this directive, and the health sections of the 1960 version of the Twelve-Year Agricultural Programme, see SCMM(S) 22, pp. 10, 12.

[31] *JMJP*, 30 June 1958.

[32] At least, it was the only poem of 1958 that he released.

[33] From the translation in Ch'en, *Mao and the Chinese Revolution*, p. 349; the translators explain that the Cowherd is a constellation. There is a second verse.

[34] On medical education reforms, see 'Monstrous crimes of urban "lords"' Health Ministry in opposing 26 June "directive"', *Hung I Chan Pao* (Red Medicine Combat News) and *Pa I-pa Chan Pao* (18 Aug. Combat News), 26 June 1967, trans. in SCMP(S) 198, p. 33. On the promotion of Chinese medicine, see SCMM(S) 22, pp. 10–11.

[35] David M. Lampton, 'Health policy during the Great Leap Forward', *CQ*, No. 60 (Oct.–Dec. 1974), pp. 668–98.

[36] *Mao, Miscellany*, I, p. 141. TLC, pp. 31–2.

[37] Mao, *Critique*, p. 123.

[38] See for instance 'History of struggle between the two lines (on China's machinery front)', *Nung-yeh Chi-hsieh Chi-shu* (Agricultural Machinery Technique), No. 9, 1968, trans. in SCMM 633, p. 7.

[39] Po I-po, 'Respect and remembrance—Marking the 60th anniversary of the founding of the CCP', *HC*, No. 13, 1981, trans. in FBIS-CHI-81-145, p. K33; 'Revisionist trumpeter', *Pei-ching Kung-she* (Peking Commune), 26 May 1967, p. 3, col. 1.

[40] *Pei-ching Kung-she*, 26 May 1967, p. 3, col. 1.

[41] See Chou, *The Chinese Inflation, 1937–1949*, especially ch. VIII, 'A comparison of the Chinese and other inflations'.

[42] See Hsia, *Price Control in Communist China*.

[43] See *Origins*, I, pp. 87–8.

[44] *Mao Tse-tung ssu-hsiang wan sui* (1969), p. 151.

[45] Ibid., pp. 146, 151–2. TLC, pp. 11–13. See also *Origins*, I, pp. 87–9.

[46] *Mao Tse-tung ssu-hsiang wan sui* (1969), pp. 148–9, 151–2.

[47] Ibid., p. 149; the actual phrase used by Mao for the Politburo was *piao-chueh chi-ch'i*, literally 'voting machine', but the comparison makes clear the implication.

[48] CB 892, pp. 9–10.

[49] Ibid., p. 10.

[50] Donnithorne, *China's Economic System*, p. 365; see also Barnett, *Cadres, Bureaucracy and Political Power in Communist China*, p. 21.

[51] Donnithorne, *China's Economic System* p. 517.

[52] Ibid., p. 365.

[53] For a brief resumé of Wu Po's career see Li, *Chung Kung Shui-shou Chih-tu*, Appendices, pp. 17–18.

[54] Mao, *SW*, V, pp. 334–5.

[55] *Mao Tse-tung ssu-hsiang wan sui* (1969), p. 149; for a discussion of the importance of Mao's preface, see *Origins*, I, pp. 26–7.

[56] *Mao Tse-tung ssu-hsiang wan sui* (1969), p. 157. This source apparently summarizes Mao's speeches to the SSC on 28 and 30 Jan. A partial text of the speech on the 28th is included in *Mao chu-hsi tui P'eng, Huang, Chang, Chou fan-tang chi-t'uan-ti p'i-p'an*, pp. 1–3; it is translated in *CLG*, I, No. 4, pp. 10–14.

[57] *Mao Tse-tung ssu-hsiang wan sui* (1969), p. 154. The version of the dictum that was published in the first issue of the theoretical journal *Red Flag*, 1 June 1958, p. 3, was slightly different and was drawn from an article written in April 1958, not from this speech; for a translation, see Schram, *The Political Thought of Mao Tse-tung*, p. 352.

[58] Ibid., p. 158. Kao Kang and Jao Shu-shih were senior party members—Kao was among the top half dozen in the Politburo—purged in 1954–5.

[59] Ibid., p. 159. According to *A Comprehensive Glossary of Chinese Communist Terminology*, p. 194, the concept of red and expert education was discussed by the President of the Academy of Sciences, Kuo Mo-jo, in 1957. Liu Shao-ch'i had stressed the importance of the combination of red and expert in a speech on 6 Nov. 1957; *Pol. Docs*, p. 400.

[60] See *Origins*, I, p. 298.

[61] *Huai-nien Mao Tse-tung T'ung-chih*, pp. 208–13.

[62] *CLG*, I, No. 4, pp. 13–14.

[63] Ibid., p. 14.

[64] CB 892, p. 1.

[65] Ibid., p. 14.

[66] Mao's preface to the Sixty Articles was dated 31 Jan. The document was apparently issued by the CC's general office on 19 Feb. (ibid. p. 1) and, to judge by Kiangsu's experience, it was distributed down to the level of county secretary during the second half of February (according to an article by Kiangsu 1st secretary, Chiang Wei-ch'ing, in *JMJP*, 14 May 1958, trans. in CB 509, p. 6). It is not possible to tell from internal evidence whether Mao's preface was written for the conference that discussed the Sixty Articles or for the general office's mailing list. On the assumption that Mao required a little time for 'pondering' (CB 892, p. 1) and drawing up the document after the Nanning conference, that he probably had little time for this while he was still travelling in the south, that the SSC session probably ruled out a separate conference from 28 to 30 Jan., and that the commencement of the NPC session on 1 Feb. would have made the convening of a high-level conference thereafter difficult albeit not impossible, I would speculate that the meeting which discussed the Sixty Articles met on 31 Jan.

[67] CB 892, p. 1.

[68] Ibid.

[69] Ibid., p. 4. For use of the term 'great leap forward' in connection with the water conservancy drive, see Oksenberg MS, ch. 13. See also note 99 below.

[70] For a description of the first 'leap' in 1956, see *Origins*, I, Pt 1.

[71] CB 892, p. 3.

[72] Ibid., pp. 5–7.

[73] Ibid., p. 7. Apart from Mao's statement that Liu was responsible for an article on rules and regulations, Liu's authorship is also indicated by the reference in the article to the Shihchingshan power station. Liu had visited this enterprise on 6 Sept. 1957 (ECMM 115, pp. 1–4).

[74] CB 892, pp. 7–8.

[75] Cf. Li Fu-ch'un's speech to the CCP's 8th Congress, quoted in *Origins*, I, p. 124.

[76] CB 892, p. 7.

[77] Ibid., p. 7.

[78] Ibid., p. 2.

[79] Article 8; ibid., p. 3.

[80] Li, *The Statistical System of Communist China*, p. 71.

[81] CB 892, p. 3.

[82] Li, *Statistical System*, p. 72. Li describes (p. 71 ff.) how the new targeting system was imposed on the State Statistical Bureau amid accusations that the old system was conservative and passive.

[83] The CC published a directive on experimental plots on 14 Feb. 1958; see SCMP 1720, p. 5. The experimental plot movement arose in Hungan *hsien*, Hupeh province, where cadres, transferred to the grass roots, set aside small plots on

which they attempted to find better methods of cultivation; ibid., pp. 5–12. The movement was encouraged by the CC as a means of uniting cadres and masses and helping production, embodying the twin goals of redness and expertise; see the *JMJP* editorial, 15 Feb. 1958, in ibid., pp. 12–15.

84 CB 892, p. 13.

85 See *Origins*, I, pp. 105–7, 152–6.

86 For Chou's role in the rectification campaign, see ibid., pp. 33–5, 180–3, 218–19, 231–40, 274–8.

87 CB 493, p. 5 (Li); CB 494, p. 6 (Po).

88 CB 493, p. 6.

89 CB 494, p. 9; *HHPYK*, No. 5, 1958, p. 15.

90 Po's targets are in CB 494, p. 15; I have calculated the percentage increases for 1957 over 1956 on the basis of Po's figures for output increases in 1957 (ibid., p. 3) and the 1956 figures as given in *Ten Great Years*, p. 95. (The 1957 figures in the latter source do not correspond to Po's; since what I am interested in here is not actual output but the basis on which Po drew up his 1958 targets, I have ignored the 1957 figures in *Ten Great Years*, even though they are presumably more accurate.)

91 CB 494, p. 2. According to Po, more major projects were completed in 1957 than in any other year of the 1st FYP (ibid.).

92 CB 493, p. 11.

93 In his speech on contradictions; *Pol. Docs*, p. 294.

94 Oksenberg MS, ch. 11 (1 mou = 0·1647 acre).

95 Ibid., ch. 13.

96 See Po's speech to the 1958 NPC in CB 494, p. 4.

97 Ibid. Li Hsien-nien estimated the investment value of the water conservancy work at 6,000 million yuan (CB 493, p. 12), or over twice the projected state expenditure on agriculture for 1958.

98 Grey Chou, III, pp. 40–1.

99 *JMJP* editorial, 'A congress that strove for a great leap forward', 12 Feb. 1958. Po I-po revealed after Chou's death that the Premier had proposed the slogan; when Mao asked a group of colleagues, among them Chou, where the phrase had come from, the Premier remained modestly silent and it was left to others to tell the Chairman (Grey Chou, III, p. 33). But it is not clear whether Chou himself devised the slogan or simply adopted it. The phrase 'great leap forward' was used in a story about a mountainous area in Chi-yuan *hsien* carried on p. 2 of the *Honan Jih-pao* on 17 Nov. 1957; it was again used in a front page headline on cotton production in the same paper on 1 Dec. 1957. Less than a month before the use of the phrase 'great leap forward' on 17 Nov., the *Hunan Jih-pao* was still using the 1956 slogan 'high tide'; see the report on the expanded 6th plenum carried by the paper on 20 Oct. Presumably the phrase 'great leap forward' was coined some time between those dates. I have not found the phrase used in other provincial papers of this period, though the incompleteness of Western holdings of these papers make it impossible to state categorically that it did not appear elsewhere. However, in view of the trail-blazing role played by Honan in the great leap forward, it seems reasonable to assume that the phrase did originate there. See also note 69 above.

3.   The Chengtu conference

1 Chi, *Key Economic Areas in Chinese History*, pp. 96–7; Tregear, *A Geography of China*, pp. 76–8.

2 Smedley, *The Great Road*, p. 71.

³ Chengtu was not among the first dozen Chinese cities in terms of population, being outnumbered even by the other great Szechwanese city, Chungking; *Ten Great Years*, p. 12.

⁴ See ibid., p. 11, for provincial population figures for 1957. For the political importance of grain surplus provinces, see 'Evidence of crime of T'ao Chu and Chao Tzu-yang of following Liu Shao-ch'i in rural work', *Fan-hsiu Chan Pao* (Anti-revisionism Combat News), 8 July 1967 (SCMP 4018, p. 3), where T'ao, the one-time party leader of central-south China, is quoted as saying 'At a central work conference, whoever holds the largest stock of the food crop can out-talk anybody else'. See also 'A shocking case of political persecution', *Hung-se Tsao-fan-che* (Red Rebel) (Canton?) 4 Jan. 1968 (SCMP 4123, p. 2).

⁵ Hunan, the native province of Mao and Liu Shao-ch'i, was best represented on both the CC and Politburo. For the CC proportions, see Derek J. Waller, 'The evolution of the Chinese Communist political elite, 1931–56', in Scalapino (ed.), *Elites in the People's Republic of China*, p. 58.

⁶ For speculation that Mao sent the outsider Ho Lung into Szechwan in an attempt to provide a counterpoise to the popularity of the native Liu Po-ch'eng, see Whitson, *The Chinese High Command*, p. 19.

⁷ See ibid., Charts A, C, D.

⁸ See *Origins*, I, pp. 109, 254.

⁹ See *Szechwan Jih-pao*, 5 Dec. 1957, where a revised draft of the Szechwan programme was published after the national programme was revised.

¹⁰ See David S. G. Goodman, 'Li Jingquan and the South-West Region, 1958–66: The life and "crimes" of a "local emperor"', *CQ*, Jan.–March 1980, pp. 74–5.

¹¹ See Mao's speech to the Chengtu conference on 20 March 1958 in *Mao Tse-tung ssu-hsiang wan sui* (1969), p. 166, where the Szechwanese leader denoted by 'X X X' must be Li Ching-ch'üan. Li seemed to demonstrate some embarrassment at the 8th Congress at the relative slowness of collectivization in Szechwan; Mao's remark at Chengtu may have been calculated to reassure Li that he had not thereby suffered in the Chairman's esteem.

¹² K'o Ch'ing-shih had been a member of Mao' party fraction in Yenan; see Ho Teh-ch'uan, 'With Chairman Mao at a party fraction', SCMP 1905, p. 1.

¹³ See *JMJP*, 11, 12, 15 and 27 April 1958; *Szechwan Jih-pao*, 6 and 7 April 1958.

¹⁴ *JMJP*, 15 April 1958.

¹⁵ They were delivered on 10, 20 and 22 March; see *Mao Tse-tung ssu-hsiang wan sui* (1969), pp. 159–80. They are translated in *Issues & Studies*, Nov. 1973 (speech of 10 March), pp. 95–8, and Dec. 1973 (speeches of 20 and 22 March), pp. 103–12. The speech of 22 March is also included in *Mao Chu-hsi Wen-hsuan* (Chairman Mao's Selected Writings), pp. 78–83, and this version is translated in JPRS 49,826 (12 Feb. 1970), pp. 45–52. In his speech on 10 March, Mao referred to saying something 'yesterday' (*Issues & Studies*, Nov. 1973, p. 97), but if he did make a speech on 9 March we have no record of it.

¹⁶ *Issues & Studies*, Nov. 1973, pp. 95–6.

¹⁷ Ibid., pp. 96, 98.

¹⁸ Ibid., p. 96.

¹⁹ Ibid. Mao's criticism of copying Soviet educational practices was later alleged to have been aimed at Liu Shao-ch'i and Lu Ting-yi. (See 'Chronology of the two-road struggle on the educational front of the past 17 years', *Chiao-yü Ko-ming* (Educational Revolution), 6 May 1967 (JPRS 41,932, p. 27). If this is correct then it was presumably because Liu and Lu were in overall charge of education and propaganda; but then Mao's criticisms of copying Soviet econo-

mic practices must equally have been aimed at Chou En-lai. In other words, it seems unlikely that Mao's attack on copying from the Soviet Union was meant as a major personal attack on some of his senior colleagues even if he did feel some of them had gone to extremes. It should be noted anyway that the quotation in JPRS 41,932, p. 27, does not correspond to Mao's speech as carried in *Issues & Studies*, Nov. 1973, p. 96. Moreover the JPRS quotation suggests Mao also attacked Liu and Lu for encouraging emulation of Soviet-style journalism, whereas we know that as early as 1956 Liu was scathingly critical about Soviet press methods (see *Origins*, I, p. 76).

[20] See MacFarquhar, *Hundred Flowers*, pp. 26, 27, 46, 64, 78, 80, 92, 220.

[21] *Issues & Studies*, Nov. 1973, p. 97.

[22] Ibid.

[23] Grey Chou, III, p. 59.

[24] *Issues & Studies*, Nov. 1973, p. 97.

[25] Ibid.

[26] Ibid., p. 98.

[27] Ibid., p. 97.

[28] See *Origins*, I, pp. 99–109, 157–9.

[29] *Issues & Studies*, Nov. 1973, p. 98. See also Dedijer, *Tito Speaks*, p. 331.

[30] *Issues & Studies*, Nov. 1973, p. 98.

[31] Ibid. By 'colonies' Mao was referring to the creation of Sino-Soviet joint-stock companies in Manchuria and Sinkiang in 1950, together with the agreements on the joint management of the Chinese Changchun railway, and the garrisoning of Soviet troops in the naval base of Port Arthur (Lüshun) which was to be jointly used. To the best of my knowledge this speech by Mao was the first revelation that the Russians had insisted also on banning third country nationals from these areas.

[32] See 'A chronicle of events in the life of Liu Shao-ch'i (1899–1967)', CB 834, p. 19, and below pp. 283–92.

[33] *Issues & Studies*, Nov. 1973, p. 98.

[34] Ibid., p. 97. For discussions of the Kao Kang affair, see the relevant chapter in Frederick Teiwes, *Politics & Purges in China*, and Harold Hinton, *The 'Unprincipled Dispute' within the Chinese Communist Top Leadership*.

[35] *Issues & Studies*, Nov. 1973, p. 98. See also *Origins*, I, p. 316. In his discussions of this issue, Mao stated that the *NYT* published the full text of his speech. This is welcome confirmation that the version of the speech on contradictions obtained by the paper through Polish sources and published on 13 June 1957 was accurate. But the *NYT* never claimed that it was publishing a complete text and it is clear that it did not. Probably Mao at Chengtu was just talking loosely when he referred to a complete text, but it is conceivable that he had been misinformed in 1957 as to the extent of the *NYT* revelations in order that he should be induced to publish an official, revised version. (See *Origins*, I, pp. 266–7.)

[36] Borisov & Koloskov, *Soviet-Chinese Relations, 1945–1970*, p. 152.

[37] *Issues & Studies*, Nov. 1973, p. 97; for a discussion of this speech, see *Origins*, I, pp. 61–74.

[38] *Kuan-yü T'an Chen-lin wen-t'i-ti ch'u-pu tsung-ho ts'ai-liao* (A preliminary synthesis of material on the problem of T'an Chen-lin) (Liaison station for thoroughly smashing T'an Chen-lin's capitalist, counter-revolutionary, restorationist adverse current, 17 March 1967), p. 22.

[39] *Issues & Studies*, Nov. 1973, p. 98.

[40] Cf. the excerpts in the *NYT*, 13 June 1957, with the relevant section (7) of the official text in *Pol. Docs*, pp. 287–8.

[41] *Issues & Studies*, Dec. 1973, p. 107.

[42] *Mao, Miscellany*, I, p. 85.

[43] See *Teng Hsiao-p'ing fan-tang fan-she-hui-chu-i fan-Mao Tse-tung ssu-hsiang-ti yen-lun chai-pien*, p. 17; *P'eng Chen Fan-ko-ming hsiu-cheng-chu-i yen-lun chai-pien* (Selection of P'eng Chen's counter-revolutionary revisionist utterances) (Peking: China People's University's New People's University Commune and Mao Tse-tung's Thought Red Guards, May 1967), pp. 7, 8, 11, 13; *Counter-revolutionary revisionist P'eng Chen's towering crimes of opposing the party, socialism and the Thought of Mao Tse-tung*, trans. in SCMM 639, pp. 6, 8, 16; *Ts'ui Chiu Chan Pao* (Destroy the Old Combat News), 25 May 1967, pp. 2, 3; *Tung Fang Hung Chan Pao* (East is Red Combat News), p. 5, no. 71, p. 6, no. 81; 'Criticism of Ch'en Pei-hsien's five sham self-examinations', *Kung-jen Tsao-fan Pao* (Workers' Rebellion Journal), 10 Feb. 1968, trans. in SCMP 4131, p. 6—K'o Ch'ing-shih's slogan, reported here, was 'The rectification movement may come to an end for the moment, but the spirit of rectification must never be lost.' Renewed wooing of the bourgeoisie has been foreshadowed by Liu Shao-ch'i at a conference of directors of united front work departments in Dec. 1957; see *Completely purge Liu Shao-ch'i for his counter-revolutionary revisionist crimes in united front, nationalities, and religious work*, trans. in SCMM 645, pp. 7, 8, 12, 13, 15.

[44] Klochko, *Soviet Scientist in Red China*, pp. 74–6.

[45] *Issues & Studies*, Dec. 1973, pp. 108–9.

[46] Ibid., pp. 109, 110.

[47] Sun Yeh-fang, 'Consolidate statistics work, reform the statistics system', *Ching-chi Kuan-li* (Economic Management), 15 Feb. 1981, trans. in FBIS-CHI-81-058, p. L5.

[48] *K'o Chi Ko-ming*, Aug. 1967, pp. 14–17. For Ch'en's relationship to Mao, see *Origins*, I, pp. 17–18.

[49] *Issues & Studies*, Dec. 1973, pp. 108, 110.

[50] Ibid., p. 111.

[51] Ibid., p. 112. Tu Fu and Li Po of the T'ang dynasty are accepted by most Chinese as the greatest classical poets their culture has produced. Tu Fu has been particularly beloved of 'leftist' and communist intellectuals because of his trenchant criticism of the contemporary court, but in 1971 Kuo Mo-jo, China's leading intellectual and President of the Academy of Sciences, dethroned Tu Fu from his position as the people's poet; see Kuo, *Li Po yü Tu Fu*, and the review of this volume by Wen-djang Chu in *CQ*, Oct.–Dec. 1973, pp. 796–8.

[52] See *Origins*, I, pp. 178–80.

[53] For a discussion of what the author called the 'multimillion-poem movement', see S. H. Chen, 'Multiplicity in uniformity: poetry and the Great Leap Forward', *CQ*, July–Sept. 1960, pp. 1–15; see also Goldman, *Literary Dissent in Communist China*, pp. 244–7, and Fokkema, *Literary Doctrine in China and Soviet Influence, 1956–1960*, pp. 202–8.

The famous poet Ho Ch'i-fang noted the following peasant stanza after an inspection tour in Honan during which 'we were obliged to compose several pieces of doggerel':

Chairman Mao's eyes are like stars in the sky,
Even people living deep in the mountains see their light.

Ho dedicated a poem of his own to the peasant poet which illustrated the degree to which even the country's leading literary lights had to bow to the new movement:

Of all the stars in the skies, Venus shines the brightest,
Among poets from the distant past, Li Po and Tu Fu are celebrated most.
Who is it writes the best poems today?

The multitudes of laboring people.
Both poems are quoted in Hsu, *Literature of the People's Republic of China*,
p. 530.
    In one of his Chengtu speeches, Mao attacked comrades who had failed to
criticize sufficiently erring bourgeois intellectuals (*Issues & Studies*, Dec. 1973,
p. 109). During the cultural revolution it was alleged that the comrades referred to included P'eng Chen and two senior propaganda officials, Lu Ting-yi
and Chou Yang (*Hung-se P'i-p'an-che* (Red Critic), 16 June 1967, p. 2, col.
3), but I have not found any other evidence to corroborate this suggestion. Indeed these men were likely to have been sterner critics than Mao of 'bourgeois
intellectuals'—P'eng and Lu because of their position on rectification, Chou
Yang because of the antipathy felt towards him by some of the intellectuals
cited by Mao; see *Origins*, I, pp. 190–1, 201, 203.

54 *Ku-tsu kan-ching, li-cheng shang-yu, to, k'uai, hao, sheng*; see *Mao Tse-tung
    ssu-hsiang wan sui* (1969), p. 166. (This is the official translation as given in
    Han-Ying Shih-shih Yung-yü Tz'u-hui, p. 141; the translation in *Issues & Stu-
    dies*, Dec. 1973, p. 104, is somewhat different.)
        '*To, k'uai, hao, sheng*' had been the slogan adopted by Mao for the 1956
    leap; see *Origins*, I, pp. 30–2. According to various accounts, Chou En-lai
    was responsible for suggesting 'more, faster, better' as a slogan at the end of
    1955. It was approved by Mao, and then Li Fu-ch'un, Chairman of tne State
    Planning Commission, suggested adding 'more economically', which Mao also
    accepted. (See Grey Chou, III, p. 33; SWB/FE/6014/BII, pp. 3–4; Ku Cho-
    hsin et al, 'The tremendous contribution of Comrade Li Fu-ch'un to economic
    planning work', *JMJP*, 22 May 1980, p. 2.)
        '*Li-cheng shang-yu*', according to Mao, ante-dated the 1958 leap (*Mao Tse-
    tung ssu-hsiang wan sui* (1969), p. 219), but I have not been able to trace its
    origins. Only '*ku-tsu kan-ching*' was evolved specially for the 1958 leap and
    there was apparently some discussion as to whether it should be *ku-tsu* or *ku-
    ch'i* that preceded *kan-ching*; *ku-ch'i kan-ching* would have simply meant
    'summon up one's energies' and Mao preferred *ku-tsu kan-ching* or 'summon
    up all one's energies' because it introduced the dimension of quantity to the
    slogan (see ibid., and *Mao, Miscellany*, I, p. 117).
        To go by Mao, *Ku-tsu kan-ching* and *li-cheng shang-yu* were probably first
    combined in the *JMJP* New Year editorial, 1 Jan. 1958 (*Mao, Miscellany*, I, p.
    157); but, if so, it was at that stage only a happy turn of phrase rather than an
    agreed slogan. (In this editorial the phrase 'great leap forward' was used to re-
    fer to the enonomic advance of 1956.)
        The Shanghai party secretary, K'o Ch'ing-shih, may have been the first to
    use *ku-tsu*; see his report to the Shanghai party on 25 Dec. 1957 where he
    advocated *ku-tsu ko-ming-ti* (revolutionary) *kan-ching* (*JMJP*, 25 Jan. 1958,
    p. 4). In his speeches on 28 and 30 Jan. 1958, to the SSC, Mao used *ku-ch'i* in
    the phrase *ku-ch'i yung-ch'i* (summon up bravery); see *Mao Tse-tung ssu-
    hsiang wan sui* (1969), p. 155. In his speech to the NPC on 1 Feb. 1958, Fi-
    nance Minister Li Hsien-nien copied K'o in inserting *Ko-ming* in advocating
    ku-ch'i ko-ming kan-ching (*HHPYK*, No. 5, 1958, p. 12). The *JMJP* editorials
    on the NPC session (3 and 12 Feb. 1958) shortened this to *ku-ch'i kan-ching*.
    Presumably Mao opted for *ku-tsu kan-ching* at some point in the following five
    weeks. Thereafter *ku-tsu* became current; see for example a headline in *JMJP*,
    10 April 1958, p. 4, and the front-page banner headlines in the same paper on
    May Day which carried the complete leap forward slogan.

55 See *Mao Tse-tung ssu-hsiang wan sui* (1969), p. 166. My interpretation of this
    passage differs from that in *Issues & Studies*, Dec. 1973, p. 103. The passage
    starts off: '*Honan t'i-ch'u i-nien shih-hsien ssu, wu, pa,...*', which *Issues &*

Studies renders 'Honan has proposed April, May and August harvests...' on the assumption that *ssu, wu, pa* refer to the fourth, fifth and eighth months of the year. I believe, however, that it refers to the key article on grain yields in the Twelve-Year Agricultural Programme in which it was proposed that areas roughly north of the Yellow River should increase yields from 150 catties per mou to 400 catties, south of the Yellow River and north of the Huai River from 208 catties to 500, and south of the Huai River from 400 catties to 800; see clause 2 of the revised programme, *JMJP,* 26 Oct. 1957.

Issues & Studies renders *shui-li-hua* simply as 'water conservation' which loses the sweep of the original proposal. Most importantly, the magazine fails to indicate the grandiose nature of Honan's aims by omitting to reveal that all of them were to be achieved within one year as opposed to the 12 sanctioned in the Twelve-Year Agricultural Programme.

[56] See the brief memoir in *HHYP,* No. 1, 1979, p. 103, which draws a merciful veil over Wu's activities during the great leap, saying only that he made positive contributions to the development of Honan's economy in the post-1949 period. The precise date of Wu's effective takeover from his disgraced predecessor is uncertain; see Chang, *Power and Policy in China,* pp. 45–6.

[57] SCMP 1722, p. 1. Even in February, Honan had been the most ambitious province in the campaign against the four pests.

[58] See *Origins,* I, pp. 86–8.

[59] *Mao Tse-tung ssu-hsiang wan sui* (1969), p. 166; *Issues & Studies,* Dec. 1973, pp. 103–4. It was at this point that Mao cited collectivization and contrasted Chou Hsiao-chou's helter-skelter approach to the movement in Hunan unfavourably with the more relaxed pace set by Li Ching-ch'üan in Szechwan in order to demonstrate that he did not insist on a breakneck pace.

[60] *Mao Tse-tung ssu-hsiang wan sui* (1969), p. 166.

[61] Ibid., p. 167. See also SWB/FE/5995/BII, pp. 6–7.

[62] At one conference in June, T'an Chen-lin revealed the increases considered probable at Chengtu; see his article in *HC,* No. 6, 1958, in ECMM 144, p. 2. At another conference, he revealed what the 'leftist' targets had been at the time of Chengtu; see *P'i T'an Chan Pao* (Criticize T'an Combat News), 5 Aug. 1967, p. 2, col. 1.

[63] See *Kuan-yü T'an Chen-lin wen-t'i-ti ch'u-pu tsung-ho ts'ai-liao* (*hsu chi*) (Preliminary general material on the problem of T'an Chen-lin [further collection]), 6 April 1967, p. 3, No. 22. Mao's suggestion as reported by T'an does not appear in so many words in the records available of the Chairman's speeches at Chengtu, but it is clearly hinted at in his speech of 20 March (*Issues & Studies,* Dec. 1973, pp. 103–4).

[64] 'Completely settle the heinous crimes of China's Khrushchev and company in undermining agricultural mechanisation', *Nung-yeh Chi-hsieh Chi-shu* (Agricultural Machinery Techniques), No. 5 (8 Aug. 1967) (SCMM 610, p. 19).

[65] Perkins, *Agricultural Development in China,* p. 56. See also the *JMJP* editorial, 6 May 1958 (SCMP 1771, p. 7).

[66] Perkins, *Agricultural Development in China,* pp. 57–8.

[67] See the article by Huang Ching, then director of the State Technology Commission, quoted in Chao, *Agricultural Production in Communist China,* pp. 95–6.

[68] For a description of this dispute, hostile to Liu, see 'History of struggle between the two lines [on China's farm machinery front]', *Nung-yeh Chi-hsieh Chi-shu,* No. 9, 1968 (SCMM 633, pp. 7–10). For a description of the collectivization drive, see *Origins,* I, pp. 15–19.

[69] *Pol. Docs,* p. 100.

[70] For a discussion of this error, see W. K.[Werner Klatt], 'Soviet agriculture as

a model for Asian countries', *CQ*, Jan.-Mar. 1961, pp. 116-30, and Chao, *Agricultural Production in Communist China*, pp. 91-3.

[71] SCMM 633, p. 10.

[72] The report was submitted on 12 March 1957; ibid.

[73] Ibid.

[74] See Perkins, *Agricultural Development in China*, pp. 59-60.

[75] Shortage of labour on the Mao family farm was the occasion of one of the many quarrels Mao had with his father. Mao chose to help his father's tenants rather than his father in an emergency during the autumn harvest (see Ch'en, *Mao and the Chinese Revolution*, p. 22).

[76] Kenneth R. Walker, 'Organisation for agricultural production' in Eckstein, Galenson & Liu (eds), *Economic Trends in Communist China*, pp. 405-13.

[77] SCMM 633, p. 10. It is not clear from this account that K'ang's investigation was conducted at Mao's instance, but the implication is that it was sympathetic in intent and findings. This source certainly indicates that the shortage of man-power during the busy periods was a major plank in Mao's argument; ibid., p. 11. For K'ang's support of mechanization, see SCMM 610, p. 28. For a possible explanation of K'ang's close ties with Mao, see *Origins*, I, p. 148.

[78] Quoted in Chao, *Agricultural Production in Communist China*, p. 96; a full text of this article is translated in ECMM 120, pp. 34-43. Huang Ching, who died in 1958, allegedly preceded Mao as the husband of Chiang Ch'ing; see Hao-jan Chu, 'Mao's wife—Chiang Ch'ing', *CQ*, July-Sept. 1967, pp. 148-9.

[79] Chao, *Agricultural Production in Communist China*, pp. 96-8, and Huang Ching, 'Simultaneous development of industry and agriculture and the question of agricultural mechanisation', *Hsueh-hsi* (Study), 18 Jan. 1958 (ECMM 128, pp. 42-56).

[80] SCMM 610, p. 23.

[81] *Issues & Studies*, Dec. 1973, p. 103.

[82] SCMM 610, p. 23.

[83] SCMM 633, p. 12.

[84] SCMM 610, p. 20.

[85] SCMM 633, p. 13.

[86] Chao, *Agricultural Production in Communist China*, p. 109.

[87] Ibid.

[88] Schwartz, *The Soviet Economy since Stalin*, pp. 115-16.

[89] 'Summing up report on the national conference of tractor station masters (excerpts)', *Chung-kuo Nung Pao* (Chinese Agriculture), No. 5, 1958 (ECMM 147, p. 21); SCMM 633, p. 13.

[90] See Schwartz, *The Soviet Economy since Stalin*, pp. 116-18 for an account of the issues in the debate on the abolition of the MTS's in the Soviet Union.

[91] SCMM 633, p. 13.

[92] Ibid., p. 22; SCMM 610, p. 11. The allegation in the latter source that Liu was being hypocritical in advocating this policy is unconvincing. What does seem clear is that he was cost-conscious; see ibid., p. 5.

[93] ECMM 157, p. 22. A quotation in the cultural revolution account of this conference (SCMM 633, p. 13) seems to correspond to part of the last para. of section III of the report on the conference issues at the time (ECMM, loc. cit.). But even the cultural revolution version does not suggest that the conference was a major turning point.

[94] SCMM 600, p. 3.

[95] ECMM 147, p. 16.

[96] The number of collectively owned tractors went up from 2,416 in 1957 to 17,380 in 1958; on state farms the increase was from 10,177 to 16,955. The decrease in the numbers owned by agricultural machine stations was from 12,036

to 10,995. (Chao, *Agricultural Production in Communist China*, p. 109.) The total number of tractors in use in China went up from 24,629 in 1957 to 45,330 in 1958, but less than 1,000 tractors were produced domestically in the latter year (ibid., p. 107). Perhaps there was some truth in the cultural revolution allegation that T'an Chen-lin was indifferent to commune-managed mechanization (SCMM 633, p. 22) among all his other concerns.

97 Schwartz, *The Soviet Economy since Stalin*, p. 117.

98 SCMM 610, p. 27.

99 For an account of the Soviet decentralization measures see Schwartz, *The Soviet Economy since Stalin*, pp. 87–91.

100 SCMM 610, p. 22.

101 See *Origins*, I, p. 90.

102 The editorial from the *Chekiang Daily* is reproduced in *HHPYK*, No. 7, 1958, pp. 127–9.

103 See SCMM 610, p. 24.

104 A summary of Liao's speech (which provided the basis for a *People's Daily* editorial on 16 April) is contained *HHPYK*, No. 7, 1958, pp. 126–7.

105 SCMM 633, p. 6. Other leaders cited as opposing the ploughs in this account were P'eng Chen and Po I-po; another account indicates that the head of the CC's Rural Work Department, Teng Tzu-hui, also criticized them (see SCMM 610, p. 24).

106 See *Mao Tse-tung ssu-hsiang wan sui* (1969), p. 142; this admission was excised when the speech was officially published (Mao, *SW*, pp. 511–21).

107 *HHPYK*, No. 7, 1958, p. 126.

108 SCMM 610, p. 24. I have not found this quotation in Mao's speeches to the conference as printed in *Issues & Studies*, Nov. and Dec. 1973.

109 See *JMJP* editorial, 16 April 1958.

110 SCMP 1758, p. 11.

111 For the relevant article (11) in the Jan. 1956 version, see *Pol. Docs*, p. 123. For the Oct. 1957 revised ve ion, see CB 479, p. 6 (art. 7). The May 1958 version was never published (for a discussion of this see below p. 377, n. 33) but T'an Chen-lin's report on it to the congress makes no mention of the ploughs in a fairly lengthy passage on the amendments to the article on mechanization; see CB 508, p. 7. The final version of the Twelve-Year Programme, approved by the NPC in April 1960 towards the end of the great leap and well after the euphoria of 1958 had died down, also made no mention of the ploughs: CB 616, p. 8 (art. 7). For a fuller discussion of the question of mechanization and tool improvement at this time, see Stavis, *The Politics of Agricultural Mechanisation in China*, pp. 93–101, 109–125.

112 The conference was not attended by all central and provincial leaders; see *JMJP* editorial, 29 Aug. 1959.

113 See the report in *Yomiuri Shimbun*, 25 Jan. 1981, trans. in FBIS-CHI-81-049, Annex, p. 5.

114 In his speech on 22 March, Mao praised a couple of letters which were 'against him' and commended the outspokenness of men who had criticized his 100 flowers policy; see *Issues & Studies*, Dec. 1973, p. 11, and *Origins*, I, pp. 179–80. Teng stated that it was permissible to hold viewpoints different from those of the Chairman; see for instance *Teng Hsiao-p'ing fan-tang fan-she-hui-chu-i fan-Mao Tse-tung ssu-hsiang-ti yen-lun chai-pien* (Excerpts from Teng Hsiao-p'ing's anti-party, anti-socialist, anti-Mao Tse-tung Thought utterances) (Peking: Capital Red Guard Congress, China People's University Three Reds, First Detachment of the Seize Liu Teng Army, April 1967), p. 1. During the cultural revolution, Teng's remark was held against him, but I do not believe that it would have been regarded as *lèse majesté* by Mao at the time since the

Chairman himself was smiling on his critics. (See also *Origins*, I. pp. 4–5.) This source dates Teng's remark 7 April, but the Chengtu conference lasted from 9 to 26 March (*Chung-kuo Pai-k'o Nien-chien*, 1981, pp. 562–3); however, another source dates it 25 March which would mean that Teng made the remark before Mao left Szechwan and perhaps in his presence (see 'Record of Teng Hsiao-p'ing's counter-revolutionary revisionist black utterances', *Chin Chün Pao* (Advancing Army News), 14 June 1967, p. 1, col. 1).

[115] See *Teng Hsiao-p'ing fan-tang fan-she-hui-chu-i fan-Mao Tse-tung ssu-hsiang-ti yen-lun chai-pien*, p. 4.

Chapter 4. The leap is launched

[1] See p. 17 above. The CCP's new constitution, adopted at the first session of the 8th Congress in Sept. 1956, had stipulated that there should be annual congress sessions. It had been intended to hold a second session late in 1957, but, as already argued (p. 19), it had been postponed to allow Mao and his colleagues to mobilize cadres and people first. This second session turned out to be the only annual session held by the 8th Congress, and indeed the 9th Congress, which should have been held five years after the 8th, was not called until 1969, after the cultural revolution.

[2] See *Origins*, I, pp. 113–21, 160–4.

[3] Ibid., pp. 184–217.

[4] The rectification campaign was launched at the SSC on 30 April 1957. This session of the SSC was never publicly announced; even today very little is known about what Mao said on that occasion, and that little is a matter of controversy; see *Origins*, I, pp. 210, 278, 380 (note 53), 396 (note 41). The rectification campaign was launched with a CC directive, but even this was a subject of controversey and was to some extent implicitly disavowed by the *JMJP* editorial that commented on it; see ibid., pp. 212–17.

[5] For opposition to the Chairman on rectification from provincial party officials, see ibid., p. 249.

[6] Ibid., pp. 100–5.

[7] See Liu Shao-ch'i, *On the Party*, pp. 8–10.

[8] *Pol. Docs*, pp. 419, 424–6. Liu clearly indicated, for instance, that Mao's collectivization speech in 1955 and his contradictions speech in 1957 were individual initiatives; indeed, he did not refer to the latter as a speech, but as an article, which emphasized that he approved only of the revised published version. (See *Origins*, I, pp. 261–9, for a discussion of the changes introduced into the speech before publication.)

[9] See *Origins*, I, pp. 26–7.

[10] Ibid., pp. 30–2.

[11] Ibid., pp. 27–9.

[12] Ibid., pp. 57–74. Interestingly, Liu stated that the speech on ten great relationships had provided the basis for his own report to the first session of the 8th Congress (*Pol. Docs*, p. 426). This was perhaps designed as a justification or conciliatory gesture in view of the dislike that Liu must have known Mao had for parts of that report.

[13] *Pol. Docs*, p. 426.

[14] Ibid., p. 425.

[15] Ibid., p. 422.

[16] Ibid., pp. 422–3.

[17] Ibid., pp. 423–4.

[18] Ibid., p. 424.

[19] Ibid.

[20] Ibid., p. 436.

[21] Ibid., pp. 436-7.

[22] Ibid., pp. 430-1

[23] Ibid., p. 437.

[24] *Mao, Miscellany*, I, p. 95; *Mao Tse-tung ssu-hsiang wan sui* (1969), p. 192.

[25] *Mao, Miscellany*, I, pp. 105, 115; *Mao Tse-tung ssu-hsiang wan sui* (1969), pp. 204, 216.

[26] *Mao Tse-tung ssu-hsiang wan sui* (1969), pp. 218-19.

[27] *Mao, Miscellany*, I, p. 107; *Mao Tse-tung ssu-hsiang wan sui* (1969), p. 206.

[28] See Stuart Schram, 'Mao Tse-tung and Liu Shao-ch'i, 1939-1969', *Asian Survey*, April 1972, pp. 277-8.

[29] *Mao, Miscellany*, I, pp. 92-5; see also p. 41 above.

[30] See for instance Mao's statement in 1949: 'If there is to be a revolution, there must be a revolutionary party. Without a revolutionary party, without a party built on the revolutionary theory and style *of Marx, Lenin and Stalin*, it is impossible to lead the working class and the broad masses of the people to defeat imperialism and its running dogs.... With the birth of the Communist Party of China, the face of the Chinese revolution took on an altogether new aspect.' Quoted in Schram, *The Political Thought of Mao Tse-tung*, pp. 318-19.

[31] The quotation is from Liu's speech on 6 Nov. at the Peking celebration of the 40th anniversary of the Bolshevik revolution; see *Pol. Docs*, p. 399.

[32] Ibid., pp. 424-5.

[33] Ibid., pp. 426-7.

[34] Ibid., p. 427.

[35] *Pol. Docs*, p. 429.

[36] *Mao, Miscellany*, I, pp. 102, 105, 106.

[37] Ibid., p. 106; *Mao Tse-tung ssu-hsiang wan sui* (1969), p. 205.

[38] *Mao, Miscellany*, I, p. 107. See also ibid., p. 155. For Teng at Chengtu, see *Teng Hsiao-p'ing fan-tang fan-she-hui-chu-i fan-Mao Tse-tung ssu-hsiang-ti yun-lun cha pien* (Collection of Teng Hsiao-p'ing's anti-party, anti-socialist, anti-Mao Tse-tung Thought utterances) (Peking: Capital Red Representative Congress China People's University Three Red Expel Liu-Teng Army's No. 1 Detachment, April 1967), pp. 18-19.

[39] *Mao, Miscellany*, I, p. 105.

[40] See *Origins*, I, pp. 88-9. For a discussion of Mao's relationship with Chou En-lai and Teng Tzu-hui, see ibid., pp. 7-9, 326 (note 36). Li Fu-ch'un's wife Ts'ai Ch'ang, a CC member in her own right, was the sister of one of Mao's earliest and most intimate friends, Ts'ai Ho-sen, who had died during the revolution (see Schram, *Mao Tse-tung*, p. 37).

[41] See *Origins*, I, pp. 88, 315.

[42] Ibid., pp. 58, 338 (note 3).

[43] Ibid., pp. 18-19.

[44] See Roderick MacFarquhar, 'On Photographs', *CQ*, April-June 1971, pp. 296-7, and subsequent correspondence in *CQ*, July-Sept. 1971, p. 552. Photographs including Ch'en Yun were taken at the congress. *Jen-min Hua-po* (People's Pictorial), No. 7, 1958, published a picture of Liu Shao-ch'i addressing the congress session in which Ch'en Yun is clearly visible.

[45] *Origins*, I, Pts 3, 4, *passim*.

[46] *Chin Chün Pao* (Advancing Army News), 26 March 1967, p. 4, col. 2.

[47] *Mao, Miscellany*, I, pp. 103, 105. In the same speech (ibid., p. 102), Mao referred to tide-watching as lasting into 'the first half' (i.e. until June) of 1957.

[48] See *Origins*, I, p. 315.

[49] For Liu, see *Pol. Docs*, p. 427; for Mao, see *Mao, Miscellany*, I, p. 116.

[50] *Mao, Miscellany*, I, p. 109. The identity of the mysterious 'X X X' is unclear.

[51] Ibid., p. 113.

[52] See *Origins*, I, p. 311. Significantly, it was only in reference to possible splits that Mao singled out the party for special mention.

[53] Ibid., pp. 67–8.

[54] The three decrees are translated in SCMP 1665, pp. 1–10; cf. *CYWK*, pp. 60–9. According to Mao (*Mao, Miscellany*, II, p. 311), he was still working on decentralization after the second session of the 8th Congress.

[55] See Nicholas R. Lardy, 'Centralization and decentralization in China's fiscal management', *CQ*, Jan.–March 1975, pp. 28–9.

[56] Ibid., p. 29.

[57] Ibid., pp. 51–3. For the figures, see Ch'en Yun's speech to the CC's 3rd plenum, *CYWK*, p. 59; the remarks given in this source are presumably only an extract from the full speech. For an extensive discussion of decentralization issues, see Schurmann, *Ideology and Organization in Communist China*, pp. 175–8, 188–219.

[58] *CYWK*, pp. 58–9; TLC, p. 94. For the cultural revolution accusation, see *Pei-ching Kung-she* (Peking Commune), 28 Jan. 1967, p. 2, col. 3; *P'ao-hung Li Hsien-nien* (Bombard Li Hsien-nien) (8th Fighting Force, Peking Commune, Central Finance Institute, Red Representative Conference, April 1967), pp. 31, 33. Another lengthy attack on Ch'en Yun which referred to the great leap forward made no mention of any errors committed by him in 1958; *Ts'ai-mao Hung Ch'i* (Finance and Trade Red Flag), 8 Feb. 1967, trans. in SCMP(S) 172, p. 14.

[59] Grey Chou, III, p. 32.

[60] Why T'an could not simply have replaced Teng as the head of the CCP's Rural Work Department is unclear and the best hypothesis would seem to be Mao's reluctance to demote a man who had served him loyally during critical early struggles within the party; *Origins*, I, p. 326 (note 36). The choice of T'an to take over from Teng may also have been tactful; the two men had worked together during the 1930s and T'an might have been readier than others to help preserve Teng's *amour propre*. (See the biographies of T'an Chen-lin and Teng Tzu-hui in Klein & Clark, *Biographic Dictionary*.) Yet it must be noted that T'an had been as forceful as anyone in the disapproval he expressed of 'account-settlers' in his speech to the congress on the latest version of the Twelve-Year Agricultural Programme; CB 508, p. 2. It is also worth noting that at the beginning of the cultural revolution, T'an Chen-lin allegedly attempted to direct criticism of deviations from 'Maoist' agricultural policies at Teng Tzu-hui; see *Kuan-yü T'an Chen-lin wen-t'i-ti ch'u-pu tsung-ho ts'ai-liao* (Preliminary collection of material on the problem of T'an Chen-lin) (Liaison station for totally routing T'an Chen-lin's capitalist counter-revolutionary reactionary current, 17 March 1967), p. 11.

[61] It is possible that P'eng Chen was effectively a member of the PSC; see SCMM 639, p. 18. In 1966, T'ao Chu acted as secretary of the PSC before becoming a member of it; SCMP(S) 232, p. 19. Perhaps P'eng Chen played that role in the late 1950s and early 1960s.

[62] The quoted phrase was first used by the UK Prime Minister Harold Wilson to describe the leaders of the striking National Union of Seamen in the mid-1960s. It has since passed into the British political vocabulary, though normally used more ironically (because of the hyperbole in Wilson's depiction of the seamen's leaders) than is here intended.

[63] For Teng, see *Origins*, I, pp. 140–5; T'an Chen-lin had been one of Mao's

earliest adherents, participating in the Autumn Harvest Uprising in 1927 and following him thereafter to Chingkangshan.

[64] Ibid., p. 146.

[65] Gold Chou, p. 70.

[66] Chang, *The State Council in Communist China: a Structural and Functional Analysis, 1954–65*, p. 57.

[67] Ibid., p. 68.

[68] Ibid., p. 33.

[69] See Lardy, 'Centralization and decentralization', p. 56.

[70] *Origins*, I, ch. 18.

[71] See MacFarquhar, 'On photographs', where I suggest that Ulanfu's inclusion may have also been a propitiatory gesture towards the national minorities.

[72] See Frederick C. Teiwes, 'The purge of provincial leaders, 1957–1958', *CQ*, July–Sept. 1966, p. 17.

[73] In one of his speeches at the Chengtu conference, in the context of a discussion of rival personality cults, Mao referred to the *already completed* purge in Chekiang where 1st secretary Chiang Hua had ousted the provincial governor Sha Wen-han and others, asking: 'Is Chiang Hua a dictator, or Sha Wen-han a dictator?' (*Issues & Studies*, Nov. 1973, p. 97). This remark was surely very damaging as far as the victor Chiang Hua was concerned; but Mao added that similar problems were occurring in seven other provinces, all but two of which also had the results of their purges confirmed at the congress session. (For documents on the Chekiang purge, see CB 487.)

[74] Among the sins attributed to the purge victims were localism and individualism; see Teiwes, 'Purge of provincial leaders', pp. 22–30. These were errors denounced by Mao at Tsingtao; see *Origins*, I, pp. 285–9.

[75] *Mao, Miscellany*, I, p. 114.

[76] Ibid., p. 121. Mao suggested that it was better not to discipline Ku Ta-ts'un and Feng Pai-chü, senior Kwangtung cadres accused of local nationalism (see *JMST*, 1959, p. 16, and Teiwes, 'Purge of provincial leaders', pp. 23–4), and P'an Han-nien (sic, see below). If the analysis presented in *Origins*, I, p. 312, regarding the antipathy of Mao for the Kwangtung party 1st secretary T'ao Chu is correct, then Mao may have wanted to protect Tao's local critics Ku and Feng, especially if they had had anything to do with the resignation of T'ao from his concurrent post as Kwangtung governor the previous year (ibid.). Kwangtung was one of the provinces listed by Mao at Chengtu as being the scene of a struggle for power (see note 73 above).

P'an Han-nien was a Shanghai party official who had been arrested as a counter-revolutionary in July 1955 (see his biography in URI, *Who's Who in Communist China*). It is extremely unlikely that his case was reviewed along with the totally unconnected provincial purges of 1957–8; nor is his name mentioned in the list of cases reviewed that was given in the congress communiqué, though he would have been important enough to have merited mention if he had been discussed (*JMST*, 1959, p. 16). It seems more likely that P'an Han-nien was a slip and that Mao meant P'an Fu-sheng, the Honan party 1st secretary. In a later speech at the congress, Mao referred to P'an X X as a wrongdoer who should be allowed to correct himself (*Mao, Miscellany*, I, p. 115). This kind of concealment or partial concealment of names in collections of Mao's works issued for limited distribution during or after the cultural revolution seems normally to have been used to save the face of someone in trouble at the time of Mao's reference to him but who had been rehabilitated by the time the collection was distributed. P'an Fu-sheng could certainly fall into this category. After his dismissal from his provincial posts he was not heard of until 1962 but then he reappeared as Acting Director of the All-

China Federation of Supply and Marketing Cooperatives. In 1969, when this collection of Mao's writings was circulated, he was promoted from alternate to full membership of the CC at the 9th Congress.

Why Mao should have defended P'an Fu-sheng is unclear, especially as he praised his incoming successor Wu Chih-p'u (see the version of Mao's speech in *Ta Hai*, p. 24). However, in the documentation on his case, there is a reference to P'an daring to 'cheat Chairman Mao face to face' in the late summer of 1957 (CB 515, p. 11). This could mean that Mao had commended P'an when he visited Honan and that he only reluctantly agreed at the congress session that P'an should be purged after strong representation from the Honan delegation (CB·515, p. 14). It was only after the congress session that the Honan party was able speedily to proceed with the purge of P'an even though he had effectively given up his job and retreated to Peking ten months earlier (ibid.). (The official Honan account of P'an's activities alleged that he returned to the province after a prolonged sick leave when he saw the chance of mischief-making in the spring of 1957 (ibid., p. 12); could Mao, desperately needing supporters among the provincial party leaders for his rectification campaign, have encouraged P'an Fu-sheng to return to his post?)

Mao may have been compelled to list P'an Fu-sheng and the two Kwangtung officials as splitters at the congress session, but if he did their names have since been expunged from the record (*Mao, Miscellany*, I, p. 114). What is certain is that these three men were among eight purged individuals still described as 'comrades' in the final communiqué of the congress session (*JMST*, 1959, p. 16), and so Mao's wishes were in part respected. Interestingly, Mao made his recommendation of leniency not to the congress in plenary session but at a meeting restricted to heads of delegations, possibly because he wished to test their reactions first. See also Chang, *Power and Policy in China*, pp. 40–6.

[77] *Origins*, I, pp. 66–74.
[78] Ibid., p. 69.
[79] Quoted in Hsieh, *Communist China's Strategy in the Nuclear Era*, pp. 109–10.
[80] SCMP 1786, p. 6.
[81] Ibid.
[82] Ford, 'Modern weapons and the Sino-Soviet estrangement', *CQ*, April–June 1964, p. 162. Two days after the programme was published the Russians and Chinese signed the agreement to cooperate on science and technology. It was perhaps this event that confirmed Mao in his belief that with Soviet assistance for Chinese nuclear technology guaranteed he could set about reshaping the PLA.
[83] SCMP 1719, pp. 26–31.
[84] Cf. *Origins*, I, p. 242.
[85] SCMP 1719, p. 26; *HHPYK*, No. 6, 1958, p. 116.
[86] *JMJP*, 23 Feb. 1958.
[87] A still controversial instance was the famous Hundred Regiments Battle against the Japanese in 1940. It was not till 1967 that P'eng Teh-huai was openly accused of disobeying Mao's strategy on this occasion (*The Case of Peng Teh-huai*, p. 212), but an examination of the contemporary documents indicates that the accusation was probably justified and not just a retrospective attempt to blacken his name.

In an article dated 6 Nov. 1938, Mao had divided the anti-Japanese war into three phases: defensive, stalemate, counter-offensive; he stated that during the stalemate period guerrilla warfare would be primary and regular warfare supplementary (Mao, *SW*, II, p. 229). On 10 Oct. 1939, he had written that the stalemate had now been reached and that it could be broken only by the

Japanese or by the KMT, while the communists must use it for preparing for counter-offensive (ibid., pp. 297-9). On 11 March 1940, in one of his last articles before the launching of the Hundred Regiments Battle, Mao reaffirmed that the present period was one of strategic stalemate (ibid., p. 421). Yet only five months later the communists threw 115 regiments (400,000 troops) into a major conventional assault upon the Japanese. While the offensive had considerable initial effect, it brought upon the communists a fierce counter-attack and by 1941 the 8th Route Army had been reduced by virtually a quarter to 305,500 men. (See Johnson, *Peasant Nationalism and Communist Power*, p. 215; Gittings, *The Role of the Chinese Army*, p. 303). For a discussion of Mao's difficulties in getting his military theories accepted during the 1930s and 1940s, see Whitson, *The Chinese High Command*, ch. 1.

88 For a report of a conversation with Chou En-lai in which he testified to the antipathy of P'eng Teh-huai and Lin Piao, see *Foreign Relations of the United States, 1949*, VIII, p. 359.

89 For a discussion of the rise of Lin Piao and the estrangement between Mao and P'eng Teh-huai, see *Origins*, I, pp. 142-3, 146-8, 357-8 (note 29), and ch. 1 above. In *Origins*, I, I suggested that Mao, in view of his successive differences with Liu Shao-ch'i, may at the back of his mind have seen Lin Piao and Teng Hsiao-p'ing as more congenial alternate candidates for the succession.

90 For accounts of the period of dormancy of the MAC, see Ralph L. Powell, 'The Military Affairs Committee and party control of the military in China', *Asian Survey*, July 1963, pp. 349-50, and Gittings, *Role of the Chinese Army* pp. 282-5.

91 *The Case of Peng Teh-huai*, p. 176

92 We cannot be absolutely sure that Lin Piao was at this time a member of the MAC, although it seems highly probable. Some biographical volumes say he became a member in 1951 (see URI, *Who's Who in Communist China*). As of 1961, all China's marshals with the exception of the aged Chu Teh, Foreign Minister Ch'en Yi and the disgraced P'eng Teh-huai were members (Gittings, *Role of the Chinese Army*, p. 287), and it seems reasonable to assume that a similar situation prevailed in 1958. According to another source, Ch'en Yi was a nominal member of the MAC who did not attend meetings; SCMM 637, p. 38.

93 Chou En-lai, from whom Mao took over charge of the army in 1935, stayed on as his deputy (*Chung-kuo Jen-min Ko-ming Chan-cheng Ti-t'u Hsuan*, p. 22), but he seems to have relinquished that post by 1949. It is unclear whether Teng Hsiao-p'ing addressed the 1958 enlarged MAC simply as General Secretary or additionally as a MAC Vice Chairman. If he did hold the latter post concurrently, it was further evidence of his closeness to Mao; see *Origins*, I, pp. 140-5 and *Khrushchev Remembers*: the last testament, p. 253. For the later composition of the MAC, see Powell, 'The Military Affairs Committee', p. 350, Gittings, pp. 286-7, 310. For the original source of the quotation from the Chairman, see Mao, *SW*, II, p. 224.

94 SCMP 1900, pp. 5-10. For Liu Ya-lou's connections with Lin Piao, see his biography in Klein & Clark, *Biographic Dictionary*.

95 *CLG*, I, No. 4, pp. 15-21. Even extracts of other speeches made are not available.

96 The standard work on this topic is Joffe, *Party and Army: Professionalism and Political Control in the Chinese Officer Corps, 1949-1964*. The ensuing discussion relies heavily on this monograph.

97 Ibid., pp. 57-72, 121-9.

98 Ibid., pp. 72-80, 106-13.

[99] Ibid., pp. 133–8. Another characteristic of the new officer class was the privileged position of its members and their families *vis-à-vis* civilians. The party had already taken steps to curb these privileges in late 1957 (ibid., pp. 80–4, 129–33). For a pre-leap instance of Mao's emphasis on the need for egalitarianism in the PLA, see Mao, *HC*, V, pp. 328–9.

[100] It had been P'eng, for instance, who had proposed the excision of references to Mao's thought in the new party constitution in 1956; *Origins*, I, pp. 100–2.

[101] An extract from his speech is reproduced in *Documents on Disarmament*, II, pp. 967–8. The Americans clearly noted the hint and took it seriously as Dulles later revealed (*American Foreign Policy*, 1958, p. 1306).

[102] *Documents on Disarmament*, II, pp. 978–80.

[103] Ibid., p. 981; cf. SCMP 1753, p. 45.

[104] *Documents on Disarmament*, II, p. 982.

[105] *American Foreign Policy*, 1958, p. 1304.

[106] *Documents on Disarmament*, II, p. 985.

[107] See ibid., pp. 1003–4, for the letter of 22 April; ibid., p. 1038 for the letter of 9 May. 'Surprisingly' is the comment of George Quester in *Nuclear Diplomacy*, p. 183.

[108] SCMP 1753, p. 43; Hsieh, *Communist China's Strategy in the Nuclear Era*, p. 107. Ford, 'Modern weapons and the Sino-Soviet estrangement', p. 165, implies that there was some significance in the failure of the Chinese to reply for ten days. This may be so; the Chinese could have wanted to reassure themselves that the US response would be negative. But it should be noted that the reply of the UK Prime Minister was not delivered in Moscow until 21 April.

[109] This possibility became even stronger after the Eastern and Western experts met in July and Aug., for they produced a report that 'at first glance showed greater agreement and promise on new forms of policing for a test ban'; Quester, *Nuclear Diplomacy*.

[110] Hsieh, *Communist China's Strategy in the Nuclear Era*, pp. 107–8; Mehnert, *Peking and Moscow*, p. 304; SCMP 1772, p. 57. Khrushchev's 9 May letter was not delivered in Washington till the morning of 10 May, and so Ch'en Yi would only have known its contents if he had been given advance warning.

[111] SCMP 1900, pp. 9–10.

[112] See the quotation from his 2 Aug. article in Ford, 'Modern weapons and the Sino-Soviet estrangement', p. 163.

[113] Ch'en, *Mao Papers*, p. 84.

[114] CB 514, pp. 1–4.

[115] Ibid., p. 6.

[116] The identification of Liu Ya-lou is not 100 per cent certain since the *JMJP* picture caption does not give the names of Mao's two companions and there are few pictures of Liu Ya-lou available for comparison. The third man in the picture is almost certainly Wu Fa-hsien, then Political Commissar of the Air Force, later Liu's successor as Commander.

[117] This section draws heavily on Zagoria, *The Sino-Soviet Conflict*, pp. 172–99.

[118] I do not follow Zagoria in believing that this important omission indicated that the Chinese had already decided upon the Taiwan Strait adventure of the late summer of 1958.

[119] CB 492, p. 2.

[120] Ibid., p. 7.

[121] See Zagoria, *Sino-Soviet Conflict*, pp. 178–80.

[122] Quoted in Zagoria, *Sino-Soviet Conflict*, p. 180.

[123] *Kuang-ming Jih-pao*, 2 Feb. 1958, quoted ibid., p. 181.

[124] Zagoria, *Sino-Soviet Conflict*, p. 183.

[125] Ibid., pp. 187–8.

[126] Ibid., p. 183.

[127] See *Origins*, I, p. 315.

[128] *HC*, No. 1, 1958, pp. 11-18.

[129] The party propagandists were Wang Li, later a leading leftist in the early period of the cultural revolution, and Yao Chen, an associate of P'eng Chen. The Foreign Ministry official was Assistant Minister Ch'iao Kuan-hua, a former journalist and long-time associate of Chou En-lai who would himself rise to be Foreign Minister in the mid-1970s, fall from grace after the purge of the 'gang of four' and only re-emerge in public view in 1981. For the identification of 'Yü Chao-li', see 'What is Wang Li?' *Yeh Chan Pao* (Open Warfare Bulletin), Nos. 12-13 (March 1968), trans. in SCMP 4158, p. 9.

[130] Halpern MS, ch.6.

[131] SCMP 1772, p. 42.

[132] For discussions of these issues, see Halpern MS, ch. 9; Matsumoto Shigeharu, 'Japan and China', in Halpern (ed.), *Policies toward China*, pp. 132-4; Hinton, *Communist China in World Politics*, pp. 376-7.

[133] Halpern MS, ch. 6.

[134] Klein & Clark, *Biographic Dictionary*.

[135] Halpern MS, ch. 8. See also *NYT*, 19 Nov. 1959, where the rude treatment of Dr Subandrio is mentioned but Ch'en Yi is not cited by name as the man responsible.

[136] Quoted in Maxwell, *India's China War*, p. 170.

[137] See Lall, *How Communist China Negotiates*, pp. 84-9.

[138] SCMP 4007, pp. 1-3.

[139] Ch'en Yi was with Chou En-lai in the group of young Chinese that went to France on a work/study course after World War I and is said to have struck up a friendship there with his fellow Szechwanese, Teng Hsiao-p'ing. In 1926, Ch'en joined Chou's staff at the Whampoa Military Academy. After the KMT broke with the CCP, Ch'en was among the first to rally to Mao's banner on Chingkangshan. Later, during the 1940s, Liu Shao-ch'i was for a time political commissar of the army Ch'en commanded. (See the biography of Ch'en in Klein & Clark, *Biographic Dictionary;* Whitson, *The Chinese High Command*, pp. 36-7 and ch. 4; Huang, *Chung Kung Chün Jen Chih* (A Directory of Chinese Communist Military Personnel), pp. 365-71.

[140] Lieberthal, p. 112.

[141] *WWAR*, p. 192 ff.; Grey Chou, III, pp. 20, 47; Green Chou, p. 379 ff. *PR*, No. 18, 1958, pp. 12-14.

[142] *Lao I-pei Wu-ch'an-chieh-chi Ko-ming-chia Shih-tz'u Hsuan-tu* (A Selection of Poems by the Older Generation of Proletarian Revolutionaries), pp. 136-7.

[143] Mao's nostalgia for roughing it, Yenan-style, is noticeable in his speech to the CC's 2nd plenum in Nov. 1956; see Mao, *SW*, V, p. 336.

Chapter 5.   The coming of the communes

[1] Cf. Mao's speech to the CC's 6th (Wuchang) plenum on 19 Dec. 1958, when he said the communes were 'undiscovered' until Aug. (*Mao, Miscellany*, I, p. 140), with the *JMJP* editorial, 29 Aug. 1959 (CB 590, p. 23), after P'eng Teh-huai's attacks on the communes, where the emphasis is on the development of the commune in theory and practice prior to Aug. 1958. For the latter approach, see also ECMM 210, pp. 13-16.

[2] See his speech to the SSC on 13 Oct. 1957; *Mao Tse-tung ssu-hsiang wan sui* (1969), p. 136: Mao, *HC*, V, p. 487, and *SW*, V, p. 504.

³ See Schran, *The Development of Chinese Agriculture*, p. 30, Table 2.6. For the scale of the conservancy campaign, see Oksenberg MS, ch. 13. Interestingly, a year earlier, when Premier Chou had expressed scepticism about the viability of larger APCs to a high-level Indian agricultural mission, he had revealed that one such APC into whose efficiency he had ordered an investigation was reported to be working satisfactorily because 'there was a joint water conservancy project which unified the people'. Despite this encouraging report, Chou still retained 'serious doubts' about larger APCs. (The one investigated had 30,000 inhabitants, which would have qualified it as a healthy-sized commune in 1958 terms.) (See *Report of the Indian Delegation to China on Agricultural Planning and Techniques*, pp. 25–6.)

⁴ See HHPYK, No. 19, 1957, pp. 135–8; Walker, 'Organisation of agricultural production', in Eckstein, Galenson & Liu (eds), *Economic Trends in Communist China*, p. 439. Walker points out (note 22) that as late as Dec. 1957 T'ao Chu, the Kwangtung 1st secretary, was still advocating the preservation of small APCs for ten years.

⁵ See JMJP editorial, 'Long live the People's communes!' (29 Aug. 1959) trans. in CB 590, p. 23. Mao later claimed that mess halls had been set up in Honan as early as 1956; see CLG, I, No. 4, p. 37.

⁶ CB 590, p. 23.

⁷ *Chung-kuo Kung-ch'an Tang Chien Shih Chiang-yi* (Canton, 1981), II, p. 345.

⁸ C13 590, p. 23.

⁹ Ibid. See also T'an Chen-lin's article on the bumper summer harvest, JMJP, 11 Aug. 1958, trans. in SCMP 1834, p. 21. T'ao Chu later claimed that a commune had been set up in Kwangtung in April 1958, as the result of a federation of eight APCs and two handicraft cooperatives; see SCMP 1939, p. 2.

¹⁰ HC, No. 3, 1958, p. 10.

¹¹ Ibid., No. 4, 1958, p. 8.

¹² I here assume that if Mao had talked in these terms before Ch'en's article in HC, No. 3, had gone to press Ch'en would have quoted him in it. Since HC is a fortnightly publication it seems reasonable to suppose that the 1 July issue would have gone to press no earlier than half-way between that date and the date of publication of the previous issue, 16 June. This leads one to the hypothesis that Mao's endorsement was given some time between 23 and 30 June. (There was a Politburo meeting on 20 and 21 June to discuss the wage system, but the evidence suggests Mao did not attend; see Lieberthal, pp. 115–16.)

The evidence that it was Ch'en who conceived the commune idea was reinforced after his post-cultural-revolution disgrace. An attack on him (not by name but contemporary evidence makes it clear that he was the target) in JMJP, 15 Aug. 1971, attributed to him the exaggerated ideological claims made for the commune in 1958. The commune idea itself could not be attributed to him without discrediting the communes themselves; but the evidently close involvement of Ch'en with various aspects of the idea make it legitimate to draw the conclusion that he also spawned it, particularly when it is remembered that he was the first Politburo member to promote it.

Mao's disclaimer was made at the Lushan plenum on 23 July 1959; see CLG, I, No. 4, p. 41. For a post-Mao attack on Ch'en Po-ta's leftism at this period, see Lu Wei, 'Don't the problems of "leftism" and rashness exist in socialist construction?', HHYP—WCP, No. 2, 1980, pp. 49–50.

¹³ See for instance Chu Li & Tien Chieh-yun, *Inside a People's Commune*, p. 9.

¹⁴ See Wen-shun Chi, 'The ideological source of the People's Communes in Communist China', *Pacific Coast Philology*, II (April 1967), pp. 62–78. Ch'en Po-ta, having worked closely with Mao for two decades (*Origins*, I, p. 325, note 25) would certainly have been aware of his respect for K'ang Yu-wei.

[15] Cf. article by T'an Chen-lin (SCMP 1834, p. 21) and Mao's introductory note in *HC*, No. 1, 1958, p. 4. There is nothing in the accompanying article on the APC (ibid., pp. 4–10) to suggest that it inspired the commune idea; it exemplified only the customary virtues of hard work, resilience, initiative and solidarity. It is in *PR*, No. 19, 1958, p. 5, that it is said that Mao met the APC director in late June.

[16] The quote in Ch'en Po-ta's article from the words '*ying-kai chü-pu-ti*' to the words '*ch'eng-wei wo kuo she-hui-ti chi-pen tan-wei*' (*HC*, No. 4, 1958, p. 8) is identical with the quote in T'an Chen-lin's. These were presumably the words attributable to Mao. For the attribution of a longer passage to Mao, see *K'o Chi Ko-ming* (Science and Technology Revolution), July 1967, p. 21. The account given in *PR*, No. 19, 1958, of Mao's chat with the director of the APC gave no indication that the Chairman mentioned the word 'commune'.

[17] *HC*, No. 3, 1958, p. 17.

[18] Ibid., p. 12.

[19] *HHPYK*, No. 15, 1958, p. 114; referred to in Roy Hofheinz, 'Rural administration in Communist China', *CQ*, July–Sept. 1962, p. 154. The eight-day conference ended on 14 July.

[20] At the second session of the 8th Congress, Mao praised Ch'ang-ko *hsien* in Honan for its successes with deep ploughing, but he made it clear that he had not been there, only read about it (*Mao, Miscellany*, I, pp. 103, 123).

[21] The Chinese press reported that Mao was in Hopei on the 4th (*JMJP*, 11 Aug.), Honan from the 6th to the 8th (ibid., 12 Aug.), Shangtung on the 9th (ibid., 13 Aug.), Tientsin from the 10th to the 13th (ibid., 16 Aug.) and that he visited the APCs on the outskirts of Peking on his way back from Tientsin by car on the 13th (ibid., 16 Aug.). The director of Ch'iliying commune informed an Indian demographer later in 1958 that it was set up on 20 July, the day following Mao's visit; see Chandrasekhar, *Communist China Today*, p. 53.

[22] *JMJP*, 12 Aug. 1958. A translation of a report on this visit in the *Kung-jen Jih-pao* (Workers' Daily), in SCMP 1847, p. 5, puts the word 'cooperative' into the mouths of Mao and Wu Chih-p'u in this exchange. Ch'iliying was in the same district, although a different *hsien*, as the APC introduced by Mao in *HC*, No. 1, 1958. For Mao's Hopei visit, see *PR*, No. 31, 1958, pp. 21–2.

[23] *JMJP*, 13 Aug. 1958. The first sentence reads: '*Hai-shih pan jen-min kung-she hao.*'

[24] *CLG*, I, No. 4, p. 41; see ch. 10 below. It is not clear whether the major quotation from Mao on the communes used in the press during the leap—'*Jen-min kung-she hao*' (People's Communes are good)—was taken from the exchange between Mao and T'an Ch'i-lung or from some other exchange between Mao and a journalist as the Chairman claims. The phrase was first used as a front-page headline in the *JMJP* on 18 Aug.

[25] It was this report that sparked me to write my first dispatch on the communes in the London *Daily Telegraph* on 21 Aug. 1958.

[26] See the report of his conversation with some students on the night train from Tientsin to Tsinan on 12 July; *JMJP*, 30 July 1958, trans. in SCMP 1829, p. 5.

[27] *Pei-ching Jih-pao* (Peking Daily), 8 June 1967, p. 5.

[28] *JMJP*, 23 July 1958.

[29] I deduce that the articles were published with a view to influencing the mood of the conference because, although printed in the main CCP organs in August, they related to events—an East China Farm coordination conference and the size of the summer harvest—which took place in June and July and could thus have appeared weeks earlier. See T'an Chen-lin, 'Strive for a bountiful life in 2–3 years', *Red Flag*, No. 6, 1958, trans. in ECMM 144, pp. 1–7; and idem., 'On China's unprecedented bumper summer harvest this year', *JMJP*, 11 Aug.

1958, trans. in SCMP 1834, pp. 15–21. (Indeed, a fullish report of T'an's speech to the East China conference had already appeared in *JMJP*, 28 June 1958.)

30 *P'i T'an Chau Pao* (Criticize T'an [Chen-lin] Combat News), 5 Aug. 1967, p. 2, col. 1. For T'an's reminiscences about his early life, see SCMP 2362, pp. 7–11.

31 See p. 357 (note 60) above.

32 See Roy Hofheinz, 'Rural administration in Communist China', *CQ*, July–Sept. 1962, pp. 150–5. T'an was present at the Honan party meeting in July 1958 at which Wu's predecessor as provincial 1st secretary, P'an Fu-sheng, was officially purged (ibid., p. 154); see also p. 358 (note 76) above.

33 See the biography of T'an in Klein & Clark, *Biographic Dictionary*, where this point is made.

34 Ibid.

35 Whitson, *The Chinese High Command*, p. 204. Cultural revolution gossip suggested that, despite his toughness, T'an was henpecked; SCMP(S) 238, p. 3.

36 *CLG*, I, No. 4 (Winter 1968/9), p. 41. The quotation, which reads oddly because Mao appears to have started by addressing T'an and then talked about him to the rest of the audience, is from the Chairman's speech to the Lushan plenum on 23 July 1959.

37 'Gangsters' speeches by T'an Chen-lin', *Hung Ch'i* (Red Flag; a Red Guard paper, not the central party organ), 21 March 1967, trans. in SCMP(S) 178, p. 33 (I have tidied up the translation). The text is also available in *Pa Pa Chan Pao* (8 Aug. Combat News), 29 March 1967, p. 8, and *Kuan-yü T'an Chen-lin wen-t'i-ti ch'u-pu tsung-ho ts'ai-liao* (Preliminary collection of materials on the problem of T'an Chen-lin's capitalist, counter-revolutionary restorationist adverse current), pp. 35–6. The speech was made at a Shensi/Sian cadres' conference which was held either on 11 Nov. (according to the latter source) or in Dec. (according to idem. (*hsu chi*) (further collection), 6 April 1967), pp. 10, no. 84, 12, no. 102. For a commentary on the speech, see *Chin Chün Pao* (Advancing Army News), 15 March 1967, p. 3.

38 SCMP 1834, p. 21.

39 SCMP 1839, p. 2.

40 *Kuan-yü T'an Chen-lin wen-t'i-ti ch'u-pu tsung-ho ts'ai-liao* (*hsu chi*), p. 14, no. 115. For Mao, see SCMP 1915, p. 1.

41 See 'Report on investigation of Teng Hsiao-p'ing's crimes', *Hung Wei-ping* (Red Guard), No. 2, 1967, trans. in SCMM 590, p. 13. No precise date is given for Teng's elaboration of his vision of communism, but internal evidence in this source indicates it must have been during one of two visits to Tsunyi, in Kweichow province, and the tenor of his remarks suggests they were made during his first visit (Nov. 1958) rather than his second (Nov. 1965).

42 See for instance the resolution on the establishment of people's communes in the rural areas (*JMJP*, 10 Sept. 1958); five directives on aspects of agriculture (ibid., 11 Sept. 1958); the directive on combining education and work (ibid., 20 Sept. 1958); and the decision that cadres should spend one month a year doing manual labour (ibid., 30 Sept. 1958).

43 According to P'eng Teh-huai; see 'Some notes of P'eng Teh-huai's', *Chin-tai Shih Yen-chiu* (Studies in Modern History), No. 4, 1980, trans. in JPRS 77,668, pp. 8–9.

44 See the Peitaiho communiqué in SCMP 1846, p. 1.

45 SCMP 1853, pp. 1–2.

46 Hofheinz, 'Rural administration in Communist China', pp. 142–6.

47 SCMP 1853, p. 2.

48 *JMJP*, 10 Sept. 1958.

[49] SCMP 1853, pp. 1–2.
[50] See Walker, *Planning in Chinese Agriculture*, pp. 23–41, especially p. 41.
[51] SCMP 1853, pp. 3–4.
[52] Ibid., p. 4.
[53] See ch. 2, p. 31, above.
[54] *CLG*, I, No. 4, pp. 41–2.
[55] During the Lushan conference in July 1959; see Wu Leng-hsi's confession, SCMM 662, p. 7.
[56] *JMJP*, 30 July 1958, trans. in SCMP 1829, p. 5; this is an account of a discussion that Liu Shao-ch'i had on a train journey between Tientsin and Tsinan as early as 12 July.
[57] The quotation is from a report of his visit to Shantung in mid-July carried by the *Kuang-ming Jih-pao* on 4 Aug. 1958, reprinted in *HHPYK*, No. 16, 1958, pp. 39–40. See also a report of his visit to Honan in mid-Sept. during which he advocated full-time care for children in nurseries and the development of boarding schools at the primary level so that social education rather than family upbringing could be stressed; SCMP 1911, p. 12. This explains why a cultural revolution source was able to accuse Liu with some justification of exaggerated demands during the leap; see *San-fan fen-tzu Liu Shao-ch'i tsui-o shih*, pp. 35–6.
[58] *Origins*, I, p. 59.
[59] There seems to be no doubt about the size of the summer harvest even though some areas reported the worst floods on the Yellow River in a century. See *Chou Tsung-li-ti Ku-shih*, pp. 66–69; Green Chou, pp. 202 ff., 307 ff.
[60] Mao correctly proclaimed the victory of collectivization in Jan. 1956, long before its actual completion, and set about planning the first leap forward (*Origins*, I, pp. 26–7). At the same time, he incorrectly (as he later admitted) proclaimed the victory of socialism and set about planning an amelioration of the domestic political atmosphere (ibid., pp. 15–16, 33–8, 160–4).
[61] *Mao Tse-tung ssu-hsiang wan sui* (1969), p. 243.
[62] SCMP 1846, p. 1.
[63] Ibid.
[64] *Tzu-liao hsuan-pien*, p. 230.
[65] *CLG*, I, No. 4, p. 39. See also FBIS-CHI-81-145, p. K33, where Po I-po confirms that Mao set the 10·7 million ton target before Peitaiho.
[66] SCMP 1846, p. 1. Interestingly, the sea breezes of Peitaiho seemed regularly to conjure up optimistic, long-range visions of increased steel production in the minds of the Politburo. There in the summer of 1955, a figure of 15 million tons was set as the 2nd FYP target, but at the 8th Congress a year later this had been reduced to 10–12 million tons; *Mao, Miscellany*, I, p. 80.
[67] Liu Sui-nien, 'Some problems that need to be investigated in order to get the overall balance of the national economy right', *HHYP–WCP*, No. 5, 1980, p. 17.
[68] *CLG*, I, No. 4, pp. 39, 41, 42–3.
[69] Ibid., p. 38. For a brief account of the impact of the leap on the transport system, see Wu, *The Spatial Economy of Communist China*, pp. 130, 187, 194, 206, 289.
[70] *CLG*, I, No. 4, pp. 38, 40.
[71] 'Down with "three-anti" element and big renegade Po I-po, sinister despot on the industrial and communications front', *Tung-fang Hung* (East is Red), 15 Feb. 1967, trans. in CB 878, p. 6; and 'Forty charges against Po I-po', *Hung Wei-ping Pao* (Red Guard News), No. 8 (22 Feb. 1967), trans. ibid., p. 16.
[72] *Mao Tse-tung ssu-hsiang wan sui* (1969), pp. 228, 230, 240.
[73] Ibid., p. 264.

74 Ibid., p. 252.
75 Ibid., p. 240.
76 Ibid., p. 264.
77 Ibid., p. 240.
78 Ibid., p. 235.
79 Ibid., pp. 24, 34. It will be interesting to see if Mao's exaggerated forecasts are allowed to survive in the texts of his speeches when subsequent volumes of Mao, *HC*, are published. The forecast cited here was in one case (p. 24) omitted when Mao, *HC*, V, appeared (cf. idem., p. 216), and in the other case disappeared with the rest of the speech which was not reprinted.
80 The party secretariat, chaired by Teng Hsiao-p'ing, partook of the euphoria when it decided shortly after Peitaiho to celebrate the revolution's tenth anniversary by building ten great buildings and expanding T'ienanmen Square; *Mien-huai Liu Jen T'ung-chih*, pp. 204–5. The Great Hall of the People and the Museum of Chinese History, which stand opposite each other on T'ienanmen Square, are the two most prominent monuments to that massive construction drive. They were completed on time by 1 Oct. 1959; the construction took ten months! Chou En-lai decided that there was no need for a new building to house the SC; Grey Chou, III, p. 21.

Chapter 6.   High tide

1 *Chin Chün Pao* (Advancing Army News), 14 June 1967, p. 3, cols 2–3. Teng was speaking on 15 July at a national united front conference. For quotations on foreign policy from his speech on 11 July to the same conference, see *Teng Hsiao-p'ing fan-tang fan-she-hui-chu-i fan-Mao Tse-tung ssu-hsiang-ti yen-lun chai-pien*, pp. 49–50.
2 For an account of the Middle East crisis see Barraclough, *Survey of International Affairs, 1956–8*, ch. VIII.
3 Quoted ibid.
4 This paragraph is based on the analysis of Zagoria, *The Sino-Soviet Conflict*, pp. 195–9.
5 SCMP 1827, p. 28.
6 Ibid., p. 26.
7 On 30 Nov. 1958; see *Mao, Miscellany*, I, p. 135. Mao made his remark to illustrate how the West became alarmed about supposed Chinese influence even when China had done nothing. In this case, he was deriding Western comment which had assumed that Khrushchev abandoned his summit proposal because of Chinese pressure. It is not clear whether Mao's reference to a four-power summit was a slip of the tongue (East–West summits then were normally four-power) or if he was hinting to party members his disapproval of the Soviet suggestion of India as a fifth participant. What does seem unlikely is that Mao would have chosen to minimize the effectiveness of Chinese pressure to this audience and so one must surely accept the accuracy of his statement.
8 Quoted in Barraclough, *Survey of International Affairs*.
9 Quoted in Zagoria, *Sino-Soviet Conflict*, pp. 203–5.
10 See Mao's speech to the CC's 10th plenum in Sept. 1962 (*Mao Tse-tung ssu-hsiang wan sui* (1969), p. 432, and *CLG*, I, No. 4, p. 88) and Khrushchev's memoirs (*Khrushchev Remembers*, pp. 258–61).
11 *Khrushchev Remembers*, p. 258. It is not absolutely clear from either this source or Mao's speech when the Russians first made this request. Some Western analysts have stated that it was in April 1958, but the source they all quote —a Chinese official in Japan whose remarks on the subject, made in Japan in

1964, were picked up by the BBC (SWB/FE 1488, p. A2/1)—makes no reference to any month. Correspondence with two of the analysts concerned uncovered only hazy recollections of where 'April' came from, the most likely source apparently being a UK diplomat, now dead. 'April' may be correct, but in view of the heated Chinese reaction and the alarm it engendered in Moscow, it seems unlikely that the Soviet leaders would have delayed at least four months before flying to Peking. However, if they did, then the scenario that would fit best with both Mao's and Khrushchev's accounts would be that the radio station proposal was made in April, but the 'joint fleet' proposal not till the meeting in July–Aug.

12 Ibid.

13 Ibid., p. 290.

14 Ibid., p. 258–9. The Khrushchev visit disrupted air communications between Moscow and Peking for three days; Klochko, *Soviet Scientist in Red China*, p. 105.

15 *Khrushchev Remembers*, p. 259.

16 Ibid., pp. 259–60.

17 *CLG*, I, No. 4, p. 88.

18 SWB/FE 1488, p. A2/1.

19 See p. 64 above.

20 *Mao, Miscellany*, I, p. 135.

21 In *Khrushchev Remembers*, p. 261, Khrushchev, having failed to mention the Taiwan Strait issue during his very full account of his talks with Mao, states in a new section that 'in 1958' the Chinese requested military aid for use against the Nationalists. The implication is that it was in 1958 at a time other than the meeting. Allen Whiting refuses to believe Mao's assertion that Taiwan was not mentioned but makes no comment on the fact that Khrushchev effectively confirmed this; see his 'Quemoy 1958: Mao's miscalculations', *CQ*, June 1975, p. 269.

22 Hsieh, *Communist China's Strategy in the Nuclear Era*, pp. 71–2; Griffith, *The Chinese People's Liberation Army*, pp. 224–5.

23 *NYT*, 3 Aug. 1958; *Christian Science Monitor*, 9 Aug. 1958.

24 *Khrushchev Remembers*, pp. 261–2.

25 Ibid., pp. 260–1.

26 Zagoria, *Sino-Soviet Conflict*, pp. 201, 209.

27 *Mao, Miscellany*, I, p. 138. In Zagoria's excellent study, pp. 206–8, a whole series of reasons, seven in all, some overlapping, are given for the Chinese decision to initiate the bombardment of Quemoy. It is quite possible that some of these were aired in the Peitaiho discussions, but I think this type of analysis greatly overestimates the degree to which comprehensive cost-benefit calculations enter the heads of political leaders, and especially Mao's. The Chairman would seem to have been far simpler in his approach, focusing on a specific objective for a single reason. If his colleagues and followers felt it necessary to justify their support to themselves and each other with a more sophisticated rationale, that would be their concern.

28 Hinton, *Communist China in World Politics*, pp. 266–7, suggests that the date was chosen because it was the anniversary of the Hitler–Stalin pact and thus a reminder to the Russians of the danger of compromising with imperialism.

29 Zagoria states that most analysts agree that no invasion was intended. The artillery barrage began shortly before the onset of the typhoon season when amphibious operations would have been extremely difficult. Moreover, the requisite equipment for an amphibious operation was never assembled; Zagoria, *Sino-Soviet Conflict*, p. 206.

[30] The US State Department issued a text of the Chinese broadcast on 28 Aug.; it was reproduced in *The Times*, 29 Aug.

[31] The text of Dulles' comments is in MacFarquhar, *Sino-American Relations, 1949–71*, p. 159.

[32] For reports on the blockade, see dispatches from Frank Robertson in the *Daily Telegraph*, 3 Sept., Hanson Baldwin, *NYT*, 5 Sept., and Greg MacGregor, ibid., 6 Sept. An Associated Press dispatch of 5 Sept. (*New York Herald Tribune*, European edition, 6–7 Sept.) talked of 'persistent but unconfirmed' reports that ships of the US 7th Fleet would 'soon start escorting Nationalist supply vessels; Robert Franklin (*Observer*, 7 Sept.) stated that the Americans had already offered escort facilities but that the Nationalists had so far not taken up the offer.

[33] Text in MacFarquhar, *Sino-American Relations*, pp. 159–62.

[34] The main reason for the summoning of the SSC would appear to have been to communicate to senior officials outside the CCP the various decisions taken and plans formulated for the economy at Peitaiho. But, somewhat unusually, the announcement of the opening session listed those attending by name, perhaps to present an image of national unity at a time of crisis.

[35] *Mao Tse-tung ssu-hsiang wan sui* (1969), p. 233.

[36] Ibid., pp. 236–7.

[37] This visit was only revealed to Westerners relatively recently by the leading Soviet Foreign Ministry China specialist, M. S. Kapitsa, who accompanied Gromyko; see Doak Barnett, 'Peking and the Asian Power balance: The 1958 Quemoy crisis—the Sino-Soviet dimension', *Problems of Communism*, July–Aug. 1976, pp. 38–9.

[38] Zagoria, *Sino-Soviet Conflict*, pp. 211–13; John K. Thomas, 'The limits of alliance: the Quemoy crisis of 1958', in Garthoff (ed.) *Sino-Soviet Military Relations*, pp. 124–7, 131–2. For an opposing view which argues that the Russians actually did all that the Chinese wanted, see Morton H. Halperin and Tang Tsou, 'The 1958 Quemoy crisis', in Halperin (ed.) *Sino-Soviet Relations and Arms Control*, pp. 265–303.

[39] *Mao, Miscellany*, I, p. 136.

[40] See Zagoria, *Sino-Soviet Conflict*, pp. 213–14.

[41] *Mao Tse-tung ssu-hsiang wan sui* (1969), pp. 238–40; the quotation about Khrushchev is on p. 240.

[42] Quoted in Borisov & Koloskov, *Soviet-Chinese Relations, 1945–1970*, p. 155.

[43] Quoted in Gittings, *Sino-Soviet Dispute*, p. 92.

[44] The further development of the crisis is described by Zagoria, *Sino-Soviet Conflict*, Thomas, 'The limits of alliance' and Halperin and Tsou, 'The 1958 Quemoy crisis'.

[45] See Zagoria, *Sino-Soviet Conflict*, pp. 217–21.

[46] *Mao, Miscellany*, I, p. 125.

[47] Su Yü returned to office as a Deputy Defence Minister in the aftermath of the dismissal of P'eng Teh-huai in Sept. 1959. This conceivably could mean that he had been dismissed by P'eng Teh-huai for obeying Mao's orders when P'eng himself had refused to collaborate, but this seems improbable. More likely, Su voiced his unhappiness at the humiliation suffered by the PLA as a result of political bungling. For the allegation of P'eng's refusal to collaborate with Mao, see Green Chou, p. 197.

[48] *Mao Tse-tung ssu-hsiang wan sui* (1969), p. 231.

[49] Ibid., pp. 237, 255.

[50] The first 'everyone a soldier' banner headline appeared in *JMJP* on 13 Sept., and on that day the paper reported that the movement had started within the last few days. However, arms were issued to commune members in Hsushui,

Hopei, in Aug. as a result of Mao's on-the-spot instructions (CB 520, p. 1). For an eye-witness account by an English writer of an anti-US rally in Chengtu, see Wollaston, *China in the Morning*, pp. 107–10.

[51] CB 530, p. 20.

[52] Ibid., p. 12.

[53] Ibid., p. 7.

[54] Ibid., p. 3.

[55] Ibid., p. 6.

[56] Chandrasekhar, *Communist China Today*, pp. 51–2 (emphasis in the original).

[57] *Mao Tse-tung ssu-hsiang wan sui* (1969), p. 237.

[58] See Gittings, *The Role of the Chinese Army*, pp. 209–15.

[59] See Griffiths, *The Chinese People's Liberation Army*, p. 271; for a more extended discussion, see Hsia, *Metaphor, Myth, Ritual and the People's Commune*, pp. 1–15.

[60] Gittings, *The Role of the Chinese Army*, pp. 211–12.

[61] Quoted ibid., p. 211.

[62] Quoted in Joffe, *Party and Army*, p. 90.

[63] Ibid., pp. 87–91.

[64] CB 538, p. 2. Though mess halls were popularized nationally during the high tide of the leap, provinces had been experimenting with them earlier in the year; see ibid., pp. 5–6.

[65] *JMJP*, 10 Nov. 1958; ibid., pp. 20–3. Prof. Chandrasekhar (*Communist China Today*, p. 56) quotes a poem from a Chinese newspaper illustrating the worst of commune cooking:

> At the sound of the cease-work bell,
> We enter the mess hall to eat.
> Taking one mouthful of rice,
> We find sand between our teeth;
> Helping ourselves to the vegetable,
> We find grass stalks in it.
> We lay down the chopsticks,
> And go to work again.

[66] Quoted in A. V. Sherman, 'The people's commune', in Hudson, *The Chinese Communes*, p. 36.

[67] T'ien Sheng, 'The outlook of communism as seen from the people's communes', *Cheng-chih Hsueh-hsi* (Political Study), No. 10, 1958, trans. in ECMM 151, p. 8.

[68] For the revelation by Li Hsien-nien that free food was discussed at Peitaiho, see *PR*, No. 37, 1958 p. 13. For the attribution of the suggestion to K'o Ch'ing-shih, see TLC, p. 53.

[69] SCMM(S) 25, p. 26.

[70] Sherman, 'The people's commune', pp. 36–8.

[71] SCMP 1867, p. 3. Yao Wen-yuan, who was to publish the first blast of the cultural revolution seven years later, also rejected the idea that the system would encourage idlers: SCMP 1900, pp. 2–5.

[72] See Lu Chung-chien, 'Loopholes in Hua Kuo-feng's assessment of Mao Tsetung', *Cheng-ming* (Contend) (Hong Kong), 1 Sept. 1980, pp. 24–31.

[73] See *Origins*, I, pp. 86–90, and ch. 2 above.

[74] *PR*, No. 37, 1958, p. 13.

[75] *Chung-kuo Ch'ing-nien Pao* (Chinese Youth News), 25 Oct. 1958, trans. in CB 540, p. 11.

[76] Ibid., pp. 9–10.

[77] Chandrasekhar, *Communist China Today*, pp. 55, 57.

[78] *Hung Wei-ping*, No. 2, 1967, trans. in SCMM 590, p. 13.

[79] Chandrasekhar, *Communist China Today*, pp. 55–6 for a description.

[80] Wollaston, *China in the Morning*, p. 48. Liu Shao-ch'i, touring Kiangsu, visited a new village in the course of construction and wondered why there were no windows in the rear walls to improve ventilation. The local party secretary made an instant architectural decision and undertook to have such windows put in (SCMP 1911, p. 4).

[81] Chandrasekhar, *Communist China Today*, p. 51. For T'an Chen-lin's comments on this subject, see p. 84 above.

[82] Trans. in *PR*, No. 38, 1958, p. 6. For an identification of Wang, see p. 362 (note 129) above.

[83] See Wu Leng-hsi's confession trans. in *CLG*, II, No. 4, p. 74.

[84] CB 537, p. 2.   [85] Ibid., p. 3.

[86] *Mao Tse-tung ssu-hsiang wan sui* (1969), p. 248; *Mao, Miscellany*, I. p. 233. No date is given in the original for this item—'Opinions on the free supply system'—but its tone suggests 1958 as the year of origin and not 1960 as suggested in *Mao, Miscellany*. It is possibly an extract from Mao's Peitaiho speech, but is more likely to have been a more private communication, perhaps to K'o Ch'ing-shih, Chang Ch'un-ch'iao and other Shanghai supporters. Had Mao expressed these views at Peitaiho or some such major party occasion, it seems unlikely that so many people would have been bold enough to pour cold water on Chang Ch'un-ch'iao's views.

[87] For the attribution of the note to Mao, see *CLG*, II, No. 4, p. 74.

[88] Ibid., pp. 17–24.

[89] See Charles Hoffman, 'Work incentive policy in Communist China', *CQ*, Jan.–March 1964, pp. 101–3; Perkins, *Market Control and Planning in Communist China*, pp. 150–1. For other articles in the debate initiated by Chang Ch'un-ch'iao, see CB 537, pp. 8–17, 33–7. One of these articles revealed that some piece-rate workers had been earning up to double their basic wages in the earlier part of 1958 and that this had caused contradictions between them and hourly-wage workers; ibid., p. 5.

[90] During the cultural revolution, an attempt was made to suggest that Mao's prescription of part-work, part-study was meant to be universal in application. This was done by quoting one sentence of the relevant clause of the Sixty Articles out of context. See for example *Liu Shao-ch'i fan-tang fan-she-hui-chu-i fan-Mao Tse-tung ssu-hsiang yen-lun i-pai lieh* (A hundred examples of Liu Shao-ch'i's anti-party, anti-socialist, anti Mao Tse-tung Thought utterances) (Canton: Study Chairman Mao's Works Office, Revolutionary Committee of the Canton City Military Affairs Control Committee, May 1967), p. 7. The difference in the prescription ('could' and 'should') is accounted for by the fact that agricultural school students and teachers would participate in labour as a matter of course on their school farms.

[91] CB 892, p. 12; Mao, Untitled Collection, p. 37.

[92] *Origins*, I, p. 197.

[93] See Ch'en Tao-yuan et al., 'To restore the good name of the "two track educational system"', *HHYP—WCP*, No. 6, 1980, p. 198, col. 2.

[94] Robert D. Barendsen, 'The agricultural middle school in Communist China', *CQ*, Oct.–Dec. 1961, p. 111 (note 7). These figures were revealed by Lu Ting-yi in an open letter dated 14 March 1959, published on the first anniversary of the founding of the agricultural middle schools (ibid.) The enormous gap between the two figures starkly illustrated the extent of educational deprivation in China.

[95] *HHYP—WCP*, No. 6, 1980, p. 198, col. 1.

[96] Quotations from the 7 May speech can be found in SCMM 653, pp. 29–30,

and *Liu Shao-ch'i fan-ko-ming tsui-o shih* (History of Liu Shao-chi's counter-revolutionary crimes), p. 33. Quotations from the 30 May speech are in SCMM 653, pp. 22–3, 29; 'Chronology of the two-road struggle on the educational front in the past 17 years', trans. in JPRS 41,932, p. 30; in *T'i Yü Chan-hsien* (Physical Education Front), 6 May 1967, p. 3, Nos. 74, 77–8; in *San-fan fen-tzu Liu Shao-ch'i tsui-o shih* (History of the crimes of the three-anti element Liu Shao-ch'i), p. 34; and in *Liu Shao-ch'i ts'ai-liao hui-pien* (A collection of material on Liu Shao-ch'i) (1st collection) (Tientsin, April 1967), pp. 127–8, 131–2. (This latter source, pp. 127–32, also contains quotations from Liu's utterances on this subject made on other occasions in 1958, as well as in later years.) It is probable that part-work, part-study was also discussed at the two national conferences on educational work in April and June 1958 although our knowledge of their agendas may be incomplete (see Lieberthal, pp. 109, 116); certainly Lu Ting-yi conveyed the essence of Liu's speech of 30 May to the June conference (*Lu Ting-yi fan-tui Mao Tse-tung ssu-hsiang t'ui-hsing hsiu-cheng-chu-i chiao-yü lu-hsien yen-lun chai-pien* (Selection of Lu Ting-yi's sayings opposing Mao Tse-tung's thought and promoting the revisionist educational line) (Peking: Joint committee of the capital for criticizing reactionary academic 'authorities', May 1967), p. 4, No. 10, p. 18, no. 80, p. 19, no. 86).

97 SCMM 653, p. 22.

98 Ibid., pp. 29–30.

99 *San-fan fen-tzu Liu Shao-ch'i tsui-o shih*, p. 34.

100 *HHYP—WCP*, No. 6, 1980, p. 199, cols 1–2.

101 For the early development of agricultural middle schools, see Barendsen, 'The agricultural middle school', pp. 107–8; for the secretariat meeting, see Lieberthal, p. 108.

102 Barendsen, 'The agricultural middle school', pp. 111–12, 115–17. According to Barendsen, '[t]he need for 'junior agricultural technical personnel' in the communes is seen as being very urgent. Lu Ting-yi, in his Feb. 1960 article in *Jen-min Chiao-yü* stated that China would need 1,840,000 agricultural machine operators and 440,000 "technical farming cadres" in order to complete the task of mechanization and modernization of agriculture. These are the people who will be counted upon to drive the tractors and combines, maintain the electric motors powering irrigation equipment, perform skilled tasks in local fertilizer and insecticide factories, act as surveyors, veterinary assistants, and bookkeepers, and do similar lower-level technical work in commune farms and factories'. (Ibid., p. 112.) As to the accomplishments of graduates of agricultural middle schools, Barendsen (p. 118) quotes an NPC delegate as saying that they were behind on book knowledge, but excelled in productive labour.

103 Ibid., p. 112; SCMM 653, p. 23.

104 Barendsen, 'The agricultural middle school', p. 110.

105 See *Origins*, I, p. 217, for a discussion of Liu's overlordship of the fields of press and propaganda; the field of propaganda, as the activities of the propaganda chief, Lu Ting-yi, confirmed, embraced education. However, the tone of Liu's remarks to the YCL CC indicate a personal rather than just a party responsibility; *Liu Shao-ch'i fan-ko-ming tsui-o shih*, p. 33 (this source states that Liu's remarks were made at a central work conference, but the quotation itself indicates that this was the meeting with the YCL). Years later, Chou En-lai was to claim that even he as Premier was unable to prevent Lu Ting-yi from controlling the Ministry of Education; *Shou-chang chiang-hua chi* (Collection of leaders' speeches), No. 4 (Peking: Tsinghua University Defend the East Combat Corps, Nov. 1966), p. 68.

106 CB 892, p. 12; Mao, Untitled Collection, p. 37.

[107] See for instance 'Chronology of the two-road struggle', JPRS 41,932, p. 30, and SCMP 4100, p. 2, where the system is called 'double-tracked'. During the cultural revolution, it was alleged that Liu's statements on part-work, part-study made in Tientsin were in opposition to Mao's on the same subject, that they ignored Mao's instructions to Wuhan and Kiangsi Communist Universities, and that Liu claimed the role of pioneer because of his statement; see CB 834, p. 17, *Liu Shao-ch'i fan-tang, fan-she-hui-chu-i fan-Mao Tse-tung ssu-hsiang yen-lun i-pai lieh*, p. 7, and *Liu Shao-ch'i fan-ko-ming tsui-o shih*, p. 33.

Significantly no actual quotations from Liu's Tientsin statement were given; nor was any date ascribed to it. Unfortunately, there is also no evidence in contemporary material as to when Liu said what in that city. However, we do know that Liu boarded a train at Tientsin on 12 July 1958, and it is legitimate to assume that this was when he inspected the city (SCMP 1829, p. 1). If so, then Liu cannot be accused of ignoring Mao's instructions, for the Chairman had not yet issued them. Mao visited Wuhan University on 12 Sept. (CB 891, p. 31), while his instructions to Kiangsi Communist University are dated 1961 (ibid., p. 36), although Chou En-lai said that Mao had written to the University in 1959 but decided against publication of that letter (*Shou-chang chiang-hua chi*, p. 68).

The other evidence adduced, coupled with cultural revolutionaries' reluctance to quote from Liu's Tientsin statement, strongly suggests that Liu did not contradict Mao's line. It can be asserted with greater certainty that cultural revolution quotations from remarks made by Liu in 1964 do not bear out the allegations that he claimed a pioneering role for his Tientsin statement; indeed he did not even say what his Tientsin statement was about, and remarked only that popular enthusiasm was high in the city at that time (*Liu Shao-ch'i fan-tang, fan-she-hui-chu-i fan-Mao Tse-tung ssu-hsiang yen-lun i-pai lieh*, p. 7).

[108] For the joint directive, see *HHPYK*, No. 19, 1958, pp. 1–4; the pre-Peitaiho origins of the directive are attested to by references in it to APCs rather than communes (ibid., pp. 2, 3). (The failure to amend these references here and in Lu Ting-yi's article, 'Education must be combined with productive labour' (*HC*, No. 7, 1958; *CB* 516), was presumably a reflection either of the hectic pace of life or the rigidity of the bureaucratic process.) For the directive's encouragement of the two types of schools, see *HHPYK*, No. 19, 1958, p. 3., col. 1. For an important example of cultural revolution approval of the directive, see JPRS 41,932, p. 29.

[109] An example of the contradictory nature of cultural revolution criticisms is that attacks by Mao in 1958 on previous educational policies are praised as denunciations of Liu Shao-ch'i and Lu Ting-yi ('Chronology of the two-road struggle', JPRS 41,932, p. 27), whereas similar attacks by Liu and Lu are rejected for being denunciations of Mao (ibid., p. 30; *Lu Ting-yi fan-tui Mao Tse-tung ssu-hsiang*, p. 4, no. 10).

[110] For Mao, see p. 108 above; for Liu, see SCMP 4100, p. 21; for Teng Hsiao-p'ing, see Lieberthal, p. 108; for Lu Ting-yi, see 'Chronology of the two-road struggle', JPRS 41,932, p. 30.

[111] *Lu Ting-yi fan-tui Mao Tse-tung ssu-hsiang*, p. 19, No. 19.

[112] *Mao Chu-hsi chiao-yü yü-lu*, p. 20 (two items).

[113] *Mao Tse-tung ssu-hsiang wan sui* (1969), pp. 241–2.

[114] 'Chairman Mao's instructions (1934–66) concerning revolution and education', trans. in SCMM(S) 19, p. 31. See also reports on Mao's visits to educational institutions in Hupeh and Anhwei trans. in SCMP 1906, pp. 1–10.

[115] *Pei-ching Jih-pao*, 8 June 1967, p. 5.

[116] SCMP 1863, p. 3.

[117] SCMP 1867, p. 3.

[118] For an attempt to attack Lu Ting-yi's article on the basis of a few short, isolated quotations, see 'Chronology of the two road struggle', JPRS 41,932, p. 30. Lu's reference (CB 516, p. 8) to attempts during 1957 to promote the combination of education with productive labour suggested that his department had been promoting the policy even before Mao had again thrown his weight behind it in Jan. 1958; if so, Lu may have been trying to exculpate himself from any charge of laggardness. Even Chou En-lai, when he was obliged to attack Lu Ting-yi's educational line during the cultural revolution, could not fault Lu's words and had to resort to the device of alleging that only now was it possible to discern in them a hidden heretical significance that had not been noticed at the time; *Shou-chang chiang-hua chi*, p. 67.

[119] See SCMP 4100, p. 2; the date of the quotation from Lu Ting-yi is not given, but 1958 is implied.

[120] *HHPYK*, No. 19, 1958, p. 3, col. 2.

[121] See Donald J. Munro, 'Egalitarian ideal and educational fact in Communist China', in Lindbeck (ed.), *China: Management of a Revolutionary Society*.

[122] 'Destroy the "three-family village" black gang in Wuhan University, carry the educational revolution to the end', *Yang-ch'eng Wan Pao*, 11 July 1966, trans. in SCMP 3747, p. 8.

[123] 'Down with anti-three element Chang Tsai-wang', *Hung-se Tsao-fan Pao* (Red Rebel News) (Lhasa), 9 Sept. 1967, trans. in SCMP(S) 231, p. 21.

[124] Wollaston, *China in the Morning*, pp. 91–2.

[125] Ibid., p. 87.

[126] Ibid., p. 90.

[127] SCMP 1862, pp. 16–17.

[128] SCMP 1887, pp. 18–21.

[129] SCMM 653, p. 30.

[130] Gold Chou, p. 68.

[131] Grey Chou, II, p. 287.

[132] Ibid., pp. 287–8.

[133] Trans. in SCMP 1857, pp. 16–18.

[134] Trans. in SCMP 1855, pp. 4–8, 22–4.

[135] *Tzu-liao hsuan-pien* (Selection of materials), p. 232.

[136] SCMP 1855, p. 41.

[137] *CLG*, I, No. 4, pp. 39, 41.

[138] *Chin-tai Shih Yen-chiu*, No. 4, 1980, trans. in JPRS 77,668, pp. 8–9.

[139] SCMP 1855, p. 14.

[140] *PR*, No. 40, 1958, p. 6. Liu Shao-ch'i had advocated amateur steel-making as early as July; SCMP 1829, p. 5.

[141] Grey Chou, II, pp. 361–2. Chou is said to have come sleepless from an all-night conference on the morning of 20 Sept. This dating suggests that some of the masses were mobilized, perhaps on a trial basis, even before the *JMJP* editorial of 4 Oct. SC permission had been necessary to allow Peking University students to enter the steel campaign, and this had apparently been granted on 16 Sept. (ibid.).

[142] *PR*, No. 34, 1958, p. 3.

[143] Wollaston, *China in the Morning*, p. 115. For a more jaundiced 'inside' account of the steel campaign by a US Korean war defector who was working in a paper mill in Shantung province during the great leap, see Karnow, *Mao and China*, pp. 101–2.

[144] Wollaston, *China in the Morning*, p. 118. After seeing a performance of *Twelfth Night* during this period, Chou En-lai advised a Shanghai troupe to put on plays reflecting current struggles; Grey Chou, II, pp. 519–20.

[145] *Wen-Ko Feng-yun* (Cultural Revolution Storm), No. 9, 1967, p. 28.
[146] SCMP 1960, pp. 6–8.
[147] In mid-Oct., during an inspection tour in Hopei, Teng was advocating transforming native-style iron smelters into foreign-style ones; SCMP 1963, p. 4.
[148] JPRS 77,668, p. 8.
[149] SCMP 1930, pp. 17–20.

PART TWO: RETREAT

Chapter 7. Withdrawal at Wuhan

[1] Klochko, *Soviet Scientist in Red China*, p. 82. Klochko, who defected while on a visit to Canada in 1961, was generally sympathetic to the Chinese though scornful of what he saw as the aberrations of the leap forward.

[2] T'ao Lu-chia (Shansi 1st secretary), 'On the new developments in worker-peasant relations and urban-rural relations', *JMJP*, 16 May 1958, trans. in CB 509, p. 23.

[3] *TGY*, p. 3183.

[4] Despite a tripling of the industrial labour force in 1958, the number of workers *and* clerical and other staff covered for labour insurance only increased by 20 per cent from 11·5 million to 13·8 million (a much smaller increase than between 1956 and 1957), and the number eligible for free medical care only increased by 5 per cent from 6·6 million to 6·9 million (*TGY*, pp. 218–19). For a report on how the system worked in Szechwan, see SCMP 1795, pp. 28–9.

During the cultural revolution, Liu Shao-ch'i and junior officials were criticized for the use and expansion of the contract labour system, but while resentment at ineligibility for welfare benefits probably existed and was understandable, it is difficult to see how the state could have afforded the extra financial burden for genuinely temporary workers; see 'Information about Liu Shao-ch'i in the system of temporary and contract labour', SCMM 616, pp. 21–30. Certainly it is not apparent that Liu's role was any more reprehensible than Chang Ch'un-ch'iao's attempt to do away with piece rates (see ch. 6 above). For a post-cultural revolution defence of Liu and the contract labour system, see Huang Cheng-shen, 'Is implementing the "two types of labour system" a restoration of capitalism?', *HHYP—WCP*, No. 5, 1980, pp. 26–7.

[5] For Szechwan, see Li Ta-chang, 'Report on the work of the Szechwan Provincial People's Council', *Szechwan Jih-pao*, 24 June 1959, trans. in SCMP 2109, p. 26; for Honan, see Wu Chih-p'u, 'Consolidation and development of people's communes', *HC*, No. 1, 1960, trans. in ECMM 197, p. 2.

[6] For the loss of work days to agriculture in 1958, see Ch'en Cheng-jen, 'Speed up the technical transformation of agriculture', *HC*, No. 4, 1960, p. 10. I have calculated that this was the equivalent of one-third of the days devoted to grain production on the basis of figures given in T'an Chen-lin, 'On certain problems to do with realising the mechanisation of our country's agriculture', *HC*, No. 6, 1960, p. 4. T'an calculated the total number of work days devoted to agriculture as 60 billion of which about 50 per cent were spent on water conservancy, forestry, subsidiary food crops, fish farming, etc.

[7] CB 509, p. 24.

[8] See Marion R. Larser 'China's agriculture under communism', in *An Economic Profile of Mainland China*, I, p. 201.

[9] Hopei's slogan was 'Learn from Honan, catch up with Honan'; see the report of Hopei governor Liu Tzu-hou trans. in SCMP 1949, p. 11. For the impact of competitiveness on Chao Tzu-yang in Kwangtung, see SCMP 4123, p. 3.

[10] ECMM 197, pp. 2–3.

[11] Trans. in SCMP 1886, pp. 17–18.

[12] *JMJP* editorial, 9 Oct. 1958, trans. in SCMP 1875, pp. 1–3. See also *JMJP* editorial, 12 Oct., which signalled increased alarm at the suggestion that the harvest might be even bigger than anticipated and might demand even greater efforts.

[13] *JMJP* editorial, 9 Nov. 1958, trans. in SCMP 1898, p. 12.

[14] SCMP 1913, pp. 6–7.

[15] Cf. SCMP 1829, p. 4, and CB 834, p. 18.

[16] SCMP 1698, p. 14. In Kwangtung, lack of rest led to a measles epidemic among children; see White Chou, III, p. 36.

[17] *Mao, Miscellany*, II, p. 284.

[18] See report of Deputy Governor Chao Che-fu to the Shantung Provincial People's Congress, 22 May 1959, trans. in SCMP 2062, p. 36.

[19] See his 1958 work report ('Continue to advance under the banner of the general line'), *Anwhei Jih-Pao*, 12 Feb. 1959, trans. in JPRS 2005-N, p. 8.

[20] See report of Governor Li Ta-chang to the Provincial People's Congress, *Szechwan Jih-pao*, 24 June 1959, trans. in SCMP 2109, p. 21.

[21] 'Forty charges against Po I-po', *Hung-wei-ping Pao* (Red Guard News), No. 8 (22 Feb. 1967), trans. in CB 878, p. 16.

[22] See Conclusions.

[23] Li Ta-chang estimated the increase in peasant living standards at between 20 and 30 per cent; SCMP 2109, p. 26. Mao referred to under-reporting in his speech to the 6th plenum, although he regarded this as less serious than over-reporting; *Mao, Miscellany*, I, p. 140.

[24] See Li Choh-ming, *The Statistical System of Communist China*, pp. 69–188, and pp. 31–2 above.

[25] Li Choh-ming, *The Statistical System*, pp. 93–4. For the attribution of cadre competitiveness to Mao, see p. 43 above.

[26] 'Dossiers of Teng Hsiao-p'ing', SCMM(S) 27, p. 12.

[27] The other parts are Hankow and Hanyang. For a summary description of the meetings, see Lieberthal, pp. 123–7.

[28] *Mao, Miscellany*, I, pp. 134–5.

[29] Ibid., pp. 140, 147. There is a misprint on p. 147 (and in the original Chinese text: *Mao Tse-tung ssu-hsiang wan sui* (1969), p. 268), where Mao suggests publishing an output figure of 730 (rather than 750) million catties; other figures given in the same passage show that this is incorrect, and this is confirmed by another version of this passage, in *Mao, Miscellany*, I, p. 223; *Mao Tse-tung ssu-hsiang wan sui* (1967), p. 148. The date of Mao's speech is also given incorrectly as 19 Dec., i.e. well after the conclusion of the plenum; the correct date is presumably 9 Dec. which is the one given in the list of contents.

[30] *JMJP*, 24 Oct. 1958.

[31] CB 479, p. 5, art. 4.

[32] CB 892, p. 2, art. 3.

[33] CB 508, p. 7. The 1958 version of the Programme was never published, perhaps because it already seemed out of date in the context of the leap!

[34] SCMP 1798, p. 14.

[35] *JMJP*, 10 June 1958, sections III and IV.

[36] SCMP 1815, p. 14; *HHPYK*, No. 15, 1958, pp. 113, 114.

[37] SCMP 1834, p. 16.

[38] *JMJP*, 11 Sept. 1958; SCMP 1857, pp. 1–13. Even now the ordering of the items did not seem sacrosanct. In the list of directives issued, water conservancy was correctly listed first, but deep ploughing was incorrectly placed second above fertilizer.

[39] *JMJP*, 6 Oct. 1958.

[40] *JMJP*, 20 Oct. 1958; the conference took place from 10 to 18 Oct. The eight

items were said to have been 'put forward' (*t'i-ch'u*) by Mao. On the same day the paper also published an article by a senior Honan party official in which he advocated a seven-item formula, omitting the reference to disease and pests.

41 Ibid.

42 Cf. ibid. and *JMJP*, 10 and 12 Nov. 1958. These latter issues contain reports of three further multi-province agricultural conferences (north-western, eastern, and southern and south-western), all starting on 27 Oct. and ending on either 4 or 5 Nov.; since it is highly unlikely that each conference simultaneously and coincidentally arrived at the final formula for the agricultural charter, it seems legitimate to assume that it was honed to its final form and description prior to the opening of the conferences, but after the closing of the first conference on 18 Oct. A further illustration (see note 40 above) of the confusion in the media was provided by a report in *PR*, No. 35, 1958, p. 4, on the Sian conference. The report, which was published on 28 Oct. as the second set of conferences got under way, referred to an agricultural charter, but listed only the five Peitaiho items as its components. See also ibid., pp. 8, 10–11.

43 Chao, *Agricultural Production in Communist China*, pp. 78–80.

44 *Mao, Miscellany*, I, pp. 103–4.

45 Mao seems to have had a penchant for pinning his faith on model units and workers; for instance, he had the Hupeh labour model Kuan Mu-sheng to stay at his home. Kuan was apparently denounced in 1963, but it is not clear from cultural revolution attacks whether the output achievements claimed for his rural unit were phoney or not. See 'Arrest political pickpocket Wang Jen-chung', trans. in SCMM(S) 29, pp. 38–40.

46 See T'an Chen-lin, 'Strive for a bountiful life in two or three years', *HC*, No. 6, 1958, pp. 10–11; ECMM 144, p. 5.

47 SCMP 1857, p. 7.

48 URI, *Communist China, 1958*, p. 74.

49 *Mao, Miscellany*, I, p. 144. Mao attributed the system to the people but the *JMJP* editorial on 24 Oct. stated that it was put forward by Mao.

50 See the discussion of Shansi's experience in the work report of the provincial government; *Shansi Jih-pao*, 8 Dec. 1958, trans. in SCMP 1946, p. 8. See also the description of Shansi as the pioneer of this system in an NCNA report of 17 Dec. 1958, SCMP 1920, pp. 17–18.

51 For the conference report, see *JMJP*, 20 Oct.; for the editorial and the eulogies to the high-yielding areas, see *ibid.*, 24 Oct. 1958, and *PR*, No. 35, 1958, pp. 8–10.

52 *JMJP*, 20 Oct. 1958.

53 Ibid., editorial, 24 Oct. 1958.

54 Ibid., 10 Nov. 1958.

55 SCMP 1912, pp. 8–9.

56 Ibid., p. 6; *JMJP*, 10 Nov. 1958.

57 SCMP 1912, p. 11; *JMJP*, 12 Nov. 1958.

58 SCMP 1893, pp. 22–3; ibid. 1920, p. 17.

59 Ibid. 1893, p. 23.

60 Ibid. 1903, p. 23.

61 Ibid.

62 These calculations are made on the basis of the various provincial statistics collated in *Provincial Agricultural Statistics for Communist China*, pp. 1–2, 30, 50, 60, 139, 159, 179–80. The Wuhan plenum endorsed reducting cultivated acreage by two-thirds; see *Pol. Docs*, p. 496, where the translation uses the term 'sown' but the context makes it clear that 'cultivated' is intended.

63 See *Chung-kuo Nung-yeh Nien-chien* (China Agricultural Yearbook), 1980, p. 34.

64 *Mao, Miscellany* I, pp. 133, 144.

65 Anthony M. Tang, 'Policy and performance in agriculture', in Eckstein, Galenson & Liu (eds), *Economic Trends in Communist China*, p. 497.

66 See his extolling of Anhwei's achievements in *Mao, Miscellany*, I, p. 142.

67 Lu Chung-chien, 'Loopholes of Hua Kuo-feng's assessment of Mao Tse-tung', *Cheng-ming* (Contention) (Hong Kong), No. 35, 1980, trans. in JPRS 76,736, p. 20.

68 *TGY*, p. 121.

69 JPRS 76,736, p. 20.

70 Most of the attacks on T'an's activities at this period refer to speeches he made in Sian and Shantung; see *P'i T'an Chan Pao* (Criticise T'an [Chen-lin] Combat News), 5 Aug. 1957, p. 4, cols 2–3. The context suggests that the Sian speech referred to was made at the multi-province agricultural conference in Oct. (see p. 123 above) and not at the Shensi/Sian cadres conference in Nov. or Dec. at which T'an outlined his vision of communism (see p. 84 above). An allegation that T'an pushed the use of an untested, experimental rope-drawn tractor in Sept. ('T'an Chen-lin's crime of sabotage against farm mechanisation must be reckoned with', *Nung-yeh Chi-hsieh Chi-shu* (Agricultural Machine Technique), No. 6 (8 June 1968), trans. in SCMM 624, p. 4) must be seen against the background of Mao's advocacy of the extensive promotion of the same tool in the same month (SCMP 1874, p. 4).

71 At the first Chengchow conference in mid-Nov. *Mao, Miscellany*, I, p. 131.

72 For attacks on Liu, see *San-fan fen-tzu Liu Shao-ch'i tsui-o shih*, p. 35, *Liu Shao-ch'i fan-ko-ming tsui-o shih*, p. 33, and 'A chronicle of events in the life of Liu Shao-ch'i (1899–1967)', trans. in CB 834, p. 17. In 'A supplementary biography of Liu hsiu', JPRS 41,858, p. 188, in which Teng Hsiao-p'ing is also attacked, it is asserted that a more rational line was introduced when Mao wrote to rural cadres; but this was not until April 1959. (See CB 891, pp. 34–5, where the date is incorrectly given as Nov. 1959; for a discussion of the text of this important letter, see pp. 170–1 below.

73 *Mao, Miscellany*, I, p. 147.

74 See pp. 89–90 above.

75 *Mao, Miscellany*, pp. 141, 144–5, 210. It is not clear whether the 30–40 million target (p. 141) refers to 1960 or 1961; Mao says 'within three years', but this could mean either within the scheduled three years of the leap (i.e. by 1960) or three years from when he was speaking (i.e. by 1961).

76 Ibid., p. 133.

77 Ibid., p. 210.

78 Ibid., pp. 145–6.

79 Ibid., p. 134; Donnithorne, *China's Economic System*, pp. 253, 258–9. In 1959–60 coal accounted for 40 per cent of the total volume of railway freight.

80 See Lieberthal, pp. 123–4, for a list of leaders who did not attend all or even part of the Chengchow conference.

81 See Hsi Chung-hsun's account in Grey Chou, III, pp. 18–19.

82 See ch. 10 below.

83 See Wang Chen et al., 'Remember and carry on', HHYP, No. 2, 1981, p. 61.

84 *Mao, Miscellany*, I, pp. 133, 139. Yang had been made an alternate member of the CC at the May congress session. In Feb. 1958, Yang's Ministry of Urban Services had been renamed the 2nd Ministry of Commerce, and Ch'en Yun's Ministry of Commerce had been renamed the 1st Ministry. In September, the two ministries had been combined as the Ministry of Commerce with Ch'eng Tzu-hua as Minister. In Nov. 1958, Ch'en Yun became Chairman of the newly created State Capital Construction Commission, but Yang was

dispatched to a minor post in distant Tsinghai and only surfaced again in the Chinese heartland as Vice Governor of Hopei province in 1962–3. See Donnithorne, *China's Economic System*, pp. 518–19, and the biography of Yang in Klein & Clark, *Biographic Dictionary*.

85 *Mao, Miscellany*, I, p. 133.

86 Ibid., p. 138.

87 Ibid., pp. 133, 139.

88 According to *Khrushchev Remembers*, pp. 274–5, Chou En-lai flew to Moscow to request advice on China's problems with the steel industry 'after the beginning of the Great Leap Forward'; the Russians dispatched a deputy chairman of their State Planning Commission, Deputy Premier Zasyadko, who allegedly told Khrushchev on his return 'after a few weeks' that the main problem was that experienced steel men had been dispatched to the countryside leaving the steel plants to be run by veterinarians among others. Khrushchev's account gives the impression that Chou's visit was an emergency one, some time in 1958, and was occasioned entirely by the steel crisis. While such a secret trip by the Chinese Premier to Moscow to ask assistance in this field cannot be ruled out, it seems likely that the Soviet premier dramatized the episode in recalling it. Zasyadko visited China publicly in mid-June 1959 for nine days (*Pravda*, 11 and 20 June 1959; *PR*, No. 26, 1959, p. 22); if this was the visit Khrushchev was referring to, it seems more likely it was arranged when Chou En-lai attended the 21st congress of the CPSU in Jan.–Feb. 1959. If so, the length of time before the visit took place and its comparative shortness do not confirm Khrushchev's suggestion of emergency aid. (Khrushchev also dilates on how Zasyadko probably drank his way through the long train journey to China, whereas on the official visit he flew both ways.) Later in the year, Zasyadko was among those receiving an important Chinese delegation which included a number of deputy ministers connected with industry; *Pravda*, 11 Sept. 1959.

89 Grey Chou, III, p. 6; for a contemporary account of the visit see *HHPYK*, No. 24, 1958, p. 19.

90 *Mao, Miscellany*, I, p. 131. See also Tuan Chün-yi et al., 'Comrade Shao-ch'i, Honan's people remember you!', *JMJP*, 21 May 1980.

91 *Mao, Miscellany*, I, p. 128.

92 Ibid., p. 132

93 Ibid., p. 131.

94 Ibid., p. 132.

95 Li Jui, 'Remember T'ien Chia-ying', *HHYP—WCP*, No. 4, 1980, p. 172; 'Comrade Teng Li-ch'ün gives guidance lecture on studying the "Resolution"', *Chung-kuo Ch'ing-nien Pao*, 11 July 1981, trans. in FBIS-CHI-81-143, p. K17.

96 *Huai-nien Liu Shao-ch'i T'ung-chih*, p. 377.

97 *HCPP*, No. 20, pp. 185–7, 242; An Tzu-wen, 'Construct our party well', *JMJP*, 8 May 1980.

98 *Mao, Miscellany*, I, pp. 142–3.

99 *Pol. Docs*, pp. 492–5.

100 *Mao, Miscellany*, I, p. 138, *Mao Tse-tung ssu-hsiang wan sui* (1969), p. 257.

101 *Pol. Docs*, p. 492.

102 SWB/FE/5990, p. BII/1.

103 *Mao, Miscellany*, I, p. 142; *Mao Tse-tung ssu-hsiang wan sui* (1969), p. 261.

104 Zagoria, *Sino-Soviet Conflict*, pp. 109–33, has an extended discussion of Soviet reactions to the communes and Chinese ideological claims. Zagoria points out that the decision to hold a special congress of the CPSU was announced on 5 Sept. 1958, after the passage of the Peitaiho resolution

although before its publication. It seems likely that the Russians would have had some knowledge of the resolution before its publication.

[105] *Teng Hsiao-p'ing fan-tang fan-she-hui-chu-i fan-Mao Tse-tung ssu-hsiang-ti yen-chai-pien* (Selection of Teng Hsiao-p'ing's anti-party, anti-socialist, anti-Mao Tse-tung Thought utterances) (Peking: First Detachment of the People's University Three Red Pluck out Liu-Teng Army, Capital's Red Representative Conference (ed.), April 1967), p. 47.

[106] For the announcement of Mao's resignation see *Pol. Docs*, pp. 487–8.

[107] The last two paragraphs are based in large part upon the analysis and, except where indicated separately, quotations in Zagoria, *Sino-Soviet Conflict*, pp. 128–32.

[108] Ibid., p. 133.

[109] *Pol. Docs*, p. 490.

[110] Ibid., p. 492.

[111] Ibid., p. 502.

[112] *Mao, Miscellany*, I, p. 129. There has been some confusion as to when Mao made his comments on Stalin's text, 1958 or 1959; see ibid., pp. 129, 191. In TLC, pp. 29–30, it is confirmed that Mao discussed it in a speech at the opening of the first Chengchow conference.

[113] Ibid., p. 130. For Stalin's reply to the economists, see his *Economic Problems of Socialism in the U.S.S.R.*, pp. 93–104. For a brief commentary on the political background to Stalin's treatise, see Leonhard, *The Kremlin since Stalin* pp. 36–9. Despite Mao's attack, Chinese party members continued to be adjured to read works by the late Soviet dictator, as well as other Marxist classics; see *Ta hai hang-hsing k'ao to-shou*, pp. 33–4, and *Mao, Miscellany*, I, pp. 234–5.

[114] *P'eng Chen fan-ko-ming hsiu-cheng-chu-i yen-lun chai-pien* (Excerpts from P'eng Chen's counter-revolutionary revisionist utterances) (Peking: China People's University, New People's University Commune and Mao Tse-tung Thought Red Guards, May 1967), p. 40. This remark, as its source suggests, was used against P'eng during the cultural revolution, but set beside Mao's speech at Chengchow any accusation of it proving that P'eng was a pro-Khrushchev revisionist is plainly illegitimate. P'eng Chen was also denounced during the cultural revolution for ideas contained in the introductory message he apparently wrote for the inaugural issue of the Peking theoretical journal *Ch'ien Hsien* (Front Line) on 25 Nov. 1958, but an examination of it does not suggest it was aimed against either Mao or the great leap forward. Its second sentence proclaimed that Mao's thought would be the journal's guide. (For the text of the message, see *JMJP*, 26 Nov. 1958. For criticisms, see 'Introductory statement in Ch'ien Hsien's inaugural issue is a revisionist manifesto', *Yangch'eng Wan Pao*, 29 May 1966, trans. in SCMP 3711, pp. 4–8; *Counter-revolutionary revisionist P'eng Chen's towering crimes of opposing the party, socialism and the Thought of Mao Tse-tung* (10 June 1967) trans. in SCMM 639, pp. 7–8; *P'eng Chen fan-ko-ming hsiu-cheng-chu-i yen-lun chai-pien*, p. 34; 'Destroy the black back-stage manager of "Three family village"', *Kuang-ming Jih-pao*, 18 June 1967, trans. in SCMP 3977, pp. 12–13.

[115] See *Origins*, I, pp. 61–3, and ch. 3 above.

[116] *Pol. Docs*, p. 147.

[117] For a report on the new textbook, see *PR*, No. 35, 1958, p. 18. Presumably the researchers working on it would have been expected to provide the 'systematization' of Mao's 'rich' economic thought called for by Teng Hsiao-p'ing earlier in the year; see *Chin Chün Pao*, 14 June 1967, p. 2, col. 1.

[118] 'Ho Lung's crimes in mountaineering activities', *T'i-yü Chan-hsien* (Physical Education Front), 9 Feb. 1967, trans. in SCMP(S) 175, p. 19. Ho, who

became Chairman of the Physical Culture and Sports Commission in Sept. 1959, had presided over the preparatory conference of the Chinese Mountaineering Association in 1958.

[119] Zagoria, *Sino-Soviet Conflict*, pp. 99, 126.

[120] *PR*, No. 7, 1959, p. 12. For Chou's remarks on the communes in his address to the CPSU 21st congress, see Floyd, *Mao against Khrushchev*, p. 260. For Chou's support for Happiness Homes for the aged and nurseries during a visit to a Hopei commune after the Wuhan plenum, see *Cheng-jung Sui-yueh* (Eventful Years), pp. 22-5.

[121] SCMP 1932, pp. 22-5.

Chapter 8.   Mao Veers Right

[1] *Pol. Docs*, p. 502

[2] *JMST*, 1959, p. 44. For a brief discussion of the translation, see Hsia, *The Commune in Retreat as Evidenced in Terminology and Semantics*, p. 24.

[3] See Lieberthal, pp. 130-8; *P'eng Teh-huai Tzu-hsu* (P'eng Teh-huai's Autobiography), p. 299. Lieberthal argues (p. 131) that the Peking conference referred to by Mao is likely to be the national conference of directors of CCP Rural Work Departments held from 12 to 26 Jan., but this seems unlikely. Mao referred to the January Peking conference as one of a number of meetings prior to the Lushan conference in July-Aug. 1959 at which critics of the communes and the leap could have aired their doubts (*Mao, Miscellany*, I, p. 195; II, p. 311). But there is no reason why Defence Minister P'eng Teh-huai and the three other major critics at Lushan should have attended a conference of relatively junior officials like rural work directors, and there is no evidence that they did. The only senior officials who appear to have attended were T'an Chen-lin, Teng Tzu-hui and Ch'en Cheng-jen who had national responsibility for rural work. Presumably, therefore, the Peking meeting was another Politburo meeting. I have dated it the 27th because according to Mao (*Mao, Miscellany*, I, p. 179) there were thorough discussions of commune management problems on that day. This may also have been the occasion, referred to by Mao seven years later (CB 891, p. 71) as lasting less than a day, to his dissatisfaction.

[4] For post-Wuhan provincial meetings, see for instance SCMP 1938, pp. 6-17, and SCMP 1945, pp. 7-16.

[5] *Mao Tse-tung ssu-hsiang wan sui* (1967), p. 41

[6] Hsia, *The Commune in Retreat*, p. 25.

[7] Ibid., pp. 29-35; idem, *Metaphor, Myth, Ritual and the People's Commune*, pp. 3-15. The official version of the *san hua* was 'organizing along military lines, working as if fighting a battle and living the collective way' (*Pol. Docs*, p. 501); '*tsu-chih chün-shih-hua, hsing-tung chan-tou-hua, sheng-huo chi-t'i-hua*' (*JMST*, 1959, p. 44).

[8] *Pol. Docs*, p. 501

[9] Hsia, *The Commune in Retreat*, pp. 34-5

[10] SCMP 1938, pp. 6-7.

[11] Ibid., pp. 12, 14; SCMP 1945, pp. 13, 14, 16.

[12] SCMP 1938, pp. 7, 11, 14.

[13] See for example SCMP 1938, pp. 6-17; SCMP 1945, pp. 7-16, *passim*.

[14] SCMP 1965, p. 11.

[15] Walker, *Letters from the Communes*, p. 16

[16] Ibid., p. 18.

[17] Ibid., pp. 18-19.

[18] Ibid., p. 39.

[19] Ibid., p. 17.

[20] Ibid., p. 18.

[21] Ibid., p. 20.

[22] Ibid., p. 23.

[23] Ibid., p. 34.

[24] Ibid., p. 38.

[25] Ibid., p. 30.

[26] Ibid., pp. 36–7.

[27] Ibid., p. 41.

[28] Ibid., p. 42.

[29] Ibid.

[30] Ibid., p. 19.

[31] Hsueh Kuang-chün, 'The just spirit of heaven and earth lives on—in memory of Comrade T'ao Chu', *HC*, No. 1, 1979, trans. in JPRS 73,074, p. 83.

[32] See the longer version of T'ao's remarks in *Wen Hui Pao* (Hong Kong), 13 Jan. 1959, trans. in SCMP 1939, pp. 9–10. The *PR* version is in *PR*, No. 9, 1959, pp. 6–9.

[33] Trans. in SCMP 1913, pp. 8–9.

[34] Vogel, *Canton under Communism*, p. 258. For Chao's age, and other background details, see 'Chao Tzu-yang's record', *Yeh Chan Pao* (Field Combat News) (Canton), 13 Oct. 1967, trans. in SCMP 4085, p. 13.

[35] Trans. in SCMP 1971, pp. 26–40.

[36] *Mao Tse-tung ssu-hsiang wan sui* (1967), pp. 39, 41.

[37] SCMP 1971, p. 33

[38] SCMP 1971, pp. 27–8, 29.

[39] Ibid., p. 33.

[40] Ibid., pp. 32, 33.

[41] Red Alliance, Hsuwen, 'A shocking case of political persecution', *Hung-se Tsao-fan-che* (Red Rebel), 4 Jan. 1968, trans. in SCMP 4123, pp. 1–11.

[42] Ibid., p. 11.

[43] Ibid., p. 4.

[44] Ibid., pp. 4–5.

[45] Ibid., p. 5. The implication of this cultural revolution account is that there was no hoarded grain; this was not Mao's belief at the time, as we shall see.

[46] Ibid., pp. 5–7.

[47] Ibid., p. 7.

[48] Ibid., p. 6. Chao set a target of 5,000–6,000 million catties of concealed grain to be uncovered in Kwangtung. The claimed grain output for 1958 was 62,000 million catties; SCMP 1974, p. 32.

[49] SCMP 4123, p. 11; see also p. 6 for confirmation that Chao believed that concealment of grain was endemic throughout the province.

[50] *HHPYK*, No. 8, 1959, p. 33. Liu Shun-huan, a Kiangsu party secretary, also placed opposition to departmentalism in the context of the chess game policy in a work report to a provincial party conference on 29 Jan., but he did not link it to a grain concealment problem; *HHPYK*, No. 7, 1959, pp. 20–1. Shu T'ung, the Shantung 1st secretary, made a strong attack on departmentalism in his work report to the provincial party conference on 24 Jan., but he was concerned exclusively with long-existing political problems within the top leadership of the provincial party; *Ta Chung Jih-pao* (Great Masses Daily), 7 Feb. 1959.

[51] *HC*, No. 5, 1959 (published on 1 March), pp. 25–9.

[52] Ibid., p. 26. The Honan provincial party paper stressed a similar priority of interests in an editorial on the chess game policy when it stated that the production brigade must serve the commune, the commune must serve the *hsien*

federation of communes, and the *hsien* federation must serve the province and the country (*Honan Jih-pao* (Honan Daily), 13 Feb. 1959).

53 *HC*, No. 5, 1959.

54 *JMJP*, 24 Feb. 1959.

55 Ibid.

56 *HC*, No. 4, 1959, pp. 9–12.

57 Ibid., p. 12. The importance of the policy to Shanghai was further underlined when both Teng Hsiao-p'ing and Li Fu-ch'un, Chairman of the State Planning Commission, praised it at the city party's industrial conference on 20 Feb.; *SCMP* 1972, pp. 17–18. The difficulty of implementing the policy, despite such heavyweight support, was illustrated at the national commodity exchange fair held in Shanghai at this time, when the head of the Canton delegation apparently refused to allow commodities produced in his city to be allocated elsewhere unless his hard bargaining terms were met; see 'Down with Tu Cheng-hsiang, top party power holder and capitalist roader in the Canton Municipal finance and trade system', trans. in *SCMM* 628, pp. 19–20.

58 *P'eng Teh-huai Tzu-hsu*, p. 299.

59 *Mao Tse-tung ssu-hsiang wan sui* (1967), pp. 39, 47.

60 *Mao Tse-tung ssu-hsiang wan sui* (1969), p. 278; the 'one ounce' in the trans. of this passage in *Mao, Miscellany*, I, p. 157, is in fact a Chinese ounce (*liang*), equivalent to 50 g. For emergency action taken, see *SCMP* 1933, pp. 2–12.

61 *Mao Tse-tung ssu-hsiang wan sui* (1967), p. 39. An example of Mao's night owl habits is provided by the story of his writing to a former junior cadre of the central guards unit at 4 am on 28 Jan. 1959; see *Mao Tse-tung T'ung-chih Pa-shih-wu Tan-chen Chi-nien Wen-hsuan*, pp. 204–5.

62 *Mao Tse-tung ssu-hsiang wan sui* (1967), p. 60. During the cultural revolution Mao expressed dissatisfaction that this meeting lasted less than a day (ibid., p. 45; CB 891, p. 71), but he seemed satisfied at the time.

63 *Mao Tse-tung ssu-hsiang wan sui* (1969), pp. 271–9; *Mao, Miscellany*, I, pp. 151–8. Although the speech is headlined 2 Feb., in the text Mao says: 'Now it is 1 February.' However the context (and the fact that Mao did not say 'today') suggests that he is merely emphasizing that a new month has started rather than giving the date when he is actually speaking.

64 *Mao Tse-tung ssu-hsiang wan sui* (1967), p. 60. For reports on this commune, see Lü Hung-pin's report to the NPC (*HHPYK*, No. 11, 1959, pp. 87–8 and *PR*, No. 20, 1959, pp. 9–10. The Shangtung 1st secretary Shu T'ung was on an inspection visit in the countryside from 13 to 23 Feb.; *Ta Chung Jih-pao*, 6 May 1959.

65 *Mao Tse-tung ssu-hsiang wan sui* (1967), pp. 3–7; the title of this speech refers to the districts as 'Hsin, Lo, Hsu, Hsin', which I assume to be Hsinhsiang, Loyang, Hsuch'ang and Hsinyang.

66 *Mao, Miscellany*, I, p. 151.

67 Ibid., p. 153. Both messages were passed on to a wider audience by a *JMJP* editorial, 10 Feb. 1959. In fact, provincial parties were already busy with fertilizer accumulation campaigns: see *Ta Chung Jih-pao*, 23 Jan. 1959; *Anhwei Jih-pao*, 3 Feb. 1959.

68 *Mao, Miscellany*, I, p. 153

69 Ibid., p. 154

70 Ibid., p. 156.

71 Ibid., p. 157.

72 Ibid.

73 Ibid., p. 158.

74 *Mao Tse-tung ssu-hsiang wan sui* (1967), pp. 4–5.

[75] Ibid., p. 39.

[76] Ibid., pp. 8–49.

[77] Lieberthal, p. 133.

[78] *Mao Tse-tung ssu-hsiang wan sui* (1967), pp. 16, 17, 25, 36.

[79] Po I-po, 'Respect and remembrance—marking the 60th anniversary of the founding of the CCP', *HC*, No. 13, 1981, trans. in FBIS-CHI-81-145, p. K34.

[80] *Mao Tse-tung ssu-hsiang wan sui* (1967), pp. 10, 20.

[81] Ibid., p. 47.

[82] Ibid., p. 40; see also pp. 18, 39, 42.

[83] Ibid., pp. 34, 36, 39, 40, 41, 44; on p. 19, the last part of the phrase is varied to read *san shou-k'uan* (and see also p. 10). The note on the whole phrase in *A Comprehensive Glossary of Chinese Communist Terminology*, p. 229, indicates that this was the first occasion it was used. (The *Glossary's* reference is to the much shorter version of Mao's speeches to the conference contained in *Mao Tse-tung ssu-hsiang wan sui* (1969), pp. 279–88.) For the later employment of this slogan by Lin Piao, see Domes, *Socialism in the Chinese Countryside*, pp. 68–9.

[84] *Mao Tse-tung ssu-hsiang wan sui* (1967), p. 19.

[85] Ibid., p. 44.

[86] Ibid., pp. 34, 39.

[87] Ibid., p. 36.

[88] Ibid., p. 40.

[89] Ibid., p. 22.

[90] Ibid., p. 21.

[91] Ibid., p. 9. For an earlier attack on rural departmentalism, when Mao was on the other side, see *Origins*, I, pp. 293–4.

[92] *Mao, Miscellany*, I, p. 159.

[93] *Mao Tse-tung ssu-hsiang wan sui* (1967), pp. 14, 22–3.

[94] Ibid., p. 21; see also p. 11.

[95] Ibid., pp. 23, 36, 38, 45. For a description of the Wang Kuo Fan APC, see Mao, *Chung-kuo Nung-ts'un-ti She-hui-chu-i Kao Ch'ao*, I, pp. 13–14, 16–26, trans. in *Socialist Upsurge in China's Countryside*, pp. 24–25, 67–81.

[96] *Mao Tse-tung ssu-hsiang wan sui* (1967), p. 9.

[97] Ibid., p. 14. For Honan's approach to this problem see SCMP 1965, p. 15.

[98] *Pol. Docs*, pp. 455–6; *JMST* (1959), p. 33.

[99] Crook & Crook, *The First Years of Yangyi Commune*, pp. 38–9.

[100] Ibid., pp. 42–3.

[101] Ibid., p. 43.

[102] *Mao Tse-tung ssu-hsiang wan sui* (1967), p. 41.

[103] Ibid., p. 19.

[104] Ibid., pp. 6, 14, 22, 29.

[105] Ibid., p. 40.

[106] Ibid., pp. 15, 40.

[107] Ibid., p. 40. For a passing reference by Mao to the blind flow of labour to the cities, a subject he said had not been discussed at the Chengchow conference, see ibid., p. 48.

[108] Ibid., p. 15.

[109] Ibid., pp. 6, 11, 12, 15, 21–2, 23–4, 31–2, 41.

[110] Ibid., p. 11.

[111] Ibid., p. 41.

[112] For an account of Chang Chih-tung's role in China's early modernization programme, see Teng & Fairbank, *China's Response to the West*, pp. 164–74, 195–207.

[113] *Mao Tse-tung ssu-hsiang wan sui* (1967), p. 15

[114] Ibid.
[115] Ibid., p. 32.
[116] Ibid.
[117] Ibid., pp. 15, 21, 24, 32, 41.
[118] Ibid., pp. 15, 24.
[119] Ibid., p. 21.
[120] Ibid., p. 14.
[121] Ibid., p. 41.
[122] Ibid., pp. 10, 11.
[123] Ibid., pp. 44, 45.
[124] Ibid., p. 10.
[125] Ibid., p. 44. For a brief account of Wang An-shih's reforms, see Reischauer & Fairbank, *East Asia: The Great Tradition*, pp. 206–8.
[126] *Mao Tse-tung ssu-hsiang wan sui* (1967), p. 9; see also p. 10.
[127] Ibid., p. 34.
[128] Ibid., p. 42.
[129] CB 562, p. 7.
[130] Crook & Crook, *The First Years of Yangyi Commune*, p. 57.
[131] CB 562, pp. 3–4.
[132] *Mao Tse-tung ssu-hsiang wan sui* (1967), p. 11.
[133] Ibid., p. 26.
[134] Ibid., p. 44. For other critical comments on Stalin, see ibid., pp. 5, 48–9.
[135] See Fainsod, *How Russia Is Ruled*, pp. 530–2.
[136] *Mao Tse-tung ssu-hsiang wan sui* (1967), p. 26.
[137] Ibid., p. 18; see also p. 21.
[138] Ibid., p. 16.
[139] Ibid.
[140] Ibid., pp. 10, 11, 18, 21, 26, 41, 47.
[141] Ibid., pp. 21, 29, 38.
[142] Ibid., pp. 26, 45.
[143] Ibid., p. 38.
[144] Ibid., pp. 9, 26, 45.
[145] Ibid.
[146] Ibid., p. 4.
[147] Ibid., p. 47. For the particular worries of basic-level cadres, see ibid, pp. 36–7.
[148] Ibid., p. 29. Mao also portrayed the cadres in the upper ranks of commune administration (commune level and management district level) as being neutral or ambivalent in the confrontation between the upper levels and the grass roots; see ibid., p. 26.
[149] Ibid., p. 39; Mao's words were *min hsin pu an, chün hsin yeh chiu pu an*.
[150] Ibid.
[151] Ibid., p. 48
[152] Ibid., p. 41
[153] Ibid., p. 27. Mao slightly underestimated the longevity of the Ch'in dynasty (221–206 BC) and slightly overestimated that of the Sui (AD 589–618).
[154] Ibid., p. 9.
[155] Ibid., p. 36.
[156] Ibid., pp. 11, 13.
[157] Ibid., pp. 13, 38, 45
[158] Ibid., p. 27.
[159] Ibid., pp. 13, 16, 26, 31, 38.
[160] Ibid., p. 13.
[161] Ibid., p. 42.
[162] Ibid., p. 41.

[163] Ibid., pp. 35, 36, 441. During the cultural revolution Foreign Minister Ch'en Yi was criticized for cautioning *Poetry* magazine in April 1959 against becoming a vehicle for the masses' verses; *Tung-fang Hung Chan Pao* (East Is Red Combat News), 15 June 1967, p. 7, no. 91. Yet is seems likely that Ch'en Yi, a noted poet in his own right (see *Ch'en Yi Shih-tz'u Hsuan-chi* [Selected Poems of Ch'en Yi]), had been chosen by Mao to pass on this particular element of the views he enunciated at the second Chengchow conference.

[164] *Mao Tse-tung ssu-hsiang wan sui* (1967) p. 40

[165] Ibid., p. 22

[166] Ibid., p. 12; see also p. 9.

[167] Ibid., pp. 12, 20, 28, 30–1, 37.

[168] On occasion, Mao indicated that that this 15–year period might be inclusive of the period of transition from brigade to commune ownership; ibid., p. 49. Elsewhere he stated that the transition to communism might take 20 years or a little longer and would be in addition to the brigade–commune transition; ibid. p. 20. Mao's vagueness is understandable.

[169] See p. 131 above.

[170] *Mao Tse-tung ssu-hsiang wan sui* (1967), pp. 19, 30–1, 37.

[171] Ibid., p. 26.

[172] Ibid., p. 22

[173] Ibid., p. 23.

[174] Ibid., p. 22

[175] Ibid., p. 10.

[176] Ibid., p. 22.

[177] Crook & Crook, *The First Years of Yangyi Commune*, p. 59.

[178] *Mao Tse-tung ssu-hsiang wan sui* (1967), pp. 8, 13–14, 45. For an earlier, more imprecise analysis, see p. 6.

[179] Ibid., p. 10.

[180] Ibid., pp. 16, 24, 26, 33, 36, 45. The precise relationship of accumulation to consumption could be calculated in at least three ways; see Fukien Province Economic Planning Committee's Agriculture Office, 'Preliminary views on the methods of computing the accumulation and consumption in people's communes', *Chi-hua yü T'ung-chi* (Planning & Statistics), No. 5 (8 March 1959), trans. in ECMM 173, pp. 44–5. In the one example cited, perhaps typical of Fukien communes, consumption varied between 72·61 per cent and 51·65 per cent according to the method of calculation. A major difference between the Fukien analysis and the manner in which Mao presented the Honan figures was that Mao apparently did not count any of the welfare expenses as consumption.

[181] *Mao Tse-tung ssu-hsiang wan sui* (1967), p. 35.

[182] Ibid., pp. 30, 35, 45.

[183] Ibid., pp. 24, 31. For a latter-day confirmation of Mao's emphasis on overall balance at this time, see Liu Sui-nien, 'Some problems in the research necessary to get overall balance in the national economy', *HHYP-WCP*, No. 5. 1980, p. 16

[184] *Mao Tse-tung ssu-hsiang wan sui* (1967), p. 10.

[185] Ibid., p. 24.

[186] Ibid., p. 36.

[187] Ibid., p. 39.

[188] Ibid., p. 40. Mao's summary of Anhwei's policy is elliptical but the meaning seems clear.

[189] Ibid., pp. 39–40.

[190] Ibid., p. 39. See also his earlier speech to the Honan cadres, ibid., pp. 4–5.

[191] Chao Tzu-yang, 'A communist of noble character', *JMJP*, 23 March 1979,

reproduced in *HHYP*, No. 4, 1979, pp. 56–7. Chao goes on to list a number of measures T'ao took but he appears to have telescoped the events of 1959–61 because these policies were almost certainly not adopted till after the CC's 9th plenum in Jan. 1961. The text of T'ao Chu's speech released at the time (*HHPYK*, No. 13, 1959, pp. 1–6) contains admissions of error by the Kwangtung party, but no self-criticism or admission of hot-headedness or mention of mistaken opposition to grain concealment. Perhaps the most pointed oblique reference to this latter issue comes in a passage where T'ao points out that subjective error, preconceived ideas, can vitiate the conclusions drawn from on-the-spot investigations (ibid., pp. 5–6).

[192] Mao, *Critique of Soviet Economics*, p. 123.

[193] The article was also included in a collection of articles by T'ao Chu published under the title *Li-hsiang Ch'ing-ts'ao Ching-shen Sheng-huo* (Ideals, Sentiments, and Spiritual Life) (first published in 1962).

[194] Yao Wen-yuan, 'Comments on T'ao Chu's two books', *China Reconstructs (Supplement)*, Nov. 1967, pp. 17–18.

[195] Goldman, *China's Intellectuals: Advise and Dissent*, pp. 84–5.

[196] I have used the translation from Legge, *The Four Books*, p. 588. Interestingly, Yao Wen-yuan made no attempt to suggest that T'ao's quotation was meant to draw his readers' attention to the immediately prior sentences which read: 'Moreover, when the superior men of old had errors they reformed them. The superior men of the present time, when they have errors, persist in them, (ibid., pp. 587–8)!

[197] *HHYP*, No. 4, 1979, pp. 57–8.

[198] Yao Wen-yuan, 'Comments on T'ao Chu's two books', p. 17.

[199] Ibid.

[200] This is suggested in Goldman, *China's Intellectuals*, p. 85.

[201] See ch. 10 below.

[202] From the first issue of *HC* in 1958 to the end of 1965, the year before the cultural revolution, only the more senior Politburo member K'o Ch'ing-shih of Shanghai, among top provincial officials, equalled T'ao Chu's record of five articles published (T'ao Lu-chia of Shansi had four; Tseng Hsi-sheng of Anhwei, Wu Chih-p'u of Honan and Wang Jen-chung of Hupeh had three each). Perhaps even more significantly, in 1959 T'ao Chu had six articles or speeches reproduced in *HHPYK* as compared with five for Tseng Hsi-sheng and four each for K'o Ch'ing-shih and alternate Politburo member Ulanfu of Inner Mongolia. And few provincial 1st secretaries, surely, would have attracted the galaxy of senior party officials that T'ao got to attend the Kwangtung party meeting in Feb. 1959: Deputy Head of State, Marshal Chu Teh; Politburo standing committee member, Marshal Lin Piao; CC members, Marshal Yeh Chieng-ying and Wang Chen (Minister of State Farms and Land Reclamation); and alternate CC member and Deputy Director of the party's rural work department, Ch'en Cheng-jen (*Nan-fang Jih-pao*, 1 March 1959). See also SCMM(S) 27, p. 17, on a Kwangtung tour by top party officials and their families.

[203] See *Origins*, I, especially Pts 3 and 4.

[204] Yao Wen-yuan, 'Comments on T'ao Chu's two books', points out that P'eng Teh-huai's attack at Lushan occurred not long after the publication of T'ao Chu's article, but does not attempt to make any closer connection.

Chapter 9. Chairman Liu

[1] *Mao Tse-tung ssu-hsiang wan sui* (1967), p. 45.

[2] Ibid., pp. 104–6; *Mao, Miscellany*, I, pp. 164–5, where 'tide-watchers and account-reckoners' are translated 'observers and auditors'.

³ *Mao, Miscellany*, I, p. 165.

⁴ Ibid., pp. 168–9; *Mao Tse-tung ssu-hsiang wan sui* (1967), pp. 108–9; *P'eng Teh-huai Tzu-hsu*, pp. 299–300.

⁵ *Mao Tse-tung ssu-hsiang wan sui* (1967), p. 35.

⁶ Ibid., pp. 106–7; *Mao, Miscellany*, I, pp. 166–7.

⁷ *Mao Tse-tung ssu-hsiang wan sui* (1967), p. 50.

⁸ Ibid., p. 263. See also *The Case of Peng Teh-huai*, pp. 17–18, 406–7.

⁹ Lieberthal, p. 135.

¹⁰ *PR*, No. 18, 1958, p. 13.

¹¹ TLC, p. 11.

¹² Ibid., p. 13.

¹³ Ch'en Yun, 'Several serious problems in capital construction work at present', *HC*, No. 5, 1959, pp. 1–16, reproduced in *CYWK*, pp. 70–92; citations are from the latter source. Translations have appeared in ECMM 166, pp. 1–15, and (in abbreviated form) in *PR*, No. 10, 1959, pp. 6–8.

¹⁴ TLC, pp. 78–9.

¹⁵ *CYWK*, pp. 70–3.

¹⁶ Ibid., pp. 74–6; cf. *Origins*, I, pp. 63–6.

¹⁷ *PR*, No. 6, 1958, pp. 9–11.

¹⁸ *CYWK*, pp. 77–89.

¹⁹ Ibid., p. 94. For Mao's use of the slogan in Yenan, see Compton, *Mao's China*, p. 65; for the importance attached to it then by Ch'en, see TLC, p. 104. It is of course much in vogue in China today.

²⁰ For Ch'en's version, see *CYWK*, p. 84. For Mao's version, see *Mao Tse-tung ssu-hsiang wan sui* (1969), p. 294; for the identical, official Chinese translation, see *Ma-k'o-ssu En-ko-ssu Ch'üan Chi* (Collected Works of Marx and Engels), XX, p. 125. The concept comes from *Anti-Dühring* and the full passage represents a salutary commentary on the philosophy of the great leap forward: 'Hegel was the first to state correctly the relationship between freedom and necessity. To him, freedom is the appreciation of necessity. "Necessity is *blind* only *in so far as it is not understood*." Freedom does not consist in the dream of independence of natural laws, but in the knowledge of these laws, and in the possibility this gives of systematically making them work towards definite ends. This holds good in relation both to the laws of external nature and to those which govern the bodily and mental life of men themselves—two classes of law which we can separate from each other at most only in thought but not in reality. Freedom of the will therefore means nothing but the capacity to make decisions with real knowledge of the subject.... Freedom therefore consists in the control over ourselves and over external nature which is founded on knowledge of natural necessity; it is therefore necessarily a product of history.' (From the translation in *A Handbook of Marxism*, p. 255.)

²¹ *CYWK*. p. 93.

²² *PR*, No. 35, 1959, p. 14.

²³ *CYWK*, pp. 93–4. An interesting aspect of Ch'en's figures is that they represented only a small percentage of claimed and projected output; in the case of pigs, these were 180 million in 1958 and 280 million in 1959 (see *PR*, No. 17, 1959, p. 18.)

²⁴ *CYWK*, p. 94.

²⁵ Ibid., pp. 94–5.

²⁶ See ch. 10 below.

²⁷ *Mao Tse-tung ssu-hsiang wan sui* (1967), p. 244.

²⁸ *Pol. Docs*, pp. 485–6.

²⁹ *JMST*, 1959, p. 45.

[30] See Chou En-lai's speech (CB 559, p. 7) and Li Fu-ch'un's speech (CB 562, p. 10).

[31] Lieberthal, p. 137.

[32] *CYWK*, pp. 97, 102.

[33] Ibid., p. 97.

[34] TLC, p. 116.

[35] Ibid.; *CYWK*, p. 98. Liu Shao-ch'i's presence at this conference is indicated in Ch'en Yun's letter to Mao on this topic; the content of this letter makes it clear Mao could not have attended.

[36] See ch. 2 above.

[37] *CYWK*, p. 98.

[38] Ibid., pp. 97–8.

[39] Ibid., p. 99.

[40] Ibid., pp. 100, 102, 106.

[41] Ibid., p. 101.

[42] TLC, pp. 83–4.

[43] *CYWK*, pp. 104, 106. For an indication of the way in which Ch'en Yun's authority had suffered even in his area of special responsibility, commerce, presumably as a result of Mao ignoring him during the leap, see TLC, p. 107.

[44] Kenneth Lieberthal has suggested to me that perhaps only the letter was submitted to Mao, but it seems unlikely that Ch'en would have risked rejection of his case for want of the supporting evidence contained in his report. Whether the Chairman read the report is another matter.

[45] *CYWK*, pp. 106–7.

[46] *Mao Tse-tung ssu-hsiang wan sui* (1967), p. 244. Mao's placing of the decision in June confirms that the Politburo conference reached no conclusion for it met in May.

[47] Grey Chou, III, p. 19,

[48] See ch. 10 below.

[49] TLC, p. 116.

[50] *CYWK*. p. 97.

[51] *Mao, Miscellany*, I, p. 170.

[52] Ibid., pp. 170–1.

[53] Ibid., p. 171.

[54] Ibid., p. 172.

[55] Ahn, *Chinese Politics and the Cultural Revolution*, p. 45.

[56] TLC, pp. 54–5.

[57] Lieberthal, pp. 135–8; *Chung-kuo Kung-ch'an Tang Chien Shih Chiang-Yi* (Canton, 1981), II, p. 351; *Mao, Miscellany*, II, p. 242.

[58] *Mao Tse-tung ssu-hsiang wan sui* (1967), pp. 51–3, 58–62; *Mao, Miscellany*, I, pp. 175–81. Comparison of Mao's speech at the 7th plenum and the subsequently issued 16 articles indicates that the first was the basis for the second. The Shanghai plenum devoted particular attention to the first three of Mao's 'methods'; *Chung-kuo Kung-ch'an Tang Chien Shih Chiang-yi*, II, p. 351.

[59] Teng Hsiao-p'ing was accused of suggesting in the winter of 1958 that a general revolt in Tibet was the least likely of three possibilities; see *Sheng Chih Hung Ch'i* (Provincial Organs Red Flag), Jan. 1968, p. 4. See also 'How the revolt in Tibet broke out', trans. in SCMP 4086, pp. 6–12.

[60] There is a considerable literature on this topic. See Lattimore, *Inner Asian Frontiers of China*; Joseph Fletcher, 'Ch'ing Inner Asia c. 1800' and 'The heyday of the Ch'ing order in Mongolia, Sinkiang and Tibet', *The Cambridge History of China*, 10, *Late Ch'ing, 1800–1911*, Pt 1, pp. 35–106, 351–408. On the Tibetan revolt, see Patterson, *Tibet in Revolt*; Moraes, *The Revolt in Tibet*; Hutheesingh (ed.), *Tibet Fights for Freedom*; *Tibet, 1950–1967*; Ginsburgs &

Mathos, *Communist China and Tibet*. For a general overview of CCP policies towards the national minorities, see Dreyer, *China's Forty Millions*.

[61] Confirmation that Mao retired to the second front at this time was provided during the cultural revolution; see *Liu Shao-ch'i fan-ko-ming tsui-o shih*, p. 34.

[62] For a fuller discussion, see *Origins*, I, pp. 105–7, 152–6.

[63] Ibid., pp. 154–5.

[64] Ibid., p. 155.

[65] *HCPP*, No. 20, p. 172.

[66] Ibid., p. 277.

[67] Ibid., pp. 227, 272–3.

[68] Ibid., p. 227.

[69] Ibid., p. 40.

[70] Ibid., p. 228. This source does not specify that this episode took place in connection with the 8th Congress, but circumstantial evidence suggests that it must have been the occasion.

[71] Ibid., p. 277.

[72] Ibid., pp. 175, 228.

[73] Ibid., p. 273.

[74] See Ernest J. Simmons, 'The organisation writer (1934–46)', in Hayward & Labedz (eds), *Literature and Revolution in Soviet Russia, 1917–1962*, p. 85.

[75] *HCPP*, No. 20, p. 112.

[76] This description was of course originally applied to Robespierre.

[77] Liu's party branch apparently consisted of his household and office staff.

[78] *HCPP*, No. 20, pp. 231, 276.

[79] Ibid., pp. 231–2; *Huai-nien Liu Shao-ch'i T'ung-chih*, p. 378. For an allegation that Liu departed on two occasions from his rule about gifts, see CB 834, p. 21.

[80] *HCPP*, No. 20, pp. 211–13

[81] Ibid., pp. 204–6, 263–4. During the cultural revolution, it was alleged that Liu had given landlord members of his family advance warning of land reform plans. It seems more likely that they appealed for information, which he supplied without giving them exemptions; see 'Strike down Liu Shao-ch'i, pious scion of the landlord class', *Liu Shao-ch'i Tsui-hsing Lu* (A record of Liu 'Shao-ch'i's crimes), trans. in SCMM(S) 26, pp. 23–30. Only one member of Liu's large family had approved of his joining the revolution; see Liu Ai-ch'in, *Nü-er-ti Huai-nien*, (Memories of a Daughter), p. 17.

[82] *HCPP*, No. 20, pp. 233, 264–5; *Huai-nien Liu Shao-ch'i T'ung-chih*, p. 381.

[83] *HCPP*, No. 20, p. 265.

[84] Ibid., p. 269; *Nü-er-ti Huai-nien*, p. 52.

[85] *Nü-er-ti Huai-nien*, p. 58.

[86] *HCPP*, No. 20, p. 269.

[87] *Nü-er-ti Huai-nien, passim*, but especially pp. 63–72.

[88] *Huai-nien Liu Shao-ch'i T'ung-chih*, p. 380. According to this account, Liu had chronic stomach problems dating back to his early days in Anyuan.

[89] Ibid., p. 381.

[90] *HCPP*, No. 20, p. 265.

[91] Ibid., pp. 209–10, 230, 274–5; *Huai-nien Liu Shao-ch'i T'ung-chih*, p. 379.

[92] *HCPP*, No. 20, pp. 226, 254–6, 270–2.

[93] For the bonhomie of the marshals, see ch. 10 below; for the camaraderie of the SC, see ch. 12 below.

[94] *Huai-nien Liu Shao-ch'i T'ung-chih*, p. 2. See also *Foreign Relations of the United States*, 1949, VIII, p. 359.

[95] *HCPP*, No. 20, p. 32.

[96] Gold Chou, p. 21. Lo published this article after the purge of the 'gang of four' but before the rehabilitation of Liu Shao-ch'i.

[97] *HCPP*, No. 20, p. 32; *Huai-nien Liu Shao-ch'i T'ung-chih*, p. 12.

[98] *HCPP*, No. 20, pp. 174-5, 242-3, 277; *Huai-nien Liu Shao-ch'i T'ung-chih*, p. 373. But Liu made sure never to disturb Mao!

[99] *HCPP*, No. 20, p. 181.

[100] For Liu as a 'tool' of the party, see ibid., p. 171, and SCMP(S) 173, p. 16. For Liu's readiness to self-criticize, see An Tzu-wen, 'Let us build our party well', *JMJP*, 8 May 1980, and Li Wei-han, 'Comrade Liu Shao-ch'i's direction of united front work', *JMJP*, 10 May 1980. For further comparison of Liu with Mao and Chou, see *Origins*, I, pp. 3-9.

[101] Li Po-jen, 'Unsurpassed contributions, paragon of study', *JMJP*, 20 May 1980. Liu also appears to have directed people towards the study of Chinese medicine before Mao; see *HCPP*, No. 20, p. 257. Against these claims one has to put the claim that wherever possible Liu consulted Mao in advance on all major issues; ibid., pp. 121-2.

[102] *Hsin-wen Chan-hsien* (News Battleline), 13 May 1967, p. 4, col. 1. See also 'Big political struggle on the News Front', ibid., 30 June 1967, trans. in SCMP(S) 203, p. 32. For Chou En-lai's version, see *Ko-ti T'ung-hsun* (Correspondence from All Parts of the Country), No. 4 (13 Sept. 1967), p. 1, trans. in SCMP 4081, p. 2). For a discussion of the importance of photographs as clues to Chinese political developments, see MacFarquhar, 'On photographs'.

[103] The pamphlet *'Maniacs' of the New Era*, trans. in SCMM 603, p. 30.

[104] In fact, anyone over 35 was eligible. *Liu Shao-ch'i fan-ko-ming tsui-o-shih*, p. 33; *Chu Teh fan-tang fan-she-hui-chu-i fan-Mao Tse-tung ssu-hsiang-ti tsui-hsing*, p. 13. For another allegation of Chu literally stepping out of line and pushing himself forward, see the latter source, p. 150.

[105] Ting Wang, *P'eng Teh-huai Wen-t'i Chuan Chi*, p. 394.

[106] *The Case of Peng Teh-huai*, p. 37.

[107] *CLG?* I, No. 4, p. 81.

[108] *The Case of Peng Teh-huai*, p. 37; Ting Wang, *P'eng Teh-huai Wen-t'i Chuan Chi*, p. 394.

[109] *Origins*, I, pp. 100-102, 147-8.

[110] Ting Wang, *P'eng Teh-huai Wen-t'i Chuan Chi*, p. 394.

[111] See the article by Liu Lan-t'ao, an alternate member of the party secretariat, in which he alleged that 'right opportunists' (i.e. P'eng Teh-huai and his colleagues) knew nothing about the harmonization of collective leadership and the role of the individual; *The Case of Peng Teh-huai*, p. 103. But P'eng was not the only one to feel that the elevation of Liu would not solve the problem of ensuring collective leadership; see the remark attributed to another alternate secretary, Hu Ch'iao-mu, in *Teng Hsiao-p'ing fan-tang fan-she-hui-chu-i fan-Mao Tse-tung ssu-hsiang-ti yen-lun chai-pien*, p. 2.

[112] *Origins*, I, pp. 100, 136-8

[113] Ibid., pp. 334-5 (note 59). For an excellent extended discussion of the Kao Kang case, see Teiwes, *Politics & Purges in China*, pp. 166-210.

[114] *The Case of Peng Teh-huai*, p. 41.

[115] The kind of attitude probably characteristic of most PLA marshals and generals was revealed by Ho Lung when, early in 1959, he visited an exhibition commemorating the Nanchang uprising, the event officially constituting the founding of the PLA. Ho commented: 'At the time of the 1 Aug. uprising, I depended on the party politically, but the party depended on me militarily' (*Wen Ko Feng-yun* (Cultural Revolution Storm), No. 8, 1967, p. 34). Alleged-

ly Ho Lung had earlier stated that the abolition of the old military regions in 1954 was due to fear on the part of the CC and Mao that the PLA would revolt; SCMM(S) 27, p. 29.

116 *Ko-ti T'ung-hsun*, No. 4, p. 1, trans. in SCMP 4081, p. 2. See also *Chingkangshan* (Chingkang Mountains), 18 April 1967, trans. in SCMP 3946, p. 2. For the suggestion that Liu was responding in anger to P'eng, see Moody, *The Politics of the Eighth Central Committee* p. 142.

117 Teiwes, *Politics & Purges in China*, p. 412.

118 One of the problems associated with analysing this episode is that the evidence is provided by cultural revolution papers whose concern was to prove collusion rather than conflict between Liu Shao-ch'i and P'eng Teh-huai. Chou En-lai managed to avoid committing himself on the issue; see SCMP 3946, p. 2.

119 See pp. 51–5 above.

120 Quoted in the pamphlet *'Maniacs' of the New Era*, SCMM 602, p. 10.

121 See for instance *'Selected edition on Liu Shao-ch'i's counter-revolutionary revisionist crimes*, trans. in SCMM 651, pp. 32–6.

122 See for instance 'Look at Liu Shao-ch'i's sinister features!' *Ching-kang Shan*, 1 Jan 1967, trans. in SCMP(S) 162, p. 7; 'Knock down the head of the great renegade clique—Liu Shao-ch'i', *Hung Ch'i* (Red Flag), 8 March 1967, p. 5; 'Utterly smash Liu Shao-ch'i's renegade clique', *Ch'un Lei* (Spring Thunder), 13 March 1967, trans. in SCMP 3951, pp. 1–6.

123 P'eng Chen's 'clique', for instance, is suggested in Moody, *Politics of the Eighth Central Committee*, p. 62. For P'eng Chen's closeness to Liu, see SCMM 651, p. 38.

124 *Tzu-liao Hsuan Pien*, p. 232. During his visit to Shaoshan in the summer of 1959, Mao re-emphasized the importance of the educational revolution, yet also spoke approvingly of students obeying teachers; see *Shaoshan Hung Jih*, p. 263.

125 Grey Chou, II, pp. 404–5. This incident must have occurred after Chou's return to Peking on 7 Dec. (Lieberthal, p. 126).

126 *Lu Ting-yi fan-tui Mao Tse-tung ssu-hsiang t'ui-hsing hsiu-cheng-chu-i chiao-yü lu-hsien yen-lun chai-pien* (Selected utterances of Lu Ting-yi that opposed Mao Tse-tung Thought and promoted the revisionist educational line) (Peking: Capital Liaison Committee for criticizing the bourgeois reactionary scholarly 'power holders', May 1967), p. 17, nos 75–6. See also SCMM(S) 18, pp. 15–16.

127 *HHYP*, No. 8, 1980, pp. 144–5. At the 1959 NPC, Chou told educationalists of the need to correct, consolidate and raise educational work standards on the basis of the achievements of 1958; Grey Chou, II, p. 349.

128 Chou En-lai, *Kuan-yü Wen-yi Kung-tso-ti San-tz'u Chiang-hua*, pp. 1–5.

129 *Ko Chi Ko-ming*, No. 2 (Aug. 1967), pp. 20–3.

130 SCMP 4139, p. 12.

131 *Liao Lien Chan Pao* (Liaoning Alliance Committee Combat News), 21 July 1967, p. 3, col. 1; *Ts'ui Chiu Chan Pao* (Destroy the Old Combat News), 25 May 1967, p. 2; SCMM 639, p. 6. See also SCMM 619, pp. 59, 75. In Jan. 1959, a senior united front work official, Hsu Ping, proclaimed the 'five won't changes' to reassure both businessmen and non-communist intellectuals; the five were: fixed interest, high salaries, academic ranks, political arrangements, educational reform (see *HHYP*, No. 4, 1980, pp. 52–3).

132 *Strike down the top capitalist-roader in the party—Liu Shao-ch'i* (Fourth Series) (Peking: Institute of Chemical Engineering, Mao Tse-tung Thought Propaganda Team, 10 April 1967), pp. 62–3.

Appendix 1

[1] Waley, *The Analects of Confucius*, p. 171
[2] Ibid., p. 21-2; Creel, *Confucius. The Man and the Myth*, p. 240.
[3] Reischauer & Fairbank, *East Asia: The Great Tradition*, p. 70.
[4] See p. 214.
[5] Much of the ensuing discussion is based on the stimulating analysis in Hsia, *The Commune in Retreat as Evidenced in Terminology and Semantics*, pp. 29–35. However, when Hsia wrote, he did not have at his disposal Mao's speeches at the second Chengchow conference; regrettably he died without being able to read the further evidence of semantic confusion contained therein.
[6] *Pol. Docs*, pp. 455-6; *JMST*, 1959, p. 33.
[7] Hsia, *The Commune in Retreat*, p. 36.
[8] *JMST*, 1959, p. 43.
[9] *Pol. Docs*, p. 501:
[10] *Mao Tse-tung ssu-hsiang wan sui* (1967), p. 19
[11] Ibid., p. 13. There is a similar reference to four levels on p. 10, although the *hsiao* has been dropped, clearly inadvertently, from the lowest level.
[12] See Crook & Crook, *The First Years of Yangyi Commune*, pp. 39–40, 196, 227.
[13] *Mao Tse-tung ssu-hsiang wan sui* (1967), pp. 40, 47.
[14] Ibid., p. 18.
[15] Ibid., p. 107.
[16] Walker, *Planning in Chinese Agriculture*, pp. 18–19; Dutt, *Rural Communes of China*, p. 35.
[17] Hsia, *The Commune in Retreat*, pp. 37–8.
[18] Ibid.; with his perception of the importance of the presence or absence of an adjective to modify *sheng-ch'an tui*, Hsia thought that the use of the unmodified term at Lushan indicated a weakening of the commune level taking place at that time, whereas with the material now at our disposal it is clear that that weakening took place at Chengchow.
[19] *Pol. Docs*, p. 500; *JMST*, 1959, p. 43; Hsia, *The Commune in Retreat*, p. 36.
[20] *Pol. Docs*, p. 500.
[21] Hsia, *The Commune in Retreat*, pp. 37–8.
[22] See for example *Mao Tse-tung ssu-hsiang wan sui* (1967), pp. 15, 22, 23, 29, 32.

PART THREE: CLASH

Chapter 10. High Noon at Lushan

[1] *Shaoshan Hung Jih*, p. 241. There are curious discrepancies about reports of Mao's arrival time which are unimportant in themselves, but which shed an interesting light on the imprecision with which an official body concerned to record every detail of this red-letter day performed its task. The 5.44 pm timing is given in an article written by a group of guards and reception personnel who handled Mao's various visits to Hunan. But, in one version of the account of the visit by the staff of the Exhibition Hall of Comrade Mao Tse-tung's Old Home in Shaoshan, the Chairman's arrival is given as 4 pm; see *Mao, Pa-shih-wu Tan-ch'en*, p. 263. When this latter article was being prepared for publication in *Shaoshan Hung Jih*, the editor of the book must have noticed the discrepancy and in an otherwise identical version of the article the time was changed to 'after 5 pm' (p. 266). Another account describes the arrival more poetically as taking place at dusk; *Nan-wang-ti Chi-yi*, p. 5. All the available accounts of the visit are somewhat reverential, but this is probably the right flavour to be conveyed.

[2] At Changsha, Mao had swum in the Hsiang River accompanied by members of the Hunan swimming team (*Shaoshan Hung Jih*, pp. 246, 264–5) and inspected a school (*ibid.*, pp. 261–3). This volume also includes a brief impression of the visit by Mao's chauffeur (pp. 287–9).

[3] *Nan-wang-ti Chi-yi*, p. 5. Reminiscences about Lo Jui-ch'ing suggest that as Minister for Public Security he regarded Mao's safety as his personal responsibility; see for instance *Shen-ch'ieh Huai-nien Lo Jui-ch'ing T'ung-chih*, p. 205. Lo Jui-ch'ing had sufficient confidence in his relationship with Mao to be able to tell students at a Public Security Institute that they could doubt anyone's words, even the Chairman's; see 'Lo Jui-ch'ing deserves to die ten thousand times for his crimes', *Chingkangshan* and *Kwangtung Wen-yi Chan Pao* (Chingkang Mountains and Kwangtung Literature and Arts Combat News), 5 Sept. 1967, trans. in SCMP 4046, p. 2.

[4] *Shaoshan Hung Jih*, p. 242. Unusually for so important a visit, there is no report of Mao being accompanied by the then Hunan provincial 1st secretary, Chou Hsiao-chou, although Chou had accompanied Defence Minister Marshal P'eng Teh-huai on his Hunan tour in Dec. 1958 (*Heng Tao Li Ma P'eng Chiang-chün*, p. 156). Possibly Chou was with Mao, but his rehabilitation was not as assured as that of Lo Jui-ch'ing when *Shaoshan Hung Jih* was going to press in 1978. If Chou was unable to accompany Mao for good if unexplained reasons, this may account for the presence of Hupeh 1st secretary Wang Jen-chung in Mao's party; see *Arrest Political Pickpocket Wang Jen-chung*, trans. in SCMM(S) 29, pp. 1–2.

[5] Chou Li-po's account did not appear at the time, presumably because shortly thereafter the conflicting on-the-spot assessments of Hunanese reality made by Mao and P'eng Teh-huai had made the Chairman's return to Shaoshan a subject for controversy rather than celebration. When Chou Li-po's account finally did appear in 1966, he got into trouble partly, it was alleged, because he

mentioned Mao's first wife, Yang K'ai-hui, and so offended his current wife, Chiang Ch'ing, and partly doubtless because Lo Jui-ch'ing had recently been purged; see *Nan-wang-ti Chi-yi*, pp. 1–4.

[6] *Nan-wang-ti Chi-yi*, p. 5.

[7] *Shaoshan Hung Jih*, p. 241. His chauffeur states that he made an inspection tour including a visit to the school that same evening (ibid., p. 287), but this conflicts with other accounts which indicate that Mao did little on the evening of the 25th.

[8] Ibid., p. 247.

[9] Ibid., pp. 244–5.

[10] Ibid., p. 242.

[11] *Tsai Mao . . . Shen-pien*, pp. 200–201.

[12] *Shaoshan Hung Jih*, p. 242. The five styles were: communist style, boastfulness, blind directives, commandism and special privileges (ibid.).

[13] See *Hua Kuo-feng . . . Chi-ch'eng-che*, p. 141.

[14] According to Chou Li-po's account (*Nan-wang-ti Chi-yi*, p. 6), Mao's mother and father died in the same year, aged 53 and 49 respectively, but another report of this visit gives their ages as 52 and 50 (Mao, *Pa-shih-wu Tan-ch'en*, p. 265).

[15] For Liu see *Huai-nien Liu Shao-ch'i T'ung-chih*, pp. 343, 358; for Chou see White Chou, III, pp. 85–6; *WWAR*, pp. 20, 164–5; *Chou Tsung-li-ti Ku-shih*, p. 138; for P'eng Teh-huai, see *Tsai P'eng Tsung Shen-pien*, p. 49. The dropping of the reference to Mao Tse-tung's Thought in the 1956 party constitution had little impact on the cult of Mao at the popular level.

[16] *Shaoshan Hung Jih*, p. 270; *Nan-wang-ti Chi-yi*, pp. 10–11.

[17] *Shaoshan Hung Jih*, pp. 270–1. In another striking example of the discrepancies surrounding what should have been a meticulously recorded visit, Chou Li-po states that Mao visited the reservoir before his midday meal; *Nan-wang-ti Chi-yi*, p. 11.

[18] This appears to have been Mao's routine; see *Nan-wang-ti Chi-yi*, p. 11.

[19] Ibid.; *Shaoshan Hung Jih*, pp. 272–3.

[20] *Shaoshan Hung Jih*, p. 243.

[21] Ibid., pp. 274–5.

[22] Ibid., p. 243.

[23] 'Return to Shaoshan', as trans. by Michael Bullock and Jerome Ch'en, *Mao and the Chinese Revolution*, p. 350. Wang Jen-chung also composed a poem after this visit implying disapproval of the sentimentality of Mao's visit in view of his achievements since leaving Shaoshan; see *Arrest Political Pickpocket Wang Jen-chung* (SCMM(S) 29, p. 2).

[24] *Nan-wang-ti Chi-yi*, pp. 9–10. Although the morning of 27 June seems the most likely timing for Mao's visit to his parents' grave, it is conceivable that it was the 26th, for this source states that he went from the graveside to the school. However, Chou Li-po also states that Mao spent two days but only one night in Shaoshan (ibid., p. 11), and this may be how the confusion arose in his account. Two more circumstantial, less impressionistic, accounts agree that he was in Shaoshan for the nights of 25 and 26 June (*Shaoshan Hung Jih*, pp. 242–3, 275). Mao's chauffeur endorses that but introduces new confusion by asserting that the Chairman did not leave Shaoshan until 28 June (ibid., p. 288)! Again one is mystified by the inconsistency in accounts (in the latter case in the same volume) of so important an occasion. The dating of the graveside visit is complicated because one of the two best sources on Mao's return to Shaoshan does not mention it, while the other is totally opaque as to when it occurred (ibid., p. 273).

[25] *Shaoshan Hung Jih*, pp. 273–4; *Nan-wang-ti Chi-yi*, p. 11.

[26] *Shaoshan Hung Jih*, pp. 243-4, 288.

[27] From the Bullock and Ch'en translation in Ch'en, *Mao and the Chinese Revolution*, p. 351.

[28] Ross H. Monro, 'Lu-shan: Quiet retreat for China's poets and politicians', *Christian Science Monitor*, Weekly International Edition, 1 Aug. 1977.

[29] Li Jui, 'Remembering T'ien Chia-ying', *HHYP—WCP*, No. 4, 1980, pp. T172-3. T'ien was Mao's principal private secretary for some years; Li Jui, author of a book about Mao's early life, *Mao Tse-tung T'ung-chih-ti Ch'u-ch'i Koming Huo-tung* (Comrade Mao Tse-tung's Early Revolutionary Activities), was one of T'ien's assistants.

[30] *Mao, Miscellany*, I, p. 182.

[31] Ibid., p. 184.

[32] See *Origins*, I, pp. 86-91.

[33] *Mao, Miscellany*, I, pp. 182-3.

[34] Ibid., p. 183.

[35] *Ts'ai-mao Hung Ch'i* (Finance and Trade Red Flag), 15 Feb. 1967, trans. in SCMP(S) 177, p. 9. See below.

[36] Li Jui, 'Remembering T'ien Chia-ying', pp. 172-3.

[37] *Mao, Miscellany*, I, p. 182.

[38] See the memorial article written on the occasion of the 80th anniversary of Li's birth entitled 'Comrade Li Fu-ch'un's enormous contributions to economic planning work', *JMJP*, 22 May 1980.

[39] See *Origins*, I, pp. 146-8. The death of Mao's eldest son, An-ying, in the Korean War is mentioned there; for a fuller account, see Chin, *Mao An-ying*, pp. 148-57, where it is revealed that although he was killed on 25 Nov. 1950, no one dared tell the Chairman until P'eng Teh-huai returned home two months later to report to him on the conduct of the war. P'eng is quoted as saying that 'we didn't look after him well' (p. 156), but there is of course no indication as to whether Mao blamed P'eng personally for his loss. For an account of the dismal fates of Mao's three sons by his first wife, Yang K'ai-hui, see *Nan-wang-ti Chi-yi*, p. 124 ff. For discussions of problems between Mao and P'eng in the 1920s and 1930s, see Rue, *Mao Tse-tung in Opposition, 1927-35*, pp. 115, 205; Schwartz, *Chinese Communism and the Rise of Mao*, pp. 173-4, 176.

[40] The opinion of Kung Chu, one of his subordinate commanders in the 1930s; see *The Case of Peng Teh-huai*, p. i. For the toughness of Peng's constitution during the rigours of the Korean war, see *Tsai P'eng Tsung Shen-pien*, pp. 14-15.

[41] *Heng-tao-li-ma P'eng Chiang-chün*, pp. 20-21, 53-4, 69 ff.

[42] See P'eng's autobiographical fragments in *HHYP—WCP*, No. 3, 1980, p. 72; also *Heng-tao-li-ma P'eng Chiang-chün*, p. 6.

[43] Klein & Clark, *Biographic Dictionary*, p. 728.

[44] For Kung Chu's appraisal of P'eng's military abilities, see *The Case of Peng Teh-huai*, p. ii. Conventionally, the Chinese communists reckon Marshal Liu Po-ch'eng their greatest strategist and Marshal Lin Piao their greatest tactician. For an example of P'eng's bravery under fire, see *Heng-tao-li-ma P'eng Chiang-chün*, pp. 13-14. For Mao's poem to P'eng, see ibid., p. 13; according to this account, P'eng changed the words 'our great General P'eng' to 'our heroic Red Army'. For a rough dating of the poem, see *The Case of Peng Teh-huai*, p. xiii. For Mao's admiration for and criticism of P'eng's military talents, cf. *Mao, Miscellany*, II, pp. 341, 345.

[45] *Tsai P'eng Tsung Shen-pien*, pp. 49-51.

[46] *Heng-tao-li-ma P'eng Chiang-chün*, p. 19. P'eng Teh-huai again alluded to his penchant for cursing people during moments of lucidity which punctuated the

coma he was in for the last two months of his life; see Ch'en Yun-hao, 'The deathbed utterances of Chief P'eng', *HHWC*, No. 1, 1981, p. 169.

[47] *Heng-tao-li-ma P'eng Chiang-chün*, pp. 17-18.

[48] *CLG*, I, No. 4, p. 81.

[49] *Heng-tao-li-ma P'eng Chiang-chün*, p. 148. This is a curious account (pp. 148-52) bearing in mind that it was published in Dec. 1979. There is no real hint of the disquiet aroused in P'eng's mind by what he saw, as is brought out in the account of his bodyguard (see below).

[50] *Tsai P'eng Tsung Shen-pien*, p. 69.

[51] Ibid., pp. 69-70.

[52] Ibid., pp. 70-1.

[53] Ibid., p. 71.

[54] *P'eng Teh-huai Tzu-hsu*, p. 265. P'eng Teh-huai states that he only attended one of the two Chengchow conferences. Since he discusses the proceedings of that conference in advance of his discussion of the Wuchang conference and plenum, I have assumed that it was the first Chengchow conference which he attended; certainly it was then that criticism of the 'communist wind' began (Lieberthal, p. 124). P'eng's absence from all but the final day of the first Chengchow conference (10 Nov.) may thus have been due to his travels in Kansu.

In a statement in captivity during the cultural revolution, P'eng said: 'On the train to Chengchow, we held a meeting to oppose the "Communist Style"' (*The Case of Peng Teh-huai*, p. 120), which suggested that the Marshal had held a meeting of his staff on the basis of his Kansu tour. This may have been the case, but it seems more likely that cultural revolutionaries tampered with P'eng's account of the session summoned by Mao on the train *from* Chengchow.

The Wuchang conference and plenum lasted from 21 Nov. to 10 Dec. 1958. According to Lieberthal (pp. 125-6), P'eng was in Peking from 21 to 24 Nov. and 1 to 6 Dec. See also 'Great General P'eng returns to his native place', *HHYP—WCP*, No. 4, 1979, p. 144. (The description 'great general' is a quotation from the poem by Mao lauding P'eng.)

[55] 'Great General P'eng returns,' *HHYP—WCP*, No. 4, 1979, p. 144.

[56] Ibid.; *Tsai P'eng Tsung Shen-pien*, p. 72.

[57] *HHYP—WCP*, No. 4, 1979, p. 245.

[58] Ibid.

[59] *Tsai P'eng Tsung Shen-pien*, p. 72.

[60] Ibid., p. 73.

[61] Ibid., p. 72.

[62] *HHYP—WCP*, No. 4, 1979, p. 145.

[63] Ibid.

[64] *Tsai P'eng Tsung Shen-pien*, p. 73.

[65] *HHYP—WCP*, No. 4, 1979, p. 145.

[66] Ibid., p. 144.

[67] Ibid., p. 145.

[68] Ibid., p. 144.

[69] Ibid. While there is no significant contradiction between the two accounts of P'eng's visit to the Happiness Home, they vary interestingly in mood. P'eng's bodyguard paints the peasants as trusting and bewildered; the *Chung-kuo Ch'ing-nien* (China Youth) reporters (whose account was reprinted in *HHYP—WCP*, No. 4, 1979) depict them as angry and outspoken.

[70] *HHYP—WCP*, No. 4, 1979, p. 145.

[71] Ibid., p. 146.

[72] Ibid., p. 145.

[73] Ibid., p. 146.

[74] Ibid.; *Tsai P'eng Tsung Shen-pien*, p. 74.

[75] *HHYP—WCP*, No. 4, 1979, p. 145; *Tsai P'eng Tsung Shen-pien*, pp. 73, 74.

[76] *HHYP—WCP*, No. 4, 1979, p. 146.

[77] *The Case of Peng Teh-huai*, p. 120. During the period of the second Cheng-chow conference P'eng was seen in Peking on a number of formal occasions so spaced as to suggest that he could only have attended that meeting for a few days, if at all.

[78] *P'eng Teh-huai Tzu-hsu*, pp. 266–7; *Tsai P'eng Tsung Shen-pien*, p. 75; *The Case of Peng Teh-huai*, p. 38. P'eng tried unsuccessfully to persuade Chief of Staff Huang K'o-ch'eng to go in his place.

[79] See *I-chiu-wu-chiu nien fei ch'ü tzu-jan tsai-hai ch'ing-k'uang tiao-ch'a* (Investigation into the natural disasters in the bandit areas in 1959) (hereafter *Tsai-hai tiao-ch'a*), pp. 7–8.

[80] Ibid., pp. 9–14. For official reports on the Kwangtung floods, including an assessment of them by party 1st secretary T'ao Chu, see *JMJP* 21, 23, 25 and 27 June and 1 July 1959. For T'ao Chu's parlous physical condition at the time, see Chao Tzu-yang, 'The noble character of a communist', *HHYP— WCP*, No. 4, 1979, p. 58.

[81] See for instance *JMJP*, 12 and 27 June 1959.

[82] Ibid., editorial, 7 July 1959.

[83] *Tsai-hai tiao-ch'a*, pp. 4–7.

[84] This was revealed when a number of issues of a secret military magazine reached the West in the 1960s; see Cheng, *The Politics of the Chinese Red Army*, pp. 15–19, 209, 213.

[85] *P'eng Teh-huai Tzu-hsu*, pp. 266–7; *The Case of Peng Teh-huai*, p. 37.

[86] See Walker, *Hunger in China*, pp. 19, 33.

[87] Ibid., pp. 28, 41. These figures are so low as to verge on the incredible; perhaps the letter writers exaggerated their plight in order to excite sympathy.

[88] Ibid., pp. 26, 39. One letter from a city-dweller talks of a 12 lb monthly ration; ibid., p. 21.

[89] Ibid., pp. 23, 30.

[90] Ibid., pp. 26, 28, 39.

[91] The importance of the Lushan conference has sparked considerable academic investigation and some insightful analyses. See for instance Teiwes, *Politics Purges in China*, ch. 9; Joffe, *Between Two Plenums*, pp. 8–22; Chang, *Power and Policy in China*, pp. 110–19; Ahn, *Chinese Politics and the Cultural Revolution*, pp. 38–44; Moody, *The Politics of the Eighth Central Committee*, pp. 139–46.

[92] *The Case of Peng Teh-huai*, p. 4.

[93] Ibid., p. 2. This comment seems to echo the remark of the resident at the Happiness Home quoted above, p. 197, providing a useful confirmation of the accuracy of the memory of P'eng Teh-huai's bodyguard.

[94] Ibid., p. 394.

[95] Ibid., pp. 2, 3, 4.

[96] Ibid., pp. 1, 2, 3, 5.

[97] Ibid., p. 2.

[98] Ibid., pp. 2–3.

[99] Ibid., p. 1. It is worth noting that Mao toured China's villages more assiduously than P'eng Teh-huai, and the Chairman may have felt that Marshal's comments were based on a superficial understanding. But on the other hand, no one in the villages was likely to be as frank in conversation with Mao as with any other leader; see the comment of one Chinese on the uselessness of Mao's

tours as a means of gathering facts, quoted in MacFarquhar, *Hundred Flowers*, p. 108.

[100] *CLG*, I, No. 4, pp. 44-5.

[101] *Tsai P'eng Tsung Shen-pien*, pp. 75-6.

[102] *The Case of Peng Teh-huai*, p. 36; *P'eng Teh-huai Tzu-hsu*, pp. 267-8.

[103] Chang Wen-t'ien had translated works by English, Russian, French and Italian authors. He was an early friend of Kuo Mo-jo, the dominant cultural figure in post-1949 China. See Klein and Clark, *Biographic Dictionary*, pp. 61-7.

[104] Much of the information of this brief sketch is derived from Klein and Clark, *Biographic Dictionary*, and *Huai-nien Chang Wen-t'ien T'ung-chih* (Remember Comrade Chang Wen-t'ien), pp. 32-4, 104-6, but much of the interpretation is my own. In *Origins*, I, p. 140, I indicated that Mao took over the chairmanship of the MAC at Tsunyi, but this latter source indicates that his position was not formalized as early as that.

[105] *The Case of Peng Teh-huai*, p. 420; *Huai-nien Chang Wen-t'ien T'ung-chih*, pp. 106-8. Teiwes points out that the two men had collaborated during the preparation for the Warsaw Pact (*Politics & Purges in China*, p. 389).

[106] Chang flew to Moscow on 23 April (SCMP 2001, p. 43), P'eng on 24 April (SCMP 2002, p. 35). Both men flew on to Warsaw on the evening of 24 April (SCMP 2002, p. 35; SCMP 2004, p. 40) and I am assuming that they must have been on the same plane. P'eng was guest of honour at a banquet given on 27 April by the Chinese ambassador to Poland for the military delegation the marshal was leading; also present were the delegates to the Warsaw Pact Foreign Ministers meeting which Chang was attending as an observer (SCMP 2004, p. 39). The following evening, P'eng was a guest at a Polish dinner for the Warsaw Pact Foreign Ministers (SCMP 2005, p. 48). However, the two men are unlikely to have had many other opportunities of meeting in the Polish capital for P'eng was visiting Szczecin, Gdynia and Gdansk from 25 to 27 April (SCMP 2004, pp. 37-8), and he left for East Germany on the morning of 29 April (SCMP 2005, p. 42).

[107] *The Case of Peng Teh-huai*, p. 420.

[108] The final split between Chang Wen-t'ien and the most senior of the Soviet-trained group, Wang Ming, appears from Mao's account to have occurred at the 7th Congress; but at Lushan, the Chairman accused Chang of not genuinely turning over a new leaf on that occasion. See *CLG*, I, No. 4, p. 62, where Mao refers to Chang by his one-time alias Lo Fu.

[109] *The Case of Peng Teh-huai*, p. 36. In later years, admitting that memory no longer served him, P'eng was to give a far blander, more circumspect account of his dealings with Chang Wen-tien; see *P'eng Teh-huai Tzu-hsu*, pp. 268-9.

[110] *Tsai P'eng Tsung Shen-pien*, p. 75.

[111] See *Wu Han ho 'Hai Jui Pa Kuan'* (Wu Han and 'The Dismissal of Hai Jui'), pp. 2, 137. The description 'unbending moralist and fearless remonstrator' is applied by Howard J. Wechsler to Wei Cheng (see *Cambridge History of China*, Vol. 3, Pt 1, p. 197) but it applies equally well to Hai Jui. The precise dates of the Shanghai work conference were unclear, but it is now said to have lasted from 25 March to 4 April 1959; see *P'eng Teh-huai Tzu-hsu*, p. 300.

[112] *Mao, Miscellany*, I, p. 176.

[113] Ibid. For a brief account of Yueh Fei, see Hucker, *China's Imperial Past*, pp. 276-7. Ironically, the Yueh Fei model was used against Mao after his death. In what seemed like a clear reference to the late Chairman, a writer in the *Pei-ching Wan Pao* (Peking Evening News), 11 Sept. 1980, argued that the real killer of Yueh Fei, the man behind the official normally excoriated by Chinese historians for the crime, had been the emperor of the day, Chao Kou. 'Before, I could not understand why Qin Gui [Ch'in Kuei] dared to kill a high

official like Yue Fei on groundless charges. Later, I understood. Qin Gui succeeded in doing so because of the backing of Zhao Gou, [Chao Kou]'. In other words, behind Lin Piao and the 'gang of four' stood Chairman Mao. Yueh Fei could stand for any victim of the cultural revolution, but since he was a general perhaps the author of this article had P'eng Teh-huai particularly in mind even though the 'gang of four' had nothing to do with his dismissal. But whoever he had in mind as the victim, the author concluded with a clear hint that Mao's culpability should be brought into the open: 'In our socialist state, there should be no taboos. We must restore the real features of history and tell the students and youth that both Zhao Gou and Qin Gui killed Yue Fei. We must get Zhao Gou to kneel down before Yue Fei's grave.' (See Wu Zhao, 'We should get Zhao Gou to kneel down, too', trans. in FBIS-CHI-80-195, pp. L9–10.

[114] See *Pei-ching Hsin Wen-yi* (Peking New Literature and Art) 8 June 1967, p. 2, col. 1. For a quotation from Chou Yang's promotional activities regarding Hai Jui in Shanghai, see *Hung-se P'i-p'an-che* (Red Critic), 24 May 1967, p. 4, col. 4. For the triple authorship of the play, see Thomas S. Fisher, '"The play's the thing": Wu Han and Hai Jui revisited', paper presented to the California regional seminar, Center for Chinese Studies, Univ. of California, Berkeley, 1 Dec. 1974, pp. 29–30. For details on Chou Hsin-Fang, see URI, *Who's Who*, I, pp. 166–7. According to the cultural revolution polemic, the principal writer was Hsu Ssu-wen; see 'Criticism of *Hai Jui relieved of his office* and *Hsieh Yao Huan* gradually deepens', *Hsi-chu Pao* (Drama News), 10 March 1966, trans. in SCMM 528, p. 49. According to Fisher ('"The play's the thing"') the third author was T'ao Hsiung, who was a leading figure in the Shanghai Academy of Peking Opera (URI, *Who's Who*, II, p. 606).
Charles Hucker gives the following account of the occasion on which Hai Jui presented his memorial: 'On one celebrated occasion in the reign of Shih-tsung (Chia-ching r. 1521–67), Hai apparently presented himself at the palace gate to submit a memorial denouncing some of the emperor's notorious idiosyncrasies. The emperor flew into a rage and ordered that Hai not be permitted to escape. "Never fear, sire", the eunuch go-between told the emperor. "He has said goodbye to his family, and has brought his coffin with him, and waits at the gate!" Shih-tsung was so taken aback by this news that he forgave Hai for his impertinence' (*China's Imperial Past*, p. 306). For a full account of the life of Hai Jui, see the entry by Chaoying Fang in the *Dictionary of Ming Biography*, I, pp. 474–9; for another interesting account, see the chapter on Hai Jui in Huang, *1587, A Year of No Significance*.

[115] Fisher, '"The play's the thing"', p. 28.

[116] *Wu Han ho 'Hai Jui Pa Kuan'*, p. 2.

[117] This account of Wu Han's career leans heavily on his biography in *BDRC*, III, pp. 425–30. See also Pusey, *Wu Han: Attacking the Present Through the Past*, pp. 1–7. I have substituted 'locust tree' for 'ash' as a more accurate rendering.

[118] For a description of the united front, see Van Slyke, *Enemies and Friends: the United Front in Chinese Communist History*; see also *Origins*, I, pp. 48–50.

[119] Fisher, '"The play's the thing"', pp. 9–10. According to *BDRC*, III, p. 427, he appears to have published only two original historical articles during the period 1949–58.

[120] See *Origins*, I, pp. 271–2, 276, 277–8. Pusey describes one of Wu Han's speeches during the anti-rightist campaign as being the 'one piece of Wu Han's writing I have seen in which there is no trace of Wu Han' (*Wu Han*, p. 11). For the date of Wu Han's entry into the CCP, see *Wu Han ho 'Hai Jui Pa Kuan'*, p. 137.

[121] For a brief account of Ts'ao Ts'ao, see Hucker, *China's Imperial Past*, pp. 132–4; for the Empress Wu, see *Cambridge History of China*, Vol. 3, Pt 1, chs 5, 6. Kuo Mo-jo had led the way in reassessing these historical personalities.

[122] Fisher, "'The play's the thing'", pp. 18–19.

[123] Pusey, *Wu Han*, pp. 15–17.

[124] Quoted in Schram, *Mao Tse-tung Unrehearsed*, p. 237. For a typical cultural revolution account underlining the sinister coincidence between P'eng Teh-huai's actions at Lushan and Wu Han's studies of Hai Jui, see SCMP 3698, p. 5.

[125] *Wu Han ho 'Hai Jui Pa Kuan'*, pp. 2, 137. I think it highly unlikely that this account of Mao's encouraging the emulation of Hai Jui and Wei Cheng would have been concocted after the Chairman's death to provide a posthumous vindication of Wu Han. The nearest approach to a confirmation of Mao's role in the origins of the Hai Jui affair to be found in cultural revolution sources occurs in *Counter-Revolutionary Revisionist P'eng Chen's Towering Crimes of Opposing the Party, Socialism and the Thought of Mao Tse-tung*, trans. in SCMM 640, p. 5. According to this pamphlet, the Peking party 2nd secretary, Liu Jen, consulted his notebook in Jan. 1966 at the height of the assult on Wu Han and told a colleague: 'When the Shanghai conference was held in 1959, the Chairman adopted the attitude of affirming this historical figure—Hai Jui.' However, this did not indicate that Mao had taken the initiative on this topic, and the comments of the editors of the pamphlet implied that Liu Jen was lying (which they possibly believed to be the case).

[126] *Wu Han ho 'Hai Jui Pa Kuan'*, pp. 2, 137. Wu Han's claim to have been encouraged to write about Hai Jui by 'leading comrades[sic]' is also mentioned in the cultural revolution source cited in the previous footnote: SCMM 640, p. 5; but again the implication is that Liu Jen, who reports this claim, is lying.

[127] As Wu Han had joined the CCP by this time, P'eng Chen was his superior in both the government and party hierarchies within the capital.

[128] See *Origins*, I, pp. 33–5.

[129] Grey Chou, III, p. 5. For Mao's poem, see Wong Man, *Poems of Mao Tse-tung*, pp. 50–3. Memorial volumes devoted to Chou are dotted with other references to the Premier's careful attention to Mao's commands. See for instance Grey Chou, II, pp. 457–8.

[130] Schram, *Mao Tse-tung*, p. 48.

[131] See Ch'en, *Mao and the Chinese Revolution*, pp. 359–60.

[132] Mao, *SW*, V, pp. 176–83.

[133] Pusey, *Wu Han*, p. 9.

[134] Ibid., pp. 15–16.

[135] For a cultural revolution allegation that P'eng Teh-huai said he had to act like Hai Jui, see Moody, *The Politics of the Eighth Central Committee*, p. 143. But Hu Ch'iao-mu did not actually say that it had been the right opportunists who had raised Hai Jui's name at Lushan. For Hu Ch'iao-mu's role, see *Pei-ching Hsin Wen-yi* (Peking New Literature and Art), 8 June 1967, p. 2, col. 1. In one cultural revolution 'source, Hu Ch'iao-mu is indicted under a blanket accusation of inspiring all Wu Han's writings. It is therefore possible that Hu was the mysterious 'leading comrade'. However, the source does not inspire confidence and is inaccurate in dating one of the two most important of Wu Han's pieces on Hai Jui (CB 874, p. 42). Moreover, if Hu was the 'leading comrade' in question there seems to be no reason why this was not used against him more explicitly during the cultural revolution and not acknowledged in post-cultural revolution writings. For the date of completion of Wu Han's article, see Wu Han, *Teng-hsia Chi*, p. 168. For an account of Wu Han's further writings, see Fisher, "'The play's the thing'", pp. 19–20, 25–6.

[136] For a contrary view, see Goldman, *China's Intellectuals: Advise and Dissent*, pp. 33–4.

[137] Fisher remarks that at least four plays on Hai Jui were produced prior to Wu Han's; Fisher, '"The play's the thing"', pp. 29–30.

[138] *Tsai P'eng Tsung Shen-pien*, p. 75; *P'eng Teh-huai Tzu-hsu*, p. 269–71.

[139] *The Case of Peng Teh-Huai*, pp. 14, 120.

[140] Ibid., pp. 36–7.

[141] *Tsai P'eng Tsung Shen-pien*, p. 76.

[142] *The Case of Peng Teh-huai*, p. 7.

[143] Ibid., p. 7.

[144] Ibid., pp. 8–9.

[145] Ibid., p. 121.

[146] Ibid., p. 9.

[147] Ibid., p. 121. Mao's comments in this regard validated 'Kremlinology' as one legitimate tool for the analysis of Chinese politics; see *Origins*, I, p. 407, and MacFarquhar, 'On photographs'. For P'eng Teh-huai's disclaimer and the latest version of his letter of opinion, see *P'eng Teh-huai Tzu-hsu*, pp. 268, 283.

[148] *The Case of Peng Teh-huai*, pp. 9–10.

[149] Ibid., p. 10.

[150] See 'The confession of Wu Leng-hsi', *CLG*, II, No. 4, pp. 75–6; *P'eng Teh-huai Tzu-hsu*, p. 267.

[151] *The Case of Peng Teh-huai*, p. 11.

[152] See above pp. 130–1.

[153] *The Case of Peng Teh-huai*, p. 11. In his excellent analysis of the Lushan conference, with much of which the present author agrees, Frederick Teiwes suggests (*Politics & Purges in China*, p. 412) that P'eng Teh-huai and his fellow-critics sought to win Mao over to their views rather than launch a frontal attack on him. This was certainly P'eng's best line of defence and he may well have in part believed it. But since Mao had already initiated a far-reaching reform of the communes taking account of issues P'eng raised at Lushan, and since Ch'en Yun was already at work reining in the leap forward, a comprehensive, root and branch attack on the policies of the previous 18 months was an unnecessary manoeuvre from the point of view of convincing the Chairman.

[154] *The Case of Peng Teh-huai*, pp. 11, 400.

[155] See the translation in Tucker, *The Lenin Anthology*, p. 559.

[156] *Heng-tao-li-ma P'eng Chiang-chün*, pp. 9–10.

[157] P'eng observed that this was one of the phrases that had particularly irked the Chairman; *The Case of Peng Teh-huai*, p. 121.

[158] The precise words of Mao's order are: 'Yin-fa ko t'ung-chih ts'an-k'ao'; see *Kuang-hui-ti li-shih wen-hsien*, Sept. 1967, p. 43. The semi-secret nature of. this publication is indicated on the final page along with its source. For the remarkable resemblance between P'eng's confession and Red Guard propaganda denouncing him, cf. *The Case of Peng Teh-huai*, pp. 14, 120–1. For P'eng's later version see *P'eng Teh-huai.Tzu-hsu*, p. 276.

[159] There seems little doubt from the Chinese text of P'eng Teh-huai's speech at the 8th plenum that Chang Wen-t'ien had made two speeches, but it is conceivable that one of the dates in the text is a mistake, that only one speech was made, that P'eng did not know what was to be in it in advance, but that when he read it he found that it reflected the discussions the two men had had; see *The Case of Peng Teh-huai*, pp. 420–1. See also *Huai-nien Chang Wen-t'ien T'ung-chih*, pp. 35, 108. For a confirmation that Chou Hsiao-chou and Huang K'o-ch'eng spoke, see *P'eng Teh-huai Tzu-hsu*, pp. 269–70.

[160] According to P'eng, Chang sent over only an outline and took it back after

P'eng had read it, so presumably there was only one copy; ibid., p. 421.
[161] *Wen-ko Feng-yun*, No. 10, 1967, p. 12; ibid., No. 5, 1967, p. 23.

[162] See 'Down with 'three-anti' element and big renegade Po I-po, sinister despot on the industrial and communications front', *Tung-fang Hung* (East Is Red), 15 Feb. 1967, trans. in CB 878, p. 7; 'Ten great crimes committed by the counter-revolutionary Po I-po', *Chingkangshan* (Chingkang Mountains), 1 Jan. 1967, trans. in SCMP(S) 162, p. 14. Ch'i Wei-tung, 'Dig out the economic black line of the 30s and its backstage boss—Liu Shao-ch'i, China's Khrushchev', *Wei Tung* (Defend the East), 15 June 1967, trans. in SCMP(S) 207, p. 13. To be fair to Po, his absence in Peking from 11 to 16 July may have meant that he returned to Lushan with little time to finalize the original draft before Mao launched his counter-attack; for Po's presence in Peking, see Lieberthal, p. 141.

[163] *P'ao-hung Li Hsien-nien* (Bombard Li Hsien-nien) (Peking: Red Representative Conference, Central Finance and Banking Institute, April 1967), pp. 25, 33. Two scholars (Domes, *The Internal Politics of China*, p. 112, and Dittmer, *Liu Shao-ch'i and the Chinese Cultural Revolution*, p. 40) have cited *China News Analysis* (Hong Kong), No. 761, p. 4, to suggest that two votes were taken at the Lushan conference. This may have been the case—though there is little evidence to suggest that the CCP's leading bodies actually take decisions in that way—but the Red Guard source quoted by *China News Analysis* neither confirms nor denies this. It merely quotes Li Hsien-nien as saying: 'On the first day I agreed with the views of P'eng Teh-huai but on the second day I opposed them.'

[164] *CLG*, I, No. 4, p. 33.

[165] The fact that Mao spoke in the morning is mentioned in 'Liu and Teng are the revisionist chiefs on the agricultural front', *K'o Chi Chan Pao* (Science and Technology Combat News), 2 June 1967, p. 8, col. 3.

[166] *CLG*, I, No. 4, pp. 27-9.

[167] Ibid., pp. 28, 35. For a discussion of the 1957 anti-rightist campaign, see *Origins*, I, Pt 4; for Chang Po-chün's Political Planning Institute proposal, see especially ibid., pp. 273, 275-6. Lo Lung-chi's good friend P'u Hsi-hsiu, a journalist who like Lo came under attack during the anti-rightist campaign, was the sister of P'eng Teh-huai's wife, P'u An-hsiu; see ibid., pp. 225, 262-3. Pu Hsi-hsiu was banned from journalism and eventually went to work for the Cultural History Materials Committee of the CPPCC; she died of cancer in 1970 at the age of 60. (See Hsin Po, 'Able lady general, P'u Hsi-hsiu', *HHYP*—*WCP*, No. 12, 1980, p. 181.)

[168] *CLG*, I, No. 4, pp. 29-33. For Mao's claims to be a middle-of-the-roader, see ibid., pp. 37, 38, 39, 40.

[169] *The Case of Peng Teh-huai*, pp. 3, 8.

[170] *CLG*, I, No. 4, pp. 33-6.

[171] *The Case of Peng Teh-huai*, p. 2.

[172] *CLG*, I, No. 4, pp. 37-8.

[173] Ibid., p. 41.

[174] Ibid., pp. 39, 41, 42-3. For K'o Ch'ing-shih's support for Mao during the 100 flowers period, see *Origins*, I, pp. 200, 281-2, 290-2.

[175] *CLG*, I, No. 4, pp. 38, 40, 41, 42. I am assuming that 'X X X of the Ministry of Agriculture' (the name was excised by Red Guard editors) was the Minister, Liao Lu-yen. Two other excised names in this passage cannot be so readily hypothesized.

[176] Ibid., p. 37. In view of the subsequent disgrace of Hunan 1st secretary Chou Hsiao-chou for collaboration with P'eng Teh-huai, Mao's reference to this province may have been a slip of the tongue; alternatively, he may have been pre-

paring the ground for an attack on Chou for hypocritically denouncing leftism when he himself had been a prominent leftist.

[177] Ibid., p. 43.

[178] Ibid., p. 42. This translation says 26,000 li; the original source says 25,000 li.

[179] Ibid., p. 40; see also p. 33.

[180] *Mao Chu-hsi tui P'eng, Huang, Chang, Chou fan-tang chi-t'uan-ti p'i-p'an*, p. 9. The translation of this important passage in *CLG*, I, No. 4, p. 35, does not in my judgement quite capture its flavour. Mao made this remark in an almost tangential passage, but the import was very clear.

[181] *CLG*, I, No. 4, p. 26. This version would appear to have been made as part of a written comment appended to P'eng's letter of opinion. If so, Mao's threat was given more enduring significance and wider distribution. For P'eng's recollection of this passage under questioning during the cultural revolution, see *The Case of Peng Teh-huai*, p. 121. Chang, *Power and Policy in China*, p. 117, says that many high-ranking PLA officers were reported to have endorsed P'eng's letter; the assertion is based on the reports of two refugees. Chang, in his chapter in Whitson (ed.), *The Military and Political Power in China in the 1970s*, p. 49, says that 'a large number of PLA officials signed the memorandum in support of P'eng's action' but gives no source.

[182] One piece of evidence indicating the crucial roles of Liu and Chou at Lushan is provided by the post-plenum photograph which showed Mao flanked by them alone, and not, as was normal, by any other members of the Politburo standing committee. Ch'en Yun and Teng Hsiao-p'ing were absent, but Marshals Chu Teh and Lin Piao were not. My hypothesis is that Chu was excluded because of his defence of P'eng at the plenum, but that it was thought unwise to antagonize him further by appearing to isolate him by placing Lin Piao on the podium. Nevertheless Lin Piao is clearly visible in the audience, in what looks like a highly doctored photograph, whereas Chu Teh is not. See *JMJP*, 27 Aug. 1959, and MacFarquhar, 'On photographs'.

Mao indicated that Chou was on his side in a passage in which he talked about working with the Premier during the leap; see *CLG*, I, No. 4, p. 38. A number of other names of party leaders, apparently those under a cloud, were excised from the text of Mao's speech by cultural revolution editors; one of these (e.g., ibid., p. 42) may well have been Liu's. P'eng Teh-huai's angry exchange with Liu at Lushan is another indication that the state chairman had sided with the party chairman; see ch. 9 above.

[183] Mao had prepared the justification for this in his speech by underlining how long he had spent listening to his critics with stiffened scalp; *CLG*, I, No. 4, pp. 27-28, 33. For P'eng's explanation of why he chose not to speak in plenary session, see *P'eng Teh-huai Tzu-hsu*, p. 275.

[184] *The Case of Peng Teh-huai*, p. 19.

[185] *The Case of Peng Teh-huai*, pp. 205, 480. The operative word has been delicately removed, but the full meaning of the bowdlerized text is crystal clear. There is an apparent contradiction between Mao's statement that he had exhibited forbearance for 20 days (*CLG*, I, No. 4, p. 36) and P'eng later reference to 18 days. Mao presumably was referring to the period from P'eng's first intervention in the north-west group (3 July) to the day he was speaking (23 July). If P'eng was being precise, he would have had to have uttered the quoted phrase on 21 July; but we know P'eng did not attend the conference session that day because he missed Chang Wen-t'ien's speech (see above p. 217). My assumption is, therefore, that in the heat of the moment, P'eng picked a figure out of the air.

The 40 days of criticism P'eng underwent in Yenan presumably had to do with his military disagreements with Mao as mentioned in his self-examination at Lushan (*The Case of Peng Teh-huai*, pp. 33-4). Mao implied later that this prolonged criticism session took place just before the CCP's 7th Congress in 1945 and was primarily concerned with P'eng Teh-huai's conduct of the 100 Regiments Battle (*Mao, Miscellany*, II, p. 345).

186 The precise closing date of the work conference was 30 July. At one point in his speech Mao stated 'now the conference will soon be adjourned', only to add that it might as well go on until the end of the month (*CLG*, I, No. 4, p. 36). In his speech to the subsequent 8th plenum, Mao described the work conference as follows: 'First, small meetings were held for nine days, then we met in plenary session, and finally resolutions were adopted' (ibid., p. 61; I have adjusted the translation slightly). This suggests that the small group meetings may have started on 2 July (the day Mao issued his second directive at the outset of the conference; *Mao, Miscellany*, I, pp. 182-4) and continued until midday on 10 July (P'eng Teh-huai made his last intervention at the north-west group meetings on the morning of the 10th). On 10 July Mao made a speech which presumably represented his preliminary response to what he had heard of the criticisms voiced at the group meetings; this speech may have been his opening remarks at the plenary sessions, which one could thus assume began on the afternoon of the 10th (*CLG*, I, No. 4, p. 44). The debate at the plenary sessions would, I suggest, have been ended by Mao's speech on 23 July; thereafter the discussions probably focused not on the leap but on what to do about P'eng (i.e. what resolutions to pass on him), discussions that would have given a chance for conference participants to scramble to Mao's side of the argument. Presumably, Mao had his secretaries draw up the indictment of P'eng's career which the Politburo Standing Committee endorsed on 1 Aug.; *Chungkuo Kung-ch'an Tang Chien Shih Chiang-yi* (Canton, 1981), II, p. 3530.

187 *Tsai P'eng Tsung Shen-pien*, p. 77.

188 *Kuang-hui-ti li-shih wen-hsien*, p. 12. Two more CC members seem to have arrived before the end of the session if one compares the figures announced by Mao at its commencement with those issued in the official communiqué at its completion; cf. Lieberthal, p. 145. In addition, these sources indicate that either 14 or 15 non-members also sat in on the sessions. It is also clear that some CC members who had not attended the conference turned up for the plenum; see *CLG*, I, No. 4, p. 61.

189 For P'eng's criticism of exaggeration, see *The Case of Peng Teh-huai*, pp. 10-11; for Mao's speech, see *CLG*, I, No. 4, p. 60. It is of course possible that this is not a complete text of Mao's speech.

190 *CLG*, I, No. 4, pp. 60-3.

191 Ibid., pp. 54-5.

192 There is no indication that Mao's letter to Chang Wen-t'ien was circulated as a conference document.

193 Ibid., pp. 47-9.

194 For P'eng's disclaimer, see *Kuang-hui-ti li-shih wen-hsien*, p. 46.

195 *The Polemic*, p. 77.

196 *Khrushchev Remembers*, pp. 268-70.

197 For Nixon's account of the visit and the debate, see idem., *Six Crises*, pp. 243-81; for Khrushchev's, see *Khrushchev Remembers*, pp. 364-7.

198 For the announcement of the visit—actually an exchange of visits was envisaged, but Eisenhower's return visit never took place—see *The Public Papers of the Presidents of the United States: Dwight D. Eisenhower, 1959*, pp. 560-4. At his press conference, Eisenhower simply said he had initiated the correspondence leading to the visit in early July. Khrushchev states that the invitation was carried by First Deputy Premier Kozlov on his return from a visit to the United States (*Khrushchev Remembers*, pp. 368-9); Kozlov left for

home on 13 July (*Department of State Bulletin*, XLI, No. 1049 (3 Aug. 1959), pp. 157-8).

[199] Nixon, *Six Crises*, pp. 284-7.

[200] Zagoria, *Sino-Soviet Conflict*, pp. 134-5. The attack was not reprinted in the *JMJP*.

[201] *CLG*, I, No. 4, p. 52.

[202] See p. 132 above.

[203] *CLG*, I, No. 4, p. 53.

[204] For Wang's behaviour at Tsunyi, Mao's acknowledgement of it and Wang's handling of the arrangement for the Chairman's ex-wife, see Wang Chen et al., 'Recollections and inheritance—In memory of Comrade Wang Chia-hsiang', trans. in FBIS-CHI-81-038, pp. L10-11. (There is some question as to whether Ho Tzu-ch'en was in what might properly be called an asylum; she is apparently now living in Shanghai.) At Tsunyi, Wang became, along with Chou En-lai, one of Mao's two deputies on the small group set up to run the army, the base from which Mao outflanked General Secretary Chang Wen-t'ien and eventually rose to become party Chairman; this makes Wang's subsequent demotion even more puzzling. For other biographical data on Wang Chia-hsiang, see his biography in Klein & Clark, *Biographic Dictionary*, pp. 895-900.

[205] *The Case of Peng Teh-huai*, p. 180.

[206] Ibid., pp. 39-44. This text of the 8th CC resolution which was only released during the cultural revolution is officially described as 'excerpts'. It is conceivable that there was an additional section on P'eng's links with Khrushchev, but there seems no reason why such a section, if it existed, should not have been released at a time of animosity between Peking and Moscow.

[207] See for instance ibid., p. 180. In the heat of anger at the Bucharest party congress in June 1960, Khrushchev reportedly accused the Chinese of sending P'eng Teh-huai to a labour camp because he had dared criticize the policy of the communes in a letter to the CPSU (Crankshaw, *The New Cold War: Moscow v. Pekin*, p. 109). However accurate this account of Khrushchev's remarks, it is inconceivable that cultural revolutionaries would not have denounced any such if it had in fact been sent. Perhaps the Soviet leader was attempting to sow confusion within the ranks of the CCP and to persuade fraternal delegates at the Romanian congress that there was a rebel faction within the CCP ready and willing to deal more rationally with the CPSU.

[208] 'Down with Ch'en Yun, old hand at opposing Chairman Mao', *Ts'ai Mao Hung Ch'i* (Finance and Trade Red Flag), 15 Feb. 1967, trans. in SCMP(S) 177, p. 9. As late as June 1959, provincial leaders were still promoting the policy of taking the country as a coordinated chess game, which had been Ch'en Yun's slogan for restoring balance and organization to the economy; see the report on the work of the Kirin provincial government given by Li Yu-wen on 7 June, *Kirin Jih-pao*, 10 June 1959, trans. in SCMP 2082, p. 32.

[209] See Teng's confession (*Teng Hsiao-p'ing tzu-pai shao*) reproduced by Kwangtung province Shang-shan-hsia-hsiang ch'ing-nien 'fu-chi' chan-tou tui, p. 4. I deduce that the accident happened at Lushan, because another cultural revolution source states that Teng 'slipped away on the pretence of ailing legs' (*The Case of Peng Teh-huai*, p. 205), implying that he was there for part of the work conference but left before the plenum. For a brief account of Teng's appreciation of the problems caused by the attempt to do everything at the same time, see *Chin Chün Pao* (Advancing Army News), 14 June 1967, p. 2, col. 3.

[210] See *Origins*, I, pp. 146-8, and p. 65 above.

[211] According to Chou En-lai; see *Foreign Relations of the United States*, VIII,

The Far East: China, p. 359. See also *Tsai P'eng Tsung Shen-pien*, p. 68.

212 For details of the relationship between Chu Teh and P'eng Teh-huai, see *Tsai P'eng Tsung Shen-pien*, pp. 66–7.

213 *Chu Teh fan-tang fan-she-hui-chu-yi fan Mao Tse-tung ssu-hsiang-ti tsui-hsing* (Chu Teh's crimes against the party, socialism and Mao Tse-tung's Thought), Second Collection (Peking: Capital Liaison Station for thoroughly criticising Chu Teh, 15 April 1967), p. 13. For Chu's remarks about mess halls, see *Hsin Pei-ta* (New Peking University), 23 Jan. 1967, p. 3, col. 2; for a statement that the communes were set up too early, see *Tung-fang Hung* (East is Red), 11 Feb. 1967, trans. SCMP(S) 172, p. 22.

214 See *Exposing the towering crimes of counter-revolutionary revisionist Li Ch'i against the party, socialism and Mao Tse-tung Thought*, trans. in SCMM(S) 23, p. 10. Li Ch'i was at this time 1st secretary of Taiyuan in Shansi province; ibid., p. 1.

215 Since P'eng Teh-huai occupied such a prominent place in the demonology of the cultural revolutionaries, I have assumed that anyone who uttered a remotely sympathetic word on his behalf at Lushan would have been nailed by them. Chu Teh's is the only real defence that I have found. Foreign Minister Marshal Ch'en Yi, who was not at Lushan, was the first to call on P'eng when the latter returned to Peking. However, he appears to have reproved P'eng for getting into the scrape and counselled him to speak less hastily in the future; see *Tsai P'eng Tsung Shen-pien*, pp. 67–8.

216 Apart from Mao's speeches at Lushan and his letter to Chang Wen-t'ien, see for instance the comments on his temper by Ch'en Yi, *Wen-ko Feng-yun* (Cultural Revolution Storm), No. 9, 1967, p. 28, and Edgar Snow, *Red Star over China*, p. 84.

217 The problem is obviously not peculiar to China. The present author's wife Emily MacFarquhar once asked a member of Mrs Indira Gandhi's Congress Party, an Indian politician of independent standing, why he had not criticized her Emergency Rule at the time. He answered with disarming frankness: 'In my case, it was fear'!

218 Even if peasants were too nervous to tell Liu the facts, he had access to reality through his household staff. For instance, one of his children's nurses returned from a visit home in the summer of 1959 and blurted out to Liu's wife Wang Kuang-mei her observation of rural food shortages and other hardships; see *HCPP*, No. 20, pp. 280–1.

219 *CLG*, II, No. 4, pp. 76–7.

220 See *Origins*, I, p. 312.

221 'Knock down old-line counter-revolutionary P'eng Teh-huai', *Hsin Pei-ta* (New Peking University), p. 3, col. 2.

222 *K'o Chi Chan Pao*, 2 June 1967, p. 8, col. 3.

223 See *Origins*, I, pp. 334–5 (note 59).

224 Jao Shu-shih, allegedly Kao Kang's principal accomplice, occupied the key position of Director of the party's Organization Department when he was purged in 1954; prior to that he had been head of the party's East China Bureau and secretary of its Shanghai committee; see Klein & Clark, *Biographic Dictionary*, pp. 408–11.

225 *Hsin Pei-ta*, 9 Aug. 1967, p. 3, col. 3. See also *CLG*, I, No. 4, p. 74.

226 For Liu's view that P'eng's links with Kao Kang deprived him of the right to speak out, see *San-fan fen-tzu Liu Shao-ch'i tsui-o shih*, p. 36. For Liu's description of P'eng as a left-over evil of the Kao–Jao alliance, see 'A record of the criminal activities of anti-party, army-usurping chieftain, P'eng Teh-huai', *Chingkangshan* (Chingkang Mountains), 1 Aug. 1967, p. 6, col. 4. According to this source, Liu was criticized by Mao for an insufficiently strong character-

ization of P'eng's role in the Kao Kang affair. For Liu's high appraisal of P'eng's strength of character, see the article by Liu's bodyguards, 'Around Comrade Shao-ch'i', *HCPP*, No. 20, pp. 243−4.

[227] Fang Chih-ch'un, 'An unforgettable day', *JMJP*, 16 May 1980.

[228] Li Jui, 'Remembering T'ien Chia-ying', *HHYP—WCP*, No. 4, 1980, p. 173. The episode of the poem-writing was very traditional. The four companions came upon a pavilion in which there was a large stone on which was engraved a poem by Wang Yang-ming. When they noticed there was no answering verse inscribed on the pillars of the pavilion, T'ien was urged to provide one. To write it, he used a charred pine branch which Li Jui had picked off the ground.

[229] See *Origins*, I, pp. 86−91, 312−15. For Chou's disputes with P'eng Teh-huai, see Grey Chou, II, pp. 205−6, 231−5.

[230] *Mao chu-hsi tui P'eng, Huang, Chang, Chou fan-tang chi-t'uan-ti p'i-p'an*, p. 19. These criticisms were quoted by Mao in a note/speech on 15 Aug., almost at the conclusion of the plenum. The fact that he did not cite them earlier suggests that they were made, probably by the outspoken P'eng, during the plenum. Another possibility is that for reasons of debating tactics, Mao was not prepared to repeat such fundamental criticisms, even to deride them, until his victory was assured.

[231] See *Origins*, I, pp. 7−9. In a sense Chou seems also to have seen himself as Mao's personal aide as well as one of his senior colleagues; at Lushan, for instance, he felt he had to take personal charge of ensuring that Mao's quarters were not too hot (Green Chou, p. 396).

[232] Grey Chou, II, p. 288.

[233] Post-Mao Chinese assessments of the importance of Lushan as a turning point in Chinese party norms include An Tzu-wen's statement that after 1959 the CCP departed from democratic centralism (*JMJP*, 8 May 1980), and the description by the Peking party school's theoretical investigation group of post-Lushan political life as abnormal (*HHWC*, No. 3, 1981, p. 71, col. 1). For a perceptive Western analysis, see Teiwes, *Politics & Purges in China*, pp. 436−40.

[234] *Tsai P'eng Tsung Shen-pien*, p. 78. P'eng Teh-huai's self-criticism is in *The Case of Peng Teh-huai*, pp. 31−8. How he came to write it is in *P'eng Teh-huai Tzu-hsu*, pp. 276−8.

[235] The suicide of Kao Kang, by contrast, may have seemed suspicious to many, but probably worried few; for a discussion of the Kao Kang affair, see Teiwes, *Politics & Purges in China*, pp. 166−210. Chang Wen-t'ien's secretary feared he would take an overdose of sleeping pills at Lushan, and removed them; *Huai-nien Chang Wen-t'ien T'ung-chih*, p. 108.

[236] *Tsai P'eng Tsung Shen-pien*, pp. 77−8.

[237] The CC resolution on the 'anti-party clique' was not published until the cultural revolution and then only in the form of excerpts. It is contained in *The Case of Peng Teh-huai*, pp. 39−44. David A. Charles pointed out that Huang K'o-ch'eng and Chou Hsiao-chou had worked together when the former was a Hunan party secretary in the early 1950s; see 'The dismissal of Marshal P'eng Teh-huai', *CQ*, Oct.−Dec. 1961, p. 69.

[238] *Tsai P'eng Tsung Shen-pien*, p. 81. The texts of P'eng's letter and Mao's comment on it are in *Mao, Miscellany*, I, pp. 187−8.

[239] *Tsai P'eng Tsung Shen-pien*, pp. 81−2, 84. Despite the potential political hazards of staying with P'eng, his bodyguard appears to have felt he could not desert him in his hour of need; his only worry was that he, like P'eng, would have to resign from the PLA, but the Marshal was able to avert this. For the date of P'eng's move, see *HHWC*, No. 5, 1981, pp. 174−5.

The Yuan Ming Yuan (the Garden of Perfection and Light) had once been a 'showpiece of the Italian baroque' designed in the 18th century by Jesuit advisers of the Emperor Ch'ien Lung. It had been looted and then destroyed by an Anglo-French force in 1860. For a brief description of its appearance today, see Bonavia, *The Chinese*, p. 84. See also the pictures accompanying the article 'Yuan Ming Yuan', *China Pictorial*, No. 5, 1981, pp. 36-43. In one section of the Yuan Ming Yuan is a compound surrounded by high walls which is probably the Wu Jia Hua Yuan where P'eng Teh-huai was confined.

240 *Tsai P'eng Tsung Shen-pien*, pp. 84, 91.

241 Ho Ch'eng, 'Comrade Fu Lien-chang—from a Christian to an outstanding communist', *JMJP*, 6 March 1981, trans. in JPRS 77,968, p. 15. The translation refers to Chou En-lai's 'sparkling eyes'; I have assumed they could not have been sparkling with joy or amusement.

242 *Tsai P'eng Tsung Shen-pien*, pp. 82, 86-90, 91-2, 94-5. But P'eng Teh-huai kept his distance from the guards to 'avoid suspicion'! (ibid., p. 93).

243 For P'eng's earlier reading habits, or lack of them, see 'Dossiers of P'eng Teh-huai', trans. in SCMM(S) 27, p. 22. For a more sympathetic view suggesting that during the revolutionary years he would read pamphlets whenever he got a spare moment, see *The Case of Peng Teh-huai*, p. ii.

244 *Tsai P'eng Tsung Shen-pien*, pp. 106-7, 109. In addition to sending P'eng state documents, the CC detailed Yang Shang-k'un, an alternate member of the party secretariat, to be its liaison officer with him; see *Heng-tao-li-ma P'eng Chiang-chun*, p. 71. P'eng's name appeared in print on 29 May 1960 (NCNA) as a member of the funeral committee for his fellow Politburo member Lin Po-chü, but otherwise he dropped totally out of sight after Lushan.

245 *Mao, Miscellany*, I, p. 186.

246 *Tung-fang Hung Chan Pao* (East Is Red Combat News), 15 June 1967, p. 6, no. 80. (The year of the conference is given incorrectly as 1957.)

247 Sun Yeh-fang et al., 'A meticulously scholarly attitude', *HHYP*, No. 8, 1967, p. 18; 'Resolutely discredit and knock down Chang Wen-t'ien, a major anti-party element', *Chin Chün Pao* (Advancing Army News), 31 May 1967, trans. in SCMP(S) 194, p. 32. According to another account, Chang was assigned the task of investigating the theories of the Soviet economist Liberman who sought to establish profit as a measure of performance; see 'Record of the crimes of counter-revolutionary revisionist element Yang Shang-K'un', *Tung-fang Hung Pao* (East Is Red News), 23 June 1967, p. 3, col. 1.

248 *HHYP*, No. 5, 1979, pp. 63-4.

249 See *Hua Kuo-feng T'ung-chih shih Mao Chu-hsi Ko-ming Lu-hsien-ti Cho-yueh Chi-ch'eng-che* (Comrade Hua Kuo-feng is the brilliant continuer of Chairman Mao's revolutionary line), p. 17. See also *Hua Chu-hsi tsai T'ai-yang Sheng-ch'i-ti ti-fang* (Chairman Hua in the place where the sun rises), p. 73, and *Hua Chu-hsi tsai Hunan* (Chairman Hua in Hunan), p. 5. A comparison of these three sources suggests that a standard formulation was devised to emphasize Hua's links with Mao, the sole source of legitimacy for his succession, but this does not mean that it was a fabrication. P'eng Teh-huai had not yet been rehabilitated when these works were published.

250 *Hua Kuo-feng T'ung chih... Chi-ch'eng-che*, pp. 136-42, especially p. 141.

251 For an account of Hua Kuo-feng's early career, see Michel Oksenberg and Sai-cheung Yueng, 'Hua Kuo-feng's pre-Cultural Revolution Hunan years, 1949–66: the making of a political generalist', *CQ*, Jan.–March 1977, pp. 3–51. For hagiographical but nevertheless useful Chinese accounts of Hua's career, see the works cited in note 249 above.

252 The precise dating of the MAC conference is uncertain. P'eng Teh-huai said it lasted from late Aug. to early Sept., but another source has it stretching into

Oct. Cf. *P'eng Teh-huai Tzu-hsu*, p. 278; *HHWC*, No. 3, 1981, p. 70. For Liu Shao-ch'i's order, see *The Case of Peng Teh-huai*, p. 47.

253 *Kuang-hui-ti li-shih wen-hsien*, Sept. 1967, p. 22. The fact that this was an article not a speech is attested to in ibid., pp. 47–8, which also records P'eng Teh-huai's angry comments on Ch'en Po-ta's analysis. For Mao's version of the question, see *Mao Chu-hsi tui P'eng*, p. 21.

254 See *Kuang-hui-ti li-shih wen-hsien*, Sept. 1967, pp. 49–56 for some of P'eng's early offending works; for Mao's attack on them, see *CLG*, I, No. 4, pp. 79–80.

255 *CLG*, I, No. 4, pp. 83–4.

256 Ibid., pp. 7–9. Ch'en Po-ta criticized P'eng Teh-huai's pre-1949 views at much greater length; see *Kuang-hui-ti li-shih wen-hsien*, Sept. 1967, pp. 23–8.

257 *CLG*, I, No. 4, pp. 80–1.

258 *Kuang-hui-ti li-shih wen-hsien*, Sept. 1967, pp. 22–30.

259 *CLG*, I, No. 4, pp. 81–2.

260 Ibid., p. 82–3.

261 Ibid., p. 84.

262 *Mao, Miscellany*, I, p. 187. *P'eng Teh-huai Tzu-hsu*, pp. 278–9.

263 'P'eng Teh-huai's notes on the Lushan plenum published', *Chin-tai Shih Yen-chiu* (Researches in Modern History), No. 4, 1980, trans. in JPRS 77,668, pp. 6–10.

264 For the committee of inquiry, see 'Towering crimes of Ho Lung, anti-party element and army usurper', *T'i-yü Chan-hsien* (Physical Education Front), 28 Jan. 1967, trans. in SCMP 3912, p. 12; for Ho's reluctance to criticize P'eng Teh-huai, see 'Dossiers of Ho Lung', trans. in SCMM(S) 27, p. 27.

265 This was the Wuhan regional commander, Gen. Ch'en Tsai-tao; see *Steel 2nd HQ* (Wuhan), No. 38 (22 Aug. 1967). At the height of the cultural revolution, in the summer of 1967, Gen. Ch'en was involved in the 'Wuhan incident', an event that eventually led to the suppression of the worst Red Guard excesses; see Philip Bridgham, 'Mao's Cultural Revolution in 1967: the struggle to seize power', *CQ*, April–June 1968, pp. 24–7.

266 *CLG*, I, No. 4, p. 82.

267 This remark is quoted in a number of cultural revolution sources; see for instance *Selected edition on Liu Shao'ch'i's counter-revolutionary revisionist crimes*, trans. in SCMM 651, p. 20. Unfortunately only a few quotations from this speech were made available during the cultural revolution, presumably because the rest of the speech would have disproved Red Guard allegations. However, I believe it is possible to infer Liu's objectives in this speech.

268 As in the preceding footnote, this quotation appears in many places; see for instance *San-fan fen-tzu Liu Shao-ch'i tsui-o shih*, p. 36.

269 Quoted in *Liu Shao chi's reactionary speeches* trans. in SCMM(S) 25, p. 21. Another possibility is that this remark was made by Liu at the first SSC that he chaired on 24 Aug., or even earlier, at Lushan.

270 Ibid., p. 3.

271 *Origins*, I, p. 108.

272 See for instance 'Two Khrushchevs as reflected in the magic mirror of Mao Tse-tung's Thought', *Tou-p'i-kai* (Struggle-criticism-transformation), 15 May 1967, trans. in SCMM(S) 22, p. 18. This source, like others in which this quotation is to be found, states that the remark was made at the Lushan conference on 17 Aug. Since the plenum ended on 16 Aug., one must assume that this was another example of mis-dating in Red Guard sources.

273 *Origins*, I, pp. 100–104.

274 Some Red Guard sources only cite Liu's approval of the cult of Teng Hsiao-p'ing for obvious political reasons; see for instance *Liu Shao-ch'i fan-ko-ming*

tsui-o shih, p. 34. But in at least one source, the names of Chou En-lai and Lin Piao are also mentioned; see *'Maniacs' of the new era*, trans. in SCMM 603, pp. 18, 24. (On p. 18, Lin Piao and X X X are cited; on p. 24, both Lin Piao and Chou En-lai are cited, but not the occasion of the remark; I have assumed that the X X X is Chou, and that the uncited occasion must be this MAC conference.)

[275] SCMM(S) 25, p. 4.

[276] Ibid. p. 3. The relatively low esteem in which Liu was held in the PLA was underlined a month later when a PLA propagandist urged colleagues to give greater publicity to his role during the revolutionary period and his contribution to military victory; see 'The towering crimes of counter-revolutionary double-dealer Chao I-ya', *Hsin Jen Ta* (New People's University), 21 Sept. 1967, trans. in SCMP(S) 221, p. 32.

[277] For the dating of Lin Piao's speech see *Chung Kung Chung-yang Wen-hsien* (Documents of the Chinese Communist Party Centre), No. 1, 1974, p. 10.

[278] *Illustrations of Liu Shao-ch'i's opposition to Mao Tse-tung's Thoughts in his sinister book 'On self cultivation'*, trans. in SCMM 592, p. 21.

[279] 'Vice Chairman Lin's talk (excerpts) about P'eng Teh-huai', *Ko-ming Tsao-fan Pao* (Revolutionary Rebel Paper), 25 Nov. 1967, trans. in SCMP(S) 218, pp. 19-20.

[280] Huang K'o-ch'eng, who was not dismissed formally as a secretary of the CC secretariat until 1962 (SCMM 651, p. 34; URI, *Who's Who*, p. 307), was rehabilitated in time for the 50th anniversary of the PLA on 1 Aug. 1977 (*Free China Weekly*, 8 Aug. 1977). He became the secretary of the Central Discipline Inspection Committee set up at the 3rd plenum of the 11th CC in Dec. 1978.

[281] See 'Dossiers of Lo Jui-ch'ing', trans. in SCMM(S) 27, pp. 48-9.

[282] See p. 187 above and *Shen-chieh Huai-nien Lo Jui-ch'ing T'ung-chih*, pp. 170-2, 199-201.

[283] For Lo Jui-ch'ing's career, see Klein & Clark, *Biographic Dictionary*, pp. 642-5.

[284] See David A. Charles, 'The dismissal of Marshal P'eng Teh-huai', *CQ*, Oct.-Dec. 1961, p. 73.

[285] See ibid. and the biography of each in Klein & Clark, *Biographic Dictionary*, pp. 233-6, 524-6.

[286] See Klein & Clark, *Biographic Dictionary*, pp. 826-8. Confirmation that Teng Hua was dismissed because of the P'eng Teh-huai affair was only provided years later, after his death; see *HHYP*, No. 7, 1980, pp. 49-50.

[287] See the biographies in Klein & Clark, *Biographic Dictionary*, pp. 103-4 (Ch'en Hsi-lien), 113-16 (Ch'en Keng), 359-61 (Hsu Shih-yu), 632 (Liu Ya-lou), 774-8 (Su Yu); and in URI, *Who's Who*, I, p. 158 (Ch'iu Hui-tso).

[288] See *Origins*, I, pp. 146-8 and p. 65 above. It has been argued (J. D. Simmonds, 'P'eng Teh-huai: a chronological re-examination', *CQ*, Jan.-March 1969, pp. 120-38) that steps taken during May and the first half of June 1959, during P'eng's absence abroad, to render the Defence Minister powerless, and that his dismissal at Lushan was virtually a *fait accompli* before the conference started. (The analogy is with the organization of the dismissal of Marshal Zhukov while he was abroad in the autumn of 1957.) However, the argument relies too heavily on conjectural timings of or motivations for transfers of responsibility in the PLA and the security field. For instance, mid-June is suggested for Teng Hua's removal (p. 127); but the new evidence cited in note 286 confirms that he was dismissed as a result of the campaign against P'eng's anti-party group, i.e. after Lushan. Without doubting Mao's long-term desire to get rid of P'eng, it would seem on balance more consistent

with the evidence to see Lushan as a heaven-sent opportunity to accomplish that objective at a stroke rather than as the culmination of a two-month process of personnel changes carefully designed to achieve it.

[289] For a brief discussion of Mao's 'clique' during the 1930s and its political importance, see *Origins*, I, pp. 142-3. Much of the biographical detail about Lin Piao is culled from Klein & Clark, *Biographic Dictionary*, pp. 559-67.

[290] Robinson, *Political-Military Biography of Lin Piao*, II, 1950-71, p. 148.

[291] Ibid., pp. 154-6, and Klein & Clark, *Biographic Dictionary*. These sources disagree on whether or not Lin Piao went to Korea; Chinese consulted by the present author have asserted that he did not. Some Chinese written sources imply that although Lin Piao pleaded illness at the outbreak of the Korean war this was just an excuse; see *Heng-tao-li-ma P'eng Chiang-chün*, p. 123, and JPRS 77,968, p. 16.

[292] JPRS 77,968, p. 16.

[293] *Hung-se Hsuan-ch'üan Ping* (Red Propaganda Soldier), 25 May 1967, p. 3, col. 4.

[294] *Ten Glorious Years*, p. 74.

[295] *Mao Chu-hsi Yü-lu*, pp. 198-9.

[296] *Origins*, I, p. 8.

[297] 'Dossiers of P'eng Teh-huai', trans. in SCMM(S) 27, p. 24. No evidence is given to back up this allegation, but it does not seem unlikely that P'eng chafed at the provisions for party control. According to his bodyguard, P'eng saw a lot of his fellow marshals (*Tsai P'eng Tsung Shen-pien*, pp. 66-8); perhaps the Defence Minister thought this was a more appropriate group of men with whom to discuss the running of the armed forces.

[298] See CB 589, p. 2, 6.

[299] See for instance CB 588 *passim*; *JMJP*, editorial, 27 Aug. 1959, trans. in CB 589, pp. 11-15; CB 590 *passim*.

[300] *CLG*, I, No. 4, pp. 64-5.

[301] Ibid., p. 67.

[302] Ibid., p. 69.

[303] Ibid., p. 72.

[304] Ibid., p. 81.

[305] 'Overcome rightist-inclined sentiment and endeavor to increase production and practise economy', *JMJP*, 6 Aug. 1959, trans. in SCMP 2074, p. 4 ff. The manner in which the attacks on rightism gradually escalated was first pointed out by David A. Charles, 'The dismissal of Marshal P'eng Teh-huai', p. 69.

[306] 'Defeat calamities and strive for a bumper harvest', *JMJP*, 7 Aug. 1959, quotation trans. in SCMP 2076, p. 22.

[307] For a discussion of the 1955 context, see *Origins*, I, pp. 26-7.

[308] Charles, 'The dismissal of Marshal P'eng Teh-huai', pp. 69-70. Philip Bridgham has perceptively suggested that the fact that Chou, the pragmatist, opened the attack on right opportunism would have greatly increased its impact.

[309] Trans. in SCMP 2090, p. 17. Jürgen Domes argues that Lushan witnessed a retreat on the communes; see Domes, *Socialism in the Chinese Countryside*, pp. 44-5. My belief is that the retreat took place at and after the second Chengchow conference; see Lin Tian, 'Inquiry into the system of people's communes', *Ching-chi Kuan-li* (Economic Management), No. 1, 1981, trans. in FBIS-CHI-81-048, pp. L20-21.

[310] *JMJP*, editorial, 'Let us put an end to the theory "What you have lost is more than you have gained"'; quotation trans. in SCMP 2091, p. 1. See also an NCNA report by Wu Chi-kan on 'China's small blast furnaces' (4 Sept. 1959) trans. in SCMP 2094, p. 2 ff.

[311] *JMJP* editorials, 'Refutation of the absurd view that "the balance of the economy has been upset"', 17 Sept. 1959, trans. in SCMP 2105, pp. 9–11; and 'Community dining halls have a boundless future', 22 Sept. 1959, trans. in ibid., pp. 12–17.

[312] CB 589, p. 2.

[313] See their articles trans. in *Ten Glorious Years*, pp. 1–66, 90–104.

[314] Ibid., pp. 192–3.

[315] Ibid., p. 217. For evidence that Li Ching-ch'üan criticized P'eng Teh-huai at Lushan, see 'Severe criticism of "Khrushchev" of Szechwan', Kweiyang regional service, 17 June 1967, FBIS, 20 June 1967, Chicom Regional Affairs, p. ddd 17.

[316] *Ten Glorious Years*, p. 223.

[317] Ibid., p. 237.

[318] T'ao Chu's article on revolutionary resoluteness, originally published in a Kwangtung magazine, was reprinted in *JMJP*, 2 Sept. 1959; for a translation, see SCMP 2103, pp. 1–4. Eight years later, at the height of the cultural revolution, this article was denounced by Yao Wen-yuan as counter-revolutionary! See Yao Wen-yuan, 'Comments on T'ao Chu's Two books', *China Reconstructs, Supplement*, Nov. 1967, p. 12. For an example of the recollectivization of private plots, see *CYWK*, p. 144.

PART FOUR: DEFEAT

Notes to pages 255–61

Chapter 11.   The Sino-Soviet split emerges

[1] Quoted in *The Sino-Soviet Dispute*, p. 58.

[2] *Khrushchev Remembers*, p. 263.

[3] Maxwell, *India's China War*, pp. 76–80. The account in the next three paragraphs relies heavily on that in pp. 67–134 of this source.

[4] The Indian discovery of the Chinese road across Aksai Chin and the subsequent correspondence between the two Premiers had been kept secret by both sides; ibid., p. 116.

[5] Gittings, *Survey of the Sino-Soviet Dispute*, p. 114.

[6] Borisov & Koloskov, *Soviet-Chinese Relations, 1945–1970*, p. 157 (emphasis added).

[7] Gittings, *Sino-Soviet Dispute*, p. 327.

[8] Ibid.

[9] Ibid., p. 112.

[10] *Khrushchev Remembers*, pp. 368–75.

[11] See the analysis of a veteran observer of the Soviet scene, Edward Crankshaw, in *The New Cold War: Moscow v. Pekin*, pp. 84–5.

[12] Quoted ibid., p. 85.

[13] Khrushchev misremembers—deliberately?—the timing of the Tass statement, suggesting that it was not issued until after his US visit; ibid., p. 307.

[14] Gittings, *Sino-Soviet Dispute*, p. 114. Chou's letter had been handed to the Indian ambassador in Peking on the evening of 8 Sept.; Nehru received it on the evening of 9 Sept. (*The Statesman* (Calcutta), 10 Sept.). The Chinese broadcast the letter—for the first time apparently—in English to Europe on 9 Sept. at 1020 GMT, i.e. 6.20 pm Peking time, 3.50 pm New Delhi time. FBIS, Far East, No. 126, p. AAA1. Assuming the *Statesman* report to be accurate, it would seem that Europeans were apprised of the contents of the letter before Mr Nehru had a chance to see it.

[15] *JMJP*, 6 May 1959, trans. in CB 570, pp. 2–16.

[16] Gittings, *Sino-Soviet Dispute*. The Chou letter was broadcast at 1020 GMT, the Tass statement at 1600 GMT (FBIS, USSR and East Europe, No. 177, 1959, pp. BB1).

[17] Borisov & Koloskov, *Soviet-Chinese Relations*, p. 158. This quotation is unfootnoted, but presumably comes from a Chinese note to Moscow, since Peking issued no public statement to this effect at that time.

[18] *NYT*, 17 Sept. 1959.

[19] *Public Papers of the Presidents: Dwight D. Eisenhower*, 1959, pp. 670–1.

[20] Ibid., p. 697.

[21] *NYT*, 7 Oct. 1959.

[22] Ibid., 1 Nov. 1959.

[23] *The Sino-Soviet Dispute*, p. 58.

[24] Gittings, *Sino-Soviet Dispute*, p. 332.

[25] *Khrushchev Remembers*, p. 308.

[26] Gittings, *Sino-Soviet Dispute*, p. 114.

[27] *JMJP*, 3 Oct. 1959. The absence of party General Secretary Teng Hsiao-p'ing,

who would play a major role in the Sino-Soviet dispute in the months ahead, is presumably accounted for by his leg injury, although he did attend the anniversary parade on 1 Oct.; alternatively, he may have been in attendance on some other major dignitary in Peking for the anniversary.

[28] Gittings, *Sino-Soviet Dispute*, pp. 114-15.

[29] *Khrushchev Remembers*, p. 308.

[30] For a commentary on Khrushchev's debating technique by one who had to counter it, see Nixon, *Six Crises*, pp. 250-71. Ch'en Yi's temperament was best revealed during his combative confrontations with Red Guards during the cultural revolution; see for instance 'Collection of Ch'en I's speeches', trans. in SCMM 636, p. 28.

[31] *Khrushchev Remembers*, pp. 308-9. If Khrushchev's report is accurate, it is unclear whether Ch'en Yi was referring when talking of British seizure to the McMahon line or Aksai Chin which the British only 'captured' cartographically; see Maxwell, *India's China War*, pp. 26-36.

[32] *Khrushchev Remembers*, p. 308.

[33] Gittings, *Sino-Soviet Dispute*, p. 115.

[34] Tatu, *Power in the Kremlin*, p. 46.

[35] *Khrushchev Remembers*, p. 311.

[36] Ibid., pp. 255, 260-1.

[37] Ibid., p. 269-70.

[38] Ibid., p. 283.

[39] Ibid., pp. 271-5.

[40] Ibid., pp. 275-8. For a discussion of the Bulgarian 'leap', see Liliana Brisby, 'Bulagaria: leaping forward without communes', *CQ*, July-Sept. 1960, pp. 80-4. For comment on the East German, Hungarian and Polish responses to Chinese developments at this time, see Martin Esslin, 'East Germany: Peking-Pankow axis?', Tamas Aczel, 'Hungary: glad tidings from Nanking', and Leopold Labedz, 'Poland: the small leap sideways', ibid., pp. 85-103.

[41] Gittings, *Sino-Soviet Dispute*, p. 117.

[42] Ibid., pp. 118-19. Even in public Khrushchev made no mention in Peking of the liberation of Taiwan, peaceful or otherwise, only reasserting the need to unseat the Nationalist regime from the UN; see A. M. Halpern, 'Communist China and peaceful coexistence', *CQ*, July-Sept. 1960, p. 18.

[43] See *Origins*, I, pp. 316-17.

[44] Gittings, *Sino-Soviet Dispute*, p. 118.

[45] *JMJP*, 2 Oct. 1959.

[46] Crankshaw, *New Cold War*, p. 87.

[47] Lieberthal, pp. 155-7.

[48] Halpern, 'Communist China', pp. 18-20.

[49] Quoted ibid. pp. 20-1.

[50] Quoted in Zagoria, *Sino-Soviet Conflict*, p. 244.

[51] Ibid., pp. 281-3.

[52] Maxwell, *India's China War*, pp. 110-11.

[53] Zagoria, *Sino-Soviet Conflict*, pp. 270-2.

[54] Ibid., p. 273.

[55] Ibid., pp. 284-6. During the cultural revolution, a Red Guard publication alleged that the Chinese delegate to the Hungarian Party Congress, T'an Chen-lin, went along with Khrushchev's view of the world situation. In fact, T'an paid only the customary Chinese courtesies to Khrushchev's peace moves and then, after a 'but' (*tan-shih*), devoted many more words to why these moves would be abortive because of the activities of American imperialism; cf. quotes in *Kuan-yü T'an Chen-lin wen-t'i-ti ch'u-pu tsung-ho ts'ai-liao* (*hsu chi*), pp. 13-14, no. 114, with full text in *HHPYK*, No. 24, 1959, pp. 149-50.

[56] Crankshaw, *New Cold War*, p. 91.

[57] In a speech to a cultural work conference on 27 Dec. 1959. See *Tung-fang Hung Chan Pao* (East Is Red Combat News), 15 June 1967, p. 4, no. 45. Ch'en Yi also conceded that Khrushchev could be right in some things (ibid., no. 40).

[58] *Teng Hsiao-p'ing fan-tang fan-she-hui-chu-i fan-Mao Tse-tung ssu-hsiang-ti yen-lun chai-pien* (Selections from Teng Hsiao-p'ing's anti-party, anti-socialist, anti-Mao Tse-tung Thought utterances) (No. 1 unit of the China People's University's Three Red Seize Liu-Teng Corps of the Capital's Red Representative Conference, April 1967), p. 60.

[59] Zagoria, *Sino-Soviet Conflict*, pp. 288–90; Halpern, op. cit., p. 21.

[60] Quoted in CB 619, p. 6. See also Zagoria, *Sino-Soviet Conflict*, pp. 290–2; Halpern op. cit., p. 21.

[61] Crankshaw, *New Cold War*, p. 91.

[62] *Liu Shao-ch'i ts'ai-liao hui-pien* (Compilation of materials on Liu Shao-ch'i) (1st collection), p. 112. Liu was talking to members of the family of his brother-in-law, Wang Kuang-ying.

[63] For a brief discussion of this mystery, see Hudson, Lowenthal & MacFarquhar, *The Sino-Soviet Dispute*, pp. 58–9.

[64] See ibid. and the text of the Chinese announcement about the departure of their delegation in SCMP 2192, p. 44.

[65] K'ang Sheng spent about four years in Moscow in the 1930s, Wu was there from 1926 to 1931; see their biographies in Klein & Clark, *Biographic Dictionary*.

[66] During the cultural revolution Wu Hsiu-ch'üan was accused of failing to report Khrushchev's abuse of Mao at the Warsaw Pact meeting; *Hung Wei Chan Pao* (Red Guard Combat News), 13 April 1967, p. 4, col. 2. If this abuse was contained in a speech Khrushchev made—and the remarks were allegedly 'public'—it is not clear why the accusations was made since it could presumably also be levelled at one of the Red Guards' heroes, K'ang Sheng.

[67] *The Sino-Soviet Dispute*, p. 64.

[68] The analysis in the succeeding three paragraphs is based on that ibid., pp. 59–61; the texts of the declaration and K'ang Sheng's speech are contained ibid., pp. 63–77.

[69] The three other items were the creation of a permanent UN committee for the peaceful exploration of outer space; the 1959 East–West agreement on the peaceful use of the Antarctic; and the cessation of nuclear testing over a considerable period (ibid., p. 60).

[70] Tatu, *Power in the Kremlin*, p. 46.

[71] A full report of all the ceremonies, messages, etc., is carried in CB 613.

[72] Ibid., pp. 21 (Liu's toast), 23–4 (Chu Teh's speech), 25–7 (Chervonenko's speech).

[73] Ibid., pp. 11–12.

[74] *Wen-ko Feng-yun* (Cultural Revolution Storm), No. 9, 1967, p. 42. The date of this remark of Ch'en's and the identity of the Foreign Minister's interlocutor are not given, but the context indicates that the latter was a Russian.

[75] Lieberthal, pp. 155–6.

[76] Ibid., pp. 156–7. There is no confirmation in the sources that Mao's speech was made at the Hangchow meeting, but the timing and context make it highly likely that it was.

[77] *Mao, Miscellany*, I, p. 226.

[78] Ibid., p. 227.

[79] *Liu Shao-ch'i ts'ai-liao hui-pien* (1st collection), p. 112.

[80] *Mao, Miscellany*, I, p. 226.

[81] Maxwell, *India's China War*, pp. 135, 142.

[82] Ibid., pp. 137, 139–51; SCMP 2209, pp. 30–1.

[83] 'Quarterly chronicle and documentation', *CQ*, April–June 1960, p. 90. Chou En-lai is said to have researched the Sino-Burmese boundary personally; FBIS-CHI-81-136, p. K5.

[84] Arnold C. Brackman, 'The Malay world and China', in Halpern (ed.), *Policies towards China: Views from Six Continents*, pp. 277–8.

[85] See *Wen-ko Feng-yun*, No. 9, 1967, p. 39.

[86] Brackman, 'The Malay world and China', pp. 278–9. For Chinese reporting on these events, see CB 605.

[87] Brackman, 'The Malay world and China', p. 279.

[88] For a fuller discussion, see A. M. Halpern, 'The Chinese communist line on neutralism', *CQ*, Jan:–March 1961, pp. 90–115.

[89] 'Quarterly chronicle and documentation', *CQ*, April–June 1960, p. 93; SCMP 2224, pp. 35–40; idem. 2228, pp. 40–8; idem. 2245, pp. 40–4.

[90] Maxwell, *India's China War*, pp. 155–69.

[91] 'Chairman Mao Tse-tung's several talks with guests from Asia, Africa, Latin America, *HC*, No. 10, 1960, trans. in SCMM 211, pp. 1–3.

[92] SCMP 2223, pp. 1–5.

[93] Young, *Negotiating with the Chinese Communists*, p. 227.

[94] 'Long live Leninism!' *HC*, No. 8, 1960, trans. in *The Sino-Soviet Dispute*, pp. 82–112; 'Forward along the path of the great Lenin', *JMJP* editorial, 22 April 1960; Yü Chao-li, 'Imperialism—source of war in modern times—and the path of the people's struggle for peace', *HC*, No. 7, 1960, trans. in *PR*, No. 15, 1960; and Lu Ting-yi's speech at the Lenin anniversary meeting, reproduced in *PR*, No. 17, 1960.

[95] Quoted in *The Sino-Soviet Dispute*, p. 82.

[96] The analysis of 'Long Live Leninism!' here is based on that in ibid., pp. 78–81.

[97] See pp. 7–8 above.

[98] One of the drafters was Wu Leng-hsi, Editor in Chief of *JMJP* and Director of the NCNA; see Wu's confession in *CLG*, II, No. 4, p. 77.

[99] *The Sino-Soviet Dispute*, p. 90.

[100] Ibid., p. 98.

[101] Ibid., pp. 96–8.

[102] Ibid., pp. 99–110.

[103] Ibid., p. 99.

[104] Ibid., p. 100.

[105] Ibid., p. 107.

[106] For a discussion of communism in Kerala, see Harrison, *India: The Most Dangerous Decades*, pp. 193–9.

[107] *The Sino-Soviet Dispute*, p. 119.

[108] Here is Kuusinen's stab at doctrinal innovation on nuclear weapons: 'Such are the dialectics of military-engineering progress: a new weapon created for war begins to exert an influence in favor of peace' (ibid., p. 119).

[109] *Teng Hsiao-p'ing fan-tang fan-she-hui-chu-i fan-Mao Tse-tung ssu-hsiang-ti yen-lun chai-pien*, p. 49.

[110] See Zagoria, *Sino-Soviet Conflict*, pp. 320–5; for the proceedings, see CB 620 and 621; for the official report of Liu Ch'ang-sheng's speech, see *The Sino-Soviet Dispute*, pp. 123–6.

[111] See the speech of Maurice Thorez at the Nov. Moscow conference in Dallin, *Diversity in International Communism*, pp. 842–3.

[112] See Tatu, *Power in the Kremlin*, pp. 104–5.

[113] For a summary of events see *NYT: Index, 1960*, pp. 523–7.

[114] See two articles excerpted in *The Sino-Soviet Dispute*, pp.127–31.

[115] *The Polemic*, p. 496; see also Tatu, *Power in the Kremlin*, p. 48, who gives the date as 11 May.

[116] *The Polemic*, pp. 79–80.

[117] *The Sino-Soviet Dispute*, pp. 132–40.

[118] Crankshaw, *New Cold War*, pp. 97–103, includes a long and extremely useful account of the letter of information but without the text it is impossible to judge its calibre.

[119] *The Polemic*, p. 80; according to Crankshaw, *New Cold War*, p. 104, the secret session started on 25 June.

[120] Crankshaw, *New Cold War*, pp. 104–6.

[121] *The Polemic*, p. 80; for the indication that Chinese 'Trotskyism' referred to behaviour at the WFTU meeting, see Crankshaw, *New Cold War*, p. 109.

[122] Crankshaw, *New Cold War*, p. 107. It was probably on this occasion that Khrushchev asserted that China's economic problems were directly due to Mao's undemocratic work-style and cult of personality; see *P'eng Chen fan ko-ming hsiu-cheng-chu-i yen-lun chai-pien* (A selection of P'eng Chen's counter-revolutionary, revisionist utterances) (Peking: New People's Great Commune and the Mao Tse-tung Thought Red Guards of China People's University (eds), May 1967), p. 3. No date is given for Khrushchev's vilification of Mao, but the fact that P'eng Chen reported it suggests it was at the Bucharest congress.

[123] Charles, 'The dismisal of Marshal P'eng Teh-huai', *CQ*, Oct.–Dec. 1961, p. 75.

[124] *Liu Shao-ch'i fan-ko-ming tsui-o shih*, p. 34. This source does not give a date for Khrushchev's praise of P'eng Teh-huai, but so provocative a comment fits in with other reports of his behaviour at Bucharest, although one cannot rule out the possibility that he made the remark when he visited Peking nine months earlier.

[125] Crankshaw, *New Cold War*, p. 109. I have found only one cultural revolution criticism of P'eng Chen's conduct at Bucharest in which he was described as passive and slow to riposte, but this seems unconvincing in the light of all the other evidence; see *San-fan fen-tzu Liu Shao-ch'i tsui-o shih*, p. 37.

[126] *The Polemic*, pp. 109–10.

[127] Ibid., pp. 111–12.

[128] Ibid., p. 81.

[129] Tatu, *Power in the Kremlin*, pp. 79–80.

[130] Zagoria, *Sino-Soviet Conflict*, p. 327; Tatu, *Power in the Kremlin*, pp. 110–11.

[131] Tatu, *Power in the Kremlin*, pp. 103–4.

[132] Borisov & Koloskov, *Soviet-Chinese Relations*, p. 212. The Russians also closed down the magazine *Druzhba* (Friendship), which the Chinese published in Moscow, on the ground that it was printing tendentious editorials; ibid., p. 186.

[133] *Chung-kuo Pai-k'o Nien-chien, 1981*, p. 563.

[134] Klochko, *Soviet Scientist in Red China*, p. 65.

[135] Ibid., pp. 177–8.

[136] Borisov & Koloskov, *Soviet-Chinese Relations*, p. 212. Klochko's recollection was that the Chinese note was dated between 23 and 26 July; *Soviet Scientist in Red China*, p. 178.

[137] Klochko, *Soviet Scientist in Red China*, p. 178.

[138] Ibid., pp. 164–5.

[139] Ibid., pp. 122–3, 105–2, 154–6, 159.

[140] Ibid., pp. 146–8.

[141] Ibid., pp. 152–4.

[142] Ibid., pp. 165–9.

[143] Ibid., pp. 171–6, 180–1, 190.
[144] Ibid., pp. 181–7. Klochko comments acidly that the grievance underlying all of Chervonenko's complaints was that China had 'ceased to be an obedient tool of Moscow's policy'; ibid., p. 186. The immediate response to the withdrawal by the Chinese was that they withheld their delegation from a Congress of Orientalists, held in Moscow from 9 to 16 Aug.; see Roderick MacFarquhar, 'The 25th International Congress of Orientalists', *CQ*, Oct.–Dec. 1960, pp. 114–16.
[145] Klochko, *Soviet Scientist in Red China*, pp. 188–90.
[146] Ibid., pp. 187–8.
[147] Ibid., pp. 179–87. Klochko's personal opinions cannot be taken as typical; disenchanted enough with the Soviet system to seek political asylum in Canada the year after he was in China, he is unlikely to have shared the nationalist sentiments aroused in many of his countrymen by the dispute with Peking. But the tenor of his book suggests that he would not have mis-reported his scientific colleagues' views.
[148] Gittings, *Sino-Soviet Dispute*, p. 139.
[149] Ibid., p. 140.
[150] Grey Chou, II, pp. 245–6, 249. See also Gold Chou, p. 82.
[151] Gittings, *Sino-Soviet Dispute*, p. 140.
[152] See 'History of struggle between the two lines', *Nung-yeh Chi-hsieh Chi-shu* (Agricultural Machinery Technique), No. 9, 1968, trans. in SCMM 633, p. 25; 'A chronicle of events in the life of Liu Shao-ch'i (1899–1967)', in CB 834, p. 211.
[153] Klochko, *Soviet Scientist in Red China*, pp. 178–9.
[154] *Pa I-san Hung Wei Ping* (13 Aug. Red Guard), 17 April 1967, p. 4, cols 3–4.
[155] *Tung-fang Hung Chan Pao*, 15 June 1967, p. 3, no. 36.
[156] *Wen-ko Feng-yun*, No. 9, 1967, p. 38. A year earlier, Liu Shao-ch'i reportedly told a foreign delegation that the US aim was not war but 'seizure' of the neutral zone; *Wai-shih Hung Ch'i*, 14 June 1967, p. 2, col. 2.
[157] *Wen-ko Feng-yun*, No. 9, 1967, p. 42. This remark is dated 30 July.
[158] *The Polemic*, pp. 84, 113–14.
[159] Ibid., p. 337.
[160] Crankshaw, *New Cold War*, pp. 113–14.
[161] *Chung-kuo P'ai-k'o Nien-chien, 1981*, p. 563.
[162] William E. Griffith, 'The November 1960 Moscow meeting: a preliminary reconstruction', *CQ*, July–Sept. 1962, p. 47.
[163] Borisov & Koloskov, *Soviet-Chinese Relations*, pp. 186–7; for the number of parties at the drafting conference, see Crankshaw, *New Cold War*, p. 115.
[164] *The Polemic*, pp. 84–5; Griffith, 'The November 1960 Moscow meeting', p. 40; Crankshaw, *New Cold War*, pp. 116–17.
[165] Crankshaw, *New Cold War*, p. 120.
[166] *The Polemic*, p. 85.
[167] Crankshaw, *New Cold War*, p. 117.
[168] Griffith, 'The November 1960 Moscow meeting', p. 48, suggests that the absence of the Italian communist leader Togliatti could be attributed to his canny reluctance to be personally involved in 'so potentially hazardous an international meeting'.
[169] The facts regarding the 'defection' of Chang Fan, the husband of a sister of Liu Shao-ch'i's wife, are not totally clear. Chang Fan married Wang Kuang-p'ing in 1952 and went to study in the Soviet Union in 1955 where, in October 1960, he 'betrayed' his country. In 1962, despite representations from Peking, the Soviet authorities refused to repatriate Chang Fan and other Chinese students on the grounds that they had sought political asylum; see 'Looking at

Liu Shao-ch'i's treacherous countenance from the standpoint of Chang Fan's treason', *Ch'ien-chun-pang* (Massive Cudgel), No. 2, April 1967, trans. in JPRS 41,858, pp. 78-82.

[170] *San-fan fen-tzu Liu Shao-ch'i tsui-o shih*, p. 38. According to another source, Liu's son and daughter-in-law were first separated in 1959, as a direct consequence of Sino-Soviet tension; see *A Chronicle of Events in the Life of Liu Shao-ch'i*, trans. in CB 834, p. 19. This son, Liu Yun-pin, was the child of an early wife who was killed in the 1930s. Yun-pin and his brother and sister were sent to the Soviet Union for safety whence he returned in 1957 aged about 32. He committed suicide during the cultural revolution. See his sister's account in Liu Ai-ch'in, *Nü-er-ti Huai-nien*, pp. 18, 24 ff., 66, 92.

[171] *Na-han Chan Pao* (Outcry Combat News), Feb. 1968, trans. in SCMP 4140, pp. 4-5. Liu Yun-jo, the younger brother of Liu Yun-pin, returned to China without completing his studies; possibly his growing commitment to the Soviet Union had been realized in Peking and it was decided to recall him in case an open split between the two communist super powers found the son of the Chinese head of state aligning himself with the wrong side. At any rate, Liu Yun-jo remained a source of concern to his father; ibid., pp. 6-15. See also *HCPP*, No. 20, pp. 127-38; *Huai nien Liu Shao-ch'i T'ung-chih*, pp. 363-71. For Liu's own student days in Moscow, see ibid., pp. 83-9.

[172] *The Sino-Soviet Dispute*, p. 157; SCMP 2376, pp. 27-32; idem. 2377, pp. 3840.

[173] Crankshaw, *New Cold War*, p. 118.

[174] Ibid., pp. 119-21.

[175] Ibid., p. 122.

[176] Ibid., p. 118.

[177] Ibid., pp. 123-4.

[178] Griffith, 'The November 1960 Moscow meeting', p. 40.

[179] Ibid., pp. 43-4; Crankshaw, *New Cold War*, pp. 125-6.

[180] Crankshaw, *New Cold War*, pp. 126-7.

[181] *Ch'e-ti ch'ing-suan Teng Hsiao-p'ing fan-tang fan-she-hui-chu-i fan-Mao Tse-tung ssu-hsiang-ti t'ao-t'ien tsui-hsing* (Thoroughly expose and criticize Teng Hsiao-p'ing's monstrous anti-party, anti-socialist, anti-Mao Tse-tung Thought crimes) (Materials group of 'Red Liaison Station' and East Is Red commune of the CC's United Front Department [eds], 4 Feb. 1967), p. 7. This source does not attribute this remark specifically to either of Teng's speeches only to what he said at the conference. Another source says that Teng advocated 'humanism' (*jen-tao-chu-i*) in class struggle in his speech on 14 Nov.; *Teng Hsiao-p'ing fan-tang fan-she-hui-chu-i fan-Mao Tse-tung-ssu-hsiang-ti yen-lun chai-pien*, p. 16.

[182] *The Polemic*, p. 338. This source does not attribute the remark to Teng, only to the CCP delegation, but the congruence of this quotation with reports elsewhere (Crankshaw, *New Cold War*, pp. 128-9; Griffith, 'The November 1960 Moscow meeting', p. 44) of Teng's remarks on this topic suggests that it comes from his speech.

[183] Zagoria, *Sino-Soviet Conflict*, pp. 346-7; Crankshaw, *New Cold War*, pp. 128-9. Ch'en Yi told a foreign guest in late Sept. that only the Soviet Union could lead the bloc; see *Tung-fang Hung Chan Pao*, 15 June 1967, p. 3, no. 39.

[184] Dallin, *Diversity in International Communism*, p. 841; the date of Thorez' speech is suggested in ibid., p. 830.

[185] Ibid., p. 842.

[186] Ibid., p. 832.

[187] Griffith, 'The November 1960 Moscow meeting', p. 46.

[188] Crankshaw, *New Cold War*, pp. 131–2.

[189] Ibid., p. 113.

[190] Dallin, *Diversity in International Communism*, pp. 848–50.

[191] Ibid., p. 855.

[192] Crankshaw, *New Cold War*, p. 133.

[193] Ibid., p. 128.

[194] Ibid., pp. 132–3.

[195] Ibid., p. 133.

[196] A participant at the conference informed the present writer that one humourous interclude occurred during an impassioned attack on Khrushchev by P'eng Chen, who was sitting across the table from him. P'eng's interpreter, a Chinese, entered into the spirit of this tirade and the Russian version was delivered in the same tone as the Chinese original, until Khrushchev, with uncharacteristic mildness, asked P'eng to stop his interpreter shouting at him.

[197] Se Wu Leng-hsi's confession in *CLG*, II, No. 4, p. 78.

[198] Crankshaw, *New Cold War*, p. 134, says the CCP had the support only of the Albanian, Burmese, Malayan and Australian parties; Gittings, *Sino-Soviet Dispute*, p. 146, suggests that 'the Asian parties (except for India) leant towards the Chinese side, but the Indonesian, North Korean, and North Vietnamese delegates expressed varying degrees of neutrality, although of a pro-Chinese tinge'.

[199] *The Sino-Soviet Dispute*, p. 174.

[200] See *Origins*, I, ch. 4, for a discussion of the impact of the CPSU's 20th Congress on the CCP; for Mao's concessions in Moscow in 1957, see ch. 1 above.

[201] For the Chinese admission that they had conceded on these points, see *The Polemic*, pp. 87–8.

[202] *The Sino-Soviet Dispute*, p. 202.

[203] *CLG*, II, No. 4, p. 78.

[204] CB 34, p. 19.

[205] For the Chinese assessment of their 'victories' in the final version of the Statement, see *The Polemic*, pp. 86–7. For outside assessments of the balance struck in Moscow, see *The Sino-Soviet Dispute*, pp. 174–6 (the Statement itself is reproduced on pp. 177–205); Griffith, 'The November 1960 Moscow meeting', pp. 54–6; Zagoria, *Sino-Soviet Conflict*, pp. 343–69; Gittings, *Sino-Soviet Dispute*, pp. 145–6.

[206] The photograph that formed part of a six-page picture feature devoted to Sino-Soviet friendship in the Chinese magazine *Jen-min Hua-pao* (People's Pictorial), No. 1, 1961, is reproduced in *CQ*, Jan.–March 1961. The men portrayed are Khrushchev, Kozlov, Suslov, Mikoyan, Liu Shao-ch'i, Teng Hsiao-p'ing and P'eng Chen.

[207] *Tung-fang Hung Chan Pao*, 15 June 1967, p. 3, no. 37, p. 4, no. 41. The second of these quotes gives 14 Aug. rather than 14 Dec. as the date of Ch'en Li's speech. Unless there were two identical conferences within four months, Dec. appears to be the more likely timing.

[208] Tatu, *Power in the Kremlin*, p. 105.

[209] *CLG*, II, No. 4, pp. 78–9.

[210] In the projected third volume of this study.

[211] *The Polemic*, pp. 415–80.

Chapter 12.   The end of the leap

[1] *Mao, Miscellany*, I, p. 238.

[2] For instance the Anshan constitution; see 'The confession of Wu Leng-hsi', *CLG*, II, No. 4, pp. 77–8.

[3] See Lieberthal, pp. 154–64.

[4] Leaving aside P'eng Teh-huai and Chang Wen-T'ien, whose disgrace had excluded them from the Politburo in all but name, there were at this time 24 full and alternate members of that body.

[5] See Mao's speech to the CC's 9th plenum, *Mao, Miscellany*, II, p. 238; and 'Along the socialist or the capitalist road?', reproduced in *China Reconstructs*, Nov. 1967, p. 8, col. 1; 'Look at T'ao Chu's ugly face', *Hung Wei Pao* (Red Guard News), No. 3 (22 Jan. 1967), trans. in SCMP 3937, p. 2; 'T'ao Chu's report to higher intellectuals', *Kuang-ya Pa-san-i* (Kuang-ya 31 Aug.), April–May 1968, trans. in SCMP 4200, p. 9.

[6] *HCPP*, No. 20, pp. 182–3. For further details of Liu's complaint, which necessitated him taking sleeping pills, see ibid., pp. 214, 247–51. Liu's visit was the first paid to Hainan by a senior central leader; ibid., pp. 239–40. Chou En-lai was also ill during 1959, and spent time in hospital; see Grey Chou, II, p. 520.

[7] *HCPP*, No. 20, p. 182. For Mao's opinions on this Soviet text, see pp. 295–8 above.

[8] *HCPP*, No. 20, pp. 182–3; Hsueh Mu-ch'iao, 'Remember the great Marxist, Comrade Shao-ch'i', *HC*, No. 10, 1980, p. 9; *Huai-nien Liu Shao-ch'i t'ung-chih*, p. 375.

[9] *URI, Who's Who*, II, p. 676.

[10] Klein & Clark, *Biographic Dictionary*, p. 372. Hsueh regained his vice chairmanship of the Planning Commission while giving up his vice chairmanship of the Economic Commission in Dec. 1960; ibid.

[11] Choh-ming Li, 'China's industrial development, 1958–63', *CQ*, Jan.–March 1964, p. 36.

[12] See p. 218 above.

[13] See 'Thoroughly eradicate the black flag from economic circles, Hsueh Mu-ch'iao', *Chin Chün Pao* (Advancing Army News), 11 March 1967, pp. 2–3, for a cultural revolution version. For a post-Mao explanation of Hsueh's setback, see Ch'iu Chien, 'An economist's approach to learning—profile of China's noted economist Hsueh Mu-ch'iao', *Kuang-ming Jih-pao* 12 Feb. 1981, trans. in FBIS-CHI-81-042, p. L18. For a comparison of Hsueh's views with Ch'en Yun's, see Dorothy J. Solinger, 'Economic reform via reformulation in China: where do rightist ideas come from?', *Asian Survey*, Sept. 1981, pp. 947–60.

[14] Support for this hypothesis is provided by the fact that Hsueh's departure from the State Statistical Bureau does not appear to have resulted in a massive reorganization designed to install more pliant statisticians. Hsueh was replaced by one of his deputies, Chia Ch'i-yun, who was also denounced during the cultural revolution; URI, *Who's Who*, I, p. 130.

[15] 'Dig out the economic black line of the 30s and its backstage boss—Liu Shao-ch'i', *Wei Tung* (Defend the East), 15 June 1967, trans. in SCMP(S) 206, p. 27.

[16] *HCPP*, No. 20, p. 183. This date may be inaccurate as there is some confusion as to Liu's movements during Nov. 1959. He is also reported to have been in Shanghai on the 13th; see *Chieh-fang Jih-pao* (Liberation Daily), 17 May 1980, p. 2. If this report is accurate, presumably Liu went to Hainan thereafter; it seems unlikely that he would have broken his vacation and made the long journey north to Shanghai just to visit a factory. Liu was missing from public view from 26 Oct. to 10 Dec.

[17] *Huai-nien Liu Shao-ch'i t'ung-chih*, p. 375.

[18] *HCPP*, No. 20, pp. 247–9. Liu was persuaded to do special exercises for his complaint; ibid., pp. 250–1. He also required weekly dental treatment, which was given him by a physician on his staff; ibid., p. 248.

[19] *Liu Shao-ch'i t'ung-chih yung-ch'ui-pu-hsiu*, p. 30.

[20] *HCPP*, No. 20, pp. 208-9.

[21] Ibid., p. 183.

[22] *Mao, Miscellany*, I, p. 233.

[23] SCMP(S) 206, p. 27.

[24] Kung Hsiao-chi, 'To manage the economy requires respect for objective laws', *Ching-chi Kuan-li* (Economic Management), No. 4, 1980, p. 2.

[25] Sun Yeh-fang, 'Value theory, promote democracy, respect science', *Ching-chi Yen-chiu* (Economic Research), No. 4, 1980, pp. 7-8.

[26] See p. 180 above.

[27] *Ta-tao tang-nei tsui-ta-ti tsou tzu-pen-chu-i tao-lu tang-ch'üan-p'ai—Liu Shao-ch'i*, pp. 62-3.

[28] The available texts of Mao's comments on the Soviet *Text-book on Political Economy* give different dates for them: 1960 in *Mao Tse-tung ssu-hsiang wan sui* (1967), p. 167; and 1961-2 in idem. (1969), p. 319. Several references in the text indicate clearly that 1960 must be the date of completion of the comments. The following are culled from the translation of the texts in Mao Tse-tung, *A Critique of Soviet Economics* (hereafter cited as Mao, *Critique*): on p. 52, there is a reference to the ten years that Shanghai has been liberated, i.e. 1949-59; on p. 77, Mao states that it has been four years since concurrent promotion of industry and agriculture was proposed, which must refer to the four years from the delivery of his speech on the ten great relationships, i.e. 1956-9; in the same passage there is a comparison of the amount of steel allocated to agriculture in 1959 and 'this year' in terms which leave little doubt that 'this year' must be 1960; on p. 90, there is a reference to the leap forward bonuses of the previous two years, evidently 1958 and 1959; on p. 91, Mao discusses iron production 'from the standpoint of 1959' suggesting that is the last year for which he has figures; the same comment applies to Mao's citation of capital accumulation percentages on p. 99, where again 1959 is the last year mentioned; on p. 122, Mao talks of the 'great experiment' of the past two years, evidently the great leap forward of 1958-9.

In addition, there are a number of references which suggest that the comments were completed early in 1960, and that the writing was started in late 1959. On p. 35, Mao says 'we can look to 1960' as a promising year; on p. 88, he refers to 'last year's all-out effort to produce steel and iron' which must refer to 1958; on p. 96, he talks of Honan 'planning after 1959 and 1960' which suggests that 1959 is not yet over as he writes; on p. 117, he says 'from 1960 on we will still have to work intensively for thirteen years' (i.e. the last three years of the current FYP, 1960-2, and two further FYPs), which suggests that he is writing before 1960 has begun, or not long after it has started.

Finally, it is inconceivable that Mao would have written about China's industrial prospects in the generally sanguine manner which characterizes this work had the withdrawal of Soviet experts begun, and equally inconceivable that he would have failed to mention that event. Thus these comments were almost certainly completed by mid-July 1960, and probably much earlier.

The third edition of the *Text-book on Political Economy* was published in a Chinese translation in Jan. 1959; see the review article by Li Yun in *HC*, No. 15, 1959, pp. 36-41, trans. in ECMM 183, pp. 13-19.

[29] See for instance, Mao, *Critique*, pp. 37, 38-9, 40-2, 48-50, 105.

[30] Ibid., p. 122. See also pp. 48, 90, 94-5, 97-8, 100-101, 107.

[31] Ibid., pp. 55-6, 57-8.

[32] Ibid., p. 80.

[33] Ibid., pp. 81-2.

[34] Ibid., p. 126.

[35] Ibid., pp. 52–3.

[36] Ibid., p. 87.

[37] Ibid., p. 119.

[38] Ibid., pp. 93–4.

[39] Ibid., pp. 95–6; see also p. 79.

[40] Ibid., p. 79.

[41] Ibid., p. 112; see also pp. 67, 70, 82–6, 98–9.

[42] Ibid., p. 75.

[43] Cf. ibid. and *Mao, Miscellany*, I, p. 172.

[44] Mao, *Critique*, pp. 51, 55, 66.

[45] Ibid., p. 88.

[46] Ibid., pp. 97–9.

[47] Ibid., pp. 102–4.

[48] Ibid., pp. 126–7.

[49] Ma Yin-ch'u, 'My philosophical thinking and economic theory', *Hsin Chien-she* (New Construction), No. 11, 7 Nov. 1959, trans. in ECMM 195, p. 43. It was generally assumed at the time that the 'good friend' referred to in the final paragraph of Ma's article (ibid., p. 46) was Chou En-lai. See also Ma Yin-ch'u, 'I repeat my request', *Hsin Chien-she*, No. 1 (7 Jan. 1960), trans. in ECMM 201, p. 15.

[50] See various articles trans. in ECMM 201, pp. 1–10, 16–19; idem. 208, pp. 1–14; SCMM 213, pp. 24–36; idem. 214, pp. 1–10.

[51] Ma's ten-year tenure of the presidency of Peking University ended on 28 March 1960; see SCMP 2244, p. 1. See also *HHYP*, No. 9, 1979, p. 71.

[52] *Mao Tse-tung ssu-hsiang wan sui* (1967), p. 252; idem. (1969), p. 319.

[53] CB 891, pp. 32–3.

[54] *Mao, Miscellany*, I, p. 171.

[55] T'an Chen-lin, 'On certain problems to do with realising the mechanisation of our country's agriculture', *HC*, No. 6, 1960, p. 3.

[56] URI, *Who's Who*, I, p. 77. For Ch'en Cheng-jen's importance to Mao during the 1955 collectivization campaign, see *Origins*, I, p. 18.

[57] Po I-po, 'Struggle for the speedy realisation of the great duty of technically transforming agriculture', *HC*, No. 20, 1959, pp. 24–5. According to cultural revolution sources, Po described Mao's assertion that the fundamental way out for agriculture lay in mechanization as 'incomplete'; see 'Completely settle the heinous crimes of China's Khrushchev in undermining agricultural mechanisation', *Nung-yeh Chi-chieh Chi-shu* (Agricultural Machinery Technique), No. 5 (8 Aug. 1967), trans. in SCMM 610, p. 18. However there is no hint of any disagreement in this Po article; and doubtless Mao, too, would have described mechanization as incomplete without his own 'eight character constitution'.

[58] See p. 149 above; Hsu Hsin-hsueh, 'High speed and proportionate development of the national economy', *HC*, No. 3, 1960, trans. in ECMM 203, p. 2.

[59] T'an Chen-lin, 'On certain problems', p. 4.

[60] Ibid., p. 3.

[61] Ch'en Cheng-jen, 'Speed up the technical transformation of agriculture', *HC*, No. 4, 1960, p. 6.

[62] Li Fu-ch'un, 'Greeting the new forward leap in 1960', *JMJP*, 1 Jan. 1960, trans. in SCMP 2172, pp. 2–11. The phrase 'right opportunism' largely disappears from the articles of major central and provincial leaders in 1960. Li and others referred instead to 'right deviation' (*yu-ch'ing*); ibid., p. 2. In his speech to the 1960 NPC, Li referred to right opportunists in the context of 1959, not as a continuing concern; CB 615, p. 7.

[63] SCMP 2172, pp. 7-8.

[64] Ibid., pp. 6-7.

[65] Ibid., pp. 2-3. *JMJP*, 31 March 1960 (CB 615, p. 39), reported that a supplementary plan for the last three years of the 2nd FYP was in preparation; none was ever issued. For the 1959 plan communiqué issued on 21 Jan. 1960, see SCMP 2186, pp. 1-8.

[66] See *Origins*, I, p. 124.

[67] SCMP 2172, p. 3.

[68] Ibid., pp. 10-11.

[69] Trans. in Hsu, *Literature of the People's Republic of China*, p. 515.

[70] Ibid., p. 513.

[71] Wu Chih-p'u, 'Consolidation and development of people's communes', *HC*, No. 1, 1960, trans. in ECMM 197, p. 1.

[72] Ibid., p. 3.

[73] According to Liu Shao-ch'i, quoted in Chi Ch'un-yi, 'The people's commune is a great creation of the popular masses of China', *HC*, No. 5, 1960, trans. in ECMM 210, p. 19. It is possible that the two figures are not strictly comparable since Wu's percentage may not include income from private plots, whereas Chi's presumably does. However, the comparison is still relevant, since income from private plots was probably squeezed as a result of post-Lushan militancy.

[74] Wu chih-p'u, 'Consolidation and development of people's communes', p. 5.

[75] Wang Wen-shih, 'The new production brigade leader', trans. in Hsu, *Literature of the People's Republic of China*, p. 481.

[76] *Facts about Liu Chien-hsun's crimes—anti-party, anti-socialist element, counter-revolutionary double-dealer*, 12 March 1967, trans. in SCMM(S) 32, p. 16. Ironically, Wu Chih-p'u and Liu Chien-hsun were both denounced as capitalist roaders during the cultural revolution.

[77] 'Comrade Shao-ch'i, the people of Honan remember you', *JMJP*, 21 May 1980, p. 2, col. 2. TLC, p. 55.

[78] *JMJP*, 21 May 1980, p. 2, col. 3.

[79] SCMP 4200, p. 9.

[80] Klochko, *Soviet Scientist in Red China*, p. 159.

[81] White Chou, III, p. 85; Grey Chou, II, p. 442.

[82] *HCPP*, No. 20, p. 202.

[83] 'A history of crimes of opposing the party, socialism and the Thought of Mao Tse-tung—Liu Shao-ch'i's true counter-revolutionary revisionist face as seen from his activities in Tientsin after Liberation', *8.13 Hung Wei-ping* (13 Aug. Red Guard), 13 May 1967, trans. in SCMM 588, p. 19.

[84] *HCPP*, No. 20, pp. 196-7. During the cultural revolution it was alleged that Liu on his tours—and he made a number of provincial visits during the first half of 1960—lived lavishly (SCMM 588, p. 19; SCMM(S) 22, p. 23). Such accounts may have been fabricated to blacken his reputation for austerity, but it is of course possible that local officials 'killed the fatted calf' in order to impress their distinguished visitor and that Liu felt unable simply to boycott such banquets. For some of Liu's visits, see 'Emperor Liu and concubine (of the first rank) Wang visit Changpakou', *Tou-p'i-kai* (Struggle-criticism-transformation), 15 May 1967, trans. in SCMM(S) 22, p. 23 (Shensi; April); 'Comrade Shao-ch'i, the people of Honan remember you', *JMJP*, 21 May 1980 (Honan, April); 'The crimes of Liu Shao-ch'i, Teng Hsiao-p'ing, and Li Ching-ch'üan at the Chengtu Tool Plant', *Erh-ch'i Chan Pao* (7 Feb. Combat News), 25 July 1967, cols 2-3 (Szechwan; May); 'Comrade Shao-ch'i, Shanghai's workers remember you', *Chieh-fang Jih-pao*, 17 May 1980 (Shanghai, May).

[85] See Li Fu-ch'un's speech to the NPC in CB 615, p. 14.

[86] See the new version, T'an Chen-lin's commentary on it and the subsequent *JMJP* editorial in CB 616.

[87] D. E. T. Luard, 'The urban communes', *CQ*, July–Sept. 1960, pp. 74–9.

[88] Quoted in '"Red Flag"—A city people's commune', *China Recontructs*, July 1960, reproduced in SCMM 218, p. 35. This article conveys well the way in which propagandists attempted to recreate in the cities the atmosphere in the countryside in the late summer of 1958.

[89] *Liao Lien Chan Po* (Liaoning Alliance Combat News), 21 July 1967, p. 3, cols 2–3; *Mao, Miscellany*, I, p. 230.

[90] *CLG*, I, No. 4, p. 69.

[91] 'Forty charges against Po I-po', *Hung-wei-ping Pao* (Red Guard News), 22 Feb. 1967, trans. in CB 878, p. 16; I have modified the translation.

[92] 'Down with "three-anti" element and big renegade Po I-po, sinister despot on the industrial and communications front!', *Tung-fang Hung* (East Is Red), 15 Feb. 1967, trans. in CB 878, p. 7. While the object of these Red Guard attacks on Po was to divert blame from Mao to him for the economic setbacks caused by the 1960 leap, there is no reason to doubt that Po deliberately adapted himself to the post-Lushan mood, if only for reasons of survival.

[93] See the translation of his speech to the NPC in CB 618, pp. 12–15.

[94] Ibid., pp. 16–18.

[95] Ibid., p. 17. Wang Ho-shou's continued 'leftism' on steel may have harmed him; he was far less visible after this speech (Klein & Clark, *Biographic Dictionary*).

[96] *Mao Tse-tung ssu-hsiang wan sui* (1967), p. 249; *Mao, Miscellany*, I, p. 230, where the Soviet steel works is incorrectly titled 'Marx' instead of Magnitogorsk.

[97] 'Chinese press condemns revisionist economic line', NCNA, 25 Aug. 1967, in SCMP 4012, p. 17; 'Smash "70 articles for industry", a revisionist black programme', *Yu-tien Chan Pao* (Post and Telecommunications Combat News), 28 June 1967, trans. in SCMP(S) 210, p. 27

[98] The precise date of Mao's comment is given in *PR*, No. 16, 1970, p. 3.

[99] *Mao Tse-tung ssu-hsiang wan sui* (1967), p. 249

[100] *Mao, Critique*, p. 124.

[101] See for instance SCMP(S) 27, pp. 27–31. Allegedly the Geology Ministry ignored the charter, its party secretary saying: 'This is the business of the Anshan Steel Works and has nothing to do with our geological contingents.' But presumably this had more to do with the ministry's lack of factories than the party secretary's revisionism. See 'Seven crimes committed by counter-revolutionary revisionist Ho Ch'ang-kung', *K'o Chi Hung Ch'i* (Science and Technology Red Flag), 11 March 1967, trans. in SCMP(S) 186, p. 27.

[102] *CLG*, II, No. 4, p. 77. For the identification of this conference as one on the machine industry, see note 106 below.

[103] T'ao Chu, 'Several questions of leadership over factories, mines and enterprises', *HC*, No. 12, 1960, trans. in SCMM 218, pp. 7–12.

[104] Ch'en Shou-chung, 'The diversified enterprises in the Paotow Iron and Steel Company, *HC*, No. 17, 1960, pp. 34–5.

[105] *WWAR*, pp. 13–14.

[106] The identification of the conference is provided in a number of sources, see for instance *Liu Shao-ch'i fan-ko-ming tsui-o shih*, p. 36, and 'The black record of quotations from the counter-revolutionary revisionist Liu Shao-ch'i', *Chin Chün Pao* (Advancing Army News), 16 April 1967, trans. in JPRS 41,889, p. 60. The date of Liu's remark is provided, as far as I can establish, only in the latter source. I have assumed that this conference is the same June Shanghai conference at which Teng Hsiao-p'ing and Wu Leng-hsi discussed the Anshan constitution, since it also related to industrial management. It would

seem likely that the May Shanghai conference on foreign affairs (Lieberthal, p. 159) spilled over into June, and that some of the conferees decided to hold an on-the-spot conference on industrial matters since they were in China's premier industrial city. (An on-the-spot conference is one held at a factory, commune or other organization at which the particular successes or failures peculiar to that unit are discussed with a view to promoting or preventing them elsewhere.)

[107] 'T'an Chen-lin's crime of sabotage against farm mechanization must be reckoned with', *Nung-yeh Chi-hsieh Chi-shu*, No. 6, 1968, trans. in SCMM 624, p. 6; 'Expose a big plot for capitalist restoration', WHP, 29 April 1967, trans. in SCMP(S) 187, p. 7. Liu appears to have raised the trust issue again in 1963 and initiated experiments in 1964.

[108] *Liu Shao-ch'i fan-ko-ming tsui-o shih*, p. 36.

[109] Mao's directive is quoted in Ch'en Shou-chung, 'The diversified enterprises', *HC*, No. 17, 1960, p. 31.

[110] Ibid., p. 31 ff.

[111] SCMP(S) 187, pp. 8–10.

[112] *Origins*, I, pp. 19–25.

[113] See *Liu Shao-ch'i's crimes in carrying out the capitulationist line for transforming the capitalists at the People's Commercial Centre*, June 1967, trans. in SCMM 619, pp. 50, 52. On p. 50, there are two references to Mao. First, there is a reference to 'Chariman Mao's instructions' on the handling of capitalists. Secondly, it is said that 'they wantonly distorted Chairman Mao's great instructions, talked only about "relaxation" but not about "strain" when dealing with the capitalists. . .' (the 'they' in the quotation refers to Tientsin officials acting in line with Liu's ideas). The giveaway in this comment is the admission that Mao, too, spoke of 'relaxation'. Moreover, it was not the case that Liu did not talk about problems in the relationship between the CCP and capitalists. The second reference is a quotation from a report on handling capitalists prepared by the appropriate CCP committee in Tientsin. The report includes the sentence: 'Hearing the guiding remarks of Manager Li, the novel ideas of Manager Wang, and the comments of the party *and the chairman*, the industrialists and businessmen are boundlessly happy' (emphasis added). Again it is the reference to the chairman, i.e. Mao, which is crucial; had he been opposed to the policy or silent about it even, the happiness of the Tientsin would certainly have known bounds!

[114] See *Origins*, I, Pts 3 and 4 *passim*, but especially pp. 285, 289.

[115] Li Wei-han, 'Comrade Liu Shao-ch'i's guidance on United Front work', *JMJP*, 10 May 1980, trans. in JPRS 75,872, p. 43.

[116] SCMP 2086, pp. 1–2.

[117] Ibid., 2100, pp. 1–2. The only difference in topics was the addition of a discussion of pardons for criminals to mark the revolution's tenth anniversary.

[118] *Ta-tao tang-nei tsui-ta-ti tsou tzu-pen-chu-i tao-lu tang-ch'üan-p'ai—Liu Shao-ch'i*, pp. 62–3.

[119] See *Mao, Miscellany*, I, p. 229; 'Chronology of important events in the struggle between the two lines in the field of higher education', *Chiao-hsueh P'i-p'an* (Criticism and Repudiation of Pedagogics), No. 2, 1967, trans. in SCMM(S) 18, p. 16.

[120] See the NCNA report in SCMP 2213, p. 1.

[121] Li Wei-han, 'Comrade Liu Shao-ch'i's guidance', p. 43.

[122] Ibid., p. 42.

[123] *Pa Pa Chan Pao* (8 Aug. Combat News), 21 April 1967, p. 8, col. 2. This source dates the Politburo conference as taking place in January. Perhaps a January conference spilled over into February, or perhaps this source is wrong.

[124] Li Wei-han, 'Comrade Liu Shao-ch'i's guidance', p. 43. During the cultural revolution, the date of this reception was sometimes given as 2 Feb., sometimes as 20 Feb. Texts of the speech are available in Liu, *Fourth Collection*, pp. 71–4, and *Liu Shao-ch'i ts'ai-liao hui-pien* (1st collection), pp. 114–18.

[125] Li Wei-han, 'Comrade Liu Shao-ch'i's guidance', p. 42.

[126] See MacFarquhar, *Hundred Flowers*, pp. 197–200.

[127] Liu, *Fourth Collection*, p. 71.

[128] Ibid.

[129] Ibid., p. 72.

[130] Ibid., pp. 72, 74.

[131] Ibid., pp. 72–3. Liu had taken a similar line in conversation with his brother-in-law's family a few days earlier; see *Liu Shao-ch'i ts'ai-liao hui-pien* (1st collection), pp. 110–11. There seems little doubt that this was a basic tenet of Liu's personal philosophy, based on his assessment of the course of his own career; see *Origins*, I, pp. 5–6.

[132] *Pa Pa Chan Pao*, 21 April 1967, p. 4, col. 2.

[133] *Liu Shao-ch'i ts'ai-liao hui-pien* (1st collection), p. 111.

[134] See the CDNCA/ACFIC plan of work in SCMP 2213, pp. 4–12; and the activities generated in Tientsin, in SCMM 619, pp. 47–59.

[135] SCMP 2213, p. 3.

[136] 'Chronology of the two-road struggle on the educational front in the past 17 years', *Chiao-yü ko-ming* (Educational Revolution), 6 May 1967, trans. in JPRS 41,932, p. 31.

[137] *Lu Ting-yi fan-tui Mao Tse-tung ssu-hsiang t'ui-hsiang hsiu-cheng-chu-i chiao-yü lu-hsien yen-lun* (Excerpts from Lu Ting-yi's speeches opposing Mao Tse-tung Thought but promoting the revisionist educational line) (Peking: Capital Liaison Committee for Criticising the Reactionary Academic 'Authority' of the Bourgeois Class, May 1967), p. 17.

[138] Ibid., p. 21.

[139] Ibid., p. 20.

[140] JPRS 41,932, p. 32.

[141] *Lu Ting-yi fan-tui Mao Tse-tung ssu-hsiang*, p. 21.

[142] The ensuing discussion draws upon Robert D. Barendsen, 'The 1960 educational reforms', *CQ*, Oct.–Dec. 1960, pp. 55–65.

[143] Quoted ibid., p. 60.

[144] Quoted ibid., p. 59.

[145] Ibid., p. 56.

[146] *San-fan fen-tzu Liu Shao-ch'i tsui-o shih*, p. 36.

[147] *Lu Ting-yi fan-tui Mao Tse-tung ssu-hsiang*, p. 20.

[148] Barendsen, 'The 1960 educational reforms', p. 58. The texts of the speeches of Lu Ting-yi and Yang Hsiu-feng to the 1960 NPC are trans. in CB 623, pp. 1–19.

[149] *Chung-kuo Ch'ing-nien Pao* (China Youth News), 16 Aug. 1966, trans. in SCMP 3772, pp. 11–12.

[150] Klochko, *Soviet Scientist in Red China*, pp. 130–1.

[151] Ibid., p. 138.

[152] *Ch'üan Wu-ti* (Completely Matchless), 20 June 1967, p. 2, col. 3.

[153] Klochko, *Soviet Scientist in Red China*, p. 153.

[154] Ibid., p. 135.

[155] Ibid., pp. 157–8.

[156] Ibid., p. 176.

[157] JPRS 41,932, p. 26; SCMM(S) 18, p. 16.

[158] *Origins*, I, pp. 100–101, 105.

[159] *How Vicious They Are!* trans. in SCMP(S) 208, p. 3; *Chin Chün Pao*, 26 March 1967, p. 4, col. 1.

[160] 'Record of Hu Yao-pang's crimes against the Thought of Mao Tse-tung', *Ch'ing-nien Chan-hsien* (Youth Battle Front), 1 June 1967, trans. in SCMP(S) 194, p. 30.

[161] 'Liu Shao-ch'i counter-revolutionary revisionist utterances on culture and art', *Hung-se Hsuan-ch'uan Ping* (Red Propaganda Soldier), 10 May 1967, trans. in SCMP(S) 205, p. 34.

[162] *Ch'üan Wu-ti*, 26 June 1967, p. 2, col. 3.

[163] *P'i T'an Chan Pao* (Criticise T'an Combat News), 5 Aug. 1967, p. 2, col. 2.

[164] Chuang Chia-fu, 'Arm our own heads with Mao Tse-tung's Thought', *JMJP*, 15 May 1966, trans. in SCMP 3707, pp. 6–9.

[165] *Wai Shih Hung Ch'i* (Foreign Affairs Red Flag), 14 June 1967, p. 4, col. 3.

[166] *Counter-revolutionary revisionist P'eng Chen's towering crimes of opposing the party, socialism and the Thought of Mao Tse-tung*, 10 June 1967, trans. in SCMM 639, pp. 1–2; *P'eng Chen fan-ko-ming hsiu-cheng-chu-i yen-lun chai-pien* (Selection of P'eng Chen's counter-revolutionary revisionist utterances) (1st collection), May 1967, p. 4; 'Wipe out the counter-revolutionary revisionist clique of the old Peking municipal committee headed by P'eng Chen', *Chingkangshan* and *Chin Chün Pao*, 20 April 1967, trans. in JPRS 41,858, p. 94. See also *Hsin Pei-ta* (New Peking University), 22 April 1967, p. 4; *Pei-ching Kung-Jen* (Peking Worker), 27 May 1967, p. 4, col. 1; *Pei-ching Jih-pao* (Peking Daily), 10 June 1967, p. 8, col. 3.

[167] *Lu Ting-yi fan-tui Mao Tse-tung ssu-hsiang*, pp. 2, 3.

[168] Yang Hsien-chen, 'The encourager and overseer of the construction of the party school—remembering Comrade Shao-ch'i', *HC*, No. 7, 1980, p. 21. K'ang Sheng is referred to in this article only by the sarcastic epithet 'the authority on theory' (*li-lun ch'üan-wei*) because he had not yet been publicly denounced.

[169] Ibid., p. 22. See also idem. No. 18, 1980, p. 23 ff.

[170] *San-fan fen-tzu Liu Shao-ch'i tsui-o shih*, p. 37. When Yang Hsien-chen had to self-criticize in Dec. 1959, he claimed that his erroneous utterances were based on what he had heard from P'eng Chen and others; SCMM 639, p. 9. For K'ang Sheng's 1958 dictum, see 'Some ways in which Mao Tse-tung Thought was presented during the past 40 years', *HC*, No. 2, 1981, trans. in FBIS-CHI-81-030, p. L13.

[171] See *Tung-fang Hung Chan Pao*, 15 June 1967, p. 5, nos 58, 63; *K'o Chi Chan Pao* (Science and Technology Combat News), 22 May 1967, p. 6, no. 44; SCMP 3933, p. 8, no. 34; SCMM(S) 18, p. 16.

[172] 'The towering crimes of counter-revolutionary double-dealer Chao I-ya', *Hsin Jen Ta* (New People's University), 21 Sept. 1967, trans. in SCMP(S) 221, p. 31. For the 'three-eight style', see Gittings, *The Role of the Chinese Army*, p. 102.

[173] See his speech at the closing session of the national militia conference, trans. in SCMP 2252, pp. 16–18.

[174] SCMM 602, p. 8.

[175] NCNA, 8 Oct. 1960, trans. in SCMP 2358, pp. 1–3.

[176] *Ch'e-ti ch'ing-suan Teng Hsiao-p'ing fan-tang, fan-she-hui-chu-i, fan-Mao Tse-tung ssu-hsiang-ti t'ao-tien tsui-hsing*, p. 2.

[177] 'Dossiers of Lu Ting-yi', trans. in SCMM(S) 27, p. 45. During the cultural revolution, a curious story was retailed about Mme Lu Ting-yi writing anonymous poison-pen letters to Lin Piao's family. The truth of this allegation and its political significance are hard to assess. See 'Exposing and accusing Lu Ting-yi and his wife—counter-revolutionary Yen Wei Ping—who have com-

mitted the counter-revolutionary crime of ruthlessly persecuting Comrade Lin Piao and his family', *Chan Pao* (Combat News), 18 Jan. 1967, trans. in SCMP(S) 165, p. 12.

[178] The article is trans. in *PR*, No. 41, 1960, pp. 6−15.

[179] Ibid., p. 15.

[180] See the articles on Mao's fourth volume translated in CB 641, 643. For an orthodox version, see Li Wei-han's speech to the non-communist parties on 14 Aug. 1960, trans. in CB 639, pp. 9−31.

[181] 'Big military competition is big exposure of Lo Jui-ch'ing's plot to usurp army leadership and oppose the party', *JMJP*, 28 Aug. 1967, trans. in SCMP 4022, p. 2.

[182] NCNA report in *JMJP*, 29 Dec. 1960, reproduced in *JMST*, 1961, p. 273.

[183] Ku Cho-hsin et al., 'Comrade Li Fu-ch'un's great contribution to economic planning work', *JMJP*, 22 May 1980.

[184] Grey Chou, III, p. 19.

[185] *Pei-ching Kung-she*, 26 May 1967, p. 3, col. 3.

[186] *Liao Lien Chan Pao*, 12 July 1967, p. 4, col. 1.

[187] Grey Chou, III, p. 19; *Ching-chi Yen-chiu* (Economic Research), No. 5, 1980, pp. 6−7; Gold Chou, p. 70.

[188] *Mao, Miscellany*, I, p. 232

[189] See the refugee report in *URS*, Vol. 28, pp. 198−200.

[190] *Kuan-yü T'an Chen-lin wen-t'i-ti ch'u-pu tsung-ho ts'ai-liao* (A preliminary collection of material on the problem of T'an Chen-lin), 6 April 1967, p. 8.

[191] Lin Tian, 'Inquire into the question of the system of the people's communes', *Ching-chi Kuan-li* (Economic Management), No. 1, 1981, trans. in FBIS-CHI-81-048, p. L20−21.

[192] The directive was never published but copies filtered out to Hong Kong and Taiwan; see for instance *URS*, Vol. 28, pp. 200−201. Lin Tian, 'Inquire into the system of the people's communes', appears to believe that the 12-point directive made the team the basic unit, but this is not the case.

Conclusions

[1] This is the way the world ends
Not with a bang but a whimper.
T. S. Eliot, 'The Hollow Men'

[2] 'Quarterly chronicle and documentation', *CQ*, April−June 1961, p. 183.

[3] CB 644, p. 1.

[4] Yang Jianbai & Li Xuezeng, 'The relations between agriculture, light industry and heavy industry in China', *SSIC*, No. 2, 1980, p. 190.

[5] Liu Guoguang & Wang Xiangming, 'A study of the speed and balance of China's economic development', *SSIC*, No. 4, 1980, p. 23.

[6] Yang & Li, 'The relations between agriculture, light industry and heavy industry', p. 190.

[7] *Ching-chi Yen-chiu*, No. 5, 1980, p. 4.

[8] Liu & Wang, 'A study of the speed and balance of China's economic development', p. 26.

[9] Lo Keng-mo, 'Analysis of the formation of China's planned economy and its course of development', *Ching-chi Yen-chiu*, No. 2, 1981, trans. in JPRS 77,793, p. 9. (I have modified the grammar.)

[10] Feng Pao-hsing, Wang Hsin & Chang Ta-chien, 'The necessity of giving priority development to light industry for a certain period of time', *Ching-chi Yen-chiu*, No. 1, 1980, p. 20.

[11] Liu & Wang, 'A study of the speed and balance of China's economic development', p. 29.

[12] Yang & Li, 'The relations between agriculture, light industry and heavy industry', p. 191.

[13] These figures are put together from ibid., pp. 195, 196.

[14] Ibid., p. 196; Lo Keng-mo, 'Analysis of the formation of China's planned economy', p. 7; TLC, p. 53.

[15] Lo Keng-mo, 'Analysis of the formation of China's planned economy', p. 7.

[16] Compiled from K. R. Walker, 'Chinese grain production statistics: a comment on Kang Chao's research note', CQ, April–June 1980, pp. 342–3; Kang Chao, 'The China watchers tested', CQ, Jan.–March 1980, p. 102; Chung-kuo Nung-yeh Nien-chien (Chinese Agricultural Yearbook), 1980, p. 34. See also Hsueh Mu-ch'iao, Tang-ch'ien Wo Kuo Ching-chi Jo-kan Wen-t'i, p. 14.

[17] Ching-chi Yen-chiu, No. 1, 1980, pp. 24–5.

[18] Yang & Li, 'The relations between agriculture, light industry and heavy industry', p. 193.

[19] Ibid., p. 207.

[20] The following quotations are taken from Cheng, The Politics of the Chinese Red Army, p. 13. The soldiers may have been misinformed but their perceptions are almost as important as the truth in assessing the political impact of the crisis.

[21] SCMM 578, p. 28.

[22] Ching-chi Kuan-li, No. 2, 1981, p. 3; Jen-k'ou Li-lun Kai-shuo (Honan, 1981), p. 83; I am indebted to John Aird for the estimates of population loss.

[23] Hsueh Mu-ch'iao, 'Speech at the First Sino-Japanese Meeting for the Exchange of Economic Knowledge', trans. in FBIS-CHI-81-123, p. K5.

[24] Sun Yeh-fang, 'Speech', trans. in FBIS-CHI-81-143, p. K12.

[25] Lo Keng-mo, 'Analysis of the formation of China's planned economy', p. 10,

[26] Cheng, The Politics of the Chinese Red Army, p. 459.

[27] Po I-po, 'Respect and remembrance—marking the 60th anniversary of the founding of the CCP', HC, No. 13, 1981, trans. in FBIS-CHI-81-145, p. K34.

[28] For the estimated loss, see TLC, p. 25; for the 1st FYP capital construction investment figure, see PR, No. 16, 1959, p. 28; for the comparison of the 1st and 2nd FYPs, see Ching-chi Yen-chiu, No. 1, 1980, pp. 24–5.

[29] PR, No. 27, p. 19.

[30] T'an Chen-lin, 'Advance from victory to victory under the firm leadership of the party central committee—commemorating the 60th anniversary of the CCP', HC, No. 13, 1981, trans. in FBIS-CHI-81-147, p. K15.

[31] Po I-po, 'Respect and remembrance', p. K33.

[32] PR, No. 27, p. 19.

[33] Lo Keng-mo, 'Analysis of the formation of China's planned economy', p. 8.

[34] Po I-po, 'Respect and remembrance', p. K32.

[35] Yang & Li, 'The relations between agriculture, light industry and heavy industry', p. 203.

[36] HHYP—WCP, No. 2, 1980, pp. 66–9.

[37] See the memorial article on Chia T'o-fu, in 1956 the Minister of Light Industry, in HHYP, No. 7, 1980, p. 60, col. 2.

[38] TLC, pp. 76–7.

[39] Lo Keng-mo, 'Analysis of the formation of China's planned economy', p. 7.

[40] They shall be nameless.

[41] This is hinted at in Mao, Critique, pp. 121–2, 124.

[42] See Richard H. Solomon, Mao's Revolution and the Chinese Political Culture.

[43] Po I-po, 'Respect and remembrance', p. K34.

[44] Ibid.

[45] *Mao, Miscellany*, I, p. 231.
[46] See *Origins*, I, pp. 270–92.
[47] Po I-po, 'Respect and remembrance', p. K34.

BIBLIOGRAPHICAL NOTE

In the Bibliographical and Methodological Note in volume I, I pointed out that the basic primary material for it was of two types: the contemporary record, reflecting events as seen by Chinese at the time; and the cultural revolution material, the main purpose of which was to denigrate disgraced leaders and thus had to be used with particular care.

Since the death of Mao and the purge of the 'gang of four' in the autumn of 1976, a third type of material has appeared, condemnatory of the cultural revolution and intended to set straight the record distorted by the cultural revolutionaries. This material is also *parti pris*, but, with the qualifications mentioned below, does not appear to be distorted in the manner of the items purveyed by the Red Guard newspapers. It takes a number of forms. The earliest consisted of heavily hagiographical collections of articles, mainly about Mao and Chou En-lai. Even these collections contain important insights and nuggets of valuable information.

A second, more abundant and more useful, set of publications began to appear after the 3rd plenum of the 11th Central Committee in December 1958, when Teng Hsiao-p'ing became the dominant figure in the post-Mao leadership. A far more determined and thorough effort was now begun to rehabilitate all party officials persecuted unjustly during the cultural revolution. In the case of officials now dead, this took the form of articles or collections of articles, and while they again leaned towards the hagiographical, the books that were produced were more informative that the earlier ones on Mao and Chou. In some cases, texts of hitherto unknown speeches and articles were published. Some of these items were intended for circulation only within China, but copies eventually become available in the West. At the same time, China's economists were unleashed and they proceeded to recount the mistakes of the past in great detail; much of their analysis dealt with the great leap forward. Thus, when examining a book produced in China in recent years, it is crucial to turn to the back to see if it was published after December 1978.

The other crucial date for evaluating the likely political thrust of post-cultural revolution material is May 1980, the month in which Liu Shao-ch'i was finally rehabilitated. Until that time it was possible for books rehabilitating other leaders to treat Liu, where he figured in the story, in the manner of the cultural revolutionaries. After that date it was in principle possible for the whole record to be set straight. The next stage will be reached if and when it is possible to publish material which treats cultural revolutionaries, for instance Lin Piao, as Mao has now been treated, i.e. as men who contributed much to the revolution but were guilty of great mistakes. Also unavailable still are the official minutes of important meetings.

What is the effect of the new materials? Clearly devastating for anyone who may have swallowed whole the version of history purveyed during the cultural revolution. More importantly, it restores light and shade to the uniformly black-and-white picture depicted by the cultural revolutionaries, a dichotomy which some observers accepted even when their sympathies were with the victims. In the Introduction to volume I, I asserted that the interaction of the Chinese leadership during the period 1956–65 was complex. The new material underlines that complexity, but facilitates its delineation.

BIBLIOGRAPHY

AHN BYUNG-JOON. *Chinese Politics and the Cultural Revolution*. Seattle: University of Washington, 1976.

American Foreign Policy: Current Documents, 1958. Washington, D.C.: Department of State, 1962.

ANDORS, STEPHEN. *China's Industrial Revolution: Politics, Planning, and Management, 1949 to the Present*. London: Martin Robertson, 1977.

BARNETT, A. DOAK. *Cadres, Bureaucracy and Political Power in Communist China*. New York: Columbia University Press, 1967.

BONAVIA, DAVID. *The Chinese*. New York: Lippincott & Crowell, 1980.

BOORMAN, HOWARD L. *Biographical Dictionary of Republican China*, I–IV. New York: Columbia University Press, 1967–71.

BORISOV, O. B. & B. T. KOLOSKOV. *Soviet-Chinese Relations, 1945–1970*. Bloomington: Indiana University Press, 1975.

BRZEZINSKI, ZBIGNIEW K. *The Soviet Bloc: Unity and Conflict*. Cambridge, Mass.: Harvard University Press, rev. & enlarged ed., 1967.

CHANDRASEKHAR, S. *Communist China Today*. London: Asia Publishing House, 1961.

CHANG, PARRIS, H. *Power and Policy in China*. University Park: Pennsylvania State University Press, 1975.

CHANG WANG-SHAN. *The State Council in Communist China: A Structural and Functional Analysis, 1954–65*. New York: Columbia University, unpubl. MA thesis.

CHAO KANG. *Agricultural Production in Communist China*. Madison: University of Wisconsin Press, 1970.

CH'EN, JEROME. *Mao and the Chinese Revolution*. London: Oxford University Press, 1965.

—— ed. *Mao Papers: Anthology and Bibliography*. London: Oxford University Press, 1970.

Ch'en Yi Shih-tz'u Hsuan-chi (The Selected Poems of Ch'en Yi). Peking: Jen-min Ch'u-pan She, 1977.

CH'EN YUN: *some major sources*

    Ch'en Yun T'ung-chih Wen-kao Hsuan-pien, 1956–62 (A Selection of Comrade Ch'en Yun's Manuscripts). Kwangtung Jen-min Ch'u-pan She, 1981.

    TENG LI-CH'ÜN. *Hsiang Ch'en Yun T'ung-chih Hsueh-hsi Tso Ching-chi Kung-tso* (Study Comrade Ch'en Yun's Way of Doing Economic

Work). Peking: Chung Kung Chung-yang Tang Chiao Ch'u-pan She, 1981.

CHI CH'AO-TING. *Key Economic Areas in Chinese History*. New York: Paragon, 1963.

CHIN CHEN-LIN. *Mao An-ying*. Shanghai: Jen-min Ch'u-pan She, 1980.

Chinese Communist Who's Who. Taipei: Institute of International Relations, 1970.

CHOU EN-LAI: *some major sources*

　Ching-ai-ti Chou Tsung-li Wo-men Yung-yuan Huai-nien Ni (Beloved Premier Chou, We Will Always Remember You). Peking: Jen-min Ch'u-pan She, 1977. (White Chou)

　Cheng-jung Sui-yueh (Eventful Years). Tientsin: Jen-min Ch'u-pan She, 1977.

　CHOU EN-LAI. *Kuan-yü Wen-yi Kung-tso-ti San-tz'u Chiang-hua* (Three Speeches on Literary and Art Work). Peking: Jen-min Ch'u-pan She, 1979.

　Chou En-lai Tsung-li Pa-shih Tan-ch'en Chi-nien Shih Wen Hsuan (A Collection of Poems and Writings on the 80th Anniversary of Premier Chou En-lai's Birth). Peking: Jen-min Ch'u-pan She, 1978. (Gold Chou)

　Chou Tsung-li-ti Ku-shih (Tales of Premier Chou). Tientsin: Jen-min Ch'u-pan She, 1977.

　Jen-min-ti Hao Tsung-li (The People's Good Premier). Shanghai: Jen-min Ch'u-pan She, 1977. (Green Chou)

　Jen-min-ti Hao Tsung-li (The People's Good Premier). Shanghai: Jen-min Ch'u-pan She, 1978 (vol. II), 1979 (vol. III). (Grey Chou)

　We Will Always Remember Premier Chou En-lai. Peking: Foreign Languages Press, 1977.

CHOU SHUN-HSIN. *The Chinese Inflation, 1937–1949*. New York: Columbia Unversity Press, 1963.

Chu Teh fan-tang fan-she-hui-chu-i fan-Mao Tse-tung ssu-hsiang-ti tsui-hsing (Chu Teh's anti-party, anti-socialist, anti Mao Tse-tung Thought Crimes). Peking: Capital's Liaison Station for thoroughly criticising Chu Teh, 15 April 1967.

CHUNG CHONG-WOOK. *Maoism and Development: The Politics of Industrial Management in China*. Seoul: Seoul National University Press, 1980.

Chung-kuo Nung-yeh Nien-chien, 1980 (China Agricultural Yearbook, 1980). Peking: Nung-yeh Ch'u-pan She, 1980.

CLEMENS, WALTER C. *The Arms Race and Sino-Soviet Relations*. Stanford: Hoover, 1968.

Communist China, 1955–59: Policy Documents with Analysis. Cambridge, Mass.: Harvard University Press, 1962.

Communist China, 1958. Hong Kong: Union Research Institute, 1959.

COMPTON, BOYD. *Mao's China: Party Reform Documents, 1942–44.* Seattle: University of Washington Press, 1952.

CRANKSHAW, EDWARD. *The New Cold War: Moscow v. Pekin.* Harmondsworth: Penguin, 1963.

CREEL, H. G. *Confucius, The Man and the Myth.* London: Routledge & Kegan Paul, 1951.

CROOK, DAVID and ISABEL. *The First Years of Yangyi Commune.* London: Routledge & Kegan Paul, 1959.

DALLIN, ALEXANDER, ed. *Diversity in International Communism: A Documentary Record, 1961–63.* New York: Columbia University Press, 1963.

DEDIJER, VLADIMIR. *Tito Speaks.* London: Weidenfeld & Nicolson, 1953.

DITTMER, LOWELL. *Liu Shao-ch'i and the Chinese Cultural Revolution.* Berkeley: University of California Press, 1974.

Documents on Disarmament, 1945–1959, II, *1957–59.* Washington D.C.: Department of State, 1960.

DOMES, JÜRGEN. *The Internal Politics of China.* New York: Praeger, 1973.

—— *Socialism in the Chinese Countryside: Rural Societal Policies in the People's Republic of China, 1949–1979.* London: C. Hurst, 1980.

DONNELLY, DESMOND. *The March Wind.* London: Collins, 1959.

DONNITHORNE, AUDREY. *China's Economic System.* London: Allen & Unwin, 1967.

DREYER, JUNE TEUFEL. *China's Forty Millions.* Cambridge, Mass.: Harvard University Press, 1976.

DUTT, GARGI. *Rural Communes of China.* London: Asia Publishing House, 1967.

ECKSTEIN, ALEXANDER. *China's Economic Revolution.* Cambridge: Cambridge University Press, 1977.

ECKSTEIN, ALEXANDER, GALENSON, WALTER and LIU TA-CHUNG, eds. *Economic Trends in Communist China.* Chicago: Aldine, 1968.

ELEGANT, ROBERT S. *Mao's Great Revolution.* London: Weidenfeld & Nicolson, 1971.

ELVIN, MARK. *The Pattern of the Chinese Past.* London: Eyre Methuen, 1973.

FAINSOD, MERLE. *How Russia Is Ruled.* Cambridge, Mass.: Harvard University Press, rev. ed., 1963.

FAIRBANK, JOHN K., *The Cambridge History of China,* vol. 10: *Late Ch'ing 1800–1911,* Pt I. Cambridge: Cambridge University Press, 1978.

FEJTÖ, FRANÇOIS. *Chine–URSS, La Fin d'une hégémonie: les origines du grand schisme communiste, 1950–57.* Paris: Plon, 1964.

FLOYD, DAVID. *Mao against Khrushchev.* New York: Praeger, 1964.

FOKKEMA, D. W. *Literary Doctrine in China and Soviet Influence,*

1956–1960. The Hague: Mouton, 1965.

Foreign Relations of the United States, 1949, VIII: *The Far East: China*. Washington D.C.: U.S. Government Printing Office, 1978.

GALE, GEORGE. *No Flies in China*. London: Allen & Unwin, 1955.

GARTHOFF, RAYMOND L., ed. *Sino-Soviet Military Relations*. New York: Praeger, 1966.

GINSBURGS, GEORGE & MICHAEL MATHOS. *Communist China and Tibet: The First Dozen Years*. The Hague: Martinus Nijhoff, 1964.

GITTINGS, JOHN. *The Role of the Chinese Army*. London: Oxford University Press for RIIA, 1968.

—— *Survey of the Sino-Soviet Dispute, 1963–1967*. London: Oxford University Press for RIIA, 1968.

GOLDMAN, MERLE. *China's Intellectuals: Advise and Dissent*. Cambridge, Mass.: Harvard University Press, 1981.

—— *Literary Dissent in Communist China*. Cambridge, Mass.: Harvard University Press, 1967.

GOODRICH, L. CARRINGTON & FANG CHAOYING. *Dictionary of Ming Biography, 1368–1644*. New York: Columbia University Press, two vols, 1976.

GRIFFITH, SAMUEL B. *The Chinese People's Liberation Army*. New York: McGraw-Hill for Council on Foreign Relations, 1967.

HALPERIN, MORTON. *China and the Bomb*. London: Pall Mall, 1965.

—— ed. *Sino-Soviet Relations and Arms Control*. Cambridge, Mass.: M.I.T. Press, 1967.

HALPERN, A. M. *The People's Republic of China in the Post-War World*. Unpubl. MS. at the Council on Foreign Relations, New York.

—— ed. *Policies toward China*. New York: McGraw-Hill for Council on Foreign Relations, 1965.

Han-Ying Shih-shih Yung-yü Tz'u-hui (Chinese-English Dictionary of Current Political Phrases and Terms). Peking: Shang-wu Yin-shu Kuan, 1964.

Handbook of Marxism, A. New York: Random House, 1935.

HARRISON, SELIG S. *India: The Most Dangerous Decades*.

HINTON, HAROLD C. *Communist China in World Politics*. London: Macmillan, 1966.

—— *The 'Unprincipled Dispute' within the Chinese Communist Top Leadership*. Washington, D.C.: USIA-IS-98-55, July 1955.

HOXHA, ENVER. *Reflections on China*. Tirana: '8 Nëntori' Publishing House, 1979.

HSIA, RONALD. *Price Control in Communist China*, New York: IPR, 1953.

HSIA, T. A. *The Commune in Retreat as Evidenced in Terminology and Semantics*. Berkeley: Center for Chinese Studies, University of California, 1964.

—— *Metaphor, Myth, Ritual and the People's Commune.* Berkeley: Center for Chinese Studies, University of California, 1961.

HSIEH, ALICE LANGLEY. *Communist China's Strategy in the Nuclear Era.* Englewood Cliffs, N.J.: Prentice-Hall, 1962.

HSU KAI-YU, ed. *Literature of the People's Republic of China.* Bloomington: Indiana University Press, 1980.

Hua Chu-hsi tsai Hunan (Chairman Hua in Hunan). Peking: Jen-min Ch'u-pan-she, 1977.

Hua Kuo-feng T'ung-chih shih Mao Chu-hsi Ko-ming Lu-hsien-ti Cho-yueh Chi-ch'eng-che (Comrade Hua Kuo-feng Is the Brilliant Continuer of Chairman Mao's Revolutionary Line). Peking: Jen-min Ch'u-pan She, 1977.

Huai-nien Chang Wen-t'ien T'ung-chih (Remember Comrade Chang Wen-t'ien). Changsha: Hunan Jen-min Ch'u-pan She, 1981.

HUANG CHEN-HSIA. *Chung Kung Chün Jen Chih.* (A Directory of Chinese Communist Military Personnel). Hong Kong: Research Institute of Contemporary History, 1968.

HUANG, RAY. *1587: A Year of No Significance.* New Haven: Yale, 1981.

HUCKER, CHARLES O. *China's Imperial Past.* Stanford: Stanford University Press, 1975.

HUDSON, G. F. *The Chinese Communes.* London: Soviet Survey, 1960.

HUDSON, G. F., LOWENTHAL, RICHARD, & RODERICK MACFARQUHAR. *The Sino-Soviet Dispute.* New York: Praeger, 1961.

HUTHEESING, RAJA, ed. *Tibet Fights for Freedom.* Bombay: Orient Longmans, 1960.

I-chiu-wu-chiu nien fei ch'ü tzu-jan tsai-hai ch'ing-k'uang tiao-ch'a (An Examination of Natural Calamities in Bandit Areas in 1959). Taiwan: Defence Ministry, Intelligence Division, Sept. 1959.

INDIA, GOVERNMENT OF: MINISTRY OF FOOD AND AGRICULTURE. *Report of the Indian Delegation to China on Agricultural Planning and Techniques.* New Delhi: Government of India Press, 1956.

JOFFE, ELLIS. *Between Two Plenums: China's Intraleadership Conflict, 1959–1962.* Ann Arbor: Center for Chinese Studies, University of Michigan, 1975.

—— *Party and Army: Professionalism and Political Control in the Chinese Officer Corps, 1949–1964.* Cambridge, Mass.: Harvard East Asian Research Center, 1965.

JOHNSON, CHALMERS. *Peasant Nationalism and Communist Power.* Stanford: Stanford University Press, 1962.

JOINT ECONOMIC COMMITTEE, CONGRESS OF THE UNITED STATES. *An Economic Profile of Mainland China.* Washington, D.C.: U.S. Government Printing Office, 1967.

KARNOW, STANLEY. *Mao and China.* London: Macmillan, 1972.

Khrushchev Remembers: The Last Testament. London: Deutsch, 1974.

KHRUSHCHOV, N. S. *Report to a Joint Session of the Supreme Soviet of the U.S.S.R., November 6, 1957.* London: Soviet News, 1957.

KLATT, WERNER, ed. *The Chinese Model.* Hong Kong: Hong Kong University Press for Institute of Modern Asian Studies, 1965.

KLEIN, DONALD W. & ANN B. CLARK. *Biographic Dictionary of Chinese Communism, 1921–1965.* Cambridge, Mass.: Harvard University Press, 1971.

KLOCHKO, MIKHAIL A. *Soviet Scientist in Red China.* Montreal: International Publishers Representatives, 1964.

KOLKOWICZ, ROMAN. *The Soviet Military and the Communist Party.* Princeton: Princeton University Press, 1967.

KUO MO-JO. *Li Po yü Tu Fu* (Li Po and Tu Fu). Peking: Jen-min Wen-hsueh Ch'u-pan She, 1971.

KUO, WARREN, ed. *A Comprehensive Glossary of Chinese Communist Terminology.* Taipei: Institute of International Relations, National Chengchi University, 1978.

LALL, ARTHUR. *How Communist China Negotiates.* New York: Columbia University Press, 1968.

Lao I-pei Wu-ch'an-chieh-chi Ko-ming-chia Shih-tz'u Hsuan-tu (A Selection of Poems by the Older Generation of Proletarian Revolutionaries). Changsha: Hunan Jen-min Ch'u-pan She, 1979.

LATTIMORE, OWEN. *Inner Asian Frontiers of China.* Boston: Beacon Press, 1962.

LEGGE, JAMES. *The Four Books.* Taipei: Culture Book Co., 1960.

LEONHARD, WOLFGANG. *The Kremlin since Stalin.* London: Oxford University Press, 1962.

LI CH'A. *Chung Kung Shui-shou Chih-tu* (Taxation System of the Chinese Communists). Hong Kong: Union Research Institute, 1969.

LIEBERTHAL, KENNETH. *A Research Guide to Central Party and Government Meetings in China, 1949–1975.* White Plains, N.Y.: International Arts and Sciences Press, 1976.

LIPPIT, VICTOR D. *Land Reform and Economic Development in China.* White Plains, N.Y.: International Arts and Sciences Press, 1974.

LIU SHAO-CH'I: *some major sources*

Collected Works of Liu Shao-ch'i, 1945–57 and *1958–67.* Hong Kong: Union Research Institute, 1969 and 1968.

Down with Liu Shao-ch'i—Life of Counter-Revolutionary Liu Shao-ch'i. Peking: Chingkangshan Fighting Corps of the Fourth Hospital, Peking Municipality, May 1967, trans. in CB 834.

Huai-nien Liu Shao-ch'i T'ung-chih (Remember Comrade Liu Shao-ch'i). Changhsa: Hunan Jen-min Ch'u-pan She, 1980.

Hung Ch'i P'iao-p'iao (Red Flags Fluttering), No. 20. Peking: 1980.

Liu Ai-ch'in. *Nü-er-ti Huai-nien* (Memories of a Daughter). Shihchia-chuang: Hopei Jen-min Ch'u-pan She, 1980.

Liu Shao-ch'i fan-ko-ming tsui-o shih (The history of the counter-revolutionary crimes of Liu Shao-ch'i). No place: Struggling morning and evening combat team and Alone and immovable combat team, 30 May 1967.

Liu Shao-ch'i ts'ai-liao hui-pien (Compilation of materials on Liu Shao-ch'i) (1st collection). Tientsin: April 1967.

Liu Shao-ch'i T'ung-chih Yung-ch'ui-pu-hsiu (Comrade Liu Shao-ch'i is Immortal). Peking: Jen-min Ch'u-pan She, 1980.

San-fan fen-tzu Liu Shao-ch'i tsui-shih (The History of the Crimes of Three-anti Element Liu Shao-ch'i). Peking: Red Guard Congress Peking Mining Institute East Is Red 'Renew the day', May 1967.

Selected edition on Liu Shao-ch'i's Counter-revolutionary Revisionist Crimes. Tientsin: Liaison Station 'Pledging to fight a bloody battle with Liu-Teng-T'ao to the end' attached to 18 Aug. Red Rebel Regiment of Nank'ai University, April 1967, trans. in SCMM 651–3.

Ta-tao tang-nei tsui-ta-ti tsou tzu-pen-chu-i tao-lu tang-ch'üan-p'ai—Liu Shao-ch'i (Strike Down the Greatest Power-holding Capitalist-Roader Clique [sic] within the Party—Liu Shao-ch'i). Peking: Peking Chemical Industry Institute's Mao Tse-tung Thought Propaganda Personnel, 4th collection, 10 April 1967.

Liu Zheng, Song Jian et al. *China's Population: Problems & Prospects*. Peking: New World Press, 1981.

MacFarquhar, Roderick. *The Hundred Flowers Campaign and the Chinese Intellectuals*. New York: Praeger, 1960.

—— *The Origins of the Cultural Revolution*, I: *Contradictions among the People, 1956–1957*. London: Oxford University Press; New York: Columbia University Press; both for RIIA, 1974.

—— *Sino-American Relations, 1949–1971*, New York: Praeger; Newton Abbot, Devon: David & Charles; both for RIIA, 1972.

Ma-k'o-ssu—En-ko-ssu Ch'üan Chi (Complete Works of Marx & Engels), XX. Peking: Jen-min Ch'u-pan She, 1971.

Mao Tse-tung: *some major sources**

Li Jui. *Mao Tse-tung T'ung-chih-ti Ch'u-ch'i Ko-ming Huo-tung* (Comrade Mao Tse-tung's Early Revolutionary Activities). Peking: Chung-kuo Ch'ing-nien Ch'u-pan She, 1957.

Mao Chu-hsi chiao-yü yü-lu (Chairman Mao's Sayings on Education). Peking: Hung Tai Hui, Pei-ching Tien-chi Hsueh-hsiao, Tung Fang Hung Kung-she, July 1967.

Mao Chu-hsi lun wen-yi yü-lu (Chairman Mao's Sayings on Literature

---

* Some additional items, with details of translations and contents, can be found in *Origins*, I, pp. 409–11.

and the Arts). Shanghai: Hsi-chu Hsueh-yuan 'Mo-ming Lou' Pien-chi Pu, no date.

Mao Chu-hsi-ti ko-ming wen-yi lu-hsien sheng-li wan sui (Long Live the Victory of Chairman Mao's Revolutionary Line on Literature and the Arts). Peking: Pei-ching Tien-ying Chih-p'ien Ch'ang Ko-ming Tsao-fan Lien-lo Tsung-pu, July 1967.

Mao Chu-hsi tui P'eng-Huang-Chang-Chou fan-tang chi-t'uan-ti p'i-p'an (Chairman Mao's Criticism of the P'eng [Teh-huai]-Huang [K'o-ch'eng]-Chang [Wen-t'ien]-Chou [Hsiao-chou] anti-party clique). (Nei-pu Wen-chien; chu-i pao-ts'un—Internal document; take security precautions). No publisher, no date.

Mao Chu-hsi wen-hsuan (Chairman Mao's Selected Writings). No publisher, no date.

Mao Chu-hsi yü-lu (The Sayings of Chairman Mao). Peking: Chung-kuo Jen-min Chieh-fang Chün Tsung Cheng-chih Pu, 2nd ed., 1966.

MAO TSE-TUNG. *A Critique of Soviet Economics*. New York: Monthly Review Press, 1977.

MAO TSE-TUNG, *Hsuan Chi* (Selected Works). Peking: Jen-min Ch'u-pan She, vols I–IV, 1960. vol. V, 1977.

MAO TSE-TUNG, *Selected Works*. Peking: Foreign Languages Press, vols I–III, 1965, vol. IV, 1961, vol. V, 1977.

Mao Tse-tung ssu-hsiang wan sui! (Long Live Mao Tse-tung's Thought). No publisher, no date.

Mao Tse-tung ssu-hsiang wan sui (Long Live Mao Tse-tung's Thought). No publisher, 1967.

Mao Tse-tung ssu-hsiang wan sui (Long Live Mao Tse-tung's Thought). No publisher, 1969.

Mao Tse-tung T'ung-chih Pa-shih-wu Tan-ch'en Chi-nien Wen-hsuan (A Collection of Writings to Mark the 85th Anniversary of the Birth of Comrade Mao Tse-tung). Peking: Jen-min Ch'u-pan She, 1979. (Mao Tse-tung: untitled collection). No publisher, no date.

Miscellany of Mao Tse-tung Thought (1949–1968), I & II. Washington, D.C.: JPRS 61269-1, -2, 1974.

Quotations from Chairman Mao Tse-tung. Peking: Foreign Languages Press, 1972.

Shao-shan Hung Jih Chao Ch'ien Ch'iu (The Red Sun of Shaoshan Illuminates a Thousand Autumns). Changsha: Hunan Jen-min Ch'u-pan She, 1978.

Ta hai hang-hsing k'ao to-shou (Sailing the Seas Depends on the Man at the Helm). No publisher, no date.

Tsui-kao chih-shih (Supreme Directives). No publisher, no date.

Tzu-liao Hsuan-pien (A Selection of Materials), No publisher, Jan. 1967.

Wo-men tsai Mao Chu-hsi Shen-pien (At the Side of Chairman Mao). Shanghai: Jen-min Ch'u-pan She, 1977.

MAXWELL, NEVILLE. *India's China War*. London: Cape, 1970.

MEHNERT, KLAUS. *Peking and Moscow*. London: Weidenfeld & Nicolson, 1963.

Mien-huai Liu Jen T'ung-chih (Remember Comrade Liu Jen). Peking: Pei-ching Ch'u-pan She, 1979.

MOODY, PETER R. *The Politics of the Eighth Central Committee of the Communist Party of China*. Hamden, Conn.: Shoe String Press, 1973.

MORAES, FRANK. *The Revolt in Tibet*. New York: Macmillan, 1960.

Nan-wang-ti Chi-yi (Unforgettable Memories). Peking: Jen-min Jih-pao Ch'u-pan She, 1979.

NIXON, RICHARD M. *Six Crises*. New York: Doubleday, 1969.

OKSENBERG, MICHEL. *Policy Formulation in Communist China: the Case of the Mass Irrigation Campaign, 1957–8*. New York: Columbia University, unpubl. Ph.D. thesis.

PATTERSON, GEORGE N. *Tibet in Revolt*. London: Faber, 1960.

P'ENG TEH-HUAI: *some major sources*

    The Case of P'eng Teh-huai, 1959–68. Hong Kong: Union Research Institute 1968.

    CHING HSI-CHEN, *Tsai P'eng Tsung Shen-pien* (At the Side of Chief P'eng). Chengtu: Szechwan Jen-min Ch'u-pan She, 1979.

    Chi-nien P'eng Teh-huai T'ung-chih (Remember Comrade P'eng Teh-huai). Peking: Wen-wu Ch'u-pan She, 1982.

    Heng-tao-li-ma P'eng Chiang-chün (Gallant General P'eng). Peking: Jen-min Ch'u-pan She, 1979.

    P'eng Teh-huai Tzu-hsu (P'eng Teh-huai's Autobiography). Peking: Jen-min Ch'u-pan She, 1981.

    TING WANG. *P'eng Teh-huai Wen-t'i Chuan Chi* (Special Collection on the P'eng Teh-huai Problem). Hong Kong: Ming Pao, 1969.

PERKINS, DWIGHT H. *Agricultural Development in China, 1368–1968*. Chicago: Aldine, 1969.

Polemic on the General Line of the International Communist Movement, The. Peking: Foreign Languages Press, 1965.

Provincial Agricultural Statistics for Communist China. Ithaca, N.Y.: Committee on the Economy of China, SSRC, 1969.

Public Papers of the Presidents, The: Dwight D. Eisenhower, 1959. Washington, D.C.: U.S. Government Printing Office, 1960.

PUSEY, JAMES R. *Wu Han: Attacking the Present through the Past*. Cambridge, Mass.: Harvard University, East Asian Research Center, 1969.

PYE, LUCIAN W. *Mao Tse-tung: The Man in the Leader*. New York: Basic Books, 1976.

—— *The Spirit of Chinese Politics*. Cambridge, Mass.: MIT Press, 1968.

QUESTER, GEORGE H. *Nuclear Diplomacy: The First Twenty-five Years.* New York: Dunellen, 1970.

REISCHAUER, EDWIN O. & JOHN K. FAIRBANK. *East Asia: The Great Tradition.* London: Allen & Unwin, undated.

ROBINSON, THOMAS W. *A Political-Military Biography of Lin Piao*, II, *1950–71.* Santa Monica: Rand Corporation unpubl. study, Aug. 1971.

RUE, JOHN E. *Mao Tse-tung in Opposition, 1927–35.* Stanford: Stanford University Press, 1966.

SCALAPINO, ROBERT A., ed. *Elites in the People's Republic of China.* Seattle: University of Washington Press, 1972.

SCHRAM, STUART R. *Mao Tse-tung.* Harmondsworth: Penguin, rev. ed., 1967.

—— ed. *Mao Tse-tung Unrehearsed: Talks and Letters: 1956–71.* Harmondsworth: Penguin, 1974.

—— *The Political Thought of Mao Tse-tung.* Harmondsworth: Penguin, enlarged & rev. ed., 1969.

SCHRAN, PETER. *The Development of Chinese Agriculture, 1950–1959.* Urbana: University of Illinois Press, 1969.

SCHURMANN, FRANZ. *Ideology and Organization in Communist China.* Berkeley: University of California Press, rev. ed., 1968.

SCHWARTZ, BENJAMIN I. *Chinese Communism and the Rise of Mao.* Cambridge, Mass.: Harvard University Press, 1951.

SCHWARTZ, HARRY. *The Soviet Economy since Stalin.* London: Gollancz, 1965.

SELDEN, MARK, ed. *The People's Republic of China.* New York: Monthly Review Press, 1979.

Shen-ch'ieh Huai-nien Lo Jui-ch'ing T'ung-chih (Deeply Remember Comrade Lo Jui-ch'ing). No place: Ch'ün-chung Ch'u-pan She, 1978.

SMEDLEY, AGNES. *The Great Road: the Life and Times of Chu Teh.* New York: Monthly Review Press, 1956.

SNOW, EDGAR. *Red Star over China.* London: Gollancz, 1937.

STALIN, J. *Economic Problems of Socialism in the U.S.S.R.* Moscow: Foreign Languages Publishing House, 1952.

STAVIS, BENEDICT. *The Politics of Agricultural Mechanisation in China.* Ithaca: Cornell University Press, 1978.

T'AO CHU. *Li-hsiang Ch'ing-ts'ao Ching-shen Sheng-huo* (Ideals, Sentiments, and Spiritual Life). Peking: Chung-kuo Ch'ing-nien Ch'u-pan She, 1964.

TATU, MICHEL. *Power in the Kremlin: From Khrushchev to Kosygin.* New York: Viking, 1970.

TEIWES, FREDERICK C. *Politics & Purges in China.* White Plains, N.Y.: M. E. Sharpe, 1979.

Ten Glorious Years. Peking: Foreign Languages Press, 1960.

Ten Great Years. Peking: Foreign Languages Press, 1960.

Teng Hsiao-p'ing fan-tang fan-she-hui-chu-i fan-Mao Tse-tung ssu-hsiang-ti yen-lun (Edited Extracts from Teng Hsiao-p'ing's Anti-party, Anti-socialist, Anti-Mao Tse-tung Thought Utterances). Peking: No. 1 Detachment of the China People's University's Three Red Seize Liu-Teng Team (attached to) the Capital's Red Guard Representative Congress, April 1967.

TENG SSU-YÜ & JOHN K. FAIRBANK. *China's Response to the West.* Cambridge, Mass.: Harvard University Press, 1954.

Tibet, 1950–1967. Hong Kong: Union Research Institute, 1968.

TREGEAR, T. R. *A Geography of China.* London: University of London Press, 1965.

TUCKER, ROBERT C., ed. *The Lenin Anthology.* New York: Norton, 1975.

TWITCHET, DENIS, ed. *The Cambridge History of China*, vol. 3: *Sui and T'ang China, 589–906*, Pt 1. Cambridge: Cambridge University Press, 1979.

WALEY, ARTHUR. *The Analects of Confucius.* London: Allen & Unwin, 1945.

WALKER, KENNETH R. *Planning in Chinese Agriculture: Socialisation and the Private Sector, 1956–62.* London: Cass, 1965.

WALKER, RICHARD L. *Hunger in China.* New York: New Leader, no date.

—— *Letters from the Communes.* New York: New Leader, 1959.

WHITSON, WILLIAM W. *The Chinese High Command: A History of Communist Military Politics, 1927–71.* London: Macmillan, 1973.

—— ed. *The Military and Political Power in China in the 1970s.* New York: Praeger, 1972.

Who's Who in Communist China. Hong Kong: Union Research Institute, rev. ed., 2 vols, 1969.

WILSON, J. TUZO. *One Chinese Moon.* New York: Hill & Wang, 1959.

WOLLASTON, NICHOLAS. *China in the Morning.* London: Cape, 1960.

WONG MAN, translator. *Poems of Mao Tse-tung.* Hong Kong: Eastern Horizon Press, 1966.

WU HAN. *Teng-hsia Chi* (Writings by Lamplight). Peking: San-lien Shu-tien, 1979.

Wu Han ho 'Hai Jui Pa-kuan' (Wu Han and 'The Dismissal of Hai Jui'). Peking: Jen-min Ch'u-pan She, 1979.

WU YUAN-LI. *The Spatial Economy of Communist China.* New York: Praeger, 1967.

ZAGORIA, DONALD S. *The Sino-Soviet Conflict, 1956–61.* Princeton: Princeton University Press, 1962.

INDEX